The Length and Depth of Acting

The Length and Depth
of ACTING

EDWIN ⌐DUERR

with a Foreword by A. M. Nagler

𐌀𐌀

HOLT, RINEHART AND WINSTON · NEW YORK

ACKNOWLEDGMENTS

For permission to quote at length from copyrighted material sincere appreciation is due:

George Allen & Unwin Ltd., for permission to quote from *The Art of the Actor* translated by Elsie Fogarty (copyright 1932) from C. Coquelin's *L'Art du Comédien*.

Appleton-Century-Crofts, Inc., for quotations from *The Rhetoric of Aristotle*, translated and edited by Lane Cooper. Copyright, 1932, Lane Cooper. By permission of Appleton-Century-Crofts, Inc.; from Corneille's *Le Cid* in Donald Clive Stuart's *The Development of Dramatic Art* (New York: Appleton, 1928) by permission of the publisher Appleton-Century-Crofts, an affiliate of Meredith Press.

G. Bell & Sons, Ltd., for permission to quote from F. M. Stawell's translation of Euripides' *Iphigenia in Aulis*.

The Trustees of the late Harley Granville-Barker, 52, Bedford Square, London, England, for permission to quote from his *The Exemplary Theatre*, copyright 1922.

Harcourt, Brace & World, Inc., for permission to quote from *The Development of the Theatre* by Allardyce Nicoll, copyright 1927, 1948.

George G. Harrap & Company Ltd., also for permission to quote from Allardyce Nicoll's *The Development of the Theatre*.

The Harvard University Press, for quotations reprinted by permission of the publisher and the Loeb Classical Library from Cicero, *De Oratore*, Volumes I and II, translated by E. W. Sutton, completed by H. Rackham, copyright 1942, 1948; and from the *Institutio Oratoria of Quintilian*, 4 volumes, translated by H. E. Butler, Cambridge, Mass.: Harvard University Press, 1921–22, 1933, 1936, 1953; quotations reprinted by permission of the publishers from W. Beare, *The Roman Stage*, Cambridge, Mass.: Harvard University Press, 1951.

The Hudson Review for permission to quote from "The Kind of Poetry I Want" by Hugh MacDiarmid. Copyright © 1961 by The Hudson Review.

The Macmillan Company for permission to quote from B. V. Varneke, *History of the Russian Theatre* translated by Boris Brasol, edited by Belle Martin, copyright 1951.

Methuen & Co. Ltd., for permission to quote from *Greek Tragedy: A Literary Study* by H. D. F. Kitto, copyright 1939, 1950; and from *The Roman Stage* by W. Beare, copyright 1951.

Oxford University Press, Inc., for permission to quote from *The Medieval Stage* by E. K. Chambers, copyright 1903, 1925, 1948, and from his *The Elizabethan Stage*, copyright, 1923, 1945, 1951; and from *The Medieval French Drama* by Grace Frank, copyright 1954.

Routledge & Kegan Paul Ltd., for permission to quote from *Theatre Drama and Audience in Goethe's Germany* by W. H. Bruford, copyright 1950.

Charles Scribner's Sons, and the author, for permission to quote from *The Flower in Drama*, copyright 1923, *Glamour*, copyright 1925, *Theatre Practice*, copyright 1926, and *Immortal Shadows*, copyright 1948, by Stark Young.

Theatre Arts Books, New York, and Geoffrey Bles, Ltd., London, for permission to quote from Constantin Stanislavsky, *My Life in Art* translated by J. J. Robbins. Copyright 1924 by Little, Brown & Co.; copyright © 1948, 1952 by Elizabeth Reynolds Hapgood for the Alexeieff Family. Published by permission of Theatre Arts Books, New York.

Stark Young for permission to quote from his book *The Theater*, published in 1927 by the George H. Doran Company.

To
STARK YOUNG

Before we can judge an art at all we have to know what it consists of and is driving at; we have to know the rules of the game.

–Stark Young.

Artists build theories round what they would like to do, but they do what they can.

–André Malraux.

Foreword

by A. M. NAGLER

Of all the elements that contribute to the theatrical experience of a playgoer, acting is the most evanescent. It is perhaps for this reason that we had to wait so long for a history of acting such as Edwin Duerr now places before us. To be sure, many of the great players have received due attention in the form of monographs, biographies, and general books on theater, some of them scholarly and critical, others gossipy and anecdotal. But general histories of the theater are almost perforce preoccupied with the tangibles—architecture, scenery, and costumes—and frequently tend to slight the players whose personalities and craft actually gave luster to the playhouse. One of the primary merits of Mr. Duerr's theatrical panorama is that the actor remains constantly in focus.

Theater historians are deeply conscious of the transitory nature of the material with which they work, an awareness pensively expressed by Ben Jonson when, after recording what happened onstage during the performance of his *Hymenaei* Masque, he lamented: "Only the envy was, that it lasted not still, or, now it is past, cannot by imagination, much less description, be recovered to a part of that spirit it had in the gliding by." Yet Jonson did not give up in despair: "That I may not utterly defraud the reader of his hope, I am drawn to give it those brief touches which may leave behind some shadow of what it was." And he finished his description. It is only because, like Jonson, many other observers of theater have felt the urge and the responsibility to record "those brief touches" that we are able, to a certain degree, to reconstruct the theatrical past.

Any historian has to be wary of his sources; the historian of acting, especially, cannot be enough of a skeptic. He knows he can rely on such star witnesses as Lichtenberg on Garrick, Böttiger on Iffland, and Hazlitt on Kean. Frequently, however, the case may be obscured by a plurality of testimonies, and the historian must then extricate the actor from a maze of contradictory statements. Or the scholar has to face the other extreme when he is haunted by a scarcity of information; he may encounter this situation not alone in dealing with antiquity, but even when he approaches so relatively recent a figure as Molière, for whom we have hardly three sympathetic eye-witness reports and numerous derogatory remarks by his enemies. The few testimonies we have about the character of Elizabethan acting have sufficed to drive the experts into two opposing camps, one school of thought stressing the protean quality of Burbage and the other regarding him as a formal actor-rhetorician who never really changed. All through the history of acting we encounter this duality: the type represented by Eleonora Duse, who transformed herself beyond self-recognition into the character she assumed, and the type exemplified by Josef Kainz, who remained Kainz in whatever part he played or—to put it differently—played on the part as if on the strings of an instrument. Estheticians (both actors and critics) have wrestled with this paradox, and Mr. Duerr has wisely given generous attention to the theories of acting as they have evolved from Plato to Brecht.

The student of acting is likely to benefit most from Edwin Duerr's volume; it also will be of tremendous value to the stage director in gaining an insight into the psychological and technical problems of the actor's profession. The playgoer, as he peruses the pages that follow, is bound to relive some of those fleeting magic moments which had the power "to steal away the spectators from themselves."

Preface

PREFACE

In 1875, critic George Henry Lewes noted "the chaotic state of opinion on the subject of acting in many minds of rare intelligence." He wrote that he'd heard "those for whose opinions in other directions my respect is great, utter judgments on this subject which proved that they had not even a suspicion of what the Art of Acting really is." Today, when larger audiences than ever before attend acting—on stages, on motion picture and television screens—the art is still too often misunderstood.

The different ways actors work—their whys, and hows, and their aims—or what they do to "make" in a special medium characters from materials furnished by a playwright and from the materials of themselves are complex and illusive. For at least two hundred years enough men of the theater have tried to explain the esoteric process and the transient product. And "more supreme bosh," according to George Jean Nathan, "continues to be written about acting than about any other topic under the sun." Even the few valuable books in the field have been nearly always narrow in scope, limited to one time, one theory, one style, one person.

What has been needed is a careful survey of all kinds of acting. After thirty years of teaching the subject in universities, and among professionals in New York City, and principally in directing actors onstage and in front of microphones and cameras, I've undertaken to lessen a little that lack. I've tried to provide for students of the theater a background, a philosophy, a "content" for their courses, for working actors an authentic record to strengthen pride in their profession, and for nonactors—for audiences—an exposition of the intricate and fascinating fundamentals of the art. This book is, accordingly, the first history of the world's acting. It is also the first summary of all the important theories of acting from Aristotle and Seami to Stanislavski and Brecht.

Any attempt to trace the evolution of acting is, however, an attempt to record the ephemeral. We can today partly preserve examples of the art on records, tapes, and films; but the characters made yesterday by actors have disappeared like statues made out of snow. We cannot personally look at or hear their work. No one now can describe or judge it. It is gone. Necessarily, then—but also by design—I've used many quotations throughout what follows: meticulously, and gratefully, I've given credit to those who were there when I was not and furnished me with evidence, as well as to those who otherwise have informed me.

My personal evaluation of the facts, my unavoidable preferences, will, I hope, provoke discussion and thus lead to clearer thinking and valid creating.

I'm happy to thank George Freedley, Curator of the Theatre Collection, New York Public Library, for his long-continued help; Professor A. M. Nagler of Yale University for his corrections, suggestions, and Foreword; the Film Library of the Museum of Modern Art, A. Cunagin of the Committee for Cultural Relations with Foreign Countries, Moscow, M. F. Christout of the Bibliothèque de l'Arsenal, Paris, and Hugo Fetting, of the Deutsche Akademie ker Künste, Abteilung für Deutsche Theatergeschichte, Berlin, for supplying needed dates.

—E.D.

Downey, California
February, 1962

Contents

Part I–THE RISE AND FALL OF ACTING

1–*The Beginnings*   5

   The Instinct   5
   First Greek Professionals   9
   "Men As They Ought to Be"   15
   Comedians   18
   Actors' Contests   20
   Euripides   21
   The Comics Mature   26
   Actors' Guilds   27
   Greek Acting   29

2–*The Rejection*   39

   Plays in Rome   39
   A Trivial Craft   41
   Theatricality   43
   Literary Interlopers   45
   Actors Take Charge   46
   Tidbits of Theory   50
   Acting in India   56

Part II–THE RENEWAL OF ACTING

3–*Roughly a Thousand Years, 476–1450*   63

   The Instinct Survives   63
   In the Churches   67

In the Towns 73
In the Far East Again 78

4–*One Hundred and Fifty Years, 1450–1600* 83

In Clubs, Castles, Courts 83
France 85
England 87
"Italy" 89
Spain 95
Public Theaters, 1550–1580 97
Acting as a Business, 1580–1600 104

5–*The Italian Professionals* 114

No Playwrights Wanted 114
The Actor Is All, Alas! 116
Slow, Significant Failure 125

6–*Play Acting Accepted, 1600–1700* 136

Actors Everywhere 136
Professionals in France 139
Set-back in England 147
Kabuki 155
Molière; La Comédie-Française 159
The Restoration 169
Acting Is Declamation 178

Part III–THE CHANGES IN ACTING

7–*The Successful Eighteenth Century* 201

Examinations 201
The Book *Betterton* 203
Before 1725 in Paris and London 209
The First Riccoboni 214
Other Lands 216
Aaron Hill, Macklin, and Garrick 219
Le Comédien (1747) 228
The Younger Riccoboni 238
The Second Hill 241
More Garrick, More Nature 246
Germany; Russia 252
Diderot 256

Elocution Triumphant 268
Elocution in English 278

8–*The Perplexed Nineteenth Century*   287

Some Rebels 287
Reflections by Talma 296
Critics and Kean 303
Macready and Others 312
Romantic Flare 317
Tinges of Realism 327
Realism After 1850 340
English Directors 346
American Actors 361
The Meininger 365
Realism Rampant by 1875 370
Nonrealism 385
Actor's Choice? 388
Coquelin's Method 396
Reality Reproduced 405

Part IV–THE VARIETY OF ACTING

9–*The Mass-Culture Century*   411

Prologue 411
From Sweden to Duse 414
To Theatricalize or Not? 419
English-Speaking Actors 425
After 1910: Copeau 434
Expressionism 438
Stanislavski Prepares 441
Mostly Box-Office 448
American Accent in the 1920's 452
Stark Young 463
Various Russians 467
Finding a "System" 474
1930–1950 479
The Years Ahead 491

Sources   499
Important Writings on Acting   543
Index   573

PART I

THE RISE AND

FALL OF ACTING

1- The Beginnings

❧ THE INSTINCT

Actors stood by, waiting to make their first professional entrance, during many well-organized civilizations: in Sumer in southern Mesopotamia (modern Iraq), in Egypt, in Crete, in India, in China, in Phoenicia and Babylonia and Assyria, among the Hittites, the Hebrews, the Etruscans, the Chaldeans, the Medes and the Persians. They waited while other talented men, as a pleasant afterthought to routine, began to transform their attitudes toward living into art by making music and songs, by dancing, by hammering metals into decorations, by drawing and painting, by carving statues, by building temples and monuments and tombs, by participating in ceremonials and rituals, and by composing poems. They waited while the Egyptians, wooing immortality, sculptured King Didufri, the Queen Nefertiti, and the Shiek-el-Beled—and constructed, near 2900 B.C., the Great Pyramid of Khufu (or Cheops) and the Great Sphinx of Gizeh. They waited while the Mesopotamians in their *Epic of Gilgamesh* (c. 2000 B.C.) tried to master experiences and to find in them a meaning. They waited during the ninth, eighth, and seventh centuries B.C. while diverse Greek poets, among them Homer, Hesiod, and Sappho, recited the "feel" and the shape of their imaginings. Then in the sixth century B.C., in Greece, the first—vaguely known—professional actors came onstage.

5

II

Actors of one kind or another, however, without scripts and nonprofessional, must have performed long before then. We can conjecture that there have been actors always, and the click that starts the surmise is our notion that people everywhere in time must have always felt an instinct for demonstrating, for pretending and imitating and performing, for beguiling others with the words, the gestures, and the movements of impersonation. Ever since Aristotle (384–322 B.C.) observed that "Imitation is one instinct of our nature," [1] we've been sure of that truth and variously defined it.

In this century, for instance, Alexander Bakshy defined the instinct as a natural flair for dramatic action common to every human being. "It is the effort," he wrote, "to appear different to what one really is; it is the practice of make-believe. In life we exercise this faculty of complete or partial disguise in order to achieve a variety of practical ends; some innocent, some sinister, some serious, some jocular. But, whatever the end, the dramatic action itself is a part of our conduct, and may be entirely unconscious. The classical example of dramatic action in real life is the courting of lovers. A man wooing a woman tries to appear in the most impressive guise, donning the robes of angelic purity, or demoniac wickedness, of enforced and resented loneliness, or irresistible, triumphant amorousness—in short, choosing the part he is going to play as the case may require. The woman, for her part, pretends to be indifferent, skeptical, inaccessible." Then in 1949 critic Francis Fergusson defined the instinct as a latent form of human perception and named it "the histrionic sensibility." When cultivated by practice, he said, it perceives and discriminates actions just as the trained ear perceives and discriminates sounds. And, like everyone else, he found it to be a basic, or primary, or primitive virtue of the human mind.[2]

Therefore, since human beings possess something like an instinct for theatricalism, for make-believe, for impersonating, for perceiving and imitating dramatic actions, we can with some justification go way back to the dawn-days, to the Stone Age when men were painting vividly colored stags, horses, and aurochs in caves, somewhere around 13,000 B.C., and imagine with Robert Edmond Jones the birth of actors:

> Ook and Pow and Pung and Glub and Little Zowie and all the rest are sitting close together around the fire. Opposite them sit the leaders of the tribe. They have killed a lion today. Suddenly the leader jumps to his feet. "I killed the lion! I did it! I followed him! He sprang at me! I struck him with my spear! He fell down! He lay still!"
>
> He is telling us. We listen. But all at once an idea comes to his dim brain. "I know a better way to tell you. See! It was like this! *Let me show you!*"
>
> [Let me show you what happened, what I did, and what the lion did? Let me show you my fear and my bravery and my joy, and the lion's

courage and cunning and pain? Let me show you how I can hold your attention by the conflict, the suspense, and the surprises? Let me show you, by skillfully reshaping the fight a little, what it all meant to me, what I find in it as truth, as essence, as idea?]

"You, Ook, over there—you stand up and be the lion. Here is the lion's skin. You put it on and be the lion and I'll kill you and we'll show them how it was."

Ook gets up. He hangs the lion's skin over his shoulders. He drops on his hands and knees and growls. How terrible he is! Of course, he isn't the real lion. We know that. . . . He doesn't even look like a lion. "You needn't try to scare us, Ook. We know you. We aren't afraid of you!"

And yet, in some mysterious way, Ook *is* the lion. . . . He is Ook all right, but he is a lion, too. . . .

Pshaw! A man can't be a lion! How can a man be a lion? But Ook can make us believe it, just the same. . . . Ook is an actor. He will always be different from the rest of us, a little apart from us. For he can summon spirits.[3]

Thus from the start of things there were actors; and for ten thousand misty years, in every cluster of people, actors showed others, however crudely and briefly, their adventures, their jokes, their beliefs, their perceptions, their imaginings.

III

By *c.* 3000 B.C. we no longer need to assume there were actors. In early Egypt and Mesopotamia the priests, while celebrating certain seasonal, coronation, or burial rites, now and then turned into reciters and with a few lines portrayed highlights in the life of a god. They became, in the dramatized portions of their ceremonials, amateur actors. They participated in semi-plays. Among the Egyptian semi-plays extant are fifty-five *Pyramid Texts*, apparently dating back to 3000 B.C. or earlier; recent reconstructions of a few *Coronation Festival Plays* and the *Memphite (Creation) Drama*, staged anywhere from 3000 to 2000 B.C.; and, in outline, the *Abydos (Osiris) Passion Play*, which was performed almost continuously from perhaps 2000 until between 569–526 B.C.

Also from about 3000 B.C. onward priests became honored amateur actors in various Babylonian and Hittite rituals. And before 1000 B.C. they sang and sometimes acted out Hindu hymns, or Vedas; they also participated in the beginnings of dramatized ceremonials in China.

The earliest known priest who, on occasion, became an amateur actor was named I-Kher-nofret. Nearly four thousand years ago, *c.* 1870 B.C., in possibly the *Abydos Passion Play*, he imitated a character and an action before an audience: he set out to defend his father, he drove back the enemy from the Neshmet Boat, he overthrew the enemies of Osiris, he performed the Great Coming Forth, and he followed the god in his footsteps.

In Greece, however, not in Egypt, the priests by happy chance became the most influential of all the early religious amateur actors. At first, as choral leader of the dithyramb, a hymn usually honoring Dionysus, the Greek priest led a chorus of fifty in narrating, largely by improvisation, some incident in the deity's life. Then sometime before 600 B.C. individual priests, such as Arion of Corinth (whose writings may have been called "dramas," or "things performed") and Epigenes of Sicyon (whose works eventually were termed "tragedies," or goat-songs, because a goat was the victor's prize in the composition contests), began to poetize the dithyramb by writing lyrics for the chorus and the leader. And then, as this literary material was added to the rituals, the priest–poet leaders of the choral group gradually separated a bit from it and soon were attempting snatches of elementary impersonation.

Thus, slowly, but conspicuously, the Greek amateur actor emerged among the religious festivals. And this poet–actor, "who spoke the lines he had been inspired to compose, was descended through the leader of the dithyramb from the priest . . . who, since the god had entered his body, *was* the god." [4]

But these rituals were still far from being genuine plays, or scripts designed for actors. Something was missing; something had to be added to them, something profane perhaps, but at least something more human. The Greeks, in short, ached to know more about themselves, to see and hear themselves, and to celebrate themselves. Some poets therefore began to compare the rituals with the crude but very human mimic sketches about daily life then being acted by peasants (like Stone Age Ook and his leader) from instinct and for fun in all the villages of the Peloponnesus. And they listened to the rituals and then to the serious myths of the people as shaped by tale-tellers. Finally they asked, "If incidents in the lives of gods can be pleasurably and significantly represented, why not also incidents in the lives of gods *and* men? Why can't we write and enact the deeds of legendary heroes, heroes who symbolize us?" Soon enough, material for their new kind of presentations was found in the popular *Iliad* and the *Odyssey*, the former probably compiled and the latter probably invented by Homer, and set down between c. 750 and 700 B.C. Greek tragedies, therefore, were indebted "to epic poetry for subject matter, dignity of treatment and of diction, and development of plot, including such technical devices as recognition and reversal of situation. . . ." [5]

Sometime before 500 B.C., then, when the zone of literate societies, accustomed to urban life and dependent on an urban economy, extended from the Atlantic coast of Spain to the Jaxartes in Central Asia and the Ganges in India, and from southern Arabia to the north coasts of the Mediterranean and the Black Sea; when the first Iron Age was already well-established north of the Alps, and was just beginning in the British Isles; when the Mayan Indians were obscurely settling in Central America; after the birth of Buddha c. 563 B.C. and Confucius c. 551; after the fall of Babylon in 539 B.C. and the extension of the Persian Empire under Cyrus from the Hindu Kesh to the Aegean and from the Caspian to the desert of Arabia; after Ezekiel and the restoration of the Jews in Palestine in 538 B.C.; and while near-plays were being "danced" in India and in China, and the *Abydos Passion Play* was being performed in Egypt, preliminary playwrights at Athens began to compose their dramatic verses about gods and men. There the first professional actor took stage in *c.* 534 B.C.

✿ FIRST GREEK PROFESSIONALS

Thespis, according to most authorities was the first professional European actor. More accurately, he was a poet–actor, since he wrote his own lines and appeared in his own plays. The titles of only four of them have come down to us: *Phorbus* (or *The Prizes of Pelias*), *Priests*, *Youths*, and *Pentheus*. Diogenes Laertius (*c.* A.D. 200–250), the only definite authority for his signal achievement, wrote: "in ancient times the chorus at first carried on the action in tragedy alone, but later Thespis invented an actor in order to allow the chorus intervals of relief." Additional facts about Thespis are few, shadowy, and even suspect. Apparently he was a peasant poet from Icaria where, before 560 B.C., he exhibited his serious choral compositions. He may have been one of the writers who effected, by a change of ingredients, the transition from dithyramb to semi-drama, from a recital of incidents in the life of a god to a recital of incidents in the life of a hero. At any rate, when he came to Athens about 560 B.C. he continued to present productions of his tragedies perhaps partially for religious purposes, but also for pastime, and maybe for profit; "and the thing, because it was new," according to Plutarch, took "very much with the multitude." [6]

Some twenty-five years later tragedies were officially recognized by beneficent "tyrant" Pisistratus (*c.* 605–527 B.C.). About 534 B.C., in order to give greater importance to the City Dionysia, the name of an annual community religious festival, he added to the customary contests in dithyramb new contests in tragedy. Thespis, it seems, promptly won the prize for playwriting, and was honored thereafter for being the first dramatic poet to employ an actor as distinct from the chorus and its leader. At the beginning, after appointing someone else as choral leader and defining his new role by donning a simple mask, or different masks for different characters, Thespis probably did no more in his tragedies than deliver some set speeches in answer to questions from the chorus. By so doing he "invented" or at least newly emphasized the actor; whatever he called himself or was called, he created the *hypokritēs* or "answerer"; he definitely portrayed a character or characters; he started the profession of acting.

For the next thirty-five years, from *c.* 534 to 500 B.C., performances of tragedies were regularly staged at the religious festivals in Athens. However, the processes by which subsequent playwrights like Pratinas, Choeriles, and Phrynichus enriched the role of the single actor in a production remain a mystery. Undoubtedly they added a semblance of story, of plot, to monologues that filled the intervals between the choral odes; and certainly they added more and more dialogue for him, the chorus leader, and the chorus. Yet all this while the productions remained exclusively the poet's. He wrote the tragedies, staged or "taught" them to the large chorus, and experimented with chanted speech, formal gesture and movement and dance as he himself impersonated the characters.

II

Then near 500 B.C. the old, old city–state of Athens, in the territory of Attica, with a population of 400,000, or less, became the political and commercial center of the Hellenic world. After it defeated the Persians at Marathon in 490 and again at Salamis in 480 B.C., it bloomed into perhaps the most civilized society that has yet existed. Active there within one hundred and fifty-five years, or two lifetimes, in an intellectual upsurge that bordered on the miraculous, were statesmen like Themistocles (c. 525–c. 460) and Pericles (c. 495–429), the historian Thucydides (c. 460–c. 400) Mnesicles and Ictinus, the architects of the Acropolis (447–432), the sculptors Phidias (c. 500–432) and Praxiteles (c. 370–c. 330), the orator Demosthenes (384?–322), the philosophers Socrates (469–399) and Plato (427?–347?). There also were four supreme playwrights who, active in creating an enduring theater, required the trained skills of professional performers; who, in providing them with wondrous things to say and do—or with characters to interpret—gave the new profession a quick stature.

There, c. 495, forty years after the "invention" of the first professional actor, soldier Aeschylus (525–456 B.C.), author of from seventy to ninety plays, of which seven are extant, took the next step in the development of the new profession by introducing the second actor (and maybe the third). The name of the original second actor, it seems, was Cleander. No more than that is known about him now. The facts as to why he was selected, when he began to wear a mask and act, and with what formal skills he recited or impersonated characters under the "teaching" of Aeschylus, who devised his gestures and movements and regulated the tones of his voice, have evaporated. Only as an honored name does Cleander come down to us. For he wasn't a poet–actor like Thespis or Aeschylus; he was an actor only, an actor paid by the city–state for his special work. He therefore can be remembered as the first known professional to act the words, to delineate a character, conceived and written by another.

For years, however, Cleander wasn't allowed to contribute much to the tragedies in which he appeared, or to his new profession. As the second actor he came onstage only intermittently and then only as an assistant player. The two earliest of the surviving tragedies of Aeschylus are close to being single-actor pieces. The Persae (The Persians) (c. 472 B.C.), a dramatization of contemporary events, and the first play preserved in its entirety, can rather easily be adapted for presentation by one actor and a chorus of twelve by allowing the role of the queen mother Atossa to revert to the chorus whenever the Messenger or Darius is onstage. In the *Supplices* (*The Suppliants*) (c. 467 B.C.), where the chorus recites considerably more than half of the lines, only two scenes—when Danaus addresses Pelasgus and when Pelasgus defies the Herald, a total of a mere seventy lines—demand the presence of two speaking actors onstage at one time. Aeschylus, of course, impersonated the faintly characterized Pelasgus; Cleander, with two masks, contributed a brief counterpoint to the lyrical progression as the Herald, and was asked to add little or nothing in the role of Danaus (although that character may have been more functional in the two lost plays of the trilogy).

In other words, Aeschylus did not add the second actor, as we might suppose, to serve as an antagonist to the first, to turn tragedy into a conflict between them. Since his plays exhibit a hero alone with his fate, a solitary man playing out an inner drama of his own soul, Aeschylus had no need for such personal relationships or clashes. He added the second actor in order to make his dramas less static, in order to make the meager plot "move longitudinally, in action, as well as vertically, in tension." A second actor came in with fresh news—as Darius does, as the Spy does in the *Septem* (*Seven Against Thebes*) (467 B.C.)—or he presented different facets of the situation to the hero—as do Oceanus and Io in *Prometheus* (c. 460).[7] A second actor also intensified the atmosphere or the emotion of a situation—as Atossa does when she listens to the Messenger's recital of the death of her son Xerxes. That for some time was all that Cleander and other second actors were required to do onstage.

Aeschylus needed only small help, for instance, when he wrote and acted the earliest tragedy of character, *Seven Against Thebes*. The hero, Eteocles, stands out from "the person" of the chorus (led by Telestes, an artist who could by his dancing make the audience see things that were being done) as the first clearly studied individual character in dramatic literature. He is a brave and wise commander, a man of profound moral insight who, because of the Curse of the House of Laius, hates his brother and thus proceeds to lose wisdom and self-control. The characterization is highly conventional, as conventionalized as the diction, the style, the mask, the plot, and the ceremony. And it is almost single-dimensioned. Aeschylus doesn't depict the attitude of Eteocles toward the Spy, or show us "how he behaves to his wife, or whether he has one." The lifelike aspects of his nature contribute nothing to his downfall. "The Greeks left it to the modern masters of characterization to exhaust the possibilities of the insignificant." [8] And, oddly enough to us nowadays, the playwright never lets Eteocles confront his enemy brother. There's no interplay or conflict between them, no mention even of Polyneices until the tragic climax. Eteocles, in short, simply recites his own destiny.

Nevertheless, Cleander or any other assistant actor to Aeschylus, by

reciting anywhere from two to four different "helper" characters per play—
Danaus and the Herald in *The Suppliants*, Darius and the Messenger in *The
Persians*, Oceanus, Io, Hermes, and maybe Crates in *Prometheus*, a male
Scout and a female Ismene in *Seven Against Thebes*—and three times that
many different characters in a day's trilogy (four times that for a tetralogy)
—must at least have become vocally proficient, and may have tackled the
rudiments of impersonation.

III

As far as we know, not until seventy-five years after the "invention" by
Thespis, and nearly twenty-five years after the introduction of the second
player, did acting advance to the tension and revelation attendant upon character clashing with character. In the *Oresteia* (458 B.C.) of Aeschylus two
actors as individualized persons first meet onstage. When this fourteen-
character trilogy was produced—with its chorus and its mutes, or "extras,"
such as Hermes, a Bodyguard, a Herald, Attendants, Citizens, and Jurymen—
the profession of acting must have truly come into its own. Then surely the
actors sensed that their peculiar province was to be the oral and visual communication of human beings in action and reaction against human beings
per se, or against human beings who personified larger forces, such as, Fate,
Evil, Pride, Authority, and so on.

The *Oresteia*, however, requires not two but three actors. Tradition has
it that Sophocles (497–405 B.C.) brought about the innovation of three actors
in perhaps 471, or at least by 468 B.C., shortly after he entered the playwriting
contests and defeated Aeschylus. Yet it is possible that "Thespis, and after
him Aeschylus, in acting their main roles were still called *tragydos*, and the
first and second *hypokritēs*, or 'answerers,' were added by Aeschylus, making
in all three actors. When Sophocles, whose voice was weak, turned over his
role to one of the *hypokritēs* he then needed to add a third, but did not
increase the number of 'actors' as we use the word." [9]

For the *Oresteia*, Aeschylus used two additional actors, Cleander and
probably Mynniscus. In *Agamemnon*, in which roughly half of the verses, or
lines, are assigned to the characters and half to the chorus, the playwright
undoubtedly acted the 330 lines of Clytemnestra; Cleander may have acted
the Herald with his 130 lines and Cassandra with her 180 for a total of 310;
leaving Mynniscus possibly to act the 40 lines of the Watchman, the 85 lines
of Agamemnon, and the 65 lines of Aegisthus for a total of 190. In the
Choephori (*The Libation Bearers*), Aeschylus interpreted the 315 lines of
Orestes, Cleander the 180 lines of Electra and the Nurse and Clytemnestra,
while Mynniscus took the 30 lines of the Servant and Pylades and Aegisthus.
In the *Eumenides* (*The Furies*) we can assume that Aeschylus memorized
the 100 lines of Orestes, Cleander the 135 lines of Apollo, and Mynniscus
the 345 lines of Athena, Pythia, and the ghost of Clytemnestra. So, for the

entire trilogy Aeschylus, impersonating two characters, intoned approximately 745 lines; Cleander, impersonating six, 620; while Mynniscus, portraying eight, delivered, 360. And the role of Clytemnestra was divided among the three of them!

In this trilogy Aeschylus increased the actors' complexity of impersonation by adding more variety, more humanity to his characters. Clytemnestra, "at first the calm, subtle, self-possessed queen, scoffing at significant dreams . . . , shifts to the woman fearing dreams, wishing to appease her husband's spirit, but afraid to approach his tomb; she sinks to the level of a human being at bay, pleading with her son for life, and lastly fades into the spirit calling upon the Furies for vengeance." Cassandra, however, isn't quite that complex, or quite that real. She's a symbol. She never exchanges words with Clytemnestra or with Agamemnon; she speaks only when she's alone with the chorus. Cleander in portraying her was asked to accentuate "at the moment of crisis, the ethical and emotional undertone of the play" in a dazzling, almost unendurable burst of lyricism. But as the Herald, Cleander could delineate a person, not merely some news being reported. The character "begins by expressing what he himself feels on his return, and his actual news comes as a parenthesis in his personal remarks. Later, still speaking as an individual, with independent rights in the play, he proceeds quite naturally to tell us what it was like at the war. He lives. . . ." And then as the Nurse, Cleander was asked to interpret "perhaps the most realistic character in the whole of Greek Tragedy." As for Mynniscus, his one enviable assignment was to portray the Watchman, a common soldier, but a living person. Structurally, the character is unnecessary; "but now the third actor is at hand, waiting to be used, and concessions can be made to naturalism." So, the ordinary figure of the Watchman "gives the scale of those who are to follow; he represents the plain Argive citizen whose sufferings are more than once contrasted with the misdeeds of their rulers; he gives, perhaps more vividly than the chorus could, certainly more tersely, an impression of the weariness of the years of waiting. . . ." [10]

But in scenes of confrontation in the *Oresteia* actors undoubtedly found their real challenge and delight. A foreshadowing of later development appears in the scene where Aeschylus as Clytemnestra fences with Mynniscus as Agamemnon, and proves her superiority. Then in the first meeting of Aeschylus as Orestes and Cleander as Electra the playwright begins to develop one of the new possibilities of his art, begins "to do what the greater number of actors in any case suggests, to take a situation in a more naturalistic way and to draw from it what it reasonably contains and not only what the theme imperatively demands." For the first time in our theater "two actors face to face . . . are treated purely as individuals for their own sakes." "Throughout Electra and Orestes are treated purely as persons placed in a certain situation, saying now this, now that, as the course of the dialogue or their inner selves suggest." "Electra is moved throughout by personal feelings—grief for her father, pity for his hateful death, despair at his present way of life. Orestes expresses other ideas. He, the son, thinks of the dishonor to his house; he prays for his father's help that he may expel the usurper and recover his inheritance." [11]

And then in the human, tensely dramatic, and shattering mother and son confrontation between Orestes and Clytemnestra actors brilliantly and irrevocably usurp the stage from the chorus. In a scene such as this a thrilling justification is found for their profession:

ORESTES

My purpose is to kill you over his body.
You thought him bigger than my father while he lived.
Die then and sleep beside him, since he is the man
    you love, and he you should have loved got only your hate.

CLYTEMNESTRA

I raised you when you were little. May I grow old with you?

ORESTES

You killed my father. Would you make your home with me?

CLYTEMNESTRA

Destiny had some part in that, my child.

ORESTES

                                  Why then
destiny has so wrought that this shall be your death.

CLYTEMNESTRA

A mother has her curse, child. Are you not afraid?

ORESTES

No. You bore me and threw me away, to a hard life.

CLYTEMNESTRA

I sent you to a friend's house. This was no throwing away.

ORESTES

I was born of a free father. You sold me.

CLYTEMNESTRA

So? Where then is the price that I received for you?

ORESTES

I could say. It would be indecent to tell you.

CLYTEMNESTRA

Or if you do, tell also your father's vanities.

ORESTES

Blame him not. He suffered while you were sitting here.

CLYTEMNESTRA

It hurts women to be kept from their men, my child.

ORESTES

The man's hard work supports the women who sit at home.

CLYTEMNESTRA

I think, child, that you mean to kill your mother.

ORESTES

                                          No.
It will be you who kill yourself. It will not be I.

CLYTEMNESTRA
> Take care. Your mother's curse, like dogs, will drag you down.

ORESTES
> How shall I escape my father's curse, if I fail here?

CLYTEMNESTRA
> I feel like one who wastes live tears upon a tomb.

ORESTES
> Yes, this is death, your wages for my father's fate.

CLYTEMNESTRA
> You are the snake I gave birth to, and gave the breast.

ORESTES
> Indeed, the terror of your dreams saw things to come clearly. You killed, and it was wrong. Now suffer wrong.

From Richmond Lattimore's translation of Aeschylus' *Oresteia*, in Grene and Lattimore, *The Complete Greek Tragedies*. The University of Chicago Press. Copyright 1953 by the University of Chicago.[12]

This Clytemnestra–Orestes scene isn't too different in essence, in strength of actions and in clash of character, from a great scene for actors which was not to be written for another two thousand years, the scene (III, iv) between Gertrude and Hamlet.

❋ "MEN AS THEY OUGHT TO BE"

The third step in the development of the professional actor dates from between 471 and 405 B.C., the playwriting years of Sophocles, a genius with a profound sympathy for the passions, vagaries, and catastrophes of men, a poet whose vision found in their sufferings a meaning and a serenity. This master-designer of pure tragedies composed more than a hundred of them, winning eighteen first prizes, and never failing to take at least second. His seven works that survive are: *Antigone* (c. 443 B.C.), *Ajax* (c. 440), the *Trachinae* (*The Women of Trachis*) (c. 440), *Oedipus Tyrannus* (*Oedipus the King*) (429), *Electra* (411), *Philoctetes* (409), *Oedipus Coloneus* (*Oedipus at Colonus*) (402, posthumous). He is the one Greek dramatist who holds a secure place in the repertoire of the contemporary theater.

Sophocles' contributions to the new profession were two, exclusive of his possible introduction of the third actor. First, recognizing the unique province and special skills of the players, he divorced acting from playwriting. He surrendered his poet's prerogative of appearing in his own productions, dropped out of the casts, and left impersonation to the professionals who by this time were becoming more numerous and more competent. At first he wrote for particular actors. Tlepolemus and Cleidemides were his favorites; possibly Nicostratus completed one of his earlier trios. In *Antigone*, for example, Tlepolemus probably acted the principal character Creon throughout, Cleidemides the parts of Antigone and the Messenger, and Nicostratus the parts of Ismene, the Guard, Haemon, and Teiresias. In *Electra* the first actor impersonated Electra, the second Orestes and Clytemnestra, and the third the Tutor, Aegisthus, and perhaps Chrysothemis—even characters as widely different as these last two. In *Oedipus the King* the first actor wore the mask of Oedipus, the second the masks of Creon and Jocasta and the Herdsman, and the third the masks of Teiresias, the Priest, and the two Messengers.

The second and salient contribution of Sophocles was his intellectual interest in and search for the true nature of man. At a time when Protagoras (*c.* 480–*c.* 410) was saying that "Man is the measure of all things," Sophocles began intensively to explore human beings. He asked his actors to interpret, with declamation and masks, certain superior persons who discover the truths about themselves. In generally abandoning the trilogy for single plays, he turned tragedy inward upon the actions of the principal *dramatis personae*. Sophocles reportedly said that he "drew men as they ought to be," that they were typical. He tried to write, he explained, "what is most expressive of character." He succeeded. "The ineffaceable impression which Sophocles makes on us today, and his imperishable position in the literature of the world, are both due to his character-drawing." He makes us feel, as he must have made his actors feel, "that his real flesh-and-blood men and women, with their violent passions and tender emotions, proudly heroic but truly human, are like ourselves and yet noble with an incomparable dignity and remoteness." [13]

Sophocles was concerned, for instance, with uncovering the motives and circumstances surrounding the actions of Electra as an individual. She is made to reveal the complicated person she is. The whole play of *Electra*, after the prologue, is a continuing attack on her by persons and events, a cumulative attack calling for an increasingly strong defense on her part. So, in a series of contrasting scenes, Electra clashes with various people, passes through a myriad of emotions, reveals herself; and then, because she does what she does, arrives at her final agony (and consolation). She doesn't suffer because of some *hamartia* (flaw or error)—an essentially Philistine conception, which implies that suffering is punishment for sin—but because in the over-all pattern of the gods suffering teaches wisdom.[14] Electra follows a main action and comes to grief, and harmony, simply because she is the kind of person she is.

Unlike Aeschylus, therefore, "Sophocles uses the greater fluidity of plot which the third actor gave" to exhibit a heroine or a hero from several points of view, to show the chief character in several different situations, to display virtues and to expose weaknesses through his actions and reactions as a member of society. No audience can understand or sympathize with the tragedy of Oedipus unless they know him as a man; and no audience can truly know him until they have "seen how he behaves to a diversity of people and (equally important) how they behave to him." The concern of Oedipus for his people, his courtesy to Creon and Teiresias which quickly passes to suspicion and rage, his attitude toward his wife and his children are by now essential to his characterization. What happens to Oedipus "is the natural result of the weaknesses and the virtues of his character, in combination with other people's. It is a tragic chapter from life. . . ." [15]

To put this another way, Sophocles used the additional characters made possible by the third actor to delineate a more complex, human hero. No longer is the latter instantaneously one-dimensional, complete, and doomed. Now he is slowly revealed as being a highly intricate individual, more balanced, more nearly normal and natural. Now only an unusual, unfortunate combination of circumstances can topple him.

Circumstances, events, happenings. Here again Sophocles improved on Aeschylus by ingeniously using the three actors for the purpose of complicating his situation, his plots. Because he saw tragedy in life as the interworking of character with circumstances, he designed plays so that the various aspects of a character combined with events to lead to disaster. What the hero and others do in a complex, conflicting, surprising, suspenseful arrangement of scenes becomes the spine of drama. *Philoctetes* and *Oedipus the King* are almost perfect examples in Greek tragedy of the interaction of events and character.

In short, Sophocles decisively changed drama from a mostly poetic, musical demonstration of emotion to a resemblance in noticeable degree of the moving actions of life. As a result, the chorus of fifteen gradually lost its lyric, but nonrealistic, function. Actors alone were needed to reveal the interlocking deeds and emotions of men.

II

Actors Tlepolemus, Cleidemides, and Nicostratus were challenged by the striking triangle scenes Sophocles devised. For instance, in *Antigone*, in the scene between Creon, the Watchman, and Antigone, the dramatic power arises from the fact that "each of the three characters has his private preoccupation, his own attitude to the central fact. Creon is faced with the incredible news that the rebel is no political agent but his own niece; Antigone, the deed now done, stands apart, out of touch with the scene, rapt in her almost mystic confidence; the Watchman, finding in the situation his own vindication and escape, is completely at his ease, struck with the wonderfully irrelevant idea that a man should deny nothing. . . ." In *Oedipus the King* the progress "of Jocasta from hope, through confidence, to frozen horror, and that of Oedipus from terror to sublime resolution and assurance, the two connected by the commonplace cheerfulness of the Corinthian (who must be extremely puzzled by the tremendous effects his simple message is creating) . . . makes as fine a combination of cross-rhythms as can well be imagined." Finally, there is the three-actor scene in *Electra* between Clytemnestra, Electra, and the Tutor. This "long and harsh wrangle between mother and daughter culminates in Clytemnestra's horrible prayer to the statue of Apollo, and immediately, as if in answer to that prayer, the Paedagogus comes in with his statement of Orestes' death," a magnificent piece of pretense, of bravura. And "as we listen to it, watching the grimness behind it, observing its effect on the two women, who, fresh from their quarrel, hang on every word, so that it comes to us through their minds, amplified—'undramatic' is the last thing we should call it." [16] And if we were the professional actors assigned such a scene, studying it, rehearsing it, performing it—we could not fail to know that this is the sort of material, the stuff of life at high pitch, for which we had been waiting.

Scenes such as these, as penetrating H. D. F. Kitto points out, are "the climax of Sophocles' manipulation of the three actors. All three have now, as it were, been disengaged from the background and stand out as free sculpture; each has, not only his own sharply drawn character, but also his own positive contribution to make to the drama of the scene; and they move so freely that from an isolated scene it might well be impossible to tell which was first, second or third, none being merely a makeweight or a foil to the other two." [17]

✺ COMEDIANS

The fourth step in the development of the profession of acting centers on comedy, on the tardy comedians. As a form of theater comedy originated and was developed apart from tragedy. So separate were the two forms that no performer in both tragic and comic roles is known until Praxiteles who appeared at Delphi in 106 B.C. as a comedian, and nine years later as a tragedian.

The evolution of comedy (etymologically a "comus-song") is as complex as it is obscure. There is some agreement, however, on three conjectures. First, the histrionic element probably was derived from vaudeville sketches publicly performed by amateurs in the sixth century B.C., and surely earlier, at Megara (the nearest Dorian city to Attica), in Sparta, Corinth, Sicily, and doubtless wherever else people congregated for merrymaking. In league with acrobats, dancers, jugglers, musicians, conjurors, and singers, amateur peasant players (like Ook and his leader) instinctively concocted and acted primitive skits which, unfettered by ritual or choruses, burlesqued mythological personages and poked ribald fun at life as they knew it. They improvised sketches, for example, in which Heracles battled a giant or tried to outwit some pygmies, in which the gossip of female temple worshippers was satirized, in which the pretentious jargon of a foreign doctor was obscenely exposed. Second, the choral element in comedy was derived from the comus, a term that denotes both a phallic revel and the band of men disguised as birds, frogs, cocks, horses, ostriches, dolphins, and the like who participated in it. The revel, part of a fertility rite, was both religious and gross; and the masqueraders as an undifferentiated mob usually formed a procession and marched from house to house improvising invectives, lampoons, and scurrilous jests. Third, and in due time, the popular farces and the comus were interspersed, with the result that individual performers were for a while submerged in the crowd. Susarian, now only another name, may have first effected this combination. Anyway, he is credited with transforming the comic choral processions into stationary but still largely improvised performances at Icaria, later bringing them to Athens where they seem to have been presented by volunteer revelers at some of the minor festivals about 560 B.C., or even by 570, ten years before Thespis arrived there with his tragedies.

Comedies, however, weren't truly recognized by the city–state until nearly fifty years after tragedies had been honored. Although they may have been added to the festival called the City Dionysia by 501 B.C., they weren't officially supported until 486 B.C. At that late time a certain Chionides won the playwriting victory in comedy. Before then the form was not taken seriously, was faintly ostracized, or at least sluffed off, as being inconsequential because of its rowdy realism. It was perhaps too close to life to be called art. But apparently by 486 B.C. a leavening ingredient—fantasy—had been added to the coarse, stinging, personal, and topical jibes of comedy. When Magnes, a successful contemporary of Chionides, used it in his comedies he gained for them a kind of respectability.

But the first comic actors weren't officially recognized for another thirty years, or about eighty years after the debut of Thespis—when Aeschylus had died, when Sophocles was nearly sixty and hadn't yet written any of his extant tragedies, and when Euripides was just beginning to compete as a playwright. The appearance of genuine professional comic actors onstage dates, if scholars are lenient, from c. 455 B.C., the time of the "old toper" playwright Cratinus. Instead of composing comedies to be performed by an undifferentiated crowd, Cratinus ended the confusion and set the number of actors at three. In short, he copied tragedies by adding to the nondescript chorus and its leaders three performers who could impersonate imaginary characters. Who these first comic actors were, in their tight-fitting and grossly padded dresses cut short so as to display a phallus, isn't certain. Cratinus himself may have been one of them; Crates was perhaps another; someone like Pherecrates may have been a third.

Next, Crates, turned playwright, subordinated the sections of his comedies to a connecting or central idea. He arranged the episodic, unrelated comic "turns" and set speeches of his predecessors into a thin play, a plot dipped in fantasy and peopled with unreal characters. Whether Crates was influenced by the example of the Sicilian Epicharmus who had added slight plots to his nonchoral mimes at Syracuse from 485 to 478 B.C. doesn't greatly matter. At least in Athens, Crates tied together the disconnected invectives and comic debates, the buffoonery and obscene jests, around a theme and illustrated it with definite and functioning characters. For example, his *Beasts* relates a simple fantasy about two people who dream of a time when they'll no longer need slaves but will be served by animals or even by utensils endowed with human intelligence. The comic actors at last had "something to play."

❀ ACTORS' CONTESTS

The fifth step in the chronological development of the profession of acting dates from the addition of competitions between actors to the competitions between playwrights at the festivals in Athens. Contests for tragic actors were inaugurated at the City Dionysia eighty-five years after tragedies had been officially recognized, and a few years before the production of Sophocles' *Antigone*, in 449 B.C. Heracleides was the first victor. These contests continued until at least the end of the third century B.C. At the less important Lenaia festival, contests for actors in tragedy were introduced c. 432, and also continued to be held until the end of the third century. And although contests for comic actors were, oddly enough, a feature of this festival as early as c. 442–440 B.C., about fifteen years after Cratinus had separated his three comedians from the crowd, they weren't included at the City Dionysia until more than a hundred years later, somewhere between 329 and 312 B.C., a hundred and sixty-five years after comedies had been officially recognized there. These comic actor competitions continued to be held until between 150 and 120 B.C.

Not enough is known about any of the competitions. For instance, why did contests for comic actors antedate those for tragic actors at the Lenaia? And why were they so tardily added at the City Dionysia? On what basis were the comic and tragic actors judged, and by whom? What was the prize? Was an honorarium awarded the victor in addition to the ivy crown? No definite answers are available. The few certainties seem to be that the prize didn't necessarily go to an actor in the winning play; that only a first actor, the protagonist—not the second or third—could win the prize; that the winner was automatically entitled to return as one of the three competitors in the following year; and finally, that "the art of delivery made its way" at least into the art of tragedy. "The art of delivery has to do with the voice: with the right management of it to express each several emotion—as when to use a loud voice, when a soft, and when the intermediate; with the mode of using pitch—high, low, and intermediate; and with the rhythms to be used in each particular case. These are, in fact, the three things that receive attention: volume, modulation of pitch, and rhythm. And it is contestants who look after these points that commonly win the prizes. . . ." [18]

So, via the contests, the chief actors of the period definitely began to compete with the playwrights for eminence. Now, of course, only their names are barely discernable in various inscriptions; but once they were regarded by audiences as theater contributors of great skill. In fact, by the time these histrionic contests were instituted some of the leading players had become so artful, or at least so popular, that the state decided it was no longer fair to allow the playwrights, in accordance with custom, to select their casts. By 449 B.C. the first actors for the tragedies and comedies to be staged at the competitions were chosen and paid by the government, and then allocated *by lot* to the competing dramatists. (Each first actor probably hired his own subordinates, the second actor, or deuteragonist, and the third actor, or tritagonist.) Under this new system, however, the actors assigned to each author continued to appear in all three or four of his plays.

Thus the state, by partly supervising the histrionic element of the festivals, by fostering contests in acting, and by centering attention upon excellence in delivery, officially recognized and enhanced the importance of the profession.

❋ EURIPIDES

"Remove Euripides" (*c.* 485–406 B.C.), it's said, "and the modern theater ceases to exist." The sixth step in the development of acting dates from the years when that unorthodox but brilliant thinker and "poet of the age of enlightenment" was a top-contending dramatist. He began to write at eighteen, entered the city contests in 455 when he was about thirty, one year after the death of Aeschylus, won his first victory in 441, the time of *Antigone*, and in all wrote some ninety plays, of which nineteen survive. The best of his tragedies are the early *Medea* (431 B.C.), in which the first actor apparently played the title role, the second Jason and the Nurse, the third Creon, Aegeus, the Tutor, and the Messenger; the also early *Hippolytus* (428 B.C.), in which the first actor impersonated the title role, the second Phaedra, Aphrodite, and Theseus, and the third Artemis, the Nurse, a Servant, and a Messenger; and his next to last composition, the stunning, puzzling *Bacchae* (405 B.C.), in which the first actor appeared as Dionysus and Teiresias, the second as Pentheus and Agave, and the third as Cadmus, the Servant, and the Messenger. In most of his other plays—and they are diversified—Euripides moved from tragedies to nontragedies. With much independence and influence he forsook the austere, lofty revelations of Aeschylus and the heroic, harmonious dooms of Sophocles and popularly turned his stories into pathos-loaded tragicomedies, psychological studies, and melodramas. He changed "a church into a cinema . . . but it is very good cinema." [19] Principally for his plays the Greeks and the Romans later built their marble theaters. Moreover, since Euripides created his chief characters not as they were supposed to function in the cosmic order of things, or as they served a myth, or as they illustrated a moral, but as he saw them with his skepticism and his vivid sense of theater, he at least tacitly made three new demands on Greek actors, demands which, after much refining, still hold for actors today.

II

First, Euripides seemed to suggest to his professional players, "Be more human." He asked them to be more lifelike, more real (within conventionalized bounds, to be sure) than actors had been in other plays. He offered them opportunities to find and convey more actuality. He assigned them the very human—even modern—task of creating divided souls, of playing "the psyche caught in the categories its reason invents" and "responding with unmitigated sharpness to the feelings of the moment." [20]

Because Euripides "drew men as they are" and brought, according to Aristophanes, "real life to the stage, men and women, just like those out there in the audience," the professional performers in his plays surely began to do something new: to shape some of their own experiences into the making of their characters. With *Medea*, among other works, Euripides marks the beginning of domestic drama. When the actor who impersonated Medea philosophized on the social position of women, when he complained against the custom that made them surrender in marriage to strange men and pay rich doweries for the privilege, or when he declared that bearing children is more dangerous than fighting battles, he was echoing words he might have heard at home the day before yesterday. And some of the most profound and wounding things said by both Medea in her boundless passion and by Jason in his boundless egotism might almost be labeled "Any wife to any husband," or "Any husband to any wife." Then with *Hippolytus*, and other plays, Euripides marks, in a sense, the beginning of the modern psychological play. Hippolytus, with his ostentatious purity, is so neurotic "he's a very monk for continence!" And "Phaedra is a normal, rather conventional woman metamorphosed into a neurotic sadist. She can set aside the moral restraints of the society in which she lives and try to seduce her step-son. When she fails, she plans his murder and makes her suicide the guaranty of his guilt." Her love "is a frenzy of madness, and, when it strikes, the victim is not accountable in terms of her former personality." [21]

In his nontragedies, however, Euripides most successfully influenced actors to "Be more human." The well-made *Alcestis* (438 B.C.), with its happy ending, is the most popular of the tragi-comedies; *Iphigenia in Tauris* (414 B.C.) is a romantic drama; *Electra* (413 B.C.)—so different in every way from the same story as manipulated by Aeschylus and by Sophocles—is the best-known melodrama; and *Helen* (412 B.C.) might be termed a high comedy. The characters in these "new" plays were emphatically more lifelike than those who heretofore had trod the stage. For example, in *Alcestis* "Admetus is drawn to the life, without mercy." In his bumbling, cowardly refusal to die as he ought instead of letting his wife die for him, this monarch "is depicted as a thoroughly respectable, convention-loving middle-class citizen. To Alcestis he makes all the proper promises: he will look after the children, he will not marry again, gone forever are the merry drinking-parties. . . . He is desperately anxious lest she should decide not to carry the business through to the bitter end, yet he is desperately afraid to be left alone. He is mightily affronted by his father, Pheres, who counsels him sarcastically to 'woo many women, so that more may die for you,' yet there is more than a trifle of shame-facedness in his talking about the whole matter with Heracles." And Electra, dressed in rags, and attending to her household chores, nags her peasant (nominal) husband, is a bit ashamed to invite strangers into her humble home, and in the end is sentimentally betrothed to Pylades! *Ion* (*c.* 412) begins "with an extended movement drawing most of its interest from sheer naturalism." Ion goes about his morning tasks, sweeps the temple steps, and chats believably until the audience can respond, "How very lifelike!" In *Orestes* (408 B.C.), the noble hero Menelaus is exposed as being human enough to fear risking the loss of his newly won happiness with Helen, his political ambitions, and his neck by saving his nephew from a threatened lynching. And in *Iphigenia in Aulis* (406 B.C.) the heart of all women is revealed in Clytemnestra's aria:

> My father pitied you, his suppliant,
> Gave me to you for wife. And a true wife I was,
> Yes, chaste and true, and cared well for your home.
> Such wives are not so common!—
> Three girls I bore you and a son, and now
> You rob me of the first! Your reason, pray,
> If men should ask it? Oh, I'll answer that,—
> To win back Helen! Your own child for a wanton,
> Your dearest for a foe! A proper bargain! . . .
> What will my heart be like, think you, at home,
> When I look on my daughter's empty chair,
> And empty room, sitting there all alone
> Companioned by my tears, still muttering,
> "Your father killed you, child, killed you himself!"
> What will your wages be when you come back?
> We who are left, we shall not want much urging
> To greet you with the welcome you deserve!
> O, by the gods, drive me not thus to sin,
> Nor sin yourself!
> If once you killed your child, how could you pray?
> What good thing ask for? Rather for defeat,
> Disgrace, and exile! Nor could I pray for you:
> We make fools of the gods if we suppose
> They can love murderers. If you come home,
> Will you dare kiss your girls? Or they dare come,
> That you may choose another for the knife?
> Have you once thought of this? Are you a man?
> Or nothing but a sceptre and a sword?
> You should have gone among the Greeks and said,
> "You wish to sail for Troy? Good, then draw lots
> And see whose child must die." That had been fair;
> Or Menelaus should have slain his own,—
> Hermione for Helen. But I, the chaste,
> I must be robbed, and she come home in triumph
> To find her daughter! Answer, if am I wrong!

From F. M. Stawell's translation of Euripides' *Iphigenia in Aulis,* in Allardyce Nicoll, *World Drama* (New York: Harcourt, Brace & World, 1950) by permission of G. Bell & Sons, Ltd.[22]

Thus, more frequently than his predecessors, and particularly in the non-tragic but pathetic central roles, Euripides indirectly encouraged his actors to be more human by building their interpretations, within formal limits, upon their own personal experience (and also encouraged his audiences to respond on the basis of theirs).

III

From what we can deduce, however, Euripides did not consider the attempt to "Be more human" as the end-all criterion of acting. It wasn't the inviolable rule that "Be natural" so often is today. He rightly sensed that acting could be, ought to be, more than merely lifelike. In all his plays he probably advised his actors, second, to "Play the playwright." In fact, they could hardly have missed his qualities of mind, his attitudes toward experience. Euripides brought onstage, in addition to a lovely lyricism, a "new middle-class tone, cold, shrewd, pragmatic, rationalist, skeptical, moralistic, and frankly sentimental." He realistically probed into the inner recesses of people and into regions of thought where ordinary citizens cared not or dared not to venture. He exposed the gods, ridiculed or condemned the heroes of legend, expressed advanced views in philosophy and sociology. He put into the mouths of his characters such unorthodox statements as: "Zeus, be thou nature's law or the mind of men . . . [The Troades, or The Trojan Women (415 B.C.), line 884], "no mortal man is free: he is the slave of money or fate, or else the mob, which rules the state, or the bonds of law keep him from living as he wishes" [Hecuba (c. 425 B.C.), line 164], and "you cities, who could remedy your troubles by reasoning, prefer to settle matters by slaughter" [The Suppliant Women (c. 421 B.C.), line 755]. In short, he taught his audiences to "think aright on things that really matter." [23]

Euripides, it appears, was more interested in the *idea* behind his characters, in the things he wanted to say, than in his characters solely as human beings. His actors must have been well aware that frequently he slighted, oversimplified, overdrew his people—even made them glaringly inconsistent—so that the idea could be more persuasively expressed.

Moreover, at a time when rhetoric was highly fashionable, he regularly turned his stage into a lecture or debating platform and his characters into purveyors of ideas, into more or less abstract orators and arguers. Sometimes, of course, the long descriptive or narrative passages, the philosophical dissertations, the wordy duels, the cascading forensics are necessary to a character or characters for the making of a thematic point or emotion. They are meant to express in vivid dramatic detail the subjective attitude of this or that character to the world-order. But in too many of his plays the verbal displays are more necessary to Euripides than to a character, and at the expense of the character. They are substitutes for action, filler-stuff, spoutings almost for the sake of spouting. They frankly transformed actors into mouth-pieces and acting into public speaking, into declamation.

Yet the indirect advice to "Play the playwright's idea" was perceptive and imperative. Euripides, we can surmise, saw clearly the essential point or purpose of acting a character. He saw it so clearly he overemphasized it.

IV

And then, third, Euripides must have confused his actors. (Or maybe he didn't!) At any rate, all the while he was asking them to be more human, and more rhetorically expressive of his ideas, he also unabashedly urged them to "Use the theater as theater." For no doubt about it, he was a playwright always aware of his medium. He exploited the resources of the art to the fullest and for their own sakes. He contrived all things cunningly; he over-crowded his plots with bold incidents; he manipulated sensational stage-pieces by stringing together whatever contrasts, surprises, or shocks would grab and hold the attention of the spectators. And, again, he had no qualms about sacrificing the true depiction of character for theatrical effect. Yes, the people in his plays ought to be human; and yes, they ought persuasively to express his ideas; but, above all else, they had to be striking. More often than not his characters serve primarily, almost exclusively, a thrilling theatrical incident. Andromache's self-sacrifice in the play with that title is "monstrous . . . designed . . . to make our blood boil." In the *Herakleidoe* (*Heracles*) (*c.* 421 B.C.) the hero in a rousing mad scene, slays his wife, his children, and very nearly his father; and then, when the fit passes, contemplates with horror what he has done. Orestes with his sword at the breast of Hermione threatens to slay her before the eyes of her father. Agave opens the bundle she carries and discovers it's the head of her son whom she's unwittingly killed. And the scenes in *The Trojan Women* when the child is torn from his mother and then returned to her dead are possibly "the most absolutely heart-rending scenes in all the tragic literature of the world." In *Hecuba* the vengeful Queen entices Polymnestor within the tent in order to put out his eyes—he crawls out on all fours. In *Medea* the Messenger's speech describing the death of the children "is sheer Grand Guignol." Of course, it can be claimed that these striking scenes, these horrors, are "meant to point to one overriding idea, the suffering which the human race inflicts upon itself through its follies and wickedness." [24] Nonetheless, they are theatrical, blatantly theatrical.

Consequently, Euripides by making several new demands upon the professional actors pulled them simultaneously in two opposite directions: he placed them forcefully between the polarities of being more human—or more theatrical. But no final harm in that. That's as it should be. How to make a character in a play both human *and* theatrical for the communication of the author's idea is every actor's basic and constant problem. We can believe that Euripides, in a way, set it up.

✳ THE COMICS MATURE

Near the end of the fifth century B.C. the form of comedy was readied for Aristophanes (c. 450–c. 380), the riotously imaginative first great comic playwright, the creator of roistering satires and caricatures, who won his first victory in 427 B.C., two years after the production of *Oedipus the King* and one year after *Hippolytus*. The earliest of his extant works, *The Acharnians* (425 B.C.), "is political lampoonery transformed into a brilliant fantasy, blending the usual coarse and vivid burlesque with the witty symbolism of an ambitious political Utopia, and enriching it by gay parodies of Euripidean tragedy." [25] That in essence is typical of the Old Comedy as perfected into literature by Aristophanes. Of his forty plays ten others survive, notably the slapstick *The Wasps* (422 B.C.), the joyous and dream-like *The Birds* (414 B.C.), the sexy, feminist, anti-war *Lysistrata* (411 B.C.), and a stinging literary satire, *The Frogs* (405 B.C.).

For these "musical" comedies with their choruses of twenty-four, Aristophanes required the services of four actors (and sometimes five) exclusive of "extras." *The Acharnians*, for example, contains one scene (lines 56–125) in which first four and then five speaking actors are onstage at one time. *The Wasps* couldn't have been performed without four actors. *The Birds* might have been staged by three actors, but the large number of roles would be more advantageously distributed among a cast of four. In *Lysistrata* four characters converse together (lines 77–253). And *The Frogs* needs one actor for Dionysus, a second for Xanthias and Aeschylus, a third for Heracles, Charon, Aeacus, the Maidservant, the Innkeeper, and Euripides, and a fourth for the small roles of the Corpse, Plathane, and Pluto.

In impersonating the characters of Aristophanes the professional comedians came of age. Although they enlivened only broad and typical and quick cartoons, they did so by using all the oral and pantomimic tricks, all the "business" and gusto and rhythms, necessary to convulse audiences. They demonstrated that comic acting, like tragic acting, depends in large measure on certain skills acquired by the performer. Not so much by being human, but by being *theatrically* expressive in comedy after comedy that criticized not only individuals, not only social foibles, but the government itself, the comic actors at last caught up with the tragic actors. They gained attention and eminence.

II

But not until sixty years after the death of Aristophanes, when Athens was under Macedonian rule (and censorship?), and the playwrights were compelled possibly to forsake invective for sentiment, fantasy for the familiar, and civic interests for the domestic, were comic actors given a chance to be more or less human onstage. Then New Comedy, poking fun at mere everyday behavior, presented them with recognizable characters they would continue to interpret, with various halts and modifications, from then on.

Among a horde of later dramatists Menander (c. 342–292 B.C.), "father of modern comedy," but unknown to Aristotle, most successfully softened the sting of satire into warmer, easier depictions of the commonplace. Influenced by Euripides and Theophrastus (c. 372–c. 287 B.C.), of whose *Characters* "no one interested in humanity ought to remain in ignorance ten minutes longer," [26] he wrote more than one hundred verse comedies (or dramas). One complete example of his work—*Dyskolos* (*The Bad-Tempered Man*) (317 B.C.)—plus considerable portions of four other scripts and fragments of a fifth, survive. They are, in a way, agitated group portraits of the ordinary people of Athens: angry fathers and gallivanting sons, young lovers, captains, cooks, and musicians, intriguing slaves, long-lost relatives, rakes and gossips and parasites, husbands, wives, and courtesans.

For the actors, who wore costumes of the day and masks that approximated stylized make-up, "Each character had its stamp and was supplied with complex motives: slaves, as well as masters, were given distinct personalities; and within the limits of the romantic story . . . people behaved with a plausibility which had not hitherto concerned the writers of comedy." [27]

❊ ACTORS' GUILDS

The seventh and final step before the Christian era in the growth of the new profession was the rather late organization of dramatic and musical performers into guilds, at Athens and elsewhere in the crumbling Macedonian empire. This is now dated about 277 B.C., nearly two hundred and sixty years, or more than three lifetimes, after the "invention" of the first actor. By that precarious, disintegrating time the leading performers were impelled to band together in order to protect their profession and their special interests. Dramatic and musical contests were no longer confined to festivals at Athens. New ones had been instituted and new theaters had been built everywhere throughout Alexander's world. To them the actors traveled to earn a livelihood. Some organization was therefore needed to handle the "bookings" and other business details. So, together with rhapsodists or reciters, chorus singers, trainers of choruses, solo instrumentalists and accompanists, costumers, and occasionally some epic and dramatic poets, the leading and secondary actors of tragedy and comedy formed a species of union called "The Craftsmen or Artists of Dionysus." In addition to managing the theater's practical matters, the guild enjoyed "monthly feasts, celebrations of the birthdays of princes and benefactors, common dinners, and wine-parties, . . . [and] took a conspicuous part in the public sacrifices of sanctuaries or towns, and might march in processions clad in purple and gold." [28] By 227 B.C. three different guilds—at Athens, Delphi, and Teos—often disputed as they divided the Hellenic world between them. (By A.D. 43 the organization of performers was virtually worldwide.)

II

This ascendancy of actors had been inevitable since the last half of the fourth century B.C. At about that time the term *hypokritēs* fell into disuse and actors began to call themselves "artists" or "artists of Dionysus." (Or as Aristotle put it, "Someone calls actors 'parasites of Bacchus'; they call themselves 'artists.'") And the term "to act" a play or a particular role became current. Such and such a play was, for instance, acted by Polus, or Theodorus, or Andronicus. So important, and skilled, did the leading performers become that the city officials decided it was unfair to continue assigning to one playwright even by lot the potentially best actor for all his plays in a contest. Therefore they changed the system. "Each of the protagonists in turn now acted one of the three tragedies of each poet, the histrionic talent at the disposal of each dramatist being thus made exactly the same. For example at the City Dionysia of 341 B.C., Astydamas was the victorious playwright; his *Achilles* was played by Thettalus, his *Athamas* by Neoptolemus, and his *Antigone* by Athenodorus. The same actors likewise presented the three tragedies of Evarstus and those of a third dramatist"—three leading roles apiece in one day! "On this occasion Neoptolemus won; a year later, under similar conditions, he was defeated by Thettalus." In comedy also, but later, the same actor sometimes served at least two poets at the contests.[29]

Aristotle noticed that in his time, 384–322 B.C., "the performers now count for more than the authors." He was right. An age of famous actors had succeeded an age of great playwrights. *Item:* Although no dependable evidence of theater payments has yet been dug up, it seems at times that the poets or composers of plays "came off worse than the performers." *Item:* Instead of appearing in only new works, leading actors, in order to enhance their reputations, revived older plays as vehicles for displaying their special talents. For example, the renowned actor Neoptolemus produced an *Iphigenia* of Euripides, and also his *Orestes*. Theodorus revived *Hecuba*; Polus revived at least three tragedies by Sophocles. *Item:* The complaint was made that "the performers suppose that unless they throw in something of their own, the audience will not understand what is meant, and hence they indulge in all sorts of bodily motions. . . ." *Item:* In order to put the actors in their proper place and to check their new-found habit of tampering with an author's text, Lycurgus, in charge of finances at Athens from 338 to 326 B.C., ordered prepared and preserved state copies of the old plays from which the actors weren't permitted to deviate; and a certain Lycon was fined ten talents for having interpolated one line in a comedy.[30]

In the fourth and third centuries B.C., the actors, not the plays, counted most. It didn't matter much to the populace if philosopher Plato, distrusting art and pleasure, and doubly distrusting any democratic pleasure, had earlier denounced acting as a kind of rhetoric addressed to women and men, slaves and free citizens, without distinction, and therefore had excluded playwrights and actors from his ideal republic. It didn't matter if both he and Aristotle had objected to the fact that the actors too often for comfort lowered themselves to the level of the ignorant portion of their audiences. It didn't matter if Aristotle wondered why it was that the Artists of Dionysus were generally men of bad character—although he may have been referring only to the lower ranks of the profession—and thought the reason was due to the vicissitudes of their fortunes and the rapid alternation between luxury and poverty, and partly to the fact that their professional duties left them no time for general culture. None of those things mattered. "The flattery of successful actors and instrumentalists in the imperial age seems to have reached the same height of absurdity as that of film-stars in the present day." The chief actors, by all accounts, garnered large incomes and held positions of honor and distinction in the community. They traveled from deme to deme in Attica, toured the Greek world, and visited the courts of Macedonian kings. They were granted immunity from hostile action, and possibly immunity from military or naval service. Aristodemus, a tragic actor, was on two occasions sent as ambassador to Macedon by the Athenians, and was largely instrumental in negotiating the peace.[31]

✤ GREEK ACTING

What, with a minimum of guesswork, can we deduce about serious Greek acting at its prime, about acting intended to appeal to crowds of people at festival times, from 17,000 to 20,000 of them, gathered together outdoors in the warmth of the sun or the chill of a breeze in an intense religious and communal mood? Well, it's easy to answer that originally the play was the thing, that the actors must have merely orated or recited it to the audience. They knew that a comedy as well as a tragedy "can produce its effect"—certainly its essential or characteristic effect—"when it is read." And the best of their serious interpretations, though oratorical, may have been "human and humanly appealing, simple, direct." [32] The comics, on the other hand, added to their scripts a personal liveliness, all sorts of vocal tricks, and some amusing, recognizably human pantomine and "stage business."

But to say only that about Greek acting isn't to say enough. We yearn for more specifics. Unfortunately, sources for those specifics are few. Lost are the several handbooks which may have touched on the subject of acting, such as the treatise on the delivery of poetry by Glaucon of Teos and the *Rules of Passion* by Thrasymachus (*c.* 480 B.C.); and lost is the seventeen-book *Theatriké Historia* compiled by the King of Mauretania, Juba II (d. *c.* A.D. 20) which undoubtedly contained material about Attic actors. Several early books on rhetoric, such as *De Elocutione Liber* by Demetrius Phalerus (*c.* 354–*c.* 283 B.C.), can be consulted; but the main facts and suppositions about ancient acting can be snipped and pasted together principally from four Greek sources: the *Ion* (*c.* 390 B.C.) of Plato, the *Poetics* and the *Rhetoric* of Aristotle (both written between 335–322 B.C.), and the battered encyclopedic *Onomastikon* of Julius Pollus (fl. A.D. 180). Aristotle, born more than twenty years after the deaths of Sophocles and Euripides and just preceding the death of Aristophanes, supplies most of the telling information. The *Poetics*, designed to furnish instructions for writing a play and an epic poem, "formulates once for all the great first principles of dramatic art." The *Rhetoric*, "one of the world's best and wisest books," and "the most helpful book extant . . . for speaking of every kind," is a practical psychology, "a searching study of the audience," "a popular treatise on the interests of men in groups and as individuals." It's also an "account of the emotions, the memory, the imagination in hope and fear, and the will." Specifically for actors it "probably deals more systematically with the means of arousing emotion in the audience than did any of its predecessors." Moreover, it examines the *ethos* of a character, his habit of choice, his disposition to do one thing, to refrain from doing another.[33]

II

The first item we encounter in the search for specifics about Greek acting is the assumption that even in those days it had potentialities—at least in tragedy—for being a craft, a science, an art. Socrates, for instance, believed that "If you are endowed by nature with a genius for speaking"—or, we can say, acting—"you will be a distinguished speaker"—or actor—"if you add thereto science and practice; but in whichever of these three requisites you are wanting, you will by so much fall short of perfection." [34]

Plato, on the other hand, with great influence maintained that reciters of poems, or actors, understand their authors and are moved to say words in the way they do not by inquiry and study, or science, and not by practice, but because they are carried out of themselves and seem to be among the persons and places of which they are speaking; in short, because they are inspired or possessed. And inspiration to Plato was a recollection of *a priori* knowledge. It couldn't be learned.[35]

Today, of course, we're disinclined to believe that inspiration descends divinely from heaven to actors. We may agree with Tyrone Guthrie that in acting "the intuitive idea is the 'alpha-plus' idea, whereas the thought-out idea is always 'beta-plus' "; but if we do, we define inspiration differently. We say that inspiration is "the sudden revealing of some possession of the mind, hidden for a time and fermented or ripened in its hiding place, suddenly upsurging and ready for immediate use." And what suddenly opens "some trap door into a subliminal area of the mind . . . may be one of several things—either special pressures from within or demands from without." The "experienced artist, the so-called professional, has mastered tricks and devices for getting it open, and so brings his subconscious mind into double harness with the rest of his cranial equipment." Or, as Stanislavski previously put it, "our art teaches us first of all to create consciously and rightly, because that will best prepare the way for the blossoming of the subconscious, which is inspiration. The more you have of conscious creative moments in your role the more chance you will have of a flow of inspiration." [36]

Aristotle borrowed something from Socrates and something from Plato in formulating his attitude toward acting as an art. At first he appears to agree with Plato by declaring that "The capacity for acting is, indeed, a natural gift, and hardly within the province of art, save in respect to the diction." But by adding "save in respect to the diction," he agrees with Socrates and those who hold that some method of procedure and much practice are necessary to the actor for the improvement of his natural talent. To Aristotle diction meant, among other things, the "modes of Spoken Utterance, including such matters as the difference between a command and a prayer, a simple statement and a threat, a question and an answer, and so forth." Knowledge of such distinctions is, he says, "the concern of the general theorist on some art like Elocution." [37]

III

The first requisite for the male Greek actor was a strong, resonant, clear voice. Not that the vast theaters in which he performed demanded excessive vocal effort: they didn't; the acoustics of most structures were quite satisfactory. But acting anywhere and of any kind demanded a better-than-average voice. Most Greek actors therefore spent years in training theirs, and usually tested them before each performance, like singers, by running over all the notes from the highest to the lowest. (A comic named Hermon once missed his cue while too conscientiously loosening up his larynx outside the theater.)

Actors in the period before Christ placed much more emphasis upon voice and enunciation than most actors do today. Today they seldom dream of learning to speak attractively or clearly. If they think about the subject at all, they may agree that they should possess voices "whose life is at once contagious to the hearer," that a stage voice should have in it a quality somehow theatrical, a quality that in some baffling way immediately clicks. They may agree that they ought to practice their alphabet until they can come before the public "able to drive a nail up to the head with one touch of a consonant." [38] But they rarely *do* anything about improving their utterance. They lazily adore flat and harsh voices and woolly execution because such faults are typical, are natural.

Voice was the prime concern of every Greek tragedian because his gestures and movements were simple and restrained, because his facial expressions were concealed behind a mask, and because his huge theater wasn't too much "a place for seeing." "The words of the dramatist were conveyed through the voice, animated by the beauty and variety of its music; and sometimes heightened further still by the music of pipes and strings that followed the voice, dilating further the poetic meaning, making it yet more poignant and unerring." No wonder that whenever an actor is mentioned by an ancient author, he is referred to in language which at the present day would seem more appropriate to . . . an operatic singer. It is always the excellence of his voice which is emphasized, little regard being paid to other accomplishments." The actor was held responsible for his voice only. Playwrights chose, or hoped for, actors with the best voices. Demosthenes declared that "Actors should be judged by their voices." [39] Neoptolemus, for one, rose to the top of his profession chiefly because of his excellent voice.

Greek actors knew something we today are likely to forget: that "the tone an actor uses can move us more than any other thing about him. The word he speaks gives the concept . . . but the voice may be anger itself or longing, and may go straight, as music does, to the same emotion in us. . . ." Words alone, even clearly articulated, can never quite express "all the half-conscious elements, delicate implications, the radiant and shadowy emanations that make up every truth." For "sound itself has significance. The articulate meaning of the word *pain* is a symbolistic accident; the sound of it goes vaguely but further in. . . ." [40]

Yet voice in the theater can be overemphasized. In the Greek theater at times it was. Many actors fell in love with their pear-shaped tones; they descended to vocal tricks by imitating claps of thunder and the sounds of winds and hail-storms, of axles and windlasses, the notes of trumpets and pipes, and all manner of instruments and all varieties of animals and birds; worse, they tried to find plays in the oratorical style where they could boom, bellow, and rant. In short, they tended to forget that the voice is neither the ultimate mark of the expert actor nor the justification of theater. Actually, it's no more than the actor's most potent instrument of expression.

A voice expressive was therefore the revised first requisite for Greek acting. Aristotle insisted that the voice must be expressive rather than merely beautiful. For him the voice of the first-rate public speaker, or actor, ought to be "significant spoken sound." A successful delivery, he knew, depends not on the exhibition of lovely tones but on the right management of such logical details as emphasis, inflection, phrasing, timing, and so on. He points out, for example, that "By not making the right pause, you may reverse the meaning";

that a particular passage "must be made dramatic, not uttered as one idea, with unvarying sentiment and tone"; and that "if your words are harsh, it is better not to make your voice harsh, too" (or perhaps that poetry needn't be spoken "poetically," that it's often better, as actors are currently fond of saying, "to play against the text"). For Aristotle a successful delivery also depends on the right management of tones as expressive of certain emotional details. And he implies—maybe too quickly—that both the logical and the emotional details will fall into place once the actor achieves a true characterization: once he adapts his voice to the personality or mood of the character, once he controls every inflection so as to express the character's mind as reflected in the text. Aristotle noted approvingly, for instance, that "Theodorus' voice as against the voices of all other actors . . . seems to be the actual voice of the person he represents." [41]

IV

An ability to characterize may have been the second specific requisite for the ancient Greek actor—although that assumption seems unwarranted when you recall that he was asked to impersonate from two to four distinctly different individuals in any one play, and from two to three times that many persons in any one day's contest. How could an actor successfully characterize, even in masks, two people as widely different, for example, as the girl Chrysothemis and the Old Pedagogue in the *Electra* of Sophocles, or be first the gracious Deianira and then her agonized husband Heracles in the same playwright's *The Women of Trachis?* And how could three different actors possibly portray Clytemnestra in a trilogy? A Greek actor, you hastily conclude, was no more than an orator or a reciter who "characterized" principally an author's poetry by appreciating and conveying to an audience its various technical merits, its meaning, and its emotion.

Yet in addition to bringing out the values of the poetry *as poetry*, the Greek actor must have instinctively pretended to be someone other than himself in each of his roles. In all probability he tried impersonation; he made characters. His characters, however, were quite unlike those in most modern plays. Classic dramatists had no desire to put completely real, minutely observed people onstage. They aimed instead to design characters functioning in the theatricalization of an idea. Only in Greek comedies do some characters retain a certain verisimilitude. In tragedies where they might be represented as "some such men as we," they are mostly depicted "as better than the men of the present day." They are ideal; they are, as Stark Young observed, "first of all, types, large forms, and afterward more or less individuals. The emotions and ideas are not so much personal as typical, powerful visitations within these human vessels of forces larger and more lasting than they, passing through them, shaking and revealing and leaving them. The images created, the diction employed in the play, are kept within the bounds of a certain size and a certain pattern of simplicity." From all this the Greek actor learned not too greatly to individualize the role; just as in turn he knew that, in so far as he was an artist, that the reactions he expressed, and the gestures he employed must have about them a certain outline quality, a pattern of universality; and just as in turn he knew "that in his recitation he must strive for line forms rather than words and phrases, and so must move toward a sonorous and impersonal and formal manner of delivery." [42]

But in interpretating these simple types or ideal forms, in characterizing them, some Greek actors may have anticipated Stanislavski. Yes, it's quite possible that the three performers of the plays of Aeschylus, Sophocles, and Euripides knew, for instance, that a tragedy—or any play—"directly presents the actions of men." They could have known from the lectures and discussions that became the *Poetics* that a play shows "human beings . . . performing or undergoing something" "as in real life." They may have seen the characters they were assigned to make, above all else, as agents, *"men in action,"* people doing things. Aristotle, for sure, defined a play in essence as "an imitation, not of men as such, but of action and life, or happiness and misery. And happiness and misery," he explained, aren't "states of being, but forms of activity; the end for which we live is some form of activity, not the realization of a moral quality. Men are better or worse, according to their moral bent; but they become happy or miserable in their actual deeds. In a play, consequently, the agents do not perform for the sake of representing their individual dispositions; rather, the display of moral character is included as subsidiary to the things that are done. So that the incidents of the action, and the structural ordering of these incidents, constitute the end and purpose" of acting. (As Stanislavski advised his students: "On the stage . . . action . . . is the basis of the art followed by the actor." "On the stage it is necessary to act," to *do*, "either outwardly or inwardly" every moment of every scene.) [43]

Greek actors may also have understood that motive is a potent ingredient of any action. Aristotle in his *Rhetoric*—and acting is a kind of rhetoric—examined "the subject of motives, with the dispositions and circumstances in which voluntary choices are made." He specifically discusses "the incentives of wrong-doers." He was sure that "we must examine any questionable word or act to see whether the motive of the agent is to secure some greater good or to avert a greater evil." In short, he said to actors who heeded him that in all impersonations "the purposes and reasonings of the agents" need to be discovered, understood, and revealed.[44]

In addition, Aristotle taught the truth that every man in a play as in life has a large motive, a dominant urge—or what Stanislavski called an "unbroken line." "Both individually and collectively," the former points out, "men have some object at which they aim in whatever they choose and whatever they avoid. This object may be summarily described as Happiness, with its constitutent parts. . . ." And "Happiness may be defined as prosperity conjoined with virtue; or as a self-sufficient existence; or as the pleasant life, with secure enjoyment thereof; or as a thriving condition of property and persons, with the ability to take care and make use of them." All things that men do toward attaining their over-all aim of happiness, he continued, are caused, shaped by: "chance, nature, compulsion, habit, reason, desire. (The first three are involuntary, the last four voluntary.)" Or, to simplify, "there are two natural causes, moral bent and thought, of the particular deeds of men" [45] in life—and therefore in a play.

Thus, according to long-ago Aristotle, an agent, or a character in a play, in order to be "true to life" and "consistent" enough, "must speak or act in a certain fashion as the necessary or probable outcome of his inward nature . . . ." He "must necessarily be endowed by the poet with certain distinctive qualities both of Moral Character . . . and . . . Intellect . . . , one might say, of heart and head"; and the actor must perceive and convey those qualities, since "it is from man's moral bent, and from the way in which he reasons, that we are led to ascribe goodness or badness, success or failure, to his acts." [46]

So, in theory at least, since such notions were "in the air," Greek actors in working out their formal characterizations may have dug from their scripts certain incentives or motivations (or justifications) for their actions in each role. While communicating the poetic quality of speeches, which frequently run to two pages, they might also have held an audience by disclosing the individual drive, the human truth, behind the magic of the words.

Greek actors were also probably aware that "the circumstances of time and occasion" are a contributing factor in every motivated action. At any rate, Aristotle in examining public speaking and playwriting emphasizes "the power of the agent to say what can be said, or what is fitting to be said, *in a given situation*" (my italics). He notes the importance of "the states of mind," the conditions, or circumstances, in which a person speaks or does something. He knew, in brief, that always there are circumstances that definitely modify the utterances or the act, such as, for instance, men's ages and their gifts of fortune; consequently, he comments briefly on the nature of young men, elderly men, men in their prime, men well-born, men wealthy, and men with power. Aristotle also knew that an action includes the receiver or object of that action, the place and time.[47]

V

Finally, in characterizing, the actors at Athens were probably aware that emotions result in the main from actions. Of course, like many actors today, some of them may have fashioned the tones of their lines toward the arousing of feelings in general and for their own sakes. They may merely have turned on the spigots of jealousy, anger, love, suffering, and so on. But some of them could easily have learned in the wake of the *Rhetoric*, where Aristotle dissects fifteen emotions, that, for instance, a man "is always angry with some particular person—Cleon or the like—and not with 'man' in general . . ."; that when a man "*is aiming at something*" (my italics), and you "cross him directly, or bother him in any other way . . . he becomes . . . angry." Hence, "people who are ailing, or needy, or in love, or thirsty—in a word, those who have any desire that is not being satisfied—are prone to anger, and are easily incensed, but above all at any one who shows indifference to their present aim." Furthermore, "the angry man aims at things (revenge) he can attain." [48] Before Stanislavski, then, Aristotle in a way advised the actor to find the emotion in an action completed or thwarted.

Then, after describing the nature of the various emotions, Aristotle furnished the Greek actor with a recipe for expressing them onstage. "The poet," he said, "should . . . assume the very attitudes and gestures appropriate to the emotions of the agents; for among authors with the same natural ability, they will be most convincing who themselves experience the feelings they represent." In other words, the poet—and why not the actor—"who himself feels distress or anger will represent distress or anger with the most lifelike reality." [49]

Some Greek actors even used what Stanislavski called "the affective memory" in order truly to find and fashion their feelings. Polus of Aegina, for one, considered by many to have been the greatest actor of his time, as Electra "took from the tomb the ashes and urn of his son, embraced them as if they were those of Orestes, and filled the whole place, not with the appearance and imitation of sorrow, but with genuine grief and unfeigned lamentation. Therefore, while it seemed that a play was being acted, it was in fact real grief that was enacted." [50]

VI

The third specific requisite of the Greek actor was "a certain natural plasticity," [51] or an ability to imagine. Obviously in characterizing general types or idealized forms he couldn't restrict himself to observing and copying all the realistic details of an action and to recalling and reproducing only personally experienced emotions. Oh, no. He went beyond doing that to design, in a nonnaturalistic style, meanings fresher and larger than those of literal facts. He imitated not life, but the playwright's imitation of life.

Here the key word, of course, is imitation, or *mimesis*. It is also a misleading word. To the Greeks it implied "the prime activity of the poet [not of the scientist, the photographer, the psychologist] . . . of the artist in the widest sense—what we might call the poetic or artistic imagination." It implied "the existence of this imagination. . . ." It signified "the copying by the poet or artist of the thing he has imagined, the representing of his image in a medium . . . which may be perceived by the senses." [52] That was its primary meaning.

Thus redefined, the stage task of the Greek actor wasn't merely the imitating of an action; it was the imagining of an action. You might even substitute, as Kenneth Burke does: " 'the miming of an action.' (Recall where Chaplin, for instance, 'imitates' a dancer by taking two forks, sticking a roll on the end of each, and acting 'lifelike' in *terms of this greatly disparate medium.*) Or: 'The ritual figuring of an action' (since Greek tragedy was built about 'qualitative' parts that, whatever their origin in nature, were as ceremonious as the processional and recessional of the Episcopalian service). Or: 'the stylizing of an action.' (The characters in Greek tragedy stood for certain civic functions somewhat as with the heroic posturing of an equestrian statue in a public park.) Or: 'the symbolizing of an action' " (a term that "aids greatly in the reclaiming of lost connotations here").[53]

And if you could have asked the Greeks why in their playwriting and consequently in their acting they didn't stop at skillfully copying honest human behavior but advanced to making something new out of it, they would have answered: Copying "can only create as its handiwork what it has seen, but imagination equally what it has not seen (or personally experienced); for it will conceive of its ideal with reference to the reality." Or they might have given Hemingway's answer: "Why be puzzled by that? From things that have happened and from things as they exist and from all things that you know, you make something through your invention that is not a representation but a whole new thing truer than anything true and alive, and you make it alive, and if you make it well enough, you give it immortality."[54]

VII

The fourth, already hinted at, and final requisite of the Greek actor must have been a perceptive sense of the whole. In his *Ion*, Plato wrote that "no man can be a rhapsode"—and he also meant an actor—"who does not understand the meaning of the poet"—or the playwright. Elsewhere he implies that in order for an actor to interpret what his author means he ought to sense somehow the harmonious functioning of his character in the design of the entire play: one can slightly paraphrase a passage in his *Phaedrus* to read as follows: " 'And what if a man were to go up to Sophocles and Euripides, and tell them that he knew how to make a very long harangue . . . on a great matter; that he could act at will [and truthfully] in a pathetic or in a bold and menacing tone; that he possessed a variety of similar accomplishments; and that thus he considered himself to be an excellent actor capable of imparting the power of tragedy?' 'Well, they, too, I imagine . . . would burst into a laugh at the notion of acting being made up of these elements [these preliminaries, as it were], without regard being paid to their consistency with one another and the whole in combination."[55]

Aristotle pointedly observed that *beginner* playwrights and actors become proficient "in the delineation of personal traits before they are able to combine the incidents of the action into an effective whole." Only later, when they are more experienced and wiser, do they understand that "before any . . . interpretations [characters] can be made," "the total object must be perceived in its own genus and species, in its own essential form. . . ." In other words, an actor should start his characterizing by turning his attention from himself and toward the play, toward the play as an idea already designed in a certain style; and he must see and understand his character as "an integral part of the whole." [56] Then, and only then, should he turn to himself as material for portraying the agent.

For the Greek actor B.C. there never was, for instance, one absolute, isolated, "real" Creon to be put together only out of his own personality and then placed alike in each of three plays of Sophocles. No Greek actor, we can assume, tried to characterize a Creon only from the actual biographical details he knew, in one way or another, about that king, or only by collating his own self-examinations or "life studies" or "emotion memories" or even imaginings. Instead, the Greek actor imagined each Creon differently; he imagined each Creon in accordance with his understanding of the organic structure, style, and point of the play. He made each Creon a uniquely different functioning agent in each of three differently designed pieces. In *Oedipus the King* Creon does certain things and is one person; in *Oedipus at Colonus* Creon does different things (and possibly in a different way, or style) and is another person; and in *Antigone* Creon is still another differently designed person. In one sense, yes, Creon is the same man in all three tragedies (and also in Anouilh's modern, very French *Antigone*); but as a character to be *acted* he is in each instance a distinctly different agent functioning harmoniously in a distinctly different whole.

To make a character only recognizably and believably "real" was, the Greeks knew, to make something without artistic point, to make virtually nothing at all. To make a character self-consistent and believable and functional *in the context and distinctive style of the play* was all.

VIII

Thus from c. 534 (the debut of Thespis) to, say, 322 B.C. (the death of Aristotle) the profession of acting was born, rapidly and intricately evolved, and achieved popularity and distinction. And thus in that time, as if in an overture, the themes of acting were announced. Some of its eternal fundamentals were discovered and discussed, mainly in examinations of play-writing and oratory, and were perchance to some degree known to actors, whose stage task was partly oratorical. Then for a long, long time those fundamentals were forgotten, lost. Not until the middle of the eighteenth century in France and in England would the themes be heard again. And not until the first half of the twentieth century in Russia and in the United States would some of them be fully developed.

2- The Rejection

✤ PLAYS IN ROME

The city-state of Athens, virtually the head of an empire by 454 B.C., was defeated in the Peloponnesian War (431-404 B.C.) by Sparta, but it retrieved most of its power and influence via the second Delian League from 378 until 338 B.C. when it was finally crushed by Philip II of Macedon. Two years later his son, and Aristotle's pupil, Alexander the Great (336-323 B.C.), succeeded to power at the age of twenty and for thirteen years spread the culture of Athens over the Mediterranean world and eastward toward India. At Alexandria, founded in 332 B.C. (and the capital of the Ptolemies from 304 to 30 B.C.), scholars collected, purified, annotated, and preserved the texts of the great Greek playwrights. And in all the old and new cities theaters were the indispensable public buildings where the tragic drama of the fifth century (not the comedy, which was too purely Athenian) was regularly performed. But by 276 B.C. Alexander's empire was broken to bits; the Hellenistic period faded away. Rome began to rule the Western world.

II

Traditionally founded in 753 B.C., Rome had become a patrician republic by c. 500 B.C., when Aeschylus was writing. During many of those years public

39

spectacles called *ludi,* or games, furnished the community with its major amusement and artistic edification. In *c.* 600 the elder Tarquin, first of Rome's Etruscan kings, built the Circus Maximus where annually the main attractions were equestrian exhibits, chariot races, beast fights, boxing matches, and the like. Then in 364–63 B.C., about sixteen years after the death of Aristophanes, actors, not playwrights, may have been awarded a first slight nod of official recognition. At that time, according to a not too reliable Livy (59 B.C.–A.D. 15), some amateur *histriones* who'd combined native Fescennine verses—the improvised banter of peasant clowns at harvest time—with Etruscan dances into a medley of repartee, song, and pantomine were permitted to appear at the games.[1] And, for all we know now, they assisted in crudely pleasing the spectators year after year while Rome subdued "Italy." A more popular festival innovation, however, was the importation in 264 B.C. of gladitorial contests.

Finally, right after the First Punic War (264–241 B.C.) against Carthage, when Rome had encountered Greek civilization, when its conquering soldiers had witnessed and envied performances of Attic plays, Roman officials as a cultural sop to the populace approved the production by professional actors of Greek tragedies and comedies as a regular feature of the *Ludi Romani.* This important date is 240 B.C., some eighty years after the death of Aristotle, some fifty years after the death of Menander.

Thus the Romans officially ignored their own faintly established, rather bawdy native theater, an actors' theater, which probably numbered some professionals among its amateur ranks, and sanctioned the aping of foreign models. They bypassed, for instance, the improvised Atellane farces—rustic, horse-play, Punch and Judy shows of a sort—which centered about such traditional, masked characters as the clowns Maccus and Bucco, the old fool Pappus, and the humpbacked, hawk-nosed, toothy Manducus; and which had been performed in the Oscan Atella (present day Aversa), and thereabouts, for at least as far back as 330 B.C. They also bypassed the largely ad-libbed Phlyax and/or Graeco-Roman mimes—brief, indecent burlesques of mythological subjects—which had been acted by amateurs since nobody knows when in the Dorian settlements of southern "Italy" and Sicily; and which by the start of the third century B.C. had perhaps been given some literary form by Rhinthon of Tarentum and been performed by such well-known players as Cleon, called "the best maskless actor among the Italian mimes," and Nymphodoros, who excelled in the memorized mime.

But these popular, indigenous, indelicate playlets couldn't be pushed aside that easily. Livy reports that "The young citizens of Rome, when forced to abandon their amateur dramatics by professional competition" after 240 B.C., "revived the old Fescennine exchange of repartee," blended it with native Atellane farces, and acted them as brief "after-pieces" at the games. In addition, the amateurs acted native mimes, probably again as "after-pieces," at the *Ludi Florales,* another festival, beginning in 238 B.C., where license permitted the appearance onstage of a mime-actress naked. Mimes were also performed at the first *Ludi Apolinares* in 212 B.C.[2]

For some time, however, these protesting efforts by Roman amateurs on behalf of a truly native drama were impotent. After 240 B.C. the theater for Roman professional actors was officially something pseudo-Greek. In that year Livius Andronicus (*c.* 284–204 B.C.), a Greek at home in Rome, translated from Greek into Latin a tragedy and produced it at the *Ludi Romani* as a supplementary attraction to the chariot races and gladitorial contests. And probably because he experienced "difficulties" in securing actors with good voices . . . he himself took the leading role." From then on similar plays supported and supervised by the government were performed there and at other celebrations. With his scripts, of which only eleven titles are known, Livius Andronicus "laid down the lines on which tragedy and comedy were to develop for a hundred and fifty years." [3] They were to be derived from Greek models. Naevius (*c.* 270–*c.* 199 B.C.), for instance, who began to earn his livelihood by writing plays in 235 B.C., and as a naturalized Roman citizen probably couldn't act in them without incurring *infamia*, composed in thirty years seven tragedies and about thirty-three comedies based on Greek originals. The comedies of Plautus and Terence are Greek in origin, have their scenes laid in Greece, deal mostly with Greek life and manners, and were acted (possibly at first by Greeks) by men dressed in Greek costumes. The tragedies of Ennius (239–169 B.C.), of Pacuvius (220–130 B.C.), and of rhetorical and melodramatic Accius (*c.* 170–86 B.C.) all followed the Greek pattern.

❀ A TRIVIAL CRAFT

Roman acting, however, from what we can gather, was un-Greek. That, of course, wasn't a fault. Acting is usually too intangible to be successfully copied; and Greek acting undoubtedly contained certain racial ingredients, or nuances, beyond the comprehension of Latins, or of any other aliens. The significant difference was something else. Professional Roman acting was un-Greek in origin, concept, and repute. Because it was only rarely and never importantly a part of sacred rituals, it was to the Romans no more than an imported novelty, like the gladitorial contests, and no more than another brand of amusement competing for audience approval with beast fights. Actors appeared onstage minus the glamor of religious tradition and minus official honors. Naevius, for example, in producing his plays, may have used pickup actors from Campania who were trained in giving Atellane farces. Actors were merely professional entertainers, wandering lower-class nobodies, like jugglers or rope-dancers or what-have-you, who tried to please a noisy, illiterate crowd. And since that crowd was also the electorate, the magistrates were anxious to satisfy it and to pay those who could supply entertainment. Men of standing in the community weren't easily induced to take up such "an extremely mean and trivial craft," especially since it promised only a sporadic livelihood. So unattractive was the calling that even after a few men had achieved wealth and distinction as actors "slaves had to be trained to take roles which self-respecting citizens refused to play."[4]

Roman acting, even at its prime, was more rudimentary than Greek acting. Cicero, for one, dismissed it as simple stuff and nonsense. He approved of actors Roscius and Aesopus, but concluded that acting on the whole was a "trivial art" of which nothing is expected save the gratification of the ear. . . ." Despite the fact that actors labor "to regulate the expression, the voice, and the movements of the body," he said, "everyone knows how few . . . there are, or ever have been, whom we could bear to watch!" or to hear! since they are such slaves to their voices they hollowly thunder words "which have no thought or knowledge behind them."[5] Roman actors, unlike Greek actors, weren't too concerned with conveying to an audience a playwright's moving or amusing idea; they were mostly interested in titillating it with cascades of rhetoric or with plenty of jokes and high-jinks. Yet in their favor you can say of them that they were forced to recognize the elementary fact that whatever else acting aims to achieve it must first of all take into account the presence, often the disinterested presence, of an audience, go out to it, grab and hold and guide its attention. This was a new fact-of-theater professional actors began to learn.

Roman acting was rarely first-rate because it lowered itself to the level of ignorant or bored audiences and was never challenged to do more than that by superior playwriting. The actors couldn't find anything of pleasure or import to communicate via the characters they made from warmed-over foreign scripts. So, pretty much on their own, they simply did the best they could with the material at hand. They saved poor plays. Terence noticed, for instance, that good acting sometimes gave a bad play an undeserved success. And Quintilian, while wincing at "the rant of an actor," the "extravagance of facial expression, gesture, and gait," and "the lascivious melodies of our effeminate stage," nevertheless appreciated the lively persuasiveness of the actor's art. He softened Aristotle's dictum that a play can produce its characteristic effect independently of a stage performance when he observed that "actors in the theater . . . add so much to the . . . poets that the verse moves us far more when heard than when read. . . . They succeed in securing a hearing even for the most worthless authors," who "repeatedly win a welcome on the stage . . . denied them in the library."[6]

II

Roman acting is worth mentioning only in comedy. In tragedy, popular not for long, it was generally something rank and weedy. Roman audiences apparently enjoyed only "melodramatic effects, volleys of rhetoric, horrific plots and descriptions, flamboyant personalities, superhuman virtue, incredible vice." They turned professional actors into incidental panderers because "they were interested not so much in the essential dramatic qualities of the performance as in externals—impressive staging, violent utterance and action, lines which might be taken as topical, the arrival of distinguished spectators and of course any mishap which might befall either the actors or any member of the audience." [7]

But crude, lively Roman comic acting could hold businessmen and nobles, women and children, and soldiers in the middle of many wars. Horse-play, broad slashing swashbuckling humor, thick color daubed on with a lavish brush could win them over. So, the "actors went before the public . . . slapstick in hand, equipped by nature with a liveliness of grimace and gesture, and prepared to act with verve, unction, and an abandon of dash and vigor that would produce a riot of merriment." [8] They succeeded. Audiences roared, applauded.

❧ THEATRICALITY

In the comedies of "Titus Maccius Plautus" (c. 254–184 B.C.), who began writing about thirty-five years after 240 B.C., the comic actors wildly pleased their audiences. No matter if Horace (65–8 B.C.) said of this slip-shod writer, "So he gets paid, his piece may sink or swim/ Huzzaed or hooted, 'tis all the same to him," and no matter if erudite critics today whine that he "wrote plays like a blacksmith mending a watch" or that reading him after Vergil is like prowling in the slums of literature,[9] Plautus was an enormously successful man of the theater. Fiction has it that he was born in Sarsina, that in his mid-twenties he came to Rome and worked as a crew member who helped set up the long and narrow platform stage—sixty feet in length was not uncommon—and hang the painted scene-cloth which nearly always represented the fronts of houses in a street. In time he became a professional actor and guild member. By c. 206 B.C. he was a playwright, and quickly became the most prolific and famous one at Rome. In the last twenty-two years of his life, Plautus put together about one hundred and thirty lively plays, of which twenty-one are extant. No other classic dramatist has survived script-wise to that extent.

Most of his works, of which the best are perhaps first, *Pseudolus* (*The Trickster*) (191 B.C.) and *Rudens* (*The Fisherman's Rope*) (189), then the better known *Miles Gloriosus* (*The Braggart Captain*) (205), *Amphitruo* (*Jupiter in Disguise*) (186), and *Menaechmi* (*The Twin Brothers*) (186), plus possibly *Casina* (*The Girl From Casinum*) (184), can easily be called musical comedies. Vigorous, colloquial, joke-loaded dialogue constitutes only about a third of each script; the rest was either recited to the incidental accompaniment of the tibia, or sung in rhymes (unknown to the Greeks). Lyrical monologues and soliloquies replaced the Greek chorus, and a kind of dancing was often added to the whole. Thus the finished product resembled a Gilbert and Sullivan operetta where verisimilitude in plot and characterization is unnecessary because undesirable.

From twelve to fifteen of the surviving comedies relate the tricky love entanglements of young men; deception is the chief element in fifteen of them, and an important element in three more. A composite-plot summary of these variations on a theme reads as follows: "A young Athenian is in love with a charming but friendless girl who is the purchased slave of a . . . professional procurer. This man is either already hiring her out to anyone who will pay, or is on the point of selling her to some unpleasant person, usually a military officer. . . . The hero is at his wits' end. He wishes to purchase her and keep her as his mistress: he cannot legally marry her, as she is not of Athenian birth. But he has not the sum demanded by the girl's owner; how then is he to rescue her? Here intervenes the slave, loyal to his young master but otherwise conscienceless, who saves the situation by an elaborate ruse either to defraud the hero's father of the needed sum or to induce the slave-owner to part with the girl. When discovery of this deception arrives, all is put right by a sudden revelation that the heroine is really of Athenian birth (but kidnapped or lost in babyhood) and can therefore marry the hero." The characters are personified traits, broad caricatures, burlesques who "may exhibit outward manifestations of grief, joy, love, anger, but their marionette nature cannot be affected thereby." [10]

II

In playing these musical comedies the actors learned the fundamental importance and peculiar joy of being theatrical onstage. For sure Plautus saw to that. He probably attended to much of the stage-directing himself; and certainly the one thing he insisted on was audience contact. He taught the five or six men in his casts, maskless at first, to acknowledge the presence of the audience and frankly to play to it. His comedies are filled with soliloquies and asides addressed to the crowd. For example, in *Casina*, Pardalisca confides to the spectators: "Didn't I play him off cleverly? For everything I've been telling him as taking place I've been telling him falsely. My mistress and the lady next door have concocted this scheme. I've been sent to fool him." In *Aulularia*, Euclio missing his treasure begs the audience: "I beseech you, give me your aid! I beg and entreat you to point out to me the person who took it! What's the matter? Why do you laugh? I know all of you; I know that there are many thieves among you . . . sitting out there as though you were honest!" And one of the slaves to Agorastocles in *Poenulus* protests, "Don't trouble about us; don't tell us. We know the whole matter, since we all learned it together in rehearsal. . . ." And later Agorastocles says to Hanno, "Cut it short, my unclest uncle, the audience wants a drink." And in *Pseudolus* when the slave boasts that he's just bamboozled the captain's servant, and Calidorus asks how, he answers: "This play is being performed for the sake of these spectators. They know how I did it; they were present when it happened. I'll tell you about it some other time." [11] Moreover, the action of a comedy by Plautus often halts while an actor, in or out of character, regales the public with the poet's humorous views on elementary philosophic matters, on the foibles of society, or on economic topics of the day—or of bygone days in Athens.

In short, Plautine actors—who must have resembled W. C. Fields (1879–1946), Bobby Clark (1888–1960), Bert Lahr (1895–), and Jimmy Durante (1893–)—weren't interested in creating illusions either of ideality or of reality. They used their skills to effect a lively presentation, to give a rousing show, a funny show. They were purely of and for the theater.

LITERARY INTERLOPERS

After Plautus, and his contemporary, Caecilius Statius (*c.* 219–*c.* 166 B.C.), Terence (*c.* 190–159 B.C.) offered the professional actors at Rome a sterner challenge. He asked them to be less broad, less loud, less frantic, less theatrical, and more human onstage. (Someone always pops up to tell us the fun we're having is all wrong!) This literary darling of the Roman aristocracy (and of medieval schoolmasters and Renaissance writers) tried to reform comedy. He tried, alas, to be an artist, to compose "new and flawless" plays that would please the intelligensia as much as the pieces by Plautus pleased the mob. His six surviving "half-Menander," sentimental comedies are: *Andria* (*The Girl of Andros*) (166 B.C.), *Hecyra* (*The Step-Mother*) (165 or 160), *Heautontimorumenos* (*The Self-Tormentor*) (163), the excellent *Eunuchus* (*The Eunuch*) (161), the well-known *Phormio* (161), and the thoroughly Terentian *Adelphi* (*The Brothers*) (160). In them he created characters "quickened into an authentic particular life. . . ." And the actors evidently achieved a wee success in humanly impersonating them—but not a long-lasting one. Terence was too chillingly superior, too elegant and urbane, too satin-like in style for the crowd. He was ahead of his time; he belonged in spirit "to eighteenth-century France and England, not to Rome of the Punic Wars." [12]

Apparently Romans were indifferent in the long run to foreign comedies. They roared at the "sure-fire" scripts by Plautus, yes; but his concoctions were almost un-Greek in the talky, speedy and rollicking use of intrigue. They admired the works of Terence, maybe; but they truly enjoyed their own homespun, lively comedies in native dress, the *fabula togata.* These playlets, made up of "loosely connected scenes taken from the everyday life of the streets, the shops, the private houses of Rome or the country towns," [13] were presented independently and in competition with the plays of Plautus and Terence. Not much is known about the *fabula togata* except a few titles: *The Lady of the Dye Shop, The Girl Who Knew Something About Law, The Butler, The Slave Set Free, Auntie, The Divorce, Off on His First*

Campaign, and so on. Written by Titinus, possibly a contemporary of Plautus and Terence, by Afranius, a successor to Terence, and by Atta, who died in *c.* 77 B.C., they outdrew literary tragedies and literary Terence.

✤ ACTORS TAKE CHARGE

Eventually, it seems, Roman theatergoers wearied of literary plays, even of the native *fabula togata.* They preferred lively actors to a well-written script. The funny, naughty, and improvised things actors did fascinated them more than the recitation of memorized words. Audiences therefore returned to liking best the indigenous, almost spurned Atellane farces and traditional mimes. As literature these pieces, of course, were abortions; "but we have reason to believe that in the life of the common people, from early times to the end of the Roman Empire, popular farce played a greater part than all the literary forms of Roman drama put together." "The farces and the mimes, while incapable of embodying careful characterization . . . , could at their best provide a vehicle for current ideas and a fruitful entertainment in skillful caricature. . . . Their descent to the lower strata of amusement was not so much the fault of the form as of the audiences that determined their content." [14]

Facts about this revived interest in Atellane farces are few. We can only suppose that professional actors, while appearing in literary plays at Rome and on tour, soon began to notice the loud success of the amateurs in arranging and presenting these largely extempore, native "after-pieces." No doubt they watched with envy the "spontaneous bits of improvised fun in which . . . , unhampered by a fixed test," [15] the amateurs freely and creatively embellished traditional, masked characters. They grew jealous of the laughs and cheers garnered by mere tyros. So, disdaining authors, the professionals also began to assemble loose and ribald farces and to show their amateur rivals a trick or two.

Later, of course, writers, tried to get in the act. Men like L. Pomponius (fl. 89 B.C.) and his contemporary Novius decided to improve the Atellane farces, to make them more literary and thus slightly more respectable. They composed brief pieces called *Maccus the Soldier, Maccus the Innkeeper, Maccus the Maid, Bucco the Gladiator, Pappus Defeated at the Polls,* and the like. But written sketches were rarely as satisfactory as the outlined ones. Actors preferred to make up their own plots, speeches, and tricks. This they continued to do, often obscenely, during the last century B.C. and the first century A.D. Then for a long time the ad lib Atellana unaccountably disappeared.

Before then, however, they were outranked in popularity by the old native mimes, a second type of nonliterary or actors' theater. These mimes originated, it's claimed, with mountebanks who had a gift for mimicry and for acrobatics; but they weren't what we today would call pantomimes. They were—oral pantomimes, or "imitations of life." [16] Mimes were like Atellane farces in that the actors, also called mimes, improvised most of their speeches and "stage business." They differed from them, it vaguely seems, in that the characters were less traditional and more varied, unmasked instead of masked, and depended for many of their effects on facial expressions, gestures, and movements. Moreover, the mimes employed actresses, usually courtesans, for the female roles—and as strip-teasers. Like the Atellane farces they were performed —first by amateurs and then by professionals—in competition with the comedies of Plautus and Terence, and especially pleased the Roman crowds because more often than not they were indecent in subject matter and language and often dealt with unnatural vice and adultery.

Mime actors earned their living by traveling from town to town—and now and then to Rome—like gypsies, setting up their simple stage in market places, and exhibiting their elementary playlets. "A rough platform served to raise them above the heads of the crowd; for scenery a portable curtain was sufficient. The actors were concealed behind the curtain till their turn came, then, parting the folds in the middle, they stepped into the public view. While they performed a colleague might be collecting coins from the spectators. . . ." At the head of each company "was the leading actor or actress (archimimus, archimima) to whom the rest were little more than foils. . . . The arch-mime would perhaps begin by announcing the title, or even summarizing the plot . . . ; he was almost continuously on the stage, and he kept the dialogue so much under his control that 'the second actor in the mime' was a phrase denoting one who . . . 'played second fiddle'. . . . The size of the companies was perhaps not so large as it later became. . . . Ovid speaks of a cast of three—the peccant wife, the foolish husband, and the foppish lover." [17]

By the beginning of the first century B.C., when the mimes were outrageously popular, actors like Decimus Laberius (106–43 B.C.) and actresses like Arbuscula and Cytheris hoped to elevate them into literature, into art. The former, most conspicuously, wrote out the dialogue for his mimes. The experiments failed. Mimes continued to be mostly improvised. Who needed a unified plot or contrived words? Who needed an author? The actors insisted on proving to audiences how essential actors were, how self-sufficient, how inventive, how expertly they could make up their own lines and then illustrate and augment them. They, and only they, were the theater.

At this same time—after Carthage had been razed and its site ploughed up; during the years of Cicero, Lucretius (c. 99–c. 55 B.C.), Vergil (70–19), Horace, and Ovid (43 B.C.–A.D. 18); and before the assassination of Julius Caesar in 44 B.C., and the establishment of the Empire in 31 B.C.—mime plays, enlarged and elaborated, virtually forced "regular" tragedies and comedies from the theaters.

No Latin mime scenarios have survived; but indications of what they were like can be gathered from "an acting edition of a Greek mime preserved from the second century after Christ, containing seven short scenes. The action takes place in front of a house. . . . The opening words show us . . . a faithless wife, trying to seduce Aesopus, one of her slaves. He is in love with a fellow-slave, Apollonia, and rejects his mistress' advances. She then orders the lovers to be taken away and left to die. A later scene shows the 'body' of Aesopus being brought in; the other slaves pretend that he has thrown himself from a height (actually they have drugged him for his own safety); his mistress mourns his death, but soon consoles herself with the company of another slave, Malacus, with whom she conspires to poison her husband, whose 'body' is presently brought in. Now comes the turning-point. The old man gets up and denounces his guilty wife and Malacus; they are led off to punishment, while Aesopus and Apollonia are found to be alive and well, and all ends happily." [18] The lascivious dialogue is in prose, and was certainly expanded at will by the actors.

During the Empire mimes were the principal form of entertainment that filled the stone structures, large and small, built by the Romans in every province. An inscription dated A.D. 169 in honor of the mime-director L. Acilius Pontinus Eutyches lists a company of sixty! As Choricius in north Africa exclaimed: "Everywhere the mimes gain fame. Rightly they get wealth from their art. They revel in their rich clothing, their store of gold, their silvery attire, and their retinues of servants." [19]

Also during the Empire pantomimes, another meretricious form of entertainment, began to compete for popularity with the mimes. In about 22 B.C., Pylades in tragedy and Bathyllus in comedy introduced these sexy dance-dramas in which they silently portrayed their roles with gestures and movements to the accompanying rhythms of seductive music. The rabble flocked to this new pornography; it applauded the lewd dancers as loudly as it applauded actors. Ever more polyglot, ever looking for novelties, ever "eager for entertainment which might exclude all possibility of having to exercise the intellect," Roman audiences "found in the lascivious pantomimes their supreme satisfaction." Horace moaned at these performances for a lazy brain; in his opinion the stage had descended to the lowest depths of infamy.[20]

Thus in less than two hundred and fifty years the Roman theater achieved the trivial and the degrading. The literary elite regarded it with something like horror. Marcus Vitruvius Pollio (fl. 70–15 B.C.), after drawing up plans for what he conceived the theater might gloriously be, put his De Architectura on a shelf where the book gathered dust for nearly fifteen centuries. Seneca (c. 4 B.C.–A.D. 65), a student of acting (and the model playwright for the Renaissance), composed his tragedies, of which nine or maybe ten are extant, only for private recitation. The last writer of tragedies known to have been produced is the consul P. Pomponius Secundus, who lived in the time of Claudius, emperor A.D. 41–54. "Most dramatic works even in his day were destined for reading. The only Roman comedy (togata) mentioned as having been played during the Empire is Afranius's Incendium [Fire!] given at a festival sponsored by Nero," [21] emperor A.D. 54–68.

II

The theater at Rome was doomed. The actors fell out of official favor; and then, as they fought frantically for survival by sinking from one indecency to another, they were increasingly ostracized. Legislation of Julius Caesar and of Emperor Augustus barred them from holding municipal *honores*, denied them the right to bring criminal action, and in particular forbade senators or their sons to take to wife women who had been, or whose parents had been, on the stage. Then Emperor Tiberius expelled *histriones* from "Italy" on moral grounds. "The example was followed by more than one of his successors, but Rome clamored fiercely for its toys, and the period of exile was never a long one." [22]

Finally, of course, the Christian church was quick to set itself against the obscene actors, and just as naturally the actors retaliated by mocking Christian sacraments—and thereby wooed defeat. If the people desire spectacles, thundered Tertullian (*c.* 150–*c.* 250), let them wait till Doomsday. Then "will be the time to listen to the tragedians whose lamentations will be more poignant for their proper pain. Then will the comedians turn and twist, rendered nimbler than ever by the sting of the fire that is not quenched." Onstage, according to Chrysostom (*c.* 347–407), "are to be seen naught but fornication, adultery, courtesan women, men pretending to be women, and soft-limbed boys." No Christian could therefore be a player, or might marry one; and a member of the unhallowed profession couldn't be baptized unless he abandoned the stage. At last, even though St. Augustine (354–430) in his *Civitate Dei* upheld the literary drama as a means of education, the church was victorious. In the fifth century, by the Code of Theodosius in 435, public performances were forbidden on Sundays. Moreover, certain sumptuary regulations were passed, which must have proved a severe restriction on the popularity as well as the liberty of the actors." Gradually the theaters of Europe were closed. The last reference to organized public entertainment is dated 533, less than sixty years after the fall of the Western Roman Empire in 476.[23]

In Constantinople (old Byzantium), the second capital of the Roman Empire since 330 B.C., censorship for a while was relaxed, possibly because the Empress Theodora (d. 548) had been a mime actress; and the government still sponsored public performances and paid the actors. The theater there perished in the seventh and eighth centuries when the Saracens devastated the East.

But, driven from their theaters, professional actors "had still a vogue, not only at banquets, but at popular merrymakings or wherever in street or country they could gather together the remnant of their old audiences. . . ." Then, however, in the words of E. K. Chambers, the *mimi* had to "rub shoulders and contend for *denarii* with jugglers and with rope-dancers, with out-at-elbows gladiators and beast-tamers. More than ever they learned to turn their hand to anything that might amuse; learned to tumble, for instance; learned to tell the long stories which the Teutons loved. Nevertheless, in essentials they remained the same; still jesters and buffoons, still irrepressible, still obscene. In little companies of two and three, they padded the hoof along the roads, traveling from gathering to gathering, making their own welcome in castle or tavern, or, if need were, sleeping in some grange or beneath a wayside hedge in the white moonlight."[24]

❀ TIDBITS OF THEORY

The first prominent actors in Rome were Pellio and Ambivius Turpio. Pellio, who specialized in buffoonery, was evidently the actor-manager who first produced and played the title roles in *Stichus* and *Epidicus* by Plautus. Turpio was a highly accomplished comedian who presented the plays of Caecilius and Terence. The outstanding actor in comedy was Quintus Roscius (Gallus) (*c.* 126–62 B.C.). A memorable Ballio in Plautus' *Pseudolus*, he did "nothing otherwise than perfectly," according to his friend Cicero, "nothing without consummate charm, nothing save in the manner befitting the occasion, and so as to move and enchant everybody." Roscius was reputedly a fine technician who thought out and practiced every gesture before employing it in public; he also taught acting to many, including the slave Panurgus, and supposedly wrote a book in which he compared acting with oratory. He's credited with having "appeared as many as one hundred and twenty-five times in a single year," and with having earned the unbelievable sum of fifty million sesterces, or nearly a million and a half dollars.[25]

In tragedies one of the top actors, and money-makers, was Claudius Aesopus (?–54 B.C.). Cicero praised him for excelling "as an emotional artist. Without attempting oratorical display or gesticulation, he read the soul-stirring lines so simply, that by his tears he roused tears and groans. . . . He was a powerful actor, not merely a skilled one." Once as Atreus deliberating the revenge of Thyestes, Aesopus "was so transported beyond himself in the heat of the action, that he struck with his scepter one of the servants who was running across the stage so violently that he laid him dead upon the place." Like many overzealous modern actors he must have really churned himself up onstage—notably as Andromache in Accius' tragedy of that name and again as Agamemnon in the same playwright's *Iphigenia*. When he died, he left a fortune of some twenty million sesterces, or well over five hundred thousand dollars.[26]

Two later comic actors, Demetrius and Stratocles, are remembered from a passage by Quintilian. It's one of the earliest critiques of acting. The two actors, he reports, "win their success by entirely different methods. But that is the less surprising owing to the fact that one was at his best in the roles of gods, young men, good fathers and slaves, matrons and respectable old women, while the other excelled in the portrayal of sharp-tongued old men, cunning slaves, parasites, pimps and all the more lively characters of comedy. For their natural gifts differed. For Demetrius' voice, like his other qualities, had greater charm, while that of Stratocles was the more powerful. But yet more noticeable were the incommunicable peculiarities of their action. Demetrius showed unique gifts in the movements of his hands, in his power to charm the audience by the long-drawn sweetness of his exclamations, the skill with which he would make his dress seem to puff out with wind as he walked, and the expressive movements of the right side which he sometimes introduced with effect, in all of which things he was helped by his stature and personal beauty. On the other hand, Stratocles' *forte* lay in his nimbleness and rapidity of movement, in his laugh (which, although not always in keeping with the character he represented, he deliberately employed to awaken answering laughter in his audience), and finally, even in the way in which he sank his neck into his shoulders. If either of these actors had attempted any of his rival's tricks, he would have produced a most unbecoming effect." [27]

Roman theorists examined the efforts of these and other competent actors; then in writings on the art of oratory they here and there hinted, as the Greeks did, at what acting at its best could be, should be. Their advice, unfortunately, did little to check the inevitable degeneration. But some of the points they made are worth glancing at today.

II

We can piece together a few tidbits for a Roman theory of acting from early writers on rhetoric, from Horace, Lucian (*c.* 120–200), Donatus (fl. 333), and so on. Our most fruitful sources of information, however, are Cicero (106–43 B.C.) and Quintilian (*c.* A.D. 35–95). Cicero's *De Gestu Histrionis* has been lost, but he more than touches on the subject of acting in his *De Oratore (On the Making of an Orator)* (55 B.C.). As "a not quite incompetent critic" of an accomplishment not his own, Cicero explains, "I do not take a very different line when I am discussing the orator from the line I should take if I had to speak about the actor." [28] And Quintilian in the *Institutio Oratoria* (*c.* A.D. 88) can't separate the education of the orator from the education of the actor.

That serious Roman acting was closely allied to oratory is clear enough. It may have been even more oratorical than Greek acting. Actors today talk to each other *and* sometimes to the audience; Roman actors declaimed to the audience. "They stood, where possible, well to the front of the stage," in W. Beare's guess; "they faced the audience, they kept their eyes on the audience, they aimed above all things at making their words carry even to the farthest seats. . . . The art of the actor lay not in naturalism or in mimicry but in clear utterance conveying the appropriate emotion and supported by appropriate gesture. It seems probable that the actor made no attempt to alter his voice according to whether he was taking the part of a gentleman or a slave, a man or a woman. . . ." You can listen across the centuries and hear the voices of the tragedians "raised in rhythmical declamation," and imagine the flute-player stepping up "now to one, now to another, playing the accompaniment for each actor in turn." [29]

Comic acting, the best or most typical Roman acting, was less oratorical than tragic acting. Consequently, it isn't often mentioned by the critics of public speaking. Perhaps it was judged unworthy of any theory or rules. Even today many consider comic acting simply a flair for "playing the situation. It's rhythm—timing, people call it." [30]

Therefore, acting to Roman theorists usually meant serious acting; and in their examinations of the subject they agreed in the main with the findings of the Greeks. They believed, for instance, that acting ought to be governed by art, by a kind of science, by the study of principles. Cicero, though wary of too much theory, and an advocate of practice and still more practice for the perfection of inborn talent, knew that any man who studies his craft, "who applies his mind to finding out the reason why some speak better [or act better] than others, may succeed in discerning it." Quintilian maintained that "Without natural gifts technical rules are useless. Consequently the student who is devoid of talent will derive no more profit" from study "than barren soil from a treatise on agriculture." But natural gifts, he continued, "are of no profit in themselves unless cultivated by skillful teaching, persistent study, and continuous and extensive practice. . . ." [31]

Both men also agreed on the paramount importance of the voice in acting. "The voice," wrote Quintilian, "has the first claim on our attention" since it is "the intermediary between ourselves and our hearers," since it "is the index of the mind, and is capable of expressing all its varieties of feeling." [32]

Meaningful reading was recognized, especially by Quintilian, as the next essential for acting. Correctness of phrasing, he suggested, "may seem but a trivial merit, but without it all the other merits of oratory [or acting] are nothing worth." An actor must discover when he "should take a breath, at what point he should introduce a pause into a line, where the sense ends or begins, when the voice should be raised or lowered, what modulation should be given to each phrase, and when he should increase or slacken speed, or speak with greater or less energy." Furthermore, he said, the orator–actor must avoid monotony, take care of subordinations, and be conscious of rhythms. He must know that emphasis is a way of "revealing a deeper meaning than is actually expressed by the words," that intonation is the "singular and unrivaled . . . prop of eloquence" because it's "by the raising, lowering or inflection of the voice that the orator stirs the emotions of his hearers. . . ." And in order to perfect himself in these details, the actor need follow but one golden rule: he "must understand what he reads." [33]

Next, impersonation, or the assumption of a role, the displaying of "the inner thoughts" of another was called by Quintilian "the most difficult of tasks." The "differences of character," he wrote, "require careful observation . . . . For example, . . . Caecilius makes the father of his comedy speak in quite a different manner from the father in the comedy by Terence." Therefore, he insisted, quoting Cicero, "we require [in the actor] a man of sharpness, ingenious by nature and experience alike, who with keen scent will track down the thoughts, feelings, beliefs and hopes of his fellow-citizens." Only, as later Lucian knew, "When every one of the spectators identifies himself with the scene enacted, when each sees . . . as in a mirror the reflection of his own conduct and feelings, . . . and not till then," [34] is the actor's success complete.

Quintilian also underlined the point that "not only what we say and how we say it [in character] is of importance, but also the circumstances under which we say it." The actor, he implies, ought to know that "In regard to every action the question arises either Why or Where or How or by what means the action is performed." "It is sagacity that teaches us to adapt our speech to circumstances of time and place and to the persons with whom we are concerned," and to "introduce numerous modifications to suit" [35] the differences.

III

Emotions, in the opinion of Cicero, ought to be communicated to an audience "not by technique, as to which I know not what to say," but under the stress of the emotions themselves. No man, he was sure, can make others feel "who is not on fire with passion, and inspired with something very like frenzy." Quintilian echoed Aristotle and Cicero when he insisted that "The prime essential for stirring the emotions of others is . . . first to feel those emotions yourself." Horace agreed; he wrote, "set the example, pray,/And weep yourself, then weep perhaps I may," or, more popularly, "If you wish me to weep, you yourself must grieve first." His ultimatum is worded a bit differently, however, in another translation: "If you would have me weep you must first express the passion of grief yourself." [36] (The word "express" changes things, doesn't it?)

For a later Greek, however, for Plutarch (A.D. 46?–c. 120), "he that only represents excels him that really feels." Plutarch, you see, perceived that in acting we "are delighted and admire everything that is artificially and ingeniously contrived. . . . And therefore, because he that is really affected with grief or anger presents us with nothing but the common bare passion, but in the imitation some dexterity and persuasiveness appears, we are naturally inclined to be disturbed at the former, whilst the latter delights us." [37]

And Lucian, writing in Greek, sided with the antiemotionalists by remembering the performance of an admirable actor who ran aground upon the reef of uncontrolled enthusiasm: "He was acting the madness of Ajax, just after he had been worsted by Odysseus; and so lost control of himself, that one might have been excused for thinking his madness was something more than feigned. He tore the clothes from the back of one of the iron-shod time-beaters, snatched a flute from the player's hands, and brought it down in such trenchant sort upon the head of Odysseus, who was standing by enjoying his triumph, that, had not his cap held good, and borne the weight of the blow, poor Odysseus must have fallen a victim to histrionic frenzy. . . ." And "the illiterate riff-raff, who knew not good from bad . . . regarded it as a supreme piece of acting; and the more intelligent part of the audience . . . saw only too clearly that it was not Ajax but the actor who was mad. . . ." They "suspected that his ultra-realism had culminated in reality." Later, another actor played a similar role, "played it with admirable judgment and discretion, and was complimented on his observance of decorum, and of the proper bounds of art." [38]

Thus began the debate on whether or not the actor while performing should feel the emotions he depicts. It would reach its climax in the eighteenth century with Diderot's dictum that the actor's "talent depends not, as you think, upon feeling, but upon rendering so exactly the outward signs of feeling. . . ." It would reach its anti-climax in the twentieth century when Stanislavski taught that the actor "*must live the part every moment [he is] playing it, and every time.*" [39]

Quintilian concludes his remarks on the emotions by saying that what "assists us to form mental pictures of things" and thus generates our emotions is the "force of the imagination." There are, he explains, "certain experiences . . . [or] *visions* whereby things absent are presented to our imagination with such extreme vividness that they seem actually to be before our very eyes. It is the man who is really sensitive to such impressions who will have the greatest power over the emotions." And the student "who gives least promise [as an actor] is one in whom the critical faculty develops in advance of the imaginative." Only by imagining, he declares, will the actor "not always be like himself," and "never unworthy of himself." [40]

IV

In addition to accepting several Greek findings about acting, Roman theorists developed one new point, and sniffed at a few more. First, the Romans stressed the importance in acting of the visual, the look of things, or characters in motion. Because they believed that the actor seen is almost as significant as the actor heard, they discussed more extensively than the Greeks did facial expressions (when masks weren't worn), gestures, and movement. They knew that "feelings . . . are mirrored by the face and by the eyes," that "gestures . . . are capable of imparting a wealth of varied meaning to the same words." They knew that an actor ought to be no stranger to the science of boxing and wrestling since his frame "must be at once supple and well-knit" [41] in order to move gracefully and with meaning.

Gestures especially attracted the attention of the Romans. Quintilian, for instance, in his *Institutio Oratoria* spends fifteen pages on the voice and nineteen on gesture. He taught that gesture, like the voice, ought to obey "the impulse of the mind," that actors should, for instance, use their hands in order to *express* something. In life, he asked, "Do we not use them to demand, promise, summon, dismiss, threaten, supplicate, express aversion or fear, question or deny? Do we not employ them to express joy, sorrow, hesitation, confession, penitence, measure, quantity, number and time? Have they not power to excite and prohibit, to express approval, wonder, or shame? Do they not take the place of adverbs and pronouns whén we point at places and things?" Yet Quintilian was aware, as was Cicero, that too much gesticulation can spoil acting. His comments on speakers "whose hands are sluggish or tremulous or inclined to saw the air" anticipated some of Hamlet's advice to the players. He also knew that much physical action onstage was obvious or trite. "Smite your hands together," he explains, "stamp the ground, slap your thigh, your breast, your forehead, and you will go straight to the hearts of the dingier members of your audience." [42]

And yet Quintilian erred. He turned pedant. He agreed with Cicero's observation that "nature has assigned to every emotion a particular look and tone of voice and bearing of its own," [43] and dissected and catalogued gestures. But as soon as he listed models for orators and actors to follow—with never an impulse for the gesture—he ossified platform and stage delivery. And for nearly two thousand years afterward various theologians of elocution, like Pollux, Engel, and Delsarte, continued to ossify it.

Standardized, prescribed gestures—or foot positions, or facial expressions, or tones of voice—may have fitted the actors of India in their aim to communicate the abstract quality or essence of things. They didn't fit Western actors in whatever it was they were searching to do onstage.

But if Quintilian was for set gestures he was faintly against set speeches and lines. He hinted that the orator—and why not the actor?—ought to try for an apparent spontaneity, for the Illusion of the First Time. The avoidance of a "display of art," he said, "itself requires consummate art; and the consummate art" in reading, in speaking, in acting is to "seem simple and unpremeditated." Words, sentences, and speeches "should spontaneously follow the thought. . . ." The actor, in short, ought to appear to say "what the instant demands." [44]

Quintilian also nudged forward another new notion about acting. He suggested that "every man must get to know his own peculiarities and must consult not merely the general rules of technique, but his own nature as well with a view to forming his delivery." And he went from there to suggest that acting is "the production and communication to the audience of all that the speaker has conceived *in his mind*" [my italics]. He very nearly insisted echoing Demosthenes, that the actor ought to convey to an audience "only what he has *carved into shape*" [45] [again my italics]. Though rather tentative, those are seminal remarks. They approach idea and design in acting.

Finally, Quintilian said of oratory, and by inference of acting, that "it involves an element of display," or a bit of heightening. "In this connection" he continued, "I may cite the practice of comic actors, whose delivery is not exactly that of common speech, since that would be inartistic, but is on the other hand not far removed from the accents of nature, for, if it were, their mimicry would be a failure; what they do therefore is to exalt the simplicity of ordinary speech by a touch of stage decoration." [46] Or by an awareness of the medium.

❀ ACTING IN INDIA

As the acting examined principally by Cicero and Quintilian was disappearing in the West, professional players began to perform in a newly evolved theater in India. Theatricals there, born of earlier religious dances and mimetic recitals, and fed by two great epic poems, *Ramayana* and *Mahabharata*, composed between the fifth and second centuries B.C., blossomed into the excellence of court entertainments somewhere near 320 B.C. (Before then there had been a treatise, now lost, on the histrionic art, the *Natasūtra* of Silālin and Krśaśva, dating from as far back as maybe 500 B.C.) Then in the second century A.D. Aśvaghosa was an important professional playwright; and in the next century the *Nātya-śāstra* (*Dramatic Science*), one of the earliest works on the theory and practice of the stage, was compiled by the symbolic Bharata.

As a climax to its theatrical efforts, India produced in the fourth and fifth centuries A.D. two masterpieces often included in anthologies of the world's great plays. The first is the lengthy *Mrichhakatikā* (*The Little Clay Cart*), based on earlier writing by Bhāsa, and usually attributed to the legendary King Śūdraka (and sometimes to an unknown court poet). The second is the exotic and lyrical *Śakuntalā* (*The Fatal Ring*) by Kalidāsa. Both plays, with their emphasis on romance and adventure, are almost future European in plot. *The Little Clay Cart* is the love story of a courtesan and a poor Brahman spun out via the rivalry of a wicked prince who desires her, a jewel robbery, the rescue of a disguised heir to the throne, the apparent strangulation of the courtesan, the conviction of the Brahman for the crime, and then an inevitable happy ending for the two sweethearts. *Śakuntalā* dramatizes with much humor the love of a King for a beautiful maiden, their marriage, a separation and a curse that cause him to forget her, a lost ring that might have brought them together again, her agonized rejection by everyone, and the various adventures, some of them celestial, that finally unite the pair with their baby son.

In fully developed romances like these, in intricate dramas about gods and kings, and in farces about the intrigues and tricks of low characters, the new-born Hindu actors (*nata*), both male and female, successfully entertained audiences. For more than five centuries, until *c.* A.D. 1000, while the West was without an organized theater, they formed a distinct professional class whose social status, however, was probably not very high because they spent their lives wandering in troupes from city to city, or from court to court, and begging for the patronage of royalty, festival officials, or wealthy connoiseurs. And their acting—not so much the plays in which they appeared—differed essentially from the acting once known in the West. They held tenaciously, aristocratically, to some of the theatrical forms which Westerners at first had almost adopted, and then had discarded under potent democratic pressures.

In the first place, Hindus believed that a theater audience expected of actors "not the statement of fact but the experience of joy." (And you might linger to examine and admire those words for their simplicity, their purity, their rightness.) Consequently, the stage task of actors wasn't primarily to imitate an action, or the emotion of people, but primarily to imitate grace-fully the *quality*—the larger, quieter, essential spirit—hidden in the events and the feelings. Actors aimed by rhythmic expression to convey to an audi-ence certain flavors or moods or *rasas* in a given play. And these moods, eight permanent ones, were listed as "the erotic, the comic, the pathetic, the furious, the heroic, the terrific, the repulsive, and the marvelous." [47]

As a result, and in the second place, the actors of India trained them-selves to suppress in performance their own personal emotions as well as the emotions of the characters they portrayed. They expressed instead only the more esthetic *rasas*. In the beginning, it's true, Bharata in the *Nātya-śāstra* (with a far-flung hint from Aristotle?) had advised the actor "as far as pos-sible to assume the emotions of the persons whom he represents, and to depict them by costume, speech, movements, and gestures as his own." Later, however, more sophisticated theory, solidified by Viśvanātha in the *Sāhita-darpana*, a fourteenth-century treatise on poetics, dictated that the emotions need "not necessarily . . . be found in the actor, who often merely performs mechanically his part according to rote and rule. . . ." [48]

In the third place, Indian actors were fonder than the Romans of gestures. They relied on them. They perfected their acting technique and achieved their onstage aim by adhering to an elaborate system of controlled, highly formal movements. A play was defined by them as "a performance to be seen" (harking back to the early Greeks), or as "a performance which can be dramatized by gestures." And acting was defined as being "the representation by gestures of the condition of people as affected by their pleasurable and unpleasurable feelings." Everything necessary to a play—even the scenery—was suggested to the public by means of gestures. One chapter in the *Nātya-śāstra* "deals with methods of describing through bodily gestures natural phenomena such as dawn, night, twilight, day, the six seasons and the sky; mountains, oceans, stars, moonlight, heat, wind, and the midday and evening sun; human beings and animals; . . . gods; . . . expressions of happiness, anger, jealousy, calamity, misery, fear, intoxication, bravery, and the various emotions." And select, highly cultured audiences knew how to translate the minutest indications given by the actors into terms of *rasas*. Gestures were rarely natural, or lifelike, or real. They were artificial. They were dancelike, strictly composed, and symbolic. They were also traditional. What was required of an actor was "not his own interpretation of a play, but a representation of the same in accordance with the prescribed rules." He could no more invent new gestures or movements than a musician can invent new notes.[49]

In summary, then, acting in India at the start of the Middle Ages was more dancelike, more formalized, conventionalized, or stylized, and less intense than Western acting. It was philosophically designed, a deliberate art, the quiet product of a conscious working of the will. Nothing was left to chance during a performance. Actors were taught that the "behavior of the artist must of necessity be studied, and not impulsive," that "the actor no more yields to the impulse of the moment in gesture than in the spoken word." In essence and to repeat, "The exhibition of the Indian's art is altogether independent of his own emotional condition; and if he is moved by what he represents, he is moved as a spectator, and not as an actor." [50]

How would the Romans have responded to such a new and odd kind of acting? What today can we say about it? What can we honestly say, with our skimpy knowledge and understanding and from a Western point of view, except that at first and even fifth glance it's unusual? Or even disturbing? Certainly we can't exclaim that Hindu acting is infantile and all wrong merely because it differs from the Roman or early Western notion—or lack of notion—of what acting ought to be. No. We can only conclude that Eastern acting differs essentially from Western acting, that it is quite sophisticated, that it is esoteric and yet stimulating, and that it is just as right as ours is.

PART II-

THE RENEWAL

OF ACTING ~ ~

3- Roughly a Thousand Years, 476-1450

❀ THE INSTINCT SURVIVES

In the sixth century A.D. Choricius with his "Apology for Actors" rallied to the defense of the ostracized profession. He argued (1) that laughter in itself isn't evil since "Man is distinguished from the brutes by this god-given quality"; (2) that an actor mustn't be identified morally with the role he impersonates; and (3) that the theater ought to portray life as it is. Yes, Choricius agreed, "there are things in the mime [plays] which serious thinkers may not approve, but these are only part of the whole, and it is illogical to treat the part as if it were the whole. . . . There is adultery in the mimic drama, but then there is adultery in Homer and Aeschylus . . . but we do not condemn Homer and Aeschylus because of individual episodes. 'Of what,' he asks, 'Of what indeed can the mimes be accused—unless you charge them with the crime of not imitating the better only? And how could they be worthy of the word "mime," which is theirs because of their portrayal of life, if they were to delineate some parts of life and to neglect others? . . . Instead of blaming the mimes, blame those who do commit the evil actions which are themselves the basis of the miming, or imitation of evil. When we thus

reflect on the matter we see that the actors are not guilty of any crime.' " [1]
This defense, like others surely, was ignored. Nobody reflected. Professional
actors remained banished, and that was that.

But the deep-rooted mimetic instinct of the people couldn't be exorcised.
"The *ludi* of the folk . . . broke out point after point into *mimesis.*" [2] Acting, though forbidden like sin, was popular with the peasants and the nobles.
As amateurs, though no longer in theaters and minus official approval, they
helped save it from an impossible extinction. Apparently some professional
(or demiprofessional) mimes never ceased to perform somehow and somewhere through the ninth century since the authorities continued to condemn
them until about that time.

Principally during the Middle Ages, however, the actors were *jongleurs*
(*Istriones sunt ioculatores*), or singer-reciters. And it's important to note that
the features of the *jongleurs, ioculatores,* or minstrels (born of Latin and
Teutonic influences) from the sixth through the tenth centuries, and especially in their palmy days of the eleventh, twelfth, and thirteenth centuries,
and even during their break-up in the fifteenth and sixteenth centuries, were
"largely the features of the Roman *mimi.* . . ." These vagabonds definitely
inherited part of the ancient mimic tradition; they indulged in some form of
mimic activity; they were often enough professional "imitators of human
things." [3]

Baudouin de Condé and his son Jean, Watriquet de Couvin, Guiraut de
Riquier, Raherus, Blondel, Verconus, and hordes of unknown ministrels preserved the rudiments of acting, and carried them to northwestern Europe, as
they "sang songs, told tales, performed tricks, imitated each other, travestied
the world and its ways in various fashions." They "wandered at their will from
castle to castle, and in time from borough to borough, sure of their ready
welcome alike in the village tavern, the guildhall, and the baron's keep. They
sang and jested in the market places, stopping cunningly at a critical moment
in the performance to gather their harvest of small coin from the bystanders.
In the great castles, while lords and ladies supped or sat around the fire, it
was theirs to while away a long bookless evening with courtly *geste* or witty
sally. At wedding or bethrothal, baptism or knight-dubbing, treaty or tourna-
ment, their presence was indispensable. . . . and rich was their reward in
money and jewels, in costly garments. . . ." "Yet," as Chambers continues,
"for all the days of honor and all the rich gifts the minstrel life must have
had its darker side. Easily won, easily parted with. . . . And even that life of
the road, so alluring to the fever in the blood, must have been a hard one. . . .
To tramp long miles in wind and rain, to stand wet to the skin and hungry
and footsore, making the slow *bourgeois* laugh while the heart was bitter
within; such must have been the daily fate of many amongst the humbler
minstrels at least. And at the end to die like a dog in a ditch, under the ban
of the Church and with the prospect of eternal damnation before the soul." [4]

But acting survived. It survived during Mohammed's lifetime (570?–632), while Charles Martel and the Franks at Tours in 732 defeated the Mohammedan invaders and saved Christianity for western Europe, while the Toltec civilization rose in about 750 in Mexico and flared for some three hundred and fifty years, and while the English listened to their eighth-century *Beowulf*, placed Alfred the Great on the throne in 871, and made London their own in 886.

II

Acting survived in the Far East, too. It survived in India until about the year 1000 when the theater declined and virtually disappeared during the Mohammedan invasions. Before then, however, the theater at long last had become a recognized institution in China when ancient singing and dancing were combined with dramatized stories. This happened, apparently, during the T'ang dynasty (A.D. 618–906) while China was perhaps the most civilized country in the world. At any rate, by 720, when the theater had achieved importance under royal patronage, a school for acting, or Imperial Dramatic College, was established by the Emperor Ming Huang. There several hundred boys and girls, "Pupils of the Pear Garden," were taught to sing and impersonate for the amusement of the nobility. Later Emperors continued to subsidize and train actors.

Even so, the profession was never a respectable one. Chinese actors, like actors elsewhere, were for a long time rewarded with something near contempt. They were merely hired human toys with no honored place in the scheme of things. An ancient poem labeled acting, for moral reasons, a "defiled art," and an early Imperial Edict decreed that "no actor's offspring should be allowed to sit in government examinations until the third generation, when the stain of his birth would have faded away." [5] Finally, in the thirteenth century, actresses were banished from the indecorous stage.

Nevertheless, during the Yuan dynasty (1260–1368), founded by Kublai Khan, the theater flourished in a great outpouring of plays written in all probability for popular as well as for court consumption. The chief dramatists were Mah Chih, Pai Jên-fu, Ching Teh-hiu, Kao Wen-shieu, and Kuan Han-ching. And several of the more than one hundred extant thirteenth-century dramas are well known in the West. *Han koong tseu* (*The Sorrows of Han*), for instance, tells the story of a weak government whose Emperor falls truly in love with a girl who has been hidden from him by his corrupt, greedy, pimping Minister because her parents were too poor to pay for favors received. The Emperor therefore orders the Minister executed; but he escapes, goes to the Khan of the Tartars who are threatening the country, and suggests that the Khan demand the girl in marriage. The weak Emperor, torn between love for the girl and fear of the Tartars, finally decides to sacrifice her. She, however, is strong and won't submit; she kills herself, and thus teaches the Emperor grief and shame. *Hoei lan kin* (*The Chalk Circle*) places in conflict two wives of the same man. One falls in love with a government clerk, poisons the husband, proves by bribery that the other is guilty of the crime, and claims as her own the child who will inherit the money. Corrupt officials then condemn the accused wife to death, but at the last moment the judge with Solomon-like wisdom decides that she is the innocent mother of the child.

Basically the plots of many of these Chinese plays aren't exactly alien to Westerners. (Voltaire, for instance, in 1755 easily and successfully adapted an old Chinese play as L'Orphelin de la Chine.) But as staged, as acted, Oriental plays resembled nothing known to the Occidental theater. The Chinese had evolved out of the isolated culture of the Far East a kind of acting that differed from Roman and all subsequent Western acting in much the same way that Indian acting did. It vaguely paralleled certain ritualistic, musical, and idealized forms of early Greek acting.

Too ancient to be naive, and always philosophic, the Chinese sensed even in the Middle Ages that art was not life nor the duplication of life. They believed that in art "it is not the outward appearance as such, but rather the idea . . . or the immanent divine spirit . . . that is to be revealed by a right use of natural forms." A Chinese painter, for example, less fact-hungry than a Westerner, never stressed likeness in his works. With his imagination he aimed to create something more illusive and more rewarding than the already obvious. After he'd mastered his technique, he put aside his brushes and his easel and went off alone to contemplate nature for hours and even days until he had grasped it "from within, instead of as a . . . common-sense external object from without." Likewise, Chinese actors never sought to copy accurately actual human behavior. They aimed rather to distil that behavior into "its inherent and ideal qualities," into its "pure, esthetic immediacy." Consequently, their stage characterizations free from easy, outer verisimilitudes, "free from merely incidental matter" were "only real in the sense that great sculptures or paintings are real." [6]

In other words, the Chinese, like the Oriental generally, conceived of impersonation in the theater as the transmutation of everyday behavior. Acting, they insisted, ought to be more detached and more playful, more ingenious and more subtle, and more revealing than only living a role. Then, because of their fondness for esthetic ritual and their extraordinary feeling for style, and because of Buddhism which insisted on dogmatic symbolism and of Confucianism which emphasized ancestor worship (transferred to art as traditionalism), they stiffened their stage technique into preset, symbolic conventions. Therefore, acting became a studied, inherited pretense designed to be musically seen.

Chinese actors, unlike Roman or medieval European actors, believed that by working uncluttered in space and by acting out even the scenery and the properties, that by wearing dazzling costumes and masklike make-ups symbolically colored and detailed, that by using symbolic movements with the skill of a dancer or an acrobat and symbolic gestures that conformed even in the slightest manipulation of the long sleeves or the pheasant feathers to what always had been done before to express the emotion of the role, that by allowing music to set the tempo of their acting and to entice the voice away from actuality whenever the pitch of the dramatic idea or the feeling seemed to require it,[7] and that by accepting cliché characterizations down to the most trivial of mannerisms—they believed that by doing all these *theatrical* things they could most directly disclose for contemplation the pleasing essence, the graceful life-movement, the divine spirit.

And yet, despite its tantalizing insights into the nature of art, this highly sophisticated Oriental acting lacked something. To Westerners, at least, it almost forgot to be human. It failed to accent the nature of man. It avoided analyzing him. We Westerners "inherit from the Greek a peculiar arrogance," as well as a somber and driving curiosity, "about the species of animal to which we happen to belong." But "The Chinese . . . never, apparently, focussed their attention . . . narrowly on their own species. They . . . never lost sight of its *relative* position in the scheme of nature." "Since," they observed, "the world does not revolve round us as its center, we need not take either the world or ourselves too seriously. We can afford to play. We can play with the off-spring of our imagination. They shall be our playthings and our delight." [8] Because of this larger, passive, and more philosophic view of the universe, Chinese actors surrendered their right to discover and to shape their own intense, personal verities. They dodged probing deeply into humanity. Characterizations of a Hamlet or a Phèdre were impossible in their theater.

Western acting, of course, for all its crude but vibrant humanness, might possibly have been enriched by certain esthetic ingredients of Oriental acting if only the two styles had met and mingled in the Middle Ages. They never could. The amateurs, the mimes, and the minstrels followed on their own, and to please the crowd, the anthropocentric vision—or illusion.

❊ IN THE CHURCHES

During the tenth, eleventh, and twelfth centuries in Europe new Catholic countries were formed and older ones consolidated. In 962, Otto I headed the Holy Roman Empire, thus uniting "Italy" with Germany; a bit later Austria and Hungary began to take shape; in 987 Hugh Capet was chosen King of France and established Paris as its capital; in 1066 William the Conqueror won at Hastings; and Alfonso VIII, King of Castile in 1158, prepared to expel the Moslems from Spain. Christians embarked on the First Crusade to recover the Holy Land from Islam in 1099, on the Second from 1147 to 1149, and on the Third from 1189 to 1192, with six more to come.

Obviously, the Church influenced governments, education, everything. More to the point, its desire that the faithful should see, hear, and understand the truth of religion pervaded every artistic impulse of the period. Anonymous painters everywhere limned a multitude of holy pictures. Architects started building Gothic cathedrals shortly after 1140 at Sens, Noyon, Senlis, Notre Dame in Paris c. 1163, at Wells and Lincoln in 1191–92, at Chartres c. 1195, and so on. Then, as early as the tenth century, amateur actors,—priests and choir boys with the instincts of Stone Age Ook, the Egyptian I-Kher-nofret, and a priest of Dionysus—began to chant, possibly in character, certain Latin tropes, or independent lines of song or dialogue, added to the genuine liturgy of the Catholic Mass. Thus the serious theater, as if to emphasize the holy shine of its origin, was born again in religious ritual.

A faint, very faint, introduction of the dramatic into the Church service was made when the well-known, four-line *Quem quaeritis* was sung antiphonally preceding the Introit of the Mass for Easter morning. "Our earliest manuscript of this trope . . . comes from Limoges and is dated between 923 and 934, but its simplest and presumably most primitive version is that . . . from St. Gall which is found in a manuscript of almost as early a date. It seems possible indeed that the author of the *Quem quaeritis* was the Tutilo of St. Gall who lived in the second half of the ninth century. . . ." Translated from Latin the trope reads:

> Whom seek ye in the tomb, O Christians?
> Jesus of Nazareth, the crucified, O Heavenly Beings.
> He is not here; he has risen as he foretold.
> Go and announce that he is risen from the tomb.

Much later the clergy, or acolytes, impersonated the Angel and the Three Marys with appropriate gestures and voice changes. One of them, "vested in an alb," sits by the sepulcher "quietly with a palm in his hand." Then "the remaining three . . . vested in copes [cloaks] bearing in their hands thuribles with incense, and stepping delicately as those who seek something, approach the sepulcher. . . . When therefore he who sits there beholds the three approach him like folk lost and seeking something, let him begin in a dulcet voice of medium pitch to sing *Quem quaeritis*. And when he has sung it to the end, let the three reply in unison *Ihesu Nazarenum*. So he, *Non est hic, surrexit sicut praedixerat. Ite, nuntiate quia surrexit a mortuis*. At the word of this bidding let those three turn to the choir and say *Alleluia! resurrexit Dominus!* This said, let the one, still sitting there and as if recalling them, say the anthem *Venite et videte locum*. And saying this, let him rise, and lift the veil, and show them the place bare of the cross, but only the cloths laid there in which the cross was wrapped. And when they have seen this, let them set down the thuribles which they bare in that same sepulcher, and take the cloth, and hold it up in the face of the clergy, and as if to demonstrate that the Lord has risen and is no longer wrapped therein, let them sing the anthem *Surrexit Dominus de sepulchro*, and lay the cloth upon the altar. When the anthem is done, let the prior, sharing in their gladness at the triumph of our King, in that, having vanquished death He rose again, begin the hymn *Te Deum Laudamus*. And this begun, all the bells chime out together." [9]

From this simple *Quem quaeritis* the dramatic instinct of the people, encouraged by dabs of minstrel acting—and maybe by some Byzantine dramas —fashioned in France the *mystère* (a term whose meaning is still a matter of dispute), in England the miracle plays, in Spain the *autos sacramentales,* and much later in "Italy" the *sacre rappresentazioni.*

Thus, given a second look at the inception of theater, we can follow in some detail—as we never could in Greece—its evolution.

"Once detached from the Mass . . . and placed in a position where it formed the conclusion of vividly symbolical ceremonies, the trope lent itself admirably to expansion and development." We can imagine writers and/or actors in due time embarking "upon the imitation of reality and the individual . . . for the sake of a livelier dramatization of Biblical themes." By the twelfth century they had created several important additions to the original scene between the Angel(s) and the Marys. Some German church, perhaps, had added an apostle scene showing Peter and John hurrying to the tomb. Some French church, let's say, had included the appearance of the risen Christ to Mary Magdalene; and "The presence of the Dominica Persona bearing His Cross, the weeping Magdalene's approach to her Lord whom at first she mistakes for a gardener, her sudden recognition that it is He, her prostration at His feet with the loud cry *Rabboni,* His injunction *Noli me tangere,* all these details from the Gospels, visualized and set to music," gave the scene a new and mounting human poignancy. Then maybe a church in Prague added the nonliturgical merchant who, with an eye for a bargain, sold the Marys spices with which to annoint their Lord. At another church some minstrels or amateurs ventured into the comic by adding to the cast of characters the spice-merchant's gabby wife or Roman soldiers sent to guard the tomb, soldiers who realistically threw dice and boasted of their prowess, and then turned cowards when put to the test. The fully developed thirteenth-century French Easter play, *Ludus Paschalis,* for instance, "begins with an event that took place on the day before Easter, *i.e.* the setting of the soldiers' watch at the tomb; it includes an expanded spice-merchant scene with two merchants, a young *mercator* as well as a presumably older one; and scenes involving the three Marys at the tomb are ornamented with lyrical lamentations; Christ's Resurrection is reported to Pilate; and His appearances to Mary Magdalene and the disciples together with the Doubting of Thomas and the *Victimae Paschali* conclude a text that thus dramatizes certain events following the Resurrection as well as some of those preceding it." [10]

II

For Christmas Day the churchmen assisted by laymen devised another play, which was derived from the Easter one and paralleled its growth. The nucleus of the earliest version, the *Officium Pastorum,* is a second trope from Limoges dating from the eleventh century (the time of the *Chanson de Roland*). In it shepherds at the crib take the place of the Marys at the tomb.

The performance of a typical script from another town, Rouen, is described as follows: "As the five shepherds, suitably costumed, enter the west door of the choir, a boy up under the vaulting, representing an angel, announces the Nativity. After seven other angels have sung *Gloria in excelsis*, the shepherds begin their march to the *praesepe*, singing, as they traverse the choir, first a responsorial poem *Pax in terris*, and then, as they round the altar, the verse *Transeamus*. At the manger they find two priests in dalmatics, who represent midwives, and with whom they carry on the familiar dialogue. At the words *Adest hic pervulus*, the *obstretrices* draw aside the curtain, and point first to the Child, and then, at the words *Ecce virgo*, to the Mother. The shepherds kneel before the figure of the Virgin, singing the verses *Salve, virgo singularis*, and after obeisance to the Child, they turn to the chorus, singing the usual sentence *Iam vere scimus*." [11]

Next, this simple shepherds' playlet was incorporated into the more colorful Epiphany play of the Magi. In the earliest scripts the Three Kings "announce their gifts of gold, frankincense, and myrrh, and then one of them, singing *Hoc signum Magni Regis*, points to a moving star which they proceed to follow from the middle of the choir to the high altar. There they deposit their gifts, whereupon from behind the altar a boy, representing an angel, announces the birth of Christ. Surprised, the kings return to the sacristy, singing the antiphon *In Bethlehem natus est Rex coelorum*." Soon, however, this flat happening was enlivened by liturgical authors who added villainy, conflict, and suspense in the striking character of King Herod. In the "remarkably original, artistic, and dramatic" eleventh-century text from Compiègne "the Magi come from various directions and meet; then Herod's *legati* address them while a *nuntius* hurries to advise Herod of their approach; presently the King greets his visitors with a kiss, learns their errand, consults his scribes regarding it, and hears from them the prophecy of the birth of his rival in Bethlehem. He bids the Magi search for the boy and report back to him. They proceed on their way, are interrogated by the midwives, discover the newly born child whom they seek, and present their gifts. However, an angel consels them to depart by another route, which they do; whereupon a messenger tells the King he has been deceived, that the Magi will not come back, and a personage invented by the liturgical playwrights, Armiger, advises killing all young children so that the boy of whom they have learned may be put to death. Herod gives the order while an angel sings the antiphon, *Sinite parvulos venire ad me talium est enim regnum caelorum*." [12] (In four other texts the Slaughter of the Innocents is actually dramatized.)

Such carefully worked out Epiphany plays offered the amateur clerical actors, of course, a chance to display and develop their instinct for acting. Certainly the cruel, powerful, worldly, more and more bombastic Herod—an actual person instead of a type—was an ambitious mimic's dream role. And all the other nonsacred, nonstatuesque characters, such as Herod's son, his chief advisor, his messengers, scribes, and courtiers, the midwives, and the shepherds, could be impersonated more and more individually, and often rather realistically.

The success of these Epiphany plays—they spread all over the continent, even to Jerusalem—naturally led to the writing of plays suitable to other religious occasions. There was a *Conversion of St. Paul*, a *Play of St. Catharine*, a *Procession of the Prophets*, a German *Antichrist* (!), and so on; a *Raising of Lazarus* and a *Daniel* were written by Hilarius, a wandering twelfth-century (English?) scholar, sometime amateur actor, and one of the few known liturgical playwrights.

III

Near the end of the twelfth century the Church, for perhaps two reasons, began to produce its assorted religious plays out of doors. First, as the productions grew longer and more elaborate, with many scenes and characters (some of them more profane than sacred), the priests undoubtedly decided that theatricals were putting too much strain on church facilities. Second, they surely concluded that outdoor presentations could attract larger audiences. Plays were therefore often performed on church steps, in churchyards, in cemeteries, on streets, and wherever. Then, in line with their "desire to make the teaching of religion visible, potent, and palatable" [13] to as many common folk as possible, the clergy apparently aimed at popularization. At any rate, as the plays were moved out of doors the Latin chanting was gradually discarded in favor of vernacular speech, and the Biblical stories were sugar-coated with more realism and more fun. Some lay actors—folk-play amateurs and semi-professionals—were probably now and then pressed into service.

The most famous outdoor liturgical and partly laicized drama is *Le Mystère d'Adam* written by an Anglo-Norman somewhere between 1146 and 1174 (at the time of the Second Crusade). The three surviving episodes, or "acts"—Adam and Eve's fall, Cain and Abel, and the Old Testament prophecies about the coming of the Redeemer—comprise "one of the most delightful and original compositions of the Middle Ages." The *Adam* section, a complete short drama in itself, "could hold an audience on the modern stage" with its "quiet, peaceful opening; the foreshadowing; the gradual rise of the action so artistically shaded in ever-increasing intensity of interest and emotion; the lyricism . . . ; the insight into human nature; the tragic climax in which the woman is exalted by her sin and the man is crushed; the tenseness and power of the dialogue. . . ." [14] It is the first surviving European play written, with a few minor exceptions, in the vernacular, and to be acted rather than sung, and to entertain as much as to instruct.

Most significantly in *Adam* the Biblical event is embedded in a contemporary reality. The ancient and sublime action is designed "to become immediate and present; . . . to be a current event which could happen any time, which every listener can imagine and is familiar with; . . . to strike

deep roots in the mind and emotions of any random French contemporary."
Consequently, the three principal characters, Adam and Eve and the Devil,
were perhaps acted with an approximation of everyday reality. Adam, for
instance "talks and acts in a manner any member of the audience is accustomed to from his own or his neighbor's house; things would go exactly the
same way in any townsman's home or on any farm where an upright but not
very brilliant husband was tempted into a foolish and fateful act by his vain
and ambitious wife who had been deceived by an unscrupulous swindler" [15]
or seducer.

With this French *Adam*, a play that centered its interest via God in
man and predicted a shifting from a concern for the hereafter to a concern
for the here and now, the liturgical theater was born in Europe in the twelfth
century. With *Adam* acting began to seem important. *Adam's* author went
to great length in his stage directions to instruct the players. "Adam," he insisted, "must be well trained when to reply and to be neither too quick nor
too slow in his replies. And not only he, but all the personages must be trained
to speak composedly and to fit convenient gesture to the matter of their
speech. Nor must they foist in a syllable or clip one of the verse, but must
enounce firmly and repeat what is set down for them in due order." He advised the Devil when spurned by Adam to go "sadly and with downcast
countenance . . . to the doors of hell, and hold council with the other
demons. Thereafter he shall make a sally amongst the people, and then approach Paradise on Eve's side, addressing her with joyful countenance and
insinuating manner." The author also coached Adam and Eve to go and sit
down a while "as if wearied with toil, and anon look tearfully at Paradise,
beating their breasts. . . . And when Adam and Eve come to their tillage
and see the thorns and thistles sprung up, they shall be smitten with violent
grief and shall throw themselves on the earth and sit there, beating their
breasts and thighs and betraying grief by their gestures." [16]

This rebirth of the theater was emphasized some years later when sacred
happenings were notably layered with contemporary comic realism by Jean
Bodel (d. 1209–10), a municipal employee and *trouvère* (or educated, part-
time minstrel or poet) of Arras, in *Le Jeu de S. Nicolas* written between 1199
and 1201. To one of the many legends about that saint he added "meaty
scenes of low life and new characters created in the spirit of his day. The
three thieves drink, gamble, and quarrel in a tavern kept by a grasping host
and his rascally servant-boy. Here come criers of town and King and a messenger who joins in the drinking, gambling, and quarreling. All these people
are pure Artois; indeed there is no desire to hide the fact; their tipple is the
good wine of Auxerre. . . ." [17] About one half of this miracle play is assigned
to these tavern scenes; and surely the amateur actors impersonated the well-
defined characters from a first-hand experience which matched Bodel's powers
of observation.

Because Bodel belonged to Confrérie de la Ste. Chandelle, a "*société des jongleurs et des bourgeois d'Arras,*" [18] and probably wrote the sketch to be acted by its members, one wonders now if the coupling of roistering and real comedy to the religious tone of the Crusades and the miracle itself might not have been the contribution of Bodel's associates, the minstrels. *Le Jeu de S. Nicolas* smacks of the farces they inherited from the mimes. Very possibly by the end of the twelfth century minstrels were not only advising or coaching amateurs in church plays but also competing with them.

❀ IN THE TOWNS

During the thirteenth century—when all Christendom was startled and stimulated by Arabic, Jewish, and Latin translations of Aristotle, when Marco Polo visited China from 1275 to 1292 where a very different theater flourished —the newborn religious theater of Europe was gradually laicized. But the very slow change didn't improve matters much. For two centuries and a half dramatic art remained a poor, peaked thing, lacking vitality and maturity. From 1200 to 1450—while Brunelleschi (*c.* 1377–1446) designed churches and palaces at Florence; while Donatello (*c.* 1386–1466) sculptured, and Giotto (*c.* 1266–1337) and Massaccio (1401–1428?) painted; while Dante wrote *The Divine Comedy* (1300–1321), Petrarch his love poems, Boccaccio *The Decameron* (1353), Chaucer *The Canterbury Tales* (1387–1400), and Villon (1431–1465?) his ballads—no great talents nourished the drama. No genuine, stimulating playwrights quickly followed the authors of *Adam* and *The Play of St. Nicholas* as Aeschylus had quickly followed Thespis, or Plautus had followed Livius Andronicus. Dogma, definite and defined, plus the scatter of new nations, prevented that kind of flowering. No one, it seemed, was interested in the theater's possibilities as an adult, nonreligious art.

Once this new liturgical theater was moved out of doors, however (eventually into the market places), and had been translated into the vernacular, all sorts of unexpected consequences followed. First, what originated "as a mere spectacle devised by ecclesiastics for the edification of the laity," came in time to appeal to a deep-rooted native instinct of drama in the folk and to continue as an essentially popular thing, a *ludus* maintained by the people itself for its own inexhaustible wonder and delight"; second, what was intended to be primarily sacred was expanded by laymen into something more secular and more comic than should be; and third, what was once united in the Kingdom of God gradually separated to become variously national. In short, the new theater got out of control. By 1210, as a result, the priests were close to being forbidden by papal edict from appearing on public stages. Thereafter, townsmen began to replace them as actors. Thereafter, also, the Church, finding "no difficulty in accommodating itself to the somewhat disconcerting by-product of its own liturgy," tended more and more to produce its plays cautiously in association with devotional societies and guilds of the towns.[19]

As a play producer, however, the Church was wary of the influence of the despised professional actor. If at first some clerics had fervently evolved the liturgical drama out of a desire to counteract the licentious entertainments of the wandering *jongleurs*, they now had more reason than ever to fear them. After all, the minstrels were at the crest of their popularity. Would they intrude? Would they try to take over? Would professional actors once again be approved, accepted? It might happen. After all, Thomas Aquinas was unaccountably on the verge of writing that "The profession of an *histrio* is by no means in itself unlawful. It was ordained for the reasonable solace of humanity, and the *histrio* who exercises it at a fitting time and in a fitting manner is not on that account to be regarded as a sinner." [20]

The clergy was convinced that professional actors were deluding innocent folk by encouraging them to introduce more and more comic relief and naughtiness into play after play so that the performances might be less sermonical and boring. And today we can see that the churchmen were accurate in their hypothesis, for not all of the comic elements in the early mysteries seem to have been of amateur origin. For example, the boasting tyrant (Herod), the jealous husband (Joseph), and shrewish wife (Mrs. Noah), the comic Devil with his canvas club and warts, and other characters have their prototypes in the mimic theater.

But what could the Church do about the insidious influence of the minstrels? Nothing much. It was trapped. It couldn't condemn professional actors without also condemning the amateur actors of its own plays. So, apparently, the professionals continued to help the amateurs write and perform such unhealthy, small-cast farces as *Courtois d'Arras* (before 1228), a much too sprightly dramatization of the parable son story; the almost Atellane *Garçon et l'Aveugle* (*The Boy and the Blindman*) (between 1266 and 1282), which had absolutely no connection with anything religious; and in England the *Interludium de Clerico et Puella* (*A Clerk and a Girl*) (between 1272 and 1307), which was dangerously similar to the traditional adultery sketch of the Roman mimes.

And then the French amateurs lost their heads and began to form themselves into frivolous counterparts of the religious *confréries*: into literary *puys, sociétés joyeuses, clercs de la Basoche* (university law students), and Parisian Enfants-sans-souci, and to act out their own profane farces and *sotties* (clownlike, satirical vaudeville patters). And most shocking to the church, the professionals suddenly began to write and act their own plays and to offer them where and when they chose. For instance, that typical minstrel, the out-at-elbows Rutebeuf (?–*c.* 1285) composed his serious play, *Le Miracle de Théophile*, at Paris about 1261 and, with the assistance of a companion, took it upon himself to recite it in public. Then an Arras clerk and *trouvère*, Adam le Bossu, or de la Halle (1230–1288), composed two secular verse comedies, the *Jeu de la Feuillée* (*The Play of the Bower of Green Leaves*) in 1276–77 and *Le Jeu de Robin et Marion* somewhere between 1282 and 1285. The first includes among its characters the author's own father, his wife and his two friends, a woman of ill-repute who discovers that her stomach-ache is an unborn child, and a fantastic group of fairies instead of saints! The humorous talk is all about love, scolding wives, hen-pecked husbands, avarice, gluttony, taxes! And it was acted before the *puy* of Arras by some of the persons portrayed! The second play was filled with lively songs and dances and with rustic characters who spoke *"comme on parle au village"!* [21]

The Church did have sufficient cause to be wary of professional actors. Also without quite knowing it, the Church had reason to be wary of the influence of certain other professionals, the scholars. In the late thirteenth or early fourteenth century Nicholas Trivet (1258–1328), an English Dominican, wrote his commentary on the plays of Seneca, which rapidly became well known throughout Europe, especially in "Italy." Then at Padua in 1315 Albertino Mussato (1261–1329) imitated Seneca and wrote, in Latin, the historical tragedy *Ecerinis*, intended to be read only, not acted. Next, other men wrote other Senecan plays. (And in 1416 Poggio would discover the complete text of Quintilian; in 1422 the principal works of Cicero would come to light at Lodi; and twelve comedies by Plautus would be found in 1427.) [22]

But the Church ignored these scholars and their plays—just as it had ignored Hrotswitha and her impotent tenth-century scripts modeled on Terence. And, curbing as much as possible the minstrels (who had organized themselves into a guild at Paris in 1321), [23] it continued to produce in conjunction with religious societies its own sacred dramas until in the fourteenth century it achieved some distinction with at least forty *Les Miracles de Notre Dame* and many elaborate Passion plays.

The diverse and appealing *Miracles*, written to be produced indoors as well as outdoors on the Virgin's several holy days by guilds or *puys*, are deeply religious in the inevitable point they make but strongly secular in the suspense-developing plots that lead up to Mary's intercession (like a Greek *deus ex machina*) and the rescue of repentant sinners. For example, the fourteenth-century *Une Femme Que Notre Dame Garda d'Estre Arse* (*A Woman Notre Dame Saved from Burning*, or *Guibour*) is mostly an emotionally charged domestic melodrama with only a tacked-on religious ending. It relates how Guibour, although innocent, is accused by gossip of being her son-in-law's mistress, and is so driven to distraction that she has him murdered. When the crime is discovered and the family arrested, she confesses in order to save her husband and her daughter, and is sentenced to be burned at the stake. There she repents and prays to Notre Dame, who at the very last minute forbids the flames to touch her. With this drama, and its kind, and characters as human as the men and women in the audiences, "we are well on the way to secular theater." [24]

The Passion plays—about the last days of Christ—moved along another avenue toward secularization. Produced at Frankfort, Vienna, and all over France, they were designed as ambitious theatrical spectacles. The fourteenth-century *Las Passion du Palatinus,* for instance, calls for a "multiple staging" or a "simultaneous setting" which will include among the *mansions* (small, usually raised, curtained structures capable of supporting simple furniture) the road to Jerusalem, locales for Caiaphas, Pilate, and Herod, the house of the smith, Golgotha, and so on. The same century's *Le Jour du Jugement* lists a cast of ninety-four characters. Obviously, presentations making such enormous demands strained the time, the talents, and the coffers of churches. They needed more help from devout townsmen.

Then when the Nativity, Passion, and Resurrection plays were linked together and the action further extended to include the Ascension and Last Judgment, together with all kinds of intermediate saint and Biblical scenes, the "cosmic" cycles came into existence. They, of course, were definitely too much, too big in scope, too spectacular for the Church to continue to finance and produce. So, much of the practical control of this new amateur theater finally passed from the clergy to the laity. Town corporations with an eye to business booms assumed, via the confraternities and the secular guilds, the responsibility of financing, managing, and staging the enlarged outdoor productions. This secularization culminated in the great processional cycles of the municipal guilds in England soon after the establishment of the Corpus Christi festival in 1311. The twenty-five Chester plays (nine on one day, nine on the second, and seven on the third) date from 1328, the forty-eight York ones from between 1330 and 1378, and the similar Wakefield (Towneley) and Coventry cycles from sometime later. By 1450 in "Italy" the *divozione* had been secularized into the *sacre rappresentizioni* and were elaborately being produced by confraternities at all sorts of municipal festivals.

II

As soon as the towns took over the production of religious plays more citizens than ever turned into actors and assumed the majority of roles. Hundreds of ordinary folk now "wanted like Bottom and his crew, to amuse themselves with the delightful new toy." When open tryouts were announced, when a proclamation asked "those of *bonne volonte* to come to *le salle de la Passion,*" when a municipal corporation looked for actors best qualified in "connyng, voice or personne," the citizens gladly appeared and made a virtue of their not being "players of price" but only "Crafts men and meane men" "lackyng lyttural scyens" and "Retoryk." [25] Acting to them was easy; anyone could do it. Why should they depend on the minstrels?

Nothing much, unfortunately or fortunately, is known now about these eager amateur actors, or "players" as they were called. Mostly perhaps they performed onstage as they did in life. For instance, in *Le Jeu de la Feuillée* it was said that "Many of the characters are not even acting; they are simply being themselves." Generally, the amateur actors were described as being "an ignorant set of men, mechanics and artisans, who know not an A from a

B, untrained and unskilled in playing such pieces before the public. Their voices are poor, their language unfitting, their pronunciation wretched. No sense do they have of the meaning of what they say." When cast in a drama (lads in the female roles), they sometimes had "to bind themselves before a notary to play on the prescribed days unless ill, to be on time, accept the roles assigned them by the superintendents, attend rehearsals or pay fines, and not to find fault or get drunk. In some localities the actors paid a sum in advance in order to take part in any benefits accruing from the performances, to help defray expenses in case of need, and also to serve as a deposit against potential fines." Often they were obliged to furnish their own costumes, to double in more than one role, and to participate in parades that heralded the performances. For their services they at times received, especially in frugal France, merely food and wine; but later they were paid fees "on a scale proportionate to the dignity of their parts. Thus at Coventry one Fawston got 4d. 'for hangyng Judas,' and 4d. more 'for coc croyng.' The payment to the performer of God was 3s. 4d. A 'sowle,' whether 'savyd' or 'dampnyd,' got 20d. and a 'worme of conscyence' only 8d. At Hull, Noah was generally paid 1s., God and Noah's wife a trifle less." And like amateurs everywhere these players loved to strut and to rant, were overly dependent on the prompter, and enjoyed mixing with the audience in their costumes and make-ups when they weren't needed onstage.[26]

And yet, in their enthusiastic, untrained way they took their acting seriously. Acting wasn't merely a game, as it was to the Orientals, but something of real importance to the world. And it wasn't an art, something different from nature, but nature itself with nothing suppressed or changed and all the honesties and commonplace details of behavior scrupulously copied. These amateurs were realists. For instance, "The effect of Christ's crucifixion could not be complete unless the actor himself suffered." The man who impersonated Jesus at Metz in 1437 "would have died on the rood-tree, for he fainted and was like to have died had he not been rescued"; and a priest named Johan de Missey "took the part of Judas, but hung too long and fainted and was like dead. . . ."[27]

Competition like that threatened the very existence of the minstrel professional actors. They were virtually excluded, except in a sometime advisory capacity, from this new civic theater. And they were more thoroughly excluded when the French secular and literary societies rapidly began to steal audiences with indoor productions of *sotties*, farces, and smaller religious plays whose casts were recruited only from among the members, referred to as *"gens ignares, artisans mecaniques."* This amateur competition reached the danger point when the first French serious yet nonreligious play, *L'Estoire de Griseldis*, based on a story by Boccaccio and written by Philippe de Mézières in 1395, was produced by him with court personages and retainers as the actors! Then in 1402 those amateurs, those tradesmen, the Confrérie de la Passion et Résurrection, who may have been giving public and court per-

formances as early as 1380, or by 1398, received official recognition from
Charles VI and the right to produce religious plays whenever and wherever
they wished. The Brotherhood immediately rented a large, second-story hall at
the Hôpital de la Trinité and converted it into a kind of theater. By 1450
the Enfants-sans-souci and Basochiens, who had been playing *sotties*, farces,
and moralities in competition with the Confrérie de la Passion, seem to have
arranged some sort of partnership with them, and from that time on these
societies acted their comedies in conjunction with the religious plays at la
Trinité. Against that unequal competition the professionals were unable to
hold their own; consequently, "it is generally thought that no troupes of professional actors appeared in France before the sixteenth century." [28]

In "Italy" and in England there was "nothing corresponding to the
plentiful production of farces by amateur associations of every kind which
characterized fifteenth-century France." Nevertheless, the Italian professional
actors began to worry. The scholars were experimentally writing more and
more plays, mostly for reading purposes, in imitation of Seneca and Terence;
and they had just discovered some new comedies of Plautus. Then in 1444 at
the Ferrara carnival the dialogue of Francesco Ariosto's *Isis* was acted *"per
personatos"* who were amateurs! The English professional actors also worried.
They saw the amateurs concocting little morality plays—in which the characters were abstractions—like *The Castle of Perseverance* (1400–1440) and
trying boldly to turn professional by touring from town to town for a fee.
In short, the minstrels saw "the scanty remnants of their audiences being
filched from them by unskilled rustics who had hit upon just the one form
of literary entertainment which, unlike poetry and romance in general, could
not dispense with the living interpreter." [29]

So, at the close of the Middle Ages—with the invention of printing in
1450, and the fall of the Eastern Roman Empire in 1453—the mimetic instinct, deep-rooted in the psychology of the people, had found its outlet
in the sacred drama of the Church, and then in the festival celebrations of
the municipal guilds and in the little farces acted by all sorts of amateur
groups everywhere. But also by 1450 the minstrels, or professional actors, who
had more than faintly influenced this development, and then had been
excluded by the clergy, the town corporations, and the amateur societies, saw
books and break-up time ahead. The future looked ominous. They had to do
something. Could they possibly develop a neglected side of their own art and
somehow become again the true actors they once had been and thus participate in and contribute to this new theater—and make it pay?

❦ IN THE FAR EAST AGAIN

Near the end of the fourteenth century, while professional actors were
kept busy in China by such first-rate playwrights as Kao-Tse-ch'eng, T'ang
Hsien-tsu, and Wu Shih-chu, and had appeared, for instance, in the still

popular *Pi-pa-ki* (*Lute Song*) (1404), the theater was danced into existence in Japan. Out of Shinto religious rites, court ceremonies, varied folk mimicries and dances the Nō or *nō-gaku* (skill or accomplishment) drama was evolved for the amusement of the public on temple grounds; then, fostered by the *samurai*, or nobles, in the fifteenth century, it was performed by subsidized actors for audiences in palaces, temples, or villages, or even at festivals held in the shrines of the remotest provinces; later it became essentially an aristocratic entertainment, and is today the oldest major theatrical art still regularly played.

This theater was vaguely initiated by actors Itchū, Muma no Shirō, Mitsutarō, Kiami, and others. Then the priest, stage director, writer, and "magnificent" actor Kwanami Kitosugu (1333–1384) and his illustrious son, Seami (Zeami) Motokiyo (1363–1444), successfully wrote, produced, and set the form for Nō dramas. The important date is 1374 when Kwanami's theatrical innovations were officially recognized and encouraged by the Shōgun. Seami, ranked "as the highest in intelligence, playwriting, and acting of the age," then perfected the Nō. He knew that "The actor who has not a good play at his disposal is like any army without weapons." Of the extant repertory of some two hundred and forty Nō dramas, about one hundred, including many adaptations of older material, are his. And the fundamentals of Nō acting were first formulated by him. Then in 1429 Seami's nephew, Motoshige (On-nami), with the assistance of his eldest son, Matasaburō (Masamori), founded the still flourishing Kanze school and continued to produce and act in Nō dramas.[30]

Most Nō plays "are built upon the god-dance, or upon some local legend or spiritual apparitions, or later, on gestes of war and feats of history." The characters are usually "ghosts of past memories" and "passive in that . . . they are directed by external influences over which they have no control." Each prose–verse composition when danced, sung, and acted "presents a distilled grace and beauty of form, appealing to the senses through qualities which can only be called unearthly in their effect." In fact, most of the Nō pieces, about as long as an average one-acter, are so potent that when three (originally) or five of them—a god-drama, a man-drama, a woman-drama, a madwoman-drama, and a demon-drama—are customarily presented on one program, lasting six or seven hours, several *kyogen* (wild words), or comic interludes in the vernacular and minus masks, chorus, or orchestra, are acted between them as a relief from the music, the emotion of the idea, and the over-all ghostly magic.[31]

The vividly oriental, poetic quality of these ballet–dramas can be quickly indicated. Kwanami's *Sotoba Komachi* (*Old Komachi*), for example, relates the tragic flash-back story of the young and beautiful Komachi who becomes too proud when too many lovers court her. To one of them who comes from afar she answers that she will listen to his wooing only after he has journeyed to her a hundred times. On his final rugged trip he dies of exhaustion. Then Komachi, suffering, becomes old, ugly, bereft of her senses, and forsaken by all—except for the ghost of her persistent lover who at last possesses her body until it is spent. Seami's early *Hagoromo* (*The Feather Robe*) tells about a fisherman who finds an Angel's feather robe. She asks him to return it to her so she can fly back to Heaven. He refuses; she pleads; reluctantly he gives it to her; and in gratitude she lengthily performs "the dances that are danced in Heaven." In Seami's *Atsumori* the character Rensei reveals that once he had been a warrior, but that now, grief-stricken, he is a priest setting-out to pray for his enemy Atsumori whom he killed in battle. On his journey to the tomb he meets and talks with a reaper who turns into the ghost of Atsumori, and the fatal hand-to-hand fight is re-enacted in a dance. But just as the ghost Atsumori is about to kill the slayer, he dramatically discovers that he cannot: "No, Rensei is not my enemy. Pray for me again, oh, pray for me again."

In interpreting these plays the Nō actors, men only, who in the principal roles are beautifully masked and always richly costumed for bulk, grandeur, and increased theatrical stature, still perform as they did in the fourteenth century on a bare, in-the-round stage. They still speak or chant in their own natural voices, even when impersonating women; they move and gesture with slow, measured economy and subtle significance, and always in strict accordance with ancient, patterned practice; and they stomp the orchestral beats with their shoeless feet, and dance to accompaniments of choral singing. Like Indian and Chinese actors, they work in traditional, stylized, and symbolistic patterns instead of realistic ones.

The principal Nō actor is called *Shite* (pronounced "shtay") or "doer." The second actor, who usually explains, is called *Waki*, or "assistant." Both of them may have onstage helpers. And when the *Shite* expresses the core of his role in his dance, the words are chanted by a chorus of ten or twelve men who sit motionless at the side of the stage. This chanting is accompanied by the music of a flute, two hand-drums, and often a stick drum.

II

Japanese actors as early as the fourteenth century were most strictly trained for their profession. And now, as it did six hundred years ago, that training begins early, sometimes at the age of seven. Before the pupils reach their prime at thirty-five they are taught the "three forms of acting-fundamentals—woman, old man, and warrior." More importantly, they are taught to "feel the thing as a whole, from the inside" instead of merely "copying facts point by point." They learn, after their technique has been mastered, that "the great difficulty is to grasp the spirit of the piece," for the excellence of Nō lies not in the depiction of action, but in the expression of emotion. The "flower" of acting "consists in forcing upon the audience *an emotion which they do not expect.*" And "The emotion is always fixed upon idea, not upon personality." In other words, Japanese actors are taught to make their movements and intonations their "own possession" for the primary purpose of conveying to audiences an essence derived from the play. As Seami said, "Forget the Nō and look at the actor. Forget the actor and look at the 'idea.' Forget the 'idea' and you will understand the Nō." [32]

Nō acting, as already noted, derives almost entirely from the teachings of Seami. Beginning in 1400, when he was thirty-seven, he set down in a number of secret articles all that he had learned, mostly from his father, about the subject. Seami's writings were secret because, as he explained, "In any field, especially in the field of stage art . . . certain matters gain in usefulness by keeping them secret." These secrets were kept from nonactors until 1665 when *Hachijyōbon-Kadensho* (*Instructions on Flower in Eight Volumes*), an extremely altered version of his original *Kadensho* (*The Instructions on Flower*), was published. Finally in 1909 the *Zeami-jūrokuboshū* (*Collection of Sixteen Treaties by Zeami*), edited by Togo Yoshida, was made available to the public. No one anywhere wrote so much so early on acting.

According to Seami, the acting of Nō centers on three fundamentals. First, there is *monomane*, imitation or miming. Acting begins with that. The actor must aim at a "complete imitation of a thing," must "adjust the act of imitation to the nature of the thing." Seami advises the actor to "Imbibe what you have learned as your own and seek to be the one you are impersonating. Then you will be a 'master doer.' " But for Seami imitation isn't the end-all, and be-all of acting. "Imitation," he insists, "must not be wholly external." Something else must be added to it. A female impersonator, for instance, "would be a 'failure,' no matter how much he 'feels' himself to be a woman, if he is not proficient in her representation" onstage before an audience.[33]

Therefore, for Seami there is beyond mere imitation the second fundamental, or *yūgen*—a term that almost escapes definition in English. Yet it must be defined because Seami taught his actors "That whatever you imitate you must not lose sight of *yūgen*." This "most essential" *yūgen* hasn't been too helpfully described as "the technique of expressing the profundity of sentiment," as "phantasy coming from spiritual depth," as "transcendental insight," as "estheticism," as "grace." Seami himself attempted to explain the term in easier words by saying, "Whatever you imitate, don't forget to make it beautiful. That's the core of *yūgen*." [34] But *yūgen* is more, or deeper, than elegance, gracefulness, or beauty.

Perhaps, because we know that Seami was deeply imbued with the teachings of Zen and believed that all truth lies hidden in the heart of things, we shall decide that *yūgen* means the beautiful expression of "what lies beneath the surface; the subtle as opposed to the obvious; the hint as opposed to the statement." We may agree that *yūgen* means something like the intimation of the essence behind externals. For example, it's reported that Seami said, "If, in the part of an old man the actor, merely because he has noticed that old men walk with bent backs and crooked knees and have shrunken frames, sets about to imitate these characteristics, he may indeed achieve an effect of decrepitude," but it will be at the expense of missing something that goes deeper than exact imitation: the idea, the essential characteristic, the spirit, the beauty. "What this actor should study, Seami says, is that effect of will without the corresponding capacity for action that shows in old age, and this effect will often be given best by making all movements a little late, so that they come after the musical beat. For in old age the limbs are heavy and the ears slow; there is the will to move but not the corresponding capacity. With this in mind the actor may then be as lively as he pleases." [35]

In short, Seami meant by *yūgen* that in all acting "there should always be a tinge of the unlike. He believed that if in art we press imitations too far, it will impinge on reality. . . ." [36]

Seami's third fundamental of acting is *hana* or "flower." This term appears to be allied in meaning to *yūgen*. In one sense it can mean the conveying to an audience of *yūgen*. It's the technique for "arousing the interest of the audience," for "bewitching the audience" with "the feeling of strangeness." In another sense, "flower" can mean the communication to an audience of rarity, of novelty. As Seami explained, "We come across something like 'An oasis in the desert' " in the acting. "That's the *flower*." [37] This "flower," as we've already noticed, "consists in forcing upon the audience *an emotion which they do not expect*." In short, the best acting should aim to do more than merely let an audience recognize and verify its experiences. It should try to extend, to deepen, and to enrich these experiences.

Seami's three fundamentals eventually, after a long time, blend and become, in rare instances, *ran-i* or attained skill. This consummation has to do with "a fully matured state of artistic sense that comes from an intense cultivation of skill, and occasionally assumes a singular style of acting." It implies that a long practicing artist of, say, fifty ought to be more aware of the quality of life and of art than a younger artist, and therefore ought to have more within himself to put into his acting. Since *ran-i* results "from a lifelong effort of training and a careful winnowing of right and wrong," [38] it might almost be called a kind of sagacity and serenity in acting; it touches the spiritual.

That, in a limping Western analysis, is the gist of Seami's theory of acting. It's the gist of most Oriental acting. But in the embryonic theaters of Europe in the Middle Ages neither the clergy, nor the tradesmen at York, nor the members of the Confrérie in Paris, nor the scholars at Ferrara could be bothered with theories, especially with esoteric theories about the art of acting. They merely went onstage to recite and to behave sort of naturally. And we can wonder, along with Walter F. Kerr, how much we Westerners "may have lost as we learned to duplicate with such fidelity the conditions of life." [39]

4 One Hundred and Fifty Years, 1450-1600

✿ IN CLUBS, CASTLES, COURTS

During the Renaissance, from roughly 1450 to 1600, the people of Europe began to explore the world and themselves. At about the time that Christian I in 1448 became King of Denmark and also governed Norway, and Ivan the Great unified Russia in 1480, and Gustavus Vasa was crowned King of Sweden in 1523, explorers sailed westward until Columbus discovered America in 1492 and the Spaniards under Cortés embarked in 1519 on the conquest of Mexico. Copernicus (1473–1542) studied the stars; Vesalius (1514–1564) examined human anatomy. Palestrina (1525–1594), of course, composed his Masses; but the painters Fouquet (c. 1420–c. 1480) Giovanni Bellini (c. 1430–1516), Botticelli (c. 1444–1510), Leonardo da Vinci (1452–1519), Dürer (1471–1528), Michelangelo (1475–1564), Titian (1477–1576), Raphael (1483–1520), Holbein the younger (1497–1543), Tintoretto (1518–1594), Brueghel the elder (c. 1525–1569), and El Greco (1545–1614) vividly shaped, even in holy pictures, their individual responses to life. And writers found human things to say that advanced from Malory's *Le Morte d'Arthur* (c. 1485) to Erasmus and his *In Praise of Folly* (1509, 1512), to Machiavelli's *The Prince* (1532), Thomas More's *Utopia* (Latin

83

in 1516, English in 1551), Rabelais' *Gargantua and Pantagruel* (1532–1552), and Montaigne's *Essays* (1580–1595).

During this period, the theater, which had been revived in the churches of France and then had migrated to the market places of Europe, migrated again. It moved, as noted, into the clubrooms of the French amateur societies; it also moved into the banqueting-halls in the castles of England, and even into the households of the Tudor sovereigns, where young men from schools and colleges wrote for actors and teased them into dreaming of a repute and a security denied them by the churches; and it moved into the ducal courts of "Italy" where scholars, inspired by Greek and Latin culture, acquainted the theater with its classical heritage. Thus, having passed from the hands of the clergy to those of the people, it was variously readied to pass, after an interval of a thousand years, into those of a professional class of actors who would try to earn a livelihood by regularly performing nonreligious plays in public playhouses. But before professionals could establish their "quality" as a "recognized constituent of the polity" and win their way to economic independence [1] they had to battle in France with amateurs, in England with amateurs and the Puritans, and in "Italy" with amateurs and scholars.

II

Despite this imminent change, religious drama continued to be produced by amateurs all over Europe during the Renaissance—and often startlingly so. In Florence in 1454 the festival of St. John's Day was celebrated with a procession of twenty-two *edifici* for the enacting of episodes from the Old and New Testaments; the *Wiener Osterspiel* (*Vienna Easter Play*) and the *Hessisches Weihnachtspiel* (*Hessian Christmas Play*) were regularly and elaborately staged; and at Metz in 1468 "The personage of Saint Catherine was performed by a young girl, about eighteen years old, who was the daughter of Dédiet the glazier, and she did her duty very well indeed, to the pleasure and delight of everybody. Though this girl had 2,300 lines in her part, she had them all at her fingers' end, and . . . did speak so quickly and so pitifully that she made several people cry, and pleased everybody. And for this reason the girl made a rich match with a nobleman. . . ." In Paris the expert *Le Mystère de la Passion* by musician and "notable *bachelier en theologie*," Arnoul Greban (d. 1471?), with its 244 speaking parts plus extras, was played at least three times before 1473 by perhaps the Confrérie. In 1486 at Winchester, England, Henry VII was entertained at dinner with a schoolboy presentation of *Christi Descensus ad Infernos*; and somewhere near 1495 the Anglo-Dutch *Everyman*, or *Elckerlijk*, solemnly took the stage. In Spain the *Auto de la Pasión* by Lucas Fernandez (c. 1474–1542) was presented on Good Fridays. And at Bourges in 1536 the stupendous *Actes des Apôtres* (1452–1478?), said to have taken forty days to perform, dazzled the spectators with its "sumptuous properties and decorations, the elaborate mechanical devices employed to produce thunder, to simulate camels, serpents, ravening lions, flying owls, dragons, spouting flames, and other performing animals, the *trucs* used to lower or raise persons and beasts or to conceal them in clouds, to burn and decapitate saints, permit magicians to fly, fountains to spout milk, ships to sail across the stage." It's a wonder the actors were ever noticed. But they were; they were praised as "serious men who know so well how to feign by signs and gestures the characters they represent that most of the audience believe them to be true and not feigned." Then in 1538 the Protestant *Pammachius* by Thomas Kirchmayer (1511–1564) was played in Zwickau, Germany, and again in Latin at Christ's College, Cambridge, in 1545. In 1547 the famous *Valenciennes Passion Play* was staged on a long platform erected in the courtyard of the Duke d'Arschot's chateau.[2]

Finally, however, by a declaration of November 17, 1548, the Court of Paris, disgusted with the profane elements that nearly dominated religious plays, prohibited the amateurs of the Confrérie from producing more of them. But in the same edict the members were granted "a full monopoly on theatrical performances in the city and suburbs; and none could be given except with their permission and to their profit." As a result the society struggled along by staging farces and moralities.[3]

❁ FRANCE

The conjecture is that French professional actors weren't too interested in appearing in religious plays—even if they had been allowed to do so. How could they exhibit their skills in those crowded casts and surrounded by such spectacular accoutrements? Furthermore, they were rarely paid much, and never regularly; they certainly couldn't make a living by that kind of acting. Therefore, they must have hoped to work more or less regularly in the farces, or better yet in serious plays, since the public would hardly support a theater that was only comic.

But from 1450 to 1550 only amateur actors dabbled with the few nonsacred plays that were staged. An almost contemporary event, probably experienced by the unknown author, was dramatized in *Le Mystère du Siège d'Orléans*, in which Joan of Arc was first portrayed onstage. This two-day amateur spectacle, calling for 140 speaking roles, is believed to have been composed anywhere from 1440, nine years after her burning, to 1456, with revisions and additions dating down to 1470. Then in the early 1450's Jacques Milet (c. 1425–1466) forsook biblical themes and delved into classical myths with his *L'Istoire de la Destruction de Troye la grant* which was staged by amateurs. And an anonymous, almost chronicle history play, *Vie de S. Louis*, involving almost three hundred different characters, was produced under the auspices of the Confrérie before 1472.

Most of the time during this long period the amateurs in Paris monopolized, with legal support, the production of lively down-to-earth farces. At a time known now as "the heyday of the theater of the Basoche" the professionals were pushed aside, forgotten. Law students and other club members, so frequently and so successfully staged their programs—consisting usually of a *sottie*, a moralité, and finally a farce—that no professional companies would risk competing with them. Professionals who wanted to act banded together in little troupes and toured.

None of these amateur farces, not even that unimportant masterpiece *Maitre Pierre Pathelin*, written surely before 1470 (by Guillaume Alécis?), and probably acted by the Basochiens, contributed much toward the development of a true French theater. And nobody knows the names of those who acted such farces: amateurs are always amateurs, and no doubt they contributed generously to what has always been considered the lowest level of French acting. Outside Paris, however, where professional troupes made up of "nearly all rascals" and women who "lived in greatest licentiousness" were trying to make a living by touring plays, a few actor names began to emerge. One of them is worth noticing. It is the name of the first professional actress in the modern theater who, tardily, "arrives on the scene . . . equipped to turn cartwheels or do handsprings . . . as well as to act in regular plays." In a contract signed at Bourges in 1545 a "Marie Fairet, or Ferré, sometimes described as the wife of the town crier, Michel Fasset, agrees with Antoine l'Espéronnière, 'player of histories, to help him to play . . . ancient pieces of Rome, consisting of several moral histories, farces and *soubressaulx*.' Furthermore, the said Marie promises to do all this 'in such a way as to give joy and recreation to all present, in order to earn, amass and obtain money . . . to the profit of the said l'Espéronnière,' for which she is to receive, besides board and lodging, the magnificent sum of twelve livres Tournois a year, or approximately twelve modern dollars." And the "wily manager, apparently conscious that Marie's charms might bring her in revenues other than those supplied by himself, further stipulates that should anyone during her engagement give her clothes or money, then 'Gailharde, wife of said l'Espéronnière, should receive one half thereof.' "[4]

Professionals like her, with an aversion to menial labor, or an itch to act at all costs, were inevitably heading toward Paris, where in due time they would take the theater away from amateurs.

II

Farces, which, to repeat, almost certainly arose out of the minstrel tradition, were popularly acted by amateurs all over Europe long after 1450. In Holland a farmer was tricked by a quack at a fair, and a husband whose wife bore him a child three months after they were married was persuaded by her relatives that all nevertheless was well. In Spain Rodrigo de Cota (?–1470) was credited with the *Dialogo entrel Amor y un Viejo* (*Dialogue*

Between Love and an Old Man) (1472–1480?). And in Germany Hans Sachs (1494–1576), master cobbler, mastersinger, and master of ceremonies of the Carnival Play in Nürnberg, wrote about two hundred warm little farces, such as, *Der fahrende Schüler im Paradies* (*The Wandering Scholar from Paradise*) (1550), *Das heisse Eisen* (*The Hot Iron*) (1551), *Der Rossdieb zu Fünsing mit den tollen Bauren* (*The Horse Thief*) (1553). Moreover, he trained the amateur actors himself and staged his playlets in an old church he had transformed into a theater. So, laughing, people everywhere became more and more avid for acted plays.

❋ ENGLAND

In order to curb the amateur actors, in order to counteract the "illegitimate competition with the real minstrels" and the resulting "decay of art," English professionals did more than form themselves into a London guild in 1469. They decided to revert to being full-fledged actors. The remedy was that simple. They began to act out little sketches in the castles of the nobles; and, smarter than the amateurs, they placed themselves under the protection of various dukes and earls. By at least 1464 they were officially recognized as "players in their enterludes" (or interludes, "the normal name for plays given in the banqueting-halls of the great"); and by 1492 they had regularly entertained Richard, Duke of Gloucester (later Richard III), Henry Bourchier, Earl of Essex, the Earls of Oxford, and so on. "The Earls of Northumberland, . . . Derby, and Shrewsbury, and Lord Arundel, all had their players before the end of the century.[5]

Next, the actors became part of the royal household, since it is recorded that probably by 1485, certainly by 1493, Henry VII (1457–1509) "had four *lusores regis, alias, in lingu Anglicana, les pleyars of the Kyngs enterluds.*" Their names were John English, Edward May, Richard Gibson, and John Hammond, and each received an annual fee of £3 6s. 8d. plus additional sums from time to time as "rewards." "The royal company continued under Henry VIII (1509–1547), who appears to have increased its numbers, and doubled the charge upon the Exchequer. . . . John English, the leader, got £6 13s. 4d. Others received £3 6s. 8d. as before, and others again only two-thirds of this amount, £2 4s. 5d. By this arrangement, it was possible to maintain an actual establishment of from eight to ten" players.[6]

But these "King's men," even in their other occupations as household servants, weren't wholly dependent on royal bounty. Whenever their services were not required at Court they formed small troupes, proudly wearing "the Kinges bage," and took their interludes on the road for extra money. And the money was there. For instance, a Thomas Arthur, tailor, who had signed as an apprentice for meat and drink and 4d. a day in the hopes of learning to act and becoming a member of the King's company, couldn't wait until his year was up. After only seven weeks he and three other covenant servants skipped out, prepared a short play or two, and toured the provinces for a profit of £30! [7]

At first, of course, the interludes taken on tour by various castle troupes were only embryonic plays. Conditioned by the size of the banqueting-halls and the hour of attention the eating nobles might award them, they were short, simple, and not very scenic. A company of four men and a boy (probably in apprenticeship to one of them) for the women's parts could easily act them with some doubling now and then. *Fulgens and Lucrece* (1497), an adaptation by Henry Medwall (fl. 1490–1500), and a *Mery Play, betwene Johan Johan the Husbande, Typ, his Wyfe, and Syr Jhan the Priest* (1520–1522) by semi-minstrel John Heywood (c. 1497–1580) are typical of the interludes performed. The first is little more than a stately debate, distantly out of Cicero, in which Lucrece, the daughter of the Roman senator Fulgens, chooses between two suitors, a plebian and a patrician; but it is enlivened by a subplot in which two youthful servants scramble for the heart of a kitchen-maid. The second, possibly influenced by French actors who appear to have journeyed to England around the turn of the century, is crude and rowdy fun for fun's sake. In such would-be plays a duke's or an earl's or the King's near-professional actors, a relief from the rank amateurs, were welcomed everywhere by country folk and town *bourgeois* as they performed on village greens, in mansions and town halls, and eventually in the courtyards of inns having outside galleries.

However, this plan of the professionals for setting up a "profitable system of double performances, at Court and in the inn yards," didn't for a long while work out too well. At Court it encouraged rather than lessened the amateur competition. Professional actors had no monopoly in staging interludes there, and they soon discovered that many courtiers seeking preferment began to produce and to take part in plays; consequently they discovered in the Gentlemen and the Children of the Chapel Royal formidable rivals. Between 1506 and 1512 the Gentlemen acted in several plays a year; then from perhaps 1517 to beyond 1550 the boys performed more or less regularly at Court; and beginning in 1627 the Chapel boys competed there with the grammar school boys of St. Paul's! Next, all the schools and universities suddenly were studying and staging plays! Students took part in them "with the avowed object of practicing . . . voice and gesture, of gaining confidence and poise for disputation and all other forms of public speaking." The first English comedy, *Ralph Roister Doister*, written in imitation of the classics by headmaster Nicolas Udall (1505–1556), may have been acted by the boys at Eton between 1534 and 1541. In other words, play-acting came to be regarded as mostly a social or educational diversion. The professional actors were no more than mere stimulants, models, or perhaps sometime coaches for select amateurs. Moreover, they were mistrusted because they sold no visible commodity. No wonder that in England, almost more than in France, it remained doubtful for most of the sixteenth century "whether the future of the drama was to rest in professional or amateur hands." [8]

Outside of the Court and the universities, in halls and inn yards, the plan of the professional actors encountered a simmering Puritan opposition by village justices of the peace, by municipal officials and boards, and most importantly by the Lord Mayor and the Corporation of the City of London. Sir Thomas Elyot (c. 1490–1546) in 1531 found it necessary to defend the public presentation of comedies as no "doctrinall of rybaudrie" but a "mirrour of man's life, where in iuell [evil] is not taught but discovered." The players were protected, if just barely, by their nobleman's livery or badge from arrest as wandering, masterless vagabonds and a whipping at a cart-rail; and, eventually, when the Corpus Christi cycles faded near mid-century, Oliver Cromwell (1488?–1540) and the followers of John Calvin (1509–1564) found the professionals worthy enough to be used in the polemic interests of Protestantism. Nevertheless, the touring actors "had no free hand to play just when and where and what they liked. They were subject to certain conveniences as to times and seasons and localities, to precautions against breaches of the peace and dangers to public health and safety. Above all, in a time of political and ecclesiastical ferment, the sentiments of their plays had to be such as would stand the scrutiny of a government by no means tolerant of criticism." In short, as the temporary alliance between the Church and the stage was being dissolved, professionals felt the deep contempt of the citizen moralist for the actor.[9]

Their hopes for success were dim. They might be squashed in the coming collision of City and Crown, or else by the Church. But if only the central authority of the Privy Council would sustain them; and then if only they could rout the amateurs at Court and at the schools by finding some expert playwrights . . . !

❀ "ITALY"

From 1450 to 1550 demiprofessional Italian actors were almost obliterated by the Roman and Greek classical revival that upsurged after scholars and artists had scampered from Turkish-held Constantinople and found patronage at the wealthy principalities of Ferrara, Mantua, Urbino. Thereafter the competing courts of "Italy" (a group of independent kingdoms, republics, and cities until national unification in 1861) put together with tremendous erudite zeal an amateur Renaissance theater which set the patterns for most of Europe.

This revival—hinted at in the Senecan *Ecerinis* of 1315 and the 1450 *L'Istoire de la Destruction de Troy*—had been set in motion by the discovery in 1414 of Vitruvius' *De Architectura*, first printed in 1486 at Rome, reprinted several times later at Venice and Florence, and translated into Italian in

1521; by the reappearance of Cicero's *De Oratore* in about 1422; and by the newly discovered twelve comedies of Plautus brought from Germany to Rome in 1427 by Nicholas of Cusa (1401?–1464). It was sustained by the printing of Quintilian's *Institutio Oratoria* in 1470; by editions of the comedies of Plautus and Terence in 1472 and 1473; by Giorgio Valla's Latin translation of Aristotle's *Poetics* in 1498; by Aldus Manutius (1450–1515) who published at Venice the *Onomasticon* of Pollux and the plays of Sophocles in 1502, of Euripides in 1503, of Aeschylus in 1518; and by Dolce's 1535 translation of Horace's "The Art of Poetry."

Study of Vitruvius, and certainly of Cicero and Quintilian, led scholars "to realize that the tragedies of the pseudo-Seneca and the comedies of Terence and the recently discoverd Plautus had been not merely recited, but acted. . . . The next step was, naturally, to act them, in the original or in translations." Before 1484, and maybe as early as 1473, at least one comedy by Plautus or Terence and *Hippolytus* were revived at Rome, after more than a thousand years, by the pupils of Pomponius Laetus (1425–1498). Then at Ferrara, a leading center of arts and letters, Duke Ercole d'Este I (1431–1505) sponsored productions of *Menaechmi* in 1486, *Amphitruo* in 1487, and *Eunuchus, Trinummus,* and *Poenulus* in 1499. In 1502 *Epidicus, Bacchides, Miles Gloriosus, Casina,* and *Asinaria* were staged as part of the festivities attendant on the wedding of Alfonso I and Lucrezia Borgia. "There were in all, one hundred and ten actors, men and women" (some of them surely dancers). "The leader of the troupe appeared in the character of Plautus and explained the argument of the five plays." [10]

Interest in the classical theater quickly spread to the courts of the Gonzagas at Mantua, the Della Rovere at Urbino, and then all over Europe. By 1500 *Amphitruo* had been translated into French; in 1506 Erasmus turned *Hecuba* and *Iphigenia in Aulis* into Latin, and in 1511 he recommended "taking a class through a play by Terence"; in 1519 Henry VIII witnessed "a goodly commedy by Plautus," and in 1527 and 1528 productions in Latin of *Menaechmi* and *Phormio* were recited at Cardinal Wolsey's palace; in Spain in 1528 Fernán Perez de Oliva (1494?–1533) made an adaptation of Sophocles's *Electra*; in 1528 and 1533 the same *Electra* as well as *Antigone* were put into Italian and acted; in 1536 Aristophanes's *Plutus* was performed at Cambridge; between 1537 and 1549 several tragedies of Euripides were translated into French; in Germany Luther's friend Philip Melanchthon (1497–1560) and his pupils recited Latin translations of Greek plays; and before 1550 there was a Portuguese *Os Amphytryões*. Then in 1549 the poet Joachim Du Bellay (1522?–1560) insisted in *La Defence, et illustration de la langue francoyse* (*The Defense and Ennoblement of the French Language*) that his country's authors should "loot the Roman city and the Delphic temple" and import classical themes, myths, and stylistic devices, and that dramatists should abandon the old mystery and morality plays and compose tragedies as fine as those of classical times, but in French.[11]

II

Italy, however, preceded France and England in a burst of playwriting inspired by ancient models. In 1471 Angelo Poliziano (1454–1494), a scholar protégé of Lorenzo de' Medici, il Magnifico, composed from classical rather than biblical sources the very brief half-opera *La Favola de Orfeo* (*The Fable of Orpheus*). In c. 1490 Matteo Maria Boiardo (c. 1434–1494) versified in the vernacular Lucian's *Timon* for the stage. Then at Ferrara in 1499 Antonio Caminelli (1436–1502) wrote *Filostrato e Panfila*, the first Italian tragedy, in which he tried to fit the *Decameron* story of Guiscardo and Ghismonda into Senecan form. Previously at Ferrara, in 1498, the poet and amateur actor Lucovico Ariosto (1474–1533) wrote, in prose along Plautine lines, the first true modern comedy, *La Cassaria* (*The Casket*), which was first acted in 1508. Its plot relates the escapades of two young men who love two slave girls and try to get money enough to purchase them. In 1502–03 Ariosto followed it with *Gli Suppositi* (*The Counterfeits*), first acted in 1509 and again ten years later in Rome, with scenery by Raphael. (Translated into French, or closely imitated, by Jacques Bourgeois in 1545, and turned into English in 1566 by George Gascoigne as *Supposes*, it served Shakespeare as one of the sources for *The Taming of the Shrew*.) The story moves from complication to complication as a student of good family disguises himself as his own servant in order to outwit an old codger who outbids him for the affections of his girl. In 1520, Ariosto reworked both comedies in verse and wrote *La Lena* (*The Bawd*), a fairly accurate picture of Ferrarese society. Another play, the lifeless *Sofonisba* by Giovanni Giorgio Trissino (1478–1550), published in 1515 and often reprinted afterwards but for some reason never acted until years later, is historically important because it is based on facts taken from Livy (the account of the defeat of Syphax and the fate of his wife Sophonisba), because it's more Greek than Senecan in form, and because it's a first play written in blank verse. In 1556 it was freely translated into French by Mellin de Saint-Gelais.

By most counts the best native comedy of the period is *La Mandragola* (*The Mandrake*), written between 1513 and 1520 by Niccolo Machiavelli (1469–1527); and technically the best tragedy is the uninfluential *Orazia* (1546) by Pietro Aretino (1492–1556).

Aretino is better known for his lacerating, realistic comedies. In the best of them—*La Cortigiana* (*The Play of the Court*) (1534), a parody of Castiglione's *Libro del Cortegiano* (1518), written at Venice in ten days—"he completed the disengagement of Italian from Latin comedy." In this bitter attack on the Papal Court in which a young man comes to Rome, has his illusions destroyed, and learns to behave vilely as the sixteenth-century Romans do, Aretino vividly sketched characters drawn from his own experience. They are "reminiscences of fact." In his prologues to *Orazia* and

La Cortigiana he asks, "Why should he make Romans ape the style of Athens? His Romans will be painted from life; his servants shall talk and act like Italian varlets, not mimicking the ways of Geta or Davus. Why should he shackle his style with precedents from Petrarch and Boccaccio? He will seek the fittest words, the aptest phrases, the most biting repartees from ordinary language." [12] Unfortunately the realistic characters he limned with much verve were put into clumsy plays.

III

Where were the Italian professional actors in all the flurry of this revival and the attempt to adapt the classical stage to an indoor hall for contemporary audiences? They appear to have been snubbed. The nobles and the scholars apparently forgot them or considered them, perhaps rightly, to be too uneducated, crude, and folksy to participate in these new and rarefied court diversions. After all, the plays weren't staged in the surviving but run-down Greek and Roman theaters for hordes of just ordinary people. They were usually presented on palace grounds, in vast halls or riding-schools, or granaries which had been transformed into elegant little theaters; and they were devised to entertain cardinals, princes, aristocratic ladies, and learned guests. So, naturally at first and for a while the men at court, the amateurs, acted out the plays. Soon the lovely ladies there didn't see why "their dashing brothers, lovers, or husbands should have all the fun of this newly discovered toy. They could read and learn by heart both Latin and Italian: they could sing and dance as well as, if not better than, the men." [13] So, they, too, took part in the more select performances. Apparently acting wasn't half as important as the play scripts; and sometimes the plays didn't seem quite as important as the decorative innovations: the use of stage wings as developed from Greek *periaktoi* by Bastiano di San Gallo (1481–1551), the painting of perspective scenery by Baldassacre Peruzzi (1481–1537), and the designing of proscenium arches by Francesco Salviati (1510–1563).

Professional players, therefore, remained on the road more or less forlornly acting out little farces written by Nicolo Compani, Pietro Antonio Carcciolo, Giavan Giorgio Alione, Il Lasca (Grazzini), Vincenzo Braco, and others. They traveled as "squirting baudie Comedians" in small troupes that sometimes included "whores and common Curtizens to playe womens partes" and competed as best they could with amateurs everywhere, with such tradesmen associations as the *Rozzi* at Siena, with social groups performing at Venice, and so on. They "lived from hand to mouth practicing their art under many vexatious restrictions from church and state, taxed for the benefit of the poor, the clergy and the prince, and unable to regulate their affairs save in the narrowest limits." [14]

One of the known, but nonitinerant professional actors, employed by the chief academies of Venice between 1512 and 1529, was a certain Zan Polo (?).

Better remembered, however, is the amateur Angelo Beolco (*c.* 1501?–1542). As "Ruzzante" (the gossip), a shrewd peasant who indulged in long and amusing soliloquies, he flourished in Venice beginning about 1520. "In the Carnival season Ruzzante would take a holiday from managing the family estates and entertain his patron, Alvise Cornaro, and other friends" by collecting a few companions and devising parts for them in the Paduan dialect. His written skits range from the early *La Moschetta* (*The Strong*) and *La Fiorina* (*The Little Flower*), which deal realistically with countryside matters, to the later *La Piovana* (*The Downpour*) and *La Vaccaria* (*The Cow Barn*), in which he successfully rejuvenated old Plautine material. Andrea Calmo (1509–*c.* 1561) a Venetian gondolier, was his friendly rival actor–author and successor.[15]

In due time, however, when the amateurs at the courts wearied of learning lines and exhibiting themselves, or when special showings called for special skills, the different princes evidently commandeered professional actors and paid cheaply for their services. By 1548, for instance, when Henri II and Catherine de' Medici were entertained at Lyons with a production of the boisterous and long-popular *La Calandria* (*The Comedy of Calandro*) (1513), adapted from Plautus' *Menaechmi* by Bernardo Cardinal da Bibbiena (1470–1520), some of the "*plus excellens comédiens et comedientes d'Italie*" were surely professionals. Professionals performed frequently at the various courts. But for some time many of these genuine actors evidently shied away from "the tyranny or oppressive favor of . . . patrons"; they found it too difficult to please capricious masters; they chafed at the limited opportunities and galling restraints of appearing in tedious, declamatory, literary tragedies; they wanted more freedom and more subsistence; they longed to act regularly in comedies before the general public. They therefore attempted, with no help from any recognized actors' guild, and not always with success, to organize themselves independently. For example, at Padua on February 15, 1545, eight men (no women are mentioned), headed by Maffeo called Zanini, agreed to form free of patronage "a fraternal company" and to observe "without hate or rancor—but with love" certain rules from Easter 1545 to Carnival 1546. Their object was to play comedies "from place to place" under Zanini's direction; and a horse was to be bought from the common funds "to carry the luggage." The men agreed not to gamble with each other at cards or in other ways, except for food, to care for any sick member of the troupe from the common funds, and to fine any runaway 100 lire, of which one-third was to go to the "governors of the place where we are," one-third to the poor, and one-third to the company. They agreed further that all money gained was to be kept in a small chest with three keys held by different members of the group, that it was never to be opened and cash removed except by the consent of all. "A year later, on April 22, 1546, the company was reconstituted at Venice, with the addition of new members. . . . Trouble arose in succeeding years, but, on August 29, 1549, Maffeo . . . was still acting at Padua, and seems thence to have gone to Rome, where he was killed three years later in a brawl." [16]

Because of such yearnings by professional players for popular esteem and economic independence, and their antipathies against patronage, scholars, and literary plays, the princes were unable to attach troupes of experienced actors to their courts until the latter third of the sixteenth century. By that time some of "the more intelligent of the *comici* seem to have been persuaded that their best good in the long run was to be found in service" with "high pay and more or less regular employment on the terms of upper servants." [17]

IV

Before then, however, Italian professional players revived and experimented with a kind of performing which did much to rout amateurs and scholars. Obviously, somewhere around 1550, they were forced to rescue acting from being dangerously monitored by the unskilled, or worse, by literary men. These professionals knew that dilettantes didn't know how to act; they were convinced that researchers can't and shouldn't tell actors what they should present onstage and how to do it, or how to create.

But, high in favor at the ducal courts, the pedants were doing exactly that! First, they led too many writers of Italian tragedies to believe "that Seneca excelled the Greek dramatists in prudence, gravity, decorum, majesty and sententious maxims." Fine things, indeed, for actors to act! Oh, yes, these scholar–playwrights read Sophocles and Euripides and the *Poetics* of Aristotle; but they admired to excess the closet-play Roman who "took a Greek tragedy and discarded everything which did not lend itself to description, oratory, debate and horror." Giraldi Cinthio (1504–1573), therefore, loaded his *Orbecche* (1541) with laborious expositions, reflections on life in general, pleadings for clemency, "narrated horrors, the substitution of metaphors and harangues for action," and speeches and monologues unconnected with the plot and of unconscionable length. [18]

Second, obviously, the scholars believed that the best acting ought to be formal and oratorical. Easily, though wrongly, they found proof for their belief in their readings of *De Oratore* and the *Institutio Oratoria*. And, since in Seneca's plays the principal characters "talk at each other, rather than to each other . . . like debaters who speak one after another on different sides of a subject," the actors in the Italian tragedies of the Renaissance were instructed to describe, accuse, plead, bewail, and declaim in full rhetorical style. The critics were sure that "the drama is all in the word, and the word has no further reality behind it." [19]

In their blood and bones the Italian professional actors knew better than that. Because of their Atellane heritage they sensed that acting should never be constricted to words, that it started with words, yes, but then went behind and beyond them. They were also certain that characters in a play ought to speak *to* each other, more or less naturally, and with spontaneity. Therefore, instead of limiting themselves to the decorous declamation of academic verbiage, they impatiently forsook playwrights and improvised their own *commedia dell' arte.*

❊ SPAIN

In Spain, the earliest mention of professional actors seems to date from about 1550. Throughout the nation, nominally united under Ferdinand V and Isabella I in 1492, and soon afterward the golden mistress of the world with fleets in two hemispheres, would-be professional actors apparently encountered little competition as they rather quickly began to make a living, a meager one at first, by appearing in plays before the general public. They were encouraged by Juan del Encina (1468-c. 1537), *"patriarca del teatro español,"* who helped most in secularizing the church plays and pageants. As actor-musician-playwright in the service of the first Duke of Alba, and sponsored by the King and Queen, he originally wrote pastoral dialogues based on religious themes but enlivened by vivid touches of daily life and by characters who spoke in a familiar rustic dialect. Then, after a residence in Rome and a whiff of the new theater there, he advanced to writing more worldly *representaciones,* such as adaptations of Vergil's eclogues, which he turned into little histories of the royal family and the ducal house of Alba, and rather human dramatizations of his earlier days at Salamanca. *Representacion del Amor* (1497) and the mythical *Egloga de Placida y Victoriano* (1513) are examples of his secular plays. Although Encina's dramas and comedies were originally performed at court and in the private houses of the nobility by talented amateurs of high rank, or by their servants, they were so truly actable that, along with the religious playlets, they were soon being toured across the countryside by newly formed companies of part-time actors.

After more playwriting of merit by actor Bartolomé de Torres Naharro (c. 1480-c. 1530) and by the Portuguese Gil Vicente (c. 1470-c. 1539), whose daughter was an actress, Lope de Rueda (1510?-1565) emerged as Spain's first professional actor-manager and popular dramatist, as its first authentic man of the theater. Originally a goldsmith, he became "a brilliant actor" the hard way. He gave up his workshop, gathered together a highly regarded company of players, including Juan de Timoneda (c. 1490-1583), and earned his livelihood for years by writing brief prose plays, which happily satirized the people of his time, and toured them from one town to another. Cervantes said of him that he acted the four characters of the Negress, the Ruffian, the Fool, and the Biscayan and many others "with the greatest skill and propriety that one can imagine." Rueda's comedies, of course, were very simply presented. In most cases actors performed on a daylight stage set up quickly in market places and yards and formed "of four benches arranged in a square, with four or five boards upon them, raised about four spans from the ground. . . ." [20] What counted most were the plays, warm, idiomatic, amusing pieces like *Eufemia* (a free version of the ninth story of the second day from the *Decameron*), *Armelina*, *Medora*, *Los Enganados* (*The Cheaters*), and the famous one-act *Las Aceitunas* (*The Olives*) in which a husband and wife quarrel over the price they'll ask in a score of years for some olives which have just been planted. What counted next was the acting.

II

Spanish acting, although stilted or formalized in nonrealistic serious plays, was in comedies instinctive and simple. The players merely used their five senses—and imagined. That was all there was to it. And it was enough. By using their faculties of sight, smell, taste, hearing, and touch they vividly represented a play's situations and characters. This, it seems, was the sort of thing they'd been taught to do at their devotions by, among others, St. Ignatius of Loyola (1491–1556), the Spanish founder of the Jesuits. In his *Spiritual Exercises* he explains the need of a certain concentration and discipline in order to stimulate a dramatic mode of prayer. In one of them, for instance, he requires the exercitant "to see in imagination the length, breadth, and depth of hell . . . the vast fires, and the souls enclosed, as it were, in bodies of fire. . . . To hear the wailing, the howling, cries, and blasphemies . . . . With the sense of smell to perceive the smoke, the sulphur, the filth, and corruption. To taste the bitterness of tears. . . . With the sense of touch to feel the flames which envelop and burn the souls." In another, the believer is instructed, in his effort to enter heaven and to talk with saints personally, to see in imagination the persons, and to contemplate and meditate in detail on "the circumstances in which they are . . . to hear what they are saying, or what they might say . . . to smell the infinite fragrance and taste the infinite sweetness of the divinity . . . to apply the sense of touch, for example, by embracing and kissing the place where the persons stand or are seated." In a third exercise Catholics are thus advised to "realize" the action of the Nativity: See in imagination "the way from Nazareth to Bethlehem. Consider its length, its breadth; whether level, or through valleys and over hills. Observe also the place or cave where Christ is born; whether big or little; whether high or low; and how it is arranged." Then "as though present" look upon "Our Lady, Saint Joseph, the maid, and the Child Jesus after his birth. . . . Consider, observe, and contemplate what the persons are saying . . . what they are doing. . . ." [21]

The purpose of the *Spiritual Exercises* of Ignatius "is to reveal, through the techniques of make-believe, the potentialities of human nature and the realities of the human situation, as Loyola understood them." They furnished Spaniards with a technique, as Francis Fergusson first noticed, "like that which the Moscow Art Theatre used to train actors." [22]

❧ PUBLIC THEATERS, 1550–1580

In Paris, in 1550 the Confrérie de la Passion opened "the first permanent popular theater to be erected since classical times." This was the Hôtel de Bourgogne, a long, narrow, two-story, barnlike structure with the theater proper, or "the great hall" accommodating maybe two thousand persons, located on the second floor above the shops of grocers, orange merchants, and horse dealers. There the amateur Confrères, and the amateur Enfants-sans-souci who sometimes rented the theater, continued to act their farces and moralities. (This Hôtel remained in the possession of the Brotherhood until 1677, and continued to offer dramatic fare to the Parisian populace, with only slight interruptions, until 1783—a total lifetime of two hundred and thirty-three years.)[23]

Then in 1552 the first French tragedy and comedy along classical lines, *Cléopâtre Captive* and *Eugène*, both by Etienne Jodelle (1532–1573), were staged in the quadrangle of the Hôtel de Rheims before an audience that included Henri II and the flower of his court. In the former, Jodelle aimed merely "to discourse upon the misfortunes of a queen" and therefore dispensed with any true development of dramatic action. In the latter, he aimed to outdo the despised *farceurs* and to present "such people as we see among us." These included the priest Eugène who loved Alix who was already the wife of Guillaume and the mistress of Captain Florimond.[24] The playwright himself impersonated the Egyptian Queen, and his casts included such distinguished amateur actors as the poets Jean de La Péruse (Jean Bastier) (d. 1554) and Remy Belleau (1528–1577), and the doctor Jacques Grévin (*c.* 1538–*c.* 1570). Who needed professional actors?

II

In perhaps the same year, 1552, *Gammer Gurton's Needle* by a William Stevenson (*c.* 1521–1575) was acted by the boys at Cambridge. Then in 1553 when Thomas Wilson (*c.* 1525–*c.* 1585) published his *Rhetorique*, an English version of Ciceronian theory, the students undoubtedly began to pay better attention to their onstage delivery, to voice and gesture. They learned, for instance, that "a cleare sounding voyce, comforteth much our deintie eares, with much sweet melodie, and causeth us to allow the matter, rather for the reporters sake, than the reporter for the matters sake."[25]

In 1552, also, the eight Court interluders seem to have been George and John Birch, Richard Coke, Henry Heriot, Richard Skinner, John Browne, Thomas Southey, and John Smith (or John Young). Each received £3 6s. 8d. a year plus a livery allowance of £1, 3s. 4d.; and for Christmas they were rehearsing "a play of Esops's Crowe wherein the moste of the actors were birds." In 1555 they toured to Leicester, in 1555–56 to Ipswich, Gloucester, and Beverley, in 1556–57 to Beverley, Oxford, Norwich, and Exeter, in 1557 to Bristol, in 1557–58 to Beverley, Leicester, Maldon, Dover, Lynme Regis, and Barnstaple.[26] However, by the early years of Elizabeth's reign (1558–1603) they and their playlets had shrunk in importance at Court; there most of the performances were given by the boy companies.

But adult professionals persisted. In 1557, some unknowns began to perform in London's inns, namely at the Saracen's Head, Islington, and at the Boar's Head, Aldgate.[27] By the following year these inns were more or less regularly being used as temporary theaters which afforded accommodations for all sorts and conditions of people.

Other near-professionals, such as Lord Dudley's players, organized in or before 1559, acted at Court during the Christmas seasons of 1560–61, 1561–62, and 1562–63. Lord Rich's men performed at Saffron Walden in 1563–64, at Ipswich in 1564, at Maldon in 1564–65, at York in 1565, at Ipswich again in 1567, at Court in 1567–68, at Canterbury in 1569, and again at Saffron Walden in 1569–70. At that time also "one of the most long-lived of the theatrical organizations of Elizabeth's time," the Earl of Sussex's Men, was formed and continued to function until 1592–94.[28]

But the earliest English tragedy, the didactic and rhetorical blank verse *Gorboduc*, by two statesmen, Thomas Norton (1532–1584) and Thomas Sackville (1536–1608), was acted in 1562 before Queen Elizabeth by lawyers and their apprentices. And the comic *Supposes*, adapted in prose by soldier, courtier, and Member of Parliament George Gascoigne (c. 1542–1578), was acted in 1566 at Gray's Inn by students.

The struggle for supremacy between amateurs and professionals was nip-and-tuck.

III

Madrid by 1560 provided touring professional troupes, like Rueda's, with five corrales—open-air yards of houses—as fixed places where they could perform. Control of these rude theaters was awarded to charitable institutions, *confradías*; they shared in the profits from the shows they booked. A perhaps heightened description of the larger traveling companies that were establishing the theater in Spain is given by actor Augustin de Rojas Villandrando (d. c. 1572) in his *Viage Entretenido (Entertaining Journey)* (1603). "A *garnacha*," he explains, "consists of five or six men, a woman who plays first lady's roles and a boy who plays the second. . . . Their repertory consists of four *comedias*, three *autos*, and as many *entremeses* [topical sketches]. . . . They remain eight days in a town, sleep four in a bed, eat a stew of beef and mutton, and some evenings a fricasse well-seasoned. . . . In a *boxiganga* there are two women, a boy, and six or seven companions. . . . They are provided with six *comedias*, three or four *autos*, five *entremeses*, two chests—one containing the baggage of the company, the other the women's clothes. They hire four pack-mules—one for the chests, two for the women, and the other on which the men may alternate every quarter-league. . . . Such players dine well; all sleep in four beds, perform by night and at festivals by day, and sup mostly on hash. . . . The *farándula* . . . has three women, eight to ten *comedias*, two chests of luggage. The players travel on mules with drivers, and sometimes in carts, visit the more important towns, dine separately, wear good clothes, perform at Corpus festivals for 200 ducats, and live contentedly (that is, those who are not in love . . .). In the *companias* . . . there are very clever people . . . , men much esteemed and persons well born, and even respectable women (for where there are so many there must be all kinds). They take with them fifty *comedias*, three hundred quarters of luggage, sixteen persons to act, thirty who eat, one who takes the money at the door (and God knows what he steals). Their labor is excessive because of the great amount of study, the continuous rehearsals. . . ." [29]

IV

Italy's first public theater, the San Cassiano in Venice, wasn't erected until 1637; but at Siena in 1560 Bartolomeo Neroni (*c.* 1500–*c.* 1571) built a more or less typical private theater for the Academy of Intronati in a great hall behind the Palace of the Senate by merely setting up a proscenium and filling it with the kind of scenery prescribed by Sebastiano Serlio (1475–1554) in his *Architettura* (1537–1547). Then in 1567, Leone de' Sommi, the Jewish leader of a company of Jews, petitioned Francesco Gonzaga "for the privilege of playing in a Mantuan 'Hall' for ten years, offering cash to pay for his license and offering in addition to give to the poor of the city each year two sacks of barley or their cost." [30] Evidently he was proposing to establish a permanent public theater for a company of professionals.

Actor-director-manager de' Sommi, or di Somi (1527–1592), is remembered now as the author of four *Dialoghi in materia di rappresentazione scensche* (*Dialogues on Stage Affairs*) written between 1556 and 1564(?). In one of them, apparently derived from Quintilian, he discusses acting. The first main point de' Sommi makes is that "it is far more essential to get good actors than a good play." Yet he carefully counsels them "to give time to the auditors for appreciating the poet's words and relishing his sentences, which are by no means ordinary and commonplace." His second main point is that the actor's job is "to try as hard as he can to cheat the spectator into the belief that what he sees on the stage is true" until little by little "the audience gets the impression not of a play composed and finished by an author, but rather of a series of real events taking shape before them." His third main point is that no rules can be framed for the profession of acting. Histrionic ability "must be born in the individual . . . ; the performer must have a natural disposition for his work, otherwise he can never succeed"; feelings "cannot be learned if they do not come by nature."

De' Sommi also believed that the actor must have a good accent, good voice, and above all other things he "must be vivacious and bright in his diction, except, of course, when he has to express grief, and even on such an occasion he must express it in a vital manner so as not to bore the audience. In fine, just as the poet has to hold the attention of the audience by a seeming naturalness and a well-planned vivacious dialogue, so the actor has the business of keeping the variety of his actions appropriate to the situations, of maintaining a constant alertness, and of avoiding a tedious dullness; this last simply bores an audience in the theater and comes from cold interpretation, lacking the necessary fire and fitting power." In other words, the actor ought to "observe and imitate the natural manner of those persons whom he represents, above all avoiding as a capital crime what I shall call, for want of a better word, a pedantic manner of interpretation, after the style of school-children repeating their lessons before their master. That method of acting, I say, which makes the words seem like a passage learned by rote, must be avoided; and endeavor must be made above all other things to render whatever is spoken thoroughly effective, with suitable alternation of tones and appropriate gestures. The whole dialogue must seem like a familiar talk, wholly improvised." And since "perhaps the power of words is not more than the power of gesture," the actor must find "movements and gestures of an appropriate kind to make his part seem real." He should alter them "according to the variety of moods and . . . imitate not only the character he represents but also the stage in which that character is supposed to be at the moment." [31]

While de' Sommi was setting down these observations, other professional Italian actors were beginning to garner success with their new *commedia dell' arte*. For instance, in the 1560's one of the early professional actresses of Renaissance Europe, a Vincenza Armani (*c.* 1540–1569) was praised on tour for playing "in three different styles, in comedy, tragedy, and pastoral," and for "observing the proprieties of each so exactly that the Academy of the Intronati of Siena, which cherishes the cult of the drama, often said this lady spoke better extempore than the most finished writers after much thought." But "In 1568 the ecclesiastical authorities in Bologna listed a formidable number of reasons, typical of many urged against actors generally, why . . . the improvised plays . . . should not be encouraged." These actors, they warned, "play for the most part in lascivious and dishonest pieces which corrupt good morals; they are vagabonds of evil repute, who carry about with them women of bad life; they bear away from the city a great deal of money and give cause to youths and boys to rob their fathers in order to pay for a play." [32] All such protests, however, were impotent. The actors of the *commedia dell' arte* were readying a unique triumph.

Meanwhile, Italy's scholars and assistant scholars continued pontifically to announce their notions of what plays and acting should be. Their intentions, of course, like those of most bunglers were good. In agreement with the *commedia* actors, they sensed that scripts and characterizations ought to have more of life in them. They believed, following Julius Scaliger (1484–1558), that the details of a play ought to be "so arranged and disposed that they approach nearest to actual truth (*ad veritatem*)." "It is not sufficient," they argued, "that the spectator should be satisfied with the action as typical of certain actions of life. An absolutely perfect illusion must prevail; the spectator must be moved by the actions of the play exactly as if they were those of real life." [33]

Therefore in a well-intentioned but poor snatch at verisimilitude, they insisted that all plays ought to abide by two new unities—the unities of time and place. Playwright Giraldi Cinthio "enacted" a law to the effect that the action of a script ought, for more lifelikeness, to be confined to one day, or but little more. Then in 1570, Ludovico Castelvetro (1505–1571) in his *Poetica d'Aristotele* formulated a second law to the effect that all action ought to be confined within a very limited space, or nearly one locale, instead of moving about unnaturally in many different areas. Thus playwriting was circumscribed. And for a long, long time it remained so—especially in seventeenth-century France where critics swore unalterable allegiance to Aristotle's unity of action and to the two unities invented by the Italians.[34]

Italian scholars also circumscribed the writing and the acting of characters in a play. Here they bungled again. Instead of demanding more of the essence of life in the creation and interpretation of characters, they asked, misled by Aristotle, for *decorum*, for more and more decorum, and almost nothing but decorum. And decorum implied a standard, a hardening, a crystallization. So, the scholars insisted, for instance, that onstage "every old man should have such and such characteristics, every young man certain others, and so on for the soldier, the merchant, the Florentine, the Parisian, and the like." In other words, each character in a play, "when once discriminated and definitely formulated, became fixed as a necessary and inviolable substitute for the reality which had thus been analyzed." [35] (This standardization of characters faintly echoed, of course, the Oriental theory.) Individual transgressions by playwrights or actors were held to be in bad taste.

Oddly enough, the professional actors of the *commedias*, while rejecting many of the literary rules devised by the scholars, approved of fixed characters. They set up their own definite types by transforming the principals of the old Atellane farces into relatively new, standard, cartoon figures. "Bologna . . . contributed the Doctor. . . . Venice . . . evolved Pantaloon and the Captain. The two Bergamos . . . produced the sly booby, Harlequin, and the knave, Brighella. . . . Milan produced Beltrame and Scapin . . . ; Naples brought forth first Puncinella and then Scaramouche . . . ; and in Calabria appeared Coviello. . . ." These stock characters were then placed in improvised pieces which "in distinction to the written comedies, . . . could not be performed except by professional actors" whose stage task was to please only the motley crowd, *la molitudine rozza*. And in quick time this new form of theater, especially this new kind of acting, became so popular in Italy that most of the working men, it was said, deprived themselves of food in order to have the wherewithal to go to the play.[36]

Moreover, these *commedia dell' arte* actors soon attained an international fame. Zan Ganassa, or Alberto Naseli (fl. 1568–1583) who impersonated the Zanni and possibly Arlecchino, at Ferrara in 1570, performed with an Italian company in Paris in 1571–72. Despite the fact that the secular authorities there refused them permission to play because their comedies "teach only folly and adultery and serve as a school of debauchery to the youth of both sexes," the foreigners performed in the Salle de Bourbon with a license from the King. Ganassa's fellow actors may have been the first of the famous Gelosi troupe, of whom it was claimed that "Because they make a strong point of gesture and represent many things through action, even those who do not understand their language cannot fail to understand the subject of the piece[s]. . . ." In 1573 Ganassa may have been in London—although Drusiano Martinelli (?–c. 1607), who appeared there before Lent in 1577–78, is supposed to have been the first Italian comedian to cross the Channel. In 1575 and in 1578–79 Ganassa was performing in Seville, Madrid, and Toledo. And wherever the *commedia dell' arte* was toured, all over Italy and all over Europe, by the Gelosi and other companies "there was such a concourse and crowd of spectators that the . . . best preachers . . . , all together, did not gather so many people when they gave their sermons." [37] Italian professional actors, in short, were achieving economic independence and stature— and returning the wincing scholars to their libraries.

V

In the 1570's professional companies of French actors were still prevented from competing with the monopoly-entrenched Confrérie. Once, "hearing that arrangements were being made by some players from Bordeaux to give classical pieces at the Hôtel de Cluny . . . they required the *concierge*, under pain of fine and imprisonment, to pull down the stage within twenty-four hours." Yet by 1578, when the Enfants-sans-souci, their sometime tenant, wearied of staging plays, the Confrérie seem to have rented their Hôtel de Bourgogne briefly to a provincial company of actors headed by Agnan Sarat (?–1613).[38] But no professionals were permitted to establish themselves in the capital.

VI

By 1574 in England the Puritans were maintaining that professional actors "corrupt good moralities" and that "Great then is the errour of the magistrate to geue sufferance to these players, whether they bee minstrels, or enter-ludours who on a scaffold, babling vaine newes of the sclander of the world, put there in scoffing the vertues of honest men. . . ." Yet in the same year, after the City Corporation and the Crown had tiffed for some time over the question of who should license playing-places in London, and the former had frequently inhibited stage performances, Elizabeth completely ignored the City and issued an experimental patent to the Earl of Leicester's Men "to vse, exercise and occupie the arte and facultye of playenge Commedies, Tragedies, Enterludes, stage playes . . . aswell for the recreacion of oure loving subiectes, as for our solace and pleasure when we shall think good to see them . . . as well within oure Citie of London . . . as also within the liberties and fredomes of anye oure Cities, townes, Bouroughes &c whatsoeuer . . . thoroughte oure Realme of England." [39]

In that auspicious year of 1574 the Earl of Leicester's Men, his "daylye Oratours" (known as Lord Dudley's players from about 1559 until 1564), included James Burbage (c. 1530–1597) who, "by occupacion a joyner and reaping but a small lyving by the same, gave it over and became a common player in playes," John Perkin, John Laneham, William Johnson, and Robert Wilson. The company had been making a fair living by acting plays since 1564 at Maldon, Bristol, York, Oxford, Beverley, Leicester, Abington, Barnstaple, Gloucester, Suffron, Walden, Ipswich, Nottingham, and probably in London. They had performed at Court in 1572 and 1573.[40]

This hard-working, fortunate company wasn't too happy, however, about a code for the regulation of plays which the City Corporation drew up as soon as it realized that the theater had virtually been forced upon it. The actors were wary, as they performed in the open yards of the London inns, of depending too much on the discretion of the antagonistic Lord Mayor and Aldermen. Therefore, they looked toward the suburbs and the easier conditions afforded by lax county governments.

Then in 1576, the second auspicious date, actor Burbage, borrowing about £660 from his father-in-law, designed and built outside the City boundaries an enclosed wooden structure called the Theatre which was opened to the public in the autumn of that year. There the Earl of Leicester's Men acted their plays. "Admission was one penny for standing room on the ground, and a second penny for admission to the galleries; for a further penny one could obtain a stool, or what was described as 'a quiet standing' out of the crowd on the floor. . . ." [41]

These actors did not perform solely at their new suburban theater; they continued to play at Court and on tour. In December 1576 the men presented *The Collier* at Court. "In 1576–77 they were at Stratford-on-Avon [when Shakespeare was thirteen], in September 1577 at Newcastle, and [in] October at Bristol, where they gave *Myngo*. In 1577–78 they were also at Bath. They were at Court [in] 1577. . . . They may have been at Wanstead in May 1578 when Leicester entertained Elizabeth with Sidney's *The May Lady*." In the same year they performed "at Maldon . . . at Ipswich . . . at Lord North's at Kirtling. They played *A Greek Maid* at Court [in] 1579." In their absence the Theater was often used for exhibitions of swordplay and for athletic competitions. And in winter the company apparently continued to stage plays in the heart of the City at either the Bull Inn, the Bell Inn, the Bel Savage Inn, or the Cross Keys Inn despite the annoying municipal restrictions.[42]

In 1577 a second public playhouse, the Curtain, was built (perhaps by Burbage) on a piece of land called the Curtain very near the Theatre. But nothing definite is known about who first appeared there. In the same year a private theater within the City, the Blackfriars, was opened and used by the Children of the Chapel Royal and of Windsor Chapel until 1580.

The efforts of the boys by this time, however, were fruitless; the adults had won. The professionals had almost squashed the competition of the amateurs. From 1567 to 1576, for instance, the Paul's boys had received eleven rewards for Court performances, other boys two, and the adult companies only six; however, after the building of the first theater, between 1576 and 1583, the adult companies received thirty-nine rewards and the boys only seventeen. The royal fee for an appearance was increased to £10. Then other adult professional companies were formed. The Earl of Warwick's Men were revived, Lord Howard's Men (later the Lord Admiral's Men) appeared at Court for the first time at Christmas of 1576–77, and the Earl of Sussex's Men curtailed their touring and confined their activities mainly to London. By 1578 "eight ordinarie places" in the City were occupied by players. And they were thronged. One estimate sets the aggregate gain of the eight places, open at first but once in a week, at £2,000 a year. And the actors began to get "under gentlemen's noses in sutes of silke" and to "looke askance ouer the shoulder at euery man, of whom the Sunday before they begged an alms." [43]

The professional players had "secured the future of the drama by making it economically independent; and the copestone of their edifice was the building of the permanent theaters." But there was still trouble ahead. The Puritans, incensed at the rapid growth of professional acting as a recognized occupation, deliberately began to brand the actors with *infamia* and the more recent stigma of vagabondage. They insisted that acting, being essentially the simulation of what is not, is by its very nature "within the compasse of a lye." They labeled players "a very superfluous sort of men." [44]

❁ ACTING AS A BUSINESS, 1580–1600

During the 1580's in Paris, with the amateurs still firmly in control of the theater, no significant changes occurred in the drab condition of acting. There Odet de Turnèbe (1553–1581) wrote in 1580 (?) *Les Contens* (*The Merry Ones*), "the masterpiece of French classical comedy of the Renaissance"; and in 1583 Robert Garnier (1534–1590) wrote *Sédecie*, or *Les Juives* (*The Jews*), one of the better examples of early rhetorical tragedy. But these scripts, and others like them, were only the intermittent creations of amateurs. Although composed with a view to production, they were not written under normal theatrical conditions, in which a playwright is paid to produce something which must be enjoyed by a regular theatrical audience in order to succeed.[45] The visiting French professional actors in Paris, as they became increasingly popular, and began to worry the amateurs, needed professional playwrights to insure success. They envied, without emulating, or even wanting to emulate, the visiting *commedia dell' arte* actors who succeeded without authors.

But the amateurs, jealous of the foreigners' popularity and profits, called the Italian performances "a great evil which it is wrong to tolerate." They didn't tolerate them. They harassed them in every possible way and often sent them scurrying from the city. Then in 1588 an anonymous protest to the King wholeheartedly condemned *all* stage players, especially those "who are creating a sewer and house of Satan, named the Hôtel de Bourgogne. . . . In this place occur a thousand scandalous assignations, to the hindrance of uprightness and chastity of women and to the ruin of families of poor artisans. Of these the base hall is full; and for more than two hours before the play they pass their time in lewd activities, in dice games, in gluttony, and drunkenness, so publicly that many quarrels and fights result." [46]

Nothing of theater significance happened during these years in Spain either while the ever growing crowd of professional players waited and hoped for a top-notch playwright. In 1585, Lope Félix de Vega Carpio (1562–1635), age twenty-three, was frequenting the two theaters in Madrid, the Corral de la Cruz (1579) and the Corral del Príncipe (1582), and making plays his pastime, as did many other gentlemen of the capital. Then in 1588, de Vega joined the Spanish Armada that attempted to conquer England.

II

In "Italy" about 1582, Giordano Bruno (1548–1600) wrote a bitterly intelligent comedy on the corrupt customs of his time, *Il Candelaio* (*The Chandler*), but it was probably never staged. Then in 1584 the landmark Teatro Olimpico, designed by Andrea Palladio (1508–1580) and finished by Vincenzo Scamozzi (1552–1616), was opened at Vicenza. It accommodated 3,000 spectators. The first production staged there was *Oedipus the King* translated into the vernacular and directed by Angelo Ingegneri (1550–1613). The "show" was apparently designed by dilettantes for dilettantes.

But the *commedia dell' arte* troupes, who sometimes played at the Teatro Olimpico, weren't dilettantes. They were hard-working, profit-seeking professionals who were touring their improvisations everywhere. The Gelosi troupe, for a sampling, played in Milan in 1580, in Venice for the carnivals of 1581 and 1583, in Mantua in 1586, and in 1587 in Florence. Then in 1588 they journeyed to Paris but quickly returned because of a temporary decree that "forbade all comedians either French or Italian to perform plays, acrobatics, or any subtleties whatsoever under penalty of an arbitrary fine and corporal punishment." In 1589 they were back in Florence, Milan, Parma, and Mantua. The Confidenti troupe, for another sampling, appeared in 1580 at Mantua, Verona, Padua, and Bologna; from 1582 to 1584 they are known to have acted at Genoa, Venice, and Milan; next, they traveled to several French towns and then to Paris in a repertoire of comedies based on scenarios, as well as pastorals, tragedies, and *commedia sostenuta* (written comedies). But they were eventually expelled by the Confrérie de la Passion. The Uniti troupe was acting in 1584 at Ferrara, Mantua, and Padua; and in 1586 they were at Bologna, Mantua, Milan, and perhaps Turin.[47]

The favorite "stars" of the *commedia* were the actresses. Diana Ponti (fl. 1582–1602), for instance, who directed the Desiosi troupe in 1582, and Vittoria Piassimi (fl. 1573–1594), who would direct the Confidenti in 1590, were such feature attractions they performed temporarily with various major companies. In 1589 the latter and Isabella Andreini (1562–1604), the two most famous actresses of the time, were playing side by side, alternately as *prima* and *seconda donna* in the troupe of the Gelosi.

III

In England miracle plays reached the end of their long runs; the last complete cycle was staged at Coventry in 1580. The following year, in order to combat the growing opposition to the theater and to actors, especially on the part of the City Corporation, the Privy Council issued a commission which in part invested the Master of the Revels with authority to press workmen and wares for the service of the Revels. It also empowered him to call upon players and writers to appear before him and recite their pieces, presumably with a view to their consideration for performance at Court. "And, as it were incidentally to the exercise of such a power, the patent went on to declare in the most general terms that the Master of the Revels was thereby appointed 'of all suche showes plaies plaiers and playmakers together with their playing places to order and reforme auctorise and put downe as shalbe thought meete or unmeete unto himselfe or his said deputie in that behalfe.' "[48]

But the City Corporation wasn't placated. It continued to insist that actors were an evil in the commonwealth. Moreover, it appears to have committed itself, in the course of 1582, to the policy of a complete suppression of the stage because, as one Puritan put it, "Most of the Players haue bene eyther men of occupations, which they haue forsaken to lyue by playing, or common minstrels, or trayned vp from theire childehood to this abhominable exercise & haue now no other way to get theire liuvinge. . . . In a common-weale, if priuat men be suffered to forsake theire calling because they desire to walke gentlemen like in sattine & veluet, with a buckler at their heeles, proportion is so broken, vnitie dissolued, harmony confounded, that the whole body must be dismembered and the prince or the heads cannot chuse but sicken. . . ."[49]

The Crown was thus forced to forestall the City. In March 1583, the third auspicious date, the Crown formed and officially supported a new company of actors to be known as the Queen's Men. Very possibly this was a deliberate and to some extent a successful attempt to overawe the City by the use of the royal name. According to one account of the formation of this powerfully backed company of professional actors, the "Comedians and stage-players of former time were very poor and ignorant in respect to these of this time: but being now grown very skilful and exquisite actors for all matters, they were entertained into the service of divers great lords: out of which companies there were twelve of the best chosen, and . . . they were sworn the queens servants and were allowed wages and liveries as grooms of the chamber. . . . Among these twelve players were two rare men, *viz.*, Thomas [Robert] Wilson [from Leicester's Men], for a quicke, delicate, refined, extemporall witt, and Richard Tarleton [?–1588], for a wondrous plentifull pleasant extemporall wit, . . . the wonder of his time." The other ten members of the company were John Adams, John Bentley, Leonall Cooke, John Dutton, John Garland, William Johnson, John Laneham, Thobye Mylles, John Singer, and John Towne—seven Johns and a Johnson! Wilson (?–c. 1600) and Bentley (?–1585) were serious actors of repute, but it was Tarleton "in his threefold capacity as comedian [extempore clown], playwright, and musician [performer of the jig, a farce in rhyme that was sung and danced to a series of popular tunes] who held the company together and assured its prestige." As the Queen's Men these actors became "the first professional company to maintain any real coherence of policy, organization and personnel," and in time "the most famous of all the London companies during the decade of the eighties." In its first summer, in 1583, the company performed at Norwich, Bristol, Cambridge, Leicester, Gloucester, Aldeburgh, Nottingham, and Shrewsbury; and that winter they returned to London and played, probably, at the Bel Savage, the Bell, and the Bull Inns, and at the Curtain Theatre.[50] At once other companies of professional actors—like Leicester's, Oxford's and the Admiral's—were encouraged and set up their productions side by side with the Queen's. They all thrived.

Then in 1584, the fourth auspicious date, the City made its last stab. It tried to prohibit the companies from performing in wintertime within the boundaries of London. The attempt failed; the Crown firmly supported the actors. "Henceforth it became the settled policy of the Corporation to defer to the authority of the Privy Council." So, in England by 1584—later than in Italy, but perhaps more soundly—the occupation of acting began to take its place as a regular profession, in which money might with reasonable safety be invested, to which a man might look for a lifetime career, and in which he might venture to bring up his children. From 1584 onwards, for instance, a shrewd businessman and manufacturer of starch, Philip Henslowe (?–1616), "citizen and dyer," could become interested in acquiring theater properties, could build a theater like the Rose in 1588, and could take as his income half and then all of the proceeds of the galleries and still show a profit after paying most of the bills. From that date on top-flight talents could be enticed with appropriate remuneration into composing plays for actors—talents like the University wits: Lodge and Peele from Oxford, and Greene, Marlowe, and Nashe from Cambridge. George Peele (1556–1596) is best known for his *The Old Wives' Tale*, and Robert Greene (1558–1592) for *Friar Bacon and Friar Bungay*—both staged in the middle 1580's. (Yet, "Despite this intervention by men of superior education and refinement, the English professional theater continued to be an actor's theater, not a dramatist's theater. The playwrights accepted the authority of the actors who paid them. . . .") And finally, after 1584 a man like Edward Alleyn (1566–1626), then a member of the Earl of Worcester's Men, could hope for a rich and dignified future as a leading actor; and Burbage without misgivings could watch his son Richard (c. 1567–1619) begin his histrionic career in the bit role of "a messenger." [51]

During the palmy days of the Queen's Men, from 1584 through 1588, the lingering boy companies were finally put out of business by the professionals despite the fact that John Lyly (1554–1606) had written especially for the Paul's amateurs the elegantly literary *Endymion* (1583). After 1588, and the death of Tarleton, however, the fortunes of the Queen's company declined. From then on "the future of the stage lay with Alleyn and the Admiral's Men," whom he had joined in the preceding year. In 1585 this company, having combined with Hunsdon's, had acted at Dover; in 1585–86 it appeared in Coventry, Faversham, Ipswich, Leicester, and at Court; in 1586–87 it toured to Cambridge, Coventry, Bath, York, Norwich, Ipswich, Exeter, Southampton, Leicester, and finally settled down in London where it appears to have remained throughout the 1588–89 season. In 1589–90 it merged with Lord Strange's Men under Alleyn's leadership in order "to dominate the London stage by beating all rivals out of the fields." The new company took over the Theatre and the Curtain. [52]

Sometime before 1587, Thomas Kyd (1558–1594) provided Alleyn with one of his most celebrated roles, Hieronimo in *The Spanish Tragedy*. And success truly came to the Admiral's Men when they found a soaring playwright to compose regularly for them. His name was Christopher Marlowe (1564–1593). In c. 1587, Alleyn acted the title role in his *Tamburlaine the Great, Part I*, written for a company of about eighteen players reckoning four boys for the female parts. Then in c. 1589, he acted the leading roles in *The Tragical History of Dr. Faustus* and *The Jew of Malta*. Marlowe insured the company's success because he furnished its actors with stunning stories to tell, stunning characters to imagine and make, and stunning poetry to speak. He learned from Seneca what the Italians and French had failed to learn: he sensed "the essentials of declaimed verse." And he began to "split up the primitive rhetoric," to develop out of it "subtler poetry and subtler tones of conversation." He led the way toward the eventual mingling of "the oratorical, the conversational, the elaborate and the simple, the direct and the indirect. . . ." [53]

And a young man in his mid-twenties, newly in London from Stratford-on-Avon, watched the happy professional actors. He watched and listened. . . .

IV

In weak "Italy" in the 1590's the literary circles were surely appalled by the brash, phenomenal success of the *commedia dell' arte*. It was all so—uncouth. But the many troupes of money-making actors thumbed their noses and continued triumphantly to improvise their own rollicking scripts. (Their contribution to acting is assessed in the next chapter.)

In this same decade the French professional actors slowly began to come into their own. In about 1596 "the Confrères ceased acting themselves and relinquished the drama to . . . professional companies which had begun to pour into Paris, and which were forced to rent the Hôtel de Bourgogne for their performances. They settled down to reap the windfall of their monopoly. Collecting one écu a day from any troupe not renting their playhouse, they also sought in 1597 to increase the income from the Hôtel de Bourgogne by obtaining permission to open their doors on weekdays as well as on Sundays and holidays. . . . There was only this one permanent, public theater in the whole of France at the close of the sixteenth century, and all its profits accrued to the Brotherhood." In 1598, one of the early professional companies was headed by Valleran le Conte, who is known to have been acting in Bordeaux in 1592; he also had performed at Angers, Rouen, and Strasbourg. In early 1598, Valleran brought his *"troupe du Roi"* to Paris, joined forces with another troupe leader, an Andrien Talmy, and apparently presented plays in some hall other than the Hôtel de Bourgogne. Then in January 1599, Valleran and an actor-manager, Benoist Petit, signed an agreement by which their companies would alternate at the Hôtel.[54] Thus by the end of the century French professionals in Paris were beginning to prove that acting might pay.

In the early 1590's in Spain both the theater and Lope de Vega encountered evil, or at least indecisive, days. This "bad boy" and "monster of nature" was for a long while exiled from Madrid, lost his wife in 1595, and in the next year his daughter; but by 1596 he was back in the capital writing "all for MONEY" [55] a flock of assorted plays for the increasingly popular actors. Among his compositions were the graceful, religious *El Hijo Prodigo* (*The Prodigal Son*), *El Viaje del Alma* (*The Soul's Journey*), and *Las Bodas del Alma y el Armor Divino* (*The Marriage of the Soul and Divine Love.*)

But the great "increase in the number of theaters and actors and actresses throughout Spain . . . and the easy virtue of the theatrical profession, soon made the question of their continuance a grave concern." Toward the end of

1597, the King closed all the theaters. Two years later, however, in answer to public clamor, they were reopened. And by 1600 the many companies of players were reduced by law to four, "which . . . alone shall be licensed to represent comedies." In 1603 the number was raised to eight, and in 1613 to twelve.[56]

V

In London in 1591 Edward Alleyn, leading man of the affiliated Admiral's Men and Lord Strange's Men, quarreled with the Burbages and moved his actors from the Theatre and the Curtain to the Rose where he entered into a close business association with Henslowe. There, on February 19, 1592, the company opened a most successful season. Playing six days a week for some eighteen weeks, they presented twenty-three different plays and gave in all one hundred and five performances. Then, on account of some anti-alien riots, the theaters were closed until Michaelmas. In the same 1591–92 season a newly formed company of professional actors, including Richard Burbage, presented at the Theatre under the name of Lord Pembroke's Men two plays now known as *King Henry VI, Parts II and III*. They had been touched up, revised, "freshly flourished" with his "own colors" by a part-time actor named William Shakespeare (1564–1616). The presentations were so successful, at the time of the siege of Rouen, that rivals Alleyn and Henslowe at once commissioned the "upstart Crow," Shakespeare, to revise another play on the same subject for them. Offered to the public under the title of *King Henry VI, Part I*, it ran for fourteen performances from March 3 to June 20, 1592, to the clink of unusually large profits.[57] In the same year Shakespeare wrote, probably for the Pembroke actors, *The Comedy of Errors*, based largely on *Menaechmi*. In 1593 he patched and put together *Titus Andronicus*, derived in Seneca fashion from some medieval tale of "Rome the Great"; in *c.* 1593 he wrote the Italianate *Two Gentlemen of Verona* and, maybe for Burbage, *Richard III*; by 1594 he may have finished *The Taming of the Shrew*.

(During these few years actor Robert Browne [fl. 1583–1620] began taking relays of professional English players to Germany where various princes hired them to present in English and then in German many of the Elizabethan plays. And "the vivid acting of these professionals, masters of gestures and facial expression, supported by superb fooling, expert dancing, fencing and acrobatics, carried the day." Their "vivaciousness and self-assurance . . . , enhanced by the practice of improvisation which had reached England with the *commedia dell' arte*, raised the standard of acting in Germany for all time."[58])

Next, after the terrible plague of 1594, the Lord Pembroke Men became the Lord Chamberlain's Men with Burbage, Shakespeare, and Will Kempe (?–1603) as the leaders. "The first notice of the new organization is in June,

1594, when 'my Lord Admeralle men and my Lorde Chamberlain men' played from the 3rd to the 13th of the month, either in combination or separately on allotted days, for Henslowe" at the obscure Newington Butts theater. Soon afterward the Chamberlain company settled at the Theatre where they began to stage "a repertory derived by inheritance or purchase from antecedent companies" together with some new plays by Shakespeare. The earliest extant list of the principal members of the company included, in addition to Burbage, Shakespeare, and Kempe, Augustine Phillips (?–1605), Henry Condell (?–1627), William Sly (?–1608), John Heminge (1556–1630), and Thomas Pope (?–1604). George Bryan (?) and Richard Cowley (?–1619) were probably two more of the original group. By 1599 Robert Armin (c. 1568–1615) had joined the Chamberlain's Men.[59]

In addition to Alleyn, the principal members of the Admiral's Men, at least for 1594–97, seem to have been John Singer (?–1609), Richard Jones (?–c. 1615), Thomas Towne (?–1612), Martin Slater (?–1625), Edward Juby (?), Thomas Downton (?–c. 1623), and a James Donstone (?).[60]

The competition between these two great companies marked "virtually a fresh starting-point for the acting profession" in England. At long last the actors were assured of regular, full-time, profitable jobs. The Admiral's Men, for instance, played mostly at the Rose on weekday afternoons for thirty-nine consecutive weeks from June 15, 1594, to March 15, 1595. Then after a break for Lent, they played another ten weeks from Easter Monday, April 21, to June 26, 1595. Following a fifty-nine day vacation with visits to Bath and Maidstone, they then acted in London again for twenty-seven weeks from August 25 to February 28, 1596, rested for a forty-three day Lenten interval, and then acted for fifteen weeks from Easter Monday, April 12, to July 23, 1596. During the summer vacation of ninety-five days the company toured to towns like Coventry, Bath, Gloucester, Dunich, and so on. Performances for the 1594–97 seasons, including those at Court but not those given now and then at nights in private homes, totaled seven hundred and twenty-eight! And the actors, like all actors of the time, divided among themselves one-half of the box-office receipts. The other half went to the theater owner or "house." [61] The Chamberlain's Men, of course, at least matched that record of performances and profits.

In the same period, 1594–97, the Admiral's Men produced, on the average of one every two weeks, a total of fifty-five new plays! [62] Undoubtedly the Chamberlain's Men did as much. Among their new plays were possibly Shakespeare's King John (1594), Richard II (1595), Love's Labours Lost (c. 1596), Henry IV, Parts I and II (1596–97), The Merchant of Venice (1597), and Romeo and Juliet (1597).

During these years, however, the professional actors sensed that their future was still precarious. As the popularity of the plays and players increased so did Puritan discontent. It boiled. More and more the moralists insisted that men should not look to playing for a living. More and more, and deviously, the City tried to harass and even suppress the actors. More and more they were "piteously persecuted by the Lord Maior and the Aldermen: and [their] state . . . is now so uncertayne they cannot build upon it." Finally, in 1597, the fifth and final auspicious date, the Privy Council, after many vexing and intricate squabbles with the City, seems to have concluded that its method of regulation through the magistrates had broken down. It firmly took control into its own hands and definitely licensed two companies, and only two—the Admiral's Men and the Chamberlain's Men—to perform in London. Thus, and finally, a "complete stability was attained" for the new profession, and actors could freely and enthusiastically set about their business.[63]

For the 1597–98 season the Admiral's Men—reinforced by Samuel Rowley (?–1624), Charles Massey (?–1625), Robert Shaw (?–1603), William Bird (?–1624), Gabriel Spencer (?–1598), Humphrey (?–1618) and Anthony (?) Jeffes—played for a total of thirty-five weeks; for 1598–99 for forty-four weeks; and for 1599–1600 thirty-six weeks. In these three seasons they purchased fifty-eight new plays! One of the most durable of them was *The Shoemaker's Holiday* (1599–1600) by Thomas Dekker (*c.* 1572–1632). "In the three years 1598–1600, Dekker alone contributed eight complete plays and parts of twenty-four others to Henslowe . . . at about £6 a play. This may have brought him £30 in a good year—more than a parson or a schoolmaster, perhaps, but not enough to keep Dekker or his fellows from urgent requests to Henslowe for additional loans." The Chamberlain's Men in these three years surely performed as often as did the Admiral's Men. Their new plays included *Every Man in His Humour* (1598) by Ben Jonson (1572–1637), in which Shakespeare may have acted Knowell. And Shakespeare wrote for the company *A Midsummer Night's Dream* (1598), *Much Ado About Nothing* (*c.* 1598), and *King Henry V* (1599). No one, of course, is sure of any dates for Shakespeare's plays; but it is relatively certain that more than half of his total output was staged before 1600.[64]

In 1599 Cuthbert Burbage (*c.* 1566–1619), brother of Richard, built a new theater for the Chamberlain's Men near Henslowe's Rose and called it the Globe. For this enterprise the Burbages of the second generation hit upon the device of binding the interests of some of the leading actors more closely to their own by giving them a "share" of the profits of the "house." "To this end the site was conveyed by lease into two distinct moieties. One the Burbages held; the other was divided amongst five of the actors": Shakespeare, Phillips, Pope, Heminge, and Kempe. (Subsequently, of course, "it was several times redivided into a varying number of fractions, according as one man dropped out, or it was desired to admit another to participate in the benefits.") The actors, the best of them, became part owners of this new business. The Globe, probably initially designed by actors, opened in the autumn of 1599. It was an intimate theater although it accommodated about 2,000. "An actor standing at the front of the [forty-two feet wide] platform stood at the exact center of the tiny octagon, with spectators at his feet, on either side of him, and looking down at him from three sides of the building." He "stood among the audience, could see their faces, watch their changing expressions, nudge them, speak to them, include them in the action. . . ." One of the first plays on the new stage was *Julius Caesar*.[65]

Immediately thereafter, as a counter-move, Henslowe and Alleyn built a new theater for the Admiral's Men in their rivals' old territory. Modeled on the Globe, with almost identical dimensions, it was named the Fortune. Its stage was forty-three feet wide, and extended "to the middle of the yearde," or "pit," a distance of twenty-seven and a half feet. The seating capacity has been estimated at 2,138, at 2,350, and maybe even 2,558 in a pinch—with 800 packed into the "yard." The Fortune opened to the public in the autumn of 1600.[66]

By that time it was explicitly recognized again, after more than a thousand years, that acting "may with a good order and moderacion be suffered in a well gouerned state." Disgruntled authors like Greene may have called actors "Those burrs . . . those Puppets . . . that spake from our mouths, those Antics garnished in our colours," but the people called them "our witty Comedians and stately Tragedians . . . glorious and goodly representers of all fine wit, glorified phrase, and quaint action. . . ."[67]

5- The Italian Professionals

❀ NO PLAYWRIGHTS WANTED

Something needs to be said separately now about the unique contribution made by the *commedia dell' arte* ("that is, comedy produced by members of a guild or trade, for this is the meaning of *arte* in old Italian") to the resurgence of acting. The Italian players, crossing century marks and national boundaries, titillated the theater audiences of Europe for about two hundred years, say, from 1565 to about 1765. Especially in "Italy" and France they "quickly beat the learned elocutionists" with performances that "succeeded in being as diverting and attractive as the others were insipid and boring." Everywhere they took the stage with originality, vitality, theatricality. Moreover, these "splendid actors," as they were called, strove more or less unconsciously, more or less successfully, to better their social position, to put the actor's career on a par with the poet's and the painter's, and to bring the professional actor class into a better repute." [1]

Unfortunately, too much has been said lately in unadulterated praise of the *commedia dell' arte* players. Their work has seldom been truly evaluated. Theater researchers, who usually know little or nothing about acting, habitually hail them as the creators of "the modern theater, as theater," singling them out as "the men and women who, for the first time in Europe, made the stage their trade, their profession, and their life." They credit them with the earliest formation of professional companies "having contracts and stat-utes, masters and apprentices, families transmitting the craft from father to son and from mother to daughter." And they laud them for transforming "the technique of acting into a cultured and universal art." [2] But no one who has traced the almost parallel English progressions in the field can fairly award all the first prize honors to the Italians alone. And no one who treasures acting can say that they transformed it into anything much more than a temporary, rather exciting mess.

The significant truth about the *commedia dell' arte* actors is rarely men-tioned: they failed. As would-be transformers of acting they eventually failed. In their well intentioned revolt against the academicians and the dilettantes, in their attempts to advance the new profession by rejecting dramatists and by improvising, they made a stir, a glorious and lengthy stir in the world; but then slowly, inevitably, their so-called revolutionary kind of acting dwindled into being only a novelty, an amusing but freakish and pointless trick. Then, because it was not built upon the foundations of playwriting, it collapsed. The impromptu Italians couldn't compete in the long run with their col-leagues in other countries who were somehow always sure that actors ought to interpret a script carefully written, or designed, by an author. In due time they learned that "The actor who plays from his own head, speaks sometimes at random, spoils a scene and damns a piece." Finally, after 1750, they were compelled to agree with Goldoni who told them that playwrights and actors "require the assistance of one another, and we ought to entertain for one another reciprocal love and esteem, *servantis servandis*." [3]

II

At times, it's true, the better actors of the *commedia dell' arte* (or the *commedia istrionica, buffonesca, di maschere, or all' improvisa*) appeared in written plays; and probably their impersonations there were adequate. But the Italians were noted predominantly for their acting in comedies of intrigue peopled by stock characters, often masked, whose dialogue was largely impro-vised from a thin scenario. The majority of these comics pledged no allegiance to literature or to writing of any kind; they were antiwriting, antiauthor. For instance, Basilio Locatelli (?–1650), who gathered together one hundred and three scenarios in 1618 and 1622, wrote in a preface to his collection: "And if in these themes I have not observed all the desirable precepts of poetic art, remember that they are intended for extempore representation," and that "the player's function is one thing," surely the all-important thing, "and the poet's another"—something foreign and even inimical to the first. Or as one of the later actors, Evaristo Gherardi (1663–1700), explained, "A good Italian comedian" is one who "acts more from imagination than from memory. . . . There is not a single actor who plays *simply from memory*; not one who makes his entrance on the stage merely to unload as soon as possible everything he has learned" from a manuscript. Most of the Italian professionals, while admitting that it was "easy to act in a written play," just weren't willing, "like silly school-boys, to recite only what they had learned from a master, . . . to be mere echoes, unable to speak for themselves." They wanted to say what they pleased. They just had to be the sole creators and "improvise what the poet does premeditatedly." [4]

So, without benefit of playwriting, a company of ten or twelve comedians would make up dialogue on the spur of the moment and "keep the public in a gale of laughter for three hours or more." They "seized opportunity by the forelock and turned the least accident to profit. They drew inspiration from the times, the place, the color of the sky, or the topic of the day, and established a current between their audiences and themselves out of which the mad farce rose, the joint product of them all. It varied at each representation, seemed different every evening, with all the spirit and warmth and alertness of spontaneous creation, a brilliant ephemeral creature born of the moment and for the moment." [5]

And, as Andrea Perrucci (1651–1704) precariously hoped, "when an improvised comedy is performed by good actors, it succeeds in a way that bears comparison with a written play"! [6] And no one cries, "Author, author!" Only the actors beam and take bows.

Yet when these actors divorced themselves from playwrights and insisted on being independently creative they were, in a fascinating way, lost. They discovered for us the boundaries of acting by venturing beyond them.

❀ THE ACTOR IS ALL, ALAS!

Obviously, the Italian professionals were so intent on making the actor important that they made him all-important. They centered their attention solely on the actor's "sublime expressive spirit." Their characterizations were worked out, their skills perfected, and their scenarios devised only for the purpose of displaying "the virtuosity of the actor." The success of the *commedia dell' arte* performances depended "absolutely upon the actors who give them more or less point." [7]

But the premise, so lovely to the immature, that only the actor counts in the theater is untenable. It belittles the words of a play and results in an incomplete kind of acting. Since actors are rarely endowed with a talent for sitting in a study for months in a row and putting words together revealingly, or even interestingly, it isn't very likely they can do so on the spur of the moment onstage. Consequently, when actors aren't assigned words, they neither make up many of them nor rely on them very much. In instinctive desperation they turn to pantomime, to all sorts of physical actions, to anything that will substitute for words. Thus acting becomes only half of what it should be, only something to be watched instead of watched and heard.

Exactly this happened in the *commedia dell' arte*. Speech became an accompaniment, and a rather weak accompaniment, to gesture and movement and "stage business." Of course, the Italians boasted that "reciting plays is our profession." And actor Pier Maria Cecchini (1563–1645) worried about language, voice, about "speaking badly." Gherardi hoped for actors who could "charm their spectators with beauty of voice" and "flexibility of tone." Perrucci instructed the *innamorati* "to remember all the rules of behavior in voice," and advised them to "acquire a perfect Italian diction with the Tuscan inflections. . . . So little by little they will gain a habit of speech ready for every occasion, felicitous and pleasant." But the actors had nothing to say, nothing organized and worth the saying! Harlequin, of course, might rave to Eularia as she came from the tomb, "Alas, how grief has changed you! Your cheeks, which were once of a vermilion as beautiful as the backsides of a newly whipped child, are now so pale and gaunt they . . . seem like two dried codfish." Or he might advise a Captain with a toothache to "Take a pinch of pepper, some garlic, and vinegar, and rub it into your arse, and you'll forget your pain in no time. Wait a moment: I know a better remedy than that. Take an apple, cut it into four equal parts; put one of the pieces in your mouth, and hold your head in an oven until the apple is baked. I'll answer for it if it won't cure your headache." Harlequin could say such things, but obviously he was at his best when he forsook words and took to pantomine, when he acted little scenes like this typical one with Scaramouche: the latter, it seems, is onstage alone trying to think up ways and means of surprising Angelique. Harlequin enters, and Scaramouche, without telling him the reason for it all, begs him to start thinking, too. "They walk up and down the stage without speaking, wrapped in thought. Now and then they go up to each other and say, 'Egad, I have it!' Then they begin the same business again, saying, 'No, that won't do!' Once more they begin the same business. Finally, Harlequin turns round and faces Scaramouche, who says, 'Oh, that is sure to do the trick!' And they both leave the stage without a word of explanation." [8]

But such instances are really not needed to point out that the acting of the Italian professionals was almost entirely visual. In the main they were praised for their miming. Actor Angelo Costantini (c. 1655–1729) wrote in his pseudo-biography of the internationally famous "Scaramouche," Tiberio Fiorilli (1608–1694), that he used to speak little and expressed himself with difficulty; "but nature, on the other hand, had endowed him with the amazing talent of expressing through grimaces of his face all that he wished and, moreover, in the most original fashion." And Gherardi saluted him as "a model for the difficult and necessary art of simulating all the passions, and expressing them solely through the play of the features." Fiorilli, he said, could work on an audience "more effectively than any orator could ever hope to do, even with all the resources of the most persuasive rhetoric at his command." And "Harlequin Sacco," or Antonio Sacchi (1703–1788), was loved for his "postures wrought with symmetry, foolish but spiritual, coarse but graceful, always funny, and always revealing a state of soul in keeping with the situation and the subject portrayed." In short, "The actor . . . with effective gestures and movements was the motivating feature of all *commedia dell' arte* performances." [9] How he spoke didn't matter very much.

The result, to repeat, was only half-acting. One wonders, for instance, how the Italians Francesco Andreini (1548–1624) and Tristano Martinelli (*c.* 1557–1630) compared as full-fledged actors with their contemporaries Alleyn and Burbage; or how effectively they could have spoken a comic scene by a Dekker or a Jonson. One hardly dares wonder what they might have done with a sequence of mighty lines by Marlowe or with the verbal music of Shakespeare.

II

The premise that only the actor counts in the theater results in worse than half-acting. It disparages the story, the plot, the over-all action of a play and results (except in pure pantomime) in flabby and pointless half-acting. When actors seduce themselves into believing that the playwright counts for next to nothing, when they refuse to serve him by interpreting what he's designed with words, they can only resort to using no more than their own personalities and skills in order to please an audience, even at the cost of contributing nothing whatsoever to the play as a whole, even at the cost of obliterating it. Such actors blithely insist that in a play character is the fundamental thing, and that plot is secondary. They can't be bothered with thinking out the truth that "characters express themselves in their actions, and the sum of their actions implies the plot," and "the plot . . . can be therefore of all the elements in the play the most inclusive, and therefore most largely and completely expressive of the play's essential idea or quality." Vanity won't let them admit that the actor who does not draw his chief notion of the character he makes from *the plot of the play* is in danger of characterizing in a vacuum.[10]

The *commedia dell' arte* actors latched onto and fattened only characters in search of a play; after they had done that they put together or commissioned scenarios that would set the characters into any kind of motion. They found their crudely developed "people" not in myths, not in history, not in literature, and not in contemporary society, but in the accumulated traditions of the Doric mimes, the *fabulae Atellana*, and possibly the Byzantine mimes. The aspiring actress, for instance, merely had to decide "in limbo" whether she'd portray Flaminia, Lucinda, or Ardelia, or whatever the *innamorata* was called; or whether she'd represent someone like the confidante Francesquina or the saucy servant Columbia. The novice actor had only to decide "in limbo" which of the several available characters best suited him: the handsome lover, or *innamorato*, named Flavio, Lelio, Ottavio, or the like; or the blustering and ridiculous Captain, a duplicate of Plautus's Miles Gloriosus; or his stage relations, Scaramuccia or Giangurgolo; or Pantalone (Pantaloon) who was always "the old father, the greedy merchant, the doting husband, the silly guardian, the aged counsellor"; or the bookish Dottore or the oldish Coviello; or one of the zany servants, Harlequin, Brighella, the variously spelled Pulcinella (Punch), Pedrolina or Piero (who later became the French Pierrot), Scapino, Mezzetin; and so on. And once an actor had chosen the stock character that best fitted him, or vice versa, he almost always played it for the rest of his life. Thus, "Each individual actor or actress, if sufficiently gifted, was able to give the role of his election a characteristic form so that it bore forever the imprint of his personality." [11]

An Italian actor then proceeded to work out his authorless characterization by following some standard recipe. If, for instance, he chose to impersonate one of the zany servants, he knew from his familiarity with the stage that "The first Zanni must be clever, apt, witty, keen; one who can perplex, cheat, trick, and delude everyone; he must be cynically sharp, but *cum moderamine*, so that his witticisms . . . have in them a spice of risqueness and do not sound merely stupid"; and he knew that the second Zanni "must be foolish, clumsy, dull, so that he cannot tell his right hand from his left." If he elected to be the Dottore he remembered that "A number of years ago there was introduced a special style in the playing of the part, whereby the Dottore mutilated his words, saying for example, 'terrible urinal' for tribunal, . . . but, since it was realized that this rendered him far too stupid and clumsy, it has been abandoned." And if the actor decided to play Pantaloon he was aware that "The Actor who assumes this role should . . . try to provoke laughter at appropriate junctures by his self-importance and stupidity, and in this manner represent a man ripe in years who pretends to be a tower of strength and good counsel for others, whereas in truth he is blinded by amorous passion and continually doing puerile things which might lead an observer to call him a child, for all that he is almost a centenarian." [12]

Next, in order to "round out" his characterization, in order to give it more substance, each actor always memorized many assorted, unrelated bits which he could insert as often as convenient in the improvised dialogue. He filched "proverbs, sallies, charades, riddles, recitations, cock-and-bull stories, and songs"; he stored up "all sorts of metaphors, similies, repetitions, antitheses, cacophonies, hyperboles, tropes, . . . pleasant figures, . . . soliloquies, exclamations of despair, sallies, conceits of happy love, or jealousy, or prayer, or contempt, or friendship, or admiration." And he learned by heart a variety of *chiusette* (closings), or rhymed couplets which could be used to terminate a discourse or a sequence, and all sorts of *uscite* (exits), or prose passages ending in a rhymed couplet that would make for effective exits.[13]

Then, in order to "individualize" his characterization, each actor invented a number of *lazzi*, or irrelevant bits of stage business or tricky comic turns which he could exhibit to audiences whenever he felt in the mood, or whenever a scene dragged, or whenever the cast needed a breathing spell. A *lazzo*, for example, might consist of the acrobatic stunt of boxing a fellow-actor's ear with the foot, or the turning of a somersault with a glass of water in hand without spilling a drop. Another *lazzo* might be the sudden pretending by one actor, for no reason at all, that his hat is full of cherries; then daintily eating them and flicking the pits into another actor's face. Or the *lazzo* might be the show of "catching a fly, of clipping its wings in a comic manner, and of eating it." "The *lazzo* of weeping and laughing is when a character goes on cheating another. For instance, when the old man weeps at the departure of his son and smiles at the thought of having free opportunity of enjoying, without fear of jealousy, the woman he loves. The son does the same." The great pantomimist Domenico Biancolelli thus described one of his most famous *lazzi*: As Harlequin "I arrive on the stage; there I find Trivelin stretched on the ground. I think him dead and try to drag him to his feet; then I let my wooden sword fall down. He takes it and hits me on the buttocks. I turn round without speaking, and he gives me a kick on the back so that I tumble down. Up I get again; I seize and carry him; I lean him against the wings on the right-hand side of the stage. I look round . . . and meanwhile he gets up and leans himself against the left-hand side-wings." [14]

Some of these *lazzi* may once have been as funny as the shoe-eating scene in Chaplin's *The Gold Rush*, or the banquet scene in the Murray-Boretz *Room Service* (1936) in which three characters "guzzle, gorge, and stuff themselves" in almost dance patterns; but most of them seem now to have been the pantomimic expression of the actor's ego trying for a laugh at any cost. Most of them were so extraneous to a play's main action that the actors constantly had to be warned "not to deviate from the plot to such an extent" that they "cannot find their way back to it. It must be avoided that the audience, due to extended and obtrusive comic business, lose the thread of the plot or have difficulty in grasping it again. . . ." [15]

Finally, when the *commedia dell' arte* actor had thus completed his characterization independently from any script, he had only to receive a scenario—a standard one, a revised version of a standard one, or a new and hastily scribbled one—and talk it over with the other actors and the manager (*corago*) of the troupe. He had only to rehearse (*concertare*) in a perfunctory way, "the treatment and termination of scenes," to fix in his mind place names and proper names ("since it would be a grave error and unpardonable impropriety for one actor to speak of being in Rome and another in Naples; or that the character who comes from Spain would say Germany; or for the father to forget the name of his son or the lover that of his beloved"), and to be sure of the scenes ("for it would be too ridiculous for anyone to . . . enter into somebody else's house instead of his own: one would regard such a person as a booby or drunkard"). [16] He had only to run through a few new *lazzi* with some of his co-actors. At last, he had only to hang the scenario somewhere in the wings. The rest he invented for himself.

A scenario (*soggetto*) explained only what each scene was about, what each actor was to *do*, and no more. The actor rarely obtained "the least suggestion of dialogue" from it. Perrucci defined a scenario as "nothing but the tissue of scenes woven from a plot, containing abbreviated hints at an action, divided into acts and scenes, which have to be acted and spoken in an extemporaneous manner by the player. On the margin there are indications where each character has to enter, and a broken line indicates where the actors make their exits. At the top of each scenario is mentioned the place (e.g., Rome, Naples, Genoa, Leghorn, etc.) where the action of the play is supposed to take place. . . ." For example, the more or less typical scenario for *The Roguish Tricks of Coviello* was in part set down as follows:

ACT I. SCENE 1.

GIANGURGOLO *and* COVIELLO.
He tells Coviello that he has arranged a marriage for his daughter (Pimpinella) with the Captain who is away, and knocking is heard.

SCENE 2.

PIMPINELLA *and the aforesaid.*
Pimpinella, having understood this, acts a scene of foolishness, until the other two, tired out, make her go in, saying they will talk to each other some other time, and go off.

SCENE 3.

POLICINELLA *alone.*
His love for Pimpinella, and knocks.

SCENE 4.

PIMPINELLA *and the aforesaid.*
Amorous scene . . .

SCENE 5.

COVIELLO *and the aforesaid.*
Coviello's *lazzi* over the foolishness of the girl; she excuses herself as having acted so for love of Policinella and because she does not want the Captain; and both entreat Coviello to help them. Coviello promises, and Pimpinella goes in. Coviello tells Policinella that the Captain has arrived, and therefore plans . . . to dress [Policinella] as a Woman. Policinella, having acted *lazzi*, is pleased and goes away to dress himself. Coviello wants to pretend to be Giangurgolo, and goes in to dress himself.

SCENE 6.

THE CAPTAIN *alone.*
Says he is come for the marriage arranged by letter with the daughter of Giangurgolo, and that he does not know personally either the one or the other . . .

SCENE 7.

COVIELLO *and the aforesaid.*
Coviello as Giangurgolo, after acting a scene, makes himself known to
the Captain as Giangurgolo, and after they have acted *lazzi* of relationship Coviello calls [Policinella].

SCENE 8.

POLICINELLA *and the aforesaid.*
Policinella as a woman, acts his *lazzi*; the Captain says he does not want
her, and after a scene which develops as it befalls (in accordance with
the inspiration and action of the moment), and *lazzi*, they beat each
other, and end the first act.[17]

Almost all of the scenarios were three-act comedies based on assorted
and complicated love affairs. For example, of the fifty scenarios by actor
Flaminio Scala (fl. 1576–1620?), printed at Venice in 1611 under the title of
*Il Teatro Favole Rappresentative, overo la ricreazione comica, boscareccia, e
tragica: divisa in cinquanta giornate* . . . (*The Theater of Representative
Tales, or, Comic, Tragic, and Bucolic Entertainments, divided into Plays for
each of Fifty Days* . . .), thirty-nine are comedies "*tres-scandaleux* . . . in
which the slave and love intrigues negotiated by wily servants for unscrupulous young women outdo Plautus, . . . the remainder are termed *opera regia*,
or elaborate fantasies; only one . . . is a tragedy." Scala's best known scenario,
Il Ritratto (*The Portrait*), begins when Isabella, the wife of Pantalone, having
enjoyed an affair with Oratio, gives him her portrait, which he places in a
locket. Then when he calls on the scheming actress Vittoria, she steals it
from him, and then Pantalone is amazed when he calls on her and discovers
his wife's portrait in her possession. Isabella, reprimanded by her husband,
quarrels with Oratio and demands the return of the picture. His attempts to
recover it, the subsequent wooing of Vittoria by Pantalone in competition
with a braggart Captain and a certain Gratiano, the betrayal of the latter by
his wife Flaminia who takes a lover named Flavio, the attachment of a young
girl, Sylvia, for the Captain, plus some subordinate intrigues by the servants
Arlecchino and Petrolino, provide a complicated story "that bubbles with
action, surprise, and salacious humor." [18]

Other actors and troupe managers concocted scenarios along similar lines.
In *Non Può Essere* (*It Can't Be*) Luzio tries to put obstacles in the way of
his sister Violante, who wishes to marry Orazio, and at the same time pursues
his own courtship of Cinzia to the accompaniment of much merrymaking by
Policinella, the Dottore, and Coviello. *L'Amante Intersato* (*Love Interest*)
sets three or four groups of characters in motion: Pantalone, his daughter
Clarice, and her servant Argentina; the Dottore, with his son Oratio, his
daughter Flavia, and the son's servant, Virginio; Celio, a poor scholar, and
his servant, Zanni; Cassandro and Giangurgolo. In the beginning Cassandro

desires Clarice as his wife, but at the end he marries Flavia, while Celio takes Clarice, and Giangurgolo makes a comic match with Argentina. In *Le Tre Gravide* (*The Three Pregnant Women*), Lucinda, Ardelia, and Colombina are actually with child by Orazio, Ottavio, and Zanni confusingly.[19]

Enough! The stories, the plots, the scenarios were unimportant. They were only hastily, tritely contrived romantic and comic mix-ups in which the players could don their masks (but the *innamorati* never wore them, and Scaramouche Fiorilli never wore one), take stage, and aim to make a number of stock characters lively and funny. Evidently they succeeded in doing that.

But there was something naive, something superficial, something distressingly egotistical in that predominant, almost exclusive aim. Something was basically wrong with the attempt to make a character merely funny (or romantic, or dramatic, or tragic, or whatnot). The Italian actor of this period did not know, or want to know, that in portraying a character he ought first of all to try to relate it to life, as actors in other countries were at least faintly trying to do under the guidance of playwrights, and simultaneously to relate it to the essential idea and style of a play in which it functions.

In a superficial way, it must be admitted, the *commedia dell' arte* actors did try to make their characters human. They hoped, they said, to represent "people not of the dead and forgotten past, but of living and growing cities like Venice and Bergamo." Therefore, as the lovers they "dressed in the latest fashion of the period," as the Captains they uniformed themselves in "the contemporary styles," as the Pantalones their costumes were "symbols of the prosperity of Venice," as the Doctors their garb "was a caricatured version of the ordinary dress which the men of science and learning in Bologna wore both at the University and about the town," as the Pulcinellas they copied "the attire in general use among the peasants of Acerra," as the Harlequins they wore "a conventionalized . . . treatment of the dress of a tatterdemalion." And often the actors talked—as improvisors they had to talk— more or less naturally. However, everyday speech and contemporary dress aren't enough to achieve lifelikeness. The Italians rarely went below the surface of things; they never delineated the human actions of characters designed to serve an idea. Consequently, as Croce cautiously observed, "It may be that some of these actors at times rose above broad farce to the humorous and the human, but on this point nothing definite can be said." [20]

III

Nevertheless, even when the Italian comedians rejected playwrights, forfeited their proper job of interpretation, and exalted only themselves, they contributed more than a little to the development of acting. The temptation is to say that in their pantomime and in their improvising they were the first to separate acting from elocution, that "imitative branch of oratory, which in its turn is the oral branch of literature." [21] But that isn't quite true. The players of Plautus before them had done that. Comedians everywhere from the beginning had done that. What the *commedia dell' arte* actors did was to emphasize again, at a wordy time in the world when that emphasis was sorely needed, the truth that a play ought not be enjoyed or even evaluated only for its writing, that a play blooms best onstage instead of in the library. (They were far ahead of either the English or the French in making that point.) The Italians vividly centered Europe's attention on the lively, more-or-less natural, and skilled presence of the actors. They overaccented their own contribution to the whole thing called theater because their peculiar contribution wasn't being noticed, and somehow they had to draw attention to it.

First, by their gestures, postures, movements, and "stage business" the *commedia* players reminded audiences—and all workers in the theater—that the theater is "a place for seeing" actors as well as for listening to them. They demonstrated the truth that "Motion itself is the peculiar and exclusive property of the theater." [22] They proved that the actor's body can be the most plastic and expressive of forms, that an actor can truly create by the use he makes of it. They insisted that no dramatist was needed to prescribe, for instance, the glint in the eye, the strange smile, the anguished face, the curled finger, the hand flung outward, the tightened shoulder muscles, the weary sitting, the cocky strut, and so on. That highly important visual shaping of a character was, they believed, the exclusive stage task of the actor.

Sometimes it almost seems as if these comedians anticipated Stanislavski who was addicted to saying again and again to his students, "Mind you, only physical actions, physical truths, and physical belief in them! Nothing more!" [23] But their premise differed, differed fundamentally, from his. They were less psychological, instinctively more artful, more theatrical than ever he dreamed of being. Stanislavski believed in perfecting physical actions for the purpose of capturing "Faith and a Sense of Truth"; the *commedia dell' arte* actors polished their pantomime in order to contact an audience.

Next, by often speaking extempore, the Italian professionals first proclaimed the immediacy, the marvelous *now*, of acting. For them a staged story wasn't something that *had* happened, and which you studied and memorized and then re-did. Oh, no. It was something newly going on at any given instant. Acting, therefore, was doing for the first time, was participation in a current event, was always present tense. Consequently, the same general proceedings of a scene were always a bit new and different each time they were played. If, as Gherardi maintained, "Anyone can learn a part and recite it on the stage, but something else is required for Italian comedy," [24] that something else was an awareness of *now*. The *commedia dell' arte* actor was gladly compelled to respond to each new *now*. He had to adjust to fresh actions and circumstances, had to be resourceful and imaginative enough to "play off" the unexpected movements and words of the other characters in each scene of a scenario. Thus, in playing on and for the instant, for two or three hours of new instants, the Italians certainly discovered—and communicated, no doubt—the unique thrill of acting.

Finally, by reveling in improvisation these professionals tried, above all else, to rout the reciters and to bring onstage a kind of realism in acting. Spontaneity (instead of an apparent spontaneity, which is much harder to try for, and more rewarding) seemed to them the quickest way to achieve that realism. The Italians were positive that an improvising actor "plays in a much livelier and more natural manner than one who learns his role by heart." In an elementary way they were right. There was in their acting, in most instances, "a certain gracious, easy, natural air"; it accompanied all their movements and enveloped everything they said. As one scholar–critic admitted, "Their style may suffer from this method of playing *a l'impromptu*, but at the same time the action gains in naturalness and vividness . . . and the actors come and go, speak and act as informally as in ordinary life." [25]

❀ SLOW, SIGNIFICANT FAILURE

The long run of the *commedia dell' arte* can be divided, arbitrarily, into three fairly distinct periods. Period one, the time of the famous companies, continued for about seventy years, in the main paralleling the lives of de Vega and Shakespeare, from *c.* 1565 to *c.* 1637. And though the facts about the chief professional troupes are few and dim, often confusing and not always reliable, it is known that the Gelosi, or "the Zealous," who began performing before 1570, had become by 1578 (under the probable leadership of Flaminio Scala, who acted Flavio) "the most unified" of all the companies. In that same year thirty year old Francesco Andreini, who acted the Captain, succeeded Scala as director and married sixteen-year-old actress Isabella Canali. For the next twenty-five years as this Mantuan troupe toured its farces to all the courts of northern Italy and to France its "chief of theatrical artists" was this Isabella Andreini, "the first distinguished actress of the European theater." "Stately and beautiful, learned and virtuous," she pursued her intrigues as the *innamorata* "with unflagging energy and ready wit, disguising herself as a man, feigning madness, duping her ridiculous old lover, husband, or father, quarreling with her rivals, beating her servants, and berating her enemies, yet preserving a certain elegance and charm in spite of her violence." Evidently she was "one of those who create theater by their mere presence on the stage, by a turn of the head, an inflection of the voice, a gesture of welcome or dismissal." For her skills and her quality she was "crowned with laurel by the members of the Academy of the Intenti of Padua"; and again in Rome "she was crowned in effigy between the pictures of Tasso and Petrarch, after a banquet offered her by the Most Eminent Cardinal Cintio Aldobrandini. . . ." [26] Isabella died suddenly at Lyons in 1604 when the Gelosi were returning from their third visit to Paris, where they had performed at Court and at the Hôtel de Bourgogne. At once the thirty-four-year-old senior troupe of Italian comedians was disbanded.

The second oldest *commedia dell' arte* troupe, the Confidenti, or "the

Confident," played in two versions for over forty-five years from c. 1574 to
1621. "After a period of varying fortunes in Italy, the Confidenti came . . .
to France in 1584 and 1585 as protégés of the Medeci"; then about 1590
Victoria Piassimi and Giovanni Pellesini (c. 1526-?), a Pedrolino and perhaps
her husband, became directors of the company comprising about twelve members and toured their native land, France, and Spain. Thereafter the troupe
seems to have broken up. In about 1610, however, Scala emerged as the head
of a reborn Confidenti. But in 1620 the actors were in dire financial difficulties, begged their patron for help, and were "almost all mutinous and
holding themselves together with great difficulty, as is usual among players."
By 1621 the company had vanished.[27]

The third group of Italian players, the Uniti, or "the United," somehow
closely related at times to both the Gelosi and the Confidenti, performed for
over thirty-five years from c. 1578 to 1614. Actually, it may never have been a
separate troupe, but only a coming together of actors from different companies to present plays on special occasions.

The Accesi, or "the Flashing" or "inspired" company, acted for over
forty years from c. 1590 to c. 1632. By 1599, with the Duke of Mantua as
patron, the leaders of the dozen or so players were Tristano Martinelli, who
had left the illusive Desiosi troupe, and Pier Maria Cecchini, who may have
originally organized the actors. In 1600 the Accesi were summoned to Paris
by Henri IV. On the way there the all-star group, including Diana Ponti,
Tristano's talented brother, Drusiano Martinelli, and Scala, played for some
time at Turin, were held over for several months at Lyons, and finally arrived
at the French capital in January 1601, where they performed regularly until
at least October. The engagement was splattered with fights. Cecchini, for
instance, accused Tristano of planning to assassinate him "for fear I shall
reveal some of his bad tricks, once we are back in Italy." Harlequin Tristano,
it seems, "never hesitated to beseech and to flatter patrons if he saw the
least chance of screwing them up to the pitch of generosity," and then to
cheat his coleader and fellow actors. In 1608 the troupe, minus the temperamental and grasping Tristano, returned to Paris for a second visit and offered
their plays at Court and at the Hôtel de Bourgogne from February until
about October. In 1609 the Accesi under Cecchini appear to have joined
forces with the Fedeli troupe led by Giambattista Andreini (1576-1654),
the son of Francesco and Isabella. But constant fighting between their wives,
Orsola and Virginia, led to the eventual banishment of Cecchini. Under the
Accesi name the actors then toured Bavaria and Austria in 1614 and northern
Italy from 1615 to 1620. They were last heard of vaguely in 1632.[28]

The last of the principal professional companies of commedia dell' arte
actors, the Fedeli, or "the Faithful," was probably organized by Giambattista
Andreini in the service of Mantua in 1604. It held together for thirty-three
years. In 1613, with Tristano Martinelli again as the star and leader, the

troupe set out for Paris. At Chambéry he was paid fifty ducats for one performance of a comedy by the company, and then accused of having spent twenty of them on himself. At Lyons four public performances brought in two hundred and twenty ducats. Then, after acting at the Louvre and at Fontainebleau, the company opened at the Hôtel de Bourgogne in November 1613, and remained there, except for appearances at Court, until July 1614. The Fedeli were again in Paris and at Fontainebleau for nearly fifteen months, from January 1621 to March 1622. Early in the visit, however, Tristano complained of "the great discord in the company," got his release from the French King, returned to Italy, and continued to act until about 1626. His will of 1630 showed "how a clever and fortunate actor even in those uncertain times was able to lay up a fortune." [29]

Andreini in 1622 "was the leader of the most famous and best patronized company of actors in the world, the Fedeli." He was also—as a sign of changes to come—a playwright who wrote out dialogue for his actors. His works included La Maddalena (1617), "the most beautiful mixture of comedy-drama-tragedy-melodrama-pantomime-dance ever seen on the stage,"Lelio bandito (1620), a tragi-comedy in which he tried to make each character speak "as he would in real life," and La Centaura (1622), for which he provided some unusual stage machinery and splendid scenery. In 1623 and again in 1624 the Fedeli played in Paris; then near the end of 1627 the troupe seems to have broken up; the actors scattered to Naples, Rome, Modena, and maybe even to Germany and Hungary. By 1632 Andreini was attempting to gather together a new troupe and begging a new Duke of Mantua for favors. In the following year, however, another company was engaged in place of the Fedeli, "a terrible insult to pride as well as an infringement of privilege." By 1637— the year Corneille's Le Cid was first staged in Paris—"the Fedeli seem to have disbanded for good and their leader to have retired, not happily." Deep in debt by 1652, Andreini humbly petitioned the Duke for a promised pension. "So may pity," he wrote, "which never sleeps in Your Highness, grow for Lelio, who during forty years has managed comedies for the noble Gonzaga and who is now helpless." No help was forthcoming. Finally, in desperation he implored the Duke "to appoint him for the coming year (if it please God) to a life tenure of the Commission of Castles. . . . And because the benefice is so meager, not more than 27 or 30 lire a month, and that uncertain, he begs some other succor. . . ." [30] But nobody paid any attention to an old, used-up actor.

II

Period two in the life of the commedia dell' arte centered at Parma, Modena, and Paris, and continued from c. 1637 to 1700. One Parma troupe, organized by Antonio Fidenza, who had broken away from the Fedeli in

1627, performed from 1638 to 1646. Some of its often related and always quarreling actors included Niccolò Barbieri (?–c. 1640), also from the Fedeli, as Beltrame; Brigida Bianchi (1613–1703), the daughter of actor Giuseppe Bianchi (?–c. 1682), the wife of actor Nicolas Romagnesi (?–1660), and the mother of actor Marc' Antonio Romagnesi (c. 1633–1706) as Aurelia; and Carlo Cantù (1609–c. 1676) as Buffetto. Much later, from 1687 to 1691, another Parma company, headed perhaps by Francesco Calderoni, who had been playing there since 1664, performed with considerable success in the neighborhood of Munich, then toured Italy for nearly two years, went in 1693 to Brussels, and by the end of the century was in Vienna.

Modena's troupes seem from the scattered records to have been closely related to those at Parma; for some years their activities can hardly be dissociated. However, a definite Modena company of perhaps a dozen actors, headed by Bernardo Coris, was performing in 1651, and included his wife as the *prima donna* Florinda; Isabella Biancolelli, the daughter of actor Francesco Franchini, the mother of the famous Domenico, and the recent wife of Cantù, as Colombia; Cantù as Brighella; and Domenico Locatelli, back from France, as Trivellino. By 1675–77 the group had three new members: Antonio Riccoboni, the father of reformer Luigi, as Pantalone; and Costantino and Domenica Costantini, the parents of Giovan (?–1720) and Angelo.

In 1678 Francesco II, Duke of Modena, was arranging to dispatch a group of his players to England with the seventy-year-old Tiberio Fiorilli, called "by far the greatest actor of his time," as chief. This Scaramouche, from a poor company, had already played at Paris on five or six different occasions, in London for almost six months in 1673, and for about four months in 1675. Fiorilli didn't make the trip, however; the negotiations probably broke down because his royal patron owed him money for other trips. But a Modena company of twelve arrived in England in November 1678 with six portmanteaus, two great baskets, and twenty-one trunks. They rather quickly left there in February 1679 largely because anti-Catholic plots were fomenting.

Then in 1690, a few years before the Modena troupes seem to have fallen apart, a group of the actors embarked on a tour to Pescia, Camajore, Lucca, Livorno, Florence, and other Italian places. But business everywhere was so bad the cast wrote the Duke that "Already twenty days have passed since the company . . . arrived at Brescia, [and] our receipts are not sufficient to pay for our lodgings. Our present position, . . . after a costly journey from Genoa to this town, with a very heavy debt owed by the company for the escort, forces us to put our miseries before your Highness. . . . it will be impossible for us to leave this city without pawning our properties. . . ." [31]

France, however, flocked to the novelty of the *commedia dell' arte* foreigners. In 1639 a Parma-Modena troupe, whose director may have been Giuseppe Bianchi, performed at Paris on the invitation of Louis XIII, and returned there as the Cardinal Mazarin company for the 1644–45 season, and possibly until 1647–48. The leading players were Fiorilli, Locatelli, his wife

Luisa Gabbrielli as Lucilla, Bianchi as the Captain, his daughter Brigida as Aurelia, her husband Romagnesi as Orazio, and Lolli, as the Doctor. In 1653 Fiorilli and Locatelli came back with their company and played at the Petit-Bourbon (where the Gelosi had appeared in 1577); then again in 1658 a Fiorilli-Locatelli troupe returned to act at the same theater, and cordially allowed Molière's newly arrived provincial company to stage plays there on the less pouplar Mondays, Wednesdays, Thursdays, and Saturdays.[32] (In that year Molière caused a furore with the one-act *Les Précieuses ridicules*.)

Three years later, in 1661, a celebrated group of Italian actors headed by Fiorilli, Locatelli, and young Domenico Biancolelli (c. 1640–1688) as Harlequin arrived in Paris, discovered that the Petit-Bourbon had been demolished, proceeded to rent from Molière a share of his theater, the Palais-Royal seating an audience of six hundred, and firmly established the *commedia dell' arte* in France. They continued, with many changes in personnel, of course, to act in the capital for the next thirty-six years alongside Molière's major comedies and Racine's tragedies. In 1680, seven years after the former's death, the company was granted sole possession of the vacant Hôtel de Bourgogne, where they performed every day of the week except Friday as the Comédie-Italienne.

As competition with the new Comédie-Française increased, the Italians made several policy changes. First, they added more and more French phrases and songs, even whole scenes, to their scenarios. French actors, of course, at once protested; but Domenico (or the naturalized Frenchman Dominique) successfully persuaded King Louis XIV to allow his troupe to use a modicum of French in their presentations. Second, the Italians, at long last, began to sense the value of playwriting, of acting out a well-written script. Evidently they envied the actors in the comedies by Molière. It is true, indeed, that the *commedia dell' arte* greatly influenced him; but it's more importantly true that he took the crude Italian scenarios and beat them into shape by unifying the stories and the pranks around an idea and by creating characters functional to it. Certainly "the plays of Molière were the finest fruit of the *commedia dell' arte*." And certainly he taught the Italians the *point* of acting. So, at first, they performed a *comédie mixte*, or mixed play, in which certain passages of dialogue were carefully written out and interlarded with improvised speeches. But such bastard versions weren't worth much. Therefore, third, the Italians employed Jean-François Regnard (1655–1709), Charles Rivière Dufresny (1654–1724), and other Frenchmen to write plays for them. The acting, alas, "continued to be that of the *commedia dell' arte* and the actors were allowed complete scope for improvisation." [33]

Finally, in 1697 the long Paris success of the *commedia dell' arte* abruptly ended. Maybe it was time for that. Possibly the quaint plays were boring audiences because of their similarity and shallowness. Probably the novelty of the characters and the acting was wearing off. Perhaps the actors were trying too hard to hold their thinning audiences with indecencies and scurrilities.

For some time they had been harshly criticized for doing just that. At any rate, in early May 1697, when Paris was talking about a book published in Holland called *La Fausse prude*, which was read by some as an attack on Mme. Maintenon, morganatically married to Louis XIV, the Italians too cleverly changed the title of a comedy they were rehearsing to *La Fausse prude*. "Retribution came swiftly. On May 13 an order came to the police: 'The King has dismissed his Italian actors; his Majesty commands . . . you to shut up their theater tomorrow for good.' On the following day, accordingly, seals were set on all the doors of the playhouse, and the players departed sorrowfully with their belongings." [34] For nearly twenty years the Comédie-Italienne was banned from Paris.

III

Period three in the life of the *commedia dell' arte* extended from 1700 to about 1765. During the first years of the century troupes of professional actors continued to perform here and there in Italy and sometimes abroad. Then, after the death of Louis XIV in 1715, and a period of official mourning, Philippe II d'Orleans, regent for the six-year-old Louis XV, undertook to procure a new company of Italian comedians to play in Paris. He contacted the Duke of Parma, who assigned the task of forming it to actor-director Luigi Riccoboni (c. 1676–1753), son of Antonio, the Modena Pantalone. Luigi had acted at Modena in c. 1692 when he was about sixteen. Then, "moved by religious aspirations," he decided to leave the stage and become a monk. But the Duke persuaded him to remain a player, and he became a restless one. Apparently he was among the early few who sensed some of the weaknesses of extempore performances. He wrote, much later, for instance, that "the drawback of improvisation is that the success of even the best actor depends upon his partner in the dialogue. If he has to act with a colleague who fails to reply exactly at the right moment or who interrupts him in the wrong place, his own discourse falters and the liveliness of his wit is extinguished." Moreover, as a young man of culture and as a potential writer he believed that actors as well as audiences deserved genuine plays, even tragedies sometimes, instead of only a tired succession of hastily contrived, trite, foolish, and pointless comic scenarios. He, therefore, attempted to "reform" the Italian theater "by introducing, instead of improvised comedies, the written works of the poets, such as the *Sofonisba* of Trissino, the *Oedipus* of Sophocles, and many more. This experiment in the literary drama seems to have been successful enough at Modena, but . . . Venice, to which city he next took his company, remained faithful to its Arlecchinos, its Dottores, and its Pantalones, and Riccoboni, disappointed and discouraged, had to renounce his purpose." In 1713, however, he seems to have made a tremendous success in the tragedy *Merope* by Scipione de Maffei (1675–1755). [35] He was ready to go to France.

In May of 1716 the Italian professionals at long last returned to Paris led by forty-year-old Luigi as the lover Lelio. Because the Hôtel de Bourgogne wasn't quite ready for them, the actors opened on May 18 at the Palais-Royal in an old piece called *L'Inganno Fortunato* (*The Lucky Cheat*) and achieved an immediate success. In June the troupe moved to the rehabilitated Hôtel where the curtain displayed a painted phoenix arising from the flames with the motto beneath, "*Je renais.*" [36]

Success, however, didn't last very long; the novelty of the imported theater quickly wore off. When audiences thinned out because the Italians spoke only in their native tongue (even though "their pantomime was eloquent enough to tell a story or illustrate a character"), the company revived some of the French plays, only partly improvised, which had been performed in the years before the expulsion. Next, when some patrons objected to the vulgarities of Pantaloon and Harlequin, when too many patrons, accustomed to the works of Molière, showed definite signs of wearying of stereotyped characters, stale plots, and undisciplined impromptu acting, and when the *commedia* actors saw their phoenix heading for a speedy nose dive, Riccoboni, still at heart the reformer, saw his chance. He decided to use fully written out scripts. He asked "a friend named Jacques Autreau to write a play in French, using the traditional characters of the Italian comedy." Autreau did so, turning out *Le Port à L'Anglais* which the troupe memorized and presented on April 25, 1718, under Riccoboni's unifying direction for a box-office triumph. Thus the venture was saved—at least for a while.[37] Improvisation was nearly as dead as a doornail, but the venture was saved. And from then on the play or the script, perhaps awkwardly at first, became the thing for the Italians. In 1720 they acted *Arlequin poli par l'amour* (*Harlequin Refined by Love*), the first of a number of scripts written for them by Pierre-Carlet Marivaux (1688–1763), whose sentimental but meticulously polished dialogue was anything but spontaneous, and whose minute psychological analyses of character demanded the delicate touch instead of the slapstick. In 1721 the company acted *Arlequin sauvage* and *Timon la misanthrope* by Delisle; in the next year they acted Marivaux's *La Surprise de l'amour* (*The Unexpectedness of Love*) in which Lelio and a countess, having renounced love, spend the pleasant plot in gradually awakening to a largely unwished for affection for each other; and in 1723 they acted his *La Double inconstance* (*The Double Inconstancy*) which tells the story of Harlequin and Silvia who are affianced to each other until the Prince chooses the latter for his bride and Harlequin then discovers that it's Flavinia whom he truly loves. In that year, as a reward for their new and sound efforts, Riccoboni and his colleagues were granted a subsidy of 15,000 livres; and on the Hôtel de Bourgogne, under the arms of France, was inscribed "Hôtel of the Comédians Ordinary to the King."

By 1728 Riccoboni, now vindicated, relaxed a bit and wrote his *Histoire du Théâtre Italien* and also composed in verse a treatise on acting, *Dell' Arte*

Rappresentativa (to be examined in Chapter 7). In 1729, at perhaps fifty-three, he retired from the stage with an annual pension of one thousand francs. Four years later he, his wife, and his twenty-six-year-old son Francesco became naturalized French subjects. And in 1730 he watched with pride his actors performing a first-rate, still popular Marivaux comedy, *Le Jeu le l'amour et du hasard* (*The Game of Love and Chance*, or *Love in Livery*). In 1737 the Italians appeared in the same author's *Les Fausses confidences* (*False Confidences*), which the Renaud–Barrault Company successfully revived more than two hundred years later.

But by 1753, the date of Riccoboni's death, the Comédie-Italienne, even with a new and expert forty-three-year-old Harlequin, Carlo Antonio Bertinazzi (1710–1783) in the company, began again to lose favor with the theater-going public. In order to hold onto audiences the Italians began to specialize in parodies of plays performed by the Comédie-Française (much to the indignation of Voltaire who disliked having his tragedies made fun of). Then they began more and more frequently to introduce songs, music, and ballet into their productions. Next, when the French actors in the company outnumbered the Italians, they took to presenting light operas. Finally, in 1762, their theater having ceased to prosper, the actors merged with the Opéra-Comique. The resulting company was the last authentic Italian troupe to play in France.

In Italy also during the first half of the eighteenth century the *commedia dell' arte* died. Carlo Goldoni (1707–1793) is usually credited with the mercy killing. This lawyer and would-be actor outlined a play for a company led by Giuseppe Imer at Verona in 1734. Thereafter his "sole desire was to reform and correct the abuses of the stage of my country." He wanted to "substitute for the . . . fantastic adventure plays of the *commedia dell' arte* a regular comedy, written instead of improvised, without masks, without obscenities, without *lazzi* or horseplay and mere buffoonery. Above all he aimed at a comedy of character based on close observance of real life." Back in his native Venice in 1738, Goldoni began his reform with a comedy of characters, *Momolo Cortesan*, which he later called *L'Uomo del mondo* (*The Accomplished Man*). "This piece," he said, "was wonderfully successful, and I was satisfied. I saw my countrymen renouncing their old relish for farces; I saw the announced reform, but I could not yet boast of it. The piece was not reduced to dialogue; and the only part written out was that of the principal actor. All the rest was outline. . . . I could not reform everything at once without stirring up against me all the admirers of the national comedy, and I waited for a favorable moment to attack them boldly with greater vigor and greater safety." In 1743, in an attempt to get the actors to adhere "to the essence of the play," he wrote out all the dialogue for his comedy *La Donna di Garbo* (*The Admirable Woman*). And in 1749 he tried to show that "characters taken from nature" should be "substituted for fantastic intrigues" with his *La Famiglia dell' antiquario* (*The Family of the Antiquary*) in which he completely refashioned the stock, stupidly amorous Pantalone into a human being whose virtue, common sense, and magnanimity resolve the comedy.[38]

Finally, by 1750, in his fourth year of writing for Medebac's company which was playing at the Sant' Angelo (1676), one of the seven playhouses in Venice, the forty-three-year-old Goldoni was ready to make his bold and vigorous attack. He announced that he would compose sixteen new comedies for the coming season, and he kept his word. The first of them, a polemic prologue called *Il Teatro comico* (*The Comic Theater*), is "a confession of faith rather than a play, in which he took occasion to berate the antiquated methods of the Improvised Comedy." In this slender three-act sketch, in which a troupe of actors, under their leader Orazio, is engaged in rehearsing a Goldoni farce, he lampooned the various evils of the current theater as he saw them: "the foolish and disturbing claims of individual performers, the interlarding of improvised words . . . , the introduction of senseless vulgarity just for the sake of arousing merriment," the use of inexpressive masks, the perpetuation of absurd characters in whom nobody in an audience could see himself or someone else, and the lack of any point, or what he called moral purpose, in the playing. He implied that writers could remedy these faults. He announced that it was "now time for Italy to proclaim that in her the seed of good authorship is not dried up." [39]

But, unlike most theater reformers, Goldoni didn't despise actors. He understood and liked them. He never lost sight of the fact that "the reputation of an author frequently depends on the execution of the actors." He studied individual performers and wrote especially for them because, as he put it, "Every person has his peculiar character from nature"; and "if the author gives him a part to represent in unison with his own, he may lay his account with success." Goldoni was proud of the fact that his age "produced three great actors nearly at the same time: Garrick in England, Préville in France, and [Antonio] Sacchi in Italy." [40] He only wanted Italian actors to be less stupid, less egocentric, and more cooperative in the theater.

Goldoni wanted them, first, to be more expressive onstage. Therefore, he advised them to remove their masks, since "The mask must always be very prejudicial to the action of the performer either in joy or sorrow; whether he be in love, cross, or good-humored, the same features are always exhibited; and however he may gesticulate and vary the tone, he can never convey by the countenance, which is the interpreter of the heart, the different passions with which he is inwardly agitated." And he asked the actors to speak better. "Guard especially," he said, "against drawling and against declamation; speak naturally, as if you were talking; since comedy is an imitation of nature, everything that is done must be likely and probable." [41]

Goldoni insisted, second, that the actors tear up their traditional recipes and examine real people and then create recognizable characters. Since, he explained, we are, like the ancients, "again fishing comedies out of the *Mare magnum* of nature, men find themselves again searching their hearts and identifying themselves with the passion or the character which is being represented, [and] they know how to discern whether a passion is well depicted, whether a character is well sustained. . . ." Moreover, Goldoni had the manager in *Il Teatro comico* say to one of the company members, "Don't you see that it isn't right to address the audience? When he is alone on the stage, an actor should pretend that no one hears or sees him; for this habit of speaking to the audience is an intolerable fault that should not be permitted on any ground whatsoever." [42]

Third, and most importantly, Goldoni hoped that the actors would learn to hunt for and find "that quality of style which characterizes the production of one author." [43]

In that same 1750–51 season Goldoni put his theories into practice with the production of the other fifteen comedies, among them *Il Bugiardo* (*The Liar*), *La Bottega del caffe* (*The Coffee House*), *L'Avvocata Veneziano* (*The Venetian Lawyer*), *I Pettegolezzi delle donne* (*The Women Gossip*), and *La Finta malata* (*The Pretended Invalid*). In 1751 he wrote his world famous *La Locandiera* (*The Mistress of the Inn*). Then in 1753 he left Medebac to join Vendramin's company at the larger Teatro San Luca (1661) in Venice, remaining there for eight years and turning out scads of expert, highly popular comedies.

But Goldoni hadn't yet completely won his reform battle. In 1556 his envious and bitter enemy, Carlo Gozzi (1720–1806), also of Venice, "blew upon the ashes of the *commedia dell' arte*" and tried to revive it, tried to adapt it to the purposes of a literary theater. His first important *fiabe*, or fairy tale with a purpose, *Gli Amore delle tre melarance* (*The Love of Three Oranges*), partly written and partly improvised, was acted in 1761 by a company headed by fifty-eight-year-old Antonio Sacchi as Truffaldino (a type of Harlequin) and Cesare Darbes as Pantalone. Gozzi praised these "witty actors of the *commedia* who "improvise such graciously pleasing dialogue and action as may not be expressed in written terms and could not be emulated by any dramatic author." This extravaganza and the same year's *Il Corvo* (*The Crow*)—both "grotesque, absurd, full of theatrical wonder"—parodied Goldoni, satirized his realistic sentimentality, and in their prologues censured those actors who performed without masks and learned their roles by heart.[44] When Gozzi's barbed wit and wild imagination captured the attention of the public, Goldoni in disgust left for Paris.

In a very short time, however, the fickle audiences of Venice tired of Gozzi's *Il Re cervo* (*The King Stag*) (1762), his *Turandot* (1762), and his *L'Augellin belverde* (*The Magic Bird*) (1765). They called them too extravagant and too fantastic—certainly too old-fashioned. In 1765 Gozzi therefore retired from the theater. He'd given "the *commedia dell' arte* its final flourish; with him it 'made a good end.'" Sacchi's company "which caught and completed Gozzi's inspiration" continued to perform for perhaps another fifteen years, but it was an anachronism.[45]

Goldoni in Paris wrote plays for the Comédie-Italienne. In 1765 he finished his ingenious *Il Ventaglio* (*The Fan*). And by 1769 his work so impressed Louis XV that he was granted an annual pension of 4,000 livres. In 1771 he saw his *Le Bourru bienfaisant* (*The Beneficient Boor*), written in French, performed by the Comédie-Française.

6- Play Acting Accepted, 1600-1700

❀ ACTORS EVERYWHERE

Now we must go back a hundred and seventy years to 1600 to follow again the fortunes of the professional actors of literary plays, plays by de Vega in Madrid, Hardy in Paris, and Shakespeare in London.

The seventeenth century was a bustling one. New-world Jamestown was settled in 1607, the English Bill of Rights was accepted in 1689, and Peter I (1672–1725) united Russia by 1696. Harvey (1578–1657) published his findings *On the Motion of the Heart* in 1628, Galileo (1564–1642) the *Dialogues concerning Two New Sciences* in 1632, Descartes (1596–1650) *A Discourse on Method* in 1637, Hobbes (1588–1679) the *Leviathan* in 1651, Boyle (1627–1691) *The Skeptical Chemist* in 1661, Spinoza (1632–1677) his *Ethics* in 1677, Newton (1642–1727) the *Principia* in 1687, Locke (1632–1704) an *Essay Concerning Human Understanding* in 1690. Painter Caravaggio (1569–1609) in "Italy" preceded architect and sculptor Bernini (1598–1680), Velazquez (1599–1660) painted in Spain, Poussin (1594–1665) and Claude Lorrain (1600–1682) in France, and most excitingly Rubens (1577–1640), Van Dyck (1599–1641), Frans Hals (1580–1666), Rembrandt (1606–1669), and Vermeer (1632–1675) in Flanders and the Netherlands. Cervantes (1547–1616) wrote the first part of *Don Quixote* in 1605 and finished it in 1615, John Donne (1572–1631) composed his metaphysical poems and sermons in the first years of the century, Milton (1608–1674) *Paradise Lost* in 1667, La Fontaine (1621–1695) some *Fables* in 1668, Pascal (1623–1662) his *Pensées* in 1670, and Perrault (1623–1703) the *Fairy Tales* in 1697.

II

In Italy, during this time of the flourishing *commedia dell' arte*, the scholars and amateurs who spurned improvisations and appeared in regular or literary plays—and enough of them were written during the century—contributed nothing to the evolution of acting. Most of the scripts were born dead; the performers could only try in vain to resurrect them with a prescribed, stale, but decorous reciting.

In Spain—to whom England was an upstart, France a pretender to culture, Italy only a bunch of provinces, and the Americas potential colonies—the actors should have added something of their own to the evolving histrionic art. They were furnished with excellent plays in which they could perfect their warm skills to catch the eyes and ears of Europe. During the first half of the century, during the nation's "full bloom of literary, artistic, and military greatness," Lope de Vega, it has been claimed, turned out from 1,500 to 1,800 of them; but only 673 titles have been checked, and only 458 scripts are extant. Even so, his output was colossal and incomprehensible. "Comedy, tragedy, melodrama, farce, drama of action, lyric drama, poetry, realism and rhodomantade" poured from his pen "in plenty and profusion unapproachable and unapproached." With exuberant speed and invention Lope disdained scholarly rules and wrote plays to please a simple public; and please them he did with his ideal of honor, his bold and ingenious plot turns, his abundant surprises and theatrical thrills, his lyricism, his feeling for God and for people. His quickness, perhaps, prevented him from bringing onstage the comic flesh of a Falstaff, "the intensity of a *Hamlet*, and the wonder of a *Tempest*"; yet he was "more supple than Jonson, as splendid as Marlowe and more mature, more profound, and more graceful than Beaumont and Fletcher." Most importantly, Lope provided Spanish actors with heroic, romantic, realistic characters to impersonate and with probably every situation known to dramatic art to act. Single-handed and with undisputed skill he "took possession of the drama, subjecting and bringing under his sway all the players" and changing what had been a strolling actors' theater into a playwright's theater, a national theater. When he died in 1635 twenty instead of maybe two licensed companies of professional actors were performing in Madrid.[1]

Seven of the better, typical, but largely unread plays by Lope de Vega are the "long neglected classic," [2] *Fuente Ovejuna* (the name of a town meaning "sheep well") (*c.* 1614), *El mejor alcalde el Rey* (*The King the Greatest Justice*), *El castigo sin venganza* (*Punishment Without Revenge*) (both printed 1635), *El perro del hortelano* (*The Gardner's Dog*) (*c.* 1615), *La imperial de Otún* (*The Crown of Otún*), plus two typical cloak-and-sword comedies, *Lo cierto por lo dudoso* (*A Certainty for a Doubt*) printed 1625, and *El acero de Madrid* (*Madrid Steel*) (1603).

Inspired instead of stunned by Lope's productivity, other dramatists immediately provided the Spanish professional actors with worthy scripts. For instance, Juan Ruiz de Alarcón (*c.* 1580–1639), a native of Mexico, wrote *La verdad sospechosa* (*Truth Suspected*) (1628), the father of Corneille's *Le Menteur* and the grandfather of Molière's *Le Misanthrope*; and Tirso de Molina (Gabriel Téllez) (1584–1648) raced after Lope by composing some four hundred plays, among them *El burlador de Sevilla y concidato de piedra* (*The Deceiver of Seville and the Stone Guest*) (1630), the first presentation onstage of that legendary libertine, Don Juan.

Lope de Vega's true successor, however, was Pedro Calderón de la Barca (1600–1681), a philosophical, aristocratic, Christian craftsman. Because of his artistry in expressing the genius of Spain at a particular epoch in its development, he enjoyed for a long time a greater reputation than Lope. Today, however, his lack of vigor and his muted feelings for people sometimes deny him ranking as one of the world's great playwrights. Spanish professional actors, nonetheless, encountered the magic of literature when they performed in Calderón's many plays, which included *autos sacramentales* like the *Encantos de la culpa* (*Sorceries of Sin*); the cloak-and-sword comedy, *La dama duende* (*The Phantom Lady*) (*c.* 1629); the Othello-like *El médico de su honra* (*The Physician of His Own Honor*) (1635); the well-known telling of the life of St. Cyprian, *El mágico prodigoso* (*The Wonder-working Magician*) (1637); *El alcalde de Zalamea* (*The Mayor of Zalamea*) (*c.* 1640), akin to *Fuente Ovejuna*; and the holy *El gran teatro del mundo* (*The Great World Theater*) (*c.* 1645). Calderón's triumphant creation is *La vida es sueño* (*Life Is a Dream*) (*c.* 1636), a lyrical fantasy about dream versus reality.

"By 1700 . . . the corpus of the Spanish drama of all kinds had reached 30,000 plays." [3] And many writers in Europe read them in search of themes, situations, characters. European actors and critics, however, rarely had opportunities for examining the rather isolated Spaniards in performance; although apparently they missed nothing new or worth emulating. Standard eloquence and animation, often stagy and stereotyped, hardly distinguished the acting of such "Golden Age" leading performers as Jusepa Vaca (fl. 1602–1634), María de Heredia (?–1658), the famous María Calderón (fl. 1623–*c.* 1672), Baltasara de los Reyes (?–1675), Nicolás de los Rios (?–1610), Manuel Vallejo (?–1619), Baltasar Peñedo (fl. 1596–1621), Roque de Figueroa (?–1651), comic Cosme Perez (*c.* 1585–1673), and Damian Arias de Peñafiel (?–*c.* 1643) of whom it was reported: "The most famous orators came to hear him in order to acquire perfection of diction and gesture." [4] Yet, though details of their acting are unknown, the best actresses may have equaled the best of the *commedia* actresses, and several of the top actors might have offered competition to Alleyn and Burbage, to Montdory and Molière.

By 1648, at the end of the Thirty Years War, Spain in defeat was forced to accept the emergence of France as the leader of continental Europe. Spanish actors, lacking stability and verve, therefore remained in their retreat at the far corner of the continent and let other nationals do what they would with acting.

In Germany the actors weren't quite ready to contribute much to this new art. The best known early professional there was a university man, Johannes Velten (1640–1695), who by 1660 was a member of Carl Andreas Paulsen's strolling troupe. From 1678 until his death Velten managed the company, adding to its repertoire a version or two of *Hamlet* and several comedies by Molière. He "first definitely introduced women on the German stage. . . . In 1686 his troupe included three actresses: his wife [Catharina], his sister, and Sarah von Bosberg." [5]

✿ PROFESSIONALS IN FRANCE

For the first three decades of the seventeenth century, while the English, Spanish, and *commedia* actors were adding luster to the theater, and prospering, professional actors in France had a bad time of it. They remained poor nobodies. They couldn't get started; they couldn't oust the Confrérie from the Hôtel de Bourgogne and break its monopoly on things theatrical in Paris. Yes, the Brotherhood frequently rented its playhouse to professional troupes from the provinces, but always it strictly monitored them, mulcted them, and denied them permanance. The Confrérie also fought and routed "obstreperous companies who played at the Fairs of Sainte-Germain and Saint Laurent and who improvised playhouses at the Hôtel d'Argent, the Sabot d'Or, and in innumerable tennis courts" without paying the required fee. As a result, the French theater during the time of Shakespeare and Lope de Vega was barren. It "failed to produce a single play which still holds the stage today." And it failed to produce a single actor who came anywhere near winning the honors accorded Francesco Andreini, Alleyn and Burbage, or Arias de Peñafiel. Professional players, even though they performed now and then for wealthy aristocrats in their mansions in Paris or at their nearby châteaux, struggled hard to eke out a living and to attain respectability. According to a popular mountebank at the Fairs called Bruscambille (Jean Deslauriers) (fl. 1610–1634), the life of an actor, until after 1630, was "*une vie sans souci et quelque fois sans six sous.*" [6]

The already mentioned actor-manager, Valleran le Conte, tried for fourteen years, from 1598 to 1612, to establish himself in the capital, but his struggles ended in debt-ridden failure. In 1600 he was sharing the Hôtel de Bourgogne with a pick-up Italian company, whose farces were more popular than the ornate tragedies offered by Valleran. Then near the end of the year, when Robert Guérin (fl. 1600–1634)—a former baker who'd taken to clowning at the Fairs and would soon become famous as Gros-Guillaume —leased the Hôtel away from him for the presentation of comedies, Valleran abandoned Paris and took to the road. Early in 1606 and again in 1607 he again signed brief leases to perform serious plays at the Hôtel de Bourgogne, ran into more debts and difficulties, and retired once more to the provinces. In 1608 Valleran was back at the Hôtel for a while until it was let to the Accesi troupe of Italian comedians led by Cecchini.[7]

In 1609—when Guérin, former Valleran actor Laporte (Mathieu la Febvre) (c. 1584–c. 1621), and his wife, Marie Venier (fl. 1590–1619), were playing at the Hôtel d'Argent, and paying a fee to the Confrérie—Valleran "leased the Hôtel de Bourgogne from September until Shrove Tuesday 1610." This time he "and his fellow actors succeeded in fulfilling their obligation toward the Confrères de la Passion," but only by fusing with the Guérin-Laporte company, whose members, incidentally, included Hugues Guéru (c. 1573–1633), to be known as Gaultier-Garguille, and Pierre le Messier (c. 1573–1633), called Bellerose. (The Hôtel d'Argent may then have been used to a new company headed by Charles Le Noir [fl. 1610–1634].) By the end of 1611 Valleran was again deep in debt; in early 1612 he was again sharing the Hôtel with an Italian troupe. Soon afterward, battered but unbroken, he formed a new company of young actors and actresses and left for the provinces. Thereafter the three famous farceurs—leader Gros-Guillaume, Gaultier-Garguille, and Henri Legrand (c. 1587–1647), or Turlupin—proceeded to rock the Hôtel de Bourgogne with laughter for many years. In 1613 Valleran was in Holland "seeking the success which had eluded him in Paris."[8]

Nobody knows when or where he died. But Valleran le Conte's accomplishments as a pioneer French professional actor, though still vague, are several and deserve to be better known. First, he may have been the pioneer in introducing professional actresses to Paris; at least he championed them. His 1607 company at the Hôtel de Bourgogne included two actresses: Rachel Trépeau and an unnamed girl. His actress wife, Jehanne de Wancourt, was described as being "a beautiful creature, and when she appeared as a queen or princess, nothing was lacking in her impersonation except birth itself. By her expression, her gestures, and her speech you would have thought her a true queen."[9]

Second, Valleran was one of the first French teachers of acting. As early as 1599 he "took teen-agers under his wing to train them for the stage and its mysteries." They learned the fundamentals of this new craft by serving as apprentices in his companies. One of the beginners was Bellerose, who first impersonated bit roles under Valleran's instruction in 1609. Montdory

(Guillaume Desgilleberts) (1594–1651), "the first great actor to come out of the early public theater," was also a brief Valleran protégé.[10]

Third, Valleran in perhaps 1597 or 1598 hired sometime actor Alexandre Hardy (c. 1575–c. 1631) to write scripts for the theater. Hardy thus became the first French professional playwright, the first "dramatist whose reputation and reward depended upon his ability to interest the normal audience at the Hôtel de Bourgogne. . . . His plays had to get over to the footlights to an audience which had paid an admission fee." In thirty years Hardy wrote hundreds of plays, of which only thirty-four are extant.[11] His best known work, Mariamne (1610), was probably first staged by Valleran; other pieces, such as Frégonde (1620), Aristoclée, and Triomphe d'amour (1626), were composed for professional companies that followed Valleran in Paris.

II

Because of the serious efforts of professionals like Valleran, French actors were slowly accepted and appreciated. Sometimes their popularity exceeded that of the Italian players. For instance, "between November 1612 and February 1614 over 130 performances were given at the Court by professional actors. In this period at least fifty-seven performances . . . were given by Arlequin [Martinelli] and his company, and . . . at least another seventy-six performances were given by French actors. . . ."[12] But as yet there was no permanent French company playing for the Paris public. For thirteen years after the departure of Valleran many different companies impotently competed with each other in leasing the Hôtel and fighting the Confrérie.

Then in 1625 Le Noir, chief of the Prince of Orange's troupe, "rented the Hôtel de Bourgogne from under the nose of Bellerose," one of the leading "Comédiens du Roi" who'd been performing there. In the Le Noir troupe was Montdory. Soon, however, the so-called royal company returned as the prime occupants of the Hôtel, and the Le Noir actors were apparently allowed to set up a temporary theater in a tennis court. For the Hôtel actors young Jean Rotrou (1609–1650), who was called the true founder of the French theater, wrote two plays in 1628 and started to adapt a comedy by Lope de Vega. That same year, man of letters François Ogier (c. 1605–1670), recognizing the skills and the value of actors, insisted that in tragedies the "tiresome discourses which recount the misfortunes of others must be avoided and the persons themselves must be put into action."[13] Paris at long last was to be offered some acting, and was ready to support a permanent company of professional players.

Bellerose was one of the leaders, along with the three farceurs, of the group that took permanent possession of the Hôtel de Bourgogne by 1628. Other principal members were his wife, Nicole Gassaud (?–1680); Beauchâteau (François Mathieu Chastelet) (fl. 1625–1665) and his wife, Madeleine de Pouget (1615–1683); Mlle. Beaupré (Madeleine Lemoine) (fl. 1624–

1650); and Guillot-Gorju (Bertrand Hardouin de St. Jacques) (1600–1648). These actors at once instituted a campaign to overthrow their landlords. "They rebelled against the domination of the Confrérie and the heavy rents charged them. They wished to remodel the badly planned and antiquated theater. . . . But the Brotherhood sternly opposed any alterations whatsoever." [14]

By 1629 Le Noir appears to have left Paris and merged his company with one recently formed by his former colleague Montdory. At Rouen late that year, with Montdory as star, the enlarged group performed *Mélite*, the first play, a comedy, by Pierre Corneille (1606–1684). The venture proved so successful that the actors brought the play to Paris in late 1629 or early 1630 and exhibited it in a tennis court. Further success led them to decide to settle permanently in the capital. But they had to fight bitterly with the Confrérie for that right. Finally, inevitably, the monopoly was broken in 1632, doubtless through the intercession of Cardinal Richelieu (1585–1642), who had become fascinated with the theater. The troupe of Le Noir and Montdory was permitted to perform plays in their third tennis court, the Jeu de Paume (game of the palm) de la Fontaine. The actors in this second permanent company of professionals in Paris were Montdory; Le Noir and his wife, Isabelle Mestivier; Jodelet (Julien Bedeau) (c. 1600–1660), a popular white-faced comedian and rival of the three farceurs (who in 1658 would act under his own name in Molière's *Les Précieuses ridicules*); his brother, L'Espy (François Bedeau) (fl. 1610–1664); Jacquemin Jadot (fl. 1610–1660), who at first impersonated serious roles as La France and comic roles as Michau; Alizon (fl. 1610–1648), a man who specialized in playing female comic characters; Claude Deschamps de Villiers (1600–1681) with his wife, Marguerite Béguet (?–1670); François Mestivier; Pierre Marcoureau dit Beaulieu; and Nicolas Desoeillets.[15] Soon D'Orgemont (Adrien Des Barres) (?–c. 1665) joined the group.

The two companies promptly began competing with each other for public favor. At the Hôtel the actors as themselves appeared in Gougenot's *La Comédie des Comédiens* (1632) and tried "to obtain a position of honor that should free the theater from blame and reproach." In another play with the identical title, written by Georges de Scudéry (1601–1667), the Le Noir-Montdory actors tried to contradict the common notion that an actor's life "is nothing but libertinism, and a license for vice, impurity, laziness, and lack of control." Some actors, they said, are good and some are bad, and critical taste should be applied to them even as to "poetry, melons, and friends." The same actors in 1632 presented Corneille's comedy, *Clitandre*. In his *Examen* to it the author admitted that "the monologues are too long and too numerous"; but he gave the reason for the defect: "The actors demanded them in order to show off their ability." [16]

By 1634 Bellerose was the chief of the company at the Hôtel, and Montdory was the virtual leader of the opposition company. France at last could boast of two top-flight actors. Montdory, who never performed in farces, has been called "the first supremely great actor of the French stage." Critics reported that he had a quality of voice that "went to the heart," "dignities of . . . gestures," and a studied "self-abandonment." But evidently it was only with much forcing and exaggeration that "he imprinted upon the mind the sentiments he expressed." Bellerose, in contrast, wasn't a ranter. His style, it seems, was fairly quiet, so much so that to some it was affected, prim, and insipid where it should have been rousing. And sometimes, it was noticed, "he did not understand what he was saying" so beautifully.[17]

Also in 1634, when the company at the Hôtel was apparently receiving some financial support from Louis XIII, the opposition company, patronized by Richelieu, moved to a fourth tennis court which came to be known as the Théâtre du Marais, the second genuine public playhouse in Paris. But just before the new theater opened, the King ordered six of the actors—Le Noir and his wife, Jodelet, Jadot, L'Espy, and Alizon—transferred to the Hôtel de Bourgogne "to spite the Cardinal de Richelieu." Undaunted, however, Montdory added new actors to his troupe—among them André Baron (c. 1602–1655)—and it "was again better than the other one, for he [Montdory] alone was better than all the rest. With the exception of Rotrou, all the best playwrights of the time brought their works to Montdory." In the same year Jean Mairet (1604–1686) wrote Sophonisbe for the Marais actors. It was "the most artistic French tragedy up to the time of its production," "the first tragedy in France truly based on the rules," or the three unities. Moreover, although the play was written to be declaimed, "Mairet succeeded, where Hardy failed, in producing a tragedy in which the action develops through an interplay of external events and feelings. The dramatic struggle has begun to enter the human mind instead of using the human body as a shuttle-cock. Events in the plot have begun to follow each other psychologically, not merely temporally. Things have begun to happen because the hero and heroine think in a certain way and not merely because they are shipwrecked or captured." [18]

For the next three years at the Marais, Montdory realized an actor's dream of success. Among his many leading roles were, in 1635, Brutus in La Mort de César by Scudéry, and Jason in Corneille's first tragedy, Medée. Then early in 1637, opposite Marguerite Béguet as Chimène, he crowned his career by creating the hero Rodrigue in Corneille's masterpiece, Le Cid. In this play, derived from Spanish sources, Rodrigue within a period of twenty-four hours declares his love for Chimène, avenges an insult to his father by killing her father, puts his life in her hands when she's forced to demand vengeance, saves his country from the Moors in a tremendous battle, and wins a duel of honor for which the prize is Chimène. Yet in this hurrying parade of hectic actions Corneille brilliantly centers the interest on the conflict of love with honor and on the strong, human emotions of the characters who engage in it. He makes the tragedy almost psychological. For example, when Rodrigue comes to Chimène in the thrilling third act "The opponents are face to face; the problem is real; no *deus ex machina* can solve it. The conflict is in their souls." And there is a "touching pathos and dramatic power in their words unknown to French tragedy before the *Cid*. Tortured by their love, by their presence together, each is trying to do as honorable men and women should in accordance with the inexorable code of honor":

RODRIGUE
> In thy dead father's name, for our love's sake,
> In vengeance or in pity slay me here!
> Thy wretched lover keener pain will know
> To live and feel thy hate than meet thy blow.

CHIMÈNE
> Leave me, I hate you not.

RODRIGUE
> 'Tis my desert.

CHIMÈNE
> I cannot.

RODRIGUE
> When my deed is full known
> And men can say that still thy passion burns,
> Dost thou not fear the cruel stinging words
> Of censure and of malice? Silence them;
> Save thine own fame by sending me to death.

•   •   •   •   •

CHIMÈNE
> Depart.

RODRIGUE
> What wilt thou do?

CHIMÈNE
> The fires of wrath burn with the flames of love.
> My father's death commands my utmost zeal;
> 'Tis duty drives me with its cruel goad,
> And my dear wish is nothing to achieve.

RODRIGUE
> O miracle of love!

CHIMÈNE
> O weight of woe!

RODRIGUE
> We pay our filial debt with suffering.

CHIMÈNE
> Rodrigue, who would have thought!

RODRIGUE
> Or could have dreamed,

CHIMÈNE
> That joy so near so soon our grasp would miss.

RODRIGUE
Or storms so swift, already close to port,
Should shatter the dear bark of all our hope.[19]

From Corneille's *Le Cid*, in Donald Clive Stuart's *The Development of Dramatic Art* (New York: Appleton, 1928) by permission of the publisher Appleton-Century-Crofts, an affiliate of Meredith Press.

With scenes like that Corneille and the actors aroused a frenzy of public acclaim and a furor of controversy, both petty and pointed, among the literary set. The play "first gave distinction to the French stage." [20]

Shortly after his rousing triumph as Rodrigue, Montdory acted no more. While he was impersonating Herod with sound and fury in Tristan's biblical *Mariamne* "there fell an apoplexy upon his tongue which prevented his playing afterward. Pensioned by Richelieu, he lived in retirement for fourteen years" and watched the rapidly maturing theater of his country. In 1637 at the Marais his place as leader was taken by Floridor (Josias de Soulas, sieur de Primefosse) (1608-1672), who had joined the company after touring the provinces with Filandre. (He also had taken a group of actors to England in 1634-35.) The company at the Hôtel was strengthened in 1639 by the addition of Montfleury (Zacharie Jacob) (c. 1600-1667); soon he ranked second to Bellerose. The Marais, however, continued for a while to be the exciting and leading theater in Paris. There Corneille's next great tragedies, *Horace* (1640) and *Cinna* (1641), were huge successes with Floridor in the title roles. "Every gift required by the actor, it seems, was possessed by Floridor—ardent feeling, trained judgment, fine presence, graceful manners, and elastic voice. Like Bellerose, he was great in both branches of the drama, while the education he had received gave him an advantage in declamation. . . ." At this time the Marais company included, in addition to Floridor and his wife Marguerite Baloré, Jodelet and L'Espy, who had returned from the Hôtel; Villiers and his wife; the Beauchâteaus, who seem to have transferred there in 1635; Mlle. Beaupré, who joined by 1640; Baron and his new bride, Jeanne Ausoult (1625-1662); Philibert Robit dit le Gaulcher; and Laroque (Pierre Regnault Petit-Jean) (c. 1595-1676).[21]

In 1641 Richelieu opened in his palace an elaborate little theater, the Palais du Cardinal, afterwards the Théâtre du Palais-Royal; and Louis XII, likewise entranced by actors and plays, took the troupe at the Hôtel under his protection and granted it a pension of 1,200 livres a year. At the same time the King (or Richelieu) published an edict, "a landmark" in the progress of the French stage. According to the proclamation, "In the event of the said players so regulating the work of the theater as to render it altogether exempt from impurity, the King desired that their calling, which might innocently divert his people from various dull occupations, should not expose them to blame or prejudice their reputation in public intercourse." In short, the profession of acting was officially recognized; the social status of the actors was definitely raised. But the edict didn't remove the stigma of the Church; it didn't restore to actors the rights of the humblest citizen—communion and a hallowed burial. So, "honored and cherished by the Court, adored from this time forward by the public," and able to earn a livelihood, professional actors still found themselves in an ambiguous position.[22]

The striking contrast in the position of French and English professional actors was thus maintained. At the start of the century French actors were nobodies while their English counterparts prospered and were honored; in 1641 French actors were accepted and began to flourish, and next year English actors were called rogues and their theaters were closed.

III

Jean-Baptiste Poquelin (1622–1673) as a youngster must have seen Montdory and Floridor at the Théâtre du Marais and Bellerose at the Hôtel de Bourgogne. At any rate, Jesuit trained by 1642, he was trying at the age of twenty to reach a decision: he could practice law or follow his father's prosperous profession of furniture-maker and upholsterer, and succeed him as *valet-tapissier du roi*, a part-time position of honor at Court; or he could become an excommunicated professional actor. Before the end of the year he made up his mind to be an actor at all costs, and to enter into partnership with sometime provincial actress Madeleine Béjart (1618–1672) and form a company of ten, all older and more experienced than he, "to assist in financing it, to assume joint responsibility for a theater, to identify himself with the hazards and disabilities of a group no member of which had much or anything to lose." [23] He was twenty-one when he helped found the Illustre-Théâtre on June 30, 1643, and took from nobody knows where, or why, the stage name of Molière.

In the autumn of that year, while a tennis court was being readied for them in Paris, the enthusiastic, untried novices presented their first production, probably a play by Corneille, at Rouen. Early in 1644 the little group opened in the capital before an audience of relatives, friends, and professionals who didn't pay for their seats. The venture quickly failed; by the end of 1644 the actors had achieved nothing but a stack of debts. Yet somehow they managed to open again at another tennis court in 1645; again, and consistently, the project failed. But nothing, not even bankruptcy or arrest, discouraged Molière. With a few remnants of the not so Illustrious Theatre, including Madeleine, he left Paris to act in the provinces.

At that time there were a dozen or possibly fifteen companies of professional actors touring the hinterlands. Among the more important actor-managers who headed these troupes were the already mentioned Filandre (Jean Baptiste de Mouchaingre) (1616–1691), who may have served as model for the hero of Scarron's novel, *Le Roman comique* (1651); Dorimond

(Nicholas Drouin) (*c.* 1628–*c.* 1664); and Charles Dufresne (*c.* 1611–*c.* 1684). Twenty-three-year-old Molière, along with Madeleine Béjart and their friends, joined Dufresne's company then in service to the Duc d'Eperon, and stayed away from Paris for the next thirteen years.

Before Molière left the capital Corneille's *Polyeucte* was staged in 1642 at the Marais with Floridor topping the cast; and in 1643 he was Dorante, and Jodelet was Cliton, in the same dramatist's expert comedy, *Le Menteur*. In the latter year, Floridor also acted Corneille's *Rodogune* and *Théodore*, and in 1646 his *Héraclius*. Jodelet won stardom in 1645 in the lively comedy, *Jodelet, ou le maître-valet*, especially written to fit his talents by Paul Scarron (1610–1660).

At the Hôtel somewhere about this time Bellerose "was constrained by some painful malady to give up the exercise of a profession in which he had occupied the highest rank for at least a decade" or two.[24] Floridor from the Marais replaced him. Then in 1647 "le grand Corneille" was elected to the French Academy; and the actors at the Hôtel reopened their reconstructed theater (which, like the Marais, followed the latest Italian designs), and entered upon their most successful period.

❊ SET-BACK IN ENGLAND

In London during the first third of the seventeenth century "the problem of metropolitan stage-control may be said . . . to have reached a condition of comparative stability." The Puritans could only mutter their objections as the happy actors busied themselves entertaining the populace in several theaters. In 1601, in relative peace and prosperity, the lingering boy players performed Jonson's *The Poetaster* at the Blackfriars, the Admiral's Men revived Marlowe's *Dr. Faustus* for Alleyn, and the Chamberlain's Men produced *Hamlet* with Burbage as the Prince. At that time "eighteen to twenty-four thousand spectators a week [from a London area of about 160,000] through nine or ten months of the year were patronizing the Chamberlain's Men at the Globe, the Admiral's Men at the Fortune, and Worchester's Men at the Boar's Head or Rose. . . ."[25] The Chamberlain's Men followed *Hamlet* with *Othello* (*c.* 1604), *King Lear, Macbeth* (both 1605–06), and *Antony and Cleopatra* (*c.* 1606). Then in 1612 Thomas Heywood (*c.* 1570–1641), a one-time actor and the author of *A Woman Killed With Kindness* (1603), published his *Apology for Actors* which, despite many refutations, was somehow reassuring. At any rate, three expert boy players—William Ostler (?–1614), Nathan Field (1587–1620), and John Underwood (*c.* 1590–1624)—who appeared in *The Poetaster*—could grow up and, without too much opposition, become adult professional actors. In short, under Elizabeth's successor, James I (1603–1625), the theater was apparently approved—but only apparently. The Puritans waited; they prepared for the kill.

II

The Admiral's Men thinned out and disbanded by 1625. Lack of strong leadership, plus a continued poor choice of scripts, probably accounted for the company's slow deterioration. It couldn't quite compete with the play-rich Chamberlain's Men. Alleyn, after serving for twenty years as an actor of "sweet elocution," retired wealthy in 1603—along with unheralded John Singer who also had trod the stage the same length of time. Then the Admiral's Men became the Prince Henry's Men; and for the next nine years the responsible members of the group were Towne, Juby, Downton, Massey, Rowley, Bird, and the two Jeffes. In 1612 the company's young patron died, and it was then known as the Palsgrave's Men. By 1616, when "banker" Henslowe died, Downton and Humphrey Jeffes were the company leaders; but two years later, along with Juby, they retired. Downton and Juby had acted for twenty-four years, Jeffes for nineteen. The leader(s) for the next five years are unknown. When the company reopened its rebuilt Fortune in 1623 they seem to have been Massey and Richard Gunnell (?–1634?). After the plague of 1625, and the death of King James, there's no known reference to this forty-nine-year-old company in London. It had petered out—before a company of professionals had established itself in Paris.[26]

III

The Chamberlain's Men—Shakespeare's company—continued to act plays for forty-eight years (until the theaters were closed in 1642). After Elizabeth's death in 1603 the group became the King's Men; the patent for that year listed the actors as Burbage, Shakespeare, Phillips, Condell, Sly, Heminge, Cowley, and Armin (plus Lawrence Fletcher [?–1608?], although there's no reason to suppose he ever joined the group). Three actors—the clowns Kempe and Pope and the semi-acrobat Bryan—had dropped out by that time. After this date the changes in the company's personnel are only speculative: In c. 1604 it seems that the new additions were John Lowin (1576–1633), who had acted for Henslowe; Alexander Cooke (?–1614), who possibly had been apprenticed to Heminge; and another apprentice, Nicholas Tooley (c. 1575–1623). Phillips, primarily a musician and manager, died in 1605; Samuel Gilbourne (?), a company boy actor, took his place. Heminge may have assumed the managing duties. Condell and Sly became sharers sometime subsequent to 1606. Then in 1608 when the latter died after eighteen years on the stage the actors broke a rule, which hitherto had permitted only their own graduating apprentices to fill vacancies, by taking from the Children of the Queen's Revels the already mentioned Ostler and Underwood.

More changes, important ones, occurred in the next fifteen years. In 1611

Ostler became a sharer; and Robert Gough (?–1625), who had impersonated female roles for the group since about 1594, succeeded Gilbourne in the acting company. Cooke and then Ostler (once termed "Sole King of Actors") died in 1614, comedian Armin in 1615, Shakespeare in 1616, and Cowley, after twenty-five years of acting, in 1619. Their places were taken respectively by William Eccleston (?–1625?) and Robert Benfield (?–1649), both from other companies, John Shank (?–1636) from the Palsgrave's Men, the already famous Field, and female impersonator Richard Robinson (?–1648), who had served as a boy with the company. Also in 1619 Joseph Taylor (c. 1585–1652), a popular actor of the time, replaced Burbage, who in thirty-five years of acting "ne'er went off the stage but with applause." At about this time Condell joined Heminge at the management level. Lowin and Taylor soon became the principal players. In 1620 John Rice (c. 1596–?) took the place of Field, who at the time of his death "ranked second to Burbage," and in nineteen years as an actor-playwright had worked for four leading companies. By 1624 Thomas Pollard (fl. 1623–1664), Eyllaerdt Swanston (?–1651), and leading lady Richard Sharpe (?–1631) were regular members of the King's Men.[27]

During the first quarter of the century the (Chamberlain's) King's Men rose to a position of unchallenged supremacy over all the other companies acting in London. They staged the plays of Shakespeare and, among others, Jonson's great tragedy *Sejanus* (1603) and his great comedy *Volpone* (1606). Then, "drawn and driven toward dependence on the Court," and needing a second house for its winter quarters, the company acquired the town's most exclusive theater, the Blackfriars, whose freehold already belonged to the Burbages, but which since 1600 had been leased to a Henry Evans and occupied by the Children of the Revels. In 1609 the King's Men began acting at this rather small, indoor, private theater—"too expensive for penny-paying groundlings." The experiment was a bold one. "No adult company in London had ever before performed regularly in a private theater. For thirty years the private theaters with their superior audiences, their concerts, their comfortable accommodations, their traffic in sophisticated drama and the latest literary fads, had been the exclusive homes of the boy companies, the pets of society." But the King's Men, unabashed, hired Jonson and two socially favored, rising young authors named Francis Beaumont (c. 1584–1616) and John Fletcher (1579–1625) to join with Shakespeare in writing special plays for the Blackfriars. At their new theater the company produced Jonson's *Epicoene* in 1609, Shakespeare's *Cymbeline* in 1609–10, Jonson's *The Alchemist* together with Beaumont and Fletcher's *Philaster* in 1610, *The Tempest* in 1610–11, Beaumont and Fletcher's *The Maid's Tragedy* c. 1611, *The Winter's Tale* in 1612–13, and *The Duchess of Malfi* by John Webster (?–1634) in 1614 (and also at the Globe) with Burbage as Duke Ferdinand, Lowin as Bosola, Ostler as Antonio, Condell as the Cardinal, and Underwood as Delio. Needless to say, the venture was a success, so much so that soon the Blackfriars became the principal theater of the King's Men. In 1612, for instance, Edward Kirkham said the company "took £1,000 a winter more at the Blackfriars than they had formerly taken at the Globe." And "When Sir Henry Herbert listed receipts from the two theaters early in the reign of King Charles I (1623–1649), the receipts for single performances at the Globe averaged £6. 13s. 8d.; those for single performances at the Blackfriars averaged £15. 15s., or about two and one-half times as much." [28]

The wider, lasting consequences of this success at the Blackfriars were two. In the first place, something happened to playwriting. Beaumont and Fletcher changed it. (At least fifty-four plays are connected with their names: seven of the best to their partnership, two solely to Beaumont, fifteen solely to Fletcher, and the rest solely to Fletcher and indistinct collaborators, principally Massinger.) The pair put *their* stamp—not Shakespeare's, not Jonson's—on playwriting in English for the rest of the century—and even later. In their earlier *The Knight of the Burning Pestle*, first acted with a dull thud by the Children at the Blackfriars in 1607 and revived by the King's Men with cheers in 1635, the team wrote about real and ridiculous people. After that, however, they wrote in verse mostly small semi-tragedies, tidy romances, and shallow comedies which reflected only the sophisticated life at Court. And these plays outdrew Shakespeare and Jonson! The repertory of the King's Men from 1616 to 1642, with one hundred and seventy plays known on the active list, contained forty-seven by Beaumont and Fletcher, only sixteen by Shakespeare, and only nine by Jonson. Beaumont and Fletcher's scripts, in short, became models for writers unexcited by genius and content only to be witty in order to be popular and only to reproduce stencils in order to get rich. The comedies of Fletcher, Shakespeare's successor-dramatist for the King's Men (he supplied them with scripts for ten or twelve years), clearly set the trite pattern for most plays to come in the next three hundred years. His unimpressive comedies of manners "where character, to some extent at least, starts the action and determines the solution," and his comedies of intrigue "where character falls into the background and interest is concentrated on the ingenious complication and solution, with the attendant reversals and surprises, of an entertaining plot" are basically similar to many commercial successes in the theater of today.[29]

In the second place, something happened beginning in 1609 at the Blackfriars to play production. The small indoor theater certainly changed the methods of staging a play, and must have changed, at least a trifle, the company's style of acting. Some of the indoor scenic innovations of Court masque artist Inigo Jones (1573–1652) must have been used, in time, at the Blackfriars. We can imagine the beginnings there of a picture-stage, candlelit by chandeliers, footlights, and additional onstage lamps, scenery made of painted drops and angle wings (changed to flat wings c. 1638), and eventually a rising and falling curtain—all framed by the familiar proscenium arch of today. The changes in acting in such surroundings can only be guessed at, and will be touched on hereafter.

But amid all their new success as actors the King's Men never forgot Shakespeare and the glories he had made for them. Heminge and Condell in 1623 collected his plays and published them as the priceless First Folio. They assured his immortality.

IV

The theatrical and financial policies of the King's Men were determined by a small group composed mostly of actors (or their heirs) known as sharers. In 1608, for instance, the shares for the company's Blackfriars theater were made out to Cuthbert Burbage and Thomas Evans, managers, and to four of the actors—Richard Burbage, Shakespeare, Heminge, and Condell; and for the 1614 rebuilt Globe the fourteen shares were divided as follows: Cuthbert Burbage 3½, Richard Burbage 3½, Heminge 2, Condell 2, Shakespeare 1, Ostler 1, and Pope's executors 1. And these sharers "got Money and Liv'd in Reputation." Actor Burbage and Shakespeare, for instance, left property reckoned worth £300 a year. "Thomas Pope, Augustine Phillips, Henry Condell, all appear from their wills to have been substantial men when they died. And John Heminge is described in 1614 as 'of greate lyveinge wealth and power.'" Small wonder that many of the actors were called "copper-lace gentlemen" who "purchase land by adulterous playes," or were rebuked as those who through "long practise of playing are growne so wealthy that they have expected to be knighted." [30]

It has been estimated that a sharer in the King's company during the first decade of the seventeenth century—when £200 was a handsome annual income—earned about £140 to £200 a year. Translated into average twentieth-century purchasing power, this would about equal a substantial but not excessive $3,500 to $5,000 a year. Every aspiring actor, therefore, hoped to be offered, and to be able to buy, a theater share and thus become a part-owner of the company's assets—its costumes, properties, and play-books. A share, although no guarantee of security, rescued him "from the constant fear of unemployment and gave him status as one who had achieved excellence in his quality." [31]

By 1634–35 three regular members of the company who were nonsharers —Benfield with fifteen years of service, Pollard and Swanston with at least ten years each—earned in one year by acting £180 apiece which, as Cuthbert Burbage pointed out, "would very well keep an actor from starving." These three players, however, wanted to be sharers. They addressed a petition to the Lord Chamberlain to protest that they had for "a long time with much patience expected to bee admitted Sharers in ye Play houses of the Globe and the Blackfriars. . . ." But this hadn't happened, they protested, and it wasn't fair. They went on to point out that "The actors get only the receipts at the outer door and half the receipts from the galleries and the boxes. From this sum they must pay the wages of the hired men and boys, the cost of lights, music and other theatrical expenses. . . . In contrast to the actors, the housekeepers get half the takings from the galleries and boxes and all the receipts from the tiring-house at the Globe. From their share the house-keepers must pay only repairs and rent. . . . Even this charge is partially met by subletting the taphouse, tenement, and garden adjoining the Globe at twenty or thirty pounds a year. Moreover, the actor's share must be divided among nine men and that of the housekeepers among only six, so that 'when some of the Housekeepers share the 12s. a day at ye Globe the Actors share not above 3s.' "

According to this trio the sixteen Globe shares and the eight Blackfriars shares were divided in 1635 as follows:

	GLOBE	BLACKFRIARS
Cuthbert Burbage	3½	1
Mrs. (R. Burbage) Robinson	3½	1
Mrs. Condell	2	1
John Shank	3	2
Joseph Taylor	2	1
John Lowin	2	1
John Underwood's children		1
	16	8

(Shank had purchased his shares from William Heminge, son of John. Two years previously he'd paid £156 for one share in the Blackfriars with six years to run and one share in the Globe with two years to run; eleven months previously he'd paid £350 for one more share for five years in the Blackfriars and two more shares for one year in the Globe. Taylor and Lowin had been allowed their shares in about 1627–30 when, after deaths and alienations, actors were no longer being included among the share-holders. Underwood somehow acquired his share after 1614.)

In their petition Benfield, Pollard, and Swanston "admit that Lowin and Taylor deserve their shares, but contend that Shank got his three Globe shares by purchasing them 'surreptitiously'. . . . In conclusion, the actors request that the Lord Chamberlain order Shank, Cuthbert Burbage, and the Robinsons each to sell them one share in the Globe and order Shank to sell them one in the Blackfriars to be divided among the three. This allotment they think only just, so that others should not 'reape most or the chiefest benefitt of the sweat of their browes, & live upon the bread of their La-bours.' " [32] The decision was in their favor.

The King's company boy actors, or apprentices, who ranged from about ten to sixteen years of age, were each paid something like 15s. a week. But the sum wasn't given to the boy; it was paid to the actor with whom he lodged and boarded and from whom he learned the essentials of acting.[33]

The half-dozen or so "hired men," who were more or less regularly employed by the company to portray minor roles, received "from 5s. to 10s. a week, according to their ability and the amount of work they were given to do." Most of them probably expected to earn at least 1s. a day when working. And if the fee seems tiny, it is important to know that "a good carpenter . . . and other artisans as well did not earn any more than their shilling a day in Shakespeare's time." [34]

V

Other companies, of course—twelve or fifteen of them—competed with the Prince Henry-Palsgrave's Men and the King's Men. And in the first years of the century the quasi-professional boy actors continued to present plays. For instance, *The Malcontent* by John Marston (c. 1575–1634) was staged in 1604 by the Children of the Revels; and *Bussy d'Ambois* by George Chapman (c. 1560–1634) and *A Trick to Catch the Old One* by Thomas Middleton (c. 1570–1627) were acted by the Children of Paul's in 1604–05.

The third most important adult troupe was in all probability the Queen Anne's Company. Active mainly at the Red Bull and the Curtain from 1603 until 1619, it rose in skill and reputation as the fortunes of the Prince Henry-Palsgrave's Men declined. Its first leader seems to have been that "most popular actor" Thomas Green (?). Its chief player was Richard Perkins (1585?–1650), one of the ablest actors of the period. He performed for nearly forty years with the Queen's Men, the Players of the Revels, and Queen Henrietta's Men.

In 1612 Christopher Beeston (1570–1638), who had worked earlier with both the Admiral's and the Chamberlain's Men, became leader of the Queen Anne's Company; but five years later he ceased acting, turned manager, and acquired or built the indoor Phoenix, or Cockpit, theater. This he leased from 1617 to 1619 to the Queen Anne's players, from 1619 to 1622 to the Lady Elizabeth's Company, and from 1625 to 1636 to the Queen Henrietta Company. There in 1637 he organized his Beeston's Boys and undertook to train actors. He was in his last twenty years "probably the most important theatrical figure in London." [35] In 1638 his son William (1606?–1682) took charge of Beeston's Boys and trained, among others, Michael Mohun (c. 1620–1684) and John Lacy (?–1681) who acted at the Cockpit c. 1640.

VI

The King's Men continued after 1625, when Charles I began his reign, to be the outstanding company of professional actors in England—and perhaps in the world of that time. By "the beginning of 1625 at least thirty-five men and an unknown number of boys had an active part in the theatrical business" of the company. "That the enterprise could support such a large number at this time" and for about the next seventeen years "is a fair measure of its prosperity." [36] It's doubtful if any of the *commedia* troupes, any Spanish professional companies, or any Oriental groups of actors could vie with it in size, number of productions, skills, popularity, or profits.

But as the King's Men went about their bright business of acting plays the years darkened around them. Plagues recurred from 1636 onward; the Puritan opposition to the players, fanned in 1635 by the blasts of William Prynne's (1600–1669) *Histrio-Mastix, the players scourge or actors tragedie* . . . (more than a thousand pages long!), grew and grew until in 1641 "there was a great complaint made against Play-houses, and a motion made for suppressing them." Then in 1642 Civil War broke out; and on September 2 Parliament, with the Puritans in control, resolved that, "Whereas the distressed Estate of Ireland, steeped in her own Blood, and the distracted Estate of England, threatned with a Cloud of Blood, by a Civill Warre, calle for all possible meanes to appease and avert the Wrath of God appearing in these Judgements . . . and whereas publike Sports doe not well agree with publike Calamities, nor publike Stage-players with the Seasons of Humiliation, this being an Exercise of sad and pious solemnity, and the other being Spectacles of pleasure, too commonly expressing laciuious Mirth and Levitie: It is therefore thought fit, and Ordeined by the Lords and Commons in this Parliament Assembled, that while these sad Causes and set times of Humiliation doe continue, publike Stage-Playes shall cease, and bee forborne." [37] This resolution closed the "devil's chapels in London": the Blackfriars, the Globe, the Cockpit or Phoenix, the Fortune, the Salisbury Court, and the Red Bull. It finished the King's Men. The company was dissolved. The delighted Puritans pulled down the Globe in 1644; the Blackfriars was destroyed in 1647; the Fortune was almost demolished by Commonwealth soldiers in 1649.

The actors, of course, hoped against hope to "returne to their old harmlesse profession of killing Men in Tragedies without Man-slaughter." But the prohibition was renewed in 1647, and again in 1648 when "all stage-players, and players of interludes, and common playeers, are hereby declared to be, and are, and shall be taken to be, rogues. . . ." Then "When the Wars were over, and the Royalists totally Subdued, most of 'em who were left alive gather'd to London, and for a Subsistence endeavour'd to revive their Old Trade, privately. They made up one Company out of all the Scatter'd Members of several; and in the Winter before the King's Murder, 1648, they ventured to Act some Plays with as much caution and privacy as cou'd be, at the Cockpit. They continu'd undisturbed for three or four Days; but at last as they were presenting the Tragedy of the *Bloudy Brother*, (in which Lowin Acted Aubrey, Taylor Rollo . . . and I think Hart [of the 1641 *Cardinal*] Otto), a party of Foot Soldiers beset the House, surprised 'em about the midle of the Play, and carried 'em away . . . to . . . Prison. . . . Afterwards in Oliver's [Cromwell] time, they used to Act privately, three or four Miles, or more, out of Town, now here, now there, sometimes in Noblemen's Houses . . . where the Nobility and Gentry . . . used to make a Sum for them. . . . And Alexander Goffe [Gough], the Woman Actor at Black-friers . . . , used to be the Jackal and give notice of Time and Place. At Christmas . . . they used to Bribe the Officer who commanded the Guard at Whitehall, and were thereupon connived at to Act for a few Days, at the Red Bull; but were sometimes notwithstanding Disturb'd by Soldiers. . . ." [38]

❁ KABUKI

While professional actors were active in Spain, were finally accepted in France, and were rejected for too much success in England, a second form of theater, the Kabuki, was evolved in Japan. Unlike the Nō which belonged to the *samurai* or nobles, it was addressed to the *chonin*—that is, the trades-men, artisans, and peasants. In the seventeenth century, three hundred years after the advent of the Nō, and alongside it, the Kabuki theater grew and flowered (then wilted a bit), and in the process underlined once again the fundamental differences between Oriental and Occidental acting.

For the first half of the century the Kabuki performers tried to make their acting less abstract, less special, and less poetic than Nō acting. They tried to be more human onstage. Unfortunately these attempts depended too much on their being physically charming, and being physically charming led to exhibitions judged to be immoral. Consequently, the actors were eventually forced to return to stage behavior that wasn't as trivial as the merely personal and the merely lifelike.

II

The Onna Kabuki, or women's Kabuki, which was inaugurated shortly after 1600 by a woman dancer named O Kuni, was performed with much success after her death in c. 1610 for almost twenty years. At least seven Kabuki theaters were built by 1620 in Kyoto; and in 1624 the famous Saruwaka *za* (theater), later the Nakamura *za*, was opened in Yedo (Tokyo) by manager Kanzaburo. In 1629, however, the Shōgun issued a decree pro-hibiting women from appearing onstage "because of their adverse effect on public morals." The Onna Kabuki was thus succeeded by the Wakashu, or young men's Kabuki; and for another twenty years these soft males, leading despised and precarious lives, entertained the people with their sensuous charms in additional theaters which were concentrated, along with other diversions, in restricted districts of towns in order "to facilitate easy vigilance by the authorities." In 1652 the Wakashu Kabuki, again on moral grounds, was suppressed. Finally, two years later, in 1654, the Yaro Kabuki, or robust and adult men's Kabuki, was authorized. Then "all the players of both male and female parts were men who had to hold the attention of an audience by dint of skill alone"; they weren't allowed to "rely on mere physical charm as in the past." Their acting was acceptable to the authorities only when it was artistic, and it was considered artistic only when it was abstract. By the beginning of the Genroku era in 1688 the Kabuki "reached a pinnacle of achievement as a mature art, the theater of the common people." [39]

Shortly before then, in 1685, Takemoto Gidayu (1650–1724), a notable reciter to the accompaniment of the *samisen*, established his famous *Ningyo Shibai*, or doll theater (with puppet figures usually between three and four feet in height) at Osaka. There a year later he was joined by the outstanding Japanese playwright, Chikamatsu Monzaemon (Suginomori Nobumori) (1653–1724), who had for the nine previous years been writing scripts for the Kabuki theater in Kyoto. "The fame of the theater spread far and wide, and Takemoto Gidayu's technique made such an impression on the public that a school was born, founded on his methods." The *Ningyo Shibai*, a third form of Japanese theater, then became so popular with the people all over the country that it completely eclipsed the Kabuki. Kabuki actors couldn't regain their popularity for another seventy-five years, and then only when they "emulated and adapted the movements and gestures of the dolls," [40] only when they became less lifelike than they had ever been.

III

The first Kabuki playwrights, mostly actors or theater owner-managers, put together their scripts "as if drawing a picture." They never aimed to make a piece of literature; they tried to write something that would be effective only in the theater, and most effective in its visual appeal there. Fact and fancy were intermingled without reserve, realism and logic were ignored, and human nature was painted with bold and vivid strokes in a series of scenes which, while not always united into an artistic whole, provided the actors with opportunities for demonstrating their skills. Chikamatsu, who wrote about a hundred plays, fifty-one of which have been published, followed that pattern. His scripts, much longer than the Nō one-acters, and in most instances longer than full-length European plays, range from the comparatively simple *Koi Hakké Hashiragoyoma* (*Fair Ladies at a Game of Poem-Cards*) (c. 1714) to the complex, colossal classic, *Kokusenya Kassen* (*The Battles of Coxinga*) (1715). The former, a romance, tells with some charm and delicate comedy the almost endless story of two pairs of lovers bedeviled by an old *samurai* police superintendent who lusts for one of the girls. After courting mix-ups, a parental disapproval, a pregnancy, retreats into religion, long wanderings, much matter about beheadings, and two murders the sweethearts are saved from disaster and reunited after five years of separation by the benevolence of an Empress. In *The Battles*, an unreal, "superfilm" melodrama, seen by 240,000 people at one theater alone during the seventeen months of its initial run in a city whose population didn't exceed 300,000, "a Tartar king demands a Ming Emperor's favorite concubine as the price of friendship. This is merely a pretext for an invasion of China, the signal for which is given by a traitorous minister when he stabs out his own eye with a dagger. After sundry events in which the Emperor is deluded by his minister, the Tartars appear at the gates millions strong and are routed by the Chinese general Go Sankei [Coxinga] with a mere handful of soldiers. While he is engaged in this stupendous feat, however, the evil minister's younger brother cuts off the Emperor's head and binds his concubine. Go Sankei thereupon decapitates the murderer and releases the concubine. She is, however, killed by a bullet later on, and Go Sankei saves the child she is bearing by performing a Caesarian operation in full sight of the audience. To deceive the enemy, . . . bent upon seizing the imperial heir, he then kills his own child, which has been lashed to his spear throughout the engagement, and substitutes it for the recently delivered prince. Meanwhile the Emperor's daughter and the general's wife escape to Japan where they win the assistance of a great Japanese hero. . . . Finally, he comes to the aid of the loyal general Go Sankei who is keeping the royal prince in hiding; and what gargantuan battles ensue can easily be imagined." [41]

What counted most in such plays was the acting; and Kabuki acting was —and still is—unlike any European acting. Effective speaking, however, is almost as important to the Kabuki actor as it is to a Western actor. He learns to say his lines, archaic or colloquial, with highly stylized intonations. He becomes adept at making rhythmical sound patterns, approaching chant, rather than straightforward literary or conversational statements. And yet, unlike the Chinese actor, the Kabuki actor doesn't sing; that's done by the orchestra members who, at times, also speak some of his lines. But effective movement is much more important than effective speech. Japanese acting is largely a "thing of posture," a series of pictorial effects. "Dancing is the essence of the Kabuki theater"; [42] the actor (yakusha) must almost always be an expert dancer. Like the Nō actor, like all Oriental actors, he must be able to move, gesture, and pose nonrealistically to music.

IV

Three outstanding Kabuki actors of the seventeenth century were Sakata Tōjurō (1645–1709), for whom Chikamatsu wrote many of his early plays; the famous Ichikawa Danjūrō I (1660–1704), who created and set certain acting techniques, and was the forerunner of a long and distinguished line of actors bearing his name in unbroken succession until the death of Danjūrō IX in 1903; and Yoshizawa Ayame (1673–1729), the first great onnagata, or female impersonator, whose sayings about acting were collected by Fukuoka Yagoshiro and published under the title Ayame-gusa.[43]

In the contributions of the last two performers we can catch a glimpse of the unique quality of Kabuki acting. For instance, Danjūrō I—a contemporary of Betterton and Molière—developed aragoto, a technique of exaggeration "which emphasizes the power of the hero or the evil of the villain by extremes in costume [plus make-up], dialogue, and movement." It is a technique that forsakes copying natural human behavior or emotions and heightens them with a "bold display of rhythmical, emphasized movement and gesture." Danjūrō I insisted, it seems, via *aragoto* that the actor must go beyond verisimilitudes and find their "esthetic immediacy." He believed that acting was more than behaving naturally, that it should aim for the pictorial extraction of essence. From *aragoto* developed a technique known as *mie*, "which singularly typifies the art of the Kabuki actor." *Mie* means consciously to seek a dramatic effect, to "play to the gallery." With *mie* "the actor must impose himself upon his audience with the maximum power of his resources." He draws himself up into a pose, glares, gestures with the palms outward and the fingers outstretched, and then moves his head several times with a circular motion, the body and the shoulders remaining rigid. *Mie* is always performed to the beating of wooden clappers in a rapid tempo upon a wooden board. Associated with *mie*, and also derived from *aragoto*, is a walking or dancing technique called *roppo*. In *tobi roppo*, one of its several forms, "The actor performs a kind of hopping step which commences slowly but increases in tempo. The right arm is thrust out beyond the player who inclines forward on one leg, and the arm is flung back in a wide arc behind his head as he changes to the other foot. His left arm grasps a stave which is held to his side, and the whole action is carried out to the beating of a drum. It symbolizes a spirit of exaltation in having escaped from a difficult situation." [44] But enough of these abstract techniques. Danjūrō I, in brief, was an expert actor not because he could mimic a bandit, an official, a warrior, or a young lover but because via such techniques as *aragoto*, *mie*, *roppo*, and so on he could convey in theatrical ways to an audience the pleasing, thrilling, or moving attributes, and maybe sometimes the essence, of those characters in the artifice called a play.

Yoshizawa Ayame developed a way of impersonating women onstage that differed vastly, fundamentally, from that used by a man like Alizon in France or the boy actors in England. Unlike Western men and boys, Ayame didn't characterize by aping enough external traits to win audience acceptance as a female; and unlike famed contemporary actresses such as Marie Duclos and Anne Bracegirdle, he didn't exhibit or emphasize his personal charms. No. He subtly created a convention for femininity; he formalized it. He symbolized and idealized feminine qualities "in a way that no actress can do." He literally *"acted"* a woman, "where the actress can only fall back upon easier and more natural qualities with a loss of the power of expression. . . ." And yet in his mind Ayame *was* a woman: "You cannot be a good *onnagata*," he said, "unless you are like a woman in your daily life. The more you become conscious on the stage of playing a woman's part the more unsuccessful will you be." And no matter how many children you may have, you "must not lose . . . innocence of mind." [45]

The *chobo*, one of several different kinds of orchestral accompaniment for a Kabuki play, best embodies the non-naturalistic quality of its acting. A combination of a narrator and a *samisen* player, the *chobo* "describes when and where; it 'explains' and describes individual characters . . ."; it "helps to build up suspense by describing the movements, both real and intended, of the various characters. It also expresses the thoughts of a stage personality, his mental reactions to a certain situation." In addition, the *chobo* acts "as a conductor's baton to the actor; it sets his timing and dictates his movements and gestures" and thus assists them in acquiring "a symbolic quality which is divorced from realism." The *chobo*, in effect, turns the actor "into a puppet and then explains him to the audience." And "The audience watches the movements of the actors and listens to the descriptions simultaneously, so that there is a double effect in the scene on the stage." [46]

Kabuki acting, although perhaps not as intense or as poetic as Nō acting, emphasizes again the firm Oriental conviction that in the theater human behavior must be more than merely copied for the production of an illusion of reality; it must be rearranged and heightened, designed, in order to achieve for an audience the experience of joy.

A skilled Kabuki actor, therefore, is mainly a master of traditional, non-realistic techniques. And the process of learning and perfecting them, though severe and long, is a pride-filled one. "There is no chance for the young Kabuki actor to make his name overnight in a new play as a Western actor might do. He has to contend with an audience that knows the rules thoroughly"—that knows all about *monogatari*, the correct narration of past events; the related *gochushin*, or the report by a young warrior to his superiors of the progress of a battle; *teoi no jukkai*, the confessions of one who is dying and regretting past deeds, always in the agonies of a severe injury; *kudoki*, the depiction of the innermost feelings of a woman and the love kept secret in her mind; *kubijikken*, the inspection of the head of a decapitated warrior; *michiyuki*, a sort of dance which portrays a character or characters who are making a journey; *tate*, or purely stylized, rhythmical fighting; and so on. He has to contend with an audience that "is not so much interested in the play as the technique of the actor and his interpretation, and that all the time applies a mental criticism to his performance in the light of the masters who have held the name before him." [47]

Betterton and Molière, Mlle. Duclos and Mrs. Bracegirdle could hardly have understood or appreciated that kind of acting. But the people of Japan idolized their stage stars, and greatly honored them as artists who knew that "Art is something which lies in the slender margin between the real and the unreal," that "stylization . . . is what delights men's minds." [48]

❀ MOLIÈRE; LA COMÉDIE-FRANÇAISE

By the middle of the century in France the professional actors were almost too successful. Some of them complained bitterly when playwrights were noticed by the public, figured prominently on the playbills, and asked higher fees for their scripts. For instance, when Corneille demanded and got two hundred crowns for a play, Mlle. Beaupré of the Marais pouted, "Monsieur de Corneille has done us great mischief: formerly we could get plays at three crowns [or écus (1 écu = 9 livres)] a piece, written in a single night. That was the custom and it worked extremely well. Now, however, the plays of Monsieur Corneille cost us dear and we make very little out of them." Other actors, fortunately, knew in their hearts that a thriving theater depends upon first-rate scripts and that first-rate scripts cost first-rate money. In 1653 minor dramatist Philippe Quinnault (1633–1688) refused a pittance of only fifty crowns from the actors at the Hôtel for his *Les Rivales* and "suggested that no down payment be made but that he should receive ten percent of the receipts of the first run of the play, after which the rights were to be vested in the company." [49] The actors accepted his terms, and thereafter made royalty payments to playwrights.

By 1650 Floridor, the chief actor at the prospering Hôtel de Bourgogne, was joined there by large comedian Raymond Poisson (c. 1630–1690), known as Belleroche, the first of a family of actors who served the French stage for three generations. While his wife portrayed roles given up by Mlle. Bellerose, Poisson found fame by taking from Scarron's *Écolier de Salamanque* (1654) the character of the valet Crispin and putting him in several comedies. At the Marais, Laroque became the new leader, and piloted the theater through many difficult years with the assistance of actor Noel Jacques le Breton de Hauteroche (c. 1616–1707) who later was also a playwright. By the middle of 1658, however, the "fortunes of the Marais, its best actors gone, its situation in the rue Vielle-du-Temple more and more inaccessible, were . . . at a low ebb." [50]

Paris needed another French troupe to compete with "the great actors" at the Hôtel de Bourgogne.

II

After Molière became the acknowledged head of Dufresne's provincial troupe in c. 1651 he tried to brighten its repertory by turning casually to playwriting. In 1655, when he was thirty-three, he staged at Lyon his first comedy of importance, the five-act, rhymed *L'Etourdi, ou les Contra-temps* (*The Blunderer, or the Mishaps*). Adapted from Barbieri's *L'Inavvertito* (*The Indiscreet Man*) (1629), and employing stock characters, it pleased audiences with its story of a clever servant who thinks of one scheme after another to secure a lady for his master, only to have each one of them ruined by the blundering, bemused lover. Molière acted the servant Mascarille, who is on-stage seven-eighths of the time and speaks over a thousand lines or about half of the farce. In the following year, at Béziers, Molière again was Mascarille in his second surviving play, the verse *Le Dépit amoureux* (*Lovers' Tiff*), freely adapted from another Italian work, *L'Interesse (Self-interest)* (*c.* 1584) by Nicolo Secchi. But this time the chief character was another servant, Gros-René, acted by René Berthelot Du Parc (*c.* 1630–1664). Molière, apparently, wanted to perform in tragedies.

At any rate, his troupe of four women—Madeleine Béjart, her sister Geneviève (known as Mlle. Hervé) (*c.* 1622–1675), Du Parc's wife, Marquise-Thérése de Gorla (1633–1668), and Catherine Leclerc du Rozet (or Mlle. de Rose) (*c.* 1630–1706)—and six men—Molière, Dufresne, Madeleine's two brothers, Joseph (*c.* 1620–1659) and Louis (1625–1678), Du Parc, and Mlle. de Rose's husband, Edmé de Brie (1607–1676)—returned to Paris in 1658 after an absence of thirteen years to challenge the Hôtel de Bourgogne's way of playing tragedy. The lease Madeleine signed in July with the Marais group for their theater ("perhaps with the idea that the two troupes might be mingled") proved unnecessary when Molière, by pulling strings of one sort or another, was invited by the King's brother to act before the young Louis XIV (1638–1715) and the Queen mother. In the Guard Room of the Vieux Louvre on October 24, 1658, the "Troupe de Monsieur," as it was then called, staked its future on a performance of Corneille's tragic *Nicomède* (1651). The audience was probably no more then "very well satisfied with the charm and acting of the women." Then, as an afterpiece, the company acted a brief comedy by Molière, now lost, called *Docteur amoureaux.* And since "Little comedies had long been unheard of, this one seemed to be a new invention, and diverted as well as surprised everyone. . . . Molière played the Doctor; and the manner in which he acquitted himself of this role won him such esteem that His Majesty gave orders to establish his troupe in Paris." [51]

At once the newcomers were housed in the Petit-Bourbon along with the visiting Fiorilli and the *commedia dell' arte* players. After paying the Italians 1,500 livres as part of some expenses already incurred, they were assigned to perform on the less popular Mondays, Wednesdays, Thursdays, and Saturdays while the Italians retained Tuesdays, Fridays, and Sundays. Molière opened his public season there on November 2, and presented five Corneille tragedies in succession. All of them were failures. "Finally, with a strange reluctance," he decided "to do at last what he should have done at first." In late November he staged *L'Etourdi,* and followed it in December with *Le Dépit amoureux.* Success was "immediate and unparalleled." [52]

During 1659 Molière and his actors became firmly entrenched in Paris. When the Du Parcs deserted him for the Marais (only to return in a year), he hired another couple from the provinces, Philibert Gassot du Croisy (1626–1695) and his wife. And when Dufresne retired he replaced him with Charles Varlet La Grange (1639–1692), and then increased his company to twelve by signing Jodelet and his brother L'Espy of the Marais. By June Fiorilli returned to Italy, and Molière at once proceeded to give performances on Tuesdays, Fridays, and Sundays in direct competition with the Hôtel de Bourgogne. He produced six tragedies of Corneille, two of Du Ryer, two of Tristan, and one of Rotrou, all of which were in the repertory of the "great actors" at the Hôtel.

Finally, forgetting Italian models with their traditional characters, and observing instead "the manners of the Court and of those who stood well within or upon the edge of the social life of the time," Molière wrote in one-act and prose *Les Précieuses ridicules* (*The Affected Ladies*), valued by some as "the most profoundly original comedy since Aristophanes." It was acted by the company after Corneille's *Cinna* on November 18, 1659. Madeleine Béjart and Catherine du Rozet as Magdelon and Cathos, du Croisy and La Grange under their own names, Molière as his third Mascarille, manservant to La Grange, and Jodelet as Jodelet, manservant to du Croisy, scored a resounding triumph. The first performance brought in the highest gate yet received by the Troupe de Monsieur, and in . . . eleven months . . . the little comedy was played . . . forty-four times. 'People came from twenty leagues around' to hear it. . . ." And they laughed and laughed, "and then went out of the theater and thought, perhaps for the first time after having seen a comedy." [53]

At long last Molière had found his genius. For fourteen years thereafter he led "a life of harried activity, managing, directing, acting the star roles, and writing a total of twenty-nine plays, everything from tragi-comedy to knockabout farce." Thereafter as a great author and actor of comedy he made of it "not only an art form, but a means of . . . revealing to us the follies and absurdities of our behavior." [54]

He added enormously to his popularity in 1660 by impersonating the title role (which may have been designed for Jodelet, who died before the play's production) in his one-act farce in verse, *Sganarelle, ou le cocu imaginaire* (*Sganarelle, or the Imaginary Cuckold*). Next year, however, when the Petit-Bourbon was demolished and his company was moved to the Palais-Royal, Molière tried once again for a noncomedy success in his heroic *Don Garcie de Navarre*. It flopped. He tasted "the only complete and unambiguous failure of his career." At once he turned from the heroic to the human, donned again his Sganarelle costume, and came up with the full-length, verse *L'École des maris* (*The School for Husbands*), a genuine social-problem comedy. In the same year, 1661 (when Betterton was beginning to act in London), Molière put together quickly a comédie-ballet, *Les Facheux* (*The Bores*), "a picture of contemporary life built around a number of character types." Then in 1662 with his notable *L'École des Femmes* (*The School for Wives*), five acts in verse, he achieved perhaps the greatest success of his career. In it he "interpreted dramatic action to mean the psychological reactions produced by certain events . . . on characters who are thereby stimulated to follow a certain line of conduct." And in Arnolphe, a wealthy Parisian bourgeois, he penned and acted "the fullest portrait . . . yet attempted of a contemporary figure." [55]

But all the while that "People flocked to the Palais-Royal, to roar at

Arnolphe, as a score of years before they had flocked to the Marais to be stirred and uplifted by the heroes of tragedy," Molière was criticized by jealous professional rivals and by a resentful coterie "for his manner of acting, his technique as a playwright, his characterization, his style of writing, his construction of plots, his moral and social doctrines, the impiety and licentiousness of his attitude to serious subjects, his slavish reproductions of living persons and the manners of the day." In 1663 he brilliantly answered his detractors with *La Critique de l'École des femmes*, a brief comedy, a debate, "a conversation, always keeping the tone of real talk, easy and unacademic, flowing and graceful." This clearest statement of his purposes and methods as a man of the theater makes the point, one among many, that "When you portray heroes you can do just what you please. These are fanciful portraits; no one looks for lifelike resemblance in them. You merely have to follow the suggestions of your roving imagination, which often abandons the true in order to pursue the marvelous. But when you are painting men, you must paint from nature. Everyone insists that the likenesses resemble reality; and you haven't accomplished anything, unless you make your audience recognize the men of our own time." [56] (And you wonder how Floridor, Montfleury, Mlle. Beauchâteau, and Mlle. Desoeillets, who were appearing in Corneille's *Sophonisbe* at the Hôtel de Bourgogne, reacted to that.)

No matter. Between 1663 and 1673 Molière wrote and acted in at least twelve plays whose comic spirit, with its confidence in the nature of man, and whose comic technique, which enlarged the real into almost the poetic, are matchless: in 1664 (first) the highly controversial *Tartuffe*; in 1665 *Don Juan* in which Molière acted his third Sganarelle, La Grange Don Juan, Mme. Du Parc Elmire, du Croisy Dimanche; in 1666 a masterpiece, the stunning but not too popular *Le Misanthrope*, and also the slapstick *Le Médicin malgré lui* (*The Doctor in Spite of Himself*) with Molière again a Sganarelle; in 1668 *Amphitryon* with Molière as Sosie, La Thorillière as Jupiter, Mme. Molière as Alcmene, La Grange as *Amphitryon*, and du Croisy as Mercury; *Georges Dandin, ou le mari confondu* (*George Dandin, or The Baffled Husband*); and *L'Avare* (*The Miser*); in 1669 the comédie-ballet *Monsieur de Pourceaugnac*; in 1670 the joyously original *Le Bourgeois gentilhomme* (*The Bourgeois Gentleman*) with Molière as Jourdain; in 1671 the expert *Les Fourberies de Scapin* (*The Tricks of Scapin*); in 1672 the brief but important *Les Femmes savantes* (*The Learned Ladies*); and finally in 1773 *Le Malade imaginaire* (*The Imaginary Invalid*) in which Molière, truly sick, played Argan and collapsed and died within half an hour after the fourth performance.

Molière was also a great actor, a credit too often forgotten because his acting, like all acting, vanished. The words he wrote remain; the way he said them in motion was impermanent. But the echoes of his evanescent achievement indicate that he was always essentially an actor who, searching for scripts, took to writing them; and much of their eternal success derives surely from his love for, his living experience with, and his mastery of the art of acting. True, he never succeeded as a tragic actor, perhaps because he was far too intelligent to revel with deep emotions and to orate them as if he were posing on a rostrum; or perhaps because, as someone observed, "His voice was heavy, with hard inflections, and he had a volubility of utterance that ran away with his speeches and made him in this respect greatly inferior to the actors at the Hôtel de Bourgogne." But Molière was an expert comic actor, maybe the most expert of all before or since. It was written of his Sganarelle in the farce of the same name that "only by seeing Molière is it possible to appreciate how the playing of the actor illuminates the wit and verity of the author. . . . His face and bearing so well express the jealousy of Sganarelle that his emotions and thoughts would be plain to everyone though he never uttered a word. No actor ever had so expressive and variable a countenance. . . . I venture to maintain that Sganarelle exhibits no symptoms of jealousy, nor expresses any feeling, that the author has not personally observed in the men about him, so naturally are all these things expressed. . . . [He] may be said to have read the world as a preliminary to his revelations—a procedure which cannot successfully be followed unless the practitioner has as firm a gift of observation as Molière himself and as fine a discretion in the selection of what is best suited to his purpose." [57]

One of the absurdities of his time which Molière first poked fun at was the stilted and bellowing, pomp and circumstance, fake acting in tragedies. In Les Précieuses ridicules, for instance, Mascarille has written a play. To whom, asks Cathos, will he submit it? "A fine question!" he replies. "To the Hôtel de Bourgogne, of course. They are the only ones who can bring out what's in a text; the others are ignoramuses who read their lines the way people speak. They don't know how to thunder out a good line of verse, and stop at the right place; and how can you tell which is the fine passage, if the actor doesn't pause at it, and thus indicate that it's time to applaud?" And in the short L'Impromptu de Versailles (1663), another rebuttal for his critics, he announced several of his own perceptive notions of what acting ought to be. First, he insisted, the actor's task is basically to help "bring out a play's quality"; second, an actor must always impersonate from a real sense of character; third, he can truly demonstrate his histrionic excellence "by playing . . . well a character who is entirely the contrary" of himself; and fourth, he ought to "read the lines in the most natural manner possible" [58] (although the "natural" of then and now are hardly the same).

For most of his life, and most of the hours of it, Molière worked with actors; and though he knew them to be "peculiar creatures to manage," he was always proud of them and their craft, and continually trying to perfect the exciting things they could do in character for a play. More than anyone else he won for acting in France acceptance and respect. And when in 1672 Molière was proposed for the Academy, but only on the condition that he would renounce his profession as an actor, he declined the offer by saying,

"I will not insult a profession which I love, and to which I am so materially indebted, by purchasing personal advantages at the cost of throwing a slur upon it." [59]

Seven new players of importance were lucky enough to work before his death as members of Molière's company—where a full-share actor in 1660–73 received from 2,000 to 5,500 livres (1 livre = 1 franc) a year, or about $1,500 to $3,900 in today's money (but the purchasing powers, of course, are vastly different and almost impossible to estimate). Brécourt (Guillaume Marcoureau) (1638–1685) and François Lenoir La Thorillière (1626–1680) left the Marais in about 1660 for the Palais-Royal, although the former remained there only two years before going to the Hôtel de Bourgogne. Armande Béjart (1642–1700), raised by her sister Madeleine, first acted in La Critique soon after she married Molière in 1662. André Hubert (c. 1634–1700), "the last representative of women on the Paris stage," [60] joined the group in 1664. The Beauvals, Jeanne Olivier Bourgignon (c. 1648–1720) and her husband Jean Pital (c. 1635–1709), were hired in 1668. Then Michel Baron (1653–1739), the son of André and Jeanne, who had been treated as a son by Molière in 1666 when he had briefly acted with the company, returned to his tutor in 1670.

III

Jean Racine (1639–1699) was elected to the Academy in place of Molière. With his skills as a playwright he did almost as much for French tragic acting as the latter did for comic acting. Instead of merely complicating situations and plots as Corneille had done, Racine complicated with a rare sensitivity the psychology of his characters. He designed them as human beings who, "during acute and fatal periods of consciousness . . . recognize that conflicting passions, dispositions, and possibilities exist simultaneously within themselves." He "explored the shadowy world of the unconscious. . . ," or those "feelings which are . . . anterior to all civilization and which a supreme degree of civilization only covers but cannot alter." Therefore he asked of his actors a new and subtle humanness, that is, "the suggestion of thoughts and emotions half-recognized by the characters themselves, or sometimes not acknowledged at all by them. These are thoughts and emotions that have not yet emerged into action, or even into expression in words, and yet form the groundwork on which the action of the play is gradually built up." And the action is motivated logically in "a verbal medium almost as abstract as that of musical sound." In short, with Racine as playwright the actor had "a share . . . crucial in the creation of a part." [61]

Racine was first staged with moderate success in 1664 by Molière. The play was La Thébaïde, ou les frères ennemis (The Theban, or The Enemy Brothers). Then next year when Molière produced the same author's Alexandre le Grand with La Grange in the title role, Mme. Du Parc as Axiane, and La Thorillière as Porus, Racine secretly gave the same work to the Hôtel where the actors were better in tragedy; there two weeks later it was offered to the public in successful competition with Molière's company with Floridor as Alexandre, Mlle. Desoeillets (Alix Faviot) (1621–1670) as Axiane, and Montfleury as Porus. Thereafter the superb succession of tragedies from *Andromaque* to *Phèdre* was first acted at the Hôtel de Bourgogne.

With *Andromaque* (1667) Racine was recognized as a gifted dramatist in many ways superior to the aging Corneille. In this his first feminine tragedy, taken from Euripides, "the torrents of . . . four love-intoxicated persons" were recited in delicate, precise, tense verse by the thirty-four-year-old Mme. Du Parc (seduced away from Molière's company) in the title role, fifty-nine-year-old Floridor as Pyrrhus, forty-six-year-old Mlle. Desoeillets as Hermione, and sixty-seven-year-old Montfleury as Orestes. But it is unlikely, as gossip had it, that Racine taught Mme. Du Parc how to read her role line by line. "There are inherent improbabilities in the picture of a barely established dramatist engaged on his third play teaching her business in detail to an actress some six years his senior, with fourteen years of stage experience behind her. . . ." The powerful *Britannicus* (1669), a study of Nero's court, was followed by the simple, striking, feminine *Bérénice* (1670) in which the dramatic struggle "goes on in the hearts of the . . . lovers as they waver between the sacrifice of their love and the sacrifice of the interest of the [Roman] state." Their action is "to demonstrate the tragic life of the soul-as-rational." [62] With Marie Desmares Champmeslé (1642–1698) as Bérénice, Floridor as Tite, and Charles Champmeslé (1642–1701) as Antiochus the play proved much more successful than Corneille's same subject *Tite et Bérénice* as staged a week later by Molière with his wife as Bérénice, La Thorillière as Tite, and the newly returned Baron as Antiochus.

Before Molière's death Racine wrote *Bajazet* (1672), and afterwards, from Euripides, the brilliant *Iphigénie* (1672) for Mme. Champmeslé. Later he turned again to that Greek for *Phèdre* (1677), a tremendous *tour de force* which explored in overpowering aria after aria the inner conflict of a passion-obsessed woman unable to free herself from love and guilt. Mme. Champmeslé was the first Phèdre, Baron the first Hippolyte. She, it was said, spoke in "a kind of chant," but she knew how to use her voice with such skill, and she introduced aptly such natural inflections, that it appeared "as though she really felt in her heart a passion which is only on the lips." With *Phèdre* "French classical tragedy attained the highest degree of dramatic intensity and beauty. . . ." [63] But the tragedy's amazing merits weren't recognized at once. When a rival *Phèdre et Hippolyte* as acted by Molière's company outdrew his masterpiece, Racine in a huff quit the theater.

Today Racine's "compression of passion into one major crisis," "into an intense, inescapable, and intimate moment of human life . . . a mode of psychic being," seems to many, especially to Anglo-Saxons, like "a form of pernicious anemia"; and his "analytic approach to the emotions" seems to indicate an "atrophy of emotion." Moreover, his Alexandrines, with "the perfect balance of the rhymed couplet" and "the perfect balance of the individual line (regularly though not invariably broken in the middle)," ring out—especially in the always unfair translations—like talk too sculptured.[64] Yet on the French stage, as in theater annals everywhere, Racine is still rightly acclaimed one of the world's greatest playwrights. In *Phèdre*, certainly, he matched the terrifying grandeur of *Oedipus* and *King Lear* with the torrential, tearing sound of humanity trying in vain to find the heart's reasons.

IV

Molière's widow, helped by La Grange, was forced to reopen the Palais-Royal on February 24, 1673, only a week after his death because the King thought the troupe could not continue without a leader and planned to amalgamate it with the Hôtel actors. La Thorillière knew the lines for Argan in *Le Malade imaginaire*, Baron learned the part of Alceste in *Le Misanthrope*, and somehow the company warded off extinction. Before long, however, Baron, who decided to shine in tragedy, left for the Hôtel; he was accompanied there by La Thorillière and the Beauvals. Mme. Molière and La Grange at once hired Rosimond (Claude la Roze) (c. 1640–1686), who had come from the provinces to the Marais in 1668, to impersonate the Molière roles. But musician Lully (1632–1687) obtained the King's consent to make the Palais-Royal the home for French opera, and the Molière actors were suddenly evicted from their theater. La Grange, with a first payment of 14,000 livres of the 40,000 left to Mme. Molière, quickly bought the new Théâtre de Guénégaud. Then Louis XIV, "as though to atone for the loss he had inflicted on the actors . . . , evinced a practical interest in the success of the enterprise." He closed the floundering Marais, "which had survived the theatrical vicissitudes of nearly eighty years," and ordered its actors to join the Molière troupe. The chief Marais members at that time were: Laroque; Guérin d'Etriche (c. 1636–1728) and his girl-friend Mlle. Guiot (whom he deserted in 1677 to marry Mme. Molière); Nicholas Dauvilliers (?–1690) and his wife, Victoire (c. 1657–1733), the daughter of Raymond Poisson; Mme. Dupin (1649–1709) and her husband; Verneuil (La Grange's brother Achille) (1636–1709); and a Mlle. Auzillon. The united companies, with Mme. Molière at the head, opened at the Théâtre de Guénégaud early in July 1673 with *Tartuffe* and continued their rivalry with the Hôtel for another seven years.

By 1670 Mme. Champmeslé, after stardom in Racine's tragedies and many consequent dissensions, left the Hôtel with her husband and joined the Guénégaud company. (There they were awarded "in gratitude" in addition to a full share each an annual allowance of 1,000 livres.) At about the same time the Hôtel company was further weakened by the death of La Thorillière. A Mlle. Bélonde (Françoise Cordon) was hired to fill unsuccessfully the place of Mme. Champmeslé; comic Jean Baptiste Raisin (1653–1702) and his wife Françoise Pitel de Longchamp (1661–1721) were hired; Jean de Villiers (1648–1701) was hired. But it was too late; the fortunes of the Hôtel de Bourgogne were sinking.

In the summer of 1680 Louis XIV, with his "love of unity for its own sake" and his belief that State aid is essential to the interests of literature and art, issued an order to the effect that the Bourgogne and the Guénégaud troupes should form themselves into one, should perform their plays at the Théâtre de Guénégaud, and should be granted a subsidy of 12,000 livres (about $8,500 in today's U.S. money) a year. The object of the union was to "render the representations of comedies more complete, and to afford the players the means of perfecting themselves" in their art. And no other actors, with the exception of the Italian comedians, were allowed to ply their vocation without the King's express permission.[65]

Thus the present-day Comédie-Française, the company and the organization, was created and began to perform at the Théâtre-Français, often called "La Maison de Molière," in late August 1680.

The King himself, it's said, selected the actors and determined how each of them should be remunerated. The original troupe was composed of six persons who, after Molière's death, had continued as members of his company: Mme. Guérin d'Etriche (Molière), La Grange and his wife, Marie Ragueneau (1639–1737), du Croisy, Hubert, Mlle. du Rozet (Mme. de Brie); plus Rosimond and du Croisy's daughter Angelique (1657–1756), who made her debut there in 1673; and plus Mme. Champmeslé and her husband. The five Marais actors were: d'Etriche, Dauvilliers, Verneuil, Mme. Dupin, who was Montfleury's daughter, and Mlle. Guiot (Laroque had died in 1676). Twelve members came from the Hôtel: Baron and his wife Charlotte (1661–1730), who was the daughter of La Thorillière, Poisson, Hauteroche, who had left the Marais in 1663, Mme. d'Ennebault (c. 1640–1708), also Montfleury's daughter, Beauval and his wife, Raisin and his wife, Jean La Tuillerie (1630–1688), de Villiers, and Mlle. Bélonde.

Of these twenty-seven persons seventeen had full shares in the new company. Seven—du Croisy and his daughter, Raisin and his wife, Verneuil, Mlle. Guiot, and de Villiers had only half shares; and three—Beauval, and the wives of Baron and La Grange had only quarter shares. Thus the total was 21¼. (Before 1700 this was raised to 24¾.) [66]

From 1680 until the end of the century the success enjoyed by these professional actors in Paris was firm although not phenomenal. For instance, during the 1682–83 season over 150,000 people (from a population of something like half a million) paid to attend the 352 performances given almost every day of the year by the Comédie-Française. That's an average audience of about 426 persons per performance. The next year, however, the attendance fell to only 109,000," and there were three other bad years [1691–

92, 1693–94, and 1694–95] when it failed to reach 120,000." But "there were four years altogether [1682–83, 1695–96, 1698–99, and 1700–1701] when it rose to over 150,000, reaching 192,000 in the record season of 1698–99." In twenty years only three new plays and a revival attracted over 20,000 spectators separately.[67]

Nevertheless, the actors were happy because they were approved (except by the Church) and solidly established. They could make a living. At the end of the century the average earnings for the full-share actor, exclusive of a subsidy of about 1,000 livres, "were in the neighborhood of 4,900 livres [say, $3,500] a year"; and he could count on a pension of 1,000 livres when he retired.[68]

In 1689 the Comédie-Française moved to a new theater holding about 2,000 people, especially built for it in the tennis court of the Étoile, rue Neuve des Fossés, St-Germain-des-Prés, where it remained until 1770.

✿ THE RESTORATION

In 1650 London, with its population of over 600,000, the prohibitions against acting weren't always strictly enforced. Surreptitious performances were sometimes given even though the players risked imprisonment and the spectators a fine. William Beeston, "being bred up in the art of stage playing, and being skilled in that science," "seems to have been among the most active members of his profession in endeavoring to keep the idea of dramatic performances alive during the period of the Commonwealth." At the closing of the theaters in 1642 he apparently continued to train a company of young men at the Cockpit. Ten years later he was credited with "having brought up most of the Actors extant" with his "instructions, judgment and fancy." In that year, 1652, Beeston bought Salisbury Court (1629), a private theater, and no doubt presented some illegal shows there while he anxiously awaited legal tenants. Plays were also, as noted, now and then furtively acted at the Red Bull, one of the city's last open-air public playhouses, by some of the "old" actors—Taylor died in 1652, Lowin in 1653—headed by Michael Mohun. Prominent in this more or less pickup company were Charles Hart and John Lacy.[69]

By 1656 William D'Avenant (1606–1668), Shakespeare's godson, courtier, playwright, masque producer, and Poet Laureate, somehow wheedled permission to stage his *The Siege of Rhodes* in which "the story [was] sung in Recitative Musick." In September it was performed at Rutland House on a miniature stage "eleven foot in height and about fifteen in depth" with wings and backdrops. And a Mrs. Coleman, the wife of the composer, was "the first English actress who ever chaunted (not spoke) on the English stage," although she found it "quite impossible to learn either words or music, so she took the script with her." D'Avenant followed that presentation with a few more "operas" or "entertainments," presented at the Cockpit, until 1659 when his ventures began to receive "an unwelcome share of official scrutiny." [70]

Then in 1660, when Charles II (1630–1685) was restored to his throne eleven years after the beheading of his father, a bookseller and Keeper of the Cockpit since 1644 named John Rhodes (c. 1606–?) obtained a license to reopen that theater with a company of new, younger players. Among them were Thomas Betterton (1633?–1710), Cave Underhill (c. 1634–c. 1710), and two lads who "commonly Acted Women's Parts," Edward Kynaston (c. 1640–1706) and James Nokes (?–1696). But that license was nullified in August of that year when the King, believing that plays might "serve as innocent and harmless divertisement for many of our subjects," was pleased to grant a joint monopoly "for the setting up of two companies and for the erection of two theaters" to D'Avenant and to Thomas Killigrew (1612–1683), soldier, playwright, and Court official. The King also gave leave "that all the women's part[s] to be acted in either of the said companies for the time to come may be performed by women. . . ." Quickly D'Avenant decided to use as his actors the younger men of Rhodes' group, while Killigrew chose the older players of the Mohun company plus, for some reason, Kynaston of the first troupe. On November 5, 1660, Killigrew's company, the King's Men, began acting at the Red Bull, and three days later moved to its temporary Theatre Royal in Vere Street. D'Avenant's company, the Duke's Men, also opened on November 5 at Salisbury Court. And possibly in early December Killigrew produced *Othello* with "A Prologue to introduce the first Woman to come to Act on the Stage in Tragedy." This Desdemona may have been Mrs. Katherine Corey (?) who claimed to be "the first . . . of all the actresses that were established by King Charles the Second at His Restauration." Mrs. Hester Davenport (1642–?) was one of D'Avenant's first leading ladies, but she was quickly "by Force of love *erept* the Stage." [71]

Soon enough the two patentees moved into their newly built theaters. In June 1661, the younger actors started performing in a tennis court converted into the Lincoln's Inn Fields theater. There "D'Avenant, with his abiding interest in opera and scenery, set the model for the modern stage." His was framed by a proscenium arch with an apron that projected beyond it into the auditorium, and the scenery was "set" and "struck." The house capacity was an estimated 352 persons, "distributed as follows: pit, 100; King's box, 20; adjoining front boxes, 54; boxes in side walls, 48; gallery, assuming no partitions, 130." Then in early May 1663 Killigrew opened at the Theatre Royal, Drury Lane, the most famous of English theaters. The structure, measuring 58 feet by 112 feet, accommodated around 500 persons. Boxes cost 4s., pit 2s. 6d., middle gallery 1s. 6d., and upper gallery 1s.[72]

With this joint monopoly, of course, the actors discovered that their old right to set up and direct their own theatrical activities was abrogated. Now they were directed by company managers appointed by the King; now they were only paid employees (and sometimes sharers) at such-and-such a theater. And D'Avenant and Killigrew made sure that no one, especially actors, threatened their monopoly. In 1663 they shrewdly leased a theater license which had unaccountably been granted in 1660 to actor George Jolly (?), who had been feebly staging plays at the Cockpit, the Red Bull, and Salisbury Court. D'Avenant and Killigrew then "represented to the King that he [Jolly] had sold (not leased)" the license to them, and asked permission to erect a third theater to be used as a "nursery" or training school for young actors. After a long dispute Jolly was squashed and the license was revoked.[73]

But one can surmise that the actors were relatively content with their new lot. At least the theater had been re-established in England, they were performing again; and, as liveried servants of royalty, they were immune from arrest unless by warrant from the Lord Chamberlain. They eked things out artistically and financially. When D'Avenant died in 1668 while planning a magnificent new theater, his wife carried on the project and assigned the artistic management of the Duke's Men to Betterton and Henry Harris (?–c. 1682), an energetic, expert actor who had joined the company by 1661. The new theater, the Dorset Garden, designed by Christopher Wren (1631–1716), opened in November 1671. By 1674 some of the building sharers included Betterton, Harris, Nokes, Underhill, and William Smith (?–1696), a "judicious actor" hired in 1662.

In January 1672 Killigrew's Drury Lane was destroyed by fire, and the King's Men, in dire straits, seem to have performed at the Lincoln's Inn Fields while a new Drury Lane was being built. Also designed by Wren, with a capacity of 500, it opened in March 1674. "The stage now projected in a semi-oval right up to the front row of the pit, there were sidewings instead of boxes, and the whole action of the play took place beyond the proscenium pillars." There two years later, because Killigrew apparently proved to be a hopeless manager, actors Hart, Mohun, and Kynaston took active charge. And somewhere near this date they evidently instituted the practice of awarding the principal actors annual benefit performances.[74]

II

The almost sick feature of the English Restoration theater was its audience. Average citizens rarely attended plays; still dominated and dehydrated by Puritan doctrine, they stayed away from them as if from the plague. The audience therefore was largely an aristocratic one. Sponsored by the King and managed by courtiers, the playhouse became play-pens for gallants, their mistresses, and fashionable fops; plays were no more than the talk of animated dolls; and the actors, limited to performing in two barely paying theaters from 1660 to 1682, could hold the attention of the cream of society only by flamboyant oratory, mannered wit, and plain ribaldry.

At first, and for a few years, the theaters aimed for success with Elizabethan plays. D'Avenant produced Webster's *The Duchess of Malfi*, Middleton's *A Trick to Catch the Old One*, and maybe ten of Shakespeare's works. In 1661 at Lincoln's Inn Fields *Hamlet* was acted by Betterton; and D'Avenant "having seen Mr. Taylor of the Black-fryars Company Act it . . . taught Mr. Betterton in every Particle of it; which by his exact Performance . . . gain'd him Esteem and Reputation, Superlative to all other Plays." In 1662 Betterton was Mercutio, Harris Romeo, and Mary Saunderson (?–1712) Juliet; in 1663 Betterton was Sir Toby Belch in *Twelfth Night* and the King in *Henry VIII*, "being Instructed in it by Sir William [D'Avenant], who had it from Old Mr. Lowen, that had his Instructions from Mr. Shakespeare himself." Killigrew also offered plays by Shakespeare, Jonson, Beaumont and Fletcher, and other Elizabethan writers. His 1663 production of *Volpone* featured Mohun as Volpone and Hart as Mosca.[75]

One can easily guess, however, that most mid-seventeenth-century English playgoers, like many today, attended Elizabethan plays because it was thought to be the correct or cultural thing to do. They preferred, and soon got, easier entertainment. In 1664 John Dryden (1631–1700) in collaboration with Sir John Howard wrote *The Indian Queen*, an heroic, rhymed couplet concoction which was staged at Drury Lane and greatly admired for its elaborate scenery. Dryden followed that success next year with *The Indian Emperor* set in the same "rich scenes." The play "tells the story of the conquest of Mexico by stout Cortez (Hart), who is conquered by Cydaria (Nell Gwyn) (1650–1687). There are exciting complications, of course. For example, Montezuma (Mohun), a widower, sighs for wicked Almeria (Anne Marshall), who hates him and loves Cortez; Montezuma's two sons vie for the love of Almeria's sister, and Almeria's brother is contracted to Cydaria! [But] after much bloodshed all ends well with love triumphant and Cydaria and Cortez united." [76] Thereafter the two theaters competed with each other in producing more and more heroic plays in which the scenery almost outshouted the actors.

At about this time a new kind of comedy also took the stage: comedy "'Out of Jonson and Fletcher . . . , tempered by reminiscences of Molière, of the *commedia dell' arte* and of Calderón," but spiced by a passionless view of life. Dryden started things in 1667 by reworking *L'Etourdi* into *Sir Martin Mar-all, or The Feign'd Innocence* which, at Lincoln's Inn Fields with Nokes in the title role, proved to be one of the most popular attractions of the period. At the same theater in 1668 *The Sullen Lovers* by Thomas Shadwell (c. 1642–1692) and *She Would If She Could* by George Etherege (c. 1635–c. 1691) ushered in the comedy of manners. The brand "is realistic in that its setting is London and its characters types of that city's men and women, yet it is idealistic [or theatrical] in that the dramatist uses his skill to give its life a polish, a grace, and a turn of phrase which but rarely could have been met with in reality." Then in 1672 Shadwell's *Epson Wells*, a coarse comedy on cuckolding, was produced at the Dorset Garden; in 1675 at the Drury Lane Margery Pinchwife and the supposedly castrated Horner pranced about in *The Country Wife* by William Wycherley (c. 1640–1716); and the brittle parade was on. In 1676 Etherege's *The Man of Mode, or Sir Fopling Flutter*, "a play which has become, as it were, one of the very symbols of the comedy of manners," was staged at the Dorset Garden; and at the Drury Lane Wycherley's *The Plain Dealer* examined the effete society of London "with a withering scorn in place of cynical indifference or approval." [77]

Mostly audiences attended rough, lubricous farces decked out with "anything vulgar, scatological, or abnormal: physical deformities, beatings, . . . picturesque profanity, bawdy talk, . . . brothel scenes, topical references to famous bawds, homosexuality, flagellation, impotence, and veneral disease." Theatergoers especially enjoyed women's "Naked Necks and Shoulders," "Breasts hard and round" that panted "Hearts into an exstasy," and the shapely legs of actresses "in Boy's Clothes, or in Man's Clothes." They snickered and howled at bedroom scenes in which "an actress could appear in every variety of dress and undress, while an actor often came onstage 'unbraced' or 'unbuttoned' after a bedding, or [like Blunt in Mrs. Aphra Behn's (1640–1689) *The Rover* at the Dorset Garden in 1677] stimulated the audience's libido by undressing in his mistress's bedroom and stealing, 'in his Shirt and Drawers,' toward the bed where she lay asleep." [78]

Some relief from these adolescent—as well as artificial—sexed-up comedies was found in the simple *Scaramouch a Philosopher; Harlequin a School-Boy, Bravo, Merchant and Magician; a Comedy after the Italian Manner* by Edward Ravenscroft (fl. 1671–1697) which was presented in 1677 at the Drury Lane; by Dryden's *All For Love, or The World Well Lost*, an Antony and Cleopatra story, offered at the same theater in the same year; and by the powerful, almost great *Venice Preserved*, written by a disappointed actor, Thomas Otway (1652–1685), and staged at the Dorset Garden in 1682. Betterton acted Jaffier, William Smith Pierre, and Elizabeth Barry (1658–1713) Belvidera.

III

This "revival of the theaters saw the growth and development of a most notable [or at least hard-working] body of English actors." With some exceptions, of course, they were "a drinking, quarreling, swaggering, wenching crew, living hand-to-mouth" who practiced their profession for probably thirty to thirty-five weeks out of a year. For six days a week—Sundays excluded—they "labored mightily, rehearsing nearly every morning, playing every afternoon, and sometimes performing in the Court Theatre at Whitehall at night. In their spare time they studied their parts"; and the line studying was endless "Since revived plays were seldom kept on the boards for more than two or three days, and even a successful new play was lucky to have a run of three to six days"; and since "Once a part was given to a player he was expected to be ready with it at every subsequent revival, no matter how long the interval between performances." [79]

At least eight players with Killigrew's King's Men won either fame or notoriety before 1682. Hart shone as the gay gentleman of comedies, and in tragedies "might teach any king on earth how to comport himself." His "action," it was said, "could throw a luster round the meanest characters, and, by dazzling the eyes of the spectator, protect the poet's deformities from discernment." Hart most successfully impersonated characters like Massinissa in *Sophonisba* (1675) by Nathaniel Lee (*c.* 1653–1692), Caesario in *Gloriana* (1676), and Alexander in *The Rival Queens* (1677), by the same playwright; and "if he acted in any of these but once in a fortnight, the house was filled as at a new play." Hart in due time "possessed a considerable share in the profits and direction of the theater, which were divided among the principal performers"; and with "his salary of £3 a week, and an allowance as a proprietor, amounting to six shillings and three-pence a day . . . ," he earned "about £146 a year—or, in terms of today's purchasing power, roughly $3,000." And if, as it was said, Hart succeeded by "his natural and proper force," his colleague star Mohun succeeded by "his great skill and art." Trained by Beeston, he was praised for his "superlative knowledge of his profession" and especially for "the sublimity of his elocution." Mohun was evidently first-rate as Hannibal in *Sophonisba* and as Augustus Caesar in *Gloriana*; and he created the title role in Lee's *Mithridates* (1678) with "spirit and passion." Lacy, the top comedian of the company, "excelled in 'humours' of various kinds," and notably acted Falstaff. Kynaston in the first years of a stage career that stretched from *c.* 1658 to 1698 was "a Compleat Female Stage Beauty" and so expert in his impersonations "that it has since been disputable among the judicious, whether any woman that succeeded him so sensibly touch'd the audiences as he." Later, as various handsome heroes "he had a fierce, lion-like majesty in his port and utterance, that gave the spectator a kind of trembling admiration." [80]

Anne Marshall (?) was the leading lady at the Drury Lane from *c.* 1661 to 1677. Although she created Dryden's *The Indian Queen*, Almeria in his *The Indian Emperor*, Berenice in his *Tyrannick Love* (1669), Nourmahal in his *Aureng-Zebe* (1675), and then Lee's *Gloriana* and the Roxanna in his *The Rival Queens*, nothing much is known about her histrionic abilities. Nor is anything known about the skills of Mrs. ("Mistress") Corey who mostly acted second leads for thirty-two years until 1692. Mary Knep (?) was from *c.* 1665 to 1678 a "merry jade" so delectable onstage "in her night-gowne . . . , her bare face, and hair only tied up in a knot behind." Notorious Nell Gwyn, dotingly coached by Hart, was the most popular of the early comediennes. After a Drury Lane debut in 1665, her teasing charm and vivacity won her in the next season a first important role opposite Hart in a revival of Fletcher's *The Humourous Lieutenant*, a comedy about the efforts of a king to seduce his son's low-born sweetheart, which had opened the theater in 1663. Then in March 1667 she reached the top of her profession as Florimel who captures, with a jig and in breeches, Celadon (Hart) in Dryden's *Secret Love*. Two months later as Mirida who loves mad Philidor (Hart) in James Howard's *All Mistaken* she danced another jig. In November, again opposite Hart, in Beaumont and Fletcher's *Philaster* she wore breeches as Belario. Then, after other roles, she recited in 1669 the epilogue to *Tyrannick Love* and so captivated Charles II that he "went behind the scenes and carried her off to an entertainment that night." By 1770-71 she crowned her gay career in the unsuitable role of Almahide, with Hart as Almanzor, in Dryden's vast *The Conquest of Granada*. After that Nell Gwyn "left the stage for good. King Charles was not a sensitive man, and certainly he was not niggardly with his mistresses, but no one enjoys questioning glances, lifted eyebrows, and sly allusions. It was incredible that the mother of a royal bastard would return to the stage—actually work for a living—of her own accord!" [81]

Betterton of the Duke's Men was the outstanding actor of the period. In addition to Hamlet and King Henry VIII he admirably interpreted Brutus, Hotspur, Lear, Othello, Pericles, Timon, and Troilus. He also portrayed any number of "those interminable heroic generals who abound in . . . Restoration melodrama." Moreover, he "was evidently equally good not only in a roistering Falstaff, but in gay, light-o-love flirters. . . ." In acting all these widely different characters no one, it was claimed, equalled Betterton in "harmonious elocution." When a playwright's poetry came from his mouth "the multitude no more desired sense . . . than . . . musical connoisseurs think it essential in the celebrated airs of an Italian opera." "A further excellence in Betterton was, that he could vary his spirit to the different characters he acted. Those wild impatient starts, that fierce and flashing fire, which he threw into Hotspur, never came from the unruffled temper of his Brutus. . . ." For these talents and skills Betterton wasn't overpaid. In 1691 when he gave up his shares to the patentees, he agreed to act for £5 a week and an annual present of 50 guineas to help him through the summer. His wife was getting 50s. a week, and he was paid other sums for various duties, besides living rent free over the theater. In 1692 the Bettertons' total income for each acting week was estimated at £16, or (assuming thirty acting weeks to the year) £480—roughly equal to an annual $10,000 in 1958. [82]

Nine additional players with the Duke's Men achieved prominence before 1682. Harris ranked next to Betterton and "appears to have taken those parts which demanded pathos and amorous passion more than heroism or witty dalliance." He was a highly successful Romeo, Cardinal Wolsey, Aguecheek, and an energetic leading man in a horde of new plays. Nokes, Underhill, and Anthony Leigh (?-1692) were the company's comics. The first, "natural" and inimitable, could "sink into such a mixture of piteous pusillanimity, and a consternation so ruefully ridiculous and inconsolable, that when he had shaken you to a fatigue of laughter, it became a moot point, whether you ought not to have pitied him." He reached his highest peak of popularity as Sir Martin Mar-all. Underhill, "the most lumpish, moping mortal, that ever made beholders merry," acted boobies and won fame as Obadiah in Sir Robert Howard's *The Committee* (1662) and as the First Gravedigger in *Hamlet*. Leigh was a more mercurial comic who "had many masterly variations . . . particularly in the dotage and follies of extreme old age . . . and the toothless lawyer. . . ." Smith, popular and polished, was one of the stalwarts of the company, as was Samuel Sandford (fl. 1660–1699), "an excellent actor in disagreeable characters," who had "a peculiar skill in his look of marking out to an audience whatever he judged worth their more than ordinary notice"; and "In Dryden's plays of rhyme, he as little as possible glutted the ear with the jingle of it, rather choosing, when the sense would permit him, to lose it rather than to value it." [83]

Mary Saunderson, who married Betterton in 1662, shone for thirty years as a leading lady, the first woman to act Ophelia, Juliet, Miranda, and a thrilling Lady Macbeth. "The towering figures of tragedy were hers, and so were the gay rattling puppets of light comedy. . . . She even played Greek tragedy, being very successful as Jocasta in *Oedipus*. . . . She sang in Opera with distinction—her Ianthe (in *The Siege of Rhodes*) enchanted them all —and she could also dance divinely. . . ." She truly had every claim to be considered the first leading English actress. Elizabeth Barry, "the famous she tragedian," was the next outstanding English actress. At first, taught by D'Avenant, she was discharged from the company as untalented. But in 1675 she was seventeen and determined; and her next teacher, the Earl of Rochester (1647?–1698), made an actress of her in six months. "He instructed her in parts, taking her through line by line and impressing on her what the author meant by the words she was saying." He "took her, slowly and carefully, through the leading parts in several plays until she understood them all and could play them. Then he arranged an engagement for her. Leaving nothing to chance, he made her give thirty rehearsals of each character, twelve of which were done in costume. At length she made her debut as his pupil. She played Isabella, Queen of Hungary, in *Mustapha*. . . . Elizabeth showed herself a sound, efficient actress, with complete mastery of her art, but no more than this. She got applause, she pleased, but she did not excite. Rochester worked on, fanning the flame he knew was there, until, one evening, he was sure. She played Isabella again. The flame burst forth. Her talent, her art, suddenly flared up. She swept the audience with her and electrified the other players. At the end she was acclaimed. . . . Mistress Barry had triumphed." When she was twenty-two in 1680, after having been onstage for five years, she became a full-fledged leading lady as Monimia in Otway's *The Orphan* opposite Betterton. She went on to create an estimated one hundred and nineteen roles in the next thirty years, "her mien and motion superb, and gracefully majestic; her voice full, clear, and strong, so that no violence of passion could be too much for her; and when distress or tenderness possessed her, she subsided into the most affecting melody and softness." Anne Bracegirdle (1663?–1748) at the age of ten was a boy page who held up Elizabeth Barry's train in *Mustapha*. Then, after studying under Betterton, she became in about 1690 "the darling of the theater; for . . . scarce an audience saw her that were less than half of them lovers, without a suspected favorite among them: and though she might be said to have been the universal passion, and under the highest temptations, her constancy in resisting them served but to increase the number of her admirers." Mrs. Bracegirdle was thus more than an outstanding actress: she gave the lie to the general conviction that "actress" and "whore" were synonymous.[84]

During the Restoration "A good, experienced actor was usually paid about 50s. a week. Generally, women were paid less than men. If a young actress made good, she was put on the payroll at 10s. to 15s. a week—very little more than ten to fifteen dollars today. As late as 1694 the popular Katherine Corey, after many years in the theater, was getting only 30s. a week. At about the same time Elinor Leigh (c. 1650–c. 1710), after the death of her husband, comedian Anthony Leigh, was raised from 20s. a week to 30s. . . . ; even the great Elizabeth Barry had only 50s. a week plus a guaranteed £70 a year from a benefit performance."[85]

IV

In 1682, when the King's company under Killigrew's sons had fallen into a wretched state and the Drury Lane had finally closed, the Duke's company under D'Avenant's sons at the Dorset Garden initiated the amalgamation of the two troupes of actors. With Betterton, who for more than forty years "had dignified the actor's art" as chief, and "indisputably the master of the theatrical world," the joint company in mid-November opened at the Drury Lane. But the theater didn't prosper: the times were unsettled; Charles II died in 1685 and was succeeded by Catholic James II; the actors constantly fought with the management; and, almost significantly, they performed in 1688 *The Squire of Alsatia* in which Shadwell turned from the upper-class life of the times and depicted the middle-class citizens, thieves, and rascals of London. Then when William and Mary came to the throne in 1689 "the old intimacy between Court and stage was gone."[86]

In 1690 nineteen-year-old Colley Cibber (1671–1757) joined the Drury Lane company when the principal actors were "*Of Men,*—Mr. Betterton, Mr. [William] Mountfort (1664–1692), Mr. Kynaston, Mr. Sandford, Mr. Nokes, Mr. Underhill, and Mr. Leigh; *Of Women,*—Mrs. Betterton, Mrs. Barry, Mrs. Leigh, Mrs. [Charlotte] Butler (?), Mrs. [Susanna] Mountfort (1667–1703), and Mrs. Bracegirdle." He found them to be "all original masters in their different styles, not merely auricular imitators of one another, . . . but self judges of nature, from whose various lights they only took their true instruction." They "had not their equals, at any one time, upon any theater in Europe . . . ; no stage, at any one period, could show thirteen actors, standing all in equal lights of excellence, in their profession. . . ." [87]

But in the same year "an old snarling Lawyer . . . a waspish, ignorant pettifogger," Christopher Rich (?–1714), bought the theater patent, got complete control of the Drury Lane by 1693, and determined to make a profit for himself at the expense of the actors—including newcomers Thomas Wilks (1665–1732) and Thomas Doggett (c. 1670–1721). He soon offended Betterton by assigning the best roles to George Powell (1669–1714), a good actor who for only £2 a week, and that not regularly, "came upon the stage sometimes warm with Nanz brandy." [88]

Betterton eventually led a revolt and presented the actors' grievances to William III, who thereupon issued a license permitting the dissenters to break away from Drury Lane and to set up their own company at the Lincoln's Inn Fields. They opened on the last day of April 1695 in *Love for Love* by William Congreve (1670–1729) with Betterton as Valentine, Mrs. Bracegirdle as Angelica, Doggett as Ben, Underhill as Sir Sampson Legend, Smith as Scandal, Sandford as Foresight, and Mrs. Barry as Mrs. Frail. Thus the actors asserted themselves and proceeded during the final five years of the century to give Rich a thorough drubbing.

Changes, however, were in the offing: "a new theatrical world was in process of formation," a world "marked by the substituting of an upperclass morality for the moral code of the aristocrats." [89] In January 1696 Cibber's *Love's Last Shift, or The Fool in Fashion*, ushered in sentimental comedy. John Vanbrugh (1664–1726) coarsely and vainly parodied it in *The Relapse* (1696); and Congreve, finishing a sparkling *The Way of the World* in 1699, would discover that its artificial glitter and wit were tardy. Audiences wanted plays that were closer to their own lives, plays that were clean and simple and rosy true.

❧ ACTING IS DECLAMATION

Since no seventeenth-century book specifically examined the craft or art of acting at long last accepted in Europe as a relatively respectable human activity, we can only conjecture from scattered evidence—mostly English and French—what it was the professional actors of that hundred-year period did onstage. In general, it seems, they orated. They added some miming, some instinctive and energetic impersonation, and then very nearly like speakers in pulpits, behind rostrums, or in courts they declaimed the playwright's lines. In short, as in Cicero's time, acting in its essentials was quite similar to public speaking. Its basic elements were "an ordered voice and . . . [an] excellence of gesture." Acting was defined, for instance, as "either a certain visible eloquence or an eloquence of the body, or a comely grace in delivering conceits, or an external image of an internal mind." [90]

The speaking and the gesturing, however, weren't realistic. Characterizations weren't achieved by "naturalistic imitation," but by "a studied decorum." To act "naturally" meant to adhere "strictly to the rhetorical style." Realistic utterance and motion were deliberately rejected. Acting was "unnatural" whenever it was "so completely natural as to have its awkwardness quite unredeemed by the refinement of art." In other words, seventeenth-century acting was rarely a copying of normal human behavior; it was a conscious and studied alteration of behavior into art, since "Art . . . perfects Nature, makes her actions more dilucid, illustrious and sweet. . . ." [91] Consequently, the actor's onstage delivery in tragedies—and less carefully in comedies—was rearranged, heightened, designed; and his gestures were likewise formalized. In his nonimitative speaking and gesturing, in his elocution (a new word in this century), the Western actor a wee bit resembled the Chinese and Japanese actor who (to music) employed unrealistic, traditional, formal conventions, both oral and visual, in his performances. The Oriental and the Westerner alike sensed that somehow there ought to be some difference between life and art.

Actually, of course, the formal, oratoric acting of seventeenth-century Europe was derived from ancient Western times. In tragedies it resembled the unreal, stylized, formal reciting of the Greeks. And sometimes as you try to reconstruct out of the mists the two styles of acting they appear to have been similar. So, you say that they were, and let it go at that. Anyway, perhaps we can best, or at least more specifically, examine the first acting in the plays of Shakespeare, Molière, Racine, and Etherege—and by extension the acting in contemporary Italian and Spanish plays—by keeping in mind the four purely theoretic Greek fundamentals: (1) an expressive voice; (2) a vivid imagination; (3) an ability to characterize by the use of actions, motives, and surrounding circumstances; and (4) a sense of the play as a whole—plus two additional fundamentals emphasized by the Romans: (5) an expressive body; and (6) an awareness (especially in comedy) of the audience.

II

The Elizabethan actor performed in an intimate theater. At the unroofed Globe, for a typical instance, his platform was surrounded on three sides by spectators, and at rear stage he was apparently no more than eighty-five feet from the farthest of them. But a capacity audience numbered slightly more than two thousand, of which from seven to eight hundred were "groundlings" who paid a penny to stand in the yard. And very probably they outweighed the judicious. "Your Carman and Tinker," wrote Dekker in 1609, "claime as strong a voice in their suffrage, and sit to giue judgement on the plaies life and death, as well as the prowdest Momus among the tribe of Critick." Consequently, a primitive, loud, and bold rhetorical delivery was needed to sustain a play; "force and simplicity were cardinal virtues" for performing before a partly uncouth, mostly non-reading public. And when the actors moved to the confined quiet of a "private" theater, like the Blackfriars, many of them may not have shouted so much, and some of them may have developed new delicacies of expression, but still they clung to a rhetorical delivery in addressing a cultured audience which had been thoroughly taught in schools that eloquence is "the active part of learning, poetry the summit of eloquence." [92]

An Elizabethan company of twelve, with six or more hired men, in addition to boys (and much doubling), often presented as many as forty different plays a season, a good half of which were new (and required three weeks of rehearsing), so that a leading actor must have exhibited at least thirty roles a year. Sometimes he might appear in a different play on each of eleven successive nights! Then, for sure, like a modern stock actor, he never had time to theorize, to discuss interpretations, to experiment, to hunt for subtleties, to polish and perfect. He simply learned his lines, came onstage, and declaimed them. Such acting, of course, as someone said, may have been only "a kind of mechanical labour, yet well done 'tis worthy of praise." [93]

Therefore, the actor-sharers in charge of production, being practical businessmen instead of sophisticated arguers about the intricacies of acting, taught their apprentices not much more than the simple rudiments of rhetorical delivery. The boys, starting at the age of about ten, probably paid a premium, as all trade apprentices did, were attached one or two to a sharer, and learned how to read female roles and also, perhaps, the sharer's own particular specialty. Newcomers would serve as walk-ons or recite bit parts; the twelve-to-fourteen-year-olds would declaim secondary parts; and the fifteen-to-eighteen-year-olds would "orate" leading ladies as long as their voices and physical appearances allowed. All of them no doubt were commanded, first, to enunciate clearly, to speak briskly, and to project. Next, they were coached to acquire a pronunciation "musicall and plausive," or to speak musically by varying the voice and by feeling or at least hammering out the meter of the playwright's lines, and to speak meaningfully by observing "comma's, colons, & full poynts, . . . parentheses, . . . breathing spaces, and distinctions . . . ," and by illustrating them often with gestures. Finally, they were told "to utter euery dialogue liuely, as if they themselues were the persons which did speake in that dialogue, & so in euery other speech, to imagine themselues to haue occasion to utter the very same things." Trained thus, young boys could act successfully enough important female roles. Characters were created almost automatically since they were there in the words, the play fell into shape, and its quality and point, not always subtly, were communicated.[94]

The adult professional Elizabethan and later actors believed in the paramount potency of the human voice. They agreed with educators of their time, who had it variously from Cicero who had it from the Greeks, that acting, like rhetoric, was "the sweet framing of the voice," a skill in or "an

Arte" of "comely deliverie, whereby to work on mens affections." It was a "Garnishing of the maner of utterance" or a change "from the more simple and plaine maner of speaking"—just as poetry is a change from the ordinary usage of words—"unto that whiche is more full of excellencie and grace." Onstage, therefore, the voices of the actors differed considerably from the everyday, informal, conversational voices of Englishmen. They were enlarged, better modulated, more expressive. Actors achieved persuasiveness and delightfulness "only by transcending the speech patterns of ordinary daily converse." Like the Greeks they made their voices musical. An excellent actor was likened to "an excellent singer, who knows all his Graces, and can artfully vary and modulate his Voice, even to know how much breath he is to give to every syllable." And he rarely lapsed "into an *imitated* spontaneity, so to forfeit all the aids of form and accepted convention." [95]

Yet, "speaking finelie" wasn't enough. After all, words voiced with anger could be augmented by brows gathered into a menacing frown, the teeth clenched, the right fist closed and shaken, the feet stamped. That was the conventional emotion of anger audiences could quickly see and get, and no doubt about it. So, actors knew that acting, again like rhetoric, "hath two parts, *Voyce* and *Gesture* [bodily motion], the one pertaining to the eare, the other belonging to the eye." And "The gesture must folowe the change and varietie of the voyce, answering thereunto in euerie respect. . . ." Beautiful speaking "without a comely and elegant gesture, [which included] a gratious and bewiching kinde of action, a naturall and familiar motion of the head, the hand, the body, and a moderate and fit countenance," just wasn't acting. And "in the substance of [this] externall action, for the most part orators and stageplayers" agreed. They seem to have agreed most importantly in the emphasis they placed, as Quintilian had done, on the use of the arm, hand, and fingers in delivery. For example, John Bulwer (fl. 1644–1654) in his *Chirologia: or, the natural language of the hand* and *Chironomia: or, the art of manuall rhetorique*, which appeared together in 1644 just after the closing of the theaters, asserted that "the moving and significant extension of the *Hand* is . . . absolutely pertinent to speech. . . ." It "is fitted to distinguish the Comma's & breathing parts of a sentence." It can "explaine, direct, enforce, apply, apparell, & . . . beautifie the words men utter. . . ." So, the actors added gesture (in the narrower sense) to their declamations. They "sawed the air." But again, since art somehow had to differ from nature, the gestures weren't natural, everyday things. For platform acting as for platform speaking Bulwer suggested that the ordinary motions of the hand, "the usual gestures of Nature," should be reduced "into strict rules of Art, . . . making them more formall." And, like Quintilian, Bulwer dangerously classified and standardized gestures. *Chirologia*, which centers on the expression of the emotions, is divided into two sections: the first names and describes sixty-four hand gestures, forty-eight of which are illustrated; the second adds twenty-four finger gestures with twenty-four illustrations. *Chironomia*, which deals mainly with elocution, is divided into three sections: the first contains fifty-nine hand gestures with twenty-four illustrations; the second describes twenty-six "Canons of the Fingers" with again twenty-four illustrations; and the third is made up of warnings against "solecisms" in the use of the hand.[96]

Thus by what they thought was an artistic use of "pronunciation and gesture" fit for every word, figure or trope, sentence, aria, or emotion seventeenth-century English actors communicated to audiences a vivid experiencing of the words as words. And thus "Whatsoeuer is commendable in the grave Orator, is most exquisitely perfect in" an excellent actor (like Burbage); "for by a full and significant action of body, he charmes our attention. . . . He adds grace to the Poets labours. . . ."[97]

Problems of characterization, however, particularly those encountered by actors today, were almost nonexistent for seventeenth-century actors. Although someone, perhaps Burbage, was described as "transforming himself into his Part, and putting off himself with his Cloathes . . . until the Play was done,"[98] the praise seems to be only wishful thinking. We can almost be sure that an actor only in an instinctive but very lively way pretended to be a fictitious person onstage, perhaps only in the way a child playing a game makes-believe he's someone else. Probably he was mostly himself as he recited the lines in the various fictitious situations of a play. Probably he imagined the situations better than he imagined the character. Certainly he knew little and cared less about the actions, motives, and surrounding circumstances which had been discussed long, long before his time by Aristotle, Cicero, and Quintilian.

After all, the Elizabethan actor didn't need to know a great deal about "creating" a character. In the plays he acted, "Character is presented not for its own sake, in the interest of strict verisimilitude or internal consistency, but in the higher or more urgent one of tragic or comic effect. It is treated poetically rather than psychologically or logically." Actions and motives and circumstances, credibility or probability, counted "for less than contrasts and parallels, developments and climaxes, tempo and rhythm. . . ." Shakespeare's characters, for instance, "are situated *outside* all realism, that is to say beyond the psychological determination governed by the chain of normal cause and effect . . . , [and] we are not allowed to dispute or assess the motives of . . . behavior. . . . What motivates the action . . . is . . . an immediate, fundamental idea." The characters "are simplifications of the actual . . . are, as it were, abstracted from humanity, yet functionally related to it." They are "forms roughly correspondent with actuality" and "ultimately not human at all, but purely symbols of a poetic vision."[99]

Characters like that, of course, can sometimes in some areas be enriched, although more often they are nearly ruined, by modern methods of acting. But in the seventeenth century it was "the actor's job [only] to represent, to suggest . . . not to imitate a real person. . . ." He performed "without so much regard to a supposed inner logic of character as to the blatant outer logic of stage effects." What if for a while he talked with other characters in the play, and then later directly addressed the audience, confiding to them his intentions or his feelings toward other characters or toward the world or fate? What if, several times, he suddenly latched onto the play's idea, its general theme, moral or political, and expounded at length about that, or at another time suddenly talked about himself, his role, like someone who knew all the time he was only acting? [100] It worked. It worked in the theater.

The actor of sensibility found the individuality of his character "near the surface—in traits, not motives, in tone and manner rather than a consistent point of view." He found his more or less simple, almost type character reacting in a certain way in certain given situations, and he reacted in like fashion, speaking accordingly, without worrying about what or who (except the author) had brought about those situations. He could in any one play "pass from cruelty to pity, . . . from loyalty to treason, from love to hate and hate to love . . . gratuitously." He recited whatever was "in the lines (not between them or in some fanciful hypothesis erected on them)." He felt his character less as an individualized person "with his own psychological integrity than as an abstraction. . . ." He was aware "of the dialogue in terms of music; of the tune and rhythm of it as at one with the sense—sometimes outbidding the sense—in telling him what to do, and how to do it, in telling him, indeed, what to *be*." For example, Shakespeare in the pattern of his words gave the actor "all the material for . . . the complete and complex Antony, impulsive, and calculating, warm-hearted and callous, aristocrat, sportsman and demagogue." And Desdemona in another play is trusting; so the boy actor acted that. Othello is noble and then he is suspicious; so, the actor acted the one and then the other, and that was that.[101]

The point of all this is: the mind of the seventeenth-century actor had not "been warped by the naive incredulity of scientific naturalism." The actor playing Leontes in *The Winter's Tale*, for instance, did not hunt and hunt in vain for that character's motivation for his jealous actions; Leontes was jealous; what else did the actor need to know? The boy acting Lady Macbeth thought it unnecessary, even silly, to ask "Did she really have children, and if so how many?" The actors impersonating Cleopatra and Othello never went out of their minds in attempts to make the actions of these characters logically consistent. The actor of Falstaff didn't have to work out and discuss endlessly the character's "offstage activities, the fugitive and unexpressed impulses of his mind, the influences to which he would be exposed in boyhood as page to Thomas Mowbray, his lineage as it may be conjectured from scattered hints in the drama—inferring a priori likelihood of his courage from 'the circumstances and conditions of his whole life and character.' " Nor did the actor of Prince Hal discover in that character's development "the classic struggle of the ego to come to normal adjustment, beginning with the rebellion against his father, going on to the conquest of his superego . . . , then to the conquest of the *id* . . . , then to the identification with the father . . . and the assumption of mature responsibility." [102]

A pox on all that! When the Elizabethan actor took stage as this or that character all he knew, in most instances, was that what his character said was "more important than why it should be said," that the poetry would "float the character over the reefs of improbability," that "the audience would follow the dialogue as poetry, and not merely as the speech of a given character." [103]

Three hundred years ago the English actor's prime job wasn't to characterize but to communicate to an audience the *literary quality* of a playwright's lines. Unlike his contemporary *commedia dell' arte* players he respected words. He loved them. He delighted in the stunning ways in which writers strung them together, combined them, made them shine and soar. He seemed onstage, therefore, to be telling audiences: "The words used by my character were composed by a rather special person, a clever man, a wordsmith—and not by me, or by you, or by any other ordinary person. They are perfected talk, the like of which you and yours have never uttered and will never hear in life. They make the lovely magic of poetry. And I'll try to capture for you its tingling excellence."

In thus serving first the claims of language, the boy acting Lady Anne, for instance, never tried to "justify" her yielding to the twisted villain in Act I, scene ii of *Richard III*; he tried mostly to participate brilliantly in the "verbal fencing," in "the rhetoric of hatred, or invective and cynicism" of the scene. In Act I, scene v of *Romeo and Juliet*, when the lovers first meet and kiss, the actors never attempted to imitate dialogue characteristically or realistically; instead they aimed with a smidgeon of impersonation to convey to the audience "the figures, the images, and the metrical pattern" of a gracious and restrained sonnet wherein Shakespeare had refined "the essential meaning which the lovers' relationship expressed for him." And in Act IV, scene vii of *Hamlet* the boy Queen Gertrude reporting Ophelia's death never fussed and fumed and foolishly tried to fit the willow speech with some sort of consistency and believability into the rest of his performance. No. He recognized the speech as "a sort of cadenza," took the stage, and recited it nonrealistically, in the grand manner.[104]

In preparing his impersonation the actor carefully examined "the diction of the writer; noting any conspicuous elegance, or . . . novel usage . . . ; bringing out anything . . . involved or obscure in the phrases or sentence-forms; marking, where necessary, . . . metaphors and other rhetorical artifices. . . ." He looked for "Parallel passages . . . , similarities and contrasts in treatments. . . ." In addition, he especially concentrated on "Emphasis, which is the elevation of some word or words in the sentence, wherein the chief force lies." Then, knowing the sense of his lines and centering on key- or operative-words, and fully aware of the author's artifices, he rapped out his verses artfully and rhythmically—and quickly so as to keep them alive and going.[105]

He also delivered his speeches with much feeling since "Cicero expressly teacheth that it is almost impossible for an oratour to stirre up a passion in his auditors, except he be first affected with the same passion himselfe." The actor in a general, instinctive way let the emotion in the lines, often amplified into arias, take possession of him and come out at the audience. We can be relatively sure that he spoke in a raised voice with "a rush and impulse of feeling, as if the lines were speaking themselves," rarely pausing under the pretext of thinking them out (although that today might make him seem more intelligent and natural) lest the character come across as ornate and stupid. But we can doubt that the emotion the actor felt was the imagined emotion of an actual person in a real situation. Because he centered so much of his attention on words that recorded the *writer's* reaction, *his feelings*, toward a character in a situation, the actor in performing may have conveyed mostly the playwright's contagious emotion.[106]

With this kind of acting—a branch of rhetoric, an art of persuading an audience to appreciate the skill and quality of the playwright—the English actors of the first half of the seventeenth century were perhaps in only one respect unloyal to him. We can guess that they acted without a knowledge of, a feeling for, the "organic structure of the whole play." For instance, a Frenchman observed that "they look . . . only at one part of it after another [one scene, one speech or aria] without concerning themselves about the whole" (*san se soucier du total*). The actors, minus much direction, knew nothing about, even in synonyms, a "super-objective." But if they failed to fully understand a play, they could act it (which isn't as modern as actors who understand a play but cannot act it). They were experts at making individual histrionic effects "without regard being paid to their consistency with one another and the whole in combination." They could take the longer speeches especially and make of them stunning, though independent, displays of rhetorical delivery. They turned their voices "into the assembly for applause-sake, like a trumpeter in the fields, that shifts places to get an eccho," and they got it, got it with an expert, beautiful, amazing elocution. We can suppose, it's agreed, that their mere speaking "was a very brilliant thing, comparable to *bel canto*, or to a pianist's virtuosity." [107]

III

Acting in seventeenth-century France was also largely oratory, a branch of rhetoric, a more or less formal kind of reciting, in theaters that were neither as large as the English ones nor as well attended. At the Hôtel de Bourgogne, for instance, the actors on a stage six feet high, with less than a twenty-five-foot opening, weren't much more than fifty feet from the rear of the auditorium where possibly 1,200 patrons were distributed in a pit, two tiers of loges along the sides and rear of the house, and a third-level gallery called the *Paradis*. Molière's Palais-Royal, similar in design, accommodated an audience of between 1,100 and 1,400. Yet when the company was at the height of its popularity during the 1772–73 season it offered three performances a week for a season total of 131 and an average daily attendance of only 400. The

Théâtre de Guénégaud had a capacity of somewhere around 1,200, yet the Comédie-Française for the season of 1682–83 drew only an average house of 426 people for each of its 352 performances. At the new 1689 Théâtre-Français the actors on the stage apron, which projected twelve feet beyond the proscenium arch, were no more than fifty-nine feet from the farthest first-floor spectator. Their acting area—no wider than fifteen feet at the front—was railed off by balustrades against five rows of benches on either side of the apron for stage spectators. Next to the stage the orchestra, center, was reserved for the musicians, but about fifty patrons were seated on each side of them. Back of this orchestra was the traditional standing pit (*parterre*) for about 600 persons who "In their most complete repose . . . never cease talking, hissing, and shouting"; and back of the pit was the *amphithéâtre*, seven rows of benches on graduated steps. Two tiers of boxes extended along the sides and rear of the auditorium, each tier with nineteen boxes, eight persons to a box. A third or top gallery was open and furnished with benches. To the 100 people in the orchestra, the 600 in the pit, and the 304 in the boxes, add for the stage, the *amphithéâtre*, and the top gallery 300 more, and the theater's capacity totaled about 1,300. Yet even a phenomenal success like Florent-Carton Dancourt's (1661–1725) *Les Vendanges de Suresnes* in 1694 attracted only 33,000 patrons at forty-nine performances, or a half-house average of 674.[108]

At these theaters the actors, who insisted that they could "foretell the success or failure of a play better than all the authors and critics together," judged scripts submitted to them, cast them, and could with effort memorize a full-length one in eight days. They looked, it seems, for poets who would "excel in the Art of Rhetorick," who had studied "Oratory and Eloquence to the bottom" in order "to know all the passions, the springs that bring them on, and the way of expressing them with Order, Energy, and Judgment." They favored writers who could "transport . . . Actors into extraordinary and violent Sentiments, by which the Spectators are ravish'd." Their acting, therefore, was "an art of speaking well and elegantly, different and remote from the ways that are ordinary and natural." It was, more broadly, like English acting of the period, the oral and visual projection of the author's style to an audience.[109]

Performances of French plays were very nearly "recitals." Those by Corneille, we can conjecture, "had the character of a rather grandiose recitation," and it was almost "obligatory in the actors to stand in a rigid row and declaim their lines, each character listening in turn with silent attention to the rest." And in Racine's *Phèdre* the Queen has at least nine arias, speeches of twenty or more lines; Hippolytus has seven, Theseus and Theramenes three, Oenone two, and Aricia one. No wonder Dryden complained of the French that "their actors speak by the hour-glass, as our parsons do; nay, they account it the grace of their parts, and think themselves disparaged by the poet, if they may not twice or thrice in a play entertain the audience with a speech of an hundred or two hundred lines." But a later Englishman,

Somerset Maugham, reported that "Racine knew as few have how much drama is contained in the human voice. To me at all events," he explained, "the roll of those mellifluous Alexandrines is a sufficient substitute for action, and I find the long speeches, working up with infinite skill to the expected climax, every bit as thrilling as any hair-raising adventure of the movies." Another person, he wrote, "would have liked it to be more natural, the lines spoken as people naturally speak and the gestures less theatrical. I thought . . . [this] point of view mistaken. It was rhetoric, magnificent rhetoric, and I had a notion that it should be spoken rhetorically. I liked the regular thump of the rhymes; and the stylized gestures, handed down in a long tradition, seemed to me to suit the temper of that formal art." Maugham admired the way in which the actors contrived to be human, passionate, and true within the limitations that confined them, and concluded by observing that "Art is triumphant when it can use convention as an instrument of its own purpose." [110]

The need of a trained, expressive voice for the French orator—and perhaps by extension the actor—was notably stressed in "one of the most remarkable works of scholarship in the whole elocutionary movement and one of the finest treatises on delivery in the history of rhetorical theory," the *Traitté de l'action de l'orateur, ou de la Prononciation et du geste* (Paris, 1657) written by Protestant preacher Michel Le Faucheur (?–1657). His name, however, is nowhere attached to the book, which was seen through the press shortly after his death by Valentin Conrart (1603–1675), the first perpetual secretary of the French Academy. Le Faucheur makes action, "which consists of *Speaking* and *Gesture*," the subject of his treatise. He devotes the first three chapters to some general considerations of the topic; then "he turns to speaking or using the voice, and for the next eight chapters he successively analyzes the problems of being heard without difficulty, of being heard with delight, and of varying the voice in respect to the different kinds of subjects, to the different passions, to the different parts of the classical oration, to the various important figures of rhetoric, and to the different kinds of sentences and words." Chapters 12 and 13 examine gesture; and the final chapter discusses the application of the preceding precepts to a speaker's actual practice. "Throughout the entire treatise, Le Faucheur keeps ancient illustrations and ancient doctrine continuously before his reader's eyes, except for the mention of a few modern parallels. Thus Demosthenes, Cicero, Quintilian, and St. Augustine provide examples of difficulties to be overcome, or their doctrines are quoted to teach the proper management of voice and body, while Philostratus, Plutarch, Aristotle, Isocrates, and others are mentioned from time to time." [111]

Le Faucheur relegated gesture to two chapters; but some members of the French Academy, with nothing better to do, also examined that subject. They looked first at paintings, for instance, at Poussin's "Massacre of the Innocents" where "each figure is caught at an instant of psychological crisis, expressed in the attitudes of the actors: the executioner heedlessly raising his sword above the infant, the face of the mother a rigid mask, a second mother departing with a gesture of despair." Then, taking their cue from Quintilian, Bulwer (?), and from Descartes who in his *Passions of the Soul* (1650) had concluded that each of the six chief passions—wonder, love, hatred, desire, joy, and sadness—expresses itself psychologically by external signs, especially in the eyes and face, they began to mechanize expression. In 1675 a certain Henri Testelin (?), apparently a critic of painting, gave before the Academy "the most thorough and categorical discourse on Expression, summarizing and applying Descartes' treatise. 'One can represent the passions of the soul by the actions of the whole body,' Testelin explains: the elevation of the brows, the contour of the lips, the pose of the torso, the position of the feet. Aversion brings a recoil of the body, while the arms repulse the object; horror causes a similar gesture, but more forceful. In love the eyes are half closed, the lips red and humid; and the head is inclined toward the loved object. There are suitable 'attitudes' for laughter, fear, desire, timidity, melancholy." [112] This mechanizing, this cataloguing, of expressions spread like rot to acting. Soon pedants began artificially to classify and to standardize (to traditionalize, the Orientals would say) eye and facial expressions, gestures, postures and movements, and eventually even vocal tones suitable, even necessary, for actors to use onstage. Thereafter for well over two hundred years French acting—and most Western acting—was rather rigidly formalized in an attempt to make of it a respectable art like other arts.

But seventeenth-century Frenchmen (like most people today) could not completely define art. So, fascinated by theory, they thought and argued about it. Some of them were positive that it wasn't the mere copying of nature. Art, they insisted, "by an orderly Method . . . reforms the defect of Nature." Others reasoned that art couldn't be too unnatural; it ought somehow to retain "some resemblance of the disorder of Nature" so that it could more easily be recognized and enjoyed. In their belief that a play when designed should have in it a "truth to life," they became obsessed with the three unities: (1) the Aristotelian rule that the plot of a play should never have more than one principal action arranged in a strict cause-and-effect sequence, and the two Italian invented rules, (2) "that logically the scene should not change, and (3) that the time of the action . . . should correspond exactly to the time of the representation." Their acceptance of these rules was "based primarily on the idea of *vraisemblance*, which . . . came to mean 'likeness to reality.'" For them "The spectator was supposed to behold things as if they were actually happening at the moment." Plays, and the acting of them, were to be so "lifelike and so real that the spectator could not tell the difference between the imitation and the thing imitated." [113]

So wrote Jean Chapelain (1595–1674), poet, critic, and a founding member of the French Academy. He maintained that playwrights could the more surely succeed with audiences "by making use of the natural, or verisimilar"; he believed that verisimilitude is necessary "for the sole purpose of removing from the spectators all occasions to reflect on what they are seeing and to doubt its reality." Without it "the mind is neither moved or persuaded." Logically, then, he objected to monologues or soliloquies because they are unlifelike; he advocated the banishment of dialogue in verse because it isn't natural for persons to converse in verse; and he suggested that "no character should enter or leave [a scene] without apparent reason." [114]

Then François Hédelin, Abbé D'Aubignac (1604–1676), in La Pratique du théâtre (1657), a first and often silly manual on playwriting, said some things about verisimilitude which could have been extended and applied to acting. This precocious teacher and writer announced that since the theater "is but a Picture or Image of Humane Life," or "a sensible Image of the Actions of Humane Life," a playwright ought to "keep to the Rules of probability and decency as the only Guide to the Stage." Consequently, he continued, a play should be "acted by persons, who are to do every thing, as if they were the true persons represented . . . ," and who ought to know that "all Discourses upon the Stage are but the Accessories of Action." He opposed any acting that is a kind of "studied Recital . . . as done on purpose for the Spectators." He contended that an actor ought always to "seem to think more of that concern of his he is about, than of saying fine things. . . ." [115]

In short, D'Aubignac, having read Aristotle's Poetics and Rhetoric, as well as Castelvetro, wanted playwrights to furnish actors with things to do and say that were probable, or likely, recognizable, and believable. He worried, like Chapelain, about monologues in plays, confessing "that it is sometimes very pleasant to see a man upon the Stage lay open his heart, and speak boldly of his most secret thoughts, explain his designs, and give vent to all that his passion suggests; but without doubt it is very hard to make an Actor do it with probability." First of all, he said, monologues ought not "to shock the probability of the circumstances of time & place"; and second, the actor "on his side" ought to have "some apparent and powerful [and urgent] reason for him to tell" what he tells. [116]

Probability in acting, D'Aubignac insisted, could be approached by searching for the causes behind the actions as set down in the words of a play. The onstage "Interests" of actors, he repeats and repeats, should be "grounded upon sensible Motives." Item: Actors should "always come on, and go off of the Scene with some probable reason, which makes it more proper for them to do so than otherwise, and yet that must not be done grossly, but by nice and natural pretexts." Item: "The Cause which is to produce a Motion [of the mind, or emotion] in the Actors themselves, and then in the Audience, ought to be something true, or believ'd to be so." It ought to be "reasonable and probable, according to the receiv'd Opinions of Mankind; for if any Actor should fly into a passion of Anger, without reason, he would be look'd upon as a Mad-man." Item: "There is no Action of Humane Life so perfectly single, as not to be accompanied by many little Circumstances, which do make it up; as the Time, the Place, the Person, the Dignity, the Designs, the Means, and the Reasons of the Action." [117]

But D'Aubignac and the pleaders for some degree of probability in the theater lost the debate. Their attempts to retain for art certain recognizable remnants of nature were rejected. They were premature in calling attention to a point of view derived from ancient Greek rhetoric. For practicing seventeenth-century French playwrights probability was a petty thing. It just wasn't rich, extravagant, or superlative enough. Art, they proceeded to demonstrate in script after script, ought to be and could be larger than life—true in essence, yes, but always larger than life. Art, they contended, is more than the recollection of realistic details, of familiar and fussy and drab details, of restricting details. Therefore, in comedy they enlarged realism into caricature and in tragedy they transformed it into grandeur. They convinced audiences by a designed exaggeration, and "guaranteed truth by magniloquence." [118]

Corneille, for one, seldom worried about verisimilitude in his playwriting. He did admit once, as an afterthought, that what two of his characters said in *La Galerie du palais* (1634) "would be better said in a chamber or in a drawing-room" instead of in a street; "but this is a theatrical license which must be endured. . . . It goes a little beyond reality and even decorum; but it is almost impossible to do otherwise; and the spectators are so accustomed to it that they find in it nothing shocking." Fundamentally for him "A subject of tragedy must not be merely probable. . . . The great subjects . . . ought always to extend beyond the limits of the probable." [119] And the characters in such plays ought consistently to be acted beyond those limits.

And though Racine maintained that "nothing but what is true to life can appeal to us in tragedy," the speeches and the actions of his characters are anything but probable or natural. They were praised during his century for being "natural," but that "was almost tantamount to calling [them] reasonable and seemly," or "decorous in conduct," or so eternally human they could move men's hearts. Racine's characters are severed from and soar above normal, everyday probabilities. Like the *dramatis personae* of a Greek tragedy they live "their emotion-charged and exemplarily human lives . . . on an exalted level" where the eternally human is clearer because it is uncontaminated by the confusing and base details of daily life. Love, for instance, the core of most of his plays, is made so sublime that "there is hardly a trace of the physical and sexual." Moreover, any "references to sleeping, eating and drinking, the weather, landscape, and time of day are almost completely absent; and when they do occur they are fused into the sublime style." [120]

Racine snubbed verisimilitude and expertly composed for actors an elevated and frankly artificial talk. In many of his soliloquies, for example, wherein characters via a renaissance theatrical convention reveal their innermost thoughts and feelings, Racine substitutes "a well-wrought, clearly articulated statement, a summary of the main factors and relations such as might be presented in a court of law, for the mixture of confusion, misapprehension, and sharp illumination which [more probably] characterizes self-discovery." Speeches like his, of course, are in a way true because men and women do reason and feel and hope to behave like superpeople; they are unnatural, improbable, because men and women do not—as yet—reason or feel that lucidly, that resonantly, that perfectly. Therefore, an actor studying and de-livering a Racine soliloquy—or participating in any of his dialogues—must concentrate not on the probability of a character's behavior but on the poetic and yet very *precise* language used. Racine believed with Nicolas Boileau-Despréaux (1636–1711) that "actors must by reason be controlled"; and in his plays he controls them "as completely as Wagner does through the musical score." [121]

Verisimilitude was also ignored on the French comic stage. Molière's farces and high comedies, despite their amusing and yet profound mirroring of man, "are not realistic or naturalistic." His characters must correctly be described as being "just the opposite of everyday persons." They are, accord-ing to Louis Jouvet, "as large, as gigantic, as the characters in the tragedies of Corneille and Racine." They are "mad, not with the madness that occupies psychologists, but with . . . [a] sublime irrationality. . . ." [122]

Molière used certain physical traits of his actors—and even their own names—in creating some of his characters; he studied the Court and the city for his models; often he painted after nature so truly that his portraits were too cutting for comfort. Moreover, as we have seen, he asked his actors to play from a real sense of character. For instance, in *L'Impromptu* he instructed du Croisy to bring out a character's "pedantic air, which he keeps in the midst of frivolous society, and his sententious tone of voice, and his ex-act-ness of pro-nun-ci-ation, which gives full value to every syllable . . ."; and he asked Mlle. Béjart to "represent one of those women who entrench themselves proudly behind their prim virtue, look down on everyone, and are convinced that all the good qualities others may possess count for nothing in comparison with their own sorry honor—which no one else has any interest in." But instructions like that can't be termed deeply realistic. Molière didn't confine his genius to bringing onstage probable people. Primarily he limns the ridiculousness of human beings, which for him meant any "deviation from the normal and customary." And then he carries the ridiculous traits "to gro-tesque extremes." He makes his characters, above all else, theatrical. Tartuffe, for example, isn't at all probable; and no seventeenth-century actor could demote him to being recognizably real. (And the twentieth-century actor, especially the Stanislavski disciple, who blindly attempts to do that to the character woos failure.) Tartuffe exhibits his hypocrisy "execrably by exag-gerating it beyond all reason. . . . His intrigues are crude and simple-minded, and no one except Orgon and his mother can be taken in by him even for a moment—neither the other actors in the play nor the audience." That's some of the fun of the role! And Molière's miser, his hypochondriac, his mis-anthrope, his highbrow ladies and low valets are all just as uproariously im-probable and just as stingingly true. And most of the secondary characters are nonlifelike but lively adjuncts to the comic action of this or that cartoon. In the acting of them any "real representation . . . is . . . completely out of the question." [123]

In the best seventeenth-century French comedies, then, as in the tragedies, actors didn't try to reproduce natural behavior; they consciously aimed instead to alter that behavior into something that differed from and magnified life, into something called art. They aimed to bring out the quality of the play. Following the inspiration and intent of the playwright, upon whom they had wisely become dependent, they rearranged, heightened, and designed the probable into the true. Like their colleagues in tragedy who raised the verisimilar into the ideally true, the comics extended it into the ridiculously true. And their acting, although less formal and less grandiloquent (more "natural" according to Molière) and more visual or physical than tragic acting, remained in essentials a kind of oratory, a highly artificial way of speaking.

IV

In England, from 1660 to 1700, actors were in most instances restricted to orating before courtiers and their satellites who attended plays "to be entertained by fine language and witty sentences." The characters of Beaumont and Fletcher, for instance, moved "with motives not felt in the blood, through symmetrical designs of love and hate, loyalty and disloyalty," and produced only "dialectical displays of language." The characters in the many comedies of manners as noticed, spoke with "a polish, a grace, and a turn of phrase which but rarely could have been met with in reality." And the characters in, say, Venice Preserved were parts of only "another linguistic machine" where "declamation [was] substituted for tragic psychology." [124]

Complete characterizations, we can deduce, weren't a basic necessity. No matter if Betterton, as it was said, "from the time he was dressed, to the end of the play, kept his mind in the same temperament and adaptness, as the present character required"; and no matter if Rochester is supposed to have taught Mrs. Barry "to adapt her whole behavior to the situations of the character." Restoration actors had neither the need, the inclination, a method, nor time enough to work out deep, well-rounded characters. Frequently they performed in as many as four different full-length plays on four different nights until "how they could even have attempted to learn half of their numerous parts must be our wonder now." Well, they didn't; they were nearly "always damn'd imperfect the first night." Consequently, the majority of the actors "took up one line, and aided thus in establishing those 'stock' characters which appear in comedy after comedy, in tragedy after tragedy, during those forty years." As "stock" characters, or sometimes only as themselves, they stepped onto the stage apron, "not quite surrounded by spectators as before, but in a much more intimate position than actors of modern times," [125] and for the most part merely declaimed.

About all that any actor needed to succeed was "a good commanded voice, and limbs that move easily, and without stiffness." Voice was the main thing. If, as was pointed out, "there was no one tragedy, for many years, more in favor with the town than [Lee's The Rival Queens, or the Death of]

Alexander [*the Great*], to what must we impute this its command of publick Admiration? Not to its intrinsick Merit, surely . . . [but] plainly, [to] the grace and harmony of the actor's utterance." Betterton, whose "actions were few" and whose "attitude and aspect drew you into such an impatient gaze, and eager expectation, that you almost imbibed the sentiment with your eye, before the ear could reach it," was acclaimed mostly for his voice. Although it was "low and grumbling; yet he could time it by an artful climax, which enforced universal attention, even from the fops and orange-girls." Every actor, given "periods . . . round, smooth, spirited, and high-sounding, even in a false passion," tried to win the claps of the house with the fire and grace of his vocalizing. As Settle, the author of *The Fairy-Queen* (1692) observed, "He must be a very ignorant Player, who knows not there is a Musical Cadence in speaking: and that a Man may as well speak out of Tune, as sing out of Tune." Indeed, in England near the end of the seventeenth century it was generally agreed that "there is very near as much enchantment in the well-governed voice of an actor, as in the sweet pipe of an eunuch." The cultivation of a striking, flexible voice was undoubtedly stressed by dramatic coach Beeston, by Joseph Ashbury (1638–1720), "the best teacher of the rudiments of that science [acting] in the three kingdoms," and at the "nurseries" or training schools for young actors set up by D'Avenant and Killigrew in 1667, 1669, and in 1671

> Where Queens are formed, and future Hero's bred;
> Where Unfledged Actors learn to laugh and cry,
> Where infant Punks their tender voices try.[126]

On the Restoration stage the manner in which things were said—accompanied by supplementary movements of the body, the feet, the arms, the hands, the fingers, and the eyes—was the important reason for saying them. And the way was artificial, conventional. The actor's imagination was curbed by judgment, his feelings were controlled by judgment, and his naturalness was designed by judgment. Acting, as on the seventeenth-century French stage, was everyday utterance and behavior elevated into formal, respectable art.

Art was the main thing. Dryden made that point clear in his *An Essay of Dramatick Poesie* (1668), "the first piece of sustained and deliberate theatrical criticism in the English language." He defined a play as "A just and lively image of human nature, representing its passions and humours, and the changes of fortune to which it is subject, for the delight and instruction of mankind." But he didn't stop there. He added that "A play . . . to be like Nature, is to be set above it; as statues which are placed on high are made greater than the life. . . ." For Dryden a play was supposed to produce the illusion of a higher reality. Therefore "The plot, the characters, the wit, the passions, the descriptions . . . ," he said, should be "exalted above the level of common converse, as high as the imagination of the poet can carry them, with proportion to verisimility." Because Dryden was in love with words he believed that in a play "The converse . . . must be heightened with all the arts and ornaments of poesy; and must be such as, strictly considered, could never be supposed spoken by any without premeditation." His plays were never meant to represent persons speaking extempore. Dryden even boldly suggested that "one great reason why prose is not to be used in serious plays, is, because it is too near the nature of converse: there may be too great a likeness. . . ."[127]

Congreve, who wrote comedies, and wrote them in prose, nevertheless agreed with Dryden. He disapproved of realistic comic characters that "require little more than a good memory and superficial observation" from the writer and the actor; he wanted them to be "something larger than life. . . ." And because he also loved words and gloried in arranging them prettily and precisely he, too, was sure that the dialogue of a play ought to be designed instead of merely realistically reproduced. If a playwright, he observed, should with exactness "steal a dialogue of any length from the extempore discourse of the two wittiest men upon earth, he would find the scene but coldly received by the town." Along with Dryden he relegated the "imitation of common persons and ordinary speaking" to crude farces.[128] Only there could actors talk rather naturally and sometimes as if for the first time. Art was decorously beyond that sort of thing.

Some Englishmen, however, began faintly to object to all this non-natural, elevated writing and public speaking (as well as acting?). Scientists, for instance, didn't know anything about art, but they knew what they disliked. They balked at "this vicious abundance of Phrase, this trick of Metaphors, this volubility of Tongue, which makes so great a noise in the world." By 1667, a year before Dryden published his *Essay*, Thomas Sprat of the Royal Society exacted from its members "a close, naked, natural way of speaking; positive expressions; clear senses; a native easiness. . . ." He went on record as preferring in communication "the language of Artizens, Countrymen, and Merchants, before that, of Wits, or Scholars." And by 1678 preacher Joseph Glanville was condemning "affected Rhetorications, . . . the vanities of conceited speech," the "affectations of wit and finery, flourishes, metaphors, and cadencies." He declared that "plainness is for ever the best eloquence; and 'tis the most forcible."[129]

Even Dryden, a bright man, often worried about his strict allegiance to art over nature. He seemed to become more and more aware of the virtues of "verisimility" in playwriting. For instance, he admired the motivated, quite probable entrances of characters onto the French stage, saying that the business which brings an actor there ought to be "evident" so as to "render all the events in the play more natural"; and, following Corneille, he was sure that "there is nothing so absurd as for an actor to leave the stage only because he has no more to say." He observed of the lengthy recitations in French plays that "It is unnatural for any one in a gust of passion to speak long together, or for another in the same condition to suffer him, without interruption." He insisted that writers (and actors?) ought to know "by what springs" the passions "are to be moved," and that "To produce a villain, without other reason than a natural inclination, is . . . to produce an effect without a cause. . . ." He admired Shakespeare's scene between Brutus and Cassius because "the passions . . . are extremely natural, . . . the expression of 'em not viciously figurative." And he retreated a bit from his earlier insistence upon judgment and discretion and coolness to recommend that "The poet [and the actor?] must put on the passion he endeavors to represent: a man in such an occasion is not cool enough, either to reason rightly, or to talk calmly. Aggravations are then in their proper places; interrogations, exclamations, hyperbata, or a disordered connection or discourse, are graceful there, because they are natural." [130]

More than that, Dryden made three points about playwriting which, in a way, were to become highly important not only to the actors of the seventeenth century but to those of the twentieth. First, he expanded the term action to mean "every alteration or crossing of a design, every new sprung passion and turn of it. . . ." Second, he explained that "A character . . . cannot be supposed to consist of one particular virtue, or vice, or passion only; but 'tis a composition of qualities which are not contrary in the same person . . . yet . . . one virtue, vice, and passion ought to be shown predominant over all the rest. . . ." And third, he decided, after the French, that "every person who enters, though to others, makes . . . a new scene." [131]

In short, Dryden was saying by 1679 that the action of a play "ought to be probable" (or have in it "a likeness of truth, something that is more than barely possible"), "as well as admirable and great." In agreement with René Rapin's (1621–1687) Réflexions sur la Poétique (1674), he sensed that the basic aim of all playwriting (and acting?) ought to be "to reduce Nature into method, to trace her step by step, and not to suffer the least mark of her to escape us. . . ." [132]

Finally, faint intimations of many changes to come—oh, so slowly—in acting were evident on the English stage before the end of the seventeenth century. Actors began more and more to impersonate characters, according to Colley Cibber (who, it's true, commented some sixty years later in 1741). He was lengthy in his praise of Mountfort because that actor "could entirely change himself; could at once throw off the man of sense, for the brisk, vain, rude, and lively coxcomb, the false, flashy pretender to wit, and the dupe of his own sufficiency: of this he gave a delightful instance in the character of Sparkish, in Wycherley's Country Wife." As Sir Courtly Nice by John Crowne (c. 1640–c. 1703) Drury Lane 1685, "his excellence was still greater: there his whole man, voice, mien, and gesture, was no longer Mountfort, but another person. There the insipid, soft civility, the elegant and formal mien; the drawling delicacy of voice; the stately flatness of his address, and the empty eminence of his attitudes, were so nicely observed and guarded by him, that had he not been an entire master of nature, had he not kept his judgment, as it were, a sentinel upon himself, not to admit the least likeness of what he used to be, to enter into any part of his performance, he could not possibly have so completely finished it." Cibber also praised Mrs. Susanna Mountfort (after 1692 Mrs. Verbruggen) for her great skill in achieving characterizations different from herself. In *Don Quixote* by Thomas D'Urfey (1653–1723), staged at Dorset Garden in 1694–95, "she transformed her whole being, body, shape, voice, language, look, and features, into almost another animal: with a strong Devonshire dialect, a broad laughing voice, a poking head, round shoulders, an unconceiving eye, and the most bedizening, dowdy dress, that ever covered the untrained limbs of a Joan Trot. To have seen her here, you would have thought it impossible the same creature could ever have been recovered to what was as easy to her, the gay, the lively, and the desirable." [133]

Some actors also began to pay less and less attention to the audience and to concentrate upon the play in which they were acting. Of Hart, for example, it was said that "On the stage he acknowledged no audience; their warmest applause could never draw him into a moment's forgetfulness of his assumed character." And a relatively unimportant actor, Benjamin Johnson (1665–1742), was singled out as being "of all comedians the chastest and closest observer of nature." He "never seemed to know he was before an audience. . . ." [134]

Other actors, a few, began to speak onstage as if for the first time. They tried, evidently, to create the illusion of real talk. Cibber, for instance, noted of Kynaston in *Henry IV* that "every sentiment came from him as if it had been his own, as if he had himself, that instant, conceived it, as if he had lost the player, and were the real king he personated,—a perfection . . . rarely found. . . ." And he complimented Mountfort because "The wit of the poet seemed always to come from him *extempore*. . . ." [135]

In "the grand contest, viz. whether nature or art excelled [John] Verbruggen [fl. 1691–c. 1708?], wild and untaught," was acclaimed by some as being a better actor than "Betterton in the trammels of instruction." Nature, not decorum, directed Verbruggen's voice and action until he "was nature, without extravagance—freedom, without licentiousness, and vociferous, without bellowing. . . ." Yet the same critic could say of Susanna, his wife, that "She was all art, and her acting all acquired, but dressed so nice, it looked like nature. There was not a look, a motion, but what were all designed; and these at the same word, period, occasion, incident, were every night, in the same character, alike, and yet all sat charmingly easy on her. . . ." [136]

How to get more nature into their art of acting thus became the concern of most European actors during the next two centuries. Were the actors to lead the playwrights, or the playwrights to lead the actors? It didn't matter much. What did matter was that more nature in things theatrical was about to be demanded by a growing, very solid, very important merchant society. These average persons were already saying, "To hell with art! We want life as it is!"

PART III-

THE CHANGES

IN ACTING ~ ~

7- The Successful Eighteenth Century

During the eighteenth century—"the age of reason, healthy, manly, upstanding reason"—some critics and playwrights and even actors became thinkers and tried to define the obligations of theater to art and to life. In due time several of them, either perverse or progressive, decided that they ought to put more reality onstage, that they ought to be more "natural" there —although "no two generations of them . . . ever used the word in precisely the same sense. . . ." As a result, during this century the classic concept that acting is the exhibition of "reality molded into art" collided with the sometime modern concept that acting is the exhibition of reality freshly, personally, and recognizably felt (and apparently beyond the reach of art).[1]

Before 1750 a few theorists argued that an actor should no longer present to an audience the mere formal design of a character but instead should "forget, if possible, his own identity" and "put on the character" by using not only reason, but also his own sensibility "fed and directed by experience. . . ."[2] They also discussed one or two points about "natural" acting which, two hundred years later, would be new to ardent readers of Stanislavski's *An Actor Prepares*. As a result, some eighteenth-century acting moved slightly, tentatively, away from too much art toward a little more nature. Actors, guided by playwrights, now and then added lifelike touches to their characterizations.

Most of these examinations of form *versus* content and intelligence *versus* sensibility in acting were conducted by Frenchmen. As already noticed, they had worried since the time of *Le Cid* about the differences between art and nature. And their subsequent long debate on the topic of the three unities wasn't as barren as is commonly supposed. It made some of them think hard. It led some of them as they harped on versimilitude to prefer in the theater concrete, detailed reality to an abstract, ideal one. They began to want from plays, and consequently from acting, a greater familiarity of tone, something that could be understood and felt by the average man. In other words, the French who had succeeded best in following classic standards onstage, were the first to doubt them and to initiate a modern theory of acting.

But after a while, after much talk and a little experimentation, an influential number of reasoning men, especially in England and Germany, concluded that plain, ordinary nature reproduced, or even partly reproduced, onstage (as on canvas) just wasn't art. It couldn't possibly be art. Nature itself, they said, is too crude and mean, too unpolished, too earthy. Art, they repeated, should be nature improved upon, idealized. That opinion became fashionable late in the century after classical archaeologist and historian, Johann J. Winckelmann (1717–1768), his painter friend, Anton Mengs (1728–1799), and others revived with a fallacious profundity Greek notions of "ideal beauty." So, the tug-of-war between those for art and those for nature was won by the former. Beginning in the 1780's the "grand style" of acting was more popular than ever in many theaters of Europe.

II

By 1701, when professional actors, despite the Church, were now and then called "truly decent people, who are frequented and respected by gentle folk in many quarters," families were being elected to the Comédie-Française. Pierre La Thorillière (1659–1731), the son of François, Paul Poisson (1658–1735), the son of Raymond, and Étienne Baron (1676–1711), the son of Michel, were members; so were Charlotte Desmares (1682–1753), a niece of Mme. Champmeslé, and two daughters of Dancourt. Then in 1706 Philippe Poisson (1682–1743), the son of Paul and the grandson of Raymond, was admitted to the company. After all, the profession offered an enviable security when an actress like Fanchon, the widow of J. B. Raisin, sister of another company member, and a relative of Mme. Beauval, could retire on a pension of 10,000 livres and enjoy it for twenty years.[3]

At first these actors were too comfortable to break away from traditional theatrical practices that stressed "the *vérité générale, abstraite, et rationelle* to the exclusion of passion and imagination, and . . . [that] emphasized the *principe pensant* to the exclusion of the *sensibilité affective.*" The chief players of the Comédie-Française then were Pierre de Beaubourg (1662–1725), Marie (de Châteauneuf) Duclos (1668–1748), Ponteuil I (1674–1718), and Charlotte Desmares. Beaubourg, a son-in-law of Mme. Beauval, replaced the older Baron who had retired in 1691, and soon almost effaced any memories of his predecessor's "dignified simplicity, . . . restrained easy movement, [and] the thoughtful delicacy with which he rendered the gradations of sentiment." Beaubourg was addicted to "violent, absurd gesticulation" and roared out his feelings "in a frantic, ear-splitting fashion." Mme. Duclos, who after Mme. Champmeslé's death in 1698 impersonated some of her roles, was also a stiff and stagy declaimer. No wonder Jean Sallé (?–1706), with the troupe in 1701, was singled out for being "very natural, certainly an uncommon merit in these days." [4]

Theorists, however, still prescribed artificial tones for acting. Jean Leonor de Grimarest (1659–1713), for instance, in his *Traité du Recitatif, dans la lecture, dans l'action publique, dans la déclamation, et dans le chant* (1707) proved, by examples from Corneille and Racine, that each of the emotions had its own peculiar tone and could be expressed only in that tone. He also announced that each passion had its distinct visual form. But whereas Grimarest laid down strict rules for the use of the voice, he was curiously content to imply that an actor "who really feels will find the proper facial expression." [5]

Faint foreshadowings of *le vrai* to come, however, can be found in the amusing depiction of a contemporary social *milieu* by Jean-François Regnard (1655–1710) in *Le Legátaire universel* (*The Residuary Legatee*) (1708), in Alain-René Sage's (1668–1747) fairly realistic *Turcaret* (1709) and in *Le Curieux impertinent* (1710) where Philippe-Néricault Destouches (1680–1754) taught virtue and decried vice as he aimed for "*le simple et le naturel,*" which soon became the goal of the century. And by 1707 playwright Antoine Houdart de La Motte (1672–1731) was one of several who complained that classic tragedy, even as melodrama, had lost its power to touch the average man. [6]

❊ THE BOOK *BETTERTON*

Across the Channel in England tentative approaches were also being made toward a more simple, more natural drama. The new trading-class theater audiences didn't always enjoy heroics, or art, or whatever it was. They yearned vaguely for something onstage that was more familiar, more domestic; they could be touched by sentimental comedy. *The Fair Penitent* by Nicholas Rowe (1674–1718), although a tragedy, succeeded at the Lincoln's Inn Fields in 1703 because, as one critic observed, "The story is domestic, and therefore easily received by the imagination and assimilated to common life." Betterton, Powell, Verbruggen, Mrs. Barry, and Mrs. Brace-girdle topped the cast. Another success was Cibber's genteel and moralizing comedy, *The Careless Husband*, offered at the Drury Lane in 1704 with the author, Wilks, Powell, and Mrs. Anne Oldfield (1683–1730) in the leading roles. And at the Haymarket in 1707 *The Beaux' Stratagem* by George Farquhar (1678–1707), with Wilks as Archer and Mrs. Oldfield as Mrs. Sullen, appealed to audiences because of "an undercurrent of human feeling below the badinage." Most of the early eighteenth-century plays, however, even the horde of comedies, were weak things; "creative ability in the dramatic form was perhaps at its lowest ebb." Managers were often forced to glitter up their productions with *entr'acte* entertainment, "with Tumblers, and Rope-Dancers from France, . . . Dancing-Masters, and Dancing-Dogs" and "shoals of Italian Squallers." [7]

Soon enough the actors were again in charge of some of the theaters. Betterton managed his company at the Lincoln's Inn Fields until 1705, and then performed briefly at the new Haymarket. And in 1709 actors Cibber, Wilks, and Doggett were granted a license to form a new company and act away from Rich and his Drury Lane. The actors became so important in this period that Richard Steele (1672–1729) in his *Tatler* No. 35 (1709) resolved to publish observations from time to time on their performances; other writers followed suit in other periodicals. Acting began to be examined, criticized, discussed.

The two new stars of the time were Thomas Wilks and Mrs. Anne Old-field. Of the former it was said, "Whatever he did on the stage, let it be ever so trifling—whether it consisted in putting on his gloves, or taking out his watch, lolling on his cane, or taking snuff—every movement was marked by such an ease of breeding and manner, everything told so strongly the in-voluntary motion of a gentleman, that it was impossible to consider the character he represented in any other light than that of reality." Wilks also had no equal "in the touches of domestic woe, which require the feelings of the tender father and the affectionate husband." Mrs. Oldfield's voice "was sweet, strong, piercing, and melodious, her pronunciation voluble, distinct, and musical. . . . If she delighted more in the higher comic than in the tragic strain, it was because the last is too often written in a lofty disregard of nature. . . ." [8]

More and more frequently critics commended a regard for nature in acting. Steele, for instance, in the *Tatler* No. 68 (1709) took as his text Horace's instruction "If you would have me weep, you must first weep your-self," and said of it: "This is not literally true, for it would have been as rightly said, if you do observe nature, that 'I shall certainly weep, if you do not'. . . . Therefore, the true art seems to be, that when you would have the person you represent pitied, you must show him at once, in the highest grief, and struggling to bear it with decency and patience. In this case, we sigh for him, and give him every groan he suppresses." And in No. 138 (1710) Steele preserved a pre-Stanislavski remark attributed to Hart: "It was impossible to act with grace, except the actor had forgotten that he was before an audience. Till he had arrived at that, his motion, his air, his every step and gesture have something in them which discovers he is under restraint, for fear of being ill-received; or, if he considers himself as in the presence of those who approve his behavior, you see an affectation of that pleasure run through his whole carriage." Thus, in little ways, "Nature . . . Unerring NATURE," was slowly coming to be "At once the source, and end, and test of Art." [9]

II

The Art of keeping Nature always in view was the announced theme of the first European book on acting. This bastard claimant to that honor is *The Life of Mr. Thomas Betterton, the late Eminent Tragedian; Wherein The Action and Utterance of the Stage, Bar, and Pulpit, are distinctly consider'd* . . . , put together by Charles Gildon (1665-1724), a hack author, playwright, and editor. It was published in 1710, the year of the actor's death, as a salute to "the last of our Tragedians, . . . a Man so excellent in an Art which is now expiring." "I shall here by writing his Life," Gildon explained, "make him convey to others such Instructions, that if they are perfectly understood, and justly practised, will add such Beauties to their Performances, as may render his Loss of less Consequence to the Stage." [10]

The title is misleading; only pages 5-11 of 176 are biographical. Most of the volume consists of a compilation of "some Rules, by which the young Beginners might direct themselves to that Perfection, which every body is sensible is extremely (and perhaps always has been) wanting on our Stage." Gildon hoped that from such rules "we might form a System of Acting . . . , an Art, which has not been much cultivated in our Nation, either in the Practice or Theory. . . ." He explains his use of Betterton's name thus: "Plato and Xenophon introduce Socrates in their Discourses, to give the greater Authority to what they say. I shall, therefore, make the same Use of Mr. Betterton, on a Subject in which he may reasonably be thought a competent Judge." And, he adds, "I confess that I do make him require Qualifications, of which he was not perhaps Master himself." The fictitious frame of the account is a visit by Gildon and a friend to Betterton's country house in Reading. There, after dinner, a little walk, and a glass of wine, the three sit in the agreeable shade of the garden and fall into "the Discourse of Acting." Gildon begins the interview with two extended statements; thereafter Betterton does all the talking—or reading. At the end Gildon and his friend return to London. [11]

The book might better have been titled *The Duty and Qualifications of Actors*. Gildon announces early in its pages that he is "(as far as I know) the first, who in English has attempted this Subject [acting], in the Extent of the Discourse before you." But in order "to prevent any Objection, which may be made . . . that I have been a Plagiary, and deliver'd Rules for my own, which are taken out of other Authors," he admits "that I have borrow'd many of them from the French, but then the French drew most of them from [Cicero] Quintilian and other Authors." What he borrowed from the French has only recently been identified. Throughout the book Gildon follows the device of having Betterton, at various points in the monologue, introduce "manuscripts" from which, directly or indirectly, he quotes. The first "manuscript" is mentioned on pages 17–18: "I shall fetch you a manuscript on this Head [acting], written by a friend of mine [in Betterton's own hand, Gildon observes in an aside!], to which I confess I contributed all, that I was able." By and large this material, as Wilbur S. Howell has shown, is drawn from the *Traitté de l'action de l'orateur, ou de la Prononciation et du geste* (1657) by Michel Le Faucheur. In *c.* 1702 this work was anonymously translated and published in London as *An Essay Upon The Action of an Orator; As To His Pronunciation & Gesture.* A second "manuscript" is introduced on page 43: "I shall subjoin here the Signification of the various Natural Gestures from a Manuscript of a Friend of mine, which he assur'd me was taken from a learned Jesuit who wrote on this Subject." This matter, again as Howell discovered, is derived from Louis Crésol's *Vacationes Autumnales sive De Perfecta Oratoris Atione et Pronunciatione Libri III* (Paris, 1620).[12] A third "manuscript" appears on page 89: "Before I come to the Directions for the Beauties of Speaking, I think it will not be amiss to insert here a Paper given me by a Friend, of the Several Defects and Vices of a Voice, taken from the 26th Chapter of the Second Book of Julius Pollux's *Onomastics* . . . ," the *c.* A.D. 180 *Onomastikon Graece & Latine* (Amsterdam, 1706).

So, Gildon's French sources are two books on oratory, the newest of them more than fifty years old in 1710. Moreover, his examples or illustrations of public utterance are taken "from Oratory more than from the Drama." Yet his miscellany because it links classic oratory-acting with early eighteenth-century oratory-acting deserves more than a quick snub. In nearly 130 pages, he assembles several interesting points—and many dull ones—about acting as it is governed by "Nature" and "her Handmaiden ART."[13]

"Betterton" examines "Action" and the Face, "Gesture, and the Action of Hands, Legs, and Feet," pages 23–80, and the "Art of Speaking," pages 80–142. Action (looks, gestures, movements), he advises, should be the player's "chief Aim and Application. . . . A Patriot, a Prince, a Beggar, a Clown, &c. must each have their propriety, and Distinction in Action as well as Words and Language." Sometimes, for example, an actor "is to represent a choleric, hot and jealous Man, and then he must be thoroughly acquainted with all . . . those Motions of the Feet, Hands, and Looks of such a Person in such Circumstances. Sometimes he is a Person all dejected and bending under the Extremities of Grief and Sorrow; which changes the whole Form and Appearance of him in the Representation, as it does really in Nature." [14]

Therefore, Nature must be studied by the actor who would authenticate his Action. "Nature, if you obey its Summons, will alter your Looks and Gestures" rightly. Nature must be "the sovereign Guide and Scope" even though "there seems a Necessity of some Marks, or Rules to fix the Standard of what is *Natural*, and what not, else it is a loose vague Word of no manner of Use or Authority." Furthermore, the actor "must be Master of Nature in all its Appearances, which can only be drawn from Observation, which will tell us, that the Passions and Habits of the Mind discover themselves in our Looks, Actions and Gestures." [15]

But "Betterton" did not believe that many actors could depend for their Action solely on Nature. "Tho a great Genius may do this, yet Art must be consulted in the Study of the Larger Share of the Professors of this Art." The latter need a "certain Rule of Judgment." They need "to study the Graces of Action. . . ." They need to "understand the Art they should be improv'd in." And they "ought not to be . . . Stranger[s] to [other Arts like] Painting and Sculpture. . . ." Onstage, "Betterton" insists, there must be "Art always directing" since the Motions and Dispositions of the Body require an "Agreeableness" and a "Genteelness" not always found in Nature. The "Art of Gesture," he adds, "seems more difficult to be obtain'd, than the Art of Speaking; because a Man's own Ear may be judge of the Voice, and its several Variations, but he cannot see his Face at all, and the Motion of the other Parts of the Body, but very imperfectly." That's why Plutarch had in his House "a great Looking-Glass, before which he would stand and repeat his Orations, by that means observing how far his Action and Gesture were graceful or unbecoming." [16]

The "Art of Speaking beautifully," "Betterton" continues, is also "to be attain'd [not solely from Nature but] by Art" "and Exercise." From Art an actor's utterance may acquire "Grace and Harmony." Yes, as an actor talking in character, "the nearer you approach to Nature, the nearer you come to Perfection; and the farther you are from her, the more vicious is your Pronunciation." Yes, the less affected the better, for "a natural Variation is much the best; the easiest way of arriving at which, is a just Observation of common Discourse, and to mind how you speak your self in Conversation. . . ." And yes, "When you are . . . to speak, you ought first with Care to consider the Nature of the Thing of which you are to speak, and fix a very deep Impression of it in your own Mind, before you can be thoroughly touch'd with it your self, or able by an agreeable Sympathy to convey the same Passion to another." But the actor must also know that there are onstage certain "Beauties of Utterance," there is a "Decency of Speaking," there is the Art of Speaking well. After all, "in all good Speech

there is a sort of Music, with Respect to its Measure, Time and Tune."
Therefore, "Voices . . . proceed . . . from Nature . . . yet receive from
Art their Brightness, Improvement, and Perfection." [17]

In discussing the affections, the sentiments, the passions, or the feelings
of a role (which can only arbitrarily be separated from action and voice)
"Betterton," like everyone else in his day, quotes Horace: "We weep and
laugh as we see others do,/He only makes me sad, who shows the way. . . ."
In other words, the actor in performance ought personally to experience the
emotions he wishes to convey. And he can do so if he will "form in his Mind
a very strong Idea of the Subject of his Passion, and then the Passion it self
will not fail to follow, rise into the Eyes, and affect both the Sense and the
Understanding of the Spectators. . . ." Work "your self up by a strong
Imagination," advises "Betterton," "that you are the very Person and in the
very same Circumstances, which will make the Case so very much your own,
that you will not want Fire in Anger, nor Tears in Grief." And if that sounds
like Stanislavski, what about another suggestion "Betterton" makes? An actor,
he casually remarks, in order to bring his Emotions to a Perfection ought to
do as the Ancients did: "They kept their own private Afflictions in their
Mind, and bent it perpetually on real Objects, and not on the Fable, or
fictitious Passion of the Play, which they acted." [18]

It must be noted, however, that "Betterton" makes the customary
eighteenth-century point that "the Passions . . . ought never . . . transport
the Speaker out of himself." [19] Always onstage he must govern and shape.
Always he must employ judgment. Consequently, the actor can't entirely
be the character he's impersonating. He must also be himself, and at the
controls.

About characterization or impersonation "Betterton" offers few specifics.
He did know, to be sure, that too many actors are always the same no matter
how many different characters they exhibit. Generally speaking, he objects,
"let the Part be what it will, the Person, Mien, Action, Look, is the same,
that is, of the Player, not of the Person represented." He therefore believes
(as does Laurence Olivier today) that an actor ought to "vary his Face . . .
as to appear quite another Face; by raising, or falling, contracting, or extending the Brows; giving a brisk or sullen, sprightly or heavy turn to his Eyes;
sharpening or swelling his Nostrils, and the various Positions of the Mouth."
He also hopes that the actor might "vary and change his Figure, which would
make him not always the same . . . in all Parts." But "Betterton" predominantly seems to believe that characterization is more an internal than
an external thing. He stresses that point by quoting "the present Duke of
Buckingham: 'For they must look within to find/ Those secret Turns of
Nature in the Mind.' " [20]

All in all, Gildon's *Betterton* is more than a dull catalog of vocal tones,
facial expressions, and assorted gestures. If, of course, details are isolated like:
The "alluring voice . . . abounds in delicate Modulating, and harmonious

Warblings"; or "Eyes quiet, and calm with a secret kind of Grace and Pleasantness are the Offspring of Love and Friendship"; or "When you speak of your self, the Right not the Left Hand must be apply'd to the Bosom"; [21] and so on—and there are more than a hundred such items—one can with quick acumen prove the compilation is silly. But if, instead, one looks beyond the amusing or annoying details, he will discover that *Betterton* looked back at classic theories of acting while predicting some modern ones.

❦ BEFORE 1725 IN PARIS AND LONDON

Between 1710 and 1725, while critics and playwrights fretted about art versus nature, the century was becoming the century of actors and acting. The important French player of these years was Abraham Quinault-Dufresne (1693–1767), whose father, brother, three sisters and wife were also members of the Comédie-Française. Educated for the stage by Ponteuil, he made his debut at the age of nineteen in *Électre* (1712) by Prosper Crébillon (1674–1762). Six years later he created the title role in *Oedipe*, the first play by Voltaire (François Marie Arouet) (1694–1778), and succeeded Beaubourg as the star in both tragedies and comedies. Certainly he was an improvement over his predecessor if, as was said, "he sought to give his acting the charm of comparative truth to nature." But Quinault-Dufresne was later described as being "more dazzling than profound . . . full of warmth, but without order, without principles, without any of those general features which characterize genius. He was indebted for his success to the superior beauty of his person, and the excellence of his delivery." [22]

Near the end of 1715 the Comédie-Française was composed of seventeen full-share and ten part-share members. "In addition to his share in the company and regardless of his rank, each actor was paid a franc every time that he performed." Members of the troupe received three francs for attendance upon assemblies at which new plays were read, but they were fined for absence from such gatherings, from rehearsals, and from performances. In addition, "actors who played at Fontainebleau earned a pistole (1 pistole = 10 livres or francs) a day. . . . For playing at Versailles they were entertained at supper and received, in 1734, six francs a day." [23]

"A new actor had to invest in the company about 13,000 francs, an amount reduced in 1757 to less than 9,000 francs. If he did not have this amount, it was paid gradually out of his earnings. When he retired, he withdrew it. He then received a pension, amounting ordinarily to 1,000 francs for a full-share actor, but it might be increased by sums from the royal treasury. He could also give lessons in declamation and, if he trained an acceptable actor, he might be rewarded by the government for doing so." [24]

The company alternated in flops and successes. On May 6, 1718, only twenty-six persons paid admission to the theater; and on three days of the same year, August 26, September 12 and 24, only forty-five patrons bought tickets! But in November Voltaire's *Oedipe* was a huge success with Quinault-Dufresne in the title role, his brother Maurice (*c.* 1690–1744) as Philoctète, and Charlotte Desmares as Jocasta. It was acted thirty times from November 18 to January 21, twice in March and twice in April 1719, and then eight times in August 1720. La Motte's *Inès de Castro*, "the first genuinely success-ful French tragedy to lay its chief emphasis upon sentiment," was staged in 1723 with Baron as Alphonse, Quinault-Dufresne as Pedro, Mme. Duclos as Ines, and Mlle. Lecouvreur as Constance. By March 1725 it had been per-formed forty-three times. (The play "remained in the repertory till 1801." It was acted by the Comédie-Française 200 times, a record for eighteenth-century tragedies" surpassed only by Crébillon's *Rhadamiste et Zenobie* (1711), seven plays by Voltaire, and Ducis's 1769 adaptation of *Hamlet*.) [25]

Adrienne Lecouvreur (1692–1730) first acted at the age of thirteen, was then trained by actor-playwright Marc Legrand (1673–1728), and afterward toured the provinces for nine years before she made her debut with the Comédie-Française as Électre in Crébillon's tragedy and as Angélique in Molière's *Georges Dandin*. In 1721 she succeeded Charlotte Desmares as the company's leading lady and reigned as queen of the French stage until her sudden death in 1730. Yet, merely because she was an actress, she was refused Christian burial (in the same year that Anne Oldfield was buried in West-minster Abbey). Of Lecouvreur, who seems to have been a studied per-former as well as a vibrant personality, it was said that "She never appeared on the stage without seeming to be penetrated by her part. Her eyes told you what she was going to say—her fear, her anxiety, were pictured in her face . . . you saw nothing in her which did not seem real and genuine. It was her heart more than her voice which spoke to you." "I do not declaim," she insisted. "The simplicity of my acting is its one feeble merit." "Yet," someone less biased commented, "her delivery was the fruit of elaborate art, according to the school of Baron, with many delicate shades, transitions, and pauses. Her naturalness was method." [26]

Michel Baron at sixty-six returned to the Comédie-Française in 1720, after a retirement of almost thirty years, to introduce a manner of acting "not hitherto known on [the] tragic stage." Instead of declaiming all the time, he sometimes spoke naturally, even conversed with other characters in a scene. As one observer noticed, "When speaking, his talk is real conversa-tion. He conversed with the most delicate naturalness, without falling into any excesses, either of exaggeration to sublimity or of too realistic imitation." Furthermore, "He always listens to his fellow-actors, a thing to which actors, as a rule, pay little heed; and his attention is accompanied by such move-ments of face and body as are required by the nature of the speeches to which he listens." But sometimes, continued this critic (Elena Riccoboni [1686–1771], the actress wife of Luigi), Baron "declaims like the others, and cries out as loud as he can. This . . . makes him appear as an actor with different phases, now sublime and now commonplace, which jars on my ears. . . ." Yet, since "nature is not always beautiful, and every truth is not suitable for the stage," she admitted she preferred declamation. "It is indisputable that the tragic hero, in so far as he is a human being must not alienate himself from nature; but certainly it is also true that the great actions and high lineage or position of tragic heroes require a naturally majestic and dignified manner. . . ."[27]

The lady wasn't alone in her preference for declamation. Antiquarian J. B. Du Bos (1670–1742), not "too respectful toward the probable" in art, believed that "tragedies [are] made for declamation." In his *Réflexions critique et historique sur la poésie et sur la peinture* (1719) he devoted one of his three volumes to "a dissertation on the theatrical representations of the ancients," announced that they read their lines on the basis of a musical notation, and proudly concluded that their kind of stage recitation "must have been something bordering upon our tragic declamation." We French, he observed, insist on our actors of tragedy "speaking with a tone of voice more elevated, grave, and more sustained than that which is used in common conversation" because thus the spectators, at some distance from the stage, "are better enabled . . . to understand the verses."[28]

But Du Bos, paradoxically, is mostly remembered for his opposition to that "corectness" Boileau and others had enshrined as the main principle of art. He held that feelings, not reasons jelled into rules, were the fundamental force in all poetry, painting, and music. For instance, influenced by Quintilian and Horace, he was sure that in the theater "The chief merit of a declaimer, is to move himself. . . . The declaimer must himself be stirred by emotion, for true, inner feeling alone makes tone and gesture convincing." Hence, "the genius requisite to form an excellent declaimer, consists in a sensibility of heart, which makes him enter mechanically, but with affection, into the sentiments of the personage he acts." And this sensibility is "a qualification which is not in the power of art to give."[29]

Du Bos believed that "there is no criterion of art save feeling, which he calls a '*sixième sens*,' against which dispute is vain since in such matters popular opinion invariably wins the day over the dogmatic pronouncements of artists and men of letters." He unhesitatingly declared that "men will always prefer poetry [or a play, and its acting] which moves them, to that composed according to rule."[30]

II

In London before 1725 the actors, though not exceptional, were still more important than the plays in which they appeared. Steele in *Theatre* No. 1 (1720), the first English theater periodical—a puff for Drury Lane—wrote: "I doubt not but I shall bring the world into my opinion, that the profession of an Actor . . . ought to receive the kind of treatment and esteem, which the world is ready to pay to all other Artists." And Lewis Theobald (1688–1744) in the *Censor* No. 87 (1717) emphasized "the importance of good acting to bring out a play and also to enforce good conduct and ideals in the populace." [31]

In 1713 the "frigidly recitative" *Cato* by Joseph Addison (1672–1725) was performed at the Drury Lane for thirty-five successive nights—a tremendous run nursed by political factions—with Barton Booth (1681–1733) in the title role. Shortly thereafter, replacing Doggett, he became one of the triumvirate (with Cibber and Wilks) who managed the theater for something like twenty years. Each of them earned annually at least £1,500, "a very good sum in those days." Booth was the successor and imitator of Betterton. And though positive proof is lacking that Betterton chanted, Booth used "a musical Elocution." He was a "well-mouth'd" declaimer whose "voice was completely harmonious, from the softness of the flute to the extent of the trumpet." He was also praised for his "attitudes" in acting, his poses and gestures. Chief comedian Cibber, on the other hand, knew how "To rally pleasantly, to scorn artfully, to flatter, to ridicule," and to play to the audience "by the artful Management of the Look, Voice, and Gesture." Yet "the unnatural swelling of his words displeased all who preferred natural elocution to artificial cadence. . . ." [32]

During this period Mrs. Oldfield was still leading lady of the Drury Lane company for whom Mrs. (Mary Ann) Porter (?–1765) and Mrs. (Christina) Horton (fl. c. 1714–1750) played second leads. The former succeeded and "imitated, or, rather, faultily exceeded, Mrs. Barry in the habit of prolonging and toning her pronunciation, sometimes to a degree verging upon a chant." Mrs. Horton "acquired that unnatural mode of speaking which was in fashion at the time she came to the stage [c. 1714], but which was exploded before she left it" (in 1750). [33] The company's low comics were Benjamin Johnson, William Bullock (?–1742), and the "ad libber" William Pinkethman (?–1725).

John Rich (c. 1682–1761), after the death of his father, Christopher, managed the opposition house, the new Lincoln's Inn Fields, from late 1714 until 1732. Having failed as an actor, he was convinced that he was a master teacher of acting; and soon he found success as an expert mime in such popular pantomimes as *Harlequin Executed* (1717), *Harlequin a Sorcerer* (1724), and many more like them. The leading man of this company was Lacy Ryan (1694–1760), who for the 1724–25 season commanded a salary of £225, "part for his acting and the rest for his assistance at rehearsals." Next in order of importance were James Quin (1693–1766), a friend of Ryan's, who received approximately £180, Anthony Boheme (?–1731) who earned £160, and Thomas Walker (1698–1744) who earned £103. The leading lady, Mrs. Jane Bullock (?), was paid £135. "Only the principal actors had benefits which, more often than not, were a fine source of additional income for them. For example, at Quin's benefit on March 18, 1725, his advance sale amounted to £96 4s. In one night he earned as much as he regularly did in half the season."

For this same 1724–25 season Lincoln's Inn Fields operated on a budget of approximately £10,700 for a repertory program of 167 nights. In all, "44 actors were employed: 28 men and 16 women" including the leading players. "Five actors earned between £50 and £99, and ten between £20 and £49. A very youthful performer . . . received only £2 8s., 4d. for the whole season." Two women earned between £50 and £99, and four others between £20 and £49. While the five leading actors received £770 the five ranking actresses only got £350. The salaries of the 28 men totaled about £1,450; those of the 16 actresses £475."

The house for the entire season earned about £150 above all expenses before payments to the proprietor; but since Rich took as his share £275, plus about £210 in "extras," for a total of £485, the loss was at least £335.[34] Lincoln's Inn Fields, even with its novelty productions, just couldn't compete with the actors at Drury Lane.

At this period so many new plays were written that "you wou'd think the whole Town were turn'd Playwrights"; but most of the plays were thin things. Two of them deserve mention. Aaron Hill's (1685–1749) *The Fatal Extravagance* (Lincoln's Inn Fields 1721) is "a true bourgeois drama, set in England and without the least attempt at heroicising." It was a first domestic drama, "the one vital and creative force in the whole tragic productivity of the years 1700 to 1750." Steele's *The Conscious Lovers* (Drury Lane 1722) was an enormous hit, running for eighteen successive performances and "bringing more money to the company than any previous one presented there"—over £2,500. Cibber, Wilks, Booth, and Mrs. Oldfield were the leads in this "prime exemplar of 'sentimental comedy.'" They acted "admirable characters providing models for conduct . . . rather than the traditional witty yet debauched characters familiar in Restoration comedy," and aimed to arouse in a middle-class audience "the emotion of sympathy." Adapted from Terence's *Andria* (like Baron's *L'Andrienne*), *The Conscious Lovers* symbolized "the changing tone of the age." [35]

Changes were therefore due in acting. For example, when Anthony Boheme made his debut at Lincoln's Inn Fields "in the trifling character of Francisco" his "unaffected and natural" reading of one short speech: "'Tis bitter cold, and I am sick at heart,' completely electrified the audience, and aroused them to an instantaneous observation of his merit." And Steele in the *Spectator* No. 40 (1711) came out against "those particular Speeches" in tragedies "which are commonly known by the Name of Rants" or the "adding vehemence to words where there was no passion, or inflating a real passion into fustian." Yet Steele was as confused as everyone else about acting. He liked "the Grecian Gesture, and the Roman Tone." In the *Spectator* No. 334 (1712), after quoting Cicero on Gesture, he observed that "A good mien (a becoming Motion, Gesture, and Aspect) is natural to some Men, but even those would be highly more graceful in their Carriage, if what they do from the Force of Nature were confirm'd and heighten'd from the Force of Reason." For him "the reaching out of the Arm, and the most ordinary

Motion, discovers whether a Man ever lernt to know what is the true Harmony and Composure of his Limbs and Countenance. Whoever has seen Booth in the Character of Phyrrus march to his Throne to receive Orestes, is convinced that majestic and great Conceptions are expressed in the very Step. . . ." [36]

A rebellious comment on the acting of the time was made by Aaron Hill in his dedication to *The Fatal Vision* (L.I.F. 1716). He condemned the "horrible theatric way of speaking" and suggested that actors "should industriously forget themselves, and the spectators; and put on the nature . . . of every character they represent. They should not act, but really be." In the 1730's and 1740's Hill had much more to say on that theme.

❊ THE FIRST RICCOBONI

In 1728, twelve years after he had come to Paris with the Italian comedians and one year before he retired from the stage, Luigi Riccoboni decked out his notions about acting in a six-canto poem of nearly 1,200 lines called *Dell' arte rappresentativa* (*Of the Acting Art*). Ten years later, five years after he'd become a naturalized French subject, he introduced his *Réflexions historiques et critiques sur les différents théâtres de l'Europe* with thirty-six pages of "Pensées sur la déclamation." (They delighted Stanislavski when he read them in 1914. "Oh, the darling, the darling!" he exclaimed. "I could embrace him! I could kiss him!") [37]

In *Dell' arte rappresentativa* Riccoboni says that there is a "necessity for study on the part of the would-be actor, since it is not enough to trust only to natural instinct. . . ." His first main point—among many that are trivial, fuzzy, and badly organized—is that acting, at least in tragedy, is more than the copying of everyday behavior. "Doubtless," he declares, "there are some who say that on the stage one should imitate real life as closely as possible, and that whoever seeks or desires more than this, is a fool. But, on the contrary, they are fools who do not seek and who deny that there is anything further or better to be sought." That something extra is dignity or beauty. "The actor must show nature, yes; but in an elevated and noble form, the trivial . . . being reserved for the streets, or for the house" and, onstage, for comedy. For example, the actor must go beyond being natural and "study the delivery of verse. . . ." For another example, the actor playing a king must eliminate such natural actions as sitting and resting his elbows on his knees with his chin between his hands. Even if a king "*might* have made such gestures," and even if "all the stupid immediately . . . cry out, 'How natural, how true to life! Why, I did that myself!' " those aren't typical kingly actions onstage. [38] Art, in short, is different from life.

Luigi Riccoboni's second main point, more emphasized than it was by the ancients, is that "The actor . . . must feel what he acts . . . [must feel] love, anger, jealousy; [must] feel like a king or like Beelzebub; and if he really *feels* all these emotions, if 'with his heart he measures his movements,' they

will of themselves germinate in him and move him to the right action."
Post-Du Bos and pre-Stanislavski, he insisted that "When right feeling is
master it imparts the right feeling to the limbs." But Riccoboni, an intelligent
and experienced actor, knew that in acting right feeling isn't enough. Because
the interest of an audience is concentrated on an actor's face, he goes on to
say, the actor must learn to *show* his feelings (to express them, to communicate them), "or he will not be believed to feel, and in that case all is lost."
Therefore, the actor should practice facial expressions in front of a mirror until
what he feels is outwardly apparent, is conveyed. Also, and perceptively, Riccoboni notes that sometimes there is more art than nature involved in the
expression of feelings onstage. For example, "A woman crying in a scene with
her lover should . . . give the impression that her emotion is real to him, but
should make it appear feigned to the audience, so that they may see 'the deception joined with the truth and yet distinct.' " [39]

In his 1738 "Pensées sur la déclamation"—written for the pulpit, the bar,
and the academies as well as for the playhouse—Riccoboni again favors rules
and principles since "Nature does not bestow the Polish upon the Diamond
she forms; . . . and it is Labour and Art which gives it . . . Lustre." But he's
more loyal to Nature than he was, believing that "Art . . . derives its Principles wholly from Nature." For a pioneer instance, he announces that Rules for
the Turns of the Voice are unnecessary. How, he asks, "can one imagine himself capable to mark out the different Turns and Cadencies peculiar to so
many Millions of Men, each of whom has a different Voice adapted to his own
particular Genius, and immediately under its Direction? It would require a
great deal of Pains to point out in general those different Sounds, the
melancholy, the *cheerful*, the *furious*, &c., and I even believe it is useless to
put the Examples suitable to each in Writing." For Riccoboni the "Source of
every Modulation of the Voice" is the soul. Proper stage "Declamation is no
other than one's *feeling the thing he pronounces*. I do not by this mean that
which is commonly called Good Sense in speaking, and an intelligible manner
in delivering, because to feel is another thing. . . ." Moreover, "that which
seems to be as it were poured forth Extempore, carries with it an Air of
Truth and *Sincerity*, which prepossesses the Audience in favor of every thing
that is said." And yet the actor's lines "ought to be rendered very strong and
striking, even tho' the Rules of Nature should be a little transgressed, [so]
that the Expression and Acting may not be lost to such Spectators as sit at a
Distance from the Stage." [40]

The source for all visible expressions onstage is also the soul. "If a Man
enters strongly into a proper *Enthusiasm*," Riccoboni contends, "and speaks
in the Accents of the Soul, his Features will naturally form themselves into
an Agreement with his Subject by the Alteration both of his Colour and
Muscles." For example, "he will, without his own perceiving it, move his
Arm [as well as his entire body], for the Soul will then direct it, and therefore
his Gesture never can be unjust. . . . The Assistances he may borrow from

an assiduous Practice before his Looking-Glass, and great Application, may give him an affected, but never true, Motion of the Hand and Arm. . . ." [41]

"The great Business of the Stage," Riccoboni sums up, is "to enchant the Spectators into a Persuasion that the Tragedy they are beholding is no *Fiction*, and that they who speak and act are not *Players*, but *real Heroes*. But Theatrical Declamation in *France*," alas, "has quite a contrary Effect; the first Words that are heard evidently persuade the Audience that all is a *Fiction*, and the Players speak in Accents so extraordinary, and so removed from Truth, that it is impossible for one to be imposed upon." French audiences, Riccoboni complains, "are under an *habitual Illusion*, in which Truth has no share. All the World knows that *Caesar, Alexander, Hannibal*, &c. were Men like us; and every Body is persuaded that they felt their strongest Passions, and performed their most Heroic Actions in the same manner as the great Men of our own Age; yet the very Spectators who are convinced of this, being prejudiced in their Youth in favour of the bombast manner of *Theatrical Declamation*, form their Ideas of these Heroes according to the Appearance they make, as performed by *Players:* That is, as Men quite above the common level of Mankind, with a manner of walking, speaking, and looking, different from the rest of the World." Audiences are thus "transported beyond Truth in every thing they see and hear." [42]

❀ OTHER LANDS

Luigi Riccoboni's politically scattered and somnolent "Italy" offered little theatrical competition to England and France during the eighteenth century. In 1713 Francesco Scipione di Maffei (1675–1765) wrote his famous tragedy *Merope* "with true character delineation . . . and passion . . . not concealed by rhetoric"; [43] that same year, however, associated with Riccoboni, he failed to establish at Verona a long needed National Theater. After 1750, as noted, the *commedia dell' arte* floundered. Then beginning in the 1770's Vittorio Alfieri (1749–1803) tried, with some success, to revitalize classic tragedy. His *Saul* (1782–84) and *Mirra* (1784–86) are powerful plays. But that about sums up theatrical activity for those years. Italy influenced the rest of Europe only by its musicians and its architect-designers—like those "magicians of immensity," the Bibienas—who journeyed to all the capitals and courts of the continent.

The theater in eighteenth-century Spain dwindled to almost the academic under the influence of French classicism.

The theater in the Scandinavian countries never achieved much more than the elementary. As early as 1704 a Frenchman, René Montaigu (?) was summoned to Copenhagen to serve as manager for a company of actors, mostly students, and to present plays at court. The group performed until 1710, giving comedies by Molière, Dancourt, and Legrand, farces from Gherardi's *Théâtre italien*, and a few tragedies by Corneille and Racine. A second engagement lasted from 1715 to 1721. For the third season which began in 1722 Ludwig Holberg (1684–1754) contributed five original Danish comedies, among them *Jeppe paa Bjerget* (*Jeppe of the Hill*) and *Erasmus Montanus*. But from 1730 until 1746 there were no licensed performances in Copenhagen.[44] At Stockholm a Royal Swedish Theater was opened in 1737; it also patterned its plays and acting on French models.

II

In Germany the theater muddled along crudely for the first quarter of the century, was systematically reformed, starting in 1727, and by 1750 was ready to vie rather heavily with the theaters of England and France. The Velten touring company of actors, "little better than the mountebanks, jugglers, and quacks who swarmed at every fair" and "despised by respectable citizens," was managed by his widow, Catharina, from 1695 to *c.* 1715. In *c.* 1708 Joseph Anton Stranitzky (1676–1726) left the troupe for Vienna and in 1710 was at the Kärntnertor Theater creating the coarse, comic character of Hanswurst (out of the Pickelhäring of the old German companies and the Harlequin of the *commedia dell' arte*). He staged improvised farces and sensational tragi-comedies mostly derived from operas and often interlarded with impromptu comic scenes. By 1715 in Germany proper several new troupes of actors, offshoots of the Velten company, were touring shabbily from town to town. Nobody of education and taste took them seriously. They purveyed to the public "a completely low-brow entertainment, aiming at an immediate appeal by the readiest means to hand, mimicry and slapstick farce, crude emotionalism, the physical attractions—agility, strength, lung power, sex appeal—of the actors and actresses." The usual performance "consisted of a more or less serious play, the *Hauptaktion*, followed by a farce, the *Nachspiel*. The '*Hauptaktion*' soon came to be called '*Haupt-und Staatsaktion*,' because it employed 'state scenes' introducing people of rank and consequence, princes, noblemen, and illustrious persons, in a court setting." But almost always these serious plays were interrupted by crude comic scenes, and always they were followed by improvised farces. Because of that emphasis on the unliterary, "the extemporizing actor looked down with contempt on all those who memorized their parts and thus made themselves into the slaves of a writer." [45]

That type of theater was to some degree reformed by two actors, Carolina Weissenborn (1697–1760) and her husband-to-be, Johann Neuber (1697–1759), who in 1717 joined C. J. Spielgelberg's (?–1732) "High German Company of World-Wide Fame." Soon they were acting with the better known Elenson-Haack-Hofmann troupe, centered at Leipzig and Brunswick, and performing in a few "regular" plays like translations of Corneille's *Le Cid* and Racine's *Alexandre le grand*. At the break-up of the company in 1727 the Neubers formed at Leipzig their own group of actors, the "Royal Polish and

Electoral Saxon Court Comedians," and at once entered into an alliance with critic Johann Christoph Gottsched (1700–1766), a Prussian "Pope of literature," with the bold aim of completely reforming the German stage. Obscenities and improvisations had to go! "No *Haupt-und Staatsaktions*, no burlesque after-plays!" Gottsched wanted to replace them with more moral and more literary tragedies "which were first to be translations from the French, and then were to be the work of young German writers." Carolina Neuber wanted "to raise the status and improve the reputation of actors and actresses as a class." [46]

For some twelve years the Neubers, monitored by Gottsched, staged plays in temporary wooden halls, above a meat market, or in an unused dyer's loft at Leipzig, at Hamburg, Dresden, Nürnberg, Hannover, and elsewhere. They won the approval of the nobility and the intellectuals but found it difficult to attract the mob. So, for practical reasons, they were forced to add the despised one-act farces to their programs. At Hamburg in 1735 the actors—whose highest weekly wage was (nominally) five gulden, or about ten schillings—"in the course of two-hundred-and-three performances . . . extending over eight months, put on seventy-five different plays and ninety-three one-acters as after-pieces. . . ." [47] Over thirty of the comedies and about ten of the tragedies were French.

Four years later, in 1739, when the Neubers and Gottsched quarreled, separated, and weakened their influence, they had partly achieved their aim. Thereafter each touring company, eight or nine of them, introduced literary or "regular" plays into its repertory; and thereafter German actors worked seriously at their profession, became a bit more skilled in memorizing and reciting, and eventually were respected as craftsmen by audiences.

Though the Neubers continued to form and re-form companies and to act until 1756, the important new group of players was headed by Johann Friedrich Schöenemann (1704–1782), a tolerable comedian but an "unspeakably stiff and grandiloquent" declaimer of tragedy, who had been a member of the Neuber troupe for about ten years. In January 1740 his company staged its first performance in the riding-school at Lüneburg, a translation of Racine's *Mithridate*. Three neophyte actors were in the cast: Konrad Ackermann (1710–1771) impersonated the title role, his wife-to-be (in 1749) Sophia Schröder (1714–1792) was Momine (both for the equivalent of six schillings a week), and Konrad Ekhof (1720–1778) played a minor role (for five schillings a week). In its next two difficult years the company on tour performed about sixty-two plays and after-pieces. One of its most popular offerings was an original German comedy, *Der Bookesbeutel* (*The Book-purse*, or more aptly *The Old Routine*) by Heinrich Borkenstein (1705–1777). A fairly realistic portrayal of the humdrum daily life of Hamburg, it was performed sixteen times to full houses in that city in 1741 and frequently again in Berlin where the troupe worked from September 1742 to August 1743.[48]

Ackermann, Ekhof, and Frau Schröder were much more important than the company or any of its plays. They quickly became "the pillars of German dramatic art." And in 1744 the lady gave birth to Friedrich Ludwig Schröder (1744–1816), who made his debut in St. Petersburg at the age of three as an angel of innocence, and in due time ranked as one of the world's great actors. Ekhof prepared the way for him. Ekhof discovered "that acting did not mean strutting about on the stage in more or less magnificent attire, pouring out a torrent of rhymed verse, or—in comedy—exhibiting a multitude of droll, but senseless fooleries." He learned "that the essence of dramatic art, what justifies and makes it interesting, is the representation of human beings, their feelings, sufferings, and changing moods, through speech and gesture." So, he perfected his acting by study and observation "till from the wooden declamation and stiff posturings of Carolina Neuber's school he had evolved a supple and [more] natural style." [49]

But mechanical declamation as well as movement "with the stiff and formal grace of a dancing-master" were ominously defended in the 1740's by German theorists. Echoing the French classicists, they believed that "Art is an imitation, but not an exact reproduction of nature." They maintained that onstage a character ought to be exhibited as an oral and visual idealization of reality. Too close an approximation of life by the actor, and therefore too complete an illusion, would be destructive of esthetic enjoyment. Verse, for instance, according to playwright-critic Johann Elias von Schlegel (1719–1749), reminds an audience that what it's hearing isn't nature but art. Certainly he wished plays "to have contact with everyday life and to express the desires, the fears, the standards, the environment of the audience, but he did not feel that this necessitated realism of treatment." [50] Thus the debate on art *versus* nature continued.

A greater playwright-critic, Gotthold Ephraim Lessing (1729–1781), was attracted to the theater and first sponsored by the Neubers. At Leipzig in 1748—during the reign of Frederick the Great, when Kant was twenty-one, a year before the birth of Goethe, and two years before the death of Johann Sebastian Bach—they presented Lessing's first play, Der junge Gelehrte (The Young Scholar). Two years later Lessing "reached the conclusion that Shakespeare, Dryden, Wycherley, Vanbrugh, Cibber, and Congreve, who were known only by name in Germany, deserved admiration as well as the French poets; and he believed that if the German followed his own nature in dramatic art, the German stage would resemble the English more than the French." [51] That year, 1750, he edited the Beiträge zur Historie und Aufnahme des Theaters, a periodical; one of the first items published was his translation of a new treatise on acting by Riccoboni's son.

❊ AARON HILL, MACKLIN, AND GARRICK

New actors and a new kind of acting, not new plays, were the main attractions on the English stage from 1725 to 1750. "On the average it was possible for the London theatergoer to see fifteen or sixteen of Shakespeare's plays during a single [nine-month] season." The only important new successes —when the regulation run was about nine nights—were *The Beggar's Opera* by John Gay (1685–1732), a smash hit presented for sixty-two performances from the end of January to the middle of June 1728 at Lincoln's Inn Fields, and *The London Merchant* by George Lillo (1693–1739), staged twenty-three times at Drury Lane in 1731. The latter, "a landmark in the history . . . of European drama," was the first conscious effort to make an audience sympathize with the sorrows of a man below the rank of emperor, king, or statesman. Some critics, of course, refused to hail this and other domestic tragedies in prose; they found them flat when compared with poetic works like *Othello*, and concluded that something more than "nature" was needed onstage.[52] But "nature," or at least a sentimental realism, was the persistent theme: novelist Samuel Richardson (1689–1761) was writing *Pamela* (1740–41) and *Clarissa Harlowe* (1747–48), and Henry Fielding (1707–1754) his *Joseph Andrews* (1742) and *Tom Jones* (1749).

In 1732 when Colley Cibber, the last of the triumvirate, retired from Drury Lane, John Rich built his own new theater, Covent Garden, which seated 1,335 persons (335 more than the opposition house), and boasted a stage lighted by perhaps six overhead and proscenium-door chandeliers, each containing twelve candles in brass sockets, plus wing ladders (perpendicular battens) that held probably eight or ten candles, and some sort of floats (footlights). The house was opened in December with *The Way of the World*; James Quin at £300 a season was Fainall. By 1734 he "attained the meridian of his profession," succeeding Booth who had succeeded Betterton, when he recited the former's role of Cato. (And, on being wildly applauded for one of the soliloquies, he promptly "indulged the audience with its repetition.") That same year Quin moved for £500 a season to Drury Lane where he remained as the chief English actor, and theater despot, until the end of the 1740–41 season when he went to star in Dublin.[53]

During these years, however, Quin's formalized acting was often criticized for being old-fashioned. "With very little variation of cadence," according to observers, "and in a deep, full tone, accompanied by a sawing kind of action, which had more of the senate than of the stage in it, he rolled out his heroics" in "the grandiloquent or artificial style." "He was always a tolerably just Speaker; but then he was hardly any thing more; he recited, rather than acted." And always "his own picture he drew"; "In what'er cast his character was laid,/ Self still, like oil, upon the surface play'd . . ./Horatio, Dorax, Falstaff,—still it was Quin." Tobias Smollett (1721–1771) wrote in *Peregrine Pickle* (1751) that Quin's "utterance is a continual sing-song, like the chanting of vespers; and his action resembles that of heaving ballast into the hold of a ship. . . . The despair of a great man . . . this English Aesopus represents by beating his own forehead, and bellowing like a bull; and, indeed, in almost all his interesting scenes, performs such strange shakings of the head, and other antic gesticulations, that when I first saw him act, I imagined the poor man labored under that paralytical disorder, which is known by the name of St. Vitus's dance. . . . Yet this man, in spite of all these absurdities, is an admirable Falstaff, exhibits the character of the eighth Henry to the life, is reasonably applauded in . . . [Congreve's The] Plain Dealer [1676], excels in the part of Sir John Brute [in Vanbrugh's The Provoked Wife (1697)], and would be equal to many humorous situations in low comedy, which his pride will not allow him to undertake." 54

II

The worst features of Quin's style of acting—the "puffed, round Mouth, an empty, vagrant Eye, a solemn Silliness of Strut, a swing-swang Slowness in the Motion of the Arm, and a dry, dull, drawling Voice that carries Opium in its detestable Monotony"—were attacked by a garrulous oddity of a man named Aaron Hill, who in his mid-twenties had been a managing director at Drury Lane (1709–11) and had written two dramas produced there. Subsequently he fell in love with the theater (named his children Minerva, Urania, Astraea, and Julius Caesar), taught acting, and wrote more plays, including two profitable and two not so profitable adaptations from Voltaire. In the 1730's Hill embarked on a campaign to make English acting more "natural" —or at least more passionate. Alternately called "a bore of the first water" "without common sense or power of thought" or "a man of . . . genius," he "was almost the only critic of his age who labored assiduously to understand the art of acting, and who took incessant pains to communicate the knowledge he had been ennabled to acquire." 55

Hill believed that the true root of the decay in his country's theater was "the players' gross ignorance of their art." In 1733—influenced maybe by the Traité des Passions de l'ame (1650) of Descartes, and in full agreement with Steele's point in the Tatler No. 201 (1710) that "emotional conviction leads to automatic sureness of expression"—he latched onto the notion that a "knowledge of the passions . . . [is] the only thing necessary [beyond an effective voice and figure] to make a finished actor." In a prologue, "a playhouse lecture," to his friend William Bond's (?–1735) The Tuscan Treaty (C.G. 1733) he asked for more feeling in acting. He urged every performer to "Search his own bosom! [to] copy, from within . . . and your passions win." Also that year he vaguely had in mind "a design . . . of establishing an academical Theatre, for improving the taste of the stage, and training up young actors and actresses, for the supply of the Patent Theatres." 56

In brief, Hill believed that an actor must learn to use his own imagination and feel strongly the emotions he portrayed, and then through the intensity of those emotions lose himself in the assumed character and thus achieve more "naturalness" onstage.

In his insistence on the need for more feeling in acting Hill tossed off several naturalistic observations. *Item* (1733): "I will venture to prophecy, that, whenever you can *forget* an audience, you will charm them." And again, "In order to warm every body, who sees you act, you need only to forget that you are acting. 'Tis the thought of the *audience*, that takes away the natural air of the player: Whatever is well done on the stage, must be done with the same force, freedom, and spirit, as if it was doing in actual life. . . ." *Item* (1733): "There is another great beauty, in a Player, who enters strongly into nature, and that is, the significance of silent action, where, after he has done speaking, himself, he attends to what is answered, as if it, in good earnest, concerned him." *Item* (1734): Hill praised a portrayer of Othello for "that impressive attention, with which you listened, while spoke to, and the intent direction of your eye to its proper object, on the *stage*; whereas, it is common, among modern actors, to bestow their looks, and their language, upon the *audience*; whom, by that means, they are sure to put in mind that they are only Players, and in *jest*; and so destroy the noblest delight of the scene; which is, that we should be deceived into a supposition, that it is not *imitation*, but *reality*." [57]

From November 12, 1734, to July 1736 Hill with the assistance of William Popple (1701–1764) wrote a twice-a-week little periodical called the *Prompter* which was largely devoted to discussions of drama and the theater. A fourth of the issues, almost twenty, variously examined the topic of acting, and constitute "the most important body of criticism of the period." Hill indicted actors who through vanity had been led to claim the management of the theaters; he was sure that the actor-manager system had led to worse and worse acting rather than to better. "This same vanity," he felt, "caused the actors to neglect the study of their parts; they did not take rehearsals seriously, and hence made blunders and stood staring into the pit; they misconceived the parts they played and hence falsified them in their acting; they did not know how to play on the passions, had learned their gestures from Quintilian on oratory, and had indeed been chosen not for their ability to act nor their intelligence, but for their pleasing voices." And, demanding "a juster *art* of acting," he once again proposed to establish "a tragic academy . . . for instructing and educating actors in the practice of dramatic passions, and a power to express them strongly." [58]

In January 1736, Hill's *The Tragedy of Zara* (from Voltaire's 1732 *Zaïre*) was staged for a successful fourteen-night run at Drury Lane with his and father-in-law Colley's pupil, Susanna Maria Cibber (1714–1766), making her debut in the title role. Then *c.* 1740, flushed with success, Hill began to formulate a new system of acting. He expanded his twenty-line poem, "The Actor's Epitome," from the *Prompter* No. 113, into an eighty-line poem with the same title. It did little more than list and describe (from Grimarest?) the ten passions: joy, grief, fear, anger, pity, scorn, hatred, jealousy, wonder, and love! [59]

III

Before Hill developed the final versions of his theory something happened to English acting. First, Colley Cibber, in his *Apology* (1740) elegized, without knowing it, the Betterton school of performing. And second, Charles Macklin (c. 1699–1797) and David Garrick (1717–1779) in 1741 almost evicted traditional declamation from the stage. They changed "an elevated tone of voice, a mechanical depression of its tones, and a formal measured step in traversing the stage, into an easily familiar manner of speaking and acting." [60] Hill probably swooned—more from envy than joy.

Cibber wrote his *Apology*, "the best theatrical autobiography that exists," partly with the hope that it might "in some degree show what talents are requisite to make actors valuable." He wasn't, as Johnson is reported to have said to Boswell, "ignorant of the first principles of his art"; he was only behind the times. He idolized Betterton. Cibber believed "almost to an obsession that an actor with a well-trained voice can get all the effect that is necessary or indeed possible by playing a tune on it as a musician does on a fiddle." He maintained that "the voice of a singer is not more strictly ty'd to time and tune, than that of an actor in theatrical elocution: the least syllable too long, or too slightly dwelt upon in a period, depreciates it to nothing." Even as late at 1745, on emerging from retirement, he coached actors in "the good old Manner of singing and quavering out their tragic Notes." [61] Obviously his valuable comments on players, mostly in Chapters IV and V, were of little help to anyone concerned with getting more nature into acting.

Churlish Charles (McLaughlin) Macklin strongly opposed too much cadenced elocution in the theater. During his apprentice years in the provinces from 1723 to 1733, before he came permanently to London and made his debut in a secondary role at Drury Lane, he had decided that an actor ought sometimes to speak rather naturally onstage. In fact, in his first trial in the capital, he'd "spoken so *familiar*, . . . and so little in the *hoity toity* tone of the tragedy of that day," the manager told him "to go to grass for a year or two." Furthermore, Macklin believed that an actor ought to go beyond merely *saying* the lines of a role, that he ought to get away from himself and characterize. The actor, Macklin advised, "must take especial care not to mould and suit the character to his [own] looks, tones, gestures, and manners; if he does so, it will then become the actor's character, and not the poet's. No; he must suit his looks, tones, gestures, and manners to the character: the suiting the character to the powers of the actor, is imposture." [62]

For seven years, from 1734 until 1741, reformer Macklin and old-fashioned Quin, "naturally and professionally antagonistic," appeared together at Drury Lane; and Macklin became a favorite with the public in his endeavors at "natural" acting. Then, as deputy manager of the theater, he proposed a revival of Shakespeare's *The Merchant of Venice* which for nearly forty years had been supplanted by a comic adaptation. It was put into rehearsal with Quin as Antonio and Macklin as Shylock. The latter "doubtless intimated to . . . some of the actors his intention of playing Shylock as a serious character, though it is said that in actual rehearsal, he merely repeated his lines, and walked through his part without a single look or gesture, and without discovering the business which he had marked out for himself in his interpretation of the Jew. His friends shook their heads at his conceit." Quin bluntly told him he would be hissed off the stage for his presumption, and many of the actors went about complaining 'that the hot-headed, conceited Irishman,' who had got some little reputation in a few parts, had now availed himself of the manager's favor to bring himself and the theater into disgrace." Macklin, however, persisted with his project. He "made daily visits to the center of Business, the Exchange and the adjacent Coffee-houses, that by a frequent intercourse and conversation with 'the unforeskinned race,' he might habituate himself to their air and deportment." [63] Then on February 14, 1741, at the age of perhaps forty-two, he acted the Jew "That Shakespeare drew." The production was an extraordinary success; it ran for twenty-one nights. Everyone talked about Macklin's very "real" impersonation.

Thus Macklin, as one of his students later commented, "began this great improvement" of "getting more into nature in playing. . . ." "The pains he took while entrusted with the care of the actors at *Drury-Lane* . . . founded for us a new method of delivering tragedy . . . , and banish'd the bombast that us'd to wound our ears continually. . . ." But Macklin, contrary to the usual claims, didn't banish elocution from the stage. He "allow'd that on many [occasions], the pompous and sounding delivery were just, nay were necessary in . . . playing. . . ." [64] For him a play wasn't nature copied; it was nature elevated, designed.

IV

David Garrick, after having participated in some semiprofessional theatricals in London since 1737, and having made friends with Macklin and listening to his insistence upon a more "natural" method of speaking and moving onstage, brilliantly accelerated the change-over in English acting. When he failed to find a job at Drury Lane and Covent Garden, he went to Goodman's Fields (1733), a theater removed from the center of the city, and on October 19, 1741, eight months after Macklin's success, acted Cibber's version of Shakespeare's *Richard III* (1700). "He transformed himself into the very man. All was rage, fury, almost reality." Without the juice of an orange recommended to him as a voice-clearer he would have been inaudible after his vehemence of the first two acts. "His forcible style in speaking and acting, at first threw the critics into some hesitation concerning the novelty as well as the propriety of his manner. They had been long accustomed to an elevation of the voice, with a sudden mechanical depression of its tones, calculated to excite admiration, and to intrap applause." But after Garrick "had gone through a variety of scenes, in which he gave evident proofs of consummate art, and perfect knowledge of character, their doubts were turned to surprise and astonishment." Garrick's triumph at the age of twenty-four was immediate, "the most extraordinary and great that was ever known." All London went "horn-mad after him." After acting Richard for seven nights (and then at intervals during the winter), he astonished his audiences by stooping to comedy and impersonating Clodio in Cibber's *Love Makes a Man* (1700). For his seven-month season of about one hundred and fifty performances, Garrick invigorated nineteen different leading roles. He portrayed characters as widely different as the ardent, heroic Chamont in Otway's *The Orphan* (1680); Sharp, the wily knave in his own *The Lying Valet*; Fondlewife, the ancient Puritan banker in Congreve's *The Old Bachelor* (1693); Witwoud, the affected and ridiculous fop in *The Way of the World*; the gay Lothario in Rowe's *The Fair Penitent*; and, most successfully, the farcially conceited Bayes in Buckingham's *The Rehearsal* (1671). "Yet more; in the same evening (March and April 1742), after representing the age and weakness of tortured, maddened Lear [in Nahum Tate's (1652–1715) version], he became the young, stupid, vicious, country-lout, Master Johnny, in Cibber's [The] *School-Boy* [1702]." [65]

Versatility, obviously, was the first factor in Garrick's stunning success. He characterized. "The thing that strikes me above all others," a fan wrote him, "is that variety in your acting, and your being so totally a different man in Lear from what you are in Richard. There is a sameness in every other actor. Cibber is something of a coxcomb in everything. . . . Booth was a philosopher in Cato, and was a philosopher in everything else. His passion in Hotspur and Lear was much the same nature, whereas yours was an old man's passion and an old man's voice and action; and in the four parts wherein I have seen you—Richard, Chamont, Bayes, and Lear—I never saw four actors more different from one another than you are from yourself." Garrick's "imagination was so strong and powerful, that he transformed himself into the man he represented, and his sensibility was so quick, that every sentiment took immediate possession of him." He performed his roles "so naturally," commented one critic, "as that in Truth they are not perform'd at all. . . ." He "puts the Playhouse out of our Heads, and *is* actually to *us* and to *himself*, what another Actor would only *seem to be*." [66]

Vitality, "fire," or energy was the second factor. Onstage Garrick was dynamic: he blazed or clipped out his speeches; he was alive and busy every minute of every scene—perhaps much too active. Macklin, with some malice no doubt, complained that "Garrick huddled all passions into strut and quickness—bustle was his favorite. . . . In the performance of Lord Townly he was all bustle. In Archer, Ranger, Don Juan, Hamlet, Macbeth, Brute—all bustle! bustle! bustle!" [67]

Veracity ("Truth") was the third, and most important, factor in Garrick's leap into stage prominence. Because he lacked "that fullness of sound, that *os rotundum*, to roll with ease a long declamatory speech," he tried from the beginning "to play and speak everything directly different from Quin. . . ." He "was no declaimer," according to Johnson; "there was not one of his own scene-shifters who could not have spoken 'To be or not to be' better than he did." In *Hamlet*, for example—first acted at Dublin in 1742 and at London in November 1743—Garrick always seemed "to be engaged in a succession of affecting situations; not giving utterance to a speech, but to the instantaneous expression of his feelings, delivered in the most affecting tones of voice, and with gestures that belong only to nature." And in preparing the role of Lear he carefully studied the behavior of a man who'd lost his mind. "There it was," he said, "that I learned to imitate madness; I copied nature and to that owed my success. . . ." [68]

With versatility, vitality, and veracity Garrick freshened English acting. For the 1742–43 season he was hired by Drury Lane and impersonated some thirteen characters, several of them new to London, including Hamlet and a notable Abel Drugger in Jonson's *The Alchemist*. His earnings for that period totaled a lovely £1,130. In 1744 he expertly acted Macbeth and Sir John Brute (Quin's great role) in *The Provoked Wife*. In 1745 he failed as Othello. Then in 1746 Rich at Covent Garden, abandoning his light operas and pantomimes and "sceneries," signed Garrick for a year's contract; so, in company with Mrs. Hannah Pritchard (1711–1768), Mrs. Susanna Cibber, Lacy Ryan, and Henry Woodward (1717–1777) Garrick competed on the same stage with Quin. In November the latter, the master of the old school, as Horatio in *The Fair Penitent*, was more applauded than Garrick, the founder of the new school, as Lothario. As Falstaff Quin scored again over Garrick as Hotspur. But Garrick as Hastings in Rowe's *Jane Shore* (1714) outshone Quin's mechanical Gloster; and he triumphed as Ranger in the century's most popular comedy, *The Suspicious Husband* (1747) by Benjamin Hoadley (1706–1757). Quin snorted, "If the young fellow is right, I and the rest of the players have been all wrong." [69]

In 1747, in a partnership with layman James Lacy, Garrick took over the management of Drury Lane and enlarged the seating capacity to 1,268. For his company he hired Mrs. Cibber and Mrs. Hannah Pritchard in tragedy and Catherine ("Kitty") Clive (1711–1785) and Margaret ("Peg") Woffington (c. 1714–1760) in comedy, the four outstanding actresses of the time. As his alternate in leading roles he chose Spanger Barry (1719–1777), the only rival he was ever to know in tragedy. To support them he engaged Macklin, Henry Woodward, Richard Yates (1706–1796), William Havard (1710–1778), Edward ("Ned") Shuter (1728–1776), and Dennis Delane (1700–1759). Shortly afterward George Ann Bellamy (c. 1727–1788) and Thomas King (1730–1805) were added to the talented, but motley, group of actors. Mrs. Cibber, for instance, belonged to the old school. She "sang, or rather recitatived,"

even though Aaron Hill was her teacher. Her speaking "was so extremely wanting in contrast, that, though it did not wound the ear, it wearied it. . . ."
Mrs. Clive was an instinctive actress, "a mixture of combustibles," and in
Johnson's opinion "the best player I ever saw." (For the 1742–43 season at
Drury Lane she had earned the not inconsiderable sum in those days of
£796.) Mrs. Pritchard was a Quin-like reciter. "She . . . was so exact in her
articulation, that, however voluble her enunciation, the audience never lost a
syllable of it." But when she acted Lady Macbeth "she had never read the
tragedy . . . through. She no more thought of the play out of which her part
was taken, than a shoemaker thinks of the skin out of which the piece of
leather of which he is making a pair of shoes is cut." Peg Woffington was a
pretty hoyden; Barry was a handsome, vital-voiced hero and tender lover;
Delane was a ponderous mouther; Shuter was called by Garrick the greatest
comic genius he'd ever known; Woodward was an expert pantomimist; Yates,
a comic, would "on receiving a new part, fix on some living person who was
a little like it, study him attentively, and thus gain vitality for it"; and Mrs.
Bellamy glittered in her "Paris-dresses, *soupir étouffé* lutestrings, pink-coloured
Chambéry gauzes, foil, spangles, 'interwoven fast embroidery.' " These actors
Garrick trained and directed, "teaching them his own readings and inflections," and welding them into something like an ensemble. London liked
their acting. The average daily theater attendance rose from 1,410 in 1742 to
1,878 in 1748, and the weekly average attendance from 8,460 in 1742 to
11,268 in 1748. (The city's population in 1750 was an estimated 676,250.) [70]

By 1750, less than ten years after his professional debut, Garrick had
established the supremacy of his kind of acting, and Quin at sixty-seven was
ready to call quits to the contest. "Breaking the tones of utterance, or modulating," was "the favored method of delivery" onstage. Sing-song declamation
"was completely out of critical favor." "Nature" was the thing. Garrick had
made the point that the actor must forego traditional theatrical oratory and
turn to nature, must "re-interpret a play in the light of life itself," [71] in the
light of his own personal sensibilities and experience.

But if the new acting was fresh and personal and vivid, and termed
"natural," it was still very definitely heightened. Actors never attempted to
copy ordinary, everyday speaking or behavior. Art wasn't yet a slice of life. It
was nature intensified.

V

Aaron Hill in 1744 commented to a friend: Garrick "is natural . . . and
easy; has a voice articulate and placid: his gesture never turbulent, and often
well adapted, is untouched by affectation." But he wasn't sure that Garrick's
voice could reach "the *swells* peculiar to . . . the more agitated passions."
So, in order to keep his theory before the public he published in 1746 "a
simply absurd" poem of 416 lines called "The Art of Acting," "only the out-

lines of a sketch of a new system which the author is preparing in prose." The verses try to explain how the actor, his "will but commanding," should vigorously imagine and express the ten passions. And Hill promised to dedicate the second printing to Garrick *and* to Quin! Then in 1749, the year before his death, Hill finally finished (part of) his prose "An Essay on the Art of Acting," but decided "against printing it at all" because, as he pointed out in a letter to Garrick, "I see no promise of a likelihood, that I shall ever live to see another actor rise, with *your* capacity, to taste, improve, or even to comprehend, the *use* of such a system." The article, included in his posthumous *Works* (1754), IV, 337–396, makes the basic point that "To act a passion well, the actor must attempt its imitation, 'till his fancy has conceived so strong an image, or idea, of it, as to move the same impressive springs within his mind, which form that passion, when 'tis undesigned, and natural." The remainder of the essay consists mostly of some dull definitions and rather specific "Applications" of the same old ten passions.[72]

Hill, we can guess, was unsettled by Garrick's "natural" innovations in acting. Despite his theoretical pronouncements in favor of "nature," he truly preferred Booth's style, "a weigh'd significance" in utterance and "the grandeur of strong sentiment." "Nature" onstage to Hill always had to be something tumultuous. He wanted, it seems, only to replace formal declamation with impassioned declamation. In his campaign to abolish "flatness" from acting, to eradicate "a groveling, wearisome, bald, barren, unalarming, *Chillness* of Expression, that *emasculates* the mind, instead of *moving* it" he forced and distorted his ideal. His "system" of acting, like his adaptations from Voltaire, "raised the pitch and increased the fulness of the emotional passages . . . until the crises, often prodigally lengthened, were a pother of interrogations and exclamation points" that "throbbed with unreal but elevated emotion."[73]

Yet the excessively emotional "system" of Hill's—perhaps because it was almost a formula and at least something specific—appealed to many for a long, long time. His prose "Essay on the Art of Acting" was variously pirated, rearranged, and published anonymously until near the end of the nineteenth century.[74]

❀ LE COMÉDIEN (1747)

In France in 1730 La Motte was still theorizing about bringing tragedy closer to actuality. He wanted to abolish unnatural monologues and long speeches, and to replace verse with prose, which has a greater *vraisemblance*. Comedy, he argued, has thrown off the yoke and come close to actual life; tragedy should do likewise. Voltaire, on the other hand, aimed for *pompeux* in tragedy, for poetry, and for a manner of reciting it that soared above common everyday speaking. To him tragedies were works of art only when they were elevated. Furthermore, he believed that they would outdraw comedies because the depiction of passions is of more interest to people than the depiction of their foibles. He seemed to be right. In 1730 his *Brutus*, a Roman tragedy in verse, was the outstanding success at the Théâtre-Français. With Dufresne plus important newcomers Pierre-Claude Sarrazin (1689–1762), Charles de Grandval (1710–1784), and Marie-Anne Dangeville (1714–1796) impersonating the chief roles, it was acted fifteen times for paid admissions totaling 12,448. Then in 1732 Destouche's slightly bourgeois and often sentimental comedy, *Le Glorieux* (*The Conceited Count*), attracted for thirty performances an audience of 25,000. But Voltaire's *Zaïre*, an escapist and spectacular Turkish tragedy about the Crusades, accounted for 27,000 admissions in thirty-one showings. The leading characters were acted by Dufresne, Sarrazin, Grandval, and the daughter of Baron's valet, la Gaussin (Jeanne-Catherine Gaussem) (1711–1767). *Zaïre*, the most popular of Voltaire's plays (acted by the Comédie-Française even in the twentieth century), established him as the too flamboyant successor to Corneille and Racine.[75] Acting was almost right back where it had been.

But not quite. In 1733 a new tone was effectively added to playwriting by Nivelle de la Chaussée (1692–1754). He rather naturally mixed the serious with the amusing and thus importantly developed the *drame*. In his *La Fausse antipathie* (*The False Antipathy*) "comedy . . . began to arouse tender emotions . . . by the representation of incidents in the lives of ordinary people." Chaussée's "*l'Homme sensé* announces in the prologue to the play that "*le vrai, le naturel ont des charmes pour moi.*" Then in 1735 Marivaux wrote "*un excellent drame bourgeois,*" *Mère confidente* (*Mother the Confidante*), which detailed humanly the relations between a mother and her daughter. But Voltaire in the next year triumphed again with *Alzire*, a high-blown tragedy laid in sixteenth-century Peru at the time of the Spanish Conquest. In 1737, however, la Chaussée definitely established tearful comedy with his *École des Amis* (*School for Friends*). In 1741 he won even critical approval for *Mélanide*. Plays like these, "hovering between the tragic and the comic,"[76] called, of course, for some changes in acting. After all, many of the speeches were more conversational than declamatory. Could the two styles be mixed?

For *Silvie* (1741), a tragedy that "broke with convention on every possible point," the players were instructed by author Paul Landois (?) to be only natural, and not to go beyond being natural. With a simple story, told in prose and in one act, of a man who is wrongly convinced of his wife's infidelity, Landois tried to humanize tragedy. In the preface to the play he ridiculed "the regal heroes of tragedy, the sententious and heroic lines, the flowery figures of speech." Tragedy, he hooted, "departs so much from reality that if one saw the French king and his court acting and talking as do tragic heroes, one would think them crazy or indulging in a masquerade." French audiences, however, weren't quite ready for *Silvie*, for bourgeois tragedy. The play ran for only two performances "and was forgotten by everyone except

Diderot." Yet, because of the dramatic theories it exemplified, it stands as "one of the stones in the foundations of modern drama." [77]

Voltaire, meanwhile, though espousing more "nature" in acting, continued to overdecorate the Paris stage with his resonant, pseudo-classic plays: *La Fanatisme ou Mahomet le prophète* (1742), his third Mohammedan piece; *La Mort de César* (1743), a sort of Shakespearean tragedy; and *Mérope* (1743), partly derived from Maffei's 1713 Italian work.

In 1746 Charles Batteux (1715–1780) in *Les Beaux-Arts réduits à un même principle* (*The Fine Arts Reduced to a Single Principle*) declared that the business of art is to "select the most beautiful parts of nature in order to form them into an exquisite whole which shall be more beautiful than nature's self, without ceasing to be natural." [78] In *c.* 1749 Chardin (1699–1779), the colorist, was painting from his own immediate bourgeois surroundings; Buffon (1707–1778) was starting his monumental *Histoire naturelle*; and Rousseau (1712–1778) was announcing that man is good by nature and corrupted by civilization.

II

In 1736 Mme. Duclos retired after serving the Comédie-Française for forty-three years and was awarded pensions of 1,000 livres by both the Comédie and the Court. The outstanding newcomers to the organization were Marie-Françoise Marchand, called Mlle. Dumesnil (1713–1803), and Claire-Josèphe-Hippolyte Léris de la Tude, known as Mlle. Clairon (1723–1803). The former signed as an understudy for queen's roles at 100 francs a month in 1737; a year later she was a member of the company. Evidently she was an actress who trusted to the inspiration of the moment. Often, it's reported, she went onstage without quite knowing what to say, and three-fourths of the time she didn't know what she was saying; but *"le reste est sublime."* Mlle. Clairon made her debut at the Théâtre-Italien at the age of thirteen; seven years later, in 1743, she was elected to the Comédie-Française. An intellectual, studied actress, she was at first too artificial in her performing; her declamation was criticized as being "blown up, chanted, full of sighs and sobs, like that of the old Duclos." "For six years she struggled with her voice, as it was too loud and did not move the audience, . . . [but] by dint of constant practice she succeeded in making it express passion and rise to the sublime." [79]

III

In 1747 Pierre Rémond de Sainte-Albine (1699–1778), an editor of the *Mercure de France*, and the author of a *Mémoire sur le laminage du plomb* (*Monograph on Lead-plating*) (1731), became interested in acting, decided that since it was based on nature and reason any man of common sense might well hazard the expression of his ideas on the subject, and wrote *Le Comédien* (*The Actor*). In 307 fairly systematic yet repetitious pages "the theory of the sympathetic imagination [or "sensibility"] in acting . . . was first developed into a critical principle." Sainte-Albine, a layman, a member of the audience, struggled "to describe in eighteenth-century terms and on the basis of insufficient knowledge of psychology what we would today describe as the sensory receptivity and the emotional activity" of the actor. And his discussions, according to Lee Strasberg, two hundred years later, in 1947, "are perceptive, observant, and cogent." [80] The book was praised by Mlle. Dumesnil, went into a second edition in 1749, and a year later was anonymously translated into English, with additions, by John Hill as *The Actor: a Treatise on the Art of Playing; Interspersed with Theatrical Anecdotes, Critical Remarks on Plays, and Occasional Observations on Audiences.* In 1755 he rewrote it; in 1769 his rendering was adapted back into French; and in 1770 that version led Diderot to write *Le Paradoxe sur le comédien.*

"Part the First," pages 17–130, of *Le Comédien* is titled "Of the principal Advantages which a Player ought to have from Nature." Book I lists "the necessary Qualifications of Performers . . . in general" as Understanding, Sensibility, Fire, and (to some extent) a distinguished Figure. First, according to Sainte-Albine, via Hill's words, "a good understanding is as necessary to a player, as a pilot is to a vessel at Sea." He needs "good sense" or discernment —or Quintilian's "judgment"—in order to "join his skill to . . . raising the effects" the playwright intends. (Or, as a modern critic declares, "it is the mind which creates; emotion cannot do so"; as Delacroix's also noted, "Novelty is in the mind that creates, and not in nature . . ."; and as Croce remarked, "The work of art . . . cannot be created by a mind relaxed.") The important new point here—although it's as old as Plato's *Ion*—is Sainte-Albine's belief that the actor is an interpreter who ought to understand and follow "his author strictly and faithfully." [81]

Second, the actor needs "*le Sentiment*," translated by Hill as "Sensibility," or "a disposition to be affected by the passions." Sainte-Albine, quoting Horace, and probably influenced by Du Bos and the elder Riccoboni, maintains that "The player who wants feeling will never be allow'd by those who are judges to be a good, tho' he may be acknowledged to have the declamatory talents of some of our best orators. . . ." The actor must "imagine . . . that he for the time really is the person he represents, and that . . . he is himself in his own person betray'd, persecuted, and exposed to all the unmerited injuries, for which we are to pity him. Nay it is necessary that this voluntary error pass from his imagination to his heart, and on many occasions that a pretended distress produce from him real tears: In this case we no longer perceive in him the cold player, who by his studied tones and forc'd gestures, is labouring to interest our hearts in imaginary adventures; he is to us the person he represents. . . ." Moreover—and here Sainte-Albine makes an odd point—this sensibility is as important to the acting of comedy as it is to the acting of tragedy. "Sensibility in the comic actor . . . must be a more universal agent, and in the tragedian it must be a more powerful one. . . ." "*Dès qu'un Acteur manque de cette qualité, tous les autres présens de la nature & de l'étude sont perdus pour lui.*" (Hill: If an actor "is defective in this essential quality, all the advantages of nature, all the accomplishments he may have acquired by study, are thrown away upon him.")[82]

(John Hill, however, had a curious reservation on this point. He liked elocution, especially Quin's elocution. Therefore he argued that an actor needed either sensibility *or* skill in declaiming! "We have scenes in which a man who has nothing but a declamatory voice without feeling, nay almost without meaning, may acquit himself well enough: And Shakespeare . . . has given us many instances, in which the other quality, sensibility, alone will do. . . . The character of the old servant Adam, in *As You Like It*, is of this kind.")[83]

Third, according to Sainte-Albine, the player needs Fire, that is, "a just rapidity of thought, and vivacity of disposition" which give "the marks of reality" to a performance. "Fire" or vitality, of course, is the term used by Cicero and Quintilian, and by later writers on theatrical subjects, such as Chappuzeau (in 1674) and Brumoy (in 1749). It seems newly to mean more than speed, and more than an intensification of feeling. Sainte-Albine explains it helpfully as follows: Passions "may be exquisitively felt, and yet for want of this fire may be but very ill expressed." Apparently, then, "an actor can never have too much fire"[84] if he would *express vividly to an audience* what he, or the playwright, or the character feels.

Fourth, Sainte-Albine suggests that a distinguished figure (stressed by Riccoboni) isn't truly necessary onstage. Audiences, he says, ought not despise merit for the want of personal charms. We ought "the more applaud the art of the player, as we know it to be the less assisted by nature" or, in other words, by physical attractiveness. (Hill in his version criticizes Mrs. Woffington because "the whole mind of the lady . . . was bent upon charming the audience as *Mrs. Woffington*, not as Andromache.")[85]

Next, in one of his two "Reflections" in Book I, Sainte-Albine claims that understanding, sensibility, and fire are as necessary to the subordinate as to the leading players. Our good opinion of actors, he writes, "is not proportioned to the consequence of their parts, but to the manner in which they acquit themselves in them."[86] In short, in acting there are no small parts.

Book II of Part I lists "the Advantages" by which Leading players "should be superior to those who perform the subordinate Characters." Three of Sainte-Albine's "internal" qualifications are bosh: a "gaiety of Temper" for players in comedy, "an elevated Soul" for impersonators of heroes in tragedy, and youth plus a natural amorousness for those who perform the Parts of Lovers. The fourth, "Tenderness or Feeling," is repetitious. However, it's interesting to note that Sainte-Albine makes the reverse of a Stanislavski ("Emotion Memory") point. No actor ought to attempt to play the lover, he writes, "if he be past that period of his age in which loving would be proper in real life [which was probably a jab at the aged Baron]. The remembering of our past impressions will never prove sufficient for our expressing them as if present." ("*Le souvenir de nos impressions passées ne suffit pas pour nous les rendre.*")[87]

Saint-Albine's discussion of the Leading players' "external" qualifications (those that interest an audience) is muddily repetitious. Only on Voice is he clear: players of comedy should have "an easy and graceful" voice; and "The persons who would succeed in tragedy . . . have occasion for a voice that is strong, majestic, and pathetic."[88]

"Part the Second," pages 131–307, the more seminal half of *Le Comédien* (which one can suppose Stanislavski studied), is titled "Of those Assistances which Players ought to receive from Art." In the introductory remarks Sainte-Albine declares that many persons who go on the stage can no more entertain us "than a fat fellow wheezing at every step with an asthma" can "win the prize in a foot-race." After all, there's more to acting than "a memory, and the power of speaking, walking, and tossing . . . arms about."[89] A would-be player must diligently study his craft, and learn "In what the Truth of a Representation on the Stage consists."

In Chapter I, thus titled, he concludes with no startling originality that "All dramatic fictions please us the more, the more like they are to real adventures and occurrences. The perfection which we are most of all desirous of seeing arriv'd at in the representation . . . is . . . Truth . . . , the concourse of all those appearances which may assist in deceiving the audience into an imagination, that 'tis a scene of real life they are attending to." Therefore, "The performance of an actor, in whatever scene of character, is only true, when we perceive in him every thing that agrees with the age, condition, and situation of the person he represents."[90]

And most important, and modern, "The actor . . . , if he wou'd play his character with *Truth*, is not only to assume the emotions which that passion would produce in the generality of mankind; but he is to give it that peculiar form under which it wou'd appear, when exerting itself in the breast of such a person as he is giving us the portrait of. The rage of Achille is very different from that of Chremès. . . . And the grief of Ariane . . . is very different from that of a Bourgeoise."[91]

In Chapter II, "Of the Truth of Action on the Stage," Sainte-Albine departs from the traditional definition of "Action" and approaches the modern concept. "To exhibit *True Action* in a part," he explains, "is to do every thing allotted by the author to the character represented, in a manner exactly conformable to what the person himself wou'd or ought to have done in it, under every circumstance and in every situation thro' which the action of the play successively carries him." But the player must dig for his True Action since often it isn't easily evident, and often it's different "from that which may first present itself to the imagination." (Hill warns the actor to avoid taking "an exactly contrary part to nature, to reality, and to the intention of the poet.") Furthermore, the player must know that "Every scene produces some change in the circumstances of the character, and [that] every change of this kind demands a multitude of other variations in the actor in conformity. . . ." He must also know that there can be action even in silence, that silence "may be as eloquent as the finest form of words cou'd be." [92]

Next, in reverting to the older definition of "Action," Sainte-Albine rather weakly or wearily commends in the actor "judicious changes" in the countenance, in gesture, and in attitudes. And these visual expressions must be heightened, not distorted, in the theater because "That very degree of expression in the countenance, which is capable of affecting us elsewhere, is not enough to strike us in the player." Then Sainte-Albine gets lost; he can't find any "sure rules to go by" for telling an actor how to behave when impersonating fantastic characters, characters "invented out of mere caprice and wantoness of fancy, [which] have nothing in real life that is at all like them." Like Stanislavski actors, he believes that nature is the only yardstick for art; but when that isn't available, what is to be done? Well, Sainte-Albine lamely advises the player of a fantastic character "not to differ too much from the last person who excelled in it"! [93]

In Chapter IV, "On the Truth of Recitation," Sainte-Albine is sure, first, that players ought, in most instances, to "speak in their natural voice and accent." He's sure, second, in agreement with Riccoboni, that there is no one true tone of voice for the expression of each passion because "every one has his own peculiar inflexion of voice. . . . The anger of some men is a sort of thunder . . . that of others is a sort of still fire smother'd under ashes. . . ." Therefore, although the "tones of the voice . . . may be rang'd under different genera [and] species, . . . the truth of recitation, can never be treated methodically, or deliver'd in the form of a science." [94]

For sure, Sainte-Albine writes, "nothing in comedy is to be deliver'd in the way of declamation. . . . It is a general, and . . . an indispensable rule, that the actor, in comedy, is to recite as naturally as possible: he is to deliver what he has to say, in the very same manner that he would have spoken it off the stage, if he had been in the same circumstances in real life that the person he represents is plac'd in." To Sainte-Albine "rhyme and measure always tend to take off greatly from the air of truth, nature, and reality." (Hill suggests that it's "often necessary [even in tragedy] for the actor to sacrifice the measure of the verse to the sense.") [95]

Sainte-Albine at first seems uncertain as to what to prescribe for the delivery of tragedy. (The two forms were still damnably separated in his mind. After all, the plays by Voltaire and by Chaussée are so different!) He condemns declamation that's unmeaningful, unnatural, and monotonous, and then furtively observes, in agreement with Riccoboni, that delivery in tragedies should be elevated and pompous in harmony with the native majesty of their subjects. [96]

Next, Sainte-Albine lists four "Obstacles which impair the Truth of Recitation." The first is voice straining, which results from too much vehemence and ardor onstage. The second is monotony in delivery, of which there are three kinds: (1) a continual preseverance in the same modulation of voice, (2) a too great resemblance in the closes of speeches, and (3) a too frequent repetition of the same inflections. The third obstacle is an over-all sameness of utterance: If actors are told "they pronounced their sentences well in one speech, they will be sure to pronounce every speech in the same manner." The fourth, and significant, obstacle is the substitution by actors of their own emotions for the emotions of the characters they're portraying. Players "do not take the pains to regulate" an emotion "by the nature of the character that is supposed to feel it, but give us, instead of that, the manner in which themselves would have felt it." (Hill illustrates this point as follows: In acting the character of Marcia in *Cato* "the actresses have not felt the different emotions of love of their admirer and love of their country, as Cato's daughter would have felt them, but as themselves would; and have therefore miss'd all the noble struggles that the author has painted to us between those two passions.") After all, "The great care of the player shou'd be to let us see nothing of himself, but every thing of his character, while he is on the stage." [97]

In Chapter VIII Sainte-Albine tries to point out the value of a player's speaking with "the Illusion of the First Time," but he can't quite coin that phrase. (Hill inserts his observation that what the actor says onstage "shou'd seem the result of the occurrences that have occasioned it, not a part of a lesson got by rote, to be repeated to us at proper periods.") The Frenchman likes "the height of illusion" that improvisation furnishes, but not its lack of content. "It is indeed indisputable," he comments, "that the dramatic writings of a man of wit and genius, as they are studied and regular, are infinitely preferable to the impertinent additions that a player can be able to make them extempore." [98]

Next, in discussing "Natural Playing," in Chapter XI, Sainte-Albine loses his nerve. After having written that performers should, in the main, speak and behave naturally onstage, and after commending the "natural" improvements made in acting by Baron and Mlle. Lecouvreur,[99] he hedges. Or at least he's confused enough, or wise enough, to doubt that *all* acting ought to be "natural." And you can understand his uncertainty. He knew, as Stanislavski never clearly or consistently knew, that there is a difference between art and life (or nature). Sainte-Albine sensed that somehow speech and behavior onstage ought to be different from everyday speech and behavior. Watching, say, Voltaire's tragedies, he was sure that all plays couldn't be acted realistically. Unlike many modern actors, he didn't make the lazy, insensitive mistake of insisting that every impersonation ought to be lifelike.

So, quite frankly, Sainte-Albine explains that "If we choose to understand the term *natural* . . . in a larger sense, and to express by it an exact imitation of nature, as it appears in common in the world, we shall not scruple to affirm, that there are many cases in which a player would appear lifeless, spiritless, and insipid, by playing naturally." For instance, even in "natural" comedies "there are a great many . . . characters in which the actor approaches the nearer to truth of playing, (that is, to the expressing exactly what the author means) as he employs more of a certain set of extraordinary affections . . . ," or certain heightenings or exaggerations. Therefore, "every exaggeration, every heightening of a part by the performer" isn't always a fault; "it is very often a merit in the player, and not unfrequently is of absolute necessity." In tragedy, of course, a certain elevation in acting is demanded. "As tragedy proposes only to shew us nature on its most interesting and affecting side, the first thing the actor who proposes to excell in playing it has to consult, is how to give to every character he may be ordered to represent, the utmost air of dignity that it will bear. . . . Tho' there are many occasions in which . . . [a] plain manner of speaking has great charms, yet it is to be acknowledg'd that there are many others, in which all the pomp and dignity which the actor is able to bestow upon the words in the delivery of them, is scarce sufficient." Yet Sainte-Albine admits that some tragedies, especially those concerned with modern subjects, allow the actor to use a style of delivery between "*le ton du haut Tragique & de la simple Comédie héroique.*" [100]

In Chapter XII, "Of the Finesses in the Art of Playing in general," and in several succeeding chapters, Sainte-Albine tells actors that they need not be mere puppets dangling on a playwright's strings. Actors, he says, have the opportunity, even the duty, of using themselves, of being creative while they interpret. They can, and should at their best, add something of their own to each of their impersonations. Beyond being only "natural and just," he suggests, acting has the potentialities for being "ingenious and delicate"; and it can be those things when an actor of taste and judgment exhibits *his own individual finesses* in playing. "*Ils veulent non-seulement que le Comédien soit copiste fidele, mais encore qu'il soit créateur. C'est dans ce dernier point, que consistent les finesses de son art.*" (Hill: "These nice judges not only expect that a comedian [actor] should be a faithful copier of things; to claim a merit with them he must be able even to create; he must know how to contrive and form, as well as express things; and, indeed, in this consists all the *délicatesse* and superior merit of the profession.") "The actors of a lower class," Saint-Albine continues, "have no idea that they are to see with any other eyes than those of the author; they never imagine that there is a possibility of adding any thing to what he has said; but those of a superior class should always examine their parts with a discerning eye, and seize upon every remark, every circumstance that has escap'd the author, but would have done him credit if it had occurr'd to him, as occasions of merit toward the audience in themselves; whatever is wanting in the dialogue is expected to be added by their play." Only by *individually* creating can the player add magic to his performances.[101]

But his finesses, his attempts to make his every representation "more agreeable" and "to give it a greater air of truth and reality," ought "to arise naturally from what the author has himself thrown into the part," or at least ought not "appear far fetch'd, or forc'd into the play." [102]

With finesses, or his own *personal* perceptions and skills, the actor can add "new graces every time he plays a part, . . . in repeated representations." (As Hill elaborates this point: "Nature has not in her that creeping sameness that the player too often represents her under. If she affects the same man a hundred times with the same accidents, he will indeed have the same kind of sensations every time, but he will not every time have exactly the same motions and gestures to shew them by; nature has given us a thousand ways of expressing in our gesture, our astonishment, our grief, our anger, &c. And why is the player, because under the same circumstances a dozen nights together, to give us but one of them in constant repetition!") [103]

With his finesses, with his own individual creativity, Sainte-Albine claims, the actor can banish a certain sameness in the gallery of his characterizations. Whenever his many and various roles seem to have about them a certain resemblance, the player ought "to decompose" them [break them up into Stanislavski's "Units and Objectives"?], "and regulate himself by the several subordinate passions, of which the grand one [Stanislavski's "The Unbroken Line"?] that makes his character is form'd." The actor should "examine every subordinate passion in which ever of them he is to act, and he will naturally and necessarily, provided that he determines to act with truth, fall into a diversity of playing in them, which will in many cases quite deface the general resemblance; and give his audience variety where they will be very glad of it, tho' they did not expect it." [104]

In sum, "The reason why the modern actors are so very uniform, seems to be that they play rather from memory than from a feeling of the passions of their parts. When an actor, who has the true feeds of his art in him, who has genius, sensibility, and fire, performs a part in which he is thoroughly affected; when he has the command of himself so far that he is able to vary his manner occasionally, his better way is then *not* to attempt the varying his gestures and play as *the main end* [my italics] of what he is about; let him suffer himself to be wholly possess'd of his part, let him make the character as it were real to him, and nature will do the rest; the power he has of varying his manner will exert itself without his particular attention to it, and tho' his sense of the nature of the character will make him always appear in general the same man in it, he will yet always appear new." "*Tout au Théâtre doit être varié. Nous y portons le goût pour la diversité, à un tel point que nous voulons nonseulement que les Acteurs different entr'eux, mais encore que chaque jour ils different d'eux-mêmes, du moins à certains égards.*" (Hill: "Every thing on the stage ought to have the appearance of truth and reality. We carry our love of diversity so far on this occasion, that we expect the actors not only to be different from one another, but that every one of them, in every part he acts, shou'd differ from himself in every other part, at least in some particulars that may strike and affect us.") [105]

Sainte-Albine concludes *Le Comédien* with a few remarks on "graces in Playing" (also mentioned by Gildon). "Is an actor sensible that his playing is perfectly just and true?" he asks. "Is it natural? In fine, is it properly varied? An audience will always admire and esteem him in this case; but there will still want something more in order to their being charm'd with him whenever he appears; and he will see others of much less merit please infinitely more, unless he finds the way of joining to these advantages, the graces of delivery, and those of action." These graces are qualities that *may not exist in nature*. That is why acting, in one sense, is "the art of rendering nature elegant even in her defects, and this without changing her face." The grace in acting tragedy is *"dignity"*; the grace in acting comedy, of all kinds, is a "pleasing gloss." After all, *"Colette au Théâtre n'est pas la même que dans son Village."* Therefore, a "player is to make his character resemble that of people in the way of life out of which the author has taken it, but then he is to make the resemblance as perfect and at the same time as agreeable as he can. . . ." Everything "represented on the stage is to be represented in its fairest light," [106] in an artistic light.

All in all, Rémond de Sainte-Albine's *Le Comédien* offers a perceptive analysis of acting, not perhaps of mid-eighteenth-century acting, but of what an intelligent layman believed then it had chances of becoming. The book reminds one many times, in many of its points, of essential portions of Stanislavski's system. It is logical to conclude that his close friend and early assistant, dramatic critic Lyubov Gurevich, read or translated it (or one or both of the Hill versions, or the Sticotti version) in the libraries of St. Petersburg between 1912 and 1914 and, so bidden, brought her findings to Stanislavski. Then in formulating his system, in collating opinions on acting by the Riccobonis, Diderot, Mlles. Dumesnil and Clairon, Talma, Iffland, Ekhof, and others (but no mention anywhere of Sainte-Albine!),[107] Stanislavski apparently used more ideas from *Le Comédien* than from any other single source. Not that he was wrong in doing so. And not, on that score, to detract from his System, or from the long patience with which he molded his readings and experiences into an often contradictory shape. But in all fairness might he not have given Sainte-Albine some credit? Stanislavski can be criticized mostly for what he did *not* take from *Le Comédien*: the Frenchman's constant, huge worry about the difference between art and life.

✳ THE YOUNGER RICCOBONI

Stanislavski in 1914, it's said, was enthusiastic about *L'Art du théâtre à Madame xxx* (1750) by naturalized Frenchman Antonio Francesco Riccoboni (1707–1772), who on one important point cautiously contradicted his father, Luigi, as well as Sainte-Albine, and anticipated Diderot. Francesco, a middling, or inferior, "cold and pretentious actor" and sometime playwright, performed at the Théâtre-Italien in Paris from 1726 to 1750. In that year (although the treatise may have been written a year or two earlier) he published L'Art du théâtre as help for an unnamed lady who needed advice in order to do well in an art she found to be difficult. Francesco didn't intend to criticize, or even to improve upon, his seventy-five-year-old father's earlier writings on the subject; he highly valued and was influenced by the "Pensées." He hoped only to set down a few fundamentals that might serve as an introduction to those gentle reflections.[108]

L'Art du théâtre has been overpraised as "one of the most important documents in the history of acting," and as marking " a tremendous advance" over the contribution of Sainte-Albine because of its "analysis of feeling." Actually, Francesco only very briefly makes this analysis, and lists the basic emotions as anger and love. What he does do, however, is to emphasize strongly the point that the actor while using his feelings naturally and fully onstage should never forget that he is acting. In other words, the younger Riccoboni insists that the actor should not try to be the character, or, as stated today, to live the part. That point, and others, attracted the attention of Lessing, who, as noted, immediately translated the piece; in 1762 it was translated into Italian; and near the end of the century it served Schröder as the prime source for his lectures on the training of actors.[109] The book, however, has not as yet been translated into English.

In the 106 pages of the rare L'Art du théâtre (57 pages in the 1954 German reprint) Francesco examines acting under thirty headings that range from Gentleness, Nobility, and Rage to Uniformity, Pantomine, and Low Comedy. The principal, longer sections are titled Movement, and, most important, Expression, Declamation (each at least five pages long), Tempo, Insight (much more important than understanding), Voice, and Tone (each about three pages long). The theme of the book is blunt: "The actor must always imitate Nature" (Man muss allezeit die Natur nachahmen," in Lessing's translation.) The two corollaries are: "Affectation is the greatest, and the most common, fault" in actors, and "Good taste alone must keep us [the actors] within the narrow limits of Truth." [110]

Insight, according to Francesco, "is the first and most important prerequisite for the theater. It is this that makes the great actor; without it no one can become more than second-rate." The expert actor must (1) possess "a full knowledge of the natural reactions of others," not only of himself. And to acquire such knowledge he must observe, and see into, people—not only people of rank, because they are usually too artificial or too well-bred to disclose their true feelings, but ordinary people, because they are more likely to give themselves away with strong, genuine emotions. Once the actor perceives true feelings, he needs only "to add a bit of propriety" for expression onstage, "and everything will be all right. In short: one must express oneself like the common people and behave like the aristocrats." [111]

The expert actor must (2) understand the playwright, and then be able to see each line, each speech, in relation to the characters and the plot. The "task of the actor," for instance, "is not so much to move the audience by an exhibition of . . . fire," or tirades rousingly recited in a vacuum, "as to calculate the tempo and tone to fit the mood of the scene." [112]

The second prerequisite for the actor, Francesco says, is the ability to express his insights naturally. (*"Der Ausdruck muss naturlich sein."*) For example, an actor answering someone who had just spoken should not reply mechanically on cue, but should instead as in life momentarily sort out his possible reactions, and only then express the dominant emotion (*herrshende Empfindung*). And his tones should have in them his own "personal touch." [113]

But, because naturalness onstage can often produce indifferent or cold results, the actor must always enlarge, or amplify (or even design?) his utterance, gesture, and motion. "My father," Francesco notes, "used to say that an actor must go two fingers' width beyond the natural." [114]

Francesco's third prerequisite for the actor is the ability of "making an audience feel all those emotions by which he seems to be pervaded. I say: *seems* to be pervaded, not that he really is. Here, Madame," he continues, "I disclose to you one of the brilliant errors" that has misled audiences and even actors themselves. It's commonly believed "that the actor really feels the emotions he represents." That isn't so; the truth is the reverse: "Whoever actually feels what he has to express will be unable to act." He will be unable to act because under the stress of genuine emotion (1) he will probably not be able to control his voice (or his motions). Furthermore, (2) no actor can honestly and completely feel reactions when compelled to pass rapidly from one passion to another in the highly compressed convention of a play; and (3) no actor can ever be freshly, truly moved in an already determined situation or scene; for instance, how can he be honestly amazed or frightened when he already knows what is to be said to amaze or frighten him? [115]

Francesco was well aware that on this point about the stage expression of the emotions "my opinion is quite different from my father's, as you can see from his '*Pensées sur la déclamation.*' The respect that I owe to his declarations—for I'm bound to recognize him as my master in the theatrical art—almost convinces me that I am wrong. However, I still believe that my view, right or wrong, might be of some use. . . ." [116]

In sum, then, Francesco told Mme. xxx that a "full knowledge of the natural reactions of others, plus such *control* [my italics] of one's own soul that one can imitate them at will, are the requirements for an artistic masterpiece. Only with them can the actor create a perfect illusion which the spectators will find it impossible to resist." [117]

❋ THE SECOND HILL

Self-styled "Sir" and "Dr." John Hill (c. 1716–1775), the translator of *Le Comédien*, was an assorted character. Born, as one of his critics supposed, "like other Men," he served during his lifetime as an apothecary, gardener, astronomer, playwright, botanist, justice of the peace, columnist, physician, mineralist, amateur actor, editor, zoologist, and coxcomb. Mostly he was a hack author, "a phenomenon in literary history, . . . perhaps one of the most voluminous writers that this or any other age has produced." He spawned more than eighty books, and once was working simultaneously on seven of them. "Neither Fleas nor Royal Societies escaped him." He translated Theophrastus's *History of Stones* (1746) and Swammerdam's *The Book of Nature* (1758); he edited Berkeley's *The Naval History of Britain* . . . (1756); he addressed a letter to the Royal Society *in which it is proved . . . that a woman may conceive . . . without any commerce with man* . . . (1750); he composed an opera, a semi-novel, and several plays; he wrote *A Compleat Body of Gardening* (1757), *Urania, or a Compleat View of the Heavens* (1754), *The British Herbal* (1756), *The Management of the Gout* (1758), *The Construction of Timber* . . . (1770), *A Decade of Insects* (1773), *An Idea of an Artificial Arrangement of Fossils* (1774), and so on. From such "literature," from his "Discoveries . . . made in Moss, Mites, Cabbage-Leaves, Cherry Stones, Stinking Oysters, and Cockle-Shells," Hill reportedly earned £1,500 a year. He also continually squabbled with other men and made enemies who called him "a quack doctor and a quack author," a "blockhead," and "a little paltry dunghill." Yet Dr. Johnson said of him, that "if he would have contended to tell the world no more than he knew," Hill might have been "a very considerable man, and needed not to have recourse to such mean expedients [as scandal-mongering and vituperation] to raise his reputation." [118]

A man like that couldn't resist the bustle the new acting had produced in London's theaters; he had to take part in it, add to it. In 1744, as one of Macklin's pupils, he portrayed Lodovico in *Othello*, "and seems to have been the only person who regarded the experiment as a success." Six years later he translated Sainte-Albine's book. Then early in 1751 he conducted a column, "The Inspector," in the *London Daily Advertiser and Literary Gazette*. "Among the nineteen papers which Hill devoted to the theater during the next two years are to be found some excellent critiques. . . . In two papers he carried out a parallel between the art of painting and the art of acting, and then in a third set a number of actors off against famous painters; for example, Barry was said to be the counterpart in his art of Julio Romano, Woodward of Paul Veronese, Miss Bellamy of Tintoretto, and Garrick of Titian." [119] In 1755 Hill rewrote, again anonymously, his version of *Le Comédien* (perhaps because it had sold well?) under the same principal title and adding a greatly expanded subtitle: *The Actor: or, a Treatise on the Art of Playing. A new Work, written by the author of the former, and adapted to the present state of the theatres. Containing impartial observations on the performance, manner, perfections, and defects of Mr. Garrick, Mr. Barry, Mr. Woodward, Mr. Foot[e], Mr. Havard, . . . Mr. Ryan, &c., Mrs. Cibber, Mrs. Pritchard, . . . Mrs. Woffington, Mrs. Clive, . . . Miss Bellamy, &c. in their several capital parts,* 284 pages plus an Index of nineteen pages.

In the first, 1750, *The Actor* Hill as "An author unknown to you, and who ever shall remain so," submitted "to the opinion of the Managers of the British Theatres . . . what St. Albine laid before the *French* audiences. . . ." [120] He literally reproduced the original chapter headings but less carefully translated the body of the book. He paragraphed as he pleased, expanded about half of the sentences, and often illustrated the book's precepts by references to plays and players of London—with much praise for Quin and some for Garrick. He also deleted Sainte-Albine's ten-page Preface and four-page Introduction, and added three closing chapters—fourteen pages—of his own material on several trivial details of acting.

William Archer, in commenting on the second, 1755, *The Actor*, says that Hill "was certainly no fool. He was well read; he wrote a very fair style; and, theories apart, he was an excellent critic of acting." But Archer unfairly describes the book as "A mere recapitulation of the former argument, with some new anecdotes inserted." [121] Hill wrote a *new* work based on the first. He reorganized its design, eliminated several chapters, added some nearly new ones, condensed others, pepped them up with fresh illustrative material which included more praise for Garrick than for Quin, reworded the headings, and rewrote the material in his own instead of a translator's style. The result is a definite improvement over the first book.

Some of Hill's, 1755, new phrasings of Sainte-Albine's points merit mention. In "The Introduction," pages 1–3, he announces that "The intent of this treatise is to shew what acting truly is; to reduce to rules a science hitherto practiced almost entirely from fancy; and by that means to assist certain performers in their attempts to attain perfection in it, and some parts of an audience how they may regularly judge of it." [122]

In the new Chapter I, "Concerning the powers of nature, and their limits, and of the necessity of rules and art to form a perfect player," pages 5–18 (which compensates for his deletions from Sainte-Albine's Part II and the emphasis there upon art), Hill is sure that actors "receive and establish nature as the groundwork of all; but they raise upon this basis a structure, in which art has the most considerable share. . . . Playing is a science," he assures us, "and is to be studied as a science; and he who, with all that nature ever did, or can do for a man, expects to succeed wholly without the effects of that study, deceives himself extremely." It's "only . . . when the powers of genius are under the guidance of rule and method . . . that we acknowledge and admire the perfect player." Or, "An hundred people know how to indulge their natural faculties, for one who has the art to check them; but on such a regulation depends all the glory of the compleat performer." [123]

Then Hill gets ahead of himself, and almost into Chapter II, when he declares that it is the "characteristic manner of the author which the player is above all other things to study. . . . Here it is that the greatest discernment of an actor is shewn, in understanding the intent of the author; and his highest judgment in representing the temper of this mind as the other intended." In short, "We expect from the player, not to astonish us with his own ideas, but to represent properly to us those of the poet." [124]

In Chapter II, "Understanding," pages 18–48, three times longer than the 1750 one, Hill follows Sainte-Albine to emphasize the importance of the dramatist. "Indeed," he writes, "the not understanding an author, . . . is the greatest of all defects in the performer. . . ." While nature "deny'd to man the fur of the bear, and the talons of the eagle, the wings of the kite, and the strength of the horse, she gave him understanding." And the actor must use his; he "must first conceive perfectly well what an author meant. . . ." [125]

Specifically, the actor must understand the playwright's characters. "He who is able to excite passions in himself, and cause them in others," he says, "is yet but half qualified for shining in this part of his profession, unless he knows what passion is peculiar to the present circumstance; and what is the exact degree in which it is required." An actor must *understand*, for example, that a king's rage is not that "of a cook in his kitchen"; that "Sorrow in one person is one thing, and in another, another;" and that too often the passion actors exhibit "is their own, and not that of the character." [126] Throughout the book Hill continues to harp on the importance of the playwright's given circumstances which, above all else, the actor must find, study carefully, differentiate, and include in his impersonations.

Next, he blasts those actors who hold that imitation, or the copying of other actors (and directors?) will "supply the place of understanding." Players who only "observe in what manner another pronounces any sentence" and then "give it utterance in the same cadence—an ear answering the purpose of understanding—are setting their profession very low, [are] reducing that to a mechanical art. . . ." Imitation as a method of acting is contemptible, imperfect, mean. If imitation is to be the rule, he asks, "What is to become of the new plays . . . ?" And "if the former players should have been in any thing imperfect or false, there is an end of all advances in the art; and if this were the universal, as it is too much the general rule, to what end should such a person as Garrick have been born: a man who has struck out of his own mind a manner of playing many things, as Shakespeare's Lear, and many more that might be instanced, quite different from what ever was before seen or conceived. . . ." [127]

In Chapter III, "Sensibility," pages 48–78, twice as long as the 1750 chapter and supplemented by thirty more pages on the same topic in the next two chapters, Hill declares that "The business of a dramatic writer is to excite the passions; and that of the player is to represent in the most forcible manner what the other has written . . . this is the work of the sensibility." Unfortunately, he continues, "We find people of both sexes who have excellent understandings, and who have very little of this sensibility. Nay, perhaps, the greatest understandings of all are most exempt from it. It is, in reality, no other than giving way to the passions; and philosophy would teach us to get the better of [them]. . . . But what we wish in the compleat player, is this great sensibility joined with a great understanding; . . . we wish him . . . from his conception . . . to derive that sensibility, thro' which it is to be conveyed to us." In brief, "the judgment regulates the sensibility, the sensibility animates, enlivens, and inspires the understanding." [128]

Hill is sure that the actor needs to feel, but needs also to command himself, to control his feelings, lest he mar his communication. We in the audience "would have his manner of pronouncing his words take all that effect upon us, which the passage has on the most sensible reader; but we would not have it take that effect on himself." [129]

Sensibility, Hill believes, comes from nature; it can't be acquired; but it may be "cultivated, enlarged," or "regulated and reduced to order." However, he isn't clear in explaining how that can be accomplished. He almost seems, suddenly, to discount art or study and to rely on nature. "Whether it be a Bajazet that is angry," he writes, "or a Richard that is angry, the player who has *studied* [my italics] in what manner to express the sensibility of anger, will do the same things [in each characterization]; but he in whom expression is the offspring of the occasion, not of consideration and study, will have it different in each. In the same manner, . . . the actress who practices before her toilet is the same in each circumstance; she to whom nature dictates will be different in all." [130]

Then, like Sainte-Albine, Hill conventionally but curiously separates tragedy from comedy, and observes that "the sensibility of the comedian being no more than that of common life, needs little assistance, provided a due degree of it be had from nature; but this is not the case with the player in tragedy." Differing from Sainte-Albine, he contends that sensibility should be more perfect in the actor of tragedy. The latter needs a "greatness of mind." He must therefore incite, enlarge, and dilate his mind by much reading of "great and noble sentiments." He must banish from his mind all low thoughts.[131]

More sanely, Hill opposes too much extravagance in the show of sensibility. "Let not the proportion be too great for the event. A man would not gape to swallow a pea." After all, some of an emotion ought "to be within." And, again, after Sainte-Albine, he decries the mischief of the actor who is "possessed with some passion of his own, which has nothing to do with that of his character. . . . It might appear a terrible thing to Mr. Garrick or Mr. Barry to swallow poison, and they might be strangely disturbed at the doing of it; but it could not be such to Romeo in such circumstances. Here is one of those instances in which the judgment is to regulate and moderate sensibility: Suppressing what would naturally arise from the subject, by appropriating it to the character." [132]

In Chapter VI, "Concerning Spirit, and what is called, in an actor, Fire," pages 107–137, Hill regrets that "We have . . . some evidences, that a man may perfectly comprehend what an author means, nay, and his heart may be affected thoroughly by the passions, yet from a natural sluggishness of disposition he shall not be able to give life to his sensibility." In other words, some actors can't express what they understand and feel. They need "Fire," or "a daring spirit, a vivacity of imagination, and rapidity of thought" which aren't necessarily "noise and blustering." [133]

"The player of true spirit," Hill sums up, "when it is directed by understanding and awakened by sensibility, is no longer himself, when he assumes his character; he possesses himself that he is the king or hero he represents . . . he lives, not acts the scene." [134]

The second half of The Actor, while wandering into many repetitions and dwindling now and then to the trivial or the stupid, continues to offer some attractive reverberations of Sainte-Albine. Among the stupid items two are typical: (1) "The characteristics of the footman, are submission and attention, a cringing humility, and an observant obedience. While a footman is upon the stage, he should always be in motion. . . ." (2) The illusion of a love scene will be perfect "when those who are to protest and vow to each other on the stage, in reality sigh and doat on one another off. It is not much to the credit of the married state, that husband and wife have seldom been observed to play the lovers well upon the stage." Typical of the trivial, but true, items is: "The fullness or the emptiness of the house must not be suffered to affect" the actor's performance; "for if it be empty, is it not to his credit to play so, that those who are present shall say, it ought to have been fuller?" [135]

Principally, Hill is pleased to note that at present "We have nothing of the recitative of the old tragedy." Nowadays, he writes, "if we are to be pleased with the representation, it must come near reality." In "the strict adherence to nature's rules, tho' in an enlarged scale, lies the *truth*. . . . Observation therefore, and consideration, are the true instructors; the player is to throw himself without restraint into the circumstance, and observing what is his own natural deportment, he is to recollect that of some *other person* [my italics] of politeness and understanding, in a parallel circumstance; and on comparing his own action with that of the other, and judging, without prejudice, where either is excellent or amiss, he will be able, from both, to form a true action for the circumstance." [136]

Hill then lashes out at Mrs. Woffington for not acting in *character*. As Andromache, he reports, she "was in more pain about the setting of her ruffle than the death of Astyanax, or the ghost of Hector." No matter what

"Hector's widow might think, it did not appear to Mrs. Woffington there was any thing so terrible in the matter." And she communicated "the resolution of her death, with that sort of interrupted attention which a little girl would have discovered in repeating her lesson, when she thought some who were present admired her eyes more than her memory." [137]

For nonactor Hill, as for nonactor Sainte-Albine, "A perfection in the player is the hiding himself under his character." Neither of them would have approved the fundamental principle of the Actors Studio, namely, that the student must spend a year or two, or more, in getting to know himself so that he can the more truly exhibit himself onstage. Only "actors of the second class," writes Hill, "think they have nothing more to do than to express the passions of their part as they should feel them: but they are to remember, it is not as themselves, but as the characters they represent, would feel, that we expect to see them." For example, [Henry] "Mr. Milward (?–1741) has great merit, but he was Mr. Milward in every thing: whether he played Harry the fourth, or Mr. Sealand, Sciolto or Bajazet; it was still Mr. Milward repeating those parts . . ." For another example, as Pierre in Venice Preserved "Mr. Garrick felt as Mr. Garrick, and Mr. Quin as Mr. Quin; but Mr. [Henry] Mossop (1729–1774), as Pierre: they did it naturally with respect to themselves; but that is the false sense of the word, natural; Mr. Mossop does it as it is natural to the character. . . ." In sum, if an actor "is not different from himself on many occasions, we shall never allow him the praise of a consummate actor." [138]

Yet Hill concedes, just once, that "it is not altogether the truth" that an actor is always to "dissemble and conceal" his natural temper and assume that of the character he's impersonating. In comedy, for instance, a player must have by nature, and exhibit constantly, a "gaiety of disposition." Moreover, "Mr. Cibber, the best lord Foppington who ever appeared, was in real life . . . something of the coxcomb; and the reason why Mr. Woodward succeeds less in them is, that he has not in life the true character." [139]

✸ MORE GARRICK, MORE NATURE

Garrick didn't write or talk much about acting (actors can overdo that); he performed. He read more naturally than most of his predecessors—although with much heightening in tragedy and some perhaps in comedy where, according to many, he especially excelled. Declamation, Garrick said, "revolts my nature, does not please my judgment." He objected, for instance, to "the harmony of Racine's verses" because it "necessitates a sort of sing-song. . . ." [140]

Garrick also believed that "Racine, so beautiful and enchanting to read, cannot be acted, because he . . . leaves the actor nothing to do" except recite. He liked to "do" things onstage, to be visual as well as oral. In addition to acting "much with his features" (face always toward the audience) "so that even those who understand not a word of English comprehend without difficulty the scene enacted before them," he was "amazingly dexterous and nimble." Some people, of course, criticized Garrick for being overactive, overpantomimic, overvisual. Macklin, for one, disapproved of "his strange manner of dying and griping the carpet; his writhing, straining, and agonizing; (all of which he introduced into the profession of acting). . . ." Someone else doubted the value of his primer habit of acting out every word in a sentence: Benedick's "If I do, hang me in a bottle like a cat, and shoot at me!" doesn't require "such a variety of action as minutely to describe the cat being clapp'd into the bottle, then being hung up, and the further painting of the man shooting at it." Again, as Hamlet in the ghost scene, when Horatio says, "Look, my lord, it comes!" "Garrick turns abruptly round and, at the same moment, totters backward two or three steps, his legs giving way beneath him; his hat falls on the ground; his arms, especially the left, are almost fully spread, the hand on a level with his head, the right arm bent with the hand hanging down, the fingers wide apart, the mouth open; thus he remains in a noble attitude, . . . as if turned to stone, supported by his friends. . . ." Tableau. John Gielgud at that line of Horatio's simply turned slowly, slowly. Then upon seeing "the awful visitation with which his imagination has been dwelling for so many hours, his overwrought nerves for an instant betray him. He whirls away, hurling himself into Horatio's arms." [141] Garrick, one concludes, used too many muscles, tried too hard to prove that acting should be more than recitation.

He more effectively proved that point by his talent for impersonation—his novel contribution to acting. He could seem to *be* rather than to *recite* a character; and more, he could seem to be a wide assortment of characters all different from what he was. He was a born mimic. "The great art of David Garrick," it was said, "consists in the facility with which he abandons his own personality and puts himself in the situation of him he has to represent; and when once he has filled himself with that character, he ceases to be Garrick; and becomes the person assigned to him. . . ." And "all the changes which take place in his features come from the manner in which his deepest feelings work." Sainte-Albine might have phrased that tribute. Macklin, of course, diluted it by remarking that Garrick's "mind was busied" only "upon external . . . partial imitation of individuals. . . ." [142]

Maybe so. Garrick didn't attempt to copy ordinary human beings, to be simply realistic. He didn't "imitate nature, but modeled himself on an ideal personage who, in the particular situation, would be affected in the highest degree by the emotions of the moment. 'If you act only according to your own standard,' he said, 'or indeed according to the most perfect natural model that exists, you will never be more than mediocre.' " [143] Garrick, in other words, imagined in terms of his medium, in accordance with art.

He imagined (as Sainte-Albine prescribed) an ideal character *in the circumstances* and *in the style* set down by the playwright. And he knew that "a *fix'd* attention to the business of the scene [not to the audience] . . . is the *sine qua non* of acting." Only, for example, by concentrating upon Romeo and his surrounding circumstances could he impersonate more "naturally" than Barry that character's entrance into the Garden Scene. Barry came on "as a great Lord, swaggering about his love and talking so loud, that by G—, Sir, if we don't suppose the servants of the Capulet family almost dead with sleep, they must have come out and tossed the fellow in a blanket." But Garrick, "sensible that the family of the Capulets are at enmity with him and all his house, *he* comes in *creeping* upon his toes, whispering his love, and cautiously looking about him, *just like a thief in the night.*" [144]

In his concentration on the circumstances of the play Garrick to some degree allowed for and favored impulses of the moment. He believed "that the greatest strokes of genius have been unknown to the actor himself, till circumstances, and the warmth of the scene, has sprung the mine as it were, as much to his own surprise, as that of the audience. Thus I make a great difference between a great genius and a good actor. The first will always realize the feelings of his character, and be transported beyond himself; while the other, with great powers, and good sense, will give great pleasure to an audience, but never 'wring, inflame, soothe the heart like a magician.' " Once in discussing the acting of Mlle. Clairon, Garrick said he feared she lacked "those instantaneous feelings, that life-blood, that keen sensibility that bursts at once from genius, and, like electrical fire, shoots through the veins, marrow, bones, and all, of every spectator." She "is so conscious and certain of what she can do, that she never, I believe, had the feelings of the instant come upon her unexpectedly. . . ." [145]

Yet Garrick's technique was so potent he could say that "a man was incapable of becoming an actor who was not absolutely independent of circumstances calculated to excite emotion, adding that, for his own part, he could speak to a post with the same feelings and expression as to the loveliest Juliet under heaven." Despite his praise for spontaneity in acting, Garrick was above all a studied, well-prepared, completely controlled performer. Always, for instance, he was aware of his audience—probably because he was an expert comedian. All comedians must be aware of an audience, if only to save space for laughs, or to set their timings; and Garrick surely discovered no valid reason why an actor in serious plays should not for artistic reasons be equally aware of an audience. His calculation, his leaving little of his acting to chance, is one of the points made by Sir Joshua Reynolds (1723–1792) in "A Conversation Piece" between Dr. Johnson and Edward Gibbon (1737–1794). The former declares that "Garrick's trade was to represent passion not to feel it. Ask Reynolds whether he felt the distress of Count Hugolino when he drew it." *Gibbon:* "But surely he feels the passion at the moment he is representing it." *Johnson:* "About as much as Punch does. That Garrick gave in to this foppery of feelings I can easily believe; but he knew at the time that he lied. . . . it is amazing that any one should be so ignorant as to think that an actor will risk his reputation by depending on the feelings that shall be excited in the presence of two hundred people, on the repetition of certain words which he has repeated two hundred times before in what actors call their study—No, sir, Garrick left nothing to chance, every gesture, every expression of countenance and variation of voice, was settled in his closet before he set his foot upon the stage." [146]

II

By 1750–60 in London it was rather popularly admitted that "The Requisites to make either Painter, Poet, or Actor, are in a great Measure the same." Hence, in the years of empire building and the start of the agrarian and industrial revolutions, and in the time of John Wesley (1703–1791), David Hume (1711–1776), Adam Smith (1723–1790), of scientists Henry Cavendish (1731–1810) and Joseph Priestley (1733–1804), of Thomas Chippendale (1718–1779), of William Hogarth (1697–1764), Reynolds, and Thomas Gainsborough (1727–1788), of Johnson, Laurence Sterne (1713–1768), Thomas Gray (1716–1771), Horace Walpole (1717–1797), and Smollett, acting became "an art worthy of careful study." [147]

A stage impersonation was praised when it reproduced a partial reality, when the actor duly weighed "the different Manner in which different Characters feel and express the same Passion." Some critics even ceased to worry any more about the differences between art and nature. In his *Philosophical Inquiry into the Origin of our Ideas of the Sublime and Beautiful* (1757) Edmund Burke (1729–1797) couldn't "distinguish between a work of art and real life. . . ."; Lord Kames (1696–1792) with the *Elements of Criticism* (1762) was led "constantly into awkward confusions between art and life"; and Samuel Johnson, in his many writings, was "one of the first great critics who . . . almost ceased to understand the nature of art, and who, in central passages, treats art as life. He has lost faith in art as the classicists understood it. . . . He paves the way for a view which makes art really superfluous, a mere vehicle for the communication of moral or psychological truth. Art is no longer judged as art but as a piece or slice of life." [148]

Audiences wanted only "real" characters to amuse or to move them. An unknown writer in the *Royal Female Magazine* (1760), for instance, announced that he would form his opinion about theatrical entertainments, and about acting, "on the *feeling* of my heart, rather than the judgment of my head, if they should at any time happen to clash"; and a reporter for the *Gentleman's Magazine* (1768) responded to plays by asking "What do I feel?" rather than, "Has the author obeyed the rules?" [149] Almost any individual, in short, suddenly became a competent judge of the reality, if not of the design or the point, of an actor's characterizations.

Acting, "a topic of almost universal conversation," was the subject of numerous books during the third quarter of the eighteenth century in London. Roger Pickering's (1718?–1755) *Reflections upon Theatrical Expression in Tragedy* . . . (1755), though remembered by Boswell as being "the most ingenious and philosophical performance that we have upon the subject of acting," is only a rehash of current precepts. Thomas Wilkes (?) in *A General View of the Stage* (1759) uses Part II, seven chapters, pages 81–171, for a tired examination "Of the Art of Acting." *The Actor*, a poetical epistle . . . (1760) in 136 couplets by Robert Lloyd (1733–1764), announced that "Nature's true knowledge is his [the actor's] only Art," and that "Here lies the Golden Secret; learn to FEEL." And in 546 couplets of the highly popular *The Rosciad* (1761) Charles Churchill (1731–1764) weighed the abilities of many English actors and awarded first prize to Garrick because his passions "seem from quickest feelings caught:/ Each start is Nature; and each pause is Thought." Chiefly Churchill insisted that "The actor who would build a solid fame/ Must Imitation's servile arts disclaim;/ Act from himself, on his own bottom stand. . . ." Also he worried a bit because "the whole town, mad with mistaken zeal,/ An aukward rage for ELOCUTION feel." [150]

James Boswell (1740–1795) in *On the Profession of a Player, three essays . . . from the London Magazine for August, September, and October 1770* was certain that acting "ought to be ranked amongst the learned professions." It is, he wrote, "as laborious, and perhaps more so, than either law, physick, or divinity." Then, anticipating Diderot, he newly phrased a standard but shadowy point. A "good player," he acknowledged, "is indeed *in a certain sense* the character he represents"; but, more accurately, that player "must have a kind of double feeling. He must assume in a strong degree the character which he represents, while he at the same time retains the consciousness of his own character." [151]

Two volumes of *The Dramatic Censor* . . . (1770), collections of play reviews, are worth mention because critic Francis Gentleman (1728–1784) gives some vivid descriptions of the way the same parts were acted by different men. The anonymous *The Sentimental Spouter, or, Young Actor's Companion* (1774) is an elementary textbook for students.

Elocution insistently raised its artificial head with the anonymous publication of *The Art of Speaking; containing I. An Essay; in which are given Rules for expressing properly the principal Passions and Humours . . .* (1761) by political writer James Burgh (1714–1775). On the premise that "Art is but *nature improved upon and refined*," the author provided over three hundred pages of lessons in mechanical speaking. His "Index of Passions, or Humours" runs to thirteen pages!! Burgh's book quickly went through seven editions in England, and at least eight reprintings in America beginning in 1775. Thomas Sheridan (1719–1788), the father of Richard Brinsley Sheridan, and a studied, oratorical Irish actor-manager who had co-starred with Garrick, published *A Course of Lectures on Elocution . . .* (1763) in which he advised public speakers—and actors—to avoid affectation, or art, and to follow nature. His thesis is "That there are few persons, who, in private company, do not deliver their sentiments with propriety and force in their manner, whenever they speak in earnest. Consequently here is a sure standard fixed for propriety and force in public speaking; which is, only to make use of the same manner in the one, as in the other. And this, men certainly would do, if left to themselves; and if early pains were not taken, to substitute an artificial method, in the room of that which is natural." The topics of his seven lectures are: articulation and pronunciation, accent, emphasis, pauses or stops, pitch and management of the voice, tones, and gestures. Then in 1775 appeared *The Prosodia Rationalis; or an Essay Towards Establishing the Melody and Measure of Speech; to be Expressed and Perpetuated by Peculiar Symbols.* The author, Joshua Steele (1700–1791), believed "that the tones of the voice in speech through rhythm and melody could be set down as accurately as could the notes in song." His book introduced an "elaborate system of notation . . . for accent, quantity, and emphasis." [152]

III

With all the new interest in acting it is no wonder that audiences came to the theaters primarily to see actors instead of plays—even when the latter were augmented with *entr'acte* dances, songs, interludes by children, offerings on musical instruments, and recitations. Attention, it is said, was focused in the ratio of 70 percent on casts and 30 percent on scripts. A play in Garrick's time "was regarded almost solely as the vehicle for a 'star' performer. . . ." Actors and actresses who "possessed" certain roles accounted for the success of old and new playwrights. [153]

The companies, therefore, were relatively stable and relatively small. "An actor might come to the London stage from one of the Dublin theaters or from a provincial troupe, or occasionally he might make his first appearance at one of the London patent houses; but once he was accepted by the audiences in London, he usually remained attached to the Drury Lane or Covent Garden company until he retired from the stage. He might move from one of the patent theaters to the other, or he might go to Ireland for a season or two; but, so small was the world of the theater in eighteenth-century Britain, that he had virtually no other opportunity to display his talents." And "so stable was the membership of the acting company that the novelty of a new actor or actress was rare. . . ." Audiences loved the same faces and talents night after night—performances began at six o'clock—in a variety of roles in all kinds of plays. [154]

The actors were repertory actors. "They appeared, in theory, at all events, in a different play every night. Many of them knew two or three hundred parts that they could undertake at relatively short notice. . . ." Some of them might impersonate as many as thirty different characters on thirty different nights. It is startling to learn, for instance, that in the 1751–52 season (from mid-September until the end of May) "seventy full-length plays were performed at the two patent houses, sixteen of which were given at both Covent Garden and Drury Lane." And in the 1774–75 season ninety-eight full-length plays were presented at the same two houses, and again sixteen were acted at both.[155] Obviously, there wasn't much depth to the many characterizations exhibited by each actor.

Just as obviously there wasn't much team-work, except of a superficial kind. No one, in most instances, harmonized the acting or shaped it to the requirements of the play as a whole. "Each actor usually rehearsed by himself. Each actor, that is, worked out, regardless of the other actors, not only his physical movements on the stage, but also his understanding of the part he was going to play." [156]

In January 1761 Garrick presented the first new long comedy acted by either Drury Lane or Covent Garden in more than a dozen years, the "laughing" *The Way to Keep Him* by Arthur Murphy (1727–1805). Next year he enlarged Drury Lane to accommodate an audience of 2,362, or 1,027 more than Covent Garden. In 1773 the theater presented Oliver Goldsmith's (1730–1774) *She Stoops to Conquer* as well as *Macbeth* with Macklin, aged seventy-four, in the title role. In 1775, after Colman had sold his interest in the theater, Covent Garden staged *The Rivals* by Richard Brinsley Sheridan (1751–1816).

IV

Lewis Hallam (1714–1756), an actor at Covent Garden from 1734 to 1741 and an occasional actor at Drury Lane, had sailed in 1752 with his wife and a company of ten additional players to America where the stage was defended on the grounds that it promoted "the Circulation of Cash by employing Masons, Carpenters, Taylors, Painters, etc." [157] The company performed at Williamsburg, New York City, and Philadelphia plays by Shakespeare, Rowe, Lillo, Farquhar, Addison, Cibber, and so on. Hallam's pioneer work was carried on by David Douglass (?–1786) who built the Southwark Theatre in Philadelphia (1766), the John Street Theatre in New York (1767), as well as theaters at Annapolis (1771) and Charleston (1773).

❊ GERMANY; RUSSIA

In mid-century Germany, "not yet a nation," the actors were without a capital, or cultural center, where they could permanently settle and improve their skills. They spread themselves thin, wasted their energies touring, and found only intermittent security. Konrad Ackermann and his wife, Sophia Schröder, for instance, performed with a new company from 1753 until 1755 in Warsaw, Breslau, Halle, Magdeburg, Berlin, Danzig, and so on. And they kept in touch with Lessing (who, in 1754, when he was only twenty-five, translated a sizable portion of Sainte-Albine's *Le Comédien* for the *Theatralische Bibliothek*, and in the next year for the same publication much of volume III, "on the theatrical declamation of the ancients," from the *Réflexions* by Du Bos). In 1755 at Frankfort-on-Oder the troupe staged his domestic tragedy in prose, *Miss Sara Sampson*, with Ackermann as Mellefont, Sophia as Lady Marwood, and her eleven-year-old son Friedrich as Arabella. English-derived, it was "the first modern German play to be taken from life and written in natural and unstilted dialogue." Toward the end of that year the company performed in Ackermann's own theater at Königsberg until 1757 when the Seven Years War drove him to Switzerland and Alsace. After 1761 the players worked in Freiburg, Karlsruhe, Frankfort-on-Main, Mainz, Hannover, and finally in 1764 settled in Hamburg.[158]

The Schönemann company, after many wanderings, was performing by 1751 mostly at Schwerin and Hamburg. The repertoire "continued to be a mixture of classical French comedy, *comédie larmoyante* and Holberg, a steadily decreasing proportion of French tragedy, and an all too small number of original German plays, mostly comedies. . . ." At Hamburg in 1753 Konrad Ekhof, a member of the troupe, established an "Academy of Actors." Only thirty-three at the time, but "with an almost pedantic respect for the holiness and seriousness of dramatic art," he announced that "To . . . be an actor is not so easy a task as many consider it to be. . . . Dramatic art is copying nature by art and coming so near it that semblance is taken from reality. . . ." Mastery of this art, he continued, demands a vivid imagination, untired application, and a never idle practice. Within a year his plan of study was mocked to death.[159]

In 1757 Ekhof left the Schönemann company; a year later he took over managing its remnants in association with Gottfried H. Koch (1703–1775), who for twenty-one years had served as an actor and theater-poet with the Neubers and then had organized his own troupe *c*. 1750 in Saxony. The principal actors then were Koch's wife, Christiane (?), Johann Brandes (1735–1799) and his wife-to-be, Charlotte Koch (1746–1784), Johannes Brückner (1730–1786), and Joanne Starke (1731–1809). Seven years later, in 1764, when the group was at Leipzig, Ekhof left it to join the Ackermann company at Hamburg. By 1766, after a year at Dresden, the Koch actors were established in the first proper theater built in Leipzig—but they ran into some competition there from another troupe headed by "scene-chewer" Karl Döbbelin (1727–1793). In 1768 the Koch company was invited to Weimar and stayed there, subsidized by the court, until 1771. From 1771 to 1775 the actors played in Berlin.[160]

When Ekhof with his actress wife Sophie Schulz (?) joined the Ackermann company in 1764 he was the foremost actor in Germany, and, according to his countrymen, "the greatest master of theatrical language any nation ever possessed." Lessing said that Ekhof seemed to have served as a model for Sainte-Albine's advice to players. That praise, however, is a trifle confusing because Lessing didn't quite agree with the Frenchman's basic precept. He doubted if natural ability and a talent for feeling the passions of another person were sufficient to make a first-rate actor. Feelings, he believed, must always be under the actor's control. Control was of prime importance. And control was the product of technique.[161]

Ekhof, from most of the evidence, was a controlled player. According to actor Johann Brandes: "Seldom did Ekhof enter deeply into the emotions that the action demanded, but he deceived the spectators by his art. Without being touched by emotion himself he touched all hearts." Another critic said that "Ekhof . . . did not rely on emotion alone, either in his reading of the lines or in his acting; rather, he was careful, during the performance, not to become too much moved by emotion lest, because of lack of thought, he might play with less truth, harmony, expression and reserve." And Schröder commented: "The truth that the actor must only *seem* to be the person he is representing, if he is to remain true to the author, has been proved by Ekhof. Never have I noticed a tear in the eyes of this rare speaker, while his hearers could hardly keep their eyes dry." Ekhof himself maintained that "The actor must not enter into the real emotion that he is to represent, but must do everything by means of art." [162]

Ekhof's chief colleagues beginning in 1764 were, in addition to Ackermann and his not very active wife: Sophie Hensel (1738–1790), Johann M. Boek (1743–1793) and his wife Sophie Schulze (?), David Borchers (1744–1796), Karoline (Schulze) Kummerfeld (1745–1815), and the twenty-year-old Friedrich Schröder. And no doubt Ekhof's dedication to acting "marked a turning-point in the career of young Schröder. . . . [The] vivid interest and no less vivid criticism with which he followed all the performances of Ekhof [166 roles] during the five years they worked together, testify sufficiently to the fact that his art, in which he had hitherto lacked ambition, now appeared to him in a different light, and that he no longer regarded intelligence, reflection, and brain-work as superfluities." [163]

Schröder left the company for about a year in 1767 to join a troupe of improvising actors led by Austrian Joseph F. von Kurz (1715–1784). At that time Johann Löwen (1727–1771), the literary son-in-law of Schönemann, and merchant Abel Seyler (1730–1801), madly in love with Sophie Hensel, bought out Ackermann and started the abortive Hamburg National Theater. The venture lasted only from April 1767 to March 1769, and is remembered primarily for the *Hamburgische Dramaturgie* which Lessing as publicist and paid critic wrote for the theater.[164] His bright comedy, *Minna von Barnheim* (1767), was acted there (after its premiere at Leipzig by Döbbelin's troupe) for fifteen or sixteen performances with Ekhof, Ackermann, Borchers, Sophie Hensel, and Susanna (Preissler) Mecour (1738–1784) in the chief roles.

Schröder returned to his step-father's company at Easter 1769 when Ackermann agreed to take over the theater again. By August of that year, however, Abel Seyler persuaded Ekhof, Boek, and Brandes with their wives to join a new company he and Sophie Hensel were forming. "This Seyler company, with its strong nucleus of players, became one of the best of its time. . . ." as it toured for two years in northwest Germany. In 1772 Seyler succeeded Koch at Weimer, and his company continued to play there, subsidized by the court, until fire destroyed the theater in 1774. Again Seyler took to the road; but in 1775 the Duke of Gotha established a court theater, and hired the best of Seyler's actors. With a new troupe, the latter continued to tour in Saxony.[165]

When Ackermann died in 1771 Schröder, age twenty-seven, took charge of the Hamburg company. In 1772 he produced Lessing's *Emilia Galotti* (after its premiere at Brunswick by Döbbelin's troupe); in 1774 he staged Goethe's tempestuous, Shakespearean, "storm and stress" *Götz von Berlichingen*; and next year he was dreaming of acting Shakespeare.

By 1774 Germany boasted of at least fourteen theaters, and six were added by the following year. The principal ones were (1) Schröder's company in Hamburg, (2) Koch's company in Berlin at the Theater in der Behrenstrasse (1771), (3) Seyler's company at Gotha, (4) Döbbelin's company in Dresden and Magdeburg (which came to Berlin in 1775), and (5) Franz Schuch's (1716–1764) company, managed by his widow in Königsberg. (At Vienna in 1776 the Teusches Nationaltheater was established in the Theater an der Burg (1741), later called the Hofburgtheater.) [166]

II

In 1750 Tsarina Elizabeth (1709–1762), daughter of Peter the Great, was eager to substitute Russian professionals for the foreign and native amateur actors who for a long time had been entertaining the court. Two years later, hearing excellent reports about an amateur company at Yaroslavl, she summoned the group to St. Petersburg. In March 1752 the actors, headed by Fedor Volkov (1729–1763), exhibited their wares before her Imperial Majesty and several illustrious personages, won her approval, and began to stage public performances "at the German theater, on the Bolshaya Morskaya, where . . . there shall be tallow candles and fire pots with tallow; whilst in her Imperial Majesty's presence, not only wax candles and fire pots with tallow, but also firewood for heating the theater." In September Elizabeth provided for the education of the Yaroslavl actors: Volkov, his brother Grigóry, Ivan Dmitrevsky (1733–1821), and Aleksey Popov were by decree "to matriculate in the Corps of Cadets for the study of literature, foreign languages, and gymnastics." They were also to be taught stage technique and declamation by the officers. Volkov at once bought "six printed tragedies, a harpsichord and strings, [and] a mirror . . . for the study of gestures." [167]

Four years later, in August 1756, Elizabeth added to the brilliance of her court by inaugurating the Russian professional theater at "the Golovin stone house, on the Vasilyevsky Island. . . . For the said theater we have issued an order to engage actors and actresses: actors from among choir boys, and the Yaroslavl residents studying at the Corps of Cadets, such as may be required, and, in addition to these, actors from among other private people, as well as an appropriate number of actresses. . . . We entrust the directorship of the said Russian theater to Brigadier Alexander Sumarokov" (1718–1777), a playwright.[168] These first professional Russian actors bumbled along learning their craft by presenting comedies by Molière, Holberg, and Destouches, Corneille's *Le Cid* and *Cinna*, Lessing's *Miss Sara Sampson* and *Emilia Galotti*, as well as some comedies and tragedies by Sumarokov.

After the latter had been dismissed from his post for outspokenness in 1761, after Catherine took the throne in 1762, and after the death of Volkov in 1763, Dmitrevsky took center stage as Russia's chief professional actor. His two leading ladies were his wife, Dmitrevskaya (Agrafena Musina-Pushkina) (?–1788), and Tatyana Troyepolskaya (?–1774). In 1765 and 1767 Dmitrevsky journeyed abroad "for the improvement of his theatrical training" and studied the acting techniques of Lekain, Clairon, and Garrick.[169]

❁ DIDEROT

A "prodigious man, . . . vertiginous, stunning, electrifying," Denis Diderot (1713–1784) was the fermentive thinker of the Enlightenment. Ever "in a state of effervescence, ever anxious to learn some new thing, today taking a knitting-machine to pieces in order to explain it in the *Encyclopedia*, tomorrow discussing the discoveries of the physiologist Borden or the principles of the chemist Rouelle, then examining the metaphysics of Leibnitz or Malebranche and developing his own ideas in the same province, . . . ever flitting from subject to subject," Diderot by mid-century became interested in the theater. He thought about the style of plays that were being written, about how they were staged, how they were acted; and in no time at all ideas popped from his mind "like sparks from an anvil." Two of them were startling. First, he advocated—a hundred and fifty years too soon—a thoroughly realistic, even naturalistic, theater. Second, he argued that actors should wake to the fact that they are the lively creators of the essential play, and that as such they could be artists of intelligence—and sometimes geniuses.[170]

Nobody, however, paid much attention to Diderot as at intervals he loosely spun out his esthetics of the theater while editing the epochal, twenty-two volume *Encyclopédie; ou, Dictionaire raisoné des sciences, des arts, et des métiers* (1751–1772). The Comédie-Française went cosily along its by now well-established and fairly popular course. Between 1750 and 1770 (when the company moved to the Tuileries) an average of nearly 165,000 people per season paid their way into their theater. And, as in London, the actors, not the plays in which they appeared, attracted audiences. Actors were the bait—and the bosses; they kept the playwrights in second place. For instance, when Palissot's *Zarès* was staged in 1751 the actors changed the title from the original *Sardanapale*, altered Acts I, II, and V by suppressing a number of passages, and added a new character. When Rotrou's *Venceslas* (1647) was brought up to date by one dramatist, "star" Lekain privately employed another to rewrite his role, and, "without acquainting any of the players with his intention, played it according to the interpolations and excisions then made. Consequently, from the beginning to the end of the performance . . . the utmost confusion existed among the company." And when Diderot's *Le Père de famille* was produced in 1761, actors "Préville and Bellecourt relieved it of many superfluous speeches." [171]

Voltaire was the one playwright actors did not dominate as he continued to compose distant and ornate tragedies. His oriental *L'Orphelin de la Chine*, with Lekain, Mlle. Clairon, and Sarrazin in the leading roles, was played seventeen times before more than 17,000 spectators in 1755, and for sixteen times the following season. His chivalric and weepy *Tancrède*, with Lekain, Mlle. Clairon, and Brizard, ran for twenty-eight performances in 1760 and 1761, and became known as "Mlle. Clairon's tragedy." [172]

Perhaps only five additional plays worthy of mention were staged between 1759—when spectators were cleared from the stage—and 1775. Michel Jean Sedaine's (1719–1797) *Philosophe sans le Savoir* (*A Philosopher Without Knowing It*), "not only the finest example of the eighteenth-century *drame*, but . . . the first modern drama," attracted over 21,000 persons during its first run in 1765; but the actors treated the author badly and drove him to writing for the Théâtre-Italien. Shakespeare's *Hamlet*, in a version by J. C. Ducis (1733–1816), was acted twelve times from September 1769 to January 1770 with Molé as the Prince, Mlle. Dumesnil as Gertrude, Brizard as Claudius, and Marie-Madeleine Blouin (?–1779) as Ophelia. *Romeo and Juliet* was read, learned, rehearsed in two weeks, and presented for nineteen times in 1772 with Molé as Romeo and Mlle. Saint-Val (1743–1830) as Juliet.[173] Goldoni's *Le Bourru Bienfaisant*, as already noticed, was performed in 1771; and in 1775 *Le Barbier de Seville* by Pierre-Augustin Caron de Beaumarchais (1732–1799) offered a few intimations of the Revolution.

II

The leading actresses of the Comédie-Française were hardy. Mlle. Gaussin and Mlle. Dangerville performed with the company for thirty-three years before they retired in 1763. Mlle. Clairon "carried the art of declamation to the highest point of perfection" for the twenty-two years she served as leading lady (1743–1765). And her rival, Mlle. Dumesnil, always praised for her "fidelity to nature's laws" (although Garrick called her "visibly artificial"),[174] acted for thirty-eight years until she left the stage in 1775.

Henri Louis (Caïn) Lekain (1729–1778) began performing as a youngster, was admitted to the Comédie-Française in 1751, quickly topped Grandval, and became its star in tragedies. Short and ugly, he proved (as did Garrick) that talent plus study could delete "figure" from the traditional prerequisites for a perfect actor. Lekain, essentially a harsh-voiced declaimer, "tried to cause all his verses to be felt, even every word." Evidently he recited "*prodigiously, prodigiously* indeed!" Garrick, while admitting that the Frenchman performed with much feeling, found that his style "puts me strongly in mind of Quin. . . . I am sure, to relish him, it is either necessary to have . . . exquisite judgment which can discover the minutest beauties, or to be born in France." [175]

On the other hand, Préville (Pierre Louis Dubus) (1721–1799), who came to the Comédie-Française in 1753, was valued by Garrick as one of the most talented comedians he'd ever seen. In a word portrait of that actor he especially commended his abilities at characterization: Préville "performs no less than five different parts in a comedy (not a good one) called *Mecure galant* [by Boursault]. In the first he is a miserable, half-starved, sneaking compound of flattery and absurdity; in the second, he represents a shrewd, sly, suspicious, obstinate *campagnard*—both of which, though whimsical, are made natural by his manner of playing them; in the third, he is a Swiss soldier, most importantly drunk without grimace; in the fourth, he swells his figure and features into the full-blown pride, pomp, and passionate arrogance of a serjeant-at-law, and then in a moment changes himself totally, and enters with all the soft, smirking, self-conceited, familiar insignificance of a scribbling Abbé. . . . nor is he only excellent in the low parts of comedy; in the *petites pièces* of Marivaux, you will see him act with as much finesses as nature. . . . In short, he is not what may be called a mere 'local' actor. . . . his comic powers . . . make him a comedian of the world." [176]

Other important, or interesting, additions to the troupe included Jean-Baptiste (Britard) Brizard (1721–1791); François (Molet) Molé (1734–1802), who contrived to outwit the Church in its refusal to let an actor marry unless he swore to abandon the stage; the elder Mlle. Sainval (1743–1830); Mme. Vestris (Marie Dugazon or Françoise Gourgaud) (1743–1804), a student of Lekain's; Jean Maudit-Larive (1747–1827), a student of Mlle. Clairon's; Mlle. Raucourt (Françoise Saucerotte) (1756–1815), a student of Brizard's; the younger Mlle. Sainval (1752–1836); Jean Baptiste (Gourgaud) Dugazon (1746–1809); and Jacques Monvel (1743–1812).

By 1773 one critic was attributing "the indolence of the actors of the Comédie-Française and their unwillingness to put on new plays to lack of competition and to the guaranteed income of over 200,000 livres a year which they derived from the *petites loges*." [177]

III

Antoine Maillet-Duclairon (1721–1809) in his *Essai sur la connaissance des théâtres français* (1751) indicated the hesitant strides which had been made toward a more natural acting: "Declamation seems to have changed every ten years, and the tragedies of Corneille and Racine have been played in so many ways that it's almost impossible to find exactly the right method that ought to be used. . . . For a long time it was believed that the dramatic poem ought to be declaimed in a way that was more like singing than talking, as if the princes portrayed in a tragedy weren't accustomed to speaking as other people do." Nowadays, he continued, that is being changed. But actors still find difficulty with the *pièces larmoyantes*, because neither the comic nor the tragic tone quite fits the mood and the "everyday language of honest men" in such plays. Therefore, he noticed, many of the actors tend to overact *"le véritable dialogue"* because they feel that a too familiar tone might sound trivial.[178]

Playwright Jean François Marmontel (1723-1799), however, in 1752-53 persuaded Mlle. Clairon to lessen her pompous declaiming in tragedy. "I have an irresistible feeling," he explained to her, "that declamation, like style, may be noble, majestic, tragic, *with simplicity*; that expression, to be lively and profoundly penetrating, requires gradations, shades, unforeseen and sudden traits, which it cannot have when it is stretched and forced." The resulting experiments with his notion of "simple declamation," he said, "surpassed her expectations and mine. It was no longer the actress, it was . . . [the character] whom the audience thought they saw and heard. The astonishment, the illusion, the enchantment, was extreme." (Mlle. Clairon then decided that "the truth of declamation requires that of dress," and, with Lekain, led the players in abandoning "their fringed gloves, their voluminous wigs, their feathered hats, and all the fantastic apparel that had so long shocked the sight of all men of taste.") And Marmontel in 1754 wrote for *l'Encyclopédie* a brief article on "Déclamation" in which he professed to follow some principles he'd learned from Garrick's practice.[179]

Other Frenchmen also wrote about stage declamation—which, though simpler than it had been, was, you can be sure, still much more artistic than realistic. A vaguely recorded Graverelle (?) published a *Traité de l'eloquence dans tous les genres* (1757) which lifted verbatim almost four hundred pages from Charles Rollin's (1661-1741) *Traité des études* (1726-28, reprinted 1740). Prolific playwright Claude-Joseph Dorat (1734-1780) composed a popular *La Déclamation Théâtrale, poème didactique* . . . (1766) which went into a fourth edition by 1771. And Louis Charpentier (?), in discussing the *Causes de la Décadence du Goût sur le Théâtre* . . . (1768), titled one of his chapters *"Suite des prétendus talens du comédien & de la déclamation théâtrale,"* I, 63-85.

More significantly, Rémond de Sainte-Albine's precepts on acting were kept in circulation. In 1769 Hill's 1755 *The Actor* was roughly translated into French without any realization on the part of the anonymous scribbler that it was based on a French original! And because of the great interest in Garrick's acting, vivified by his visits to Paris in 1763-65, the tiny book of two hundred pages was titled *Garrick, ou Les Acteurs Anglois; Ouvrage contenant des Observations sur l'Art Dramatique, sur l'Art de la Représentation, & le Jeu des Acteurs* . . . No mention, obviously, is made of the anonymous Hill. At least three editions were printed in three consecutive years, and a German translation appeared in 1771. The book has been credited to Antonio Fabio Sticotti (?) who seems to have been a singer and actor of Pedrolino and Pantalone with Luigi Riccoboni's Paris company; but it may have been written by his son, Anton Giovanni Sticotti (1739–c. 1772), a player with but middling success as Pantaloon with the Théâtre-Italien and Opéra-Comique. Whichever Sticotti it was, he "gave most of his attention to the anecdotic side of his English original," translating many greenroom stories, and (in foot-notes) "adding parallel cases from French stage history. Thus Sainte-Albine himself might not at the first glance have recognized in *Garrick* a grandson of his own *Comédien*. Amid all the changes, however, his emotional extravagances were faithfully reproduced." [180]

IV

Diderot in 1770, using Sticotti's book as a springboard, dove into the debate that "was . . . started between a middling man of letters, Rémond de Sainte-Albine, and a great actor, [Francesco] Riccoboni," and came up in 1778 with *Le Paradoxe sur le comédien*. It "has remained to this day the most significant attempt to deal with the problem of acting." [181] *Philosophe* and sometime playwright Diderot supported inferior, not great, actor Francesco Riccoboni in opposing the new emphasis on rampant sensibility, or emotion, in acting. After all, someone had to speak up vigorously for intelligence—even in the theater—even in acting.

Diderot's paradox complicates the classic rule that the actor himself must feel in order to make others feel. It insists that the actor while performing must only *seem* to feel in order to rouse feelings in an audience. Whether this contradiction is true, partly true, or false doesn't immediately matter. It's at least provocative, and as such deserves careful scrutiny in something resembling a context.

Diderot was fascinated by the theater. In his slightly obscene, potboiler novel, *Les Bijoux indiscrets* (1748), he used one chapter to comment on drama and to decide that its perfection "consists in the imitation of an action, so exact, that the spectator, deceived without interruption, imagines that he is present at the action itself." Then, believing that plays ought to reflect the manners of the middle classes and depict the problems of the average man, he wrote in 1757 and 1758 two undramatic didactic domestic tragedies, or *drames: Le Fils naturel, ou les épreuves de la vertue (The Natural Son, or The Trials of Virtue)* and *Le Père de famille (The Father of the Family)*. The first, acted only once in 1771, was published in 1757 along with three lengthy "Entretiens sur *Le Fils naturel*," or duologues on the

drama between "Dorval [a character in the play] et Moi." *Le Père*, acted
with some success in 1761 and again in 1769, was published in 1758 with a
sizable essay, "De la Poésie Dramatique." In that same year Mme. (Marie-
Jeanne Laboras de Mézieres) Riccoboni (1714-1792), the wife of Francesco,
said in a letter to Diderot that he "did not know the smallest details of an art
[acting] which, like all others, has its technique"; he argued with her in his
reply.[182] He also, it seems, decided to learn more about acting.

Diderot already valued actors. Even though he knew that "Envy is worse
among them than among authors" and that they are "little and mean in
society," he said he "put a high value on the talent of a great actor; he is a
rare thing—as rare as, and perhaps greater than, a poet." Acting, he added,
demands "a great number of qualities that nature so rarely unites in the same
person, that one can count more great writers than great actors." "Nature's
[man] is less great than the poet's, the poet's less great than the great actor's,
which is the most exalted of all." Yet he was convinced that the "actor must
sometimes sacrifice himself to the poet." [183]

As the first naturalist in the theater, Diderot was convinced in 1757-58
that actors should perform in a lifelike way onstage, should "substitute real
people for the usual mannequins, walking with measured steps, acting according to wooden rules," and seeking applause "by addressing the *parterre*." He
advised them to "forget the spectator"; he said "think no more of the audience
than if it had never existed. Imagine a huge wall across the front of the stage,
separating you from the audience, and behave exactly as if the curtain had
never risen." He even encouraged actors to turn their backs now and then
on the audience; he asked them to speak their lines (which ought to be in
prose, "a transcript of speech in real life") naturally, to make those lines less
literary by pausing for thought more often, by breaking up or interrupting
utterance under the stress of emotion, by using instinctive and inarticulate
sounds, by relying more on gesture, pantomime, and silence.[184]

Because he was a naturalist, Diderot was at first an emotionalist. He
highly valued sensibility in the actor, ranking it above understanding, judgment, or intellect. A player, he maintained, should lose self-consciousness completely while portraying the passions of a character. A great actor, a genius, "is
transported into the situation of the personages he must act; he takes on their
characters; [and] if he experiences in the highest degree the great passions . . .
he creates the sublime." In the "Entretiens," for a specific instance, Diderot insists that "an actress of limited judgment, of ordinary understanding but of
great sensibility, understands without difficulty a situation of the soul, and
finds, without thinking, the accent which leads to the different sentiments
that constitute the situation, which all the sagacity of the philosophers is unable to unravel." [185]

Nearly ten years later, c. 1766, however, Diderot was less enthusiastic
about the worth of sensibility. In one of his letters to a young actress, a Mlle.
Jodin (?), he wrote that "The actor who has nothing but reason and calcula-

tion is frigid; and the one who has nothing but excitement and emotionalism is silly." He favored then "a kind of balance between calculation *and* warmth." [186] By 1770, however, he denied emphatically—perhaps too emphatically—the productive power of sensibility in the actor and argued for reason, for calculation, as the essential prerequisite for great acting.

Why did Diderot reverse himself? Nobody knows. Perhaps, stung by Mme. Riccoboni, he had in his wee spare time thought deeply about acting. Perhaps he'd been pained by the excesses of emotionalism in the theater. Certainly he'd examined the studied skills of Garrick. And certainly as he grew older and wiser as a naturalist he searched for and found some of the differences between art and nature. At any rate, Diderot eventually concluded that actors at their best could be more than mere sensitive copiers of nature, that they could be, must be, intelligent creators.

Diderot reached this conclusion after he evolved an over-all theory of creativity for the production of any work of art, even of a naturalistic one. He was sure, first, that the effect of a painting, of a poem, of a play, and of an onstage characterization "does not always spring from the exact description of phenomena [or from the exact or so-called honest exhibition of behavior?], but from the emotion felt by the genius who has experienced them, from the art with which he communicates to me the vibration of his soul, from . . . the ideas and feelings that he can awaken in me" as viewer, reader, listener. From that premise he worked out a three-fold process of creating: "The first step in the process is . . . the arousing of '*enthousiasmé*' by the perception of the meaning of a particular phenomenon. Next, imagination is energized by '*enthousiasmé*' to form a quantity of images by which that meaning is to be expressed; this is the most important moment of the process, the moment of inspiration. ("Imagination," which "imitates, composes, combines, exaggerates, enlarges, diminishes," must predominate.) Finally, reason, controlling the creator's technical equipment, brings order among the images and gives them comprehensible physical realization. If the genius is an artist, this realization is the work of art." [187]

Thus for Diderot sensibility, though essential to an artist, couldn't by itself make an artist. To be an artist a person with sensibility must do more than merely display it. After all, people with exceptional sensibility aren't automatically creative. An artist must be able to communicate to others (or only to himself?) via a medium a meaning, or a feeling engendered by the meaning. Thus for Diderot the new emphasis on sensibility in art was all wrong. Those who preached and practiced it neither understood art nor the artist.

V

Having worked out a concept of art, and of what an artist ought to aim to do, Diderot couldn't approve of Sticotti's *Garrick, ou Les Acteurs Anglois*

and its instructions on acting. He found the book "crabbed, obscure, complicated, bombastic . . . [and] full of commonplace." He discovered that almost
a third of it was pointlessly devoted to a discussion of the actor's sensibility.[188]
Therefore in his *Paradoxe* he tried to smash that misplaced, immature,
middle-class, impotent emphasis; and in setting down his own analysis of
acting, his theory of what he thought it should be, Diderot smashed so hard
and with so much rhetorical exaggeration that he seems to some to have
annihilated sensibility as a prerequisite.

The *Paradoxe*, unfortunately, is choppily organized, in some details un-
clear, and often overargued. "I have not arranged my ideas logically," Diderot
apologizes, "and you must let me tell them to you as they come to me. . . ."
And ideas came to him at intervals over a period of about eight years. The
gist of the treatise first appeared in October and November 1770 when
Diderot contributed two critical articles, "Observations sur une Brochure intitulée *Garrick ou Les Acteurs Anglais*," to Friedrich M. Grimm's (1723–1807)
Correspondance littéraire which circulated privately among courts of Germany
to furnish the latest information on Parisian letters. Three years later Diderot
apparently had completed one version of the *Paradoxe* and, via a friend,
submitted it to Garrick for his criticisms. None, however, were forthcoming.
At the Hague in 1774 Diderot probably did some additional work on his
duologue; and he may have retouched it later since there are in the final text
"allusions . . . to events which occurred in 1776 and 1778." He never published the *Paradoxe*. At his death in 1784 it was found among thirty-three
works in manuscript. The book was first printed in 1830. Then in 1902 a
furious critical battle was waged around it: "Is it, as we possess it today, really
the work of Diderot? or did his disciple and friend, Naigeon, adulterate and
spoil the original draft that appeared in *Correspondance littéraire* in 1770 by
the addition of odds and ends borrowed from different sources?" [189] No
absolutely certain answers to either question were found.

The core of the *Paradoxe* is traditionally summed up in Diderot's pat
and purposely startling sentence: "Extreme sensibility makes middling actors;
middling sensibility makes the ruck of bad actors; in complete absence of
sensibility is the possibility of a sublime actor." That sentence is unfortunate.
At least three other quotations more accurately summarize Diderot's theme,
his point. For instance: (1) "The actor who goes by Nature alone is often
detestable, sometimes excellent," usually mediocre. In addition, he "must have
a deal of judgment. He must have in himself an unusual and disinterested
onlooker." (2) The actor's "talent depends not, as you think, upon feeling,
but upon rendering . . . exactly the outward signs of feeling. . . ." (3) The
actor who can convey the sublimity of Nature is the actor "who can feel it
with his passion and his genius, and reproduce it with complete self-possession." [190]

In part Diderot may have derived his strong but often muddled opposition to onstage sensibility from the younger Riccoboni who, as noted, had

written in 1750 that "Whoever actually feels what he has to express will be unable to act." And before then, it must be remembered, "Betterton" in 1710 had suggested that the "Passions . . . ought never . . . transport the Speaker out of himself"; and in 1728 the older Riccoboni had told actors "it is not enough to trust only to natural instinct." Moreover, John Hill in 1755 had more or less constantly pointed out that the actor must "command his passions," that "There is nothing in . . . a player's art that takes more effect, perhaps nothing that takes so much, as this due regulated sensibility." Furthermore, Sticotti, while carelessly or deliberately dropping many of Hill's strictures on the need for controlling or shaping feelings, retained some of them; for instance, he wrote that "Judgment must control and modify the sensibility." Finally, Boswell in 1770, in the same month that Diderot was reviewing Sticotti's book, explained that the actor "must assume in a strong degree the character which he represents, while he at the same time retains the consciousness of his own character." [191]

Diderot so atrociously defines the term "sensibility" (in order more easily to win his case) that we can skip it and agree in all fairness that the *Paradoxe* attacks, or minimizes the importance of, Sainte-Albine's "*la facilité de faire succéder dans leur ame des diverses passions, dont l'homme est susceptible*," Sticotti's "*la facilité de s'abandonner aux passions*," [192] or, in today's words, the actor's almost exclusive dependence on feelings during a performance.

Diderot, once you organize the scatterings of his *Paradoxe*, offers four main, overlapping reasons why an actor should not entirely "play from the heart." First, he is sure that "Sensibility is by no means the distinguishing mark of a great genius." Penetration is. So is expression, or the rendering (the effective communication via a medium) of what has been perceived and felt. "Is it," Diderot asks, "at the moment when you have just lost your friend or your adored one that you set to work at a poem on your loss? No! ill for him who at such a moment takes pleasure in his talent. It is when the storm of sorrow is over, when the extreme of sensibility is dulled, when the event is far behind us, when the soul is calm, that one remembers one's eclipsed happiness, that one is capable of appreciating one's loss, that memory and imagination unite, one to retrace the other to accentuate, the delights of a past time: then it is that one regains self-possession and expression. One writes of one's falling tears, but they do not fall while one is employed in polishing one's verses; or if the tears do flow the pen drops from the hand: one falls to feeling, and one ceases writing [or creating]." [193]

Why, Diderot continues, "should the actor be different from the poet, the painter, the orator, the musician? It is not in the stress of the first burst that characteristic traits come out [that creativity is achieved]; it is in moments of stillness and self-command; in moments entirely unexpected. Who can tell whence these traits have their being? They are a sort of inspiration. They come when the man of genius is hovering between nature and his sketch of it, and keeping a watchful eye on both. The beauty of inspiration, the chance hits of which his work is full, and of which the sudden appearance startles himself, have an importance, a success, a sureness very different from that belonging to the first fling. Cool reflection must bring the fury of enthusiasm to its bearings." [194] The actor's head must control his heart.

Thus, according to Diderot, "The great actor watches appearances; the man of sensibility is his model; he thinks over him, and discovers by after-reflection what it will be best to add or cut away." [195] That is to say, the actor studies nature, and then in accord with the style of a play he significantly alters the natural behavior, the real emotions, with his taste or intelligence. He doesn't merely copy and live the model's emotions; he shapes them and continually controls them in order to exhibit his penetration, or the point he finds in them.

Second, Diderot insists that an actor overcome by emotion, or living his role, can neither judge his effects nor consistently achieve them. That kind of actor has no "full freedom of mind" for attending to those essential stage tasks. Often he "may feel strongly and be unable to express it" or worse, be unaware that he is not expressing it.[196]

"Let a consummate actor," Diderot says, "leave off playing from his head, let him forget himself, let his heart be involved, let sensibility possess him let him give himself up to it," and yes, he will intoxicate us in the audience, transport us "with a fine moment" or two or three; "but would you rather have a fine moment than a fine part?" The actor with "what we call sensibility, soul, passion, . . . may give one or two tirades and miss the rest. [But] To take in the whole extent of a great part, to arrange its light and shade, its forts and feebles; to maintain an equal merit in the quiet and in the violent passages; to have variety both in harmonious detail and in the broad effect; to establish a system of declamation which shall succeed in carrying off every freak of the poet's—this is a matter for a cool head, a profound judgment, an exquisite taste,—a matter for hard work, for long experience, for an uncommon tenacity of memory. The rule, *Qualis ab incepto processerit et sibi constet* [Let it continue as it began, harmonious with itself], rigorous enough for the poet, is fixed down to the minutest point for the actor. He who comes out from the wing without having his whole scheme of acting in his head, his whole part marked out, will all his life play the part of a beginner." The great actor, for instance, "has rehearsed to himself every note of his passion. He has learned before a mirror every particle of his despair. He knows exactly when he must. . . . shed tears; and you will see him weep at the word, at the syllable, he has chosen, not a second sooner or later." And "At the very moment when he touches your heart he is listening to his own voice." [197]

A great actress like Mlle. Clairon, for a specific example, struggles to capture and to shape the emotions of her role; but once she has done that, "she repeats her efforts without emotion" so that she can then "hear herself, see herself, judge herself, and judge also the effects she will produce." Thus onstage "she has a double personality"—the actress *and* the character she impersonates.[198] She constantly monitors the character, subjects it to her will, forces it to communicate what must be communicated.

"If an actor," Diderot asks, "were full, really full of feeling, how could he play the same part twice running with the same spirit [and harmony and unity] and success?" "Tomorrow . . . [he] will miss the point . . . [he] excelled in today; and to make up for it will excel in some passage where last time . . . [he] failed. [Alternatively], the actor who plays from thought, from study of human nature, from constant imitation of some ideal type, from imagination, from memory, will be one and the same at all performances, will be always at his best mark; he has considered, combined, learned and arranged the whole thing in his head. . . . His passion has a definite course—it has bursts, and it has reactions; it has a beginning, a middle, and an end. The accents are the same, the positions are the same, the movements are the same; if there is any difference between two performances, the latter is generally the better." [199]

In sum then, an actor can't "make himself master of others' minds" [200] (and feelings) by being beside himself with anger, or any other emotion. He can do that only when "he imitates anger," or any other emotion, and in so doing controls and designs it—in the same way that he wisely and with full command of himself imitates drunkenness instead of being truly drunk on-stage. In performance the actor in order to convey artistically his meaning to others must command his joy, his grief, or whatever the emotion, and not allow it to take command of him. In performance an actor must be fully aware of the effects he is producing—like the comic who knows when and just how long to wait for a laugh, and what to do to "fill in" before he proceeds. If he lives his role, completely feels it, he can't possibly do that.

Diderot argues, third, that an actor should not give way to his feelings "on the boards" as he does in life because a play is not life, or reality, but "a work of Art, planned and composed." A play is a convention—because it is peopled by "ideal type[s]," by characters who "are phantoms fashioned from this or that poet's special fantasy," because its dialogue is what "poetry talks like." "Do you suppose," he asks, "that the dialogue of Corneille, of Racine, of Voltaire, or, let me add, of Shakespeare, can be given with your ordinary voice and with your fireside tone?" Of course not. (But Diderot does not ask about the speaking of one of his favorite plays, the realistic Le Philosophe sans savoir by Sedaine, nor about the speaking of his own plays.) A play is a convention, third, because "The likeness of passion on the stage is not . . . its true likeness; it is . . . subject to conventional rules." And, finally, a play is a convention because "nothing happens on the stage exactly as it happens in nature." So, since the "truth of nature is out of tune with the truth of convention" or Art, "How should nature [or only feeling a role] without Art make a great actor . . . ?" [201]

Fourth, Diderot is against [too much] sensibility in the actor because in most instances it won't allow him to get away from himself, to "forget himself, distract himself from himself," [202] and impersonate someone else, the playwright's character. He seems to imply that the actor of sensibility is likely to remain himself onstage in order to revel in and to display only his own sensibility.

Diderot insists that the actor's job is to imagine and to impersonate— not to be—someone other than himself. "A sure way to act in a cramped, mean style," he warns, "is to play one's own character" all the time. Only a beginner is content to remain himself "and to prefer the narrow instinct of nature to the limitless study of art. . . ." Mlle. Clairon, for example, creates a type, "some vast specter in her own mind, . . . not herself. Were it indeed bounded by her own dimensions, how paltry, how feeble would be her play-ing!" How self-centered, too! And Garrick is summoned by Diderot, in what amounts to a speck of an ode in prose, to testify against an actor's playing only himself: "I take thee to witness, Roscius of England, celebrated Garrick; thee, who by the unanimous consent of all existing nations art held for the greatest actor they have known! Now render homage to truth. Hast thou not told me that, despite thy depth of feeling thy action would be weak if, what-ever passion or character thou hadst to render, thou couldst not raise thyself by the power of thought to the grandeur of a Homeric shape with which thou soughtest to identify thyself? When I replied that it was not then from thine own type thou didst play, confess thy answer. Didst not avow avoiding this with care, and say that thy playing was astounding only because thou didst constantly exhibit a creature of the imagination which was not thy-self?" [203]

Such, then, are the main arguments of the *Paradoxe*. They don't add up, as is commonly supposed, to the belief that the actor should not feel. They add up, instead, to the belief that the actor can convey the sublimity of nature when he "can feel it with his passion and his genius, and reproduce it with complete self-possession."

VI

Two omissions from the treatise, of course, immediately appear. First, Diderot ignores Garrick's criticism of the acting of Mlle. Clairon, his fear that she lacked "those instantaneous feelings, that life-blood, that keen sensi-bility that bursts at once from genius"; nor does he mention Garrick's opinion that the genius actor "will always realize the feelings of his character, and be transported beyond himself. . . ." [204] Diderot was unaware of, could not cope with, or disagreed with any reliance in performance upon careless rapture. Inspiration for him should come during the shaping of a character, not during its showing. Second, Diderot never once in the *Paradoxe* pleads for, or even mentions, naturalistic acting although, in 1757–58, he had strongly advocated a completely naturalistic theater. One wonders if perhaps by 1770–78 he had surrendered his belief in that style?

Now, as it was then, the *Paradoxe* is "a challenge to the actor to recognize the high nature of his art, a plea that he discipline and control the flow of his imagination and feeling." Diderot's "demand . . . for a technique of emotional experience is an essential of any acting theory or practice." [205]

Stanislavski was more than merely "interested" in Diderot's views. Occasionally he adopted them. He writes that "Our art . . . requires that an actor experience the agony of his role, and weep his heart out at home or in rehearsals, that he then calm himself, get rid of every sentiment alien or obstructive to his part. He then comes out on the stage to convey to the audience in clear, pregnant, deeply felt, intelligible and eloquent terms what he has been through." Stanislavski also notes that once when he acted "I divided myself, as it were, into two personalities. One continued as an actor, the other was an observer. Strangely enough this duality not only did not impede, it actually promoted my creative work. It encouraged and lent impetus to it." [206]

❀ ELOCUTION TRIUMPHANT

In all probability actors paid little heed to all these theories about acting. The guess is that—like many actors today—they disliked to think about the subject. They probably talked endlessly about it, but that doesn't mean they had to think about it. Nevertheless, before the last quarter of the eighteenth century they had tried performing—even in tragedies—a bit more "naturally," or with a little more correspondence to nature, or by using more personal experiences, than formerly. Nature was the source of playing.

But acting was not yet a copying of nature. It was still an art; and art, according to Winckelmann and others, was nature heightened, made graceful, beautiful, ideal. Eighteenth-century acting remained primarily a product of judgment. Whenever more nature was introduced it was quickly curbed lest the activity forfeit its distinction as an art. In most instances toward the end of the 1700's acting was ordered, refined, elevated by elocution. Elocution came to the rescue. Then, overstressed, the "grand style" of tragedy—with definite reverberations in domestic dramas and in comedies—effectively blocked for a long while the further intrusion of genuine naturalness onstage.

II

In late eighteenth-century Russia, however, acting had not advanced to the point where it could indulge in the tussle between art and nature. At St. Petersburg in 1782 the first original Russian play of merit, *Neodosl* (*The Minor*) by Denis Fonvizin (1744–1792), was staged. In this comic attack on serfdom the chief roles were acted by Dmitrevsky, Avdotya Mikhailova, Vasily Chernikov, and Yakov Shumsky (who impersonated an old woman). Next year Dmitrevsky, whose "Intellect and technical perfection . . . accounted for his success" as a comedian, was appointed overseer of plays in the Imperial Russian Theater, and soon began "to teach the pupils . . . of the dramatic school declamation and acting." He retired from the stage in 1787 with an annual pension of 2,000 rubles; then in 1791 he was appointed "principal supervisor of all Russian theatrical performances, instructor of those not yet sufficiently skilled, organizer of the second Russian company from among those persons already in the service, and director of the school to ensure its efficient operation." [207]

One of the successful new actors at St. Petersburg was Yakov Shusherin (1755–1813), who c. 1785 had been the leading man, for 1,300 rubles a year plus an apartment, of a company performing at Moscow. Conscientious and next in importance to Dmitrevsky, he insisted that "The dress rehearsal must be conducted with as much care as the performance itself. One must assume," he said, "that the play is not yet smooth; and, no matter how often it has been performed, it is absolutely necessary that on the morning of the performance it be rehearsed *mezzo-voce*, yet with all vocal inflections." Comic Anton Krutitsky (1751–1803) was another favorite of the nobility. His "ways and manners . . . , characteristic of the common people but . . . ennobled," won him special acclaim in *Yabeda* (*The Slanderer*) (1798), a satiric exposure of graft by Vasily Kapnist (1757–1824). Other principal players were Peter Plavilshchikov (1760–1812), a gifted elocutionist, and Aleksey Yakovlev (1773–1817), who with impulsive declamation eventually eclipsed Shusherin.[208]

III

The rescue of acting from being too "natural," and its preservation as an art, a thing of elevation, occurred most clearly in Germany.

At Hamburg in 1776 Friedrich Schröder with great success coached his actors, directed their movements, and set the pace and rhythm for his own adaptation of *Hamlet* in which he played the Ghost to pupil Johann Brockmann's (1745–1812) Prince; later Schröder impersonated Hamlet, Laertes, and the Grave-digger. By 1780 he had staged, like an orchestra conductor, eleven prose versions of Shakespeare's plays and acted leading roles in all of them, most expertly perhaps as Lear. Then, weary after almost ten years of managing and producing, after acting something like forty new parts a season, after adapting and translating and writing twenty-eight plays, he and his wife went in 1781 as guest stars to the Burgtheater at Vienna. There they remained four years to introduce "the Hamburg school's ideal of acting, the [so-called] convincingly natural representation of character. . . ." The expert actor, said Schröder, "conceives each character in such a way . . . that it not merely suggests a type, but distinguishes itself from kindred characters by individual features, which the performer *finds in his own experience*" (my italics). Yet the actor must impersonate characters other than himself because "it is no real art to play oneself. Any discerning nonactor, who knows how to speak well and who behaves reasonably well, can do that." [209]

Konrad Ekhof, at the Gotha Court Theater in 1777, where "everyone on the theater staff was a state servant," taught his young students a slightly less "natural," more intellectual method of depicting characters and the emotions. One of them, plump Johann Beil (1754–1794), for instance, learned from the old master that "the often misused term nature means to the real actor high, very high art," that "everything that takes place on the stage is . . . nature transformed." He believed that "the actor himself cannot . . . be passion or caprice itself, but simply the artistic imitation of them." And August Wilhelm Iffland (1759–1814), a sentimentalist who held that the stage was "a school of wisdom, of beautiful feelings," came in time "to act with more art than emotion," to exhibit "all the signs of the calculating intellectual actor." [210]

This Gotha Court Theater after the death of Ekhof in 1778 survived under the leadership of Johann Boek for only one year. The actors, along with some of Abel Seyler's troupe, were promptly hired by young, wealthy, and talented Baron Wolfgang von Dalberg (1750–1806) for the new "Court and National Theater" at Mannheim which opened in 1779. The principals of the new company, between 1784 and 1795 the best in Germany, were leading man Boek, his wife Sophia Schulze, August Wilhelm Iffland, Beil, Karoline Kummerfeld, Heinrich Beck (1760–1803), and his wife Karoline Siegler. Their acting, it seems, adhered in general to the principle, pronounced by Dalberg, that "Nature (naturalness) on the stage presumes convention, rules, and art." [211]

Among the plays performed at Mannheim were Dalberg's adaptation of *Julius Caesar*; many popular, fairly realistic comedies and domestic dramas by Iffland; and notably in 1781 the romantic *Die Räuber* (*The Robbers*) by brilliant, "vast," twenty-two-year-old Friedrich Schiller (1759–1805) with Boek as Karl Moor and Iffland as Franz. In 1784 the same playwright's *Kabale und Liebe* (*Intrigue and Love*), a domestic tragedy, was staged with Beck as Ferdinand, his wife as Luise, Boek as the President, Iffland as Wurm, and Beil as Miller.

In the 1780's and 1790's most of the larger centers of population in Germany established their own repertory theaters. The Elector of Mainz shared a "National Theater" with Frankfort-on-Main in 1787; the Prince-Bishops of Salzburg and Passau set up permanent theaters in 1793; and Linz, Innsbruck, Brünn, Augsburg, Nürnberg, Altona, Breslau, Riga, and others had theaters before the end of the century; "so that all the best actors came to be attached to some permanent theater, and the touring companies, still numerous if short-lived, were usually left with the dregs of the profession. There were German theaters in St. Petersburg and in the chief towns of Galicia and Hungary. The northern countries, especially Holland, were often visited by German troupes, so that, as Devrient says, even the French theater could hardly claim to cast its net so wide. The Theater Almanachs of the 'nineties mention at various times some seventy troupes, over half of which were permanent, or at least were settled in some center for a number of months of the year." [212]

In 1785 Schröder, then forty-one, returned to Hamburg as actor-manager. During this second, thirteen-year period, not quite as successful as his first, two of the more than routine productions included in 1787 the first performance of Schiller's verse *Don Carlos*, in which Schröder acted King Philip, and in 1789, after its premiere in Berlin, *Menchenhass und Reue* (*Melancholy and Repentance*) by August von Kotzebue (1761–1819). The latter is one of the earliest and most popular of a horde of Kotzebue sentimental comedies and melodramas, like *Die Spanier in Peru* (1796) and *Armuth und Edelsinn* (*Poverty and Nobleness*) (1798), which were acted all over Germany, and then with tremendous success in England and the United States.

During his second term at Hamburg Schröder refined his acting on so-called "strictly realistic lines." He worked out from his reading of the younger Riccoboni, it seems, an effective method of expressing the passions of characters. "Memorizing the role aloud, frequent rehearsals and performances," Schröder explained, "finally bring about a mechanism that seems to be perfectly sincere, and destroys, not the actor's effects, but his own emotion. An actor will never be overcome by his own weakness when he is able to provide himself with this mechanism." In other words, Schröder became like Iffland "the thoughtful spectator of his own acting as well as that of his colleagues." "Do you think," he asked, "that I should succeed in making the spectators forget Schröder if for one moment I myself were Lear—or make them fancy they were seeing Lear, if for one moment I forgot Schröder?" Furthermore, he insisted that he was so cold while acting "that between the scenes and acts, I play the part of manager as if I had done nothing but stand in the wings. My warmth is physical, not mental; it is the heat of bodily exertion, not of enthusiasm." [213]

In 1798 this first great German actor—who once admitted that "he would quite willingly do the work of a carpenter, a smith, or a teacher of ABC's as act King Lear or any other of his favorite parts"—retired. Finally secure financially at the age of fifty-four, he had been onstage for, say, fifty years and acted 700 roles ranging from Falstaff to Shylock, from Molière's Arnolphe and Orgon to Lessing's Odoardo and Paul Werner; he had "banished French affectation and established Shakespeare as the supreme model for the German stage"; [214] and he had raised acting in his language to an art that matched the honored achievements of Garrick and Lekain.

At Mannheim in *c.* 1790 Johann Boek was succeeded by Siegfried (Eckhardt) Koch (1754–1831), and in 1792 August Wilhelm Iffland became the company's artistic director. Four years later the latter almost decided to go to Weimar as manager but chose instead to take charge of the National Theater in Berlin, established in 1786 by Frederick William II. For some time a company there had been headed by Karl Döbbelin, who in 1783 had first staged Lessing's *Nathan der Weise*, written in blank verse as an antinaturalistic device. Then for a while the theater had been unsuccessfully managed by schoolmaster, philosopher, critic, and playwright Johann Jakob Engel (1741–1802) and expert, though tempestuous, romantic actor Johann Fleck (1757–1801). Success was at last achieved and stabilized during the eighteen-year reign of Iffland from 1796 until his death in 1814. As manager he tried to impress on his actors the importance of thinking and feeling *in character*. Furthermore, "He remarked, quite rightly, that one could easily notice whether the movements of an actor were prompted by his thoughts or if, on the other hand, they merely reflected the words of the part; and, quite wrongly [according to Theodore Komisarjevsky] that an actor could sincerely express on the stage only such feelings as he had experienced in life." But Iffland in his last years was plagued by the younger generation who protested that his domestic plays were tame and inept with all their "naturalness." "To them plain nature . . . was only . . . a cloak concealing shallowness." [215] They wanted more verve onstage.

Engel, incidentally, was a widely known authority on acting. In 1785–86 he'd spun out two verbose (Winckelmann influenced?) volumes, *Ideen zu einer Mimik*—which in 1788 and 1795 were translated into French as *Idées sur le geste et l'action théâtral*, went through at least three more German printings in the early 1800's, were turned into English by Mrs. Siddon's son Henry (1775–1815) in 1807, and reprinted in 1822, as *Practical Illustrations of Rhetorical Gesture and Action* . . . , and translated into Italian as *Lettere intorno Alla Mimica*.

The premise of the work is two-fold. In the first place (in the version by Siddons), the actor "ought to seize all occasions of observing nature. . . ." "The best digested rules, the finest picture galleries in the world, will not exempt him from the necessity of *thinking* for *himself*: for the choice and application of gestures exclusively belong to him; and nature affords a variety which the most indefatigable observation is unable to exhaust." [216] In the second place, the actor "Should never lose sight of the main end and grand design of his art, by shocking the spectator with too coarse or too servile an imitation" of nature. He must learn "What is at the same time the *most beautiful* and the *most true*." He must know attitudes and "gestures *picturesque*, and . . . *expressive*." He ought, in short, to "display the same fine discernment in the choice of his gestures [and attitudes], which an able author displays in the selection of his words. . . ." [217]

An actor learned from Engel that in imitating, for instance, choler he "ought to propose another end to himself than the natural imitation of a passion whose effects so easily become disgusting. . . ." And in the agonies of a stage death he ought to present "such an idea of death as every man would wish to feel as that crisis; though, perhaps, no one ever will have the good fortune to find that wish accomplished." An actress learned from the book the proper attitude Juliet should assume while awaiting Romeo. "Without a doubt her ear, and all her body (though still and quiet, the better to distinguish the noise she hears), should be inclined to the spot where she expects the entrance of the personage. It is only on that side that the foot will be planted with firmness, while the other rested on the point, will seem suspended in the air; all the rest of the body will be in a state of activity. The eye will be very open as if to collect a great number of visual rays, for the object which does not yet appear to it. The hand will be directed to the ear, as if it could really seize the sound. The other arm, to preserve the equilibrium of the body, will be directed towards the ground, with the palm turned downwards, as if eager to push aside every intrusion which might trouble the attention requisite for a moment so replete with interest." [218]

An even more "artistic" kind of acting was in due time emphasized at the Court of Weimar where Johann Wolfgang Goethe in 1775, at the age of twenty-six, had come as director of amateur theatricals. There he dabbled in social, histrionic diversions; he appeared, for instance, as Orestes in his 1779 prose *Iphigenia auf Taurus* (derived from Euripides, and published in a verse version in 1787). By 1783, however, Goethe was too busy with more important projects, and the theater was turned over to a company of second-rate professionals. But early in 1791, after he had announced that "Our public has no conception of art," [219] he unwillingly consented to supervise again the the Weimar Court Theater and, a few months later, with a troupe of new-comers and some resident professionals, opened it with Iffland's *Die Jäger* (*The Marksman*).

Thereafter for five years, with Goethe stressing "the proper speaking of the lines" and a relatively new notion of teamwork in performance, a "harmony of *ensemble*," or "a beautiful Whole," the cheap, mediocre company performed classics, operas (some by Mozart) or operettas, and light plays indistinguishable from the repertoire of other small German theaters. And the acting was so bumbling and ordinary that Goethe lost interest in the venture. (As a matter of fact, he rarely respected actors, never regarded them "as individual artists, each possessing a value in and for him or herself; to him they were only parts of an artistic whole, instruments in an orchestra, accessory figures in a landscape composition.") [220]

Goethe's ebbing interest in acting was stimulated by Iffland's month's visit to Weimar in 1796 and his skillful impersonations of maybe a dozen different roles. Schiller, Goethe's guest at some of the plays, didn't care for Iffland's acting; for him it lacked spirit, verve, life. Goethe, however, was excited by the wide range of characters convincingly presented in an "elaborately studied but never offensive realistic manner." He was suddenly magnetized by the problems of acting. More than ever Goethe was convinced, as he had said in *Wilhelm Meister*, that "no one is really an actor who can only play *himself.* . . ." He began teaching his Weimar company that "acting is an imaginative re-creation of character," and urged them "to free themselves as far as they could from the tyranny of the 'Fach,' the special lines of characters (jeune premier, chevalier, soubrette, etc.) for which, by tradition, actors and actresses were engaged in their contract with the management." He believed that "Even within the sphere of realism a creative art of acting was possible. . . ." [221]

But two years later, in 1798, while working with Schiller on the latter's *Wallenstein* trilogy, Goethe came out strongly—and influentially—against realism in playwriting and in acting. The two of them agreed "that though the domestic drama was good enough entertainment, it was not a high form of art, perhaps not art at all." They found no point in the sentimental pathos, the coarse humor, and the familiar details of realism—in all that petty and servile imitation of nature. What great things, asked Schiller, can happen to ordinary, recognizable people like parsons, leaders of commerce, secretaries, and the like? What great things can be accomplished by them? Yes, they can weave petty schemes, lend money, pocket silver spoons; but "where do you go then for the majesty of inevitable doom, which exalts man's soul even while it crushes him?" "Naturalism," both men academically decided, "is the death of art." Swept along by the Winckelmann wave of Greek classicism, they concluded that German acting "in aiming at the natural expression of character had neglected the esthetic appeal to the eye and ear of the audience." Worse, it had neglected "ideal beauty"; and beauty "is 'ideal' in the sense that the artist concentrates what is found only rarely in reality, and it is ideal as an image in the mind of the artist, an inner vision, an idea." [222]

Goethe, therefore, "applied new standards of dignity and beauty to every feature of the art of the theater. The previously prevailing tendency in acting had by no means neglected beauty, but it had aimed simply at beautiful reality. Now a subtle distinction was made between reality and truth, and beautiful truth was demanded. Up till now everything had been judged according to its correspondence with living nature, but now all had to satisfy a cultivated taste. The actors had to lay aside their specifically German manner and find a . . . more universal conception; they had to rise from a faithful but limited expression of individual character to imagining generalized types, from the real to the ideal." [223] No longer could they "naturally" characterize and feel. They were restricted to a kind of formal speaking, gesturing, and moving. They became elocutionists.

IV

By about 1780, a hundred years after the founding of the Comédie-Française, the French decided they had added just about enough nature to the writing and production of plays, especially of tragedies. The new characterizations, enriched by a calculated sensitivity, were an improvement over the old; but to add any more nature, they were afraid, would be to subtract considerably from the theater as an art. Reason and taste dictated, for instance, that plays like Shakespeare's were too romantic, too ungoverned; and that the native *drames* were too realistic, too inelegant. Voltaire harangued against "the barbarisms, the puerilities, the indecencies, and the extravagances" of that "drunken savage" Shakespeare who "had no regularity, no sense of propriety, no art" like civilized Racine. And Beaumarchais, at first a follower of Diderot, but with an eye ever on the box-office, gave up writing *drames* like *Eugénie* (1767) and turned to classical comedies as the models for his two masterpieces. "Portray ordinary men and women in difficulties and sorrow?" he asked, perhaps half in jest. "Nonsense! Such would only be scoffed at. Ridiculous citizens [in comedy] and unhappy kings [in tragedy], these are the only characters fit for treatment on the stage," [224] or fit for art.

French actors, therefore, were afforded few chances of acting in serious romantic plays. And if they performed now and then in *drames*, they never felt at home impersonating roles that demanded a simple realism. Ordinary, familiar, everyday speech and behavior did not match their "ideal of distinction with a touch in it of conscious elaboration or artifice." Trained from infancy to revere Corneille and Racine, the actors believed that the stage was primarily a place for exhibiting perfected language; and though they rarely wanted to pay much for that language, they did want to show they appreciated it by delivering it beautifully. They preferred the "splendid and sonorous eloquence that declamation at its height can achieve." [225]

Consequently, all that most of the French public "saw, or could bear to see, on the stage was the completely conventional presentation of completely conventionalized feelings, which had not, and never had, any relation . . . to any of the actual phenomena of human life." For them the words were almost all. "For them . . . the most beautiful verse was that which, while observing all the metrical rules, achieved the expression of a simple fact in the most ornately roundabout fashion." People "anxious to see . . . dramas of a kind different from those hallowed by critical approval" [226] would soon flock to the newly "invented," spectacular melodramas by Guilbert de Pixérécourt (1773–1844) and others.

In 1782 the Comédie-Française, after appearing at the *salle de machines* in the Tuilleries for about eleven years, moved its elocution to a new theater erected for it near the Luxembourg and appropriately opened it with Racine's *Iphigénie*. Some of the important new players then were Louise Contat (1760–1813), a comedienne pupil of Préville's, who taught her "those elements of diction, the *solfêggi* of speech, which are indispensable to a career on the stage"; Jean (Albonis) Dazincourt (1747–1809), second to Préville, and soon to teach elocution to Marie Antoinette; Abraham-Joseph Fleury (1750–1822), who "spoke as elegantly as a Marquis, and spelled like a kitchen-maid"; and Charles Joseph Vanhove (1739–1803), Talma's future father-in-law, who acted Kings and *pères nobles*.[227]

At this time the actors "still owned their theater; . . . they still nominally managed their own affairs, divided the receipts, determined expenditure, engaged and dismissed the staff, accepted and rejected plays; but all this they did under the control and supervision of the King, or, to speak more accurately, of the Court." Four Chamberlains "were in reality the absolute masters of the Theater." [228] With some fear, then, the Comédie-Française presented in 1784, after a delay of three years, *Le Mariage de Figaro* by Beaumarchais. With Dazincourt as Figaro, Molé as Almaviva, Mlle. Contat as Susanne, a Mlle. Olivier (1764–1787) as Chérubin, Mlle. Sainval as the Countess, and Préville in the minor role of Brid'oisin the comedy was an overwhelming success; it ran for seventy-five nights. And the revolutionists a-borning cheered when Figaro said to the aristocrat Count: "Nobility, wealth, rank, great employments—all these things make you so proud! But what have you done to earn all these good things? You have been born, nothing more."

In 1786 an official L'Ecole Royale de Déclamation was founded in Paris. Since the ability "to speak the mother-tongue, pure and unalloyed with dialect, with suppleness and beauty, was the one indispensable condition" for being admitted to the Comédie-Française; and since "lack of originality or mediocrity of talent might be condoned, but never defects in speech, or incorrectness, indistinctness, or lack of purity of diction," all candidates were required to study there under teachers "taken exclusively from among the tried and true experienced members of the company." One brief description of the work at this school, dating from 1788, survives: "The exercises are held in a small theater, which is constructed and arranged in miniature so as in all respects to resemble a full-sized one; in order that the pupils may get *le plancher*, as the French call it—that is, to accustom them from the beginning to stand and walk on the stage in a natural manner. Young players of both sexes who still require instruction, as well as students in training, assemble here under the guidance of Molé, Fleury, and Dugazon, each of whom has his day of the week appointed. A few of the elder actors and actresses attend the exercises, which last from ten till two every Tuesday, Thursday and Saturday. The number of pupils was large, and most of the material seemed good; at least I noticed, even in the case of the beginners, that they aimed at satisfying the ruling French taste, that for tragedy—and in tragedy, for much convulsion and contortion. Dugazon was instructor today. He made them repeat scenes here and there, and made constant remarks on voice, declamation, and gesticulation—in short, he let no fault pass without a remark. There was only one important objection which I should much have liked to make. He often made them change faulty passages and wrong movements; but he seldom told them the reasons for the alterations—so that he seemed to be training them rather as machines than as judicious reasoners." [229]

François Joseph Talma (1763–1826), one of the first students at the school under Dugazon and Molé, made his debut at the Comédie-Française in 1787 when he was twenty-four and became a *sociétaire* in 1789—the year the Bastille was stormed. A passionate and sonorous leading-man type, he was assigned because of his lack of seniority to only trifling roles. But "Impulsive, ambitious, and predisposed to innovation, he could not imitate the patience with which his predecessors had passed through a similar ordeal. He contended that the 'rights' exercised by his elders originated in a sort of 'theatrical feudalism' and ought at once to be abolished. No member of the Comédie was entitled to exclusive possession of particular characters; they should be open to all." [230] But supported only by Dugazon and Mme. Vestris, Talma was kept in his minor place.

The Revolution made trivial the actors' quarrels. It also almost put the more-than-a-century-old Comédie-Française out of business. In 1790–91 the National Assembly restored the actors to the rights of holy marriage and burial so long denied them by the Church, "determined that the theaters of Paris should be under the control of the municipality instead of the Gentlemen of the Chamber," and decreed that "Any citizen may erect a public theater, and give performances therein of plays of every description." The Constitutional Committee granted a playwrights' petition for the right of "any theater . . . to represent the works of dead authors," and for the right of living playwrights "to make their own terms with the players." [231] Thus the monopoly enjoyed by the Comédie-Française was broken.

In 1791 Talma, a thorough revolutionist, seceded from the organization and, with Dugazon, Mme. Vestris, Monvel, and others presented plays in competition to the Théâtre-Français (soon the Théâtre de la Nation) at the new Théâtre Français de la rue de Richelieu (soon the Théâtre de la République). Then in 1793 the entire company of the Théâtre de la Nation was arrested; some of them only by luck escaped beheading. Finally, however, after years of pure chaos, the conservative and revolutionary actors were in 1799 united in a reorganized Comédie-Française and began to perform at the theater in the Rue de Richelieu.

That same year Mlle. Dumesnil published her *Mémoires* (probably written by Coste d'Arnobat) in response to the *Mémoires, et réflexions sur la déclamation théâtrale* (1798) by Mlle. Clairon. The two old war-horses still argued, of course, about art versus nature in acting. Mlle. Clairon believed that an actor must "develop the intention of the author, feel the beauties of his composition, and adapt his character to the general scope of the work . . . , [and] give it that distinguishing feature it requires." This, she was sure, could be done only by an actor with "a strong and sonorous voice," a voice "clear, harmonious, flexible, and susceptible to every possible modulation." Mlle. Dumesnil didn't quibble with her on that point. But when Mlle. Clairon wrote: "What infinite pains and study must it not require to make an actor forget his own character; to identify himself with every personage he represents; to acquire the faculty of representing love, hatred, ambition, and every passion which human nature is susceptible"; and when she continued by asking, if there are "no arts or professions but have certain defined principles— Are there then none required to direct the tragedian?" Mlle. Dumesnil exploded: "What a sophism! The basis of theatrical art in tragedy is first of all

—and we must insist on this: *'D'avoir recu du ciel l'influence secrette* [That one has received from heaven its secret influence]. That is the source of pathos, of terror, and of one spontaneously forgetting oneself without any effort. It is a divine gift which can almost dispense with the beauties of art. . . . It seems to me that the principles of theatrical art may be completely summed up as follows: *Who am I under all circumstances?* What am I in each scene? Where am I? What have I done, and what am I going to do?" You, Mlle. Clairon, she continued, "You have never been criticized for *having art*—one would be mad to do so. You have been criticized for not having enough art to make one forget your art—and for being all art. You have been criticized for always allowing the great actress to show through in your so *finished* style of acting. However perfect art may be, it can never absolutely replace nature." [232]

❀ ELOCUTION IN ENGLISH

After enlivening British acting for thirty-five years David Garrick, at the age of fifty-nine, retired from the stage in 1776 (three years before he died) and sold his interest in Drury Lane to young Richard Brinsley Sheridan and others. At that theater next year Mrs. (Frances) Abington (1737–1815) was the original Lady Teazle, Tom King the Sir Peter, "Gentleman" Smith (1730–1819) Charles Surface, and John Palmer (1742–1798) Joseph in *The School for Scandal.* Also that year two important players made their London debuts: John Henderson (1743–1785) at Drury Lane, and elegant high-comedienne Elizabeth Farren (1759–1829) at the Haymarket (bought from Foote by Colman the elder). Then for five years things theatrical sagged until the two great Kembles, Sarah and John Philip, strode regally onstage, routed the more-or-less "realism" of Garrick, and for another thirty-five years—from 1782 until 1817—performed in "the grand style." English acting was thus reclaimed for art and "ideal beauty" by elocution.

Sarah Kemble's (1755–1831) grandfather had been an actor in the time of Betterton, her parents were strolling players, she faced audiences as a child, and at the age of eighteen married William Siddons (*c.* 1742–1808), a mediocre actor in her father's provincial company. Two years later, in 1775, she was engaged by Garrick, and in the last month of the year made her first appearance at Drury Lane as Portia to King's Shylock, only to be advised by one critic "that on the stage nothing is so barren as *cold correctness.*" [233] Then, in 1776, after impersonating several foolish roles, she was cast with Garrick in two of his farewell productions, as Mrs. Strickland to his Ranger in *The Suspicious Husband* and as Lady Anne to his Richard III. But she was hardly noticed alongside the final gleam of Garrick. And she wasn't rehired by Sheridan when he took over the theater next season. She failed.

At first Sarah Siddons was almost destroyed; but somehow she continued to act. What else could she do? She played away from London, chiefly at

Bath, for the next six years and portrayed an extraordinary range of characters. During that time "The deliberate processes of her thought, the gift of superhuman concentration, the masculine strength of mind and the feminine tenderness of feeling, joined to unprecedented histrionic ability," produced an artist. Mrs. Siddons learned to act penetratingly *in character*; she learned to express the feelings of a character with titanic power; and she learned to control, to unify, to shape those feelings. Control was instinctively important to Sarah, as it was to all the Kembles. She believed "that those who act mechanically, are sure to be in some sort right, while we who trust to nature . . . are dull as anything can be imagined, because we cannot feign." [234]

In 1782 a new, enriched, determined Mrs. Siddons, age twenty-seven, was engaged by Sheridan; and in October, after only two company rehearsals, having missed the third one because of a nervous hoarseness, she acted again at Drury Lane as Isabella in the version of Southerne's *The Fatal Marriage* (1694). This time her two leading men, Smith and Palmer, were almost unnoticed. Her triumph was sensational. "Her merit . . . swallowed up all remembrance of present and past performers." As one critic reported, "If there be any who still affect to doubt the superiority of Mrs. Siddons . . . let them examine her Isabella. . . . Let them observe during her progressions to madness, with what distinct shades sanity and reason are depicted, let them behold her frenzy increase till she attempts to stab her husband, let them watch the inexpressible anguish of her looks, while she clings to his body when dead, let them view her in her last agonies give her laugh of horror, for having at last escaped from such inhuman persecutors and insupportable miseries, and then while their passions are warm, let them declare who is her equal." "Garrick himself did not exceed, if he equalled her, in awaking public curiosity." Next month Mrs. Siddons compounded her triumph as the heroine in *Jane Shore* and as Calista in *The Fair Penitent*. In December she continued to fascinate audiences as she soared in the grand heroic manner that perfectly matched *Venice Preserved*. Her "tempestuous Belvidera was characterized by quick transitions of emotion particularly remarkable for their versatility of expression in her face and attitudes, where the finest shades were registered, yet under complete control." And "her meticulous attention to detail was consistent with the part: a positive instance of being 'in nature.'" By the end of the hurrah season in early June Mrs. Siddons had given eighty performances, for an average of three per week, from a repertoire of seven plays and was at once the greatest English actress: "Power was seated on her brow, passion emanated from her breast as from a shrine. She was tragedy personified." [235]

In 1785 Mrs. Siddons reached the summit of her glories by portraying a stunning, superhuman Lady Macbeth. And she did it mostly with brains. She had perceived, she said, "the difficulty of assuming a personage with whom no one feeling of common general nature was congenial or assistant. One's own heart could prompt one to express, with some degree of truth, the sentiments of a daughter, a wife, a lover, a sister, etc.; but to adopt this character, must be an effort of the judgment alone." So, with her glittering eyes she pried from Shakespeare's text more meanings and deeper emotions than anyone else had ever discovered there, and with her reasoning sense of design she related all her findings into a unified whole, and then with her vivid histrionic sensibility she created a character so overwhelming that the tragedy might more correctly have been titled *Lady Macbeth*. (Some of her amazing, memorable contributions to the acting of the role can be glimpsed today in notes taken during performances *c.* 1809 by G. J. Bell.)[236]

By 1802, although she acted at intervals until 1812, Mrs. Siddons had impersonated seventy-five different characters in twenty years at Drury Lane. They ranged from her cold and declamatory Zara in Hill's adaptation of Voltaire and her failure as the Countess Orsina in Lessing's *Emilia Galotti*, through fifteen widely different Shakespearean parts, to the realistic Agnes in Lillo's *The Fatal Curiosity* (1736) in 1797 and her original Mrs. Haller in the sentimental *The Stranger* (1798), a version of Kotzebue's *Menchenhass und Reue*. Quite possibly all her characters were almost identical. "Mrs. Siddons could lay no claim to versatility—it was not in her nature; she was without mobility of mind, countenance, or manner. . . ." But since tragic acting to her was "something above nature," she made the stage "a place that is happily divorced from the dullness of daily living, and turned it into a palpitant realm, inhabited by more luminous . . . women than this tame world knows." [237]

Mrs. Siddons, according to one nagging eighteenth-century critic, "is manifestly the child of Art; her best positions [and speeches?] convey strongly the idea of having been previously studied; they do not seem to arise out of the circumstances of the moment." Another critic noted that her "naturally plaintive" voice which "becomes at will sonorous or piercing, overwhelms in rage, or in its wild shriek absolutely harrows up the soul," didn't "approach enough to the familiar." Her "potent elocution" in bursts of indignation or grief, in sudden exclamation, in apostrophes was called, despite her frequent "pauses that endured beyond patience" and her sometimes "excessive slowness and solemnity," "a school of oratory." In short, at times in her acting "something of too much art was apparent." [238]

Today Mrs. Siddons would be spurned as an elocutionist by those naturalistic disciples of Stanislavski who, too often, cannot or will not act Shakespeare because his lines don't resemble their own everyday way of talking. She would be ostracized as old-fashioned by actors who balk at appreciating and preserving the poetry—or any carefully designed speeches—of a playwright. Indeed, Mrs. Siddons was an elocutionist. She cared very much about "the right management of the voice . . . in speaking." With her "powers of transubstantiation" she felt deeply the emotions of a character and then conveyed them to audiences via movement, gesture, and speech that were "picturesque, graceful, and dignified," "classical and correct." Her speaking was artificial or mechanical in the sense that it was *deliberately designed* instead of being left entirely to her thinking and feeling at the moment of utterance. And designed speaking can be and frequently is bad; but it need not be. If "the design is worked out by the speaker himself instead of copied from another, if it is intended to improve communicative efficacy, to achieve a norm of naturalness, or in impersonation, to represent the speech of a character unlike himself, there would seem to be no valid ground for objecting to the use of such a method. By it, as by speaking spontaneously, a speaker may or may not achieve a result that will *seem* natural and spontaneous." [239]

Mrs. Siddons, we deduce, seemed natural enough because she believed that matter was as important as manner. She went beyond "the declamation of study" and "the display of attitudes" and moved audiences with "those exact and forcible expressions of feeling that stamp reality on fiction. . . ." Critic Leigh Hunt emphasized that point when he wrote that "She unites with her noble conceptions of nature every advantage of art, every knowledge of stage propriety and effect. This knowledge, however, she displays" with a kind of "natural carelessness. . . ." Her acting, though designed, is in effect "the result of the impassioned moment; one can hardly imagine that there has been any such thing as a rehearsal." [240] She was, in short, an *expert* elocutionist, a great actress, an artist.

Mrs. Siddon's younger brother, handsome John Philip Kemble (1757–1823), was an elocutionist in the modern, derogatory meaning of the term. He put "the manner before the matter," preferred "effect rather than expression," and felt, as it were, in externals and without extemporaneousness. Mrs. Siddon said of him: "My brother John in his most impetuous bursts is always careful to avoid any discomposure of his dress or deportment; but in the whirlwind of passion I lose all thought of such matters." And Hunt admitted that he "could never admire Kemble, as it was the fashion to do. He was too artificial, too formal, too critically and deliberately conscious." And to critic William Hazlitt, Kemble seemed "as shy of committing himself with nature, as a maid is of committing herself with her lover. . . ." [241]

Kemble, after performing for seven years in the provinces and Ireland, promptly followed his sister to Drury Lane in 1783. At his debut as Hamlet, in competition with popular, Garrick-like Henderson at Covent Garden, he astonished the critics by "the many new 'readings' and novelties of emphasis and interpretation which his diligent study of the text had enabled him to think out. . . ." And though it was said that he "*acts* the part in general too much, and appears to have studied stage-effect rather too elaborately," everyone exclaimed that "his recitation . . . has no equal. His tones are beautifully modulated." That same season Kemble in his pedantic style also acted Richard III, Giles Overreach in *A New Way to Pay Old Debts*, Beverley in Moore's domestic *The Gamester* (1753), and King John—the last two roles opposite his sister. But "his monotony did not fatigue, his formality did not displease; because there was always sense and meaning in what he did." No

player, it was agreed, ever understood his authors better. His speaking therefore was "confident and exact, . . . expressive, and even powerful." [242]

And no one, apparently, ever understood art better. Acting as demonstrated by Kemble was the beautiful and noble product of intelligence. It
was something rare, ideal, and pure, something raised above all that was
common in life. Instead of identifying himself with, and thus contaminating
himself by, the characters he represented, Kemble endeavored "to raise
Nature to the dignity of his own person and demeanor." Instead of truly
feeling the emotions of a character, instead of adding "the deep, piercing,
heartfelt tones of nature," he seemed always "to be considering how he ought
to feel . . . or how he should express by rule and method what he did not
feel." And instead of lowering the language of poetry to common speech, to
"a rugged and colloquial familiarity," he declaimed with much decorum, with
a consciousness of the wording instead of a consciousness of the thoughts and
feelings behind them. In short, whatever Kemble did as an actor "was done
well and skillfully, according to the book of arithmetic." He was the "Euclid
of the stage." [243]

He alarmed a few of the critics. His sister they could accept; they recognized her vibrant greatness even while they complained now and then that
she was too methodical in manner, that she used too much artifice, and that
she tended to declaim. But the brother! This Kemble! He was all method, all
artifice, and he definitely, unashamedly, coldly declaimed! Yet audiences liked
him! They concluded that Kemble was more artistic than easy-going, lively,
"natural" Garrick had been! So, after the death of Henderson in 1785, and
the retirement of "Gentleman" Smith in 1788, this "only English actor of
distinction who by his contemporaries was not called natural," was raised to
a puzzling pre-eminence, was appointed manager of Drury Lane, and memo-
rably elocuted such characters as Coriolanus, Cardinal Wolsey, Addison's
Cato, Zanga in Edward Young's The Revenge (1721), Penruddock in Richard
Cumberland's (1732–1811) The Wheel of Fortune (1795), and—with some
dissents—Hamlet. For a span of thirty years no player was awarded "a more
universal or profound attention." [244]

The two Kembles thus effected a decisive change in English acting. They
restored Quin's declamation—with more elegance, for sure—to the stage
from which it had been ousted some forty-five years earlier. Their artificial
style, their elocution, their "splendid formal acting" superseded Garrick's
more "natural" method. A "new school, as it is called," a "grand manner"—
dynamic as exhibited by Mrs. Siddons, and static as exhibited by John Philip
Kemble—was alas "palmed on the rising generation, as an improvement of
the old one." [245]

Elocution in the 1780's and 1790's was obviously the fashion. As early
as 1781, for example, sometime actor John Walker (1732–1807) published the
Elements of Elocution: in which the principles of reading and speaking are
investigated; and such pauses, emphasis, and inflexcions of voice, as are suit-

able to every variety of sentence, are distinctly pointed out and explained;
with directions for strengthening and modulating the voice, so as to render it
varied, forcible, and harmonious: to which is added, a complete system of the
passions; showing how they affect the countenance, tone of voice, and gesture
of the body, exemplified by a copious selection of the most striking passages
of Shakespeare. This mechanical hocus-pocus was reprinted in a second
edition in 1799, a third in 1806, a fifth in 1815. In 1785 Walker published
A *Rhetorical Grammar, or a Course of Lectures in Elocution,* which went
into its seventh edition in 1823. In 1787 he brought out *The Melody of Speak-*
ing Delineated. Then in 1789 actor, critic, and playwright Thomas Holcroft
(1744–1809) translated, in three volumes, the *Essai sur la physiognomie . . .*
(1781–86) of Johann Kaspar Lavater (1741–1801).

Elocution became the fashion because "ideal beauty" was the fashion.
Nature was just too plain, too low, and too unregulated to be art. Reynolds in
fifteen "Discourses" delivered before the Royal Academy from 1769 through
1790 graciously maintained that in the art of painting, as in all the arts,
"nature itself is not to be too closely copied. There are excellencies . . . beyond what is commonly called the imitation of nature. . . ." A "mere copier
of nature," he said, "can never produce anything great; can never raise and
enlarge the conceptions, or warm the heart of the spectator." He was sure that
"The wish of the genuine painter [or actor?] must be more extensive: Instead
of endeavoring to amuse mankind with the minute neatness of his imitations,
he must endeavor to improve them by the grandeur of his ideas. . . ." Reynolds, as well as many others, believed that art is only "a partial representation
of nature," that the artist "must depart from nature for a greater advantage."
Otherwise, he argued, "we must prefer a portrait by Denner . . . to those
of Titian or Vandyck; and a landscape by Vanderheyden to those of Titian or
Reubens; for they are certainly more exact representations of nature." The
aim of art, according to Reynolds, is "to make an impression on the imagination and the feelings. The imitation of nature frequently does this," he said.
"Sometimes it fails, and something else succeeds. I think, therefore, the true
test of all the arts is not solely whether the production [or the characterization
by the actor?] is a true copy of nature, but whether it answers the end of
art, which is, to produce a pleasing effect upon the mind." Or "to supply the
natural imperfections of things, and often to gratify the mind by realizing and
embodying what never existed but in the imagination." In the theater, consequently, it can be said of "The lower kind of comedy, or farce, like the inferior style of painting, [that] the more naturally it is represented, the better;
but the higher appears to me to aim no more at imitation, so far as it belongs
to anything like deception, or to expect that the spectators should think that
the events there represented are really passing before them, than Raffaelle in
his Cartoons, or Poussin in his Sacraments, expected it to be believed, even
for a moment, that what they exhibited were real figures." [246]

Thus, toward the end of the eighteenth century acting in England—

and all over Europe—was pulled back from becoming too "natural," turned around, and pushed again in the opposite direction toward art.

However, while Reynolds was persuasively, if not originally, commending the depiction in art of ideal figures, other men via lectures, periodicals, and books were more frequently dissecting characters in Shakespeare's plays as if they were indeed flesh-and-blood figures. Thomas Whately (?–1772), for instance, wrote his minutely analytical *Remarks on some of the Characters of Shakespeare* in 1770, although it wasn't printed until 1785; William Richardson (1743–1814) published in 1774, 1784, and 1789 three volumes titled *A Philosophical Analysis and Illustration of some of Shakespeare's Remarkable Characters*; and Maurice Morgann (1726–1802) in the long and famous *An Essay on the Dramatic Character of Sir John Falstaff* (1777) decided that Shakespeare's characters "which are seen only in part, are yet capable of being unfolded and understood in the whole." Therefore, he wrote significantly, "it may be fit to consider them rather as Historic [real] than Dramatic beings; and, when occasion requires, to account for their conduct from the *whole* of the character, from general principles, from latent motives, and from policies not avowed." Morgann insisted that these characters "not only act and speak in strict conformity to nature, but in strict relation to us. . . . We see . . . [them] act from the mingled motives of passion, reason, interest, habit and complection, in all their proportions, when they are supposed to know it not themselves; and we are made to acknowledge that their actions and sentiments are, from these motives, the necessary result." [247]

All three men, it should be noted, found for some of the characters they examined an approximation of the modern over-all action or main drive— Stanislavski's "unbroken line." Whately, for instance, concluded that Richard III's "ruling passion is the lust for power." Richardson discovered that "A sense of virtue . . . seems to be the ruling principle in the character of Hamlet." And Morgann was convinced that "the leading quality of Falstaff's character, and that from which all the rest take their color, is a high degree of wit and humor, accompanied with great natural vigor and alacrity of mind." [248]

But late eighteenth-century English actors had no more time than they had taste for portraying characters that deeply, that realistically. After all, under their repertory system a play was readied and put onstage with the barest minimum of rehearsals. Cumberland's *The Jew*, for example, was placed in rehearsal on April 24, only two weeks before its premiere on May 8, 1794. And it did not have uninterrupted rehearsals. "It received . . . only four full rehearsals and six partial ones, these partial ones consisting chiefly of only one scene, not even a full act. Furthermore, all these rehearsals were at the most only about two hours long, and sometimes less. In other words, for a full-length, five-act, brand-new comedy a grand total of about fifteen hours, or only three hours for each act, or preparation." In the same year another new Cumberland play, *The Wheel of Fortune*, "was rehearsed nine times only, again for no more than an hour or so on each occasion." And

Measure for Measure was revived that season (having been acted nine years earlier) with only two rehearsals. The actors had barely time enough to bring onstage quickly memorized, resonantly delivered "specimens of improved elocution, but not personations of character." [249]

Paradoxically, however, their elevated-above-nature acting was often placed in competition with elaborate, authentic, "naturalistic" scenes and stage effects. When Kemble was manager of Drury Lane his "close attention to accuracy in text . . . led automatically to meticulousness in the details of production. In his staging of historical plays he was exact in every detail from period ironwork, to the heraldic quarterings on the banners. The . . . effect of this impressive elaboration was deteriorating to the standards of acting. Audiences . . . began to pay more and more attention to scenic effects, and correspondingly less to the work of the actors." Often, it was said, they "assembled more to witness the gorgeousness of the puppet-show, than to hear the poet's sentiment, or to enjoy the player's art." [250]

And worse, the actors had to forfeit nuances and fight broadly to enlist the audience's attention in always larger and larger theaters. In 1792 the seating capacity of Covent Garden was increased from 2,170 (in 1782) to 3,103. Two years later Drury Lane's capacity was raised from 2,362 (in 1762) to 3,611.[251]

II

Nothing much can be said about acting in the United States during the final years of the eighteenth century except that it was thoroughly British. For almost a decade beginning in 1784 professional players known as the American Company, managed by "the Columbus and Vespucius of the Drama," English actor Lewis Hallam, Jr. (c. 1740–1808), and Irish actor John Henry (1738–1794), enjoyed a virtual monopoly of things theatrical in New York City (at the John Street Theatre), in Philadelphia (at the Southwark Theatre), and in Baltimore and Annapolis. Two of the leading actors were Thomas Wignell (1753–1802) and Mrs. Owen Morris (1753–1826). In 1787 the troupe staged the first native comedy written for professionals, *The Contrast* by Boston-born Royall Tyler (1757–1826).

Then in 1794 Wignell, who with Mrs. Morris had seceded from the American Company, organized a new group of expert actors, partly recruited from England, and opened the elegant new Chestnut Street Theatre in Philadelphia. Modeled on the Theatre Royal at Bath, it seated about 2,000 persons. In 1796 one of the chief players was a twenty-year-old Englishman, Thomas Abthorpe Cooper (1776–1849), who had been briefly apprenticed to Kemble and Mrs. Siddons, and had made his London debut as Hamlet in 1795. Anne (Brunton) Merry (1768–1808), from Covent Garden, served as leading lady.

In that same year playwright William Dunlap (1768–1839) was one of the managers of the American Company. In 1798, with co-manager John Hodgkinson (c. 1765–1805), an English actor who had performed with Mrs. Siddons, he opened the also elegant new Park Theatre in New York City with *As You Like It*, soon followed it with his own *André* (1798), the first native tragedy, and then as sole manager wrote the first of many adaptations from Kotzebue. Dunlap also snatched Cooper from the Philadelphia company, paid him twenty-five dollars a week, and started him on his way to becoming the first "star" in the American theater. In December 1799, Cooper acted his favorite role, Hamlet, and was advised by one critic that "he ought to avoid all approach to rant, remembering that it is 'the sin that most easily besets him' in common with other players of no uncommon merit." [252]

◇◇

8- The Perplexed Nineteenth Century

✿ SOME REBELS

Romanticism in the arts is the unhelpful name given to the early nineteenth-century reaction in Europe against the eighteenth century's attachment to classicism and "ideal beauty," its fondness for abstract analysis, its conservative acceptance of stale, generalized experience. Essentially it was a liberal movement, a complex and energetic protest on behalf of something which seemed to have been omitted from all the accumulated dogma about reality. And, for sure, the same something was being left out of the new scientific method of explaining reality. That something was the individual. In other words, some artists finally wearied of expressing what everybody ought to express, and were disinclined to express only the rational. Each rebel yearned to express what he uniquely—newly and truly—felt or imagined. Romanticism was thus a venture away from both petrified rules and laboratory facts, a venture at creating something "out of Experience individually acquired." [1]

This movement, put simply, conveniently, was first hatched in about 1780, slowly gathered strength during the next fifty years, and boldly made itself evident in the arts from 1830 until, say, 1850. Realism, symbolism, and naturalism, all later phases of romanticism were "efforts at specialization, selection, refinement and intensification." The strong reaction to the first flare of romanticism from 1850 to 1885 was called realism; the reaction to realism from 1875 to 1905 was called symbolism—"which may also be called impressionism"; and the simultaneous reaction to symbolism was called naturalism.[2]

In the theater, in playwriting especially, romanticism lessened a little the old concern with the relationships between art and nature and with the traditional patterns and requirements for expression. It centered a new though fleeting attention upon the artist "as the major element generating . . . the artistic product." Art, it was held, "expresses but the truth of the single consciousness." Even Goethe, who disapproved of mere subjectivity, which he called "the general disease of the age," was positive that do what the artist will "he can only bring forth his individuality." [3]

Fresh thinking of this sort had an effect on acting.

II

For the first quarter of the nineteenth century the theater in Russia, handicapped by the absolute rule of the aristocracy, remained sterile as it fashionably, but with a crude vigor, echoed German, French, and English plays and stagings. But at least a second official troupe of actors, subject to supervision from St. Petersburg, was established by Imperial decree in Moscow by the end of 1805. Its members were largely secured from serf companies belonging to wealthy landowners, and their menial position was artificially maintained. Nobody who was really anybody—nobody, that is, with position or schooling—was allowed to perform professionally onstage; theater management "was compelled to look for players among social strata almost devoid of education. . . ." [4] By 1809, however, a Moscow State Dramatic School was organized. Three years later Napoleon captured and burned the city.

At St. Petersburg in the early 1800's maturing actors Yakov Shusherin, Anton Krutitsky, and especially Aleksey Yakovlev continued with their rough, mostly instinctive skills to entertain the nobility. Yakovlev, "Russia's great Lekain," impersonated with "Impulsive inspiration, rather than careful and well thought out preparation," characters such as Karl Moor in *Die Räuber*, Agamemnou in Racine's *Iphigénie*, and Meinau in Kotzebue's *Menschenhass und Reue*; he also created the title roles in the French-derived *Oedipus in Athens* (1804), in *Fingal* (1805), and in *Dmitry Donskov* (1807) by Vladislav Ozerov (1770–1816). "Like all other actors of his type, he played unevenly: within one part, along with excellent passages, there were completely unpolished scenes; and, just as he could act superbly when in high spirits, his playing when uninspired was very bad." The popular leading lady in the capital from her debut in 1804 until her retirement in 1825 was

Catherine Semyonova (1786–1849), often called "the Russian Mrs. Siddons," but more correctly "the Russian Mlle. George" because she was strongly influenced by the artificial declamation of that actress from the Comédie-Française who performed as glamorous guest-artist at both St. Petersburg and Moscow from 1808 until 1812. Mlle. Semyonova impersonated the classic heroines of Racine, Voltaire, Shakespeare, and Ozerov by learning her parts "from copybooks in which every word was either underscored or overlined . . . , depending upon whether the voice was to be raised or lowered; while between the lines, notations [by her coach] were made in brackets, such as: 'with rapture,' 'with contempt,' 'gently,' 'in delirium,' 'beating the chest,' 'raising the hand,' and 'lowering the eyes.' " In 1811 two additional leading actors attracted attention. The first was dignified, French-influenced Yakov Bryansky (1791–1858), "one of the bright stars of [the] classical constellation," so studied and correct in performing that he was advised by Pushkin to "Get stirred up, dear fellow; let yourself go." The second was Ivan Sosnitsky (1794–1871), an intelligent, elegant comedian, "the first to shake off tradition and to begin speaking like a human being" onstage.[5]

Before 1825 the variety, complexity, and contradictions in acting were vividly demonstrated to Russian audiences, and especially to theater dilettantes and critics, by two conscientious players who proved that characters in the same tragedies or melodramas could be acted with equal effectiveness in two contrasting styles: the studied or the intuitive, the designed or the impulsive, the artistic or the "natural," the classical or the romantic, the French or the English (and in English either the J. P. Kemble or the Edmund Kean manner). Of course, one critic preferred the first style, another espoused the second; but audiences enjoyed both styles enough, so that both held the Russian stage for years and, because of their differences, stimulated a closer and more fruitful study of acting.

Vasily Karatygin (1802–1853) was the technician. The son of an actor, he made a successful debut at St. Petersburg in 1820 and was promptly engaged for a lucrative 2,000 rubles a year, plus one annual benefit and lodging provided by the Crown. Two years later he was arrested and imprisoned for two days because, not noticing the arrival of the Director of the Theaters at rehearsal, he remained seated in the presence of that official. Despite this "crime," however, Karatygin with an expressive voice and a polished stateliness quickly became an outstanding actor. He and his wife, Aleksandra Kolosova (1802–1880), captivated aristocratic St. Petersburg through the second quarter of the century. In his characterizations "everything was so memorized, studied, and ordered, that even passion arose in him in tempos"; nothing was "accidental or unexpected: everything down to the most minute detail was considered and appraised beforehand." For example, he is reported to have worked on one of his roles, Louis XI (in a translation of a French melodrama), for an entire year, tirelessly perfecting it in solitude, in costume and make-up, and in front of a large mirror.

Karatygin, in short, moved his audiences not by a penetrating, profound inner power but by his finished technique. According to critic Vissarion Belinsky (1811–1848), he "knew how to show what artistic form means." "Decorativeness, elegance, noble posture, picturesque and graceful movement, mastery of declamation—such are his habitual weapons. It is useless to accuse him of excessive theatricalism: his acting is inconceivable without it." [6]

Paul Mochalov (1800–1848) was the intuitive performer. The son of a serf actor, he took stage at Moscow in 1817, confused his audiences with his talent and his lack of skill, but eventually conquered that mercantile and middle-class city with the inspired, though fitful, ardor of his impersonations. Antipathetic to any rational methods, Mochalov relied entirely on his feelings at the moment. Passion, not plan, was his primary concern. As one teacher of acting commented: "It is a misfortune when Paul . . . begins to reason: he is good only when he does not reason. . . . His is a genius of instinct. He has to learn a part and perform it; if he hits the mark, it will prove a miracle; but if he doesn't, it will be trash." "Even in the course of one performance his moods frequently changed, and he would either sink to a very mediocre level of acting, or suddenly rise to the height of dramatic perfection." This unevenness, this inability to control himself and to shape his characterizations, troubled Mochalov no end. But he could never solve the problem of nature versus art. He couldn't reconcile them. He was for nature; in character he voiced what he felt, however crude, and that was that. He aimed, he said, for emotional sincerity onstage. The proper expression, the communication, the graces or the beauties would take care of themselves. Mochalov, in competition with Karatygin, brought nature in the exciting, turbulent raw to such roles as Schiller's Don Carlos, Karl and Franz Moor, Miller in Kabale und Liebe, and Mortimer in Maria Stuart; he energized Shakespeare's Othello, Lear, Richard III, Romeo, and Coriolanus; and he created (in 1837) a highly original, personal Hamlet. According to Belinsky he demonstrated "that only in parts created by Shakespeare may a great actor prove that he is a great actor." [7]

Mochalov's fervid exhibitions were, for sure, too uncouth for a few Russian advocates of an "art" of acting, for those French-tainted intellectuals who insisted that art is nature improved. One professor, for instance, complained that Mochalov's sincere passion, or "naturalness," didn't "quite attain the ideal. Where it is necessary to express natural impulses he is superb: how a misanthrope feels indignant; how a youth dreams; how to express passion and despair. Still these are not art, but merely imitations of nature! The taste, refined decorum, and ideal expressiveness, those qualities which render grief interesting and joy noble, throwing a light poetic veil over every living situation, are all lacking: nor is there that enticement which shields one from the prosaic nature of life, luring one into the ideal realm of artistry. Here art is stripped of its ideal dignity, and made a mere mirror of nature." [8]

Yet that is precisely what native Russian acting, once freed from, or unaware of, esoteric foreign influences, slowly began to be: a mirror of nature.

And the actor who probably never heard of poetic or ideal naturalness, and who most influentially introduced a kind of "simplicity and lifelikeness" into the Slavic theater was Michael Shchepkin (1788–1863). Acting to him—at one time anyway—was relatively uncomplicated. He believed in carefully observing life, and then truthfully copying it onstage. That was almost all there was to it. Shchepkin, according to his countrymen, "was the first to become nontheatrical in the theater." Stanislavski praised him as the "pride of our national art, the man who re-created in himself all that the West could give and created the foundations of true Russian dramatic art, our great lawgiver and artist." [9]

Born a serf, Shchepkin first appeared on the stage of a public theater in his home province of Kursk in 1805 when he was seventeen. Three years later he was a full-fledged professional actor. "From Kursk he went to Kharkov and joined the local company; after that he proceeded to Poltava, Romny, Kremenchug, and other southern cities." In those days, he later wrote, "Acting was considered excellent when no one spoke in his natural voice and when acting consisted of extremely distorted declamation, words being pronounced as loudly as possible and nearly every one of them being accompanied by gestures. Especially in lover's parts they used to declaim so passionately that even the memory of it is funny." Shchepkin never questioned that imported, traditional manner of acting until about 1810 when he watched an amateur player, a certain Prince Meshchersky. At first, on noticing that the prince wasn't "acting" but merely behaving onstage as he would in real life, Shchepkin attributed the naturalness to inexperience. But slowly he discovered that the simplicity with which the prince spoke in no way impaired his performance. Shchepkin was moved by it. "I fell under the spell of real life," he confessed in his memoirs. "I saw no one on the stage except the prince. My eyes seemed to have become glued to him. His suffering struck a living chord in my soul; every word of his delighted me by its naturalness and at the same time tormented me." [10] Sometime afterward Shchepkin decided that to act expertly meant, above all else, to live a role truly, naturally, believably. And he was aiming, without much success, to speak onstage as he did in everyday life when, after buying his freedom in 1821, he was hired as an actor with the Imperial company in Moscow and made his big time debut in 1822.

In 1824, when the Maly (Small) Theatre was built there, Alexander Pushkin (1799–1857), poet, prose writer, and father of Russia's national literature, had for some time been requiring of playwrights "Truth of passions, genuineness of feelings in given circumstances," and "verisimilitude of characters." Next year he followed "the folk laws of the Shakespearean drama, and not the court etiquette of Racine's tragedy," [11] in writing Boris Godunov (unproduced until 1870), a chronicle play on the relationship between a tyrant and his people—which, though historical, examined a seething contemporary problem.

Thus by 1825 Russian actors, led by thirty-seven-year-old Shchepkin, who'd been onstage for twenty years, were ready to begin their long and wobbly exploration of realistic acting.

III

Goethe, to the contrary, maintained that acting at its best should be more than deception, more than merely natural, and more than mirror-true. For him the exhibition onstage of a "positive, actually existing, individual human nature" wasn't enough. That only titillated audiences; it never deeply pleased them with a revelation of beauty, the beauty of form and of idea. He therefore demanded that acting, first of all, be beautiful. "*Erst shön, dann wahr*" ("Beauty first; then truth"). Goethe believed that the perfect actor should rise above the purely objective copying of real behavior, above the purely subjective outpouring of individual sensibility, and aim to synthesize the particular and the universal, nature and mind. He wanted acting to be imaginative, theatrical, and symbolic. He hoped that via an "inner form" it might give audiences intimations of the ideal.[12]

Schiller continued to agree with him. In his preface to *Die Braut von Messina* (*The Bride of Messina*) (1803) he declared renewed war on "naturalism," claiming that the "vulgar idea of the natural" is destructive to art, that the artist can't use any element of reality just as he finds it, that the natural must be changed and raised and dignified. Everything, he said, in playwriting, staging, and acting "is only a symbol of the real." Yes, "Art must be true, but truth is something that leaves reality behind, becoming ideal." [13]

These two "idealists" in the first five years of the century staged at Weimar, along with a number of measley but popular plays, a notable selection from international dramatic literature which included in 1800 Goethe's version of Voltaire's *Mahomet*, Schiller's *Maria Stuart* and his rendering of *Macbeth*, in 1801 a translation of the *Adelphi* of Terence which was acted in masks, in 1802 the *Ion* of Euripides and Schiller's adaptation of Gozzi's *Turandot*, in 1803 Schiller's *Die Braut von Messina* and *Die Jungfrau von Orleans* (*The Maid of Orleans*) (1801), in 1804 Schiller's *Wilhelm Tell* and Racine's *Mithridate*, and in 1805 Schiller's version of *Phèdre*. After the latter's death at the age of forty-six in 1805, Goethe continued to direct the theater until 1817; he made Weimar the literary, cultural, and esthetic capital of Germany.

But the acting of the plays staged there was evidently a continuous dud. The company, headed by Caroline Jagemann (1777–1848), Pius A. Wolff (1782–1828), and his wife Amalie Malcolmi (1780–1851), was mediocre; and Goethe never understood acting and couldn't communicate to intellectual inferiors his conceptions of style in impersonation. He could only "suspend by fiat" any potential individuality and talent of the players by turning them into automatons. In 1803 he devised for his dullard beginners ninety-one paragraphs of "Rules" aimed at achieving a certain unity of method, a certain external form, attainable by all. In thus trying for a kind of ensemble, surface polish that could be perfected by constant drill, he taught his company "an excessively mechanical, artifical, rigidly classical style of declamation" [14] and posturing.

Goethe's "Rules" are appalling—then ludicrous. Read ten of them:

3. In "the art of the actor the clean and perfect pronunciation of each word is the basis of all higher recitation and declamation."

28. "The declaimer is free to select his own stops, pauses, and so forth; but he must guard against destroying the true meaning. . . ." (Yet Goethe insisted on pauses of varying lengths for commas, semicolons, colons, exclamation and question marks!)

38. "For the actor must constantly remember that he is on the stage for the sake of the public."

39. "Accordingly, it is mistaken naturalness for the actors to play to each other as if no third person were present; they should never play in profile, nor turn their backs to the audience. . . ."

40. "One must also be especially careful never to speak in toward the stage, but always speak out toward the public. . . ."

41. "It is a cardinal point that when two actors are playing together, the speaker always moves back [upstage], and the one who has stopped speaking moves down slightly. . . ."

59. "The player must bear in mind on which side of the theater he is standing, in order to adapt his gestures accordingly."

60. "He who stands on the right side must gesture with the left hand, and conversely. . . ."

74. "It is frightful, in the midst of an artistic production, to be reminded of . . . natural occasions" like blowing the nose or spitting.

81. "When he is learning the role by heart he [the actor] must constantly address himself to an audience; even when he sits at a table, by himself or with others, he should always strive to form a picture, taking up and setting down everything with a certain grace, as if it were on the stage. In such a manner he must always form part of a picture." [15]

Even worse, Goethe often conducted his rehearsals with a baton. "He was constantly appealing to the analogy of music in his instructions," according to his favorite actor Wolff. "The cast were trained to speak their lines in just the same way as an opera is rehearsed: the speed, the fortes and pianos, crescendos and diminuendos were determined by him and most carefully watched. . . ." And all the movements of the actors were just as meticulously, mechanically rehearsed. "On the stage marked out in squares every single position and movement was determined beforehand with the aim of producing a harmonious and pleasing spectacle." No wonder that a viewer of *Wilhelm Tell* in 1810 reported that the actors formed an ensemble only in the sense that it would make no difference if they all exchanged roles with each other, since "any one of them would have played any part pretty much like any other. . . ." [16]

Unfortunately Goethe's rules "gained wide currency in the theaters of Germany and other countries, and were taken . . . as words of an Olympian, to be strictly and literally observed. . . ." They became the unquestioned, true histrionic principles, and generated for too long a time an almost completely mechanical and externalized style of performing. Even as late as 1920 the aftereffects of Goethe's spurious teachings were clearly traceable in German acting.[17]

IV

Weimar, fortunately, wasn't the only theater in much-divided Germany in the early years of the new century. More and more state and municipal theaters were established everywhere and "looked upon as cultural institutions comparable with picture galleries, conservatoires of music, and academies of science." Professional actors, therefore, attained a certain tolerated status— although they weren't yet accepted by solid citizens as equals; they also escaped from the economic uncertainties of a touring life and latched onto something like security. Often, in fact, they became civil servants with pension rights. And that, according to one critic, was an evil. "An actor," he wrote, "grows rusty in settled conditions. As soon as it becomes his first thought how to secure for himself and his wife and children a decent living it is all over with his progress." [18]

Despite the fact that the supply of passable German actors was hardly equal to the demand, some of them were more expert or at least more interesting than Goethe's robots. Iffland, for instance, was still effectively performing in Berlin; the talented, mannered, and popular Ferdinand Esslair (1772–1840) toured from one town to another, settled briefly at Stuttgart, and in 1820 was appointed manager of the Court theater at Munich; plain, temperamental, rhetorical Sophie (Burger) Schröder (1781–1868) regularly thrilled audiences at Hamburg; and Ferdinand Raimund (1790–1836) was expertly performing at Vienna.

The most exciting German actor, neurotic, drinking Ludwig Devrient (1772–1840), was working at Breslau, the second city of Prussia. Like his contemporary, Edmund Kean, he was that rare, isolated, inexplicable phenomenon called an instinctive artist. No rules or methods fashioned his odd genius or restricted it. Devrient "heartily detested the conventional 'beauty' theory of Goethe's school" and paid little heed to the "copy nature" theory of Schröder's school. He followed his own bent. As an actor he used for his material not what he ought ideally to be, and not what he ought typically to be, but only what he himself uniquely was. He created his characters by vividly mimicking what he vividly imagined. And because "he ordinarily saw human beings in a glaring, fantastic light," his impersonations, "whether tragic or comic, had always a tinge of strangeness and morbidity." [19] But they were fresh, they were vital, and they were thrilling to behold in the theater.

Under an assumed name at the age of twenty Devrient began acting in 1804 with a company at Gera. With his skill at mimicry and make-up, and possibly because of some physical and vocal deficiences, he became a character actor. He forfeited his external qualities, but held tenaciously to his internal ones. Devrient never played any role well, he discovered, unless he had some mental or emotional affinity for it, "unless it shaped itself in his imagination into a definite figure that he could live with, as it were. . . ." A year later with a better company at Dessau Devrient worked hard at perfecting his romantic notions of what acting ought to be, even preparing a number of roles he knew he'd never be allowed to perform, such as, Richard III and King Philip in Schiller's *Don Carlos*. Meanwhile, he exhibited this character and that, every kind of character, until he was hailed as "the most *original* actor in Germany, the one whose distinguishing mark it was that the strange and living figures created by him seemed to spring direct from his own imagination, conforming to no existing school, and owing nothing to any previous stage-creation." [20]

In 1809 Devrient left Dessau for Breslau, first appeared there as Franz Moor in *Die Räuber*, and was acclaimed at once an actor of genius. By "his daemonic power, his fantastic appearance, so precisely suited to this figure, and his delivery, highly individual," he "lifted the character into a higher sphere than could ever be attained by Iffland's nicely-calculated, effective, but somewhat self-conscious virtuosity." Next year, at twenty-six, Devrient tackled the role of King Lear. Some seasons later this proved to be one of his finest creations—although "he never succeeded in rendering all the phases of the character with equal power, as . . . Schröder had done." And so acute was his sensibility and so torrential his passion that "many times . . . as early as the end of the second Act . . . he fell down in a sort of epileptic fit, and was obliged either to break off the performance altogether, or to give up for the rest of the evening all attempt to play with his full force." [21] Shylock, Falstaff, Harpagon in Molière's *L'Avare*, and Sheva in Cumberland's *The Jew* (1794) were other roles he successfully designed and energized.

Iffland on his last starring tour visited Breslau in 1814, acted with Devrient, acknowledged his amazing ability, and urged him to come to Berlin. Next year, after Iffland's death, Devrient was hired by the new Intendant-General of the Royal Stage-plays there, court official Count Karl Moritz von Bruhl. In early 1815—when the Congress of Vienna was remaking all Europe and setting up the German Confederation, when nationalism and prosperity and romanticism were in the air—Devrient made his Berlin debut as Franz Moor. But his rousing, unorthodox talent was too much for von Bruhl who, like most public officials, didn't know the difference between acting and an apple. Liking—or deciding that he ought to like—what had been done onstage at Weimar, he favored the elegantly academic reciting and posturing of his other leading man, Goethe's Pius A. Wolff. Two years later, in 1817, he appointed Wolff supervisor of tragedy and Devrient supervisor of comedy. Thereafter the latter mostly acted silly characters in empty German farces. For years "Three great creations—Iago, Mephistopheles, and Richard III—lay ready in his mind, waiting to see the light." [22] Devrient was neither encouraged nor allowed to exhibit them.

By 1825 this bungled, government-run theater in Berlin was a shambles, a bleak chaos. Devrient remained there, however, drank more and more, undertook exhausting tours in vacation time, slowly disintegrated. Finally, in 1828, four years before his death at the age of forty-eight, he acted Richard III with some of the old originality and fire; and that same year flashed to imaginative life again in several of his principal characters and heard the wild, sweet acclaim of audiences at the Hofburgtheater in Vienna.

Under the literate, artistic-minded leadership of Joseph Schreyvogel (1768–1832) this Hofburgtheater had become by 1823 the best showhouse in the German-speaking countries. In 1814 he'd been placed in charge of play selection, casting, production; and slowly he had gathered around him a company of expert actors which included Heinrich Anschültz (1785–1865), Sophie Schröder, Karl Costenoble (1769–1837), and Maximilian Korn (1782–1854). He also encouraged native playwright Franz Grillparzer (1791–1872), author of Sappho (1819), Das Goldene Vliess (1822), and König Ottokars Gluck und Ende (The Fortune and Fall of King Ottokar) (1825). These were the first German plays of interest, but not much importance, after that model for a flood of "fate" tragedies, Der Vierundzwanzigste Februar (The Twenty-fourth of February) (1808) by Zacharias Werner (1768–1823), Faust, Part I (1808), and the comic Der Zerbrochene Krug (The Broken Jug) plus the serious Der Prinz von Homburg (1811) by Heinrich von Kleist (1777–1811).

German creative genius for the years 1805–1825 was largely concentrated in Beethoven.

❈ REFLECTIONS BY TALMA

Napoleon in 1807 minimized the Comédie-Française's new competition by reducing the number of theaters in Paris to a mere handful. Two of them were located in the fairground Boulevard du Temple: the Théâtre de la Gaieté (1792), the first nonstate supported theater, presented melodramas, fairy plays, and pantomimes; and the Théâtre de l'Ambigu-Comique, a children's theater in 1769, continued to stage, as it had since 1797, melodramas by Pixerécourt and others. Then in 1810 the Théâtre de la Porte-Saint-Martin (1781), used for opera until 1794, re-opened as a house for dramas and spectacles. And in 1816 playwright-manager Louis Picard (1769–1828), who had given up acting in 1807 in order to qualify for admission to the French Academy and for the award of the Légion d'Honneur, "which Napoleon himself did not dare give to an actor, not even to Talma," [23] opened the Théâtre Royal de l'Odéon where he produced light operas and comedies with music. That same year the Théâtre des Funambules, at the Boulevard du Temple, began specializing in pantomimes and acrobatics. Shortly after 1820 the Théâtre du Gymnase-Dramatique, originally a nursery for young talent from the Conservatoire, offered vaudeville and then plays.

Actors of ability who weren't members of the Comédie-Française, and therefore rarely too classical, took stage. Popular Charles-Gabriel Potier (des Gailletières) (1774–1838), valued by Talma as the greatest comic of the period, and highly praised by Macready, made his Paris debut in 1809 at the Théâtre des Variétés, and in 1831 moved to the newly opened second Palais-Royal. (Jean-Gaspard) Deburau (1796–1846), pantomimist and creator in 1825 of a durable Pierrot, performed at the Funambules after 1816. Mlle. Dorval (Marie Delaunay) (1798–1849), a provincial actress and Conservatoire student, launched her career "as the most inspired interpreter of the women of the Romantic drama" in 1818 at the Porte-Saint-Martin. Her talent, "in which temperament was all in all, fitted her as completely for the boulevard theater, as it unfitted her for the classic stage." Mlle. Dorval was ill-equipped to act traditional, formal roles, "helpless in characters which she could not build up round her own personality. . . . Her art was accordingly a thing of fits and starts, intuitive, eruptive, uncalculated and incalculable." According to Théophile Gautier, "She had within her range screams so piercingly true, sobs that seemed so to tear the bosom, intonations so natural, tears so heartfelt and helpless, that the stage was forgotten, and it was impossible to believe that this was but a simulated sorrow." [24] Classical Joseph Isidore Samson (1793–1871), a Conservatoire student, toured the provinces before serving as leading man at the Odéon from 1819 to 1826 when he joined the Comédie-Française. And romantic Bocage (Pierre-François Touzé) (1797–1863), a provincial actor who wasn't wanted by the Comédie-Française, found success c. 1822 at the Odéon.

The important rebel, akin to Devrient and Kean, was Frédérick (Antoine-Prosper) Lemaître (1800–1876), who never performed with the Comédie-Française. Accepted at the Conservatoire at the age of fifteen, he studied under Pierre Lafon (1773–1846) for a few years; simultaneously he learned some less formal, more acrobatic and pantomimic acting at the Variétés-Amusantes, the Funambules, and the Cirque-Olympique. Then in 1820 he was hired by the Odéon to act small roles in classical tragedies. But, "having tasted the sweets of the applause in the side-show theaters," he thumbed his nose at conventional declamation and in 1823 accepted an engagement at the Ambigu-Comique. With his first new role there that year in L'Auberge des Adrets (The Inn of Adrets) by Benjamin Antier (1787–1870) he achieved a long run of eighty-five performances by transforming the villain, Robert Macaire, into a fabulously comic figure and rolling the audiences in the aisles. The colossal buffoonery of his conception carried them at once "into the region of hyperbole and Aristophanic fun which soared beyond the range of criticism. . . . In every sense of the word it was creative. A common melodrama without novelty or point became in his hands a grandiose symbolical caricature. . . ." [25]

Soon Lemaître would become "an actor for the people," a player of comedy, melodrama, and tragedy who inspired enthusiasm in the masses "by surprising, astonishing, overawing them." His romantic originality—his "great daring, great fancy, and great energy of animal passion"—rudely and sometimes vulgarly smashed the traditional molds for characters and brought onstage new, alive, exciting people. Lemaître "always *created* his parts—that is to say, gave them a specific stamp of individuality; . . . his imagination was seen in a hundred novel details." [26]

II

The differences between the acting of Lemaître and Mlle. Dorval and that of Talma and Mlle. Mars—like the differences between Delacroix (1798–1863) and Ingres (1780–1867) in painting—were born of the battle between romanticism and classicism which absorbed literary France in the 1820's. That battle, long foreshadowed, was perhaps officially launched in 1823 when Stendhal (Henri Beyle) (1783–1842) published *Racine et Shakespeare*, a pamphlet bristling with common sense. More than Mme. de Staël's (1766–1817) earlier book on German romanticism, *De l'Allemagne* (1810), it focused attention on true issues by asking the old question, "Shall we follow Racine or Shakespeare?" Racine, Stendhal declared, had written pompous tirades in rhymed hexameters "for the enjoyment of the snobbish court of Louis XIV." Shakespeare, on the other hand, had come closer to nature and, by violating the rules of pedants, created characters of flesh and blood. Must French dramatic authors, Stendhal asked, continue to imitate Racine's tone and ideas a century and a half later—after the French Revolution, the Republic, and the wars of the Empire had shaken the foundations of society? "Never has a people experienced more rapid and sweeping changes than those of 1780 to 1823, and yet they [the classicists, the French Academy] want to give us the same literature . . . the characters and forms that were enjoyed in 1670." [27] No, no, no! Let playwrights, at all cost, be *modern* and not imitators of antique models.

And let actors also be modern?

III

But the Comédie-Française, despite novel and lively competition from other theaters, and despite growing petitions for more modernity in their productions, calmly continued to perform traditional plays in traditional ways. The actors had no great itch for individualism or for innovations. After all, they were secure. Their organization had weathered the Revolution, and its old usages or regulations had been codified by Napoleon; its annual subsidy of 12,000 francs under the monarchy had been upped to 100,000 francs; and its losses and pensions for retired members were insured by a special government reserve fund of 200,000 francs. These actors were also secure in the belief that the comedies and tragedies in their repertoire were the glories of France, and secure in the inherited belief that their style of performing them elevated nature into art. The proof of the pudding, as everyone knew, was the fact that "When Talma and Mlle. Duchesnois play in tragedy, or Fleury [until he retired in 1818] and Mlle. Mars in comedy, the Théâtre-Français is always crammed." [28]

Glittering Mlle. Mars (Anne Boutet) (1779–1847), the daughter of a provincial actress and actor Monvel, came onstage as a child, was later coached by Mlle. Contat, and joined the Comédie-Française in 1799. There her progress followed the customary pattern: "beginning with the very young girls, the *ingenues*, of whom Molière's Agnes is the original type, she went on next to the parts of . . . riper maidens, in whom the 'intelligence of love' has awakened, technically known as '*les Amoureuses*,' and finally . . . to the witty, sophisticated young women of the world—*les grandes Coquettes*." From about 1805 onward Mlle. Mars was "the idol of Paris, and she deserved it." To see comedy for the next thirty-six years "meant to see Mars. She ruled in this sphere as Talma did in tragedy." In 1817 she was praised as "An actress . . . full of life, grace, *naiveté*, and charm; beautiful on the stage, though she is past her first youth." (And in 1839, at the age of sixty—two years before her retirement—she was still with "exquisite toilets" and "the finest, most exquisite diction" impersonating young girls. "The alexandrines fell from her lips like pearls." Macready, after seeing some of her performances in 1822, wrote that "Her voice was music, and the words issuing from her lips suggested to the listener the clear distinctness of a beautiful type upon a rich vellum page. . . . Nor was her voice her only charm: in person she was most lovely, and in grace and elegance of deportment and action unapproached by any of her contemporaries." Evidently Mlle. Mars was a consummate artist: onstage "her private voice—harsh, rough, abrupt"—was with great technical mastery "transmuted into the purest music"; and her private personality—rude, shrewish, frightening—was inexplicably transformed into a witchery of ideal womanliness that seemed a true and natural "emanation from the artist's own pure, gentle soul." [29]

Mlle. Duchesnois (Catherine Rafuin) (1777–1835) acted first with the Comédie-Française as Phèdre in 1802; then, though unbeautiful, she declaimed as Talma's partner for twenty-four years in a voice of profound tenderness and melodious sorrow. That same year attractive, imperious-minded, but capable Mlle. George (Marguerite Weymer) (1787–1835), a child of actors, was drilled in reciting by Mlle. Raucourt and at the age of fifteen made a stirring debut as Clytemnestra in Racine's *Iphigénie*. Then, after being Napoleon's mistress, she married a dancer in 1808 and journeyed to Russia where she acted for four seasons. In 1813 she returned to the Comédie-Française, left it again four years later to perform in London, and in 1822 came back to Paris to star at the Odéon.

Talma, Napoleon's favorite actor, was born too soon to be a romanticist; therefore, half-protesting his fate, he became early in the nineteenth century, the "most distinguished representative of the classic drama." But, like Devrient and Kean, he rebelled against traditional, formal histrionics, and especially against turgid declamation and unnaturalness. Talma succeeded, it's said, "in working out a style of diction of his own, which, avoiding the absurdity and deadly monotony of the old-fashioned method of delivery, brought the alexandrine as near as the form admitted to being a credible and natural vehicle for human emotions." He achieved a lively naturalness in tragedies by *truly* raving whereas his co-actors only pretended to rave. Sometimes, yes, Talma's readings came out sing-song and monotonous, but "into scenes of strong feeling he would throw himself with passionate intensity, rendering them with an almost pathological realism." When, for instance, he impersonated Othello in a version by Ducis in 1803, cranky classicist Abbé Geoffroy (1743–1814) reported that Talma's "triumph lies in the portrayal of passion worked up to delirium, to insanity." The actor, he added, "would do well to return again within the boundaries of art." Two years later the same critic contrasted Talma's and Lekain's acting of Voltaire's Orestes as follows: Lekain, "penetrated by the nobility of his art, . . . held that Orestes must preserve a certain dignity, even in his moments of madness. According to his view the intonations of voice, the gestures and facial expression of a tragic hero whose mind is unhinged by the excess of passion and calamity, must be other than those of a madman from the . . . Asylum. He did not consider that Orestes' frenzy should resemble an attack of epilepsy. . . . Talma employs a different method; he is more real and true to nature, but less noble, less interesting. He represents with great accuracy an unhappy human being who has gone out of his mind; he reproduces with great truth all the symptoms of common madness; he amazes, he appals. But . . . Lekain's method was . . . much more in accordance with the rules of art. . . ." In brief, Lekain with his intelligence created art, while Talma with his sensibility copied only nature. (No wonder the latter, irritated and confused, was tempted to horse-whip this critic.) [30]

As he matured as a tragedian, however, Talma pledged a little less allegiance to sensibility and a little more to intelligence. In his youth he had praised sensibility as the only requisite for an actor; he had even attacked Diderot for placing it second in importance to intelligence. But by 1814 he changed his conviction and admitted that for an actor intelligence was worth something, perhaps much. In a letter written then he confessed: "For a long time I played from direct inspiration, giving myself up to the feelings of the moment, forgetting completely that I was Talma and believing myself to be [for example] Achilles or Orosmane. But, aside from the exhaustion caused by this method, I was uneven; good when I was in good humor, bad when a personal anxiety brought me reluctantly back to reality." The actor, he decided, "must work upon a mob, and in order to succeed in this he must be master of himself." Thereafter, Talma apparently "*made notes* on all his inflections. . . . Such a practice acted as a safety device, preventing him from going wrong when he was not fully inspired." He worked out "a species of music which, once fixed in the memory, brought back . . . all the intonations which he could not have omitted without danger of losing himself, and of being led too far or on a false track." [31]

IV

Romanticism ripened in France in 1825 as Stendhal continued to demand more modernity in writing with an augmented edition of *Racine et Shakespeare*. But no one harangued vigorously for more modernity in acting. In that same year Rémond de Sainte-Albine's not very modern *Le Comédien* was reprinted in the *Mémoires* of Molé—and still explained acting better than did Mauduit-Larive's newer *Réflexions sur l'art théâtral* (1801) and *Cours de déclamation* (1804, 1810); and Talma, the year before he died, contributed to the *Mémoires de Lekain* (1801–02), edited by his son, some brief "Réflexions sur cet acteur, et sur l'art théâtral" which, though praised by Henry Irving (in 1883) as "a permanent embodiment of the principles of our art; a kind of *vade macum* of the actor's calling," [32] aren't much more modern than *Le Comédien*.

Since Talma was only fifteen when Lekain died, his comments on that actor are only flowers reverently placed on a tomb. But "Reflections on the Actor's Art" are worth reading because they tell something about how a classic actor yearning to be a nonclassic actor worked. According to Talma "truth in all art is what is most difficult to achieve," and therefore "nature ought to be the constant object of the studies of the actor." But in tragedy, if not in comedy, nature ought to be "noble, animated, aggrandized." "The comedian," he explains, "represents beings whom he sees every day—beings of his own class. Indeed, with very few exceptions, his task is confined to the representations of folly and ridicule, and to painting passions in his own sphere of life, and, consequently, more moderate than those which come within the domain of tragedy. It is . . . his own nature which, in his imitations, speaks and acts." But "the tragic actor must quit the circle in which he is accustomed to live, and plunge into the regions where the genius of the poet has placed and clothed in ideal forms the beings conceived by him or furnished by history. He must preserve these personages in their grand proportions, but at the same time he must subject their elevated language to natural accents and true expression; and it is this union of grandeur without pomp, and nature without triviality—this union of the ideal and the true, which is so difficult to attain in tragedy." [33]

It follows then, according to Talma, that "the principal faculties necessary to an actor" who would put "himself faithfully in the place of the personage he represents" and "perfect the idea of the author of whom he is the interpreter" are "sensibility and intelligence." And "between two persons destined for the stage, one possessing the extreme sensibility . . . , and the other a profound intelligence," Talma declares that he "would without question prefer the former." [34]

Talma calls sensibility that faculty "which agitates an actor, takes possession of his senses, . . . and enables him to enter into the most tragic situations, and the most terrible of the passions, as if they were his own." Its source, he says, is the imagination—*not the imagination which consists in having reminiscences, . . . [which] is only memory* [my italics], but that imagination which, creative, active and powerful, consists in collecting in one single fictitious object the qualities of several real objects." Here, Fleeming Jenkin comments, "Talma misses the very point which distinguishes the actor from other artists. All artists must have this sensibility he demands, but the *form* [my italics] which each naturally employs to express his emotion determines whether he shall be author, painter, musician or actor." But Talma knew only that "The poet or the painter can wait for the moment of inspiration to write or to paint," while the actor must be able to command it "at any moment, at his will." Therefore, he decided that because the actor's inspiration must be "sudden, lively, and prompt," he "must possess an excess of sensibility." [35]

Intelligence Talma defines as that faculty which "judges the impressions" sensibility "has made us feel; it selects, arranges them, and subjects them to calculation." And this intelligence "must always be on the watch, and, acting in concert with . . . sensibility, regulate its movements and effects"; because the actor "cannot, like the painter and the poet, efface what he does." "To Talma," according to Jenkin again, "intelligence meant a sound critical faculty, not logical, but perceptive, enabling its possessor to keep what was good in art and reject that which was less good. . . ." Thus "Talma, as we understand him, only felt the emotion once in its full intensity—that is to say, at the moment of creation during the solitary rehearsal. Subsequently the effect was produced by the aid of memory. . . ." Talma was well aware, for instance, that "there is in the art of reciting verse [and prose?] a part in some degree mechanical." [36] Scenes, speeches, sentences are, he knew, made up of many details that must be carefully worked out, practiced, perfected, and then repeated and repeated with exactness.

Next, Talma is sure that along with sensibility and intelligence the actor "must have a voice that can be modulated with ease, and at the same time be powerful and expressive." Lekain, he points out, "studied his voice as one studies an instrument." By dint of application he perfected it into "a rich-keyed instrument, from which he could draw forth at pleasure every sound he stood in need of. And such is the power of a voice thus formed by nature attuned by art, that it affects even the foreigner who does not understand the words." [37]

Finally, Talma adds to these old, general requirements for acting two also old but often forgotten specifics. First, he declares that in most instances in life thinking comes ahead of speaking, and that therefore onstage "The gesture, the attitude, and the look ought . . . to precede the words." Sometimes also pauses ought to precede the words or groups of words. But then there are other times when the words should come to the actor's lips "as rapidly as the thoughts to his mind; they are born with them, and succeed each other without interruption" in order to maintain the illusion of life. Passion, he emphasizes, doesn't "follow the rules of grammar; it pays but little respect to colons, and semicolons, and full stops. . . ." [38]

Second, and importantly, Talma assures any actor that the "observations which he has made on his own nature serve at once for his study and example." The actor preparing a characterization, he explains, "interrogates himself on the impressions *his* soul has felt, on the expression they imprinted upon *his* features, on the accents of *his* voice in the various states of feeling. He meditates on these, and clothes the fictitious passions with these real forms." Talma illustrates his point by confessing that "in any circumstance of my life in which I experienced deep sorrow, the passion of the theater was so strong in me that, although oppressed with real sorrow, and disregarding the tears I shed, I made, in spite of myself, a rapid and fugitive observation on the alteration of my voice, and on a certain spasmodic vibration which it contracted as I wept; and, I say it not without some shame, I even thought of making use of this on the stage, and, indeed, this experiment on myself has often been of service to me." [39]

❈ CRITICS AND KEAN

For the first years of the eighteenth century, the rich time of painters Turner (1775–1851) and Constable (1776–1837), novelists Walter Scott (1777–1832) and Jane Austen (1775–1817), and poets (each of whom tried playwriting) Wordsworth (1770–1850), Coleridge (1772–1834), Byron (1788–1824), Shelley (1792–1822), and Keats (1795–1821), the London stage was dominated by the Kemble clan. From 1800 through mid-1812 Mrs. Siddons thrilled audiences with "lofty tones and conscious modulations" which "seemed natural in her mouth, as expressing the beauty of all that was ideal. . . ." And stately John Philip Kemble, uninterested in new dramatists, kept before the public the plays of Shakespeare by acting them in a classic style despite the fact that many Germans and some Frenchmen envied them for being nonclassic. A third member of the family, attractive, younger brother Charles Kemble (1775–1854), who had first acted at Drury Lane in 1794, moved with part-proprietor John and Sarah to Covent Garden in 1803, painstakingly prepared lover and hero roles "with every emphatic word underlined and accentuated" lest he "should omit the right inflection in delivering the lines," [40] and charmingly decorated the stage until 1817 when he inherited the management of the theater.

Most of the other chief players of the period made their names in comedy. Of the five who took stage before 1800 Dorothy Jordan (1761–1816) was the popular star. She began acting at the age of sixteen in Ireland, came with "hey-day vivacity" and "tip-toe spirits" to Drury Lane in 1785, appeared last at Covent Garden in 1814, and was continually called "great and original," "the first living actress in comedy." A fresh personality, "the same in all her characters, and inimitable in all of them, because there was no one else like her," she captivated audiences "not as an actress, but as herself." Joseph Munden (1758–1832), "with the bunch of countenances, the bouquet of faces," came from the provinces to Covent Garden in 1790, remained there for twenty-three years, and then performed for eleven more years at Drury Lane. "Nature be damned; make the people laugh," he said as he caricatured his way through "the grand grotesque of farce." William Dowton (1764–1851), "a genuine and excellent comedian," "infinitely superior to the common run of serious actors," made his debut in 1795 at Drury Lane and then for years portrayed engagingly such characters as Sir Oliver in *The School for Scandal* and Sir Anthony Absolute in *The Rivals*. Robert Elliston (1774–1831), "the greatest actor of the present day," "the only genius that has approached [Garrick] in universality of imitation," was that rare comedian who also successfully acted tragic roles. He came from the provinces to the Haymarket in 1796, appeared at both Covent Garden and Drury Lane, and then in 1809 embarked upon an extensive actor-manager career. John Emery (1777–1822), who first performed at Covent Garden in 1798, was praised for his "representations of common rustic life. . . . But the power of his mind [like that of many realistic actors of today] is evidently that of imitation, not that of creation. He has nothing romantic, grotesque, or imaginary about him. Everything in his hands takes a local and habitual shape." [41]

London ached for an original, daring, fiery, human tragedian.

II

The skills and personalities of these English players were evaluated, and attractively preserved beyond the moment, by journalist, essayist Leigh Hunt (1784–1859). At a time when there were no new worthwhile dramatists, when farces were hack-written for specific stars, Hunt was attracted by "this strange superiority of the mimetic over the literary part of the stage" and decided to evaluate actors. He did so with grace, affectionate respect, and discernment—even though he later admitted, in his *Autobiography* (1850), that his judgments were "too often confounded with a literal instead of a liberal imitation of nature." [42] His *Critical Essays on the Performers of the London Theatres* . . . (1807, actually 1808) shine alongside dull, trite, would-be instructive tomes like *Chironomia; or a Treatise on Rhetorical delivery; comprehending many precepts, both ancient and modern, for the proper regulation of the voice, the countenance, and gesture* . . . (1806) by Gilbert Austin (?), *The Anatomy and Philosophy of Expression* (1806) by Charles Bell (1774-1842), the already mentioned *Practical Illustrations of Rhetorical Gesture and Action* (1807, 1822) by Henry Siddons out of Engel, and the 1821 reprinting of Aaron Hill's essay on acting. In thirty articles on individual actors and actresses, an essay on Tragedy and one on Comedy, and a chatty Appendix (all collected from the 1805-07 *News*) Hunt captures some of the fascination, the qualities, and the details of actual English acting of his time.

First, Hunt explains—curiously, but more clearly than anyone had ever done—the long persisting, classic difference between the acting of comedy and the acting of tragedy. Comedy, he says, is principally concerned with, and reflects, the habits of men in common life. In "comic characters we generally recognize the manners or peculiarities of some person with whom we are acquainted, or who is at least known in the world." Thus "The comedian . . . has little to do with the intellectual properties of human nature; his attention is directed to the lighter follies of man, to fashions and habits, to the familiar domestic manners, in short to trifling and adventitious qualities rather than to inherent character." He has only to observe and to copy in order to "act naturally." And "An audience when judging [these] common imitations of life have merely to say 'Is it like ourselves!' " [43]

Tragedy, on the other hand, is wholly occupied with the passions of men in uncommon life. And "It is more difficult to conceive passions than habits, principally because the former are less subject to common observation." Of "the deeper tragic passions we have only read, or heard; we never see in society an impassioned character like Macbeth, or King Lear, or Hamlet; such characters exhibit themselves on great occasions only, their very nature prevents their appearance in common life." Therefore the "idea of passion requires more imagination than that of habit." Therefore "The loftier persons of tragedy require an elevation of language and manner, which they never use in real life." And therefore in tragic acting the "imitation of life is perfect, [is natural], not as it copies real and simple manners, but as it accords with our habitual ideas of human character . . . ," with our general opinion of what it can or should be. Oh, yes, it's true that "kings . . . are not always dignified off the stage, for the late King of Naples used to smoke with his *lazzaroni*, George the Second was fond of kicking his ministers, and Charles the Twelfth combed his hair with his fingers"; but those are only the habits too undignified for and habits unessential to the expression of great passion. The tragic actor in his imaginings overleaps ordinary habits or commonplace nature and "delights in the highest intellectual pleasures: . . . he turns from the familiar vanities and vulgarities of common life to the contemplation of heroism, of wisdom, and of virtue; he is occupied with the soul only." [44]

A few years later, however, Hunt retreated a bit from his classic position and rooted, along with others, for some irresistible changes in acting, changes which tended to minimize the differences between the tragic and the comic. He wanted (1) more familiar nature added to elevated nature in tragic acting. By 1812 he admitted "that in every species of passion a sublime effect is producible by the occasional mixture of everyday action with strong feeling . . ."; and in 1815 he decided that "the great stage-desideratum" is "to unite common life with tragedy." He wanted (2) more heightening, more theatricality, added to the reproduction of common habits and feelings in comic acting. Comedian Tyrone Power (1797–1841), he wrote, "is so natural that he seems as if he could no more help what he does than a real Irishman could in his situation. . . . You think that an Irishman picked up on the quay at Dublin would do just as the actor does,—neither more nor less." But "there is too much of dry facsimile . . . , and not enough of garnish and ebullition." [45]

(These suggested changes resulted eventually in almost a complete reversal of form in the writing and the acting of tragedies and comedies. Comedies by 1950 would be so heightened, in various ways, that the so-called "Method" actors would nearly always find the acting of them—like the acting of Shakespeare's plays—beyond their naturalistic skills; and most tragedies and dramas would be lowered to the believably true where the same actors would often achieve vividly lifelike results.)

Second, Hunt comes out strongly in his *Critical Essays* against "that abstracted artifice which induces the actor to study his audience more than his character." "One of the first studies of an actor," he says, "should be to divest himself of his audience, to be occupied not with the persons he is amusing, but with the persons he is assisting in the representation. But of all simple requisites to the mimetic art, this public abstraction seems to be the least attained. Our good performers are too fond of knowing they are good ones, and of acknowledging the admiration of the spectators by glances of important expression: our bad performers are vainer still . . . because not being able to enter into the interest of the scene they must look for interest elsewhere. These men in reality never speak to one another, but to the pit and to the boxes: they are thinking, not what the person spoken to will reply, but what the audience think of their own speeches. . . ." Hunt praises, for instance, Mr. Bannister who "engages your attention immediately by seeming to care nothing about you; the stage appears to be his own room, of which the audience compose the fourth wall: if they clap him he does not stand still to enjoy their applause; he continues the action, if he cannot continue the dialogue." [46]

Third, Hunt rather tentatively believes that the "suggestions of the poet [the playwright] . . . must be invigorated by the additional ideas of the actor," that the actor ought to use *something of his own* in interpreting his characters, and that that something is his own fresh, highly individual imagination. "Imagination," for Hunt, "is the great test of genius; that which is done by imagination is more difficult than that which is performed by discernment or experience. It is for this reason, that the actor is to be estimated, like the painter and the poet, not for his representation of the common occurrences of the world, not for his discernment of the familiarities of life, but for *his* idea of images submitted to the observation of the senses" [my italics].[47]

In reviews written after the publication of the *Critical Essays*, Hunt expands his point about the importance of the actor's individuality. He insists that "an actor's talent must be modified by his own character off the stage," by all the things he is as a person. He dislikes an actor who "never commits himself." He urges him not to copy old patterns or other actors but instead to "invent like Garrick. . . . I do not say that a good passage in acting of any kind should not be adopted from former actors; it may descend like an heirloom forever and do honor to its users; but why . . . not give us the variety, the combination, the ever-shifting genius?" Why not *"re-create"*? Hunt is especially delighted "to see how excellently two actors can support the same character with their own separate originality." For example, he finds that as Benedick in *Much Ado About Nothing* William T. Lewis (1748?–1811) "excels in all the lighter parts of the character, Elliston in the more earnest and impassioned: in Elliston you have more of the frank soldier, more of the man of rank, more of the resolute lover; in Lewis you have more of the airy gallant, of the careless heyday fellow, of the merry soul who turns everything into a jest. . . ."[48]

III

Edmund Kean (1788?–1833), "a little man with an inharmonious voice," "with almost every physical disadvantage against him," partly answered Hunt's hope that more familiar nature might be added to formalized nature in the acting of tragedy, and bulged the boundaries of his belief that a player should thoroughly commit himself in his characterizations and thus freshly re-create them. The bastard son of a strumpet and a lunatic, an uneducated waif, a prodigy who had recited in public when he was only ten, a wild charmer, a complex and brooding egotist, Kean became a strolling provincial player in 1804 at the age of sixteen and climbed nine years later to a position as leading man at the theater in Dorchester. Near the end of that year, in 1813, he was hired by actor-manager Elliston of the minor Olympic Theatre in London and then immediately grabbed for £8 a week by the management of tottering Drury Lane. There, after mumbling his way through only one rehearsal with the company, Kean vividly impersonated Shylock on January 26, 1814. "The applause, from the first scene to the last, was general, loud, and uninterrupted"; and the house, less than a third full, "knew that they were privileged to be present at the birth of a new genius in the theater, the first reformer, perhaps, since the great days of David Garrick, the one who would revivify the histrionic art." [49]

Hunt, however, wasn't in the audience that opening night; he was in prison because of an outspoken article he'd written about the Prince Regent. But new critic William Hazlitt (1778–1830) was there. And "if Hazlitt was a godsend to Kean, Kean was scarcely less of a godsend to Hazlitt. The critic made the actor's reputation, but the actor made the critic's immortality as a theatrical critic. If Hazlitt had not had Kean to write about, he would certainly have written much less, with far inferior life and gusto, and would probably never have collected his articles." [50] Twenty-one often brilliantly perceptive reviews of Kean's performances, taken mostly from the 1814–16 *Examiner*, are included in *A View of the English Stage* (1818). Three additional examinations of Kean appear in the *Criticisms and Dramatic Essays of the English Stage* (1851), edited by Hazlitt's son, and made up of large portions of the *View* together with selections from the 1820 *London Magazine*.

Hazlitt watched and listened as Kean "destroyed the Kemble religion; and," as he noted a little sadly, "it is the religion in which we were brought up." He admired all of Sarah's acting and much of John Philip's. But he was compelled to admire also Kean's many new readings of individual lines and speeches, the constant workings of his face, his frequent and revealing "by-play," physical actions, or stage business. And even when Hazlitt found defects in Kean's acting—a lack of poetry, "dignity, grace, and tenderness"—he couldn't resist praising the newcomer's fiery, artful portrayals of Shylock, Richard III, Hamlet, Othello, and Iago that first season, and of Macbeth, Romeo, Richard II, Coriolanus, Lear, and Giles Overreach in Massinger's *A New Way to Pay Old Debts* in later seasons. He admired their originality, their wild force, and their occasional naturalness. "Acting," he philosophized, "is an art that seems to contain in itself the seeds of perpetual renovation and decay, . . . is always setting out afresh on the stock of genius and nature. . . . The harvest of excellence (whatever it may be) is removed from the ground, every twenty or thirty years . . . ; and there is room left for another to sprout up and tower to any equal height, and spread into equal luxuriance —to 'dally with the wind, and court the sun'—according to the health and vigor of the stem, and the favorableness of the season." [51]

The season was favorable to Kean. His acting captivated London's theatergoers because it broke with boring tradition, decorum, and artificiality. His new style, personal, highly personal, thrilled them with its fitful surges of genuine feeling and its sudden, intermittent, dazzling glimpses of truth. Patrons crowded Drury Lane, 166,742 of them for the first sixty-eight nights Kean performed—or an average of 2,305 per night. The theater, with its receipts about tripled, was thus saved from financial collapse. Kean for one reward had his salary doubled to £20; and in July he was voted five shares in

Drury Lane. In seven months in London and one in Dublin he earned over £4,000.[52]

Kean was, first, an *original* interpreter of Shakespeare's characters. People "rushed to see him in whatever famous part he chose to play, for they knew that he would at least re-create it, and they were agog to find out in what way." His manner of acting Richard III, for instance, as Hazlitt was quick to point out, "has one peculiar advantage; it is entirely his own, without any traces of imitation of any other actor. He stands upon his own ground, and he stands firm upon it." "Kean," he added, "is not a literal transcriber of his author's text; he translates his characters with great freedom and ingenuity into a language of his own." Obviously, as others later agreed, whatever Kean did onstage "came from an inner conviction. . . . He acted as he did, because his mind and emotions seized on a role in a way which was peculiar to him." Kean was thus a romantic actor. He did not "embody the poet's lines as an expression of emotion in poetry; he did not derive his tones and his movements from the structural detail of the verse, eliciting the author's poetry; instead he bestowed upon the words the poetry of his own emotion, but with such an intensity of truth in his inner identification with the character, and in his outer show of voice and pantomime, that the lines seemed to mean what he made them mean, and to glow with a quality of their own, although it came from him." [53]

Kean, it seems, had almost too much ingenuity and invention. He sometimes failed "even from an exuberance of talent." Hazlitt decided that Kean made "a distinct [theatrical?] effort in every new situation, so that the actor does not seem entirely to forget himself, or to be identified with the character." And he scolded Kean as Lear for his apparent "determination to give the passages in a way in which nobody else would give them, and in which nobody else would expect them to be given." Singularity, he warned, is not always excellence. Later, he severely criticized Kean as Richard III for frequently varying "the execution of many of his most striking conceptions," for his evident intention to be always new. "In general," he said, "we think it a rule that an actor ought to vary his part as little as possible, unless he is convinced that his former mode of playing it is erroneous. He should make up his mind as to the best mode of representing the part, and come as near to this standard as he can, in every successive exhibition. It is absurd to object to this mechanical uniformity as studied and artificial. All acting is studied or artificial. An actor is no more called upon to vary his gestures, or articulation at every new rehearsal of the character, than an author can be required to furnish various readings to every separate copy of his work." [54]

Kean was, second, an *emotional* interpreter of Shakespeare's characters, "a consummate master of passionate expression." Hazlitt reported that almost always his "acting is like an anarchy of the passions, in which each upstart humor, or frenzy of the moment, is struggling to get violent possession of some bit or corner of his fiery soul and pigmy body—to jostle out, and lord it over the rest of the rabble of short-lived and furious purposes." Such acting in most instances was thrilling; but sometimes it was also wrong. Kean's Othello, "his best character, and the highest effort of genius on the stage," for example, both amazed and troubled Hazlitt. Kean, he decided, "is in general all passion, all energy, all relentless will. . . . He is too often in the highest key of passion, too uniformly on the verge of extravagance, too constantly on the rack. This does very well in certain characters, as Zanga [in *The Revenge*] . . . , where there is merely physical passion, a boiling of the blood, to be expressed; but it is not so in the lofty-minded and generous Moor." And Kean, again according to Hazlitt, made Richard II "a character of *passion*, that is, of feeling combined with energy; whereas it is a character of *pathos*, that is to say, of feeling combined with weakness. This, we conceive is the general fault of Mr. Kean's acting, that it is always energetic or nothing. He is always on full stretch— never relaxed. He expresses all the violence, the extravagance and fierceness of the passions, but not their misgivings, their helplessness, and sinkings into despair." "Mr. Kean's imagination appears not to have the principles of joy or hope or love in it. He seems chiefly sensible to pain, or to the passions that spring from it, and to the terrible energies of mind or body, which are necessary to grapple with or to avert it." [55]

Hazlitt also missed in Kean's acting certain values he always found in Kemble's acting: grace, grandeur, and "the regularity of art." Specifically, he missed Kemble's skill at conceiving, developing, and exhibiting characters made consistent via some one "predominant feeling," "single impulse," "ruling passion," or "undeviating line"—what today is called "the unbroken line." He missed in Kean's Othello, for instance, "the *architectural* building up of the part." [56] The actor, it seems, usually ignored the over-all design of a role, its function as part of the whole. Instead of working his way thoroughly and consistently into a character, elaborating it steadily and sequentially, Kean seized upon certain aspects that immediately, instinctively appealed to him, and then gave them so much intense life that often they stuck out discordantly in performance. Thus because Kean could feel deeply but think thinly he stunned audiences by individual passages, by inspired moments, by "flashes of lightning," and left unheeded a unity of conception.

Kean was, third, a *sometime naturalistic* interpreter of Shakespeare's characters. "Nature" in his acting was a love of artistic contrast, a custom, almost a trick, "of changing suddenly from the grand style to the familiar in his speaking. On the one hand, the energy and intensity of his grand manner compelled conviction; on the other, the manner into which he changed was 'easy, conversational and *unstagey'*: the two manners, when combined, were unique in their impact." For example, as Macbeth "Kean rushed on to the stage, and shouted the command to hang out the banners on the outer walls 'in a voice like thunder.' Then he suddenly paused, 'dropped his double-handled sword to the ground and leaning on it, whispered, "The cry is still they come, they come," at the same time seeming to become ashy grey with fear.' " Theatergoers cheered points like that—all theatergoers, that is, except a few who feared that Kean was attempting "an extraordinary innovation . . . he would reduce the character and language of the drama to what he calls the *level of real life.*" [57]

But if he aimed to do that, Kean did so as a craftsman, as an artist. He as carefully designed his transitions to "naturalness" and his familiar way of speaking as he designed his rousing scenes. He "worked as hard and as methodically at the actual details of his performance as any member of the Kemble school." He wasn't a purely impulsive actor. Hazlitt, for instance, saw that "Mr. Kean's style of acting is not in the least of the unpremeditated, *improvisatori* kind: it is throughout elaborate and systematic, instead of being loose, offhand, and accidental. He comes upon the stage as little unprepared as any actor we know." [58]

All in all, Hazlitt concluded that Kean's acting "affords a never-failing source of observations and discussion." It nearly always leaves an "impression on the mind afterwards. It adds . . . to the stock of our ideas." [59] Acting, even with defects, is truly great only when it does that.

Hunt hopefully came to see Kean's Richard III early in 1815, thirteen months after the first performance. He was disappointed. Kean, he reported, "was no better than the best kind of actor in the artificial style; he dealt out his syllables, and stood finely, and strutted at the set off of a speech, just as other well-received performers do; and he is much farther gone in stage trickery than we supposed him to be. . . . On the other hand, he has occasional bursts, and touches of nature." In "particular passages, he undoubtedly goes far beyond . . . the best actors in vogue. . . ." Two years later Hunt almost decided that Kean "really is only a great actor by fits and starts." "Why," he asked, "does he not oftener use the . . . natural tone . . . ?" In due time, however, Hunt concluded that Kean "is unquestionably the finest actor we ever saw." Kemble, he wrote, "knew there was a difference between tragedy and common life, but did not know in what it consisted, except in *manner*, which he consequently carried to excess, losing sight of the passion. Kean knows the real thing, which is the height of the *passion*, manner following it as a matter of course, *and grace being developed from it in proportion to the truth of the sensation*, as the flower issues from the entireness of the plant, or from all that is necessary to produce it." [60]

"As to Garrick," Hunt continued, "whom we are told it would have taken two Keans to make, he was no doubt what Kean never was, an admirable comedian as well as tragic actor; but on the latter score we have very great doubts whether he could have been equal to Kean." [61]

From, say, 1817 onward Kean was in spurts the most discussed actor in London. Early that year he acted Othello to the Iago of Junius Brutus Booth (1796–1852), the father of Edwin, squashed that upstart pretender, and drove him to the United States. Then after John Philip Kemble at the age of sixty retired from the stage he'd dignified for thirty-five years, Kean was king, had his own way in everything, lived recklessly, often played carelessly in the new gas lighting, and added to his few successes too many flops because "neither he nor the Drury Lane subcommittee seemed capable of finding . . . new parts in which he could really shine alone." In 1819 when the theater, deep in debt, was taken over as lessee by Elliston, thirty-one year old Kean had reached a dead end. Audiences were no longer enthusiastic about him; they took him for granted. So, he squabbled with Elliston, with everyone; he arrogantly made a fool of himself. But by contract he was forced to remain one more season in London before he sailed in 1820 for the United States in search of new triumphs and troubles. He found both. When he returned to London in 1821 large audiences greeted his acting with such cheering as had never been heard before. But the glory was brief; soon the public's response to him grew more apathetic than ever. Kean became despondent; he was ill; he found some comfort in adultery. For the 1822–23 season Elliston, in desperation, signed Charles Mayne Young (1777–1856), Kemble's declamatory successor at Covent Garden, to act at Drury Lane. Kean exploded. He wrote Elliston: "I find Mr. Young . . . is engaged for thirty nights and my services are wanted to act with him—now this I call exceedingly impudent . . . the throne is mine. I will maintain it—even at the expense of expatriation. . . . no man in this profession can rob me of the character of the first English actor. . . ." [62] But once again he was forced by contract to perform, and once again he brilliantly, thoroughly squashed the new pretender. Young went back next season to Covent Garden. Elliston, afraid of a profitless "Kean unaided" policy, hired another tragedian, Charles Macready, who had been playing at Covent Garden with some acclaim for a few years. Again Kean balked. He said he was ill, dangerously ill, and for some time dodged acting alongside this third pretender. He wanted to go again to America. Then in 1825 he was sued by the husband of the woman to whom he'd written damaging letters, tried in court, found guilty of adultery, and reviled and ridiculed everywhere. His public at last found a way of persecuting him for his longtime arrogance. They slashed him to dirty shreds. Socially ostracized in London and in the provinces, Kean fled again in 1825 to the United States—for more abuse mingled with cheers.

❁ MACREADY AND OTHERS

The management of Covent Garden—where John Liston (1776–1846) and Joseph Grimaldi (1778–1837) began to clown in 1806 and William Farren the younger (1786–1861) first acted Sir Peter Teazle in 1818—introduced two new serious players to help the Kembles and Young battle the popularity of Kean in tragedies at Drury Lane. The first was Eliza O'Neill (1791–1872). The daughter of an actor-manager in Ireland, a big success in Dublin by 1810, she made her London debut as Juliet opposite the Romeo of Charles Kemble in 1814 and was at once applauded as an expert portrayer of "faultless nature, . . . a remarkable instance of self-abandonment in acting. She forgot everything for the time but her assumed character." Hazlitt at first wasn't so sure she was that natural, that great. He liked her "extreme natural sensibility"; but he also ventured to say that "there is as much a tone, a certain stage singsong, in her delivery as in Mrs. Siddons's. . . . Miss O'Neill does not in general speak in a natural tone of voice, nor as people speak in conversation." But after her continued triumphs, and her marriage and retirement in 1819, he decided that she was undoubtedly "the greatest tragic performer" since the advent of Kean. The source of Eliza O'Neill's command over public sympathy lay, he said, "in the intense conception and unrestrained expression of what she and every other woman of natural sensibility would feel in given circumstances, in which she and every other woman was liable to be placed. Her Belvidera, Isabella, Mrs. Beverley . . . were all characters of this strictly feminine class of heroines, and she played them to the life"—only now and then "pushing truth and nature to an excess. . . ." [63]

The second new serious actor was William Macready (1793–1873) who learned impersonation from his father, became a professional player in the provinces in 1810 when he was seventeen, and resonantly "arrived" in 1816 at Covent Garden as Orestes in the old, operatic *The Distrest Mother* (1712), a dull translation of Racine's *Andromaque*. Hazlitt noticed that "He declaims better than anybody we have lately heard." Three years later Macready surprised everyone with an exciting, talk-of-the-town performance in Kean's role of Richard III. "We expected to find vagueness and generality," wrote Hunt, "and we found truth of detail. We expected to find declamation, and we found thoughts giving a soul to words. We expected to find little more than showy gestures and a melodious utterance, and we found expression and the substantial Richard." And, liking much of the actor's Coriolanus in 1820, the same critic commented: "Let Mr. Macready take what character he pleases now; we venture to say that since his talents have got an opportunity of showing themselves, and have been acknowledged, he will never again be found rolling forth that mere melodious declamation which he used to deal out, sentence after sentence, like a machine turning ivory balls." [64] By 1823 Macready, frustrated with grubbing along at floundering Covent Garden, voided his contract and was promptly hired by Elliston at Drury Lane for £20 a night as co-leading man with Kean. When the latter shunned acting with him, Macready on his own appeared successfully in *Virginius* (1820) and *Caius Gracchus* by Sheridan Knowles (1784–1862), as Hamlet, Macbeth, Leontes. He began to challenge Kean's supremacy.

Plain, shrewd, cantankerous Macready carefully prepared himself for that challenge. Although he really didn't care much for his profession, he was born to it; so, he examined the performances of Mrs. Siddons, John Philip Kemble, Kean, and Talma and then slowly worked out his own notions of what acting ought to be. He studied the art; he liked to say that a man ought to think more about it and less of himself.[65]

First, Macready liked Kean's effective descents to natural readings; but he believed they should be more than only sporadic. He therefore tried to diminish his own stilted declamation and to evolve a way of speaking more frequently in a more familiar style. According to spiteful Fanny Kemble it was his "consciousness of his imperfect declamation of blank verse that induced him to adopt what his admirers called the natural style of speaking; which was simply chopping it up into prose." Macready also fought his own tendency toward loudness and violence in utterance; he decided that the flagrant display of "passion is weakness," that a "real sense of power is best expressed by a collected and calm demeanor," by acting with repressed force, by underplaying. Emotion, he concluded, ought to be powerfully present only in the eyes and in the ordinary voice.[66]

Second, Macready disliked Kean's—as well as every other actor's—custom of overlooking the "consistency and harmony of character" for the sole aim of "making points" or "isolated and startling effects to surprise an audience into applause." Therefore, taking a tip from the Kembles, he worked to create *whole* characters instead of only flashy, telling, unrelated moments for them. He looked for "the unity of design, the just relation of all the parts, . . . the mainspring of . . . actions, the ruling passion." He tried to penetrate "into the full depth of the poet's intention," to comprehend "his one large and grand idea." [67]

Third, Macready, never an inspired genius, liked the premeditated acting of the Kembles—but certainly not their formalism, their lifelessness. Always wary of the impromptu onstage, he preferred to jell the details of his characterizations carefully and not to vary them at subsequent performances in a misguided, superficial way of being natural. Macready, of course, never experienced the staleness of, say, a hundred night run—or ten days of television rehearsing, or eight or nineteen motion picture retakes; but he undoubtedly would have said that the modern actor who must be so natural he never quite knows how his lines will come out until he says them, and who must always change a bit the business of this scene or that in order to freshen his playing, is only confessing how uncertain he is of the merit of his work. Macready did say, in agreement with Talma and Hazlitt, that " 'there was only one best'—to discover that is the labor of the artist; and having once achieved this, is it reconcilable to common sense that he would endanger his credit by tampering with the truth his patient investigation had wrought out?" [68]

Fourth, Macready believed that practice makes perfect and that rehearsals (rare as they were then) offered the best chances for genuine, thorough practice and the consequent attainment of a surer relaxation in performance. "It was the custom of the London actors, especially the leading ones," he said, "to do little more at rehearsals than read or repeat the words of their parts, marking on them their entrances and exits, as settled by the stage manager, and their respective places on the stage. To make any display of passion or energy would be to expose oneself to the ridicule or sneers of the green-room.

. . . But the difficulty of attaining before an audience perfect self-possession, which only practice can give, made me resolve to rehearse with the same earnestness as I would act. . . ." Whenever another actor assured him, "Sir, I never can act at rehearsal, but I will do it tonight," Macready would bark at him, "Sir, if you cannot do it in the morning, you cannot do it at night." [69]

Fifth, Macready emphasized more than other actors did the value of concentration in acting, "the necessity of keeping, on the day of exhibition, the mind as intent as possible on the subject of the actor's portraiture, even to the very moment of his entrance on the scene." The player, he was convinced, "meditates himself, as it were, into the very thought and feeling of the being he is about to represent: enwrapped in the idea of the personage he assumes, he moves, and looks, and bears himself as the Roman or the Dane, and thus almost identifies himself with the creature of his imagination. . . . I cannot conceive the representation of character without this preliminary preparation." [70]

Thus with the beginnings of something like a method Macready evolved a faintly natural style of acting, a studied style, "wholly his own and completely attuned to the spirit of the early Victorian era whose eminent tragedian he was to be." [71]

II

Not everyone, however, was sure that this progression toward more naturalness in acting was meritorious. Coleridge, for instance, declared that the new "attempt to cause the highest delusion possible to beings in their senses sitting in a theater, is a gross fault, incident only to low minds. . . ." And Charles Lamb (1775–1834), the "Ariel of Criticism," the essayist who "proves little" but "almost always proves delightful," preferred onstage the abstract, the imaginative, the artificial, the theatrical, the unreal. "We have been spoiled," he gently protested, "with . . . the exclusive and all-devouring drama of common life . . . where, instead of the fictitious half-believed personages of the stage (the phantoms of old comedy), we recognize ourselves, our brothers, aunts, kinsfolk, allies, patrons, enemies,—the same as in life. . . . What is *there* transacting, by no modification is made to affect us in any other manner than the same events or characters would do in our relationships of life. We carry our fireside concerns to the theater with us. We do not go thither like our ancestors, to escape from the pressure of reality, so much as to confirm our experience of it. . . . We must live our toilsome lives twice over." For instance, "Sir Peter Teazle must be no longer the comic idea of a fretful old bachelor bridegroom, whose teasings (while King acted it) were evidently as much played off at you [in the audience] as they were meant to concern anybody on the stage—he must be a real person. . . ." [72]

Tragedians, Lamb rather lamely believed, should perhaps be unconscious of the presence of an audience; they ought to give their undivided attention to the stage business and perform honestly "Because our tears refuse to flow at a suspected imposition." But "Comedians," he wrote, "paradoxical as it may seem, may be too natural" and not always amusing whenever they appear wholly unconscious of the presence of spectators. Therefore they "must a little desert nature" and think of the audience. Isn't it "a proof of the highest skill in the comedian when, without absolutely appealing to an audience, he keeps up a tacit understanding with them; and makes them, unconsciously to themselves, a party in the scene?" For example, Joseph Palmer (1742–1798) wasn't believably natural when he acted Joseph Surface. "He was playing to you [in the audience] all the while that he was playing upon Sir Peter and his lady. . . . His altered voice was meant for you, and you were to suppose that his fictitious co-flutterers on the stage perceived nothing at all of it." Moreover, Lamb added, comedians can be too natural and consequently produce anything but mirth when they insist on copying a character "*to the life* upon the stage," when, for instance, they go about impersonating a very real Lord Grizzle in Fielding's *Tom Thumb the Great* (1730). Liston, he decided, acted the character the right way: he exhibits "a piece of drollery" that "is neither nature nor exaggerated nature. It is a creation of the actor's . . . a being of another world . . . an abstract idea of court qualities—an apotheosis of apathy." [73]

Lamb's final, almost casual, but modern anti-"natural" point was to the effect that the actors of Shakespeare ought to know that he drew his images of virtue and knowledge "not from a pretty inquisition into those cheap and everyday characters which surrounded him, as they surround us, but *from his own mind* [my italics], which was, to borrow a phrase of Ben Jonson's, the very 'sphere of humanit.'" If, Lamb implied, actors could only sense or feel that secret they would not try to reduce Shakespeare's characters, his imaginative vision, his poetry, to "strait-lacing actuality," to mere naturalness, where too often "nonessentials are raised into an importance, injurious to the main interests of the play." [74]

III

Acting in the United States for the first quarter of the nineteenth century was of little note and mostly British accented. A few dull facts tell everything worth telling. New York City's Park Theatre (seating 2,500 after 1807) was managed by American playwright William Dunlap until he went bankrupt in 1805; then English actor Thomas Cooper took over, assisted by Dunlap in 1806; finally American Stephen Price (1783–1840) gradually assumed full control in 1808 and inaugurated a policy of importing famous English actors. George Frederick Cooke (1756–1812), "nearly freed from . . . singsong defects," [75] acted at the Park from late 1810 until his death in 1812. Native actor-playwright John Howard Payne (1781–1852), who wrote the lyrics for "Home Sweet Home" (1823), recited a reputation for himself from 1809 onward in New York City, Boston, Philadelphia, Baltimore, Washington, Richmond, Norfolk, and Charleston; then in 1813 he went to London and appeared successfully at Drury Lane. At Philadelphia by 1811 the new Walnut Street Theatre set up competition for the excellent Chestnut Street Theatre managed by English actor William Warren (1767–1832) and American actor William Wood (1779–1861).

Near the end of 1820 Kean arrived in the United States, satisfied American curiosity, and had his London fame confirmed in New York City, Philadelphia, and Boston; then on a second visit to Boston he threw a temper tantrum and refused to perform for an audience of only twenty. The press flayed him home to England in mid-1821. In 1824 the new Chatham Theatre, seating 1,300 and lighted by gas, opened as a rival to the rebuilt Park Theatre. Among the members of the acting company were English Henry Wallack (1790–1870) as leading man, English George Barrett (1794–1860) as leading comedian, and the English first Joseph Jefferson (1774–1860). Toward the end of 1825 Kean returned smelling of scandal to New York City and was jeered as often as he was cheered. "We think," editorialized the New York Commercial Advertiser, "that no manager should allow such a lump of pollution to contaminate the boards. Every female must stay away and males hiss with indignation." In Boston Kean asked for mercy, but was greeted on his first appearance with yells of "Off, off!!" and with "nuts, pieces of cake, a bottle of offensive drugs." [76] Driven from the city, he retrieved some of his glory as an actor in New York, Philadelphia, Baltimore, and Charleston. Then, after acting in Montreal and Quebec, he returned at the end of 1826 to London with high hopes of being appointed manager of Drury Lane as successor to the bankrupt Elliston. But Stephen Price had been selected for that position.

Edwin Forrest, who had made his debut when only fourteen at the Walnut Street Theatre in 1820, acted Iago to Kean's Othello, Richmond to his Richard III, and Titus to his Brutus (in Payne's 1818 tragedy of that name) at Albany in 1825; and was complimented and encouraged by the visiting star. "I have met one actor in this country," Kean said later, "a young man named Edwin Forrest, who gave proofs of a decided genius for his profession, and will, I believe, rise to great eminence." [77]

❀ ROMANTIC FLARE

From 1825 to 1850 new French playwrights tardily took the stage from the actors and made it the most entertaining in Europe. Eugène Scribe (1791–1861), for one, impatient with the theories of the classicists, sensed from the popularity of melodramas and vaudevilles (playlets on contemporary topics interspersed with ditties) that theater audiences enjoyed most of all a cleverly told story. He therefore devised a foolproof playwriting technique, a formula for setting into motion not an idea, not a character, but a situation, and then complicating it with tricky surprises and suspense. In 1820, after he'd garnered success at the Théâtre de Vaudeville and at the Variétés, especially with a five-act comedy, *Une Nuit de la Garde Nationale* (*A Night with the National Guard*) (1814) and a buffoonery, *L'Ours et la pacha* (*The Bear and the Pasha*) (1819), Scribe was signed to write exclusively for the Gymnase —and, with permission, for the Théâtre-Français. He set up "what amounted to a play-factory, in which stories were found, invented, or paid for and turned, like sausages, into comestibles for which the public was eager to expend its money." By 1827 he'd written nearly one hundred plays for the Gymnase. That same year his full-length comedy, *Le Mariage d'argent* (*Marriage for Money*), was acted by the Comédie-Française. Scribe was well on his way to teaching "the dramatists of the nineteenth century their art of playmaking." [78]

Moreover, Scribe was soon called, too generously, "the founder of the modern art of staging, one of the first to introduce on the stage the animation and bustle of real life." Ernest Legouvé (1807–1903) wrote that "Those who never saw Scribe conjure up a dramatic work from what, for want of a better term, I may call the limbo of the manuscript, . . . know only half the real Scribe. I happened to come in at the very moment when Scribe was arranging the grand revolt in the third act of *Le Prophète* (1849) [the opera by Meyerbeer with a libretto by Scribe]. I cannot do better than ask the reader to picture to himself a general on the battlefield. He was here, there, and everywhere at the same time. He was enacting every part. At one moment he was the crowd, the next the Prophet, the next the woman, then striding at the head of the insurgents with a fierce air, his spectacles pushed up to his forehead; after that, and with his spectacles still on his forehead, rushing to the opposite side of the stage, and enacting the part of Berthe, pointing out to everyone his or her place, marking with a piece of chalk the exact spot where this or that actor had to stop; in short, coordinating so skillfully the evolution of his diverse characters as to impose order on their most animated movements and invest that order throughout with grace.

"No sooner was the third act finished than we rushed away to the Comédie-Française to attend another rehearsal, that of the second act of *Les Contes de la Reine de Navarre*, an act altogether different from the other, played by four characters only and completely intimate in effect. . . . No sooner does he set foot on the stage than, without adding a word, he sows the dialogue with gestures so telling, postures so effective, pauses so ingenious, he makes such adroit use of the chairs and tables, as if they were natural obstacles, that the situation is heightened, the interest brought out, the characters made vivid, the action given briskness and life. A magician had touched it with his wand." [79]

Another new playwright, romanticist Victor Hugo (1802–1883), thundered in his 1827 Preface to *Cromwell*, a script written for Talma but never produced, "Let us take the hammer to theories and poetic systems. . . . There are neither rules nor models; or, rather, there are no other rules than the general laws of nature, which soar above the whole field of art. . . ." Let us agree that "Shakespeare is the drama" because he blends "the grotesque and the sublime, the terrible and the absurd, tragedy and comedy. . . ." Therefore, the modern dramatist must differ from the classicists and choose to depict "not the *beautiful*," but a "union of the grotesque and the sublime," all the contrasts of present-day life, "the *characteristic*." But this characteristic needn't be, shouldn't be, the commonplace. The "vice that kills" the drama "is the *commonplace*." After all, Hugo continued, "Nature and art are two things—were it not so, one or the other would not exist." If the drama is "a mirror wherein nature is reflected," it must be more than "an ordinary mirror, a smooth and polished surface." As such "it will give only a dull image of objects, with no relief—faithful, but colorless. . . . The drama, therefore, must be a concentrating image, which, instead of weakening, concentrates and condenses the colored rays, which makes of a mere gleam a light, and of a light a flame. Then only is the drama acknowledged by art." [80]

This romantic fire was fanned by English actors in Paris. That same year, 1827, Charles Kemble and his company performed *Hamlet*, *Romeo and Juliet*, and *Othello* at the Odéon; during April 1828 Macready, at £100 a week, thrilled audiences with his productions of *Othello*, *Macbeth*, and *Virginius* at the old Théâtre-Italien; and throughout May and June at the Odéon Kean achieved a lesser success with his "flashes of lightning."

Next, in early 1829, Alexandre Dumas *père* (1803–1870) shocked the patrons of the Théâtre-Français with a romantic, tradition-breaking, flamboyant historical melodrama, *Henri III et sa cour*, written in prose that's often realistically accurate, familiar and direct, at times even humorous. Some months later Alfred de Vigny's (1797–1863) *Le More de Venise*, an adaptation of *Othello*, was acted by the Comédie and proved to be "a pretty strong dose for the conservatives to swallow. They choked and sputtered with rage in their journals. . . ." But, as de Vigny argued, "A simple question has to be answered. Will the French stage be open or not to a modern tragedy?" [81]

It finally was. Romanticism blazed in February 1830 when the Comédie-Française acted Hugo's *Hernani* with Firmin (François Becquerelle) (1787–1859) in the title role, Mlle. Mars, age fifty-one, as Doña Sol, Joanny (Jean Brissebard) (1775–1849) as Don Gomez, and Théodore (Pierre–Marie) Michaelot (1785–1851?) as Don Carlos. This "melodrama lifted to a high plane by a poet under the influence of Shakespeare" was applauded and cheered by the modernists and hissed and ridiculed by the classicists.[82] *Hernani* appealed to audiences, or horrified them, because of its exotic setting, its bold vitality, its lyric presentation of love, its rapid and surprising and coincidental action, its disguises and concealed identities, its great *coups de théâtre* or thrills and tirades arising from remarkable situations. And its stormy success at long last freed French playwrights from classic bondage.

Hernani, however, did little for the actors of the Comédie-Française except baffle them. Trained in the formal, even severe elegance of traditional declamation, they couldn't quite adjust to saying this new, irregular and un-disciplined, purely sensational, often ludicrous modern dialogue. And ac-customed to simple plot progressions, they lost their dignities amid the turbulence and the so-called inconsistent mixture of styles in this new kind of action. They therefore quickly hated romantic dramas, and wanted no more of them. So, in 1831 Hugo's *Marion Delorme*, the romantic and slightly re-alistic story of a courtesan, was acted at the Porte-Saint-Martin with Mlle. Dorval in the title role; and in the same year at the same theater Dumas' *Antony*, a marital tragedy about contemporary characters—and a hint of the problem play to come—was presented with Bocage as Antony and Mlle. Dorval as Adèle. There also was staged the same playwright's popular *La Tour de Nesle* (*The Tower of Nesle*) (1832), featuring Mlle. George and Bocage.

Frédérick Lemaître became the great actor of the romantic period in France. In 1827 at the Porte-Saint-Martin in Prosper Goubaux (1795–1859) and Victor Ducange's (1783–1833) *Trente Ans, ou la vie d'un joueur* (*Thirty Years, or the Life of a Gambler*) he literally scared audiences out of their skins as he went through "all the stages of the gambling mania, from the victim's twentieth to his fiftieth year," sinking "into poverty and crime, . . . begging, a ragged, crook-backed *lazzarone*, with nothing left of all that he once was—except his expressive eyes." The play ran four months without a break as Lemaître, along with Mlle. Dorval, "carried out a complete revolu-tion in the art of drama. The audience, used to the shrill tones of melodrama with its din of words and voice, all looked at one another in astonishment, moved and charmed by such simplicity and grace." [83]

After his next huge success as Mephistopheles in a simplified version of Goethe's *Faust* in 1828, Lemaître was invited to become a *pensionnaire* of the Comédie; but he refused that measly honor. In early 1830 he left the bankrupt Porte-Saint-Martin for the Ambigu and then the Odéon where he definitely decided to abandon classical tragedy in favor of modern drama. Back at the Porte-Saint-Martin near the end of 1831 he "at last won general recognition as the first actor of France," the successor of Talma. In 1833 as co-star with Mlle. George he broke all box office records there in *Lucrèce Borgia* by Dumas, then triumphantly toured France. In Marseilles his tragic genius was called more terrifying than Talma's. As one critic explained: "Talma never dwelt in the sphere in which we live our lives. . . . he wore a costume that was not like ours, he spoke a language that was never heard in ordinary life; to fear his anger one had to imagine that one lived in castles and palaces, or turn Greek or Roman. Frédérick, on the other hand, dresses as we do, in jacket and waistcoat; he speaks our drawing-room language. . . . We can meet the bourgeois characters he plays the very next day, in our town or country houses, involved by some dangerous hazard in our private plans and domestic affairs: the idea is enough to make us shake in our shoes. . . ." In 1834, after an enormous success in his own play, *Robert Macaire*, a sequel to *L'Auberge des Adrets*, Lemaître played the first of several highly acclaimed engagements in

Macready's London. In 1836 at the Variétés he exhibited every aspect of his many-sided genius in a three month run of *Kean, ou Désordre et Génie* by Dumas; two years later he opened the Théâtre de la Renaissance in the title role of Hugo's rousing *Ruy Blas*; and in 1840 in Balzac's savagely mauled *Vautrin* his characterization was called "prodigious, astounding, beyond all praise: in his mouth commonplace words acquire new meanings and importance, and from an apparently insignificant phrase he strikes a strange, lurid spark which lights up the whole play." Finally, in 1845, after new personal triumphs in Eugène Sue's (1804–1857) *Les Mystères de Paris* (1844) and in Philippe Dumanoir (1806–1865) and Adolphe Dennery's (1811–1899) *Don César de Bazan* (1844), Lemaître was invited by the Comédie-Française to become a *sociétaire*. But he knew that the company's established actors had no intention of relinquishing any of the leading roles in the repertoire to him. [Edmond] "Geffroy [1813–1883] clung doggedly to Tartuffe, [Jean-Baptiste] Provost [1798–1869] to Harpagon, Samson and Régnier to Scapin and Figaro. In these circumstances, with no hope of playing the parts in which he was most likely to shine, and every prospect of becoming involved in humiliating quarrels, Frédérick hesitated; before he could come to a decision the *sociétaires* withdrew their offer." Then near the end of 1850 he achieved one of his last sensational successes at the Gaieté as the broken-hearted clown in the sentimental *Paillasse* (known in English as *Belphegor the Mountebank*) by Marc Jean Fournier (1818–1879) and Dennery. The drama ran for exactly one hundred performances. Hugo said of Lemaître that "in spite of all his triumphs he never achieved the great, undisputed success he deserved. . . . Talma was perfect, Frédérick was uneven. Talma always pleased, Frédérick sometimes shocked. But Frédérick had movements, words, cries which shook audiences to their very depths, and astonishing flashes of brilliance which completely transfigured him and revealed him in all the dazzling spendour of absolute greatness. In a word, Talma had the more talent and Frédérick had the more genius." [84]

No doubt Lemaître and the other "barbarian" actors performed the new romantic plays with a new, skillful enthusiasm. But rarely, if ever, were they required to impersonate truly lifelike characters. The men and women in the works of Hugo, Dumas, and others are vivid, even vital; but most often they are vivid and vital under strange circumstances and in highly unusual situations. Even if the actors had tried, they could not have made them as recognizably real as a photograph because they couldn't possibly have known people like them. Nor were the actors in the well-made plays by Scribe asked to create genuine characters. In all his concoctions—twenty-three of them were staged at the Théâtre-Français from 1827 through 1859—Scribe was, as Dumas observed, "expert at manipulating characters that had no life." [85]

The "most human of the great romantic poets," who used "the romantic jargon only as a dandyism and rather as a joke, with tongue in cheek," was Alfred de Musset (1810–1857). After the failure of his *Le Nuit Vénitienne* at the Théâtre-Français in 1830, this "French Shakespeare brushed with Watteau wings" wrote the imaginative *Les Caprices de Marianne* (1833), *Fantasio* (1833), *Lorenzaccio* (1834), *On ne badine pas avec L'amour* (*No Trifling With Love*) (1834), and *Le Chandelier* (*The Decoy*) (1835). But de Musset wrote them only to be read. Actors didn't encounter his "artificial and sentimental analyses of the human heart," his prose poetry, his airy fantasies until after 1847. By then it was almost too late. The realists had begun to take stage. During the Second Republic under Louis Napoleon Bonaparte—Emperor in 1852—middle-class moralist Émile Augier (1820–1889) wrote *Gabrielle* (1849) to prove "that it is better for a woman to extract joy and romantic pleasure from living respectably as a wife than to snatch at the illusory delights of being a mistress." [86] His script is inept; but it's a semi-thesis play, an early problem play, a play about contemporary domestic life.

The age was becoming realistic. *Notre Dame de Paris* (*The Hunchback of Notre Dame*) (1831) by Hugo as well as *Les Trois Mousquetaires* (1844) and *Le Comte de Monte-Cristo* (1844–45) by Dumas *père* were vastly entertaining, yes, but also superficial. Fresher, more accurate scrutinies of life were published. Stendhal in *Le Rouge et le noir* (*The Red and the Black*) (1830) was primarily concerned with psychological character analysis; and Honoré de Balzac (1799–1850) in *Eugénie Grandet* (1832), *Le Père Goriot* (1835), and *La Cousine Bette* (1847) was picturing individuals of every class and profession with precise detail. Moreover, Gustave Flaubert (1821–1880) was about ready to start five years of work on that masterpiece of realism, *Madame Bovary* (1857). "It was only a matter of time before the drama . . . would follow in the footsteps of narrative fiction and study problems of everyday life, in everyday surroundings" via everyday characters.[87]

II

But before the plays of de Musset were performed, and before *Gabrielle*, the formal glories of French classicism were revived, with cheers, by actress Rachel (Elisa Félix) (1820–1858). She first appeared professionally at the Gymnase in early 1837; next year, coached by Joseph Samson, a last representative of the classical tradition and the incomparable professor of acting at the Conservatoire, she made her debut to an almost empty house at the Théâtre-Français as Camille in Corneille's *Horace*. Then, encouraged by critic Jules Janin (1804–1874), managed by her grasping father, and tutored by Samson, she acted a striking Hermione in Racine's *Andromaque*, Ériphile in his *Iphigénie en Aulide*, Monime in his *Mithridate*, Emilie in Corneille's *Cinna*, and Amenaïde in Voltaire's *Tancrède*. Finally she triumphed as Roxane in Racine's *Bajazet* near the end of 1838, and a Rachel boom began. In 1843, after two successful engagements in London, she reached the peak of her performances by giving "an ideal representation of real emotion" [88] as Phèdre.

In 1849 she created the role, especially written for her by Scribe and Legouvé, of Adrienne Lecouvreur.

Wholly unsuited for comedy, but quite possibly the most expert tragic actress of France, "Rachel was the panther of the stage; with a panther's terrible beauty and undulating grace she moved and stood, glared and sprang. There always seemed something not human about her. She seemed made of different clay from her fellows—beautiful but not lovable. Those who never saw Edmund Kean may form a very good conception of him if they have seen Rachel," according to George Henry Lewes. "She was very much as a woman what he was as a man. . . . Her range, like Kean's, was very limited, but her expression was perfect within that range. Scorn, triumph, rage, lust and merciless malignity she could represent in symbols of irresistible power; but she had little tenderness, no womanly caressing softness, no gaiety, no heartiness." [89]

Rachel's creative power and intensity were shaped by Samson along the lines of *"conventionalism"*; he perpetuated, in Macready's opinion, "the mannerism of the French stage, which is all mannerism." Sure that any dependence "on the breath of inspiration" was dangerous, Samson insisted on the actor's need for instruction, long study and practice, discipline. He taught Rachel that inspiration never discloses "the difficult secret of manipulating an undisciplined voice" or of controlling crude and excessive gestures, that inspiration "never reveals a role in its entirety," and is of no help in acquiring "the conventions of good taste, the simplicities of greatness, fine nuances." [90]

"I do not deny the divine flame," Samson wrote in *L'Art théâtral* (1863), "those sudden flashes that illuminate the spirit. . . . But should a mad vanity trust these lucky strokes and sudden flashes as guides?" No: "Inspiration, so dear to the misguided, does not replace study and work. . . ." No: each role entrusted to the actor's care "needs study in every detail." Only study prepares an actor to receive inspiration. But even when inspired, "even when abandoning himself, the artist must observe himself: so, artist, remember your lucky achievements! Art must remember what chance has not produced. The actor who wants to attain the pinnacle of talent must, when he gives his heart, retain his head. He adds to the effects, long since prepared, tones and gestures inspired by the stage." [91]

Samson taught Rachel to be, primarily, a posing reciter whose brilliant and burning effects may have been "good for the artist, but not for the illusion of a play." "In her early days nothing more exquisite could be heard than her elocution," according to one critic—"it was musical and artistically graduated to the fluctuations of meaning. Her thrilling voice, flexible, penetrating, and grave, responded with the precision of a keyed instrument." Yet Rachel was never quite real, and could never speak naturally; "deprived of the music of verse, and missing its *ictus*, she seemed quite incapable of managing the easy cadences of colloquial prose." In her later days Rachel, like many expert technicians, "grew careless; played her parts as if only in a hurry to get through them, flashing out now and then with tremendous power, just to show what she could do; and resembling Kean in the sacrifice of the character to a few points." [92]

Most of the actors of the Comédie-Française criticized Rachel for never becoming "a *sociétaire* or Member, because, once a member, she would have been obliged to share her profits with her fellow-members; she remained a *pensionnaire* [a salaried performer] because she could demand what salary she liked. The nights on which she played the receipts amounted to ten thousand francs, the whole of which went into her pocket. The next night the theater was empty." Rachel was also blamed by many "for having imparted a factitious life to tragedy and for encouraging her admirers to struggle against the advent of a new art. She obstinately confined herself to a dozen parts, in which she displayed incomparable power, and left imperishable memories. She did not lend the assistance of her genius to any of the contemporary poets, or, if she did so, it was with regret, and without decisive success." [93]

III

Just before and during Rachel's reign five new players of importance came to the Comédie-Française. Louise Rosalie (Despréaux) Allan (1810–1856) was a page in the first production of *Hernani* in 1830, continued her career at the Gymnase, acted in Russia, and returned to the Théâtre-Français in 1847 as the only rival to Rachel. Régnier (François Tousez) (1807–1885), after delineating Figaro with intelligence, verve, and skill in 1831, was quickly assigned all the leading classical comic roles. For one instance, he "took over the living tradition of the way to play Scapin [in Molière's *Les Fourberies*] from Samson" who "in turn, had seen Préville play it, who . . . must have been familiar with the way the part was taken by successive generations of the mighty acting family of La Thorillière, . . . whose founder joined Molière's company in 1662 and certainly saw how Molière played Scapin." As a professor at the Conservatoire Régnier taught Coquelin. Jeanne-Sylvanie Arnould-Plessy (1819–1897) made her debut in 1834 and for forty-two years was "well worth studying, not only because of the refined naturalness of her manner, but also on account of the exquisite skill of her elocution." [94] Edmond Got (1822–1901) expertly impersonated Mascarille in *Les Précieuses ridicules* in 1844 and became a valued member of the company in 1850. Louis Arsène Delaunay (1826–1903) entered the Conservatoire in 1844, acted briefly at the Gymnase and Odéon, and joined the Comédie-Française in 1848 to act lovers until he was nearly sixty.

And—like Mlle. Dorval, Bocage, and Lemaître—several new performers found success away from the Théâtre-Français. Hugues-Désiré Bouffé (1800–

1888), for example, was a sentimental comic noted for his naturalness, for his old-man blending of smiles and tears, at the Gaieté in 1824, in London in 1831, at the Gymnase in 1831, and at the Variétés in 1849. Pauline Virginie Déjazet (1798–1875) became one of the most popular actresses in Paris at the opening of the Palais-Royal in 1831; after playing there for thirteen years she went to the Variétés and the Gaieté. And Charles Fechter (1824–1879), born in London, made his debut with the Comédie in 1844 but immediately left for the Vaudeville, the Ambigu, and the Porte-Saint-Martin where he was free to work out untraditional characterizations.

IV

During this period French acting was examined by Aristippe F. Bernier de Maligny (?–1864) in *Theorie de l'art du comédien; ou, manuel théâtral* (1826), by J. Cresp in an *Essai sur la Déclamation Oratoire et Dramatique* . . . (1837), and by several others. But the most abortive and influential analysis of the subject was made by François Delsarte (1811–1871). His voice ruined by faulty training and his histrionic ambitions discouraged by arbitrary and contradictory instruction, he retaliated by attempting to prove by dedicated but fuzzy study that everyone else was wrong and that the laws of stage expression, chiefly pantomimic, were discoverable and could be formulated as precisely as mathematical principles. In 1839 Delsarte began demonstrating his findings in his first *Cours d'esthetique appliqué*; he attracted a number of swooning disciples, among them many nonactors, who for the remainder of the century, mostly in the United States, formed a precious, genteel cult.

Delsarte manufactured a seductive system for people looking for theorems that reduced the intangibles of acting to a science, to something they could teach, if not practice. Unfortunately, or fortunately, he completed only five chapters of his basic work, *My Revelatory Episodes*; consequently, the embarrassing gist of his method can be briefly pieced together only from the notations of his followers who, like the followers of Stanislavski, often vary in their interpretations of the master.

Delsarte neatly divided expression into all sorts of trinities. Art, for instance, is the revelation of the three principles of our being: life, mind, and soul. It isn't merely "an imitation of nature. It elevates in idealizing her; it is . . . a work of love, where shine the Beautiful, the True and the Good. . . . it is the search for the eternal." "The artist," it follows, "should have three objects: To *move*, to *interest*, to *persuade*. He interests by *language*; he moves by *thoughts*; he moves, interests and persuades by *gesture*. . . . Gesture corresponds to the soul, . . . is the chief organic agent. . . . It prepares the way . . . for language and thought; it goes before them and foretells their coming; it accentuates them." Moreover, "Nothing, is more ˙ plorable than a gesture without a motive," preferably a spiritual one. And since the actor represents man *en rapport* with (1) nature, (2) humanity, and (3) divinity, he shouldn't preoccupy an audience with his own personality but with something higher, vaster, nobler.[95]

Pre-Stanislavski, Delsarte insisted that the preliminary condition for all expression is relaxation (his term is flexibility). His "Decomposing Exercises," for example, are designed to free "the channels of expression" so that "the current of nervous force can thus rush through them as a stream of water rushes through a channel, unclogged by obstacles." Another preliminary condition, to be perfected by exercises, is an "Harmonic Poise of Bearing" or perfect, dynamic posture.[96]

Next, the actor who would learn to gesture, or mime, is taught by Delsarte that his torso has three zones: the chest for the mental (conscience, honor, manhood and womanhood), the heart for the moral (the affections), and the abdomen for the vital (the appetites); that "the shoulder is the thermometer of passion as well as of sensibility," the elbow is "a thermometer of the affections and self-will," and the wrist is "a thermometer of vital energy"; that, for specific illustrations, the thumb attracted inward signifies "indifference, prostration, imbecility, insensibility, or death"; that the nostrils contracted signify "insensibility, hardness, cruelty"; that the pupil of the eye "is mental, white is vital, iris is moral. . . ." [97]

The actor who wanted to speak well onstage learned from Delsarte that "A voice, however powerful it may be, should be inferior to the power which animates it"; that there are "three significant points of reverberation in the mouth: (1) the physical in the pharynx, (2) the moral or normal in the palatine arch, and (3) the mental back of the upper teeth"; that "Passion strengthens the voice in proportion as it rises, and sentiment, on the contrary, softens it in due ratio to its intensity"; that "quantitative shades or expressions result from the greatness or littleness of the being or objects to which the sounds relate"; that "This is a pretty dog" can be read in at least six hundred different ways.[98]

The system in many of its details dodged the fundamental problems of acting to center on an ingenious, spiritual (and often counterfeit) kind of parlor elocution. Delsarte himself, for instance, is reported to have vivified the lines "The wave draws near, it breaks, and vomits up before our eyes,/ Amid the surging foam, a monster huge of size" by concentrating "all the force of his accent" on the word *and*, endowing it with eight degrees of emphasis, "giving it, by gesture, voice and facial expression, all the significance lacking in the particle, colorless in itself." When he pronounced that word, and paused, "the fixity of his gaze, his trembling hands, his body shrinking back into itself, while his feet seemed riveted to the earth, all presaged something terrible and frightful. He saw what he was about to relate, he made you see it; his words had only to specify the fact, and to justify the emotion which had accumulated in the interval." [99]

Actors today recoil from any system that produces such obvious "solo reciting." Specifically, they jeer at Delsarte's formulas, especially the one for marking their scripts, for writing above Lady Macbeth's "We fail," for example:

> *Inflection:* Falling on 'fail.'
> *Emphasis:* On 'fail.'
> *Ellipsis* [or paraphrase]: We must resign ourselves to destiny.
> *Expression of Face:* Head bows, eyelids droop—resignation.
> *Gesture:* Arms drop in abandon.
> *Stage Business:* Stands left of Macbeth.[100]

Delsarte, in brief, made a well-meant but weird attempt to explore and emphasize the actor's *"interior memory,*—that unconscious storehouse where inherited tendencies, traits, and aptitudes are . . . found." [101] Neither he nor his followers, however, knew enough about that psychological area. In an esoteric mood they grasped at externals.

❀ TINGES OF REALISM

Toward the middle of the nineteenth century the theater in Italy moved from mediocrity to some importance as that scattered pawn of Europe fought nearer and nearer toward unification. The country had no new, first-rate playwrights, with the possible exception of Alessandro Manzoni (1785–1873), an admirer of Shakespeare, Goethe, and Schiller, who proved that dialogue need not be unnatural when written in verse, with such tragedies as *Il Conte de Carmagnola* (1820) and *Adelchi* (1822). But Italians became more and more interested in acting; they wrote a number of books about it as an art: an *Elementi de Mimica* (1829) by Domenico Buffelli, *Lezioni di Declamazione e d'Arte Theatral* (1832) by actor Antonio Morrocchesi (1768–1838), *Studii sulle Arti Imitatrici* (1844) by Carlo Blasis (1795–1878), *Dell' Arte Rappresentativa in Italia, studii riformativi* (1850) by Gaetano Gattinelli (1806–1870). And three players of stirring ability regained for their indigenous profession an international reputation.

The first of these was Adelaide Ristori (1822–1906), child of actors, who was performing professionally at the age of twelve. Two years later in actor-manager Giuseppe Moncalvo's (1781–1859) touring company she acted the title role in *Francesca da Rimini* (1815) by Silvio Pellico (1789–1854); in 1838, at sixteen, she was offered the position of permanent leading lady with the troupe, but instead signed as ingenue with the Royal Theatrical Company which centered its activities at Turin in the service of the King of Sardinia. Gaetano Bazzi (1771–1843)—who later wrote *Primi Erudimenti dell' Arte Drammatica per la Recitazione e la Mimica* (1845)—was the group's manager, and Carlotta Marchionni (1796–1861) its star. Under their tutelage Ristori learned to combine formal French reciting, which she called the "simple, familiar style . . . then greatly in vogue," with "that Italian fire which is inherent among us." [102] Ten years later, near mid-century, she had won wide fame for her studious, regal, and arresting impersonations of ideal heroines.

The second, and greatest of the trio, was Tomasso Salvini (1829–1915). Also a child of actors, he became a professional at fourteen when, along with his father, he joined the troupe of actor-manager Gustavo Modena (1803–1861) at Padua. There, he remembered, Modena at rehearsals "rarely spent much time in explaining the character, or demonstrating the philosophy of a part, or in pointing out the reasons for modesty or for vehemence of passion. He would say, 'Do it so,' and it would certainly be done in a masterly way." Two years later, in 1845, Salvini was hired to portray first- and second-lover's roles with the Royal Company of Florentines in Naples. He acted Paola in *Francesca da Rimini*, Egisto in Maffei's *Merope*, Carlo in Alfieri's *Filippo*, Romeo in *Giulietta e Romeo*, and so on. Then in 1848 in Rome with Ristori's company he won his first rousing success as Alfieri's Oreste. "From that moment," he later wrote, "my title of tragic actor was won, and I was only nineteen!'" At once he "felt the need of studying, not books alone, but men and things," especially "all the passions for good and evil which have roots in human nature. . . . I must become capable of identifying myself with one or another personage to such an extent as to lead the audience into the illusion that the real personage, and not a copy, is before them. It would then remain to learn the mechanism of my art, that is, to choose the salient points and to bring them out, to calculate the effects and keep them in proportion with the unfolding of the plot, to avoid monotony in intonation and repetition in accentuation, to insure precision and distinctness in pronunciation, the proper distribution of respiration, and incisiveness of delivery. I must study; study again, study always." [103] In 1849 Salvini enlisted in the army to fight for Italian independence.

Ernesto Rossi (1829–1896), the third important Italian actor of modern times, was just beginning his career near mid-century as a member of a strolling troupe. In 1846 he was signed as a replacement for Salvini by Modeno, and soon was that teacher's favorite pupil.

II

Before 1850 first-rate Russian playwrights began to feed their country's actors with native, frankly realistic material. In 1821–25, for instance, Alexander Griboyedov (1795–1829) wrote his landmark comedy in verse, *Gore ot uma* (*Woe From Wit*), a vivid satire of Slavic characters and customs directed against "the indolent and ignorant nobility, the stupid serf owners, the bootlicking and scheming officials, the dull and reactionary militarists." The play, banned at first for production or publication, was finally staged, minus the third act and other sections, in 1830 at St. Petersburg with Karatygin as the hero Chatsky, Ryazantsev (?) as Famusov (a role acted with great success by Shchepkin in Moscow), Semyonova as Sophia, Bryansky as Gorichev, and Kolosova (who had studied briefly with Mlle. Mars in Paris) as Natalie. The full play was not performed until 1869. Then in 1835–36 poet Mikhail Lermontov (1814–1841) realistically depicted the decadence of court society in the Othello-like verse drama *Maskerad* (*The Masquerade*). But, rejected by the censors as a "eulogy of vice," [104] it was not produced until 1852 at St. Petersburg with Karatygin as Arbenin.

Would-be actor Nikolai Gogol (1809–1852) then wrote *Revizor* (*The Inspector-General*), a masterpiece of technique and of fanciful realism, "the greatest play ever written in Russian (and never surpassed since)." What happens in this prose comedy is simple although ingenious: a young man, Khlestakov, "gets stranded in a town because he has lost all his money at cards, and the town is full of politicians, and he uses the politicians to raise some money by making them believe that he is a Government official sent from headquarters to inspect them. And when he has used them, and made love to the Mayor's daughter, and drunk the Mayor's wine, and accepted bribes from judges and doctors and landowners and merchants and all kinds of administrators, he leaves the town, just before the real inspector arrives." More important than the plot are the characters, a whole town of them, each drawn from life, deftly and recognizably limned with a Molière-like touch, elevated from the everyday into the eternal. Characters like that perplexed the actors. They didn't know quite how to impersonate them. Consequently, when the play was first performed in April 1836 at the Alexandrinsky Theater (1832) in St. Petersburg it wasn't an immediate success; no one in the cast satisfied Gogol except Sosnitsky as the Town Mayor (a role later portrayed in Moscow by realist Shchepkin as a strictly Russian, comic, "carnivorous, cunning blade . . . who knows well how to oppress and crush his inferiors, and how to crawl before his superiors"). The actor of the key role of Khlestakov evidently played it ("God forbid," the author warned) "in the usual farcical style in which braggarts and theatrical rakes are . . . impersonated." Gogol wanted fresh human truth to be added to the theatrical. An actor when studying a part, he said, should " 'get the all-human significance of it' before paying attention to the external traits and habits of the character"; then he should "make the thoughts and anxieties of the character his own, so as to have them permanently in his mind during the performance." (Gogol also believed that casts needed directing, because "there is no stronger excitement for a spectator than to witness such a harmonious concert of all the parts in a play, as until now has been achieved in an orchestra of music only.") [105]

In 1842 Gogol furnished the actors in St. Petersburg with two additional plays, a genial comedy, *Zhenitba* (*Marriage*) (1833–42), and a bitter satire, *Igroki* (*The Gamblers*) (1836–42). Both were staged, not too successfully, with Sosnitsky and Martynov in leading roles. Some critics, of course, didn't approve of Gogol's theatrical realism. They reminded him that "The

principal and sole condition of the stage is elegance and decorum. . . .
Yes, . . . nature and naturalness are requisite to the stage—but in a purified
form, in an elegant guise, expressed with delicacy and from a pleasant aspect.
. . . trivial and filthy nature is repugnant." [106]

Realism, however, could not be kept from the stage by the moans of
pedants and esthetes who believed, rightly, but too narrowly, that art should
be more than a copy of life. Novelist Ivan Turgenev (1818–1883), an inner
realist, began in about 1843 to probe the minds and hearts of Russia's upper
classes and to set down his muted findings in some plays he never expected
would be staged. But his *Kholostiak* (*The Bachelor*) was acted in 1849 by
Shchepkin in Moscow and St. Petersburg. And next year his one-act *Pro-
vintsialka* (*The Provincial Lady*) was performed with Shchepkin, Vera
Samoilova (1824–1880), and S. V. (Chesnokov) Shumsky (1821–1878) in
the leading roles. Then, influenced by Balzac, Turgenev wrote his masterpiece,
Mesiats y derevne (*A Month in the Country*) (1850), a study of people
trying to fathom themselves. It did not reach the stage, however, until 1872.
And because Turgenev in all his plays portrayed "most ordinary, most
mediocre people, . . . with delicate humor and with deep understanding of
their inner being which is not readily revealed to the superficial observer," [107]
he confronted his country's actors with the new, difficult challenge of finding
and expressing the hidden impulses of characters.

Before the Russians tackled inner realism, however, they proceeded
rather methodically to master outer realism. The latter was brought with
abundance to their stages by Alexander Ostrovsky (1823–1886), the country's
first full-time professional playwright, "the Balzac of the Muscovite merchant
class." [108] He wasn't at all interested in well-made plots, didn't give a fig for
a significant idea or theme, and was antitheatrical. He was simply an observer
of life who with an almost photographic exactness, with a multitude of external details, tried to capture the actual behavior of people. No more, no
less. Commonplace accuracies, he seemed to imply, were all that mattered.
Actors, if they desired, could advance from them to uncover inner motives
and meanings. In 1848 Ostrovsky began laying firm, realistic foundations
for Russian dramatic art with the full-length, prose *Scoi liudi—sochtemsia*
(*It's a Family Affair—We'll Settle It Ourselves*). The comedy was banned
by the Moscow censors for being too stupid; but, widely read after 1850, it
was finally produced in 1861.

In St. Petersburg this new accent on realism wasn't exactly cheered by
classical Karatygin, his wife Kolosova, and his outstanding pupil, Alexander
Martynov (1816–1860), or by theatrical Sosnitsky and his pupil, the popular
comedienne Barbara Asenkova (1817–1841). To them real-life acting in real-
life plays lacked the elegance, the purity, the form, the tradition of art.
Sosnitsky, for one, complained that "Our repertoire is controlled by the
sheepskin coat and vodka set. This is sad, very sad. But it will continue for a
long time. Every week new authors spring up, each one more vile than the

others, and they all busy themselves with realism. . . . In truth, Karatygin is right when he says, 'We lack only public baths on the stage. . . .' " [109]

The actors in Moscow weren't that conservative. They were fascinated by serious realistic acting and tried to practice and popularize it; in so doing they made their city the theatrical capital of Russia. The leading advocates of the new style were Shchepkin and Mochalov, Vera and Vasily Samoilov (1812–1887), the first of a family of thespians, Prov Sadovsky (1818–1872), whose son and grandson would also be actors, Shumsky, one of Shchepkin's prize students, and serf I. V. Samarin (1817–1885). Their first efforts, of course, were embryonic, were nowhere near as true-to-life as Russian acting eventually became. Even Shchepkin was often a bit too theatrical to be natural. And Samarin, whose system of training in declamation had many supporters, "admirably expressed tenderness, suffering, joy, offense, and so forth. But this he did to a certain extent impersonally, as it would have been done by an able elocutionist." [110]

But even as these Moscow actors recited they attempted to look and behave realistically onstage, to exhibit at least some of the externals of realism. Samoilov, for a typical example, usually prepared "a color sketch—often a finished portrait—of the character he was to impersonate." He labored—ahead of Stanislavski—over the most minute physical details of a part. He approached his roles, according to a critic, "above all from their outward aspect, . . . paying much attention to make-up and costume." [111]

Shchepkin, however, dug deeper than that, and in due time defined the true aims, perhaps rarely attained, of early Russian realistic acting. And in his uncomplicated, unartful way he furnished Stanislavski with the fertile beginnings of a system. By his teachings and his performances in the theater (which he called "the actor's temple, his sanctuary") Shchepkin demonstrated two truths: (1) that the actor's distinctive function is to represent characters, regardless of their tragic or comic stamp, and to represent them honestly, believably by finding models in life; and (2) that there are no small parts, only small actors, since everyone in a play must harmoniously convey his character's contribution to the author's work as a whole.[112]

Chiefly, Shchepkin advised the preparing actor "to mingle with society as much as time permits; study man *en masse*; do not neglect a single anecdote, and you will always discover the antecedent cause—why something happened this way and not that. This living book will take the place of all theories, which as yet, unfortunately, are nonexistent in our art." Then, he continued, when you, the actor, "are assigned a role, and must find out what kind of bird it is, . . . look into the play itself. It will unfailingly provide you with a satisfactory answer. . . ." And when examining your assigned character you must "get, so to speak, into the skin of the person . . . ; study his social environment, his educational background, any peculiar ideas he may have, and do not overlook even his past." Finally, you must begin work "with wiping out . . . self . . . and become the character the author intended [you] to be." Then "When reading a part, by all means try to compel yourself to think and feel in the manner which he whom you have to represent thinks and feels. Try, so to speak, to chew and swallow the whole part so that it may become part of your flesh and blood. If you succeed in this, genuine intonations and gestures will come to you of their own accord . . . ," and "you will without fail act correctly." Finally, and "For God's sake," all the while you are acting "don't be concerned with . . . your audience for both the ridiculous and the serious derive from a true conception of life." Concentrate instead on the scene, because "every word that you hear you must answer with your glance, with every line of your face, with all your being. . . ." And "may God help you . . . lest you glance sidewise for no good reason, or gaze at some strange object that has nothing to do with the scene. If you do, then everything will be lost!" [113]

Yet for Shchepkin this being completely real onstage wasn't the overall purpose of acting. Instinctively he knew that there was more to it than merely behaving naturally. What that something additional was he could not isolate or define. But he did warn actors that the "situations and details encountered in life . . . are only an aid, and not a goal—that they are only valuable when you understand your goal in acting." "Naturalness and true feeling are necessary in art," he explained in 1853, "but only to the extent that the general idea permits of them. That is what all art consists of, to grasp this feature [this idea] and to be true to it." [114]

III

Before mid-century in Germany at least two men tried to improve acting. Karl Immermann (1796–1840), a law-court official at Düsseldorf, reorganized in 1832 an amateur society he'd formed into a Theaterverein and demonstrated via special experimental performances the value of hard work and discipline. He believed that lazy, conceited, and extravagant acting could be made simpler and truer only by thorough rehearsing. "Lessing's Emilia Galotti, for instance, was produced by Immermann on the first of February 1833 after one reading of the play, one reading-rehearsal, four rehearsals in a room and two stage rehearsals, which was considered at the time a quite unusual amount of preliminary work." Immermann also believed, after Goethe and ahead of Scribe and Gogol, that rehearsals must be conducted by and dominated by one person. "The work of the dramatist," he said, "springs from one mind. Therefore, its reproduction must also come from one mind," from that of the stage manager, the director. "Immermann started work with his actors by reading the play to them. Then he had reading rehearsals with each actor separately, which were followed by a general reading rehearsal. He once wrote that 'when during this rehearsal I saw that the actors were still in disagreement as to their intonations, I had to explain to them how to get things right, and told them that if this wouldn't help I would read the necessary lines to them myself.' The action (positions and movements) was settled by Immermann after the reading rehearsals were over, at special rehearsals conducted in a private room. These 'often consisted of single acts or of some scenes only.' He held these rehearsals in a room 'so that the actors could train their imagination between its bare and sober walls, and so that those mean spirits which nowadays haunt every German theater—the demons of opposition, bombast, rhetorical declamation and routine—should not affect them.' " After two years of that kind of directing, Immermann in 1834 took over the management of the Düsseldorf Municipal Theater—with Felix Mendelssohn (1809–1847) as musical director. But despite the interest aroused among some intelligent people, the venture failed in early 1837.[115]

Eduard Devrient (1801–1877), Ludwig's nephew, an indifferent actor, but a keen observer of acting, and the author of the five volume *Geschichte der Deutschen Schauspielkunst* (1848–74), also yearned for less theatricality and more realism in German acting. In 1839 he visited Paris and watched Bocage at the Porte-Saint-Martin and the Gymnase "breathing triumphant life into all the extravagant characters of the new Romantic school." He wrote, "Bocage has in consummate perfection all the qualities that make serious French actors attractive. . . . His playing . . . is of the simplest, most unpretending naturalness; his movements and attitudes, his use of the furniture of the scene—a chair, a table—are . . . intimately homelike." German acting, on the other hand, he complained, is distinguished by conventions, by pretentiousness. "Everything has become theatrical: all stage business, all expressions, and all gestures are conceived and adopted with an eye to their effect. . . . The actor . . . only thinks of how he can do something striking and sensational. . . ."[116]

While Immermann and Devrient were working for more realism in acting, Georg Büchner (1813–1837) broke with romanticism and wrote a bitter, almost filmlike portrait of a revolutionist in *Dantons Tod* (*Danton's Death*) (1835); Karl Gutzkow (1811–1878) depicted the tragedy of a Jewish heretic in *Uriel Acosta* (1847); and Friedrich Hebbel (1813–1863) supplied German actors with significant new material to interpret; he perceptively analyzed middle-class morality and prejudices in *Maria Magdalena* (1844). Hebbel anticipated Ibsen at a time when the romantic ideal was fulfilled in Richard Wagner's (1813–1883) *Tannhäuser* (1845) and *Lohengrin* (1850). Between those two operas Karl Marx (1818–1883) and Friedrich Engels (1820–1895) published the world-shaking *Communist Manifesto* (1848).

IV

Slowly and unobtrusively before 1850 English acting was feeling its way to a realistic technique. As London's population increased from about one million and a half in 1825 to more than two million and a half by 1850, some twenty new theaters were built, among them the Strand (1832), the

St. James' (1835), and the Princess' (1840). Along with the Haymarket (1720, rebuilt 1821), Sadler's Wells (1765), the Lyceum (1794, rebuilt 1815, 1834), the Olympic (1806, 1813), the Adelphi (1806, 1819), the Surrey (1809), and the Coburg (1818), renamed the Victoria in 1833 and affectionately called the Old Vic, these smaller houses staged all sorts of varied entertainments, and a few plays, mostly during summers, in competition with the two Patent Houses. But legally plays could be staged during the winter seasons only at Drury Lane and Covent Garden until the monopoly was finally broken in 1843. In those two vast houses all the niceties of acting were lost upon most of the audience; the accessories of music and spectacle—especially elaborate scenic effects—and later horsemanship, aquatics, and menageries, were indispensable to keep the theaters from utter failure.

The new audiences wanted more than a constant fare of ancient Shakespeare; they wanted new plays nearer to their own time and interests, plays about people they could recognize and root for, laugh at, or cry over. They therefore got from typical dramatist Douglas Jerrold (1803–1857) at the Coburg the farcial *Paul Pry* (1827), a follow-up of John Poole's (1786?–1872) *Paul Pry* (1825) which ran 114 nights with Liston in the title role at the Haymarket, and the moral *Fifteen Years of a Drunkard's Life* (1828); at the Surrey the breezy *Black-Eyed Susan* (1829), acted 400 nights by a cast that included Thomas Cooke (1786–1864) and John Buckstone (1802–1879); and at Drury Lane a middle-class melodrama, *The Rent Day* (1832). And they got from Edward Fitzball (1792–1873), hack adapter of Scott's novels and composer of nautical dramas as well as libretti for light operas, *Jonathan Bradford; or, the Murder in the Road-Side Inn* (1833) which, with four rooms seen simultaneously onstage, ran for 260 nights at the Surrey.

During these doldrums Kean and Macready, like cat and mouse, did as much as they could to keep acting from becoming trivial; but the former was feeble and sick, and the latter at first was too often away from London on tour. Kean, after glowing triumphs in most of his famous roles at Drury Lane in 1827, fought with the management, left the theater he'd dominated for thirteen years, and deflected to Covent Garden. Then Macready, after an eight-month tour of the United States, returned to Drury Lane; there Kean's son, Charles (1811–1868), first appeared as a would-be actor. Next year Macready went to Paris, was followed there by Kean, and then spent two seasons touring the provinces. In 1829 Charles Kemble, facing bankruptcy at Covent Garden, was saved by his daughter, Frances Anne (1809–1893), who made a sensational debut as Juliet and proceeded to fill the theater for the next three years. Her acting, however, was old-fashioned. Fanny Kemble was "an artificial performer" addicted to "the regular conventional tragic style, both in voice and manner." Hunt wrote that "the moment this young lady has a tragic note to strike up, or thinks she has, then commences the declamation, the drawl, the monotony, the peremptoriness of air, and the dealing forth of stately syllables—in short, the false elevation of manner which she mistakes for exaltation of feeling." [117] Kean, of course, refused to take second place to her and promptly returned to Drury Lane (while Macready was away), played briefly to packed houses, failed miserably in the new role of Shakespeare's King Henry V because he couldn't remember lines, and retired to the country to convalesce. Macready then returned to Drury Lane to achieve one of his major successes in a new but poor play, Byron's *Werner*. There in 1832 the two top actors first met onstage: Kean played Othello to Macready's Iago for eight performances.

Near the end of 1832 American James Henry Hackett (1800–1871) boldly competed in London with the chief English actors. In the preceding six years he "had won top place as the American National Comedian as he toured from Boston to New Orleans with a trunkful of dialect parts ranging from Yankee Joe Bunker to French *emigré* Monsieur Morbleu, Kentuckian Nimrod Wildfire, and Dutchman Rip Van Winkle." At Drury Lane he acted Solomon Swap in his own version of Colman's *Who Wants A Guinea?* (1805) called *Jonathan in England* (or *Yankee in England*) (1812). The critics admitted that Hackett possessed some farcial talent, but they agreed "that Americans could not, or would not, draw the line of distinction between the advanced degree of taste and refinement at which this country has naturally arrived. . . ." [118]

In 1833 Kean, after another fight with the management at Drury Lane, this time over money, went back to Covent Garden (while Fanny and her father were being acclaimed in America), opened as Shylock, and then four days later as Othello opposite his son Charles as Iago collapsed. Two months later, penniless at forty-five (or six), he died.

Macready's fight to occupy the throne was ended. At the age of forty he was ready to lead a profession he believed "to be so unrequiting, that no person who had the power of doing anything better would, unless deluded into it, take it up." He began "more seriously . . . to apply to the study of my profession. . . ." But he was puzzled as to what exactly to aim for in acting. After all, Hunt had criticized him for being deficient "in passages where the ideal is required; where nature puts on the robe of art, and speaks her truths, as it were, in state." "Mr. Macready," he'd written, "seems afraid of the poetry of some of his greatest parts, as if it would hurt the effect of his naturalness and his more familiar passages." Other critics, however, were insisting that acting ought, above all else, to be natural. For instance, Oxford professor, later Archbishop, Richard Whateley (1787–1863) had said in his *Elements of Rhetoric* (1828) that the practical rule for speaking naturally is not to concentrate on effects, is not to pay a "studied attention to the Voice, but studiously to *withdraw* the thoughts from it [and from gestures?], and to dwell as intently as possible on the Sense [and the feelings]; trusting to nature to suggest spontaneously the proper emphases and tones. . . ." A reader—or an actor—he warned, "is sure to pay *too much* attention to his voice, not only if he pays *any at all*, but if he does not strenuously *labor to withdraw* his attention from it altogether." [119] Macready wondered what to do. Should he put more art or more nature into his acting? *Could* Shakespeare's poetry ever be beautifully spoken in an everyday manner? *Could* characters conceived beyond realism be made real?

Well, Macready was intelligent if not imaginative, he "was open to every influence that seemed advantageous to his art," and he was aware of the current pushings toward realism. He decided to try for more naturalness. He tackled "the problem of appearing natural in tragedy without dissipating too much the dignity essential to the genre." [120]

"I must endeavor to improve the colloquial groundwork of my acting," Macready wrote in 1833. "I want to consider every line, and test each by a natural standard" (but certainly not the natural standard of today). As Wolsey he liked his "More natural and yet more earnest delivery," and as Lear he hated his "crude, fictitious voice." But oh, he exclaimed, "How little do they know of this art who think it is easy!" Next year, however, he evolved the "Macready pause" as a way of indicating a character's thinking processes (although this pause soon became a longer and longer artistic trick for impressing audiences); and he was pleased because "my intercourse with Horatio, Rosencrantz, Guildenstern . . . was earnest and real, *ad homines.*" Macready tried hard to be natural onstage by turning his back sometimes on the audience or by reading every word of a "prop" letter or by actually writing one when the script called for that. Yet he fretted a little. "I think," he jotted down, that "I may play Othello well, but the prescriptive criticism of this country, in looking for particular points instead of contemplating one entire character, abates my confidence in myself." And sometimes he was discouraged. In 1836 he cried out: "Why cannot I make it [Macbeth] the very thing, the reality?" [121]

From 1833 to 1837—at Drury Lane for nearly three seasons, at Covent Garden for a season plus, and on tours in the provinces—Macready with hard work and patience, "*alias* indefatigability of mind," achieved a studied, Sunday kind of realism in the making of *whole* characters. They included Hamlet, Wolsey, Prospero, Posthumus, Othello, Iago, Hotspur, Macbeth, Lear, Antony, Jaques, and Coriolanus along with Virginius and Werner, but not many new men because he simply could not dredge up enough new, worthwhile, preferably poetic plays. Then, at meridian in 1837, Macready turned actor-manager and leased Covent Garden in an attempt to save the dying legitimate theater in London. Two of the actors he hired were Helen Faucit (1817–1898), who belonged to the ideal rather than to the realistic school, and Samuel Phelps (1804–1878), "a faultless elocutionist." Productions of more than routine interest included *The Winter's Tale,* with Macready as Leontes, the new *The Lady of Lyons* (1838) by Edward Bulwer-Lytton (1803–1873), Byron's dud, *The Two Foscari* (1838), a lovely *The Tempest,* Bulwer-Lytton's *Richelieu* (1839), and an elaborate *King Henry the Fifth.* But management was too much for Macready; in 1839 he quit and agreed to act at the Haymarket for £25 a night, four nights a week. There, *Money*, written by Bulwer-Lytton to satisfy "the craving for the realistic in measured doses," [122] proved to be wildly popular near the end of 1840 and ran for eighty nights with Macready as Alfred.

Madame (Lucia Elizabetta Bartolozzi) Vestris (1797–1856) and her husband, Charles Mathews the younger (1803–1878), just returned from the United States, succeeded Macready at Covent Garden. Madame, a mercurial, scandalous, popular singer who'd been performing in light operas since 1815, and sometimes in plays by 1824, had obtained a license to produce "burlettas" and in 1831 opened the small Olympic Theatre with Liston plus a small company of actors and a determination to raise "illegitimate" light plays to a high plane of excellence. She and her chief author, James R. Planché (1796–1880), had agreed that "the finest comic effect did not result from outrageous dressing and silly behavior, but from a contrast between personages who behaved like people in real life and the absurdities they were given to say" in "Drawing-rooms . . . fitted up like drawing-rooms, and furnished with care and taste." She'd succeeded, via French derived extravaganzas, in bringing onstage an airy, polite, winning sort of realism. Then, in two debt-ridden seasons at Covent Garden actress-manager Vestris and Mathews—who had joined her company in 1835 and married her in 1838— notably staged in 1841 for a fifty-nine night run "the most famous play of the age," *London Assurance* by Dion(ysius) Boucicault (1822–1890). The production, with its tasteful interiors (the first box-set) and "not stage properties, but *bona fide* realities," amazed audiences with its modernity.[123]

In late 1841 Macready, urged to undertake managing Drury Lane, supplemented his old company with, among others, James Wallack (1791–1864), Henry's brother, a Kemble school performer who crisscrossed the Atlantic to attitudinize in both London and New York City, pleasant Mary Anne (Goward) Keeley (1806–1899), and her husband Robert Keeley (1793–1869), and once again set to work to save the theater. He staged some of his old plays and a number of new but weak ones such as *The Patrician's Daughter* (1842) by Westland Marston (1819–1890), in which he was anxious "to invest the action with every detail of the most modern realism," and *The Blot in the 'Scutcheon* (1843) by Robert Browning (1812–1889). As a performer Macready was still determined to keep "The whole view of the character . . . constantly in sight," still convinced that acting is real only when "the feeling [is] taken directly from the part" and when he could identify himself with a character, and still on guard "against unreal tones." [124] Again management was too much, and too costly, for him; in mid-1843 he relinquished his duties as director of the theater and soon sailed for America.

Then the irony of it all! Phelps, the elocutionist, the believer in "the sovereign quality of a just delivery," "the last of the old school actors in the grand style," succeeded where Macready had failed. In 1844, the year after the theater monopoly was broken, he leased Sadler's Wells, a house of melodramas remote from London's entertainment center, opened in May with Mrs. Warner (1804–1854) in *Macbeth*, and soon made theatrical history with his artistic, financially successful revivals of English classics and his staging of thirty-two of Shakespeare's plays (in eighteen years). Phelps whisked from his stage all scripts that were trivial and all acting that was less than elevated. But in 1847 Madame Vestris and Mathews took over the Lyceum and for more than seven years, and more financial troubles than they could handle, pleased the public with nonclassic entertainments like the brief *Box and Cox* (1847) by John M. Morton (1811–1891), Planché's magical extravaganza, *The Island of Jewels* (1849), and his *The Day of Reckoning* (1850), an adaptation of a French play, which was acted to perfection, it seems, because "Vestris and Mathews were natural—nothing more, nothing less. They were a lady and gentleman such as we meet in drawing-rooms, graceful, quiet, well-bred, perfectly dressed, perfectly oblivious of the footlights." [125] Finally in 1850, when Drury Lane was in dire straits and Covent Garden had become a place for operas, Charles Kean, with his wife Ellen Tree (1806–1880), inaugurated at the Princess' Theatre a memorable nine-year management.

In late October of that year Macready began his farewell London engagement at the Haymarket and ended it in early February 1851 with *King Lear*. Audiences yelled "Bravo" night after night, and perceptive critics agreed that there may have been one or two tragedians who, "in some parts, excelled him in the sudden revelations of passion, [but] it is yet probable that he has never been excelled, if equalled, in the complete and harmonious development of character. In all his great impersonations was shown the same faculty of grasping the central idea of his part, and of making all the lights thrown upon details correspond with that idea." [126] Then at Drury Lane on February 26, 1851, a few days before his fifty-eighth birthday, Macready as Macbeth acted for the last time, wrote "Thank God" in his journal, and lived quietly until 1873.

By 1850 in London—where Mlle. Mars, Lemaître, Rachel, and Americans Forrest, Hackett, Charlotte Cushman, Edward L. Davenport, and Anna Cora Mowatt had appeared as colleagues of Macready—acting in some instances had changed slightly from what it had been. There was (almost) a new school and an old school. "The new school," in the opinion of one critic, "attaches far more importance to conception in the acting of a part, and neglects elocution, while the converse is held by others who depend most for plaudits upon good reading and discretion, or upon fiery verse and declamation and the music of potent sound." [127]

But the new acting wasn't truly realistic. It was still elocutionary—only a little less so. Beautiful tones and correct gestures were taught at the newly founded Musical and Dramatic Academy (1848). And Alexander Bell (1819–1905), Alexander Graham's father, started a run of elocutionary manuals in 1849 with his *A New Elucidation of the Principles of Speech and Elocution*.

V

Acting in the United States was also largely elocution. James Rush (1786–1869) reprinted several times *The Philosophy of the Human Voice* . . . (1827); and George Vandenhoff (1813–1885), who'd acted with Vestris and Mathews, published in New York City *The Art of Elocution* (1847).

The leading actors before 1850 were Edwin Forrest (1806–1872), as the Indian *Metamora* (1829) by John A. Stone (?–1834), the Roman *The Gladiator* (1831) by Robert M. Bird (1806–1854), and the fifteenth-century *Jack Cade* (1835) by Robert Conrad (1810–1858); comedian James Henry Hackett, powerful Charlotte Cushman (1816–1876), who made her debut at the Park Theater as Lady Macbeth in 1836; Edward L. Davenport (1815–1877), who began acting in 1836 at Providence, and, after two years in Boston and three in Philadelphia, came to New York City in 1846; and Anna Cora Mowatt (1819–1870), the author of *Fashion; or, Life in New York* (1845). Two Britishers, James Wallack's son, Lester (1820–1888), and Mrs. Louisa (Lane or Crane) Drew (1820–1897), were also finding fame on the American stage. In 1849 Edwin Booth (1833–1893) was an actor in his father's company, and Joseph Jefferson (1829–1905) was testing his histrionic skills.

Forrest was the star. The primary characteristic of his style was a strenuous, elocutionary, so-called realism. "He aimed for complete, detailed character portrayals, unchanged by any idealization." When he prepared to act Lear "he visited many asylums and old men's homes. He studied various manifestations of insanity—its approach, its full expression, its decline. He observed the walk, the gestures, the movements of old men. He read the best scientific books on old age and insanity, and discussed his ideas with eminent physicians." And when readying his role of the Indian Chief in *Metamora* he lived with an Indian tribe for several weeks, "adopted their habits, shared their food, slept in their huts, . . . smoked the pipe of peace . . . left the print of his own moccasins on the hunting ground. . . ." But some critics felt that Forrest enlarged his effects and "muscularized" them beyond the point of credibility. William Winter (1836–1917), for instance, wrote that Forrest had "a grand body and a glorious voice, and in moments of simple passion he affected the senses like the blare of trumpets and clash of cymbals, or like the ponderous, slow-moving, crashing, and thundering surges of the sea." Certainly the "truth to nature" which the public professed to see in Forrest's acting was merely truth to a crude stage convention of reality, and far removed from the realism of actual life. A ranter, a "bovine bellower," Forrest was addicted to an unimaginative "excess . . . of physical and spiritual force in the expression of passion." Yet audiences idolized "this man of handsome face and powerful physique who handled his body like an athlete" and roared magnificently. But not Walt Whitman (1819–1892).

Reporting in *The Brooklyn Eagle* in 1846 on Forrest's acting, he wrote: "It is a common fallacy to think that an exaggerated, noisy, and inflated style of acting—and no other—will produce the desired effect upon promiscuous audiences. But those who have observed things, theaters, and human nature, know better." [128]

❀ REALISM AFTER 1850

During the last half of the nineteenth century men of the theater, having freed their art from the conventions of classicism, or the traditional expression of traditional concepts, hurried to free it from the excesses of early romanticism, or rashly individual interpretations of experience. Like scientists some of them tended to say, "Let's abandon both these ways of looking at nature; let's begin with the facts; let's bring onstage via writing and production and acting the illusion of life, or life rearranged, or even life as it is so that audiences can see and hear for themselves and then decide by majority vote what is what." In short, the accent was shifted from art to nature so completely that art and the individuality of the artist were almost forgotten.

In France, to begin with, Alexandre Dumas *fils* (1824–1893) believed that a modern playwright ought above all else to be a true observer of men, like Balzac—who had ventured onstage with the clumsily realistic *La Marâtre* (*The Stepmother*) (1848) and *Mercadet* (1851). But Dumas also wanted "to preach, to instruct, or to correct people" with his scripts. "I realize," he said, "that the prime requisites of a play are laughter, tears, passion, emotion, interest, curiosity; to leave life at the cloakroom; but I maintain that if, by means of all these ingredients, and without minimizing one of them, I can exercise some influence over society; if, instead of treating effects I can treat causes; if, for example, while I satirize and describe and dramatize adultery I can find means to force people to discuss the problem, and the lawmaker to revise the law, I shall have done more than my part as a poet; I shall have done my duty as a man." [129] So, after making audiences weep buckets over the plight of a courtesan in a quick dramatization of his novel, *La Dame aux camélias* (*Camille*), staged at the Vaudeville in 1852 for more than three hundred performances with slightly known Eugenie Doche (1821–1900) as Marguerite and Fechter as Armand, Dumas at the Gymnase examined the effects of environment in *Le Demi-Monde* (*The Outer Edge of Society*) (1855), attacked unscrupulous profit-making in *La Question d'argent* (*A Matter of Money*) (1857), and preached a sermon in a genuine *pièce à thèse*, *Le Fils naturel* (*The Illegitimate Son*) (1858).

Augier was another dramatist who poked around in current problems and drew fairly lifelike pictures of contemporary society in the first-rate *Le Gendre de M. Poirier* (*Poirier's Son-in-Law*) (1854), touched on the evils of city life in *La Jeunesse* (*Youth*) (1858), showed the power wielded by newspaper owners in *Les Effrontés* (*The Impertinents*) (1861), and decried clerical meddling in politics in *Le Fils de Giboyer* (1862). And sometimes, it seems, his actors without forfeiting any of their skills at clear and stylish elocution, achieved touches of a new reality in their impersonations. In *Maître Guérin* (1864), for instance, Gôt's "make-up, gait, look, and manner" in the title role of the unscrupulous lawyer "were such as could have thrown Balzac into ecstasies." English critic Lewes noted that "Such acting is worth the study of every artist, no matter what his line, because it exhibits vividly the singular effect which is produced by truthfulness. Every gesture, every look, every tone of the actor [an expert performer in classic plays] seems instinct with the bourgeois nature. The way he uses his handkerchief, the way he sits down, the smallest detail, is prompted by an inward vision of the nature of the man represented." [130]

Finally, fiery Émile Zola (1840–1902) "invented, or rather resuscitated, the modern use of the term naturalism" and noisily attempted to save the theater from the "extravagances, lies, and platitudes" of classicism and romanticism, of melodramas and well-made plays. In 1873 he dramatized his novel, *Thérèse Raquin*; its action consists "in the inner struggles of the characters," lower middle-class shopkeepers, who "presume to participate in a drama of their own in their own home . . ."; and he made these characters forsake playing in order to "*live* before the audience" the drab life of every day.[131] But Zola's play about two lovers who drown an unwanted husband and then are driven to suicide by the accusing eyes of the dumb and paralyzed mother—the personification of conscience and remorse—ran for only nine performances at the Renaissance.

Zola himself, however, ran on and on. With *Thérèse Raquin*, "the first conscientiously written naturalistic drama," he announced his profound conviction that "the experimental and scientific spirit of the century will enter the domain of the drama, and that in it lies its only possible salvation"; and he continued to insist that "the future will have to do with the human problem studied in the framework of reality," that "The drama will either die, or become modern and realistic." He pooh-poohed Dumas' twisting of facts in order to prove a thesis and Augier's thinly selected realism. Zola wanted in the theater a complete objectivity, "the depiction of the real with almost photographic exactitude." And though *Thérèse Raquin* was a carefully constructed play, Zola eventually went all out for "abolishing every convention previously known to the drama. Exposition, intrigue, dénouement were entirely unnecessary. For the drama of invention and imagination, he would substitute a drama of observation and scientific fact. To write a play, a dramatist need only reproduce on the stage the story of a person or a group of persons taken from real life. This story might not be complete; it might be simply a *lambeau d'existence*" [132] (fragment of existence), or, in playwright Jean Jullien's (1854–1919) phrase, a *tranche de vie* (slice of life). In such fragments men and women, their feelings and thoughts, their vices and virtues, could be studied objectively, physiologically, and functionally—just as sugar and vitriol are analyzed in the laboratory.

Actors who listened to Zola must have wanted to ask him, "You mean that acting is to be only behaving naturally? You mean there should be no differences between the two?"

Those questions may have troubled five important newcomers to the French stage: Jean Bressant (1815–1886), who came from the Variétés and Gymnase to the Comédie-Française in 1852; Gustave Worms (1836–1910), who first performed with the same group in 1858; Constant-Benoît Coquelin (1841–1909), a pupil of Régnier's, who came to the company in 1860; Sarah (Bernard) Bernhardt (1844–1923), who followed him there in 1862; and Mounet-Sully (Jean Sully Mounet) (1841–1916), who made his Comédie-Française debut as Oreste in Andromaque in 1872.

Meanwhile, Samson published his traditional exposition of acting, L'Art théâtral, in 1863 and continued at the Conservatoire to emphasize the importance of studied, formal, beautiful speaking until his death in 1871. Then Régnier, after forty years of "uninterrupted service on the first stage of Europe," retired in 1872 on a pension almost as large as his salary, was admitted to the Legion of Honor, and continued to pass on to Conservatoire students the traditions of French acting and to serve as an admirable model for clarity and subtle artistry in stage speech. And Delaunay continued to be praised for his voice of love, a voice "of ineffable quavers and enchanting cadences, dying falls and semitones calculated to a hair's breadth." [133]

II

In Italy—to be united in 1870, with Rome as the capital—theater conservatives "still adhered to the tenets of pseudo-classicism or to those of the now old romantic school, and viewed with hostility all forms other than the traditional ones." [134] Some of the younger playwrights, however, began to study the society of their time in a search for new situations to put onstage. French-influenced Vincenzo Martini (1803–1862) wrote Il Cavaliere d'industria (The Captain of Industry) (1854) and inspected the problem of adultery in Il Marito e l'amante (The Husband and the Lover) (1855); Paolo Giacometti (1816–1882) tackled a thesis in La Morte civile (Civil Death) (1861); and Paolo Ferrari (1822–1889) "fought art for art's sake" and tried to correct current social evils in Il Duello (1868), Cause ed effetti (1871); Il Suicidio (1875).

Simultaneously Ristori as Alfieri's Myrrha, Giacometti's Queen Elizabeth (1853), Schiller's Mary Stuart, Legouvé's Medea (1855), Phèdre, and Lady Macbeth carried "the banner of Italian art round the world" and proved to all but the Orientals that acting is elocution. In 1853 she took her Royal Sardinian Theatrical Company, which included Rossi, to Paris for the purpose of showing "that in Italy also the dramatic art, once our boast and our glory, still exists, and is cultivated with affection and passion." After Paris Ristori went to Warsaw, to Greece, acted Lady Macbeth in Italian at Covent Garden in 1857 "so fully, indeed," as she explained, that during the sleep-walking scene "my pupils remained immovable in their sockets, until the tears came into my eyes," returned to France, went back to England, toured Austria and Germany, impersonated Phèdre in Italy in "a state amounting to delirium" and fell into the foot-lights, journeyed to Spain, Holland, Egypt, Belgium, Russia, made the first of four visits to the United States in 1866, and then performed in Portugal, Denmark, and Sweden. In 1874 she embarked on another world tour of more than twenty months to Bordeaux, Rio de Janeiro, Buenos Aires, Montevideo, Valparaiso, Santiago, Lima, Vera Cruz, Mexico, the United States including San Francisco, the Sandwich Islands, New Zealand, Sydney, Melbourne, Adelaide, Ceylon, Aden, Suez, Alexandria in Egypt, Brindisi, Rome!! [135] She never stopped touring.

Macready found Ristori's acting to be no more than "merely a melo-dramatic abandonment or lashing-up to a certain point of excitement." But for critic Lewes she always performed "with consummate skill" and with an "air of supreme *distinction*." "Ristori," he wrote, "has complete mastery of the mechanism of the stage, but is without the inspiration necessary for great acting. A more beautiful and graceful woman, with a more musical voice, has seldom appeared," but "the line which separates charm from profound emotion is never passed." She was no innovator, he concluded, only an expert "conventional actress" who employed with great art "the traditional conventions of the stage." [136]

Salvini in 1851 was acting with Ristori at the Teatro Valle in Rome and trying to overcome the "tendency to singsong in my voice, the ex-uberance of my rendering of passion, the exclamatory quality of my phrasing, the precipitation of my pronunciation, and the swagger of my motions." Five years later at Vicenza, Venice, and Rome he first acted Othello with Clementina Cazzola (1832–1868) as Desdemona and Lorenzo Piccilini (1826–1891) as Iago. By 1860, after he'd taken a half dozen plays, including the stirring Othello to Paris, Salvini served as chief actor with the Compagnia Reale de Fiorentini of Naples for several years, and then with much acclaim toured Spain, Portugal, South America, the United States, and England. In London for three months in 1875 he discovered that "Actors who devote themselves to tragedy, whether classical, romantic, or historical, no longer exist. Society comedy has overflowed the stage." But at Drury Lane he pre-sented in Italian Othello thirty times, Hamlet ten, and The Gladiator four, and was well satisfied. Lewes commented that "for the most part there has been an acknowledgment of Salvini's great qualities as an actor, even from those who think his conception of Othello false." The Italian he said, was "in certain passages manifestly inferior to Kean, [but] the representation as a whole was of more sustained excellence." Salvini's Hamlet, he admitted, was not Shakespeare's Hamlet, but it had "the greatest excellences. . . . The soliloquies were quiet, and were real soliloquisings, except that every now and then too much was *italicised* and *pointed out:* so that he seemed less one communing with himself, than one illustrating his meaning to a listener." Lewes concluded that Salvini "has a handsome and eminently expressive face, graceful and noble bearing, singular power of expressing tragic passion, a voice of rare beauty, and an elocution such as one only hears once or twice in a lifetime: in the three great elements of musical expression, tone, timbre, and rhythm, Salvini is the greatest speaker I have heard." [137]

Rossi by 1857 was in Vienna with his own troupe and beginning to tour everywhere chiefly in the tragedies of Alfieri and Shakespeare. Salvini praised him because "Many of the parts which he played, and which won renown for him, were by his fine and keen intellect, and by his unwearied study, fashioned and polished like a diamond." But too often, Salvini was afraid, audiences lost sight of the character Rossi acted and "would be reminded of the man who was . . . studying his inflections, and designing his motions." [138]

Five new Italian actors before 1875 were Edoardo Ferravilla (1846–1915), a comic character man; Flavio Andò (1851–1915); Ermete Novelli (1851–1919), a tragedian; Ferruccio Benini (1854–1916); and Eleanora Duse, daughter of actors, who in 1873, at the age of fourteen, was playing Juliet at Verona.

III

From 1853 until his death in 1886 playwright Ostrovsky dominated the Russian theater by enlivening the stage of the Maly in Moscow, and then the Alexandrinsky in St. Petersburg and probably eight provincial houses, with his mostly comic "pieces of actualism." In some ways ahead of Zola, he disregarded the rules for writing traditional or well-made plays and loosely yet subtly designed a horde of atmospheric scripts in which strongly native characters—clerks, merchants, housewives, and even fashionable folk—are truly captured, or caricatured, with a multitude of keenly observed, significantly human, minor peculiarities. In such plays as *Bednost ne porok* (*Poverty Is No Crime*) (1854), *Dokhodnoe mesto* (*A Lucrative Job*) (1856), the tragic and widely known *Groza* (*The Thunderstorm*) (1860), the serious *Grekh da beda na kovo ne zhivet* (*Sin and Sorrow Are Common to All*) (1863), *Na vsiakovo mudretsa dovolno* (*Enough Stupidity in Every Wise Man*, or *The Diary of a Scoundrel*) (1868), *Beshenie dengi* (*Mad Money*) (1870), and *Ne vse kotu maslianitsa* (*After Dinner Comes the Reckoning*) (1871) actors were challenged to study carefully the life around them and to bring to their characterizations and to the ensemble a kind of recognizable reality.

Other dramatists, of course, also tried for more truth in their plays. Alexander Sukhovo-Kobylin (1817–1903) wrote a revealing trilogy about city high society: *Svadba Krechinskovo* (*Krechinsky's Wedding*) (1856), first staged in St. Petersburg with Samoilov in the title role; *Delo* (*The Lawsuit*) 1862, an indictment of Russia's courts; and an even stronger exposure of legal corruption, *Smert Tarelkina* (*Tarelkin's Death*) (1869), banned from the stage until 1900. Alexei Pisemski (1820–1881) powerfully attacked class justice by dramatizing an actual occurrence, a serf's murder of a child born to his wife by a landowner, in *Gorkaia sudbina* (*Bitter Fate*). The play, one of many such protests, was produced in 1859, two years before serfdom was abolished. And Alexei Tolstoy (1819–1875) turned to history in a trilogy: *Smert Ivana Groznavo* (*The Death of Ivan the Terrible*) (1866), a scathing indictment of Russian monarchy, *Tsar Feodor Ivanovich* (1868), censored until 1898 when it opened the Moscow Art Theatre's first season, and *Tsar Boris* (1870).

None of these playwrights attained the realistic maturity of novelist Feodor Dostoyevsky (1821–1881) who in 1866 wrote the psychological *Prestupleniye i nakazaniye* (*Crime and Punishment*), or of Leo Tolstoy (1828–1910) and the huge *Voina i Mir* (*War and Peace*) (1865–69).

At first certain actors, "educated on translations of melodramas and vaudevilles . . . , felt incapable of coping with the [low realism of] Russian folk comedy; among them were many of outstanding talent who stubbornly opposed the infiltration of Ostrovsky's plays to the stage. This movement, curiously enough, was headed by Samarin, Shumsky and—particularly important—Shchepkin." [139] Soon enough, however, Ostrovsky pleased these holdouts since he provided them with highly popular scripts in which middle-class audiences, with peephole pride, could see themselves.

Since Shchepkin died in 1863 (soon after Constantin Alexeyev, who was to call himself Stanislavski, was born), the actor in Moscow who won most fame via Ostrovsky was Prov Sadovsky. He created a gallery of approximately thirty winning characters with such heightened realism that spectators seemed to behold people they'd met somewhere, with whom they'd dealt, but whose names they'd temporarily forgotten. Sadovsky, it was said, as it was said of others before and after him, "may truly be considered as the one who was principally responsible for the fact that simplicity and naturalness began to reign supreme on our stage. . . ." [140]

Other important Ostrovsky players were the sensitive, tender-voiced serf, Lyubov Nikulina-Kositskaya (1829–1868), who first impersonated the complex Katia in *The Thunderstorm*; S. V. Vasilyev (1827–1868) and his wife, Yekaterina Lavrova (1816–1877), I. F. Gorbunov (1831–1895), Varvana Borozdina (1813–1866), Modest Pisarev (1844–1906) who believed that "all dramatic acting is colored with the unique peculiarities of the performer. . . ," with "his aptitudes, the pattern of his mind, and his moral leanings"; his wife, P. A. Strepetova (1850–1903); and Glikeriya Fedotova (1846–1925), "developed under the influence of Samarin and Shchepkin," who created a number of Ostrovsky's characters, including the title role in the poetic

Snegurochka (*The Snow Maiden*) (1873), and who also portrayed Schiller's Queen Elizabeth, Shakespeare's Mistress Page, Cleopatra, Lady Macbeth, and Volumnia. "Through her the best traditions of the Maly Theatre reached . . . Stanislavski." [141]

Four of the leading players in St. Petersburg were V. N. Davydov (I. N. Gorelov) (1849–1925), provincially trained, who excelled in a wide variety of both comic and tragic Russian roles and also as Molière's Harpagon and Shakespeare's Shylock; comic K. A. Varlamov (1848–1915); and actresses M. G. Savina (1854–1915) and Fanya Snetkova (1838–1929).

The two stars at Moscow's Maly were the idolized Maria Yermolova (1853–1928) and the multitalented, half-Italian Alexander Lensky (Verviziotti) (1847–1908). Yermolova, "pride of the Russian stage," valued by Stanislavski as the greatest actress he'd ever known, not excepting Duse, was a classic player who made her debut in 1870 as Lessing's Emilia Galotti, and later was outstanding as Schiller's Maid of Orleans and Mary Stuart, as Laurentia in de Vega's *The Sheep Well* and Estrella in his *The Star of Seville*, as Phèdre, and Lady Macbeth. Painter and sculptor Lensky, who'd been acting in the provinces since 1865, was seen at Odessa during the 1875–76 season and immediately signed for the Maly. There he began by acting first lovers in comedy and tragedy, and later turned to character roles in plays by Pushkin, Griboyedov, Gogol, Turgenev, Ostrovsky, Shakespeare, Molière, Schiller, Hugo, and Ibsen. He was the "most talented and attractive actor" Stanislavski ever saw.[142]

❊ ENGLISH DIRECTORS

English acting from 1850 to 1875—or, say from the time of Dickens' *David Copperfield* (1850) to George Eliot's *Middlemarch* (1872)—was as enlivened by French influences as French acting had been enlivened by English influences. After the more or less traditional performances of Shakespeare's plays had contributed to the change from classicism to romanticism in Paris, the new performances in Parisian romantic melodramas helped to inspire a noticeable change from elocution toward more natural speaking onstage in London.

There, also as in Paris, the vigorous theaters were the small ones. Drury Lane was little better than a show-booth, and Covent Garden was a place for opera. But at Sadler's Wells in North London traditional Phelps continued staging and acting in stock dramas and Shakespeare's plays—all of them except *Troilus and Cressida*, *Titus Andronicus*, and *Henry VI* (3)—until 1862. The Haymarket, the foremost comedy house of the period, was managed from 1837 to 1853 by prolific playwright and actor Benjamin N. Webster (1797–1882), and from 1853 to about 1865 by an equally prolific playwright and actor, John Buckstone. The company was always firmly old-fashioned— and firmly British. The actors "one and all thoroughly understood Sheridan," as young Ellen Terry noticed. "Their bows, their curtseys, their grand manner, the indefinite *style* which they brought to their task, were something to see." [143] At this theater traditional Edwin Booth portrayed Shylock, Sir Giles Overreach, and Richelieu in 1861. That same year Buckstone struck it rich with a phenomenal run of Tom Taylor's (1817–1880) *Our American Cousin* (1858) in which Edward A. Sothern (1826–1881) as Lord Dundreary clowned as he had for 145 nearly consecutive performances in New York City. Taylor's best known play, however, *The Ticket-of-Leave-Man* (1863), was first presented to crowded houses at the Olympic.

Innovation was the theme at the small Princess' Theatre. There from 1850 through 1859 Charles Kean staged a number of Shakespeare's plays with a lavish and scrupulous historical accuracy in costumes, scenery, and stage business. He "drilled his company so that everyone, down to the merest mechanic and supernumerary, should produce the effect required of him in the most harmonious and telling manner." "Rehearsals lasted all day, Sundays included, and when there was no play running at night, until four or five the next morning. . . . Kean used to sit in the stalls with a loud-voiced dinnerbell by his side, and when anything went wrong on the stage, he would ring it ferociously, and everything would come to a stop, until Mrs. Kean, who always sat on the stage, had set right what was wrong." [144]

More significantly, however, the younger Kean, with the assistance of "his literary adviser and 'right-hand man,'" Dion Boucicault, introduced to the British stage the new Parisian plays, or "gentlemanly melodramas," or so-called "French trash." Boucicault, a French-named Irishman, had resided in Paris between 1844 and 1848 and seen Fechter performing in romantic dramas; he liked the new style in writing and acting because audiences liked it well enough to pay money for it. So, convinced "that the Elizabethan drama, either in the original or in imitation, had ceased to make a vital appeal" to Englishmen, he decided that these new serious plays in everyday dialogue could make that appeal—and also his own fortune. Boucicault therefore "flung conscience and literary ambition overboard," became a showman, or unadulterated businessman, and for Kean adapted a new Dumas *père* play as *Pauline* (1851), a script taken by Grangé and Montepin from the novel by Dumas as *The Corsican Brothers* (1852), and Casimir Delavigne's (1793–1843) *Louis XI* (1855). All three proved to be enormous successes. Audiences at the Princess' Theatre were enthusiastic about the heightened action and the easily recognized characters who, according to one critic, "use only such dialogue as they would use if actually engaged in the scenes they presented. . . ." No longer did an ordinary man "utter sentiments worthy of a divine, couched in language worthy of a scholar." [145]

Given "realistic" plays like the French melodramas, Kean, "in spite of virulent criticism and even invective," dabbled with a style of acting serious drama which, while only a compromise with the old, was fresher and more natural than London playgoers had yet seen. This new mode of representation he also applied "in part to Shakespearean plays." Critics saw in Kean's acting "the first marked change from the excesses of the old school to that of the newer melodramatic style." In *Pauline* he revealed himself "a first-rate melodramatic actor where hitherto we had known only a bad tragedian." In *The Corsican Brothers* Kean impersonated both brothers; and, as Lewes reported, "you must see him before you will believe how well and how quietly he plays them, preserving a gentlemanly demeanor and drawing-room manner, very difficult to assume on the stage, if one may judge from its rarity, which intensifies the passion . . . and gives . . . a terrible reality." "The stamping, spluttering, ranting, tricky actor, who in his 'salad days' excited so much mirth and so much blame, has become remarkable for the naturalness and forcible quietness with which he plays certain parts." [146]

But the younger Kean wasn't easily natural onstage; he wasn't, in fact, natural at all. He was continually aware of his "beautiful elocution," and "unhappily given to rant" in the expression of strong emotions; and every step he took, every point in his dialogue, every action he made use of was carefully calculated for its effect.[147] Kean only hesitantly searched for the new, only half-tried to make acting a little more Frenchlike, a bit more realistic, than it had been.

Charles Kean did something else for—or against—acting. He instituted the policy of "the long run." Because his sumptuous and melodramatically acted productions attracted large crowds, he regularly prolonged "their repetitions to unheard-of lengths." (Previous long runs had been isolated and unusual. In London in 1825 *Paul Pry* ran for 114 nights, in 1829 *Black-Eyed Susan* set a record of 400 performances, in 1833 *Jonathan Bradford* was acted 260 nights. In Paris Lemaître's *Trente Ans* in 1827 ran four months, his *Kean* in 1836 three months, and his *Paillasse* in 1850 100 nights; and in 1852 *La Dame aux camélias*, with Fechter, held the stage for more than 300 nights.) Kean's *Macbeth* in 1852 ran three times a week for twenty weeks; and in 1855 *Louis XI* was continued 62 consecutive nights. In that year *Henry VIII*, produced with unparalleled splendor, was repeated without a break for 100 performances. And *A Midsummer Night's Dream* in 1856 was acted 150 consecutive times. In due time the usual run of a Kean production approximated 100 nights.[148] His actors were assigned the new problem of sustaining for a long period the initial freshness of their characterizations. They were also limited to portraying only a few characters a season.

II

London-born Frenchman Charles Fechter did more than Kean did to popularize the shift toward the realistic, the shift away from "mere tradition and stage conventionality," away from "the utterly unnatural . . . style in which . . . tragedians were wont to enact the most ordinary movements of human life." In November 1860, a year after Kean had left the Princess'

Theatre and gone to America, Fechter acted there in *Ruy Blas, The Corsican Brothers*, and other plays; then in March 1861 he appeared in *Hamlet*. As Ruy Blas and the two brothers he was merely a winning personality, "but as the Royal Dane he flung a challenge to British tradition. . . . Never, people believed, could the broken English of a French melodramatic actor rise to the heights of poetic diction sustained by Burbage, Betterton, Garrick, Kemble, Kean the elder, Macready, Phelps, or even Kean the younger." But Fechter was a sensation; his Hamlet drew crowded houses for five full months. He triumphed not because of his charm, or his blond wig, or the novelty of his accent and intonation (which sometimes did odd things to Shakespeare's lines); he triumphed because of his acting, acting that "gave to the English stage a new principle. This principle was unconventionality." Fechter's "*Hamlet* was great because nothing in the play was done as it had ever been done before." This rebel "disregarded all the old theatrical traditions of measured stride and measured pause, the dramatic tones of unbroken gloom, the statuesque attitudes, the portentous, awe-pervading melancholy," and all the petrified "points" which "every audience expected to see properly executed, and according to the effect of which very largely they approved or condemned an actor's performance." Fechter did more than that. He impersonated the Prince with the "cohesion and coherence . . . of a distinctly conceived and executed idea." In short, he restaged *Hamlet* in the fashion of "gentlemanly melodrama." And critic "Clement Scott [1841–1904], Charles Dickens [1812–1870], and others hailed his 'natural' acting as preferable to the traditional acting of 'the mouthers and ranters and bow-wow gentlemen of the old school who had all the faults of Macready without any of his virtues!" [149]

Fechter's "reform" has been too freely called, "the nearest approach to a stage revolution in the history of English drama." But certainly his *Hamlet* "marked the decisive victory of French methods over the English stage tradition. For the time being, all doubts as to the superiority of the French art, which . . . had seemed heretical and disloyal, were dispelled." Thoughtful critics and the public at large were convinced "that the realism of melodrama, which previously had been regarded as vulgar, degenerate, and un-English, was actually . . . the mode of representation that English literary drama most needed." [150]

Fechter's acting of Hamlet was "realistic" only because it was "more conversational and less stilted than usual." Yes, "Shakespeare's grandest language seemed to issue naturally from Fechter's lips, and did not strike you as out of place, which it so often does when mouthed on the stage"; [151] but, for sure, his realism was still too artificial, a bit too artistic, to be called genuinely natural acting.

Even so, that "naturalism" was both accepted and rejected by Lewes. This critic liked Fechter's Hamlet; then, as if repenting for an inconsistency in judgment, as if clinging all the tighter to his belief that acting in tragedy ought to be elevated, he severely criticized Fechter's Othello, which took stage in late October 1861 for only a forty-night run. As the Moor, he wrote, Fechter's "naturalism, being mainly determined by his personality, became utter feebleness." The actor, in his attempt to be lifelike onstage, sank "into the *familiar*" and vulgarized the part. "In his desire to be effective by means of small details of 'business,' he has entirely frittered away the great effects of the drama. . . . Instead of the heroic, grave, impassioned Moor, he represents an excitable creole of our own day." [152]

The "desire to be natural—the aim at realism . . . works like poison. It is not consistent with the nature of tragedy to obtrude the details of daily life. All that lounging on tables and lolling against chairs, which help to convey a sense of reality in the *drama*, are . . . unnatural in tragedy. . . . When Fechter takes out his door-key to let himself into his house, and, on coming back, relocks the door and pockets the key, the *intention* is doubtless to give an air of reality; the *effect* is to make us forget the 'noble Moor,' and to think of a sepoy. When he appears leaning on the shoulder of Iago (the great general and his ensign!), when he salutes the personages with graceful prettinesses, when he kisses the hand of Desdemona, and when he employs that favorite gesticulation which reminds us but too forcibly of a *gamin* threatening to throw a stone, he is certainly *natural*,—but according to whose nature?" [153]

The question was, and still is, a perceptive one. Fechter, having tempted audiences into asking it, remained in London to manage the Lyceum and to act there from 1863 through 1867. Typical of his offerings were *The Duke's Motto* (1863), an adaptation of Paul Féval's *Le Bossu* by Irish-American actor-playwright John Brougham (1810–1880), which ran for seven months; the same adapter's *Bel Demonio* (1863), suggested by Boucicault's *Sixtus V*, which was acted for 175 nights; Fechter's version of *Trente Ans* called *Rouge et Noir* (1866); and an 1867 revival of Bulwer-Lytton's *The Lady of Lyons*, performed 151 consecutive times.

By then, however, "The pace of realism . . . was quickening. What had seemed revolutionarily real in 1860 was now regarded as melodramatic, and had already become a convention." [154] So, after a long tour of England and Ireland, Fechter sailed for the United States, and in January 1870 opened at Niblo's Garden in *Ruy Blas*. There and in Boston and Philadelphia he created a little stir, tried management again and failed, retired in 1873, and died three years later in Philadelphia.

III

In 1863, when Fechter took over the Lyceum, the management of Drury Lane in "a reaction against the 'vulgar school,' against the flood of sensation that had swept over the chief London stages, and against the inroads of translation from the French," [155] engaged Phelps and a company of "defenders of the old faith" who proceeded to act *Henry IV, Othello, Cymbeline,* revivals of Byron's *Marion Faliero* (1821), *Manfred* (1834), and so on. For a while fair-sized audiences rallied to the cause of the so-called "legitimate."

At the Princess' Theatre the successor to Kean the younger and Fechter was Boucicault, an actor who was primarily a playwright. There in 1864 he concocted a big success with *The Streets of London,* a reworking of *The Poor of New York* which he'd produced seven years earlier in New York City; and there in 1865, after a tryout in Liverpool, he staged his highly successful *Arrah-na-Pogue.* And for the first time at that house, and for almost the first time in the more than two hundred and fifty years since Shakespeare, the playwright again dominated the English stage. Boucicault's scripts helped to smash "the actor's desire to be the only figure of importance in the theater" [156] and reaffirmed the long-lost truth that the dramatist is, or should be, the prime talent, the honored original creative force, the mover and the shaper. Actors were demoted to their proper place as the interpreters of a play.

Unfortunately Boucicault re-emphasized the importance of the playwright rather shabbily. He did so not with any revealing insights and not with the power, glory, or bounce of words, but by using all the audience-drawing, old and new theatrical tricks: by clever and daring turns in the action, by cagily contrived climaxes, by rah-rah dabs of local color, by snatches at the contemporary and the natural, and by the skills of the scene-designer and the stage machinist. He virtually bypassed actors in his too frequent depictions of explosions, fires, snowstorms, avalanches, the "Interior of Newgate Prison," "a rocky Rook in the Mountains of Australia," the "Bridge of Notre Dame," a salt mine with "Solid Blocks of Salt," the hero tied by the villain to railroad tracks and rescued in the nick of time by the heroine from the wheels of a steaming, bell-ringing, painted locomotive, and so on. Shrewdly, skillfully he gave the hard-working, tired, middle-class public the thrills it wanted.

Boucicault had perfected his popular playwriting—he wrote or adapted something like one hundred fifteen full-length scripts—in the United States. After first acting under his own name in 1852, he seems to have had a falling out with Kean at the Princess' in 1853 and departed to seek his fortune in America—taking with him as sort-of wife Charles Kean's adopted daughter, Agnes Robertson (1833–1916), who had appeared in his *Prima Donna* (1851). In New York City she immediately acted at Burton's Theatre; and he now and then acted while he wrote. In 1856 they played together in his *Violet, or the Life of an Actress.* Then in 1857, when he was thirty-five, Boucicault arranged *The Poor of New York,* from *Les Pauvres de Paris* (1856) by Edouard Brisebarre and Eugene Nus, and presented it for a two-month run at Wallack's Theatre. Two years later, at the Winter Garden, of which he was co-manager, Miss Robertson and Joseph Jefferson acted in his successful *Dot,* based on a French version of Dickens' *A Cricket on the Hearth,* and in his original and even more successful *The Octoroon*. In 1860 Boucicault appeared in another of his box-office bonanzas, an adaptation called *The Colleen Braun*, at Laura Keene's Theatre.

That year Boucicault returned to London to repeat *The Colleen Braun* at the Adelphi; it was acted there, and in the provinces, about 360 times. At the same theater in 1861 he successfully repeated *The Octoroon*. In 1864 and 1865 he staged the two already mentioned plays at the Princess'. Also in 1865 he wrote a new version of *Rip Van Winkle* which Jefferson acted at the Adelphi for 170 consecutive nights before taking it to the United States.

Thus Boucicault proved that the playwright was all (if you overlooked the talent of Jefferson); and he made sure that the playwright would continue to be all. In his insistence on a definite percentage of the box-office receipts he "inaugurated an era of prosperity for dramatists—greater, perhaps, than that enjoyed by any other class of intellectual workers." For a play such as would have brought only sixty to one hundred pounds in 1850, Boucicault in 1866 received £6,500." [157]

And to rich playwright-in-control Boucicault "is to be traced the abandonment of the stock company. For it he substituted the practice, now all but universal in the English-speaking world, of engaging actors for individual productions only." [158] To him also can be traced the out-of-town tryout and touring of the single play.

IV

In 1865, two months after the premiere of *Rip Van Winkle*, a second influential playwright, more genteel and twinkling than Boucicault, and more worried about acting, offered London the first of six comedy-dramas that absolutely demanded a quiet realism in the playing. And when he announced, "I don't want actors; I want people that will do just what I tell them," he reiterated the dominance of the playwright, he stressed the need of a stage manager (or director), and he set out to establish "a school of acting excellent in its rendering of the prose . . . of modern life. . . ." [159] His name was T. (Thomas) W. Robertson (1829–1871).

Robertson had served "as a roving actor [of bit parts] on the Lincoln circuit, in London, and even in Paris"; he had been prompter for Mathews; and he had "adapted, translated, and borrowed with apology" from the French while writing a number of hack scripts. "He did much more: he caught the French delicacy and grace and acquired a profound knowledge of Parisian stagecraft. In him a love for the French methods was even stronger than his scorn for the shoddy English survivals." His first successful play was *David Garrick* (1864), taken from a French play, *Sullivan* by De Melesville, and written for Sothern at the Haymarket. Next he wrote *Society*, a comment on materialism, in which a mother advises her daughter to marry a rich dolt because "'Money can do everything." Refused by most of the London managers, it was first staged at Liverpool in May 1865, and then accepted by actress-manager Marie Wilton (1839–1921), who had performed in London since 1856 and won considerable fame at the Strand in burlesques by H. J. Byron (1834–1884). In April 1865 she opened the small Prince of Wales' Theatre with the "ambition to have every small part in a comedy played as well as possible, and after continued preparation. We began," she said later, "with three weeks' rehearsal for a play, afterwards [in 1870] extended to six, since to a couple of months, and in some cases longer." [160]

Robertson himself rehearsed *Society*, sparing "no pains . . . to have his somewhat novel type of characters understood and acted as he wished." The comedy was first presented in November 1865 with Miss Wilton, her future husband, Squire Bancroft (1841–1926), and another newcomer, John (Fairs) Hare (1844–1921), prominent in the cast. It "soon became the talk of the town" and ran for 150 nights; and it was revived by the Bancrofts—in 1868, 1874, and 1881—for a total record of nearly 500 showings. Then in September 1866 Robertson's *Ours*, after a tryout in Liverpool, began another 150-night run at the Prince of Wales'; and it was revived five times for a total of 700 performances. *Caste*, first produced in 1867, chalked up a record of 256 original performances, and with three revivals, a grand total of 650. *Play* (1868) ran 106 nights with no revivals. *School*, acted first in 1869, proved to be the record breaker with an original run of 381 performances and a total run of 800 performances. *M.P.* (1870) was acted for only 156 nights and never revived. "This calculation makes in all," according to Bancroft, "nearly 3,000 performances of the Robertson comedies, representing, in fact, the evenings, counting rehearsals and deducting Sundays, of ten years of life!" [161]

The super-success of the Bancrofts allowed them to hire actors "for special parts and runs of plays instead of for fixed and lengthened periods," to abolish the old custom of giving leading actors benefit performances each season, and to increase salaries "to an extraordinary extent." [162] They also eventually reduced a program to a single play, and first regularly scheduled midweek and Saturday matinees.

But the Bancrofts were both happy and unhappy about the long runs. They are, as Squire explained, "wonderfully remunerative to the manager, and a great relief from anxiety and work, but must be, eventually, very destructive to our art. After about fifty consecutive nights, in my poor belief, the actor has done all in his power with any part; to say nothing of having then played it to the most appreciative audiences. . . . I think I am inclined, in talking of long runs, to remember the words of the immortal Siddons, when she first entered Drury Lane Theatre, before the original enormous size of its interior was reduced. The great actress looked quietly round the vast building, and then said, with a sigh: 'Behold the tomb of the drama!' " [163]

The old-school actors in old plays couldn't compete with Robertson and the Bancrofts, nor with Boucicault who in 1868 erased the failure of his *How She Loves Him* (1867), as produced by the Bancrofts, with a long run of *After Dark* (from the French of Dennery and Grangé) at the Princess'. Therefore, in mid-1869 the management of Drury Lane surrendered and announced as its coming attraction *Formosa; or The Railroad to Ruin* by Boucicault. "I am neither a literary missionary nor a martyr," explained F. B. Chatterton in a letter to the *Times*. "I am simply the manager of a theater, a vender of intellectual entertainment to the London public and I found that *Shakespeare spelt ruin*. . . . In the extremity to which I was led by my faith in the fine taste of the upper classes for the poetic drama, I turned to the dramatist who has made the fortune of more than one manager in London. I need not say with what result. . . . the amount taken daily at my box-office before the doors open . . . to see *Formosa* exceeds the gross contents of my theater to witness *Macbeth*." *Formosa* ran for six months, with Henry Irving in the cast part of that time, and reportedly netted £12,000.[164] In 1875 Boucicault starred in the title role of *The Shaughraun* (1872), which he'd first produced in the United States. The play netted him more than $500,000.

But it was Robertson, joined with the Bancrofts, who finally established in England a realistic school of acting and production. He wasn't imaginative, even in a phoney way like Boucicault; but he was adept at copying onstage "a realism of *milieu*, a *milieu* which dictated the manners of the people who appeared in it." As perhaps the first British dramatist "who could really lay claim to belonging to the realistic school," he centered attention in his comedies on the "trappings and trifles of realistic everyday" and upon characters who, though thin and sentimentalized, and still addicted to asides and soliloquies, spoke and moved with a kind of external truth to life. He conceived "of stage realism as a complete whole. Others before him had penned scenes taken (more or less) from ordinary life; others, too, had introduced real objects, or their theatrical semblances, to the boards." Robertson coordinated all those efforts; and he did it so effectively that at his death in 1871 "The interest aroused by the novelty of seeing people behave on the stage as they did in real life, and the pleasure aroused by the careful finish in all details of mounting to make the stage resemble the surroundings of normal living, combined to discredit in large part the players who acted in the traditional repertory by traditional methods. A new ideal of realism had been set up, and audiences had been given new standards by which to judge dramatic productions." [165]

Realistic acting then, of course, was nearly a hundred years less realistic than it is today. Arthur Wing "Pinero, indeed, has pointed out that originally the Bancrofts insisted upon handling realism in theatrical terms, and did not make the mistake of their followers of trying to translate reality bodily to the stage. These 'seasoned and experienced actors and actresses,' he wrote, 'recognized that acting is an imitation of life, not a reproduction; and so at the beginning the teacups and saucers were handled in such a way as to be entertaining to the occupants of the back row of the gallery.' " The new acting at best represented "realism . . . in conscious progress." [166]

At the Prince of Wales' Robertson taught the actor (1) to replace *bravura* exhibitions of old-hat elocution with a "spirit of refinement," a "reserved force," a more natural kind of underplaying. "He . . . taught the actor not to act, not to want to act—if acting meant a sheer joy in acting, a gusto, an authority, a power of voice and body, a desire to be observed 'from tip to toe,' to rivet the audience's attention upon himself and hold it there." He taught the actor (2) to concentrate on more lifelike gestures and movement and stage business, on "doing little things well." Acting's "old expansiveness, its huge gestures, its operatic largeness, its full-fledged romanticism," were slowly "domesticated, if not altogether house-broken." He taught the actor (3) to value "the company as a whole," to concentrate on teamwork or *ensemble* in an effort to give each production "a unity of tone." "Perfection in *ensemble*," it was agreed, "is the purpose of the theater, the purpose of acting. . . ." [167]

Because of his striving for an external realism in acting and in all the departments of production, Robertson was more influential as stage manager than as playwright. Stage management, or directing, wasn't as some of his contemporaries believed "absolutely invented by him." No one man did that. Many authors before Robertson had in one way or another conducted rehearsals of their own plays. But as early as 1864, before he joined the Bancrofts, Robertson was convinced that "The Stage Manager is the man who should direct everything behind the scenes. He should be at one and the same time a poet, an antiquarian, and a costumer; and possess sufficient authority, from ability as well as office, to advise with a tragedian as to a disputed reading, to argue with an armorer as to the shape of a shield, or to direct a wardrobe-keeper as to the cut of a mantle. He should understand the military science like a drill-sergeant, and be as capable of handling crowds and moving masses as a major-general. He should possess universal sympathies, should feel with the sublime, and have a quick perception of the ludicrous. Though unable to act himself, he should be able to teach others. . . ." At the Prince of Wales' Theatre Robertson met all those requirements. Then at other theaters other men copied him. And this insistence on a "disciplinary change in the conduct of the theater," this entrusting the whole life of a play to the over-all authority of one man—to either the playwright or to his representative, the director—has been called "the most primary and significant step forward of the century." [168]

Most people, as the long runs attested, liked the novel attempt of the Robertsonians to exhibit in comedies "faithful copies of the outside manners of the time." Critics liked especially the new emphasis on *ensemble* playing; they teased for more of the same by praising the actors of the Comédie-Française, who sought refuge in London during the Franco-Prussian War

(1870–71), "as representing an ideal unapproached by even the Prince of Wales' company, and an object lesson in the realization of acting as an art." [169]

Other people, however, as always, resented the new. They objected to the "shrinkage in acting": the substitution of *ensemble* for the electricity of the gifted individual or star, of chatter for elocution, of realistic for pictorial movement. They complained, in effect, that the new acting in its laudable desire to avoid the overemphasis of the old "was rushing to the other extreme of underemphasizing points by covering them with a haze of byplay and naturalistic business." Modern actors just weren't acting any more. They could only reproduce politely observed rather than grandly imagined characters; they were not "equal to those parts in which the language rises above the commonplace." The Bancroft production in 1874 of *The School for Scandal* missed success, some said, because it was loaded with naturalistic scenery and appointments and naturalistic "touches" in the characterizations. The general effect was only "to emphasize mediocre and feeble acting, incapable of meeting the challenge of Sheridan's dialogue and characters." And the Bancroft *The Merchant of Venice* in 1875 failed bleakly because Charles Coghlan (1842–1899) acted Shylock naturally—because, according to critic Dutton Cook (1829–1883), "a school of acting has been established excellent in its rendering of the prose, the affectation, the languor, and the drawing-room undemonstrativeness of modern life and fashion, but peculiarly unsuited to present histrionic exhibitions of loftier and more heroic nature." Cook protested against "efforts to subdue the poet to the tameness of modern life, to reduce his sustained speeches to disjointed chat, and to impart to his plays generally an air of the boudoir or the drawing room." [170]

Criticism like that was disturbing. The Bancrofts never tried Shakespeare again, and never tackled tragedy. They sensed their limitations. They knew they could act "naturally" in modern comedies, and maybe in some modern dramas, but they didn't know how to be lifelike in Shakespeare or in tragedies. Perhaps they realized that acting cannot be "natural" in some plays. Certainly Salvini, they agreed, was great as Othello. His impersonation "lives in our memory as the grandest and completest tragic effort that we ever saw." [171] Yet he wasn't—"natural."

V

In 1875 critic George Henry Lewes (1817–1878) in his valuable book, *On Actors and the Art of Acting*, announced that expert players needn't be very brainy (as brainy, say, as John Stuart Mill, or John Dalton, or Disraeli). "With all the best wishes in the world," he wrote, "I cannot bring myself to place the actor on a level with the painter or the author. I cannot concede to the actor such parity of intellectual greatness. . . . Acting is an art very much more dependent on special aptitudes than on general intellectual vigor; a man may be . . . a marvellous actor with an amount of information . . . or of critical insight which would excite the pity of a quarterly reviewer." Lewes gently reminded actors that often an audience enjoys and applauds a *part*, a character as conceived by the playwright, rather than the *acting* of it.[172]

But Lewes loved acting and admired actors; he even tried the stage for a while; but in due time he apparently decided that he lacked the personal qualifications and "the mimetic flexibility of organization which could alone have enabled him to *personate* what he conceived." He also decided that "people generally overrate a fine actor's genius, and underrate his trained skill. They are apt to credit him with a power of intellectual conception and poetic creation to which he has really a very slight claim, and fail to recognize all the difficulties which his artistic training has enabled him to master." And he proceeded in his writings to search out the highly respectable, difficult, "special training necessary to make an actor." [173]

First, according to Lewes, "The very separation of Art from Nature involves . . . calculation." "Acting is an Art" because it observes "that cardinal principle in all art, the subordination of impulse to law, the regulation of all effects with a view to beauty." In acting, he continues, "Every detail is deliberative, or has been deliberated. . . . The sudden flash of suggestion which is called inspiration may be valuable, it may be worthless: the artistic intellect estimates the value, and adopts or rejects it accordingly." The actor's taste or "discretion must tell him when he has hit upon the right tone and right expression, which must first be suggested to him by his own feelings. In endeavoring to express emotions, he will try various tones, various gestures, various accelerations and retardations of the rhythm; and during this tentative process his vigilant discretion will arrest those that are effective, and discard the rest." In acting "As in all art, feeling lies at the root, but the foliage and flowers, though deriving their sap from emotion, derive their form and structure from the intellect." In an echo from Diderot he decides that the actor "is a spectator of his own tumult; and though moved by it, can yet so master it as to select from it only these elements which suit his purpose. We are all spectators of ourselves; but it is the peculiarity of the artistic nature to indulge in such introspection even in moments of all but the most disturbing passion, and to draw thence materials for art." [174]

Second, Lewes is sure that acting is symbolical, not actual, because "All art is symbolical." He says that onstage "We do not admire a man for being old, but we admire him for miming age"; he implies that we do not admire an actor for being the character, but we admire him for acting it; and that we do not admire an actor for being angry, but we admire him for communicating anger. An actor, he explains, must, for instance, familiarize himself with anger by watching not only himself but *others*, must next feel "a vivid sympathy" with that emotion, and finally must express it truly but *with art,* with calculation, with design if the result is to be more than the mere turbulence of nature. It's indisputable, he claims, "to those who know anything of art, that the mere presence of genuine emotion would be such a disturbance of the intellectual equilibrium as entirely to frustrate artistic expression." [175]

Third, Lewes separates sometime inseparables in order to emphasize the point that in acting "The powers of conception and the powers of presentation are distinct." The actor must have the ability to conceive the creation of another mind and to feel "a vivid sympathy" with what he is to represent, but he is finally required to do more than that. Acting, "because it is a *representative* art, cannot be created by intelligence or sensibility (however necessary these may be for the perfection of the art), but must always depend upon the physical qualifications of the actor, these being the means of representation." The actor's sensibility and intelligence in all their "internal workings must be legible in the external symbols. . . ." The public, hunting for the actor's *creative* contribution, "sees only the look, hears only the tone. . . ." Therefore, the actor must possess—and is only original in so far as he does possess—the rare gift or, as in most cases, the trained skill to personate, to convey to an audience vocally and visually, what he finds in a script. In short, the actor, like the violinist, is judged great, is "the creative artist," [176] primarily because of the skill with which he handles his instrument—which is himself.

In summary, Lewes declares that what the actor "can *express* [in words-plus] gives him his distinctive value." His "excellences . . . depend solely on his means of physical expression," on his tones, tempos, pauses, rhythms (and "very few seem to suspect that it is . . . a primary requisite in an actor that he should know how to *speak*"), on his looks, gestures, movement, stage business. And the actor tries to "express his feelings in symbols universally intelligible," in symbols that "have a certain grace and proportion to affect us esthetically," and in symbols uniquely his own and not those "employed for other characters by other actors." "Good acting, . . . like good writing, is remarkable for its individuality." [177]

But in his admiring analysis of the actor's peculiar skills Lewes didn't quite know what to say about the new "Natural Acting." It seems at first to have baffled him, confused him, made him defensive. Finally he took a definite stand. "I have always," he said, "emphatically insisted on the necessity of actors being true to nature in the expression of natural emotions, although the technical conditions of the art forbid the expressions being exactly those of real life. . . ." And, thinking perhaps of Shakespeare's plays, he asked if "an actor, having to represent a character in situations altogether exceptional, and speaking a language very widely departing from the language of ordinary life, would be *true* to the nature of that character and that language, by servilely reproducing the manners, expression, and intonations of ordinary life? The poet is not closely following nature; the poet is ideal in his treatment; is the actor to be less so?" "The supreme difficulty of the actor," he continued, "is to represent ideal character with such truthfulness that it shall affect us as real, not to drag down ideal character to the vulgar level. . . . [And] just as the language is poetry, or choice prose, purified from the hesitancies, incoherences, and imperfections of careless daily speech, so must [the actor's] utterance be measured, musical, and incisive—his manner typical and pictorial." [178]

Lewes also admitted that "naturalness being truthfulness, it is obvious that a coat-and-waistcoat realism demands a manner, delivery, and gesture wholly unlike the poetic realism of tragedy and comedy; and it has been the great mistake of actors that they have too often brought with them into the drama of ordinary life the style they have been accustomed to in the drama of ideal life." Yet he insisted that "Verse is not to be spoken as prose" and that "Prose is not to be spoken exactly as in the street." His final statement on the new acting reads as follows: "The nearer the approach to everyday reality implied by the author in his characters and language— the closer the coat-and-waistcoat realism of the drama—the closer must be the actor's imitation of everyday manner; but even then he must idealise, i.e. select and heighten—and it is for his tact to determine how much." [179]

VI

Like Lewes the leading new English actors had in due time to decide whether to accept or to reject "natural acting." Among them were vigorous Barry Sullivan (1824–1891); Hermann Vezin (1829–1910) and Mrs. (Jane Thomson) Vezin (1827–1902); popular Adelaide (Elizabeth Ann Brown) Neilson (1846–1880); Charles Wyndham (1837–1919); Madge Kendal (1848–1935), playwright Robertson's sister; Ellen Terry; and Henry Irving.

Ellen Terry (1848–1928), another daughter of actors, first performed professionally at the age of eight with her father and sister in Kean's 102-night run of The Winter's Tale in 1856; and appeared in ten more child roles with his company until he left the Princess' Theatre in 1859. Next she toured, acted at the Royalty, in stock at Bristol and Bath where, she said, she gained "the experience of my life," [180] and finally at the Haymarket for a season with Sothern. Then in 1863 at the age of fifteen, after impersonating forty roles, she left the theater and married painter George F. Watts. In 1866–68 she acted again, in ten new parts mostly at the New Queen's Theatre, and once more retired from the stage to "set up house" with archaeologist, architect, and scene designer Edward W. Godwin (1833–1886) and to give birth to Gordon Craig. In 1874, when she was twenty-six, Ellen Terry returned to the stage, acted Portia in the Bancroft's The Merchant of Venice, which ran for only three weeks in 1875, and remained to appear in four additional plays at the Prince of Wales'. Thus by the time she was twenty-seven she'd impersonated seventy-six different characters.

Henry (John Henry Brodribb) Irving (1839–1905) did better than that. He was driven to do better than that because, as Ellen Terry observed, he "at first had everything against him as an actor. He could not speak, he could not walk, he could not *look*. He wanted to do things in a part, and he could not do them." So, he translated his love for acting into a titanic will to succeed in that art. Beginning in 1854, when he was fifteen, he studied at the City Elocution Class in London and performed in amateur theatricals; two years later he changed his name to Irving and went to work professionally in the provinces. By 1859, when he failed in his London debut at the Princess', he had acted something like an incredible number of 400 different characters in more than 350 plays. Then for the next seven years he acted 180 new roles at Dublin, Glasgow, Birmingham, Liverpool, and for five seasons at the Theatre Royal in Manchester.[181] There with the American Edwin Booth, five years his senior, he portrayed Laertes, Cassio, Bassanio, and Buckingham.

In 1866, when Irving was twenty-eight, he was engaged as actor and stage manager at the St. James' Theatre, London. In one season he appeared in ten plays and became fairly well known to the public. During the summer of 1867 he spent a month in Paris at the Théâtre-Italien in Sothern's cast of *Our American Cousin*. And he haunted the Théâtre-Français; "he bowed in veneration before the silver-tongued Delaunay, who [at the age of fifty], with studied periods and melodious emphasis, conveyed the ardor of young love with grace and perfection, . . . before the rich profundity of Gôt's tragicomedy, and before the finished byplay between Jean-Baptiste Bressant and Madame Plessy in the most artificial of comedies. He watched with something near jealousy young Coquelin, three years his junior, yet already steeped in the delivery and posture of tradition, free to develop his genius with materials of which he was already a master." [182] Back in London for four seasons, 1867–71, Irving acted twenty-seven parts at the St. James', the New Queen's, Drury Lane. Among them were Petruchio opposite Ellen Terry as Katharine; Bill Sykes in a three-month run of *Oliver Twist*; Cool in *London Assurance* along with Mathews, Webster, Buckstone, Sothern, and Mrs. Keeley; and the villain in Boucicault's *Formosa*.

After seventeen years of unceasing study and practice Irving was an actor who knew his business. He was ready to be a star.

Near the end of 1871, at the age of thirty-three, Irving was hired as leading man and stage manager for the Lyceum Theatre. In his second month there "he directed every piece of business" of every actor and starred as Mathias in *The Bells*, a thriller about mesmerism, adapted by Leopold Lewis (1828–1890) from *Le Juif polonaise* by Émile Erckmann (1822–1899) and Alexandre Chatrian (1826–1890). The cheers and the notices were extravagant. *The Bells* ran for 150 nights, and Irving "became a personage who excited the curiosity of the literary and fashionable world." Next year he directed and starred in *King Charles I*, written in verse by Gorman Wills (1828–1891); the six-month run established him as the top-ranking English actor. In 1873 he asserted "his supremacy in the much-disputed field of higher drama" by acting for four months Macready's famous *Richelieu*. "The *Times* hailed his performance as 'tragic acting in the grandest style'; Clement Scott in the *Observer* condemned it whole-heartedly, finding it either dull or incoherent and punctuated by 'whirlwinds of noise which create applause mainly owing to an irresistible but still unhealthy excitement.' Dutton Cook dismissed the whole affair contemptuously; Joseph Knight gave it qualified praise but re-iterated his warnings against exaggeration." [183]

Then for four weeks in 1874 Irving acted Mathias at night and rehearsed his company in *Hamlet*. The tragedy ran for 200 performances, a record without precedent for a Shakespearean production. He proved that Shake-speare carefully acted, acted to the hilt, spelled success. Irving became one of Queen Victoria's celebrities—like Tennyson (1809–1892), Anthony Trollope (1815–1882), John Ruskin (1819–1900), and Matthew Arnold (1822–1888).

❦ AMERICAN ACTORS

By the time the United States was one hundred years old the stage there was flourishing. In New York City, for instance, theaters were con-tinually being built, burned, and rebuilt. After the Park was destroyed by fire in 1848, the chief houses were the Bowery (1826, 1828, 1837, 1839, 1845); the Broadway (1847, 1861), where *Caste* was staged in 1867; Burton's (1848), the first "house of Boucicault," where E. L. Davenport acted *Hamlet* in 1856; and Niblo's Garden (1828, 1849). Then in 1852 Brougham's Lyceum (1850) became (James) Wallack's; in 1856 English born American actress Laura (Mary Moss) Keene (*c.* 1820–1873) opened her own theater, seating 2,500, which in 1863 became the Olympic; and in 1859 the Metropolitan (1854), where Rachel acted in 1855, became the Winter Garden, and a New Bowery, seating 2,500, was erected. Finally, in 1869 Booth opened his theater to an audience of 1,807 with *Romeo and Juliet*, and Augustin Daly (1838–1899) took over the Fifth Avenue Theatre with Robertson's *Play*, building a second Fifth Avenue Theatre in 1873.

The plays offered to the public were, as before, mostly English. Some dramatists, however, began to put together American scripts; but their efforts were mostly shoddy; the writing did not compare with other American writ-ing, which had progressed from the "Leatherstocking Tales" (1827–41) by James Fennimore Cooper (1789–1851) to *The Scarlet Letter* (1850) by Nathaniel Hawthorne (1804–1864), *Moby Dick* (1851) by Herman Melville (1819–1891), and *Walden* (1854) by Henry Thoreau (1817–1862). A dozen of the top successes were: the 1853 dramatization of Harriet Beecher Stowe's (1811–1896) *Uncle Tom's Cabin* by actor George L. Aiken (1830–1876), which originally ran for 300 performances at the New National (1839); the poetic, artificial *Francesca da Rimini* (1855) by George H. Boker (1823–1890), produced at the Broadway with Davenport starred as Lanciotto;

Boucicault's *The Poor* (or *Streets*) *of New York* (1857) which ran for one month at Wallack's, and his *The Octoroon* (1859), acted for two months at the Winter Garden; Daly's adaptation, *Leah the Forsaken* (1863), at Niblo's Garden; English Mrs. Henry Wood's (1814–1887) tearful *East Lynne* (1861) dramatized for the Winter Garden in 1863 by Clifton W. Tayleur (1831–1887); Boucicault's *Rip Van Winkle*; the musical *The Black Crook* (1866), partly written by Charles M. Barras, which held the stage at Niblo's Garden for seventeen months or 474 performances; Daly's *Under the Gaslight* (1867) and his *Man and Wife* (1870), adapted from a novel by Wilkie Collins (1824–1889), which ran for ten weeks with a cast that included Clara (Morrison) Morris (1848–1925), English born Mrs. George H. Gilbert (1821–1904), and Fanny Davenport (1850–1898); *Saratoga* (1870), a comedy by the country's first truly professional playwright, Bronson Howard (1870–1908); and Daly's *Pique* (1875) which continued at the New Fifth Avenue Theatre for 238 performances and launched Fanny Davenport as a star at a salary of $200 a week. In the cast at $80 a week was British Maurice (Herbert Blythe) Barrymore (1847–1905), the father of Lionel, Ethel, and John. His brother-in-law John Drew (1853–1927) was paid $50 a week.

American acting in such plays was unperturbedly conventional. It pleased; it was often lively and often in good taste; but that's about all. No playwrights in a land of energized newness came forward with anything newly shaped or newly said to stretch the skills of the players beyond the ordinary. No critics, as in France, examined the art of acting and worked out theories about it. No innovators, as in England, challenged old fashions and at least tried for something more novel, more real, more truthful in impersonation. In the United States the theater as one of the arts was only a pleasant extra, a place to go for a laugh or a thrill, a place where shrewd managers could make money by offering democracy's crowds a little culture. And actors were only rather odd people who earned a soft living by being glamorous.

In the 1860's Charlotte Cushman and Edwin Forrest were eclipsed by Joseph Jefferson and Edwin Booth. The former brought his new *Rip Van Winkle* from London to the Olympic in 1866, when he was thirty-seven, acted it there again for two months in 1867, at Booth's Theatre for five months in 1869, and after that everywhere for years all over the country. Although Jefferson was expert as Asa Trenchard in *Our American Cousin*, as Caleb Plummer in *Dot*, Salem Scudder in *The Octoroon*, Bob Brierly in *The Ticket-of-Leave-Man*, and Bob Acres in *The Rivals*, he was life-long perfect and famous as the folksy Rip.

As a realistic actor of virtually one role Jefferson sensed that "The methods by which actors arrive at great effects vary according to their natures; this renders the teaching of the art by any strictly defined lines a difficult matter." He advised, "It is necessary to be cautious in studying elocution and gesticulation lest they become our masters instead of our servants. . . . But even at the risk of being artificial, it is better to have studied these arbitrary rules than to enter a profession with no knowledge whatever of its mechanism. . . . In . . . the acting of a part," he said, "nothing should be left to chance." However, "The exhibition of artistic care . . . does not alone constitute great acting. The inspired warmth of passion in tragedy and the sudden glow of humor in comedy cover the artificial framework with an impenetrable veil: this is the very climax of great art. . . ." Jefferson believed that the great error in acting is to "imagine that because we understand the matter, we are necessarily conveying it to others," and that the great aid is listening as though for the first time, and then "even . . . hesitating as if for want of words to frame the reply," without becoming "slow and prosy." Because actors "must not be natural but appear to be so." [184]

Edwin Booth, America's greatest actor, first went onstage in 1849, when he was sixteen, in such roles as Laertes, Macduff, Gratiano, and Edgar in support of his father. In 1850 he made his debut in New York City, in 1851 he impersonated Richard III, and in 1852 he went West to shine up his acting in San Francisco and the mining towns of California. Four years later, in 1856, he determined to conquer the East. At Baltimore, Richmond, Mobile, Memphis, Louisville, Chicago, Detroit, and Boston he appeared in *Hamlet*, *Richard III*, *A New Way to Pay Old Debts*, Colman's *The Iron Chest* (1791), and *Richelieu*. And in mid 1857 he returned as a star to New York City as Richard III at the Metropolitan Theatre. "Tremendous untrained power and unfocused energy, an interior nervousness that showed in his acting: these were some of the flaws, possible seeds of greatness, that the critics pointed out." [185]

Then in 1860 twenty-seven year old Booth for the first time directly competed with the actor for whom he'd been named, fifty-four-year-old Edwin Forrest, who for three decades had been the supreme American star. The latter portrayed Lear, Othello, Macbeth, Richard III, and Richelieu at Niblo's Garden; Booth portrayed Hamlet, Richard III, and Richelieu at the Winter Garden and "made his first really deep impression on New York." Since he had played there last "his acting had gained in depth and control. He still ranted occasionally, still was best in the lurid, mordant roles that gave his energy something to bite on, but his method was fining down. His individual style was forming, less noisy, more natural than his father's. . . ." Next year, when Booth feared that "his work was beginning to grow stale in commercial America, where 'art degenerates below the standard of a trade,' " he sailed for England.[186] During the first year of the Civil War he repeated Richard III, Giles Overreach, and Richelieu, and tried Shylock to fair success at the Haymarket; in Manchester and Liverpool he acted Hamlet, Shylock, and Othello.

Back in New York City with added prestige in 1862, Booth managed the Winter Garden in successful competition with Forrest at Niblo's Garden. And "While at Antietam dead men lay rotting on the blasted fields (14,000 Federal casualties, over 11,000 Confederate), the theaters were crammed to their flag-draped roofs." There in 1864 he acted Brutus for one gala evening with his brothers Junius and John Wilkes as Cassius and Mark Antony, and next night began his record one-hundred-performance run of *Hamlet*, which ended eighteen days before the surrender at Appomattox on April 9, 1865. Five days later his brother assassinated Lincoln. Edwin Booth quit the theater. In January 1866 he returned to the stage as Hamlet; and when the audience saw him seated in the middle of the Danish court "they leaped to their feet and cheered and cheered. . . . Booth trembled in his carved chair; his head drooped to his breast. After several moments of this pandemonium, he slowly stood up and bowed very deep. His eyes were swimming with tears. And as the ovation by the audience said many things, so Booth's deliberately low obeisance meant much more than the thanks of a player who must please to live. It was the acknowledgement of a man long on trial, to whom acquittal by his peers has restored his honor." Later he toured "half the states in the hard-won Union," acting for at least eighteen months in two years.[187]

In 1869 he opened the magnificently modern Booth's Theatre in New York and, like Charles Kean, directed "imaginatively and painstakingly the productions he starred in." These included *Hamlet, Richelieu, The Merchant of Venice, Othello, Much Ado About Nothing*, and the American John Payne's *Brutus* (1818). Top actors in his casts were Edwin Adams (1834–1877) and Lawrence Barrett (1838–1891), a classicist who "drew the line at realism," [188] and whose salary was soon increased from $250 to $400 a week. For a few years Booth held his own against foreigners Fechter and Salvini, and sponsored such modern attractions as Jefferson in *Rip Van Winkle* and minstrel Lotta Crabtree (1847–1924) in Brougham's *Little Nell* and the *Marchioness* (1866). But Booth wasn't a manager; and he wasn't modern enough. On his fortieth birthday, at the end of 1873, he was bankrupt and out of management. Two years later he acted Hamlet at Daly's Fifth Avenue Theatre with a cast that included Maurice Barrymore as Laertes and John Drew as Rosencrantz. Then for the first time he acted Richard II and King Lear.

Booth was no rebel, no innovator. Trained by his father in the old school of acting in the old repertory, he didn't relish new plays or the new "natural" acting. With admirable taste he undoubtedly softened and dignified the excesses of standard elocution until as "an expounder of the text" he was hailed as being eminently modern and natural. But he was neither. His readings were always theatrical. Like Lewes, Booth believed that the elevation of Shakespeare's poetry ought to be matched with an elevation of speech and gesture in the actor. Never, probably, could he have excelled in an Ibsen play; nor would he have cared to perform in one. Booth was too unconcerned with realism, too steeped in the romantic, too rooted in traditions for that. "In the main," he once wrote, "tradition to the actor is as true as that which the sculptor perceives in Angelo, the painter in Raphael, and the musician in Beethoven. . . . Tradition, if it be traced through pure channels, and to the fountain head, leads one as near to Nature as can be followed by her servant Art." [189]

Some of the other leading players of the time were Matilda Heron (1830–1877), who first took stage in Philadelphia in 1851 and then, beginning in 1855, acted her version of *Camille* all over the United States; forceful John McCullough (1832–1885), comic Edward Harrigan (1845–1911), and dreamer Steele Mackaye (1842–1894), the only restless worrier about acting. He studied and demonstrated Delsarte. At a Boston recital in 1871 he exhibited "a number of 'chromatic scales' or 'gamuts' of facial expression, as he called them. . . . In exhibiting these gamuts, he stood perfectly motionless, except in his countenance, and, starting from the normal expression, would make his face pass very slowly through a dozen grades of emotion to some predetermined phase, and thence he would descend, reversing the previous steps, to perfect repose. . . . Thus, he showed a chromatic state of emotion running through satisfaction, pleasure, tenderness and love to adoration, and, having retraced his steps, descended facially through dislike, disgust, envy, and hate to fury. Again he exhibited the transitions from repose through jollity, silliness, and prostration, to utter drunkenness; and made a most astonishing but painful spectacle of his fine face, passing through all the grades of mental disturbance to insanity, and down all the stairs of mental weakness to utter idiocy.—The impression produced was at once very lively and very profound." In that same year, in his system of Harmonic Gymnastics, Steele claimed he invented for acting the principle of *relaxation*.[190]

❋ THE MEININGER

The best and most influential ensemble acting in Europe was realized under the firm guidance of draughtsman and painter Georg II (1826–1914) of the minor Duchy of Saxe-Meiningen. In 1866, at the age of forty, he became head of his family and decided that the plays produced in his ninety-year-old, subsidized court theater "should not be as indifferently acted and staged as those he had seen in other court theaters and even in the imperial theaters." After all, he had attended and envied some of the Charles Kean productions in London; and he was sure that by long, hard work in perfecting every detail of a performance he could surpass their excellences. First, he abolished in his theater the star system which "had resulted in a massive tradition of affectations and grandiose conventions. . . ." Second, he began working out methods "to achieve an intensified reality and give remote events [in old standard plays] the quality of actuality, of being lived for the first time. . . ." Third, he announced, "My anger is and will always be, now and as long as I live, against all frivolity in art." [191]

From 1866 until 1870 disciplinarian Duke Georg experimented. His two chief assistants were his wife, the former actress Ellen Franz (Freifrau Helene von Heldburg) (1839–1923), and writer-teacher Friedrich von Bodenstedt (1819–1892), who while in Moscow in 1841–43 had been impressed by the "superiority" "of the Russian village commune and artel over unhealthy Western individualism," and may have given his chief the idea of stressing theater ensemble at the expense of stars. Georg himself, after careful study of each script—usually by Schiller or Shakespeare—and after extensive research, designed scenes with a scholarly authenticity and with a half-built, half-painted plasticity that almost compelled the actors to move about *in* them, to do more than merely stand or crisscross in front of them while delivering lines. He insisted on literalness and "on the continuous and direct relation between the design of a setting and the actor's movement within it." He designed plans for physical action. Georg II also designed many "of the costumes complete to the minutiae of hats and headdresses and such accessories as swords, canes, pikes, and helmets." [192] He worked out new color and lighting effects; and emphasized sound effects and incidental music. Ellen Franz drilled the actors in correct and pure speech, in utterance that was declamatory, because how else could poetry be read? Von Bodenstedt served as the director who attempted to transform each production into a unified and dynamic whole.

Then in 1870 Ludwig Chronegk (1837–1891), who had joined the company in 1866 as a comedian, was appointed director. And for another four years the Duke worked "consistently toward the theater forms that were to make possible realism and naturalism." Historical accuracy in scenes, costumes, and properties became almost a fetish with the Meininger, as the company was called. "In the production of *Julius Caesar*, for instance, the leading actor was made up to look as much as possible like the portraits of Caesar on coins; he was dressed exactly as the Duke was satisfied the Romans dressed; finally, the setting imitated as nearly as possible actual Roman scenes as described in old books." And once "After the Duke had made a journey to Rome, he issued orders for an entirely new *mise-en-scène* for *Julius Caesar*, based on his observations." [193]

Chronegk's talent for directing was greater than von Bodenstedt's, and essential to the company's success. A martinet, he drove himself and others toward perfection; and when, after twenty years, he collapsed in 1890, the Meininger also collapsed. Director Chronegk was more than a mere traffic sign who prevented actors from bumping into or covering each other. Along with the Duke he taught the actors, for instance, "that people of the eighteenth century tended to stand with their heels together because of the influence of the minuet, but that people of the sixteenth century stood with their feet apart, according to contemporary engravings." He sensed, we can guess, that "the very meaning of certain words will depend on what the actors do at the moment of speaking them," [194] and he therefore coordinated motion with meaning. He integrated the movements of the actors, as individuals and as groups, into compositions that visually interpreted a script.

Chronegk centered much of his drill time on directing crowd effects. Like Georg II with his scenes, costumes, and properties, he worked tirelessly with his "walk-ons" to achieve a visual authenticity, a copy of the real thing, a naturalness. First, he divided them into small groups for separate training. Then he assigned an experienced actor from the company of seventy to each of the groups. Even top actors were used as "corporals" for the "supers." Each "corporal" was responsible for his group's efficiency onstage; he stood in front of them and led them in various movements, gestures, murmurs, cries. And Chronegk rehearsed each scene again and again and again until the ensemble effect was often stunning. In Schiller's *The Maid of Orleans*, for example, "The crowd packed a shallow square under the portals of Rheims Cathedral. The stage was too small to hold them as they waited for the first sight of the cortège; they disappeared off stage, strained against soldiers trying to keep a lane free, climbed on each other's backs, stood on tiptoe, hopped up and down, packed every spare ledge on a fountain, jammed the stairways of near-by houses, leaned over window-sills on each other's shoulders. The mounting excitement was carefully timed as the royal procession crossed the stage into the cathedral and increasing bursts of cheers greeted each notable, such as Dunois, when he was recognized. The crescendo of jubilation swelled at the sight of the dauphin under his canopy. All the while trumpets repeated a single theme adopted from one of Brahms' chorales, with clarion insistence that mounted higher and higher until at the appearance of Joan it reached a climax of frenzy that usually incited an echoing ovation from the audience." [195]

Effects like that took unheard of time to prepare. But Chronegk and the Duke took time. "Every play was rehearsed until it was ready. It was not produced until it was ready. Rehearsals when the company was not playing began at four or five and continued past midnight." And almost always "Settings and costumes were ready for the first rehearsals, also essential properties such as furniture or weapons and armor that might prove unwieldy in handling. . . . Nothing was too difficult to attempt, no attempt was abandoned before it had been tried again and again. At one rehearsal an actor waiting for his cue with a candelabra of four immense tapers found, when his scene was reached, that they were burnt out. Eleven lines in the preceding scene had been rehearsed two hours." And once for a battle scene the Duke insisted on a dead horse to give an actor "a position in which he could die in convincing fashion and at the same time turn his face to the audience. Hour after hour the stuffed lummox was dragged to every possible position, and in every one its four rigid legs made acting between them or over them ridiculous. But the Duke persisted, and finally solved the problem by turning the legs upstage so that [the actor] died in an effective pose supported by the animal's caparisoned back." [196]

Finally, in 1874, after eight years of hard work, Georg II was satisfied that his productions had achieved the perfection he expected of them. He sent the company under Chronegk on tour. In May, for the first time away from home, the Meininger performed *Julius Caesar* in Berlin and the company was a sensation. Then for seventeen seasons between 1874 and 1890 the Meininger visited thirty-eight cities, twenty in Germany, five in Austria, five in Russia

(fifty-seven performances in Moscow in 1885 and 1890, and thirty performances in Odessa in 1890), two in Holland, two in Belgium (twenty-nine performances in Brussels in 1888), and one each in Switzerland, England (fifty-
six performances in London in 1881), Denmark, and Sweden. During this
time 2,591 performances were given abroad and 286 performances at home for
a grand total of 2,877 showings of forty-one plays. Nine plays by Schiller were
acted 1,250 times, six by Shakespeare 820 times, three by Kleist 222 times, two
by Grillparzer 153 times, and two by Molière 112 times. The five most frequently staged plays were *Julius Caesar* (330 times), A *Winter's Tale* (233),
Schiller's *Wilhelm Tell* (223), *The Maid of Orleans* (194), and *Wallenstein's
Camp* (176).[197]

Everywhere the Meininger uniquely triumphed "without the aid of a single
player recognized as an actor of the first rank." The chief members of the
company were adequate, maybe more than adequate, but hardly outstanding.
They were old-fashioned; they were elocutionists; as Stanislavski observed,
they "brought little that was new into the old stagy methods of acting." [198]
Only two performers, Ludwig Barnay (1842–1924) and Josef Kainz (1858–
1910), later became stars in the modern German theater.

The Meininger triumphed because of their careful scene designs, costum-
ing, lighting, staging, and most of all because of "their splendid grouping and
management of crowds. . . ." Their work showed the value, the necessity, for
an over-all talent who could plan and control and unify every detail of a
production. They impressed "the French and Russian theaters through their
stress upon the director." [199] They proved by example that the easiest (and
most unimaginative) way for a director to unify a play was to make it in every
onstage detail—and eventually in every nuance of acting—a copy of life.

But the Meininger, and their followers, "overlooked the fact that the real
function of the theater is not to copy life, but to interpret plays, in which life
and characters are recreated by the imagination of the dramatist, and to find
for each of them a suitable form of artistic expression on the stage." Duke
Georg and Chronegk reproduced the photographically true to life or to historical documents and "overlooked the necessity for artistic formality on the stage.
. . . . A strictly historical production of one of the so-called historical plays
by Schiller or Shakespeare does not by any means interpret it, because neither
Schiller nor Shakespeare intended to reproduce mere history, but took an
historical subject as a means to express their own ideas on life and history.
They gave their own interpretations of historical characters, which they often
even placed in unhistorical circumstances." [200]

II

The Meininger were nonimaginative enough to make their acting *look*
more or less natural; but they couldn't make it *sound* natural, or conversational. They couldn't do that because the plays they appeared in were written

in a language elevated above the tone, rhythm, and diction of believable every-day. Before any late nineteenth-century acting—especially in serious or tragic plays—could be made to sound more nearly natural, actors had to be assigned familiar prose to speak. Norwegian Henrik Ibsen (1828–1906) was the play-wright who most effectively, most influentially, furnished them with the speech of the average man. Almost squelching his own considerable poetic talents, he set recognizable human beings in believable conversational conflict with each other over current social problems, and thus ushered in the modern realistic drama.

Ibsen moved slowly from the old to the new. At sixteen he left his birth-place, Skien, for the shipowner town of Grimstad where he became a pharmacist's assistant and a poet who wrote and had published in 1850 a noisy Roman tragedy in verse called Catiline; that same year he went to Christiania (Oslo), saw one of his short plays produced there, and took up journalism; next year, when he was twenty-three, he accepted a job to assist as dramatic author at the new Norwegian National Theater in Bergen, and soon he was appointed stage manager. For six years, from 1851 to 1857, Ibsen assisted with the staging of 145 plays, more than half of them by French authors, twenty-one by Scribe. And he wrote several plays, among them a failure, the Scribe-influenced, historical Fru Inger til Ostrat (Lady Inger of Östråt) (1855), and his first success, the ballad-like Gildet paa Solhaug (The Feast at Solhaug) (1856), which has been described as "Scribe's Bataille de Dames [1851] writ tragic." [201] In late 1857, when he was nearly thirty, Ibsen was appointed artistic director of the Norwegian Theater in Christiania, staged there in 1858 his saga-style Haermaendene paa Helgeland (The Vikings at Helgeland), virtually gave up playwriting, and helped the theater to fail by 1862.

That same year he wrote in verse his first, though ineffective, play about contemporary life, Kjaerlighedens Komedie (Love's Comedy). In it he bit-terly and autobiographically attacked smug surburban conventionality and showed that "inevitably marriage brings with it a dulling of aspiration and a supine acceptance of conventional codes." Then in 1865 his countryman, play-wright Björnstjerne Björnson (1832–1910), turned realist with De Nygifte (The Newly-Weds), "the first prose play on a contemporary theme in the modern Norwegian drama." It was produced with much success at Copen-hagen, Christiania, and Stockholm. But Ibsen wasn't tempted by realism. He was an idealist. He "looked toward the eternal stars." For most of the next ten years he composed only large, fiery, soaring "ethical idealism plays": [202] Kongsemnerne (The Pretenders) (1864), acted by the Meininger in Berlin in 1876; the dramatic poem Brand (1866), not acted until 1885; Peer Gynt (1867), not acted until 1876; and finally the massive, two part Kejser og Galilaeer (Emperor and Galilian [1873]).

In 1869, however, Ibsen had written a completely realistic play in prose, De Unges Forbund (The League of Youth), an almost photographic picture of liberal politicians "without a single monologue, indeed, without a single aside." Soon he began to believe that "The verse form has done the art of acting a great deal of harm. . . . [It] will hardly find any place worth mentioning in the drama of the near future; for the literary purposes of the future will certainly not be reconcilable with it." By 1875, after Björnson had "put problems into debate" in Redaktören (The Editor) (1874), an attack on unscrupulous journalism, and in En Fallit (A Bankruptcy) (1874), a portrayal of a dishonest businessman, Ibsen at the age of forty-seven took his eyes from the sky and focused his penetrating glance upon man and society. He became, for a while, a relentless realist. He forced actors to speak naturally, "in concise and incisive conversation such as people ought to carry on in the given circumstances but never do, because real life is not art." [203]

❋ REALISM RAMPANT BY 1875

New playwrights in a surge dominated the European theater in the last quarter of the nineteenth century. With a startling, not always popular realism or naturalism (an excessive, less selective form of realism) they for a while baffled and almost belittled actors by asking for more and more verisimilitude in characterizations, in stage speech and movement. They cued them to make psychologic rather than histrionic interpretations.

Before 1880 Ludwig Anzengruber (1839–1889) in the first modern Austrian play, Das vierte Gebot (The Fourth Commandment) (1877), realistically exposed the depravity of middle-class parents. Then Ibsen marked the parting of the ways between old and new drama by probing marriage and human motives in Et dukkehjem (A Doll's House) (1879); and its unstagy effect, according to some, made it "less like a play than like a personal meeting —with people and issues that seized us and held us, and wouldn't let go." [204]

In the next decade Ibsen composed a daring, bruising realistic masterpiece, Gengangere (Ghosts) (1881); José Echegaray (1832–1916) wrote a Spanish thesis play about the vicious power of society and of gossip, El Gran Galeoto (1881), better known as The World and His Wife; Ibsen in En folkefiende (An Enemy of the People) (1882) laughed at ideals trapped by majority rule and profit-making; Henri Becque (1837–1899) attacked greed with a "Bible of naturalism," Les Corbeaux (The Vultures) (1882); Björnson in Over oevne (Beyond Human Power I) (1883) looked hard at religious faith; Ibsen joined symbolism to realism in Vildanden (The Wild Duck) (1884); Becque dissected La Parisienne (The Woman of Paris) (1885), which failed at the Théâtre-Français because the actors declaimed instead of getting under the skins of their characters and speaking realistically in "voices like ours"; Tolstoy wrote a grim, appalling peasant tragedy, Vlastini (The Power of Darkness) (1886); August Strindberg (1849–1912), once a would-be actor, contended that true naturalism "loves to see that which cannot be seen every day," [205] and lacerated audiences with Fadren (The Father) (1887) and Fröken Julie (Miss Julie) (1888); and Gerhart Hauptmann (1862–1946), the greatest

German playwright since Schiller, pictured the unsavory details of a family's degradation in Vor Sonnenaufgang (Before Sunrise) (1889).

During the final ten years of the century Ibsen returned to harsh realism with Hedda Gabler (1890); Arno Holz (1863–1929) and Johannes Schlaf (1862–1941) proved influential with their naturalistic portrait, Die Familie Selicke (1890); Georges de Porto-Riche (1849–1930) examined with clinical detachment the human heart in Amoureuse (A Loving Wife) (1891); Giovanni Verga (1840–1922) continued to add brutal realism to the Italian stage with La Lupa (The She-Wolf) (1891); Hauptmann expertly photographed a crowd of workers in Die Weber (The Weavers) (1892); François de Curel (1854–1928) with Les Fossiles (The Fossils) (1892) brilliantly, almost poetically, depicted a dying aristocracy; Hermann Sudermann (1857–1929) contrived Die Heimat (Home, or Magda) (1893); Arthur Schnitzler (1862–1931) explored love in Die Liebelei (1895) and Ibsen explored hate in John Gabriel Borkman (1896); Anton Chekhov (1860–1904) orchestrated the complex nuances of life in Chika (The Seagull) (1896); Curel wrote Le Repas du lion (The Lion's Feast) (1897); Eugène Brieux (1858–1932) discussed loveless marriages via Les Trois filles de M. Dupont (The Three Daughters of Dupont) (1897); and Chekhov revised an earlier script as Diadia Vania (Uncle Vanya) (1899).

To all this new realism, or naturalism, before the end of the century no English or America playwright contributed significantly.

II

Richly realistic plays obviously required a new kind of interpretation. So, bossy men, not necessarily imaginative, and not necessarily tingling with a feel for art, but with enough simple common sense to know what was lifelike, took charge of productions. Thus realism nourished the first directors. And the first directors nourished realism. They had to do that; in their opposition to the old and their enthusiasm for anything new they didn't quite know how else to do what else. They tried for the easy verisimilar.

One of the stimulating early directors was André Antoine (1858–1943). As a lad he'd served as a member of the claque and as a supernumerary at the Théâtre-Français, and been rejected as a student actor by the Conservatoire. In 1883 he was a clerk at the Compagnie Parisienne de Gaz and later a member of the "Cercle Gaulois," one of the many amateur dramatic clubs of Montmarte which once a month performed plays. Finally, "with a passionate curiosity about things of the theater," and eager to perform in scripts by unknown writers, Antoine at his own expense set up the Théâtre-Libre and in March 1887 produced, directed, and acted in one subscription performance of four short plays in a hall seating not quite 350 people. One play caused a stir. Two months later, without "the slightest idea of becoming a professional actor or director," Antoine offered a second evening of new plays, one an old-style comedy in verse, the other a naturalistic picture of Apache life; and "all literary and artistic Paris came to see what was being done by the amateurs. . . ." They were responsive, pro and con; they especially liked the "more natural than studied" acting. At once Antoine searched for more new plays and more one-hundred-franc subscribers as he planned a full theatrical season for seven one-night performances for 1887–88. He was convinced "that the actor's 'profession' [the system of traditions taught at the Conservatoire] and the complacency of audiences had stifled all simplicity, life, and naturalness" onstage. And he was eager to demonstrate what he could do to liberate and enliven the theater "by following logic and common sense. . . ." [206] (But perhaps the excitement of creating, even creation itself, begins where common sense ends?)

In October 1887, with thirty-seven subscribers and tall debts, Antoine presented his opening bill, a dramatization of a Goncourt novel and a one-act blood-and-thunder Apache horror. Next month at his second offering 3,000 people tried for the 800 seats in the group's new hall. In December Antoine caused much spirited comment, favorable and unfavorable, with a naturalistic, cynical play in which a mother and daughter are mistresses of a family tutor who is finally accepted as a son-in-law by a complacent father. In February 1888 he acted with and directed his amateurs—"an employee of the Ministry of Finances, a secretary in a precinct police-station, an architect, a chemist, a traveling salesman, a wine-merchant, a bronze-manufacturer," a woman dressmaker, a bookbinder, a post-office worker—in a new translation of Tolstoy's banned *The Power of Darkness*. "The private performance awakened such curiosity that a public one had to be given." Conservative theatergoers didn't like it much; but the notices "were unanimous in pointing out the irreproachable and adequate (*we do not say perfect*) performances of the various characters in the play." By June 1888, the end of the first season, Antoine had presented seventeen new plays, eight long ones and nine short ones, all but the Tolstoy work for only a single performance. And since many of them, at least the most striking, were crudely naturalistic, the public was convinced, "in spite of all protestations, that the Théâtre-Libre was bound hand and foot to Zola's school." Critics praised Antoine, ten thousand francs in debt, for possessing "all the qualities which go to make up an excellent director, and it is directors we lack rather than actors." He had eliminated, they said, "all the theatricality of the conventional player and inspired in his company the same simplicity and naturalness which characterized his own acting." At his *avant-garde* theater, they continued, "it seems that there is no stage, and that the raised curtain . . . discloses people in their houses going about their affairs unconsciously and without knowing that they are watched." [207] Thus encouraged, Antoine presented eight more programs in the second season, 1888–89, and eight more in the third, among them in 1890 a brilliant failure, Ibsen's *Ghosts*, in which he carefully impersonated Oswald.

Also in 1890 Antoine published a brochure, *Le Théâtre Libre,* in which, along with other topics, he discussed acting. Boldly he found fault with the Conservatoire because it taught the student to develop "his voice as a *special* organ quite different from the voice he really possesses," to speak "with exaggerated enunciation," and via "fine speaking" to "forego those infinitely numerous nuances which could illuminate a character and give it more intense life. . . ." It also taught all students to gesture and to move "technically in the same manner." Such instruction, he believed, tended to kill the would-be player's "sincerity, *élan,* conviction," and that special emotional fever which should grip him during a performance. And worse, it more often than not stifled personality by reducing all temperaments to one level. Minus such training, with only good will and intelligence, Antoine pointed out, his own untaught amateurs (sparked now and then by a professional actor or two) had effectively made "characters live their daily lives" onstage, and by so doing had exposed traditional, formal, external methods as being "perhaps dangerous —and at the very least useless . . ." [208]

Although Antoine admired classical plays, and the high comedy acting of Réjane and the calculated tragic acting of Conservatoire trained Mounet-Sully, he was sure that "Since the theatrical style in the new works tends more toward the use of everyday conversation, the performer [in many instances] will no longer have to *declaim* in the narrow and classical sense of the term but will have to *talk,* a feat which will be found to be as difficult." Moreover, he will have to look his stage partner in the eye and talk to him instead of only at the audience. The performer will also have to use "the simple gestures and natural movements" of modern people in real life—and at times even turn his back to an audience. Furthermore (and oddly), the performer in action ought to be unconscious of his character's actions, just as in real life "we ourselves do stupid and criminal things without being conscious of them," and certainly without commenting on them. Finally, the performer, even when a star, must not "think only of amplifying and developing his own role and its effect . . . at the expense . . . of throwing the play entirely out of equilibrium," of destroying its artistic harmony and wholeness. He must know (as Antoine learned by watching the Meininger in Brussels in 1888) that ensemble playing is "the most complete and the most exquisite joy in the theater." [209]

Some years later, in 1903, Antoine summed up his chief notions about acting by saying that members of the Théâtre-Libre (then the Théâtre Antoine) company "do not 'recite.' They live their parts." That was the essence of their acting; that was their method. These actors know, he continued, "That movement is the actor's most intense means of expression; That their whole physical make-up is part of the character they represent, and that at certain moments in the action their hands, their back, and their feet can be more expressive than any oral ranting; That every time the actor is revealed beneath the character, dramatic continuity is broken. . . . They know too [as

Stanislavski was soon to know] that every scene in a play has a movement [a beat] all its own, subordinated in turn to the general movement of the play. . . ." [210]

Antoine also maintained "that actors should have no theories about the works which they perform. Their business is merely to play them—to interpret, to the best of their ability, characters which they may fail to understand" and emotions which they may fail to appreciate. In no case should an actor "try to modify a character. . . ." "The absolute ideal of the actor," he explained, "should be to make himself a keyboard, an instrument, marvelously tuned, on which the author may play at will. It is sufficient for him to have a purely physical and technical training, to make his body, face, and voice more supple; and an intellectual training that will permit him to understand simply what the author would have him express." Yet even then, thus reduced to its limits, the actor's art "still remains a conspicuously honorable and difficult one." [211]

For seven years at the Théâtre-Libre Antoine championed realism and vitalized French playwriting and acting. Beginning with his fourth, or 1890–91, season he offered each of his productions three times—at one public rehearsal and two subscription performances; and his company appeared in a few public performances at the Porte-Saint-Martin and then in Brussels. But in Paris his production of Ibsen's *The Wild Duck* was a dismal failure. "Ultra-realist plays were being produced everywhere and a pronounced reaction against them was plainly visible." [212] Five hundred scripts, however, were submitted to Antoine for the fifth season, which was saved by Curel's psychological *L'Envers d'une Sainte* (*The Reverse of a Saint*) and Brieux's raw *Blanchette*. Next season, 1892–93, Antoine produced notably Curel's *Les Fossiles*, Strindberg's *Miss Julie*, the very funny *Boubouroche* by Georges Courtelaine (1860–1929), and Hauptmann's *The Weavers*. But in 1894, in the middle of the seventh season, a tired, bankrupt, and defeated Antoine gave up the battle. Near the end of 1897, however, with Firmin Gémier (1866–1934) as his chief assistant, he opened the Théâtre Antoine and for nine more years continued to stage naturalistic and some verse plays and to raise the new profession of directing to an admirable level.

III

The new realism—or its extension into naturalism—was sponsored with varying success by followers of Antoine in Germany, England (but not in the United States), and Russia. In Berlin in 1889 "the Théâtre-Libre . . . brought about the establishment of the Freie Bühne" by a committee soon headed by Doctor of Philosophy and drama critic Otto (Abrahamsohn) Brahm (1856–1912), who was assisted by actor Emmanuel Reicher (1849–1924). They set out to present at the well-equipped Lessing Theater a monthly matinee subscription performance of maybe ten naturalistic plays a season with professional actors borrowed from Ernst von Possart's (1841–

1921) company there, from Adolf L'Arronge's (1838–1908) Deutsches Theater, and from Ludwig Barnay's Berliner Theater. "We are erecting a free theater," announced Brahm, "for the new art which faces truth and contemporary life." And "The motto of the new art . . . is the one word *Truth*." Reicher, anticipating Stanislavski, explained that "We no longer wish to merely play 'effective scenes,' but rather wish to present complete characters with the whole conglomerate of qualities with which they are endowed. We don't want to be anything else but human beings who find the emotions of the character to be represented from within and who express these with a simple, natural voice—regardless of whether that voice is beautiful and resonant, regardless of whether the accompanying gesture is gracious or not, and regardless of whether it fits in with the conception of stock types." The actor's task, he summed up, is to show "with the simplicity of nature [not art] a complete human being to the audience." [213] Not the essential content of a human being as uniquely imagined (rearranged, compressed, heightened) by the playwright. Not a human being given a special theatrical form. Only a recognizable, believable human being.

Since Brahm believed Ibsen to be the "pathfinder of the new dramatic art which came most close to real life," he began the Freie Bühne in September 1889 with a pre-Antoine production of *Ghosts*, and followed it next month with the feverish excitement of Hauptmann's naturalistic *Before Sunrise*. Three additional plays of the seven presented the first season were the Goncourt *Henriette Maréchal* (1865), Tolstoy's *The Power of Darkness*, and Anzengruber's *The Fourth Commandment*. Among the offerings of the next two seasons were Zola's *Thérèse Raquin*, Becque's *Les Corbeaux*, Strindberg's *The Father* and *Miss Julie*, and Hauptmann's *The Weavers* and *Einsame Menschen* (*Lonely Men*, or *Lives*) (1891). Each was carefully supervised, though not actually staged, by Brahm who insisted that "today's theater calls for the realistic style." "Let the actor study nature," he advised, "nothing more than that. Let him study nature in all her spiritual fullness: thus will he avoid banality and triviality. Let him study her outside himself and within himself, in the world and within his own breast. Then the more purely and richly he develops his personality, the stronger his temperament through which, in Zola's magic formula, he observes nature, the more deeply too will he grasp life and reproduce life . . . and he will learn to shun all stylizing, all arbitrary mannerisms, all stage affectations. . . ." He will find "the real in its unadorned simplicity. . . . As for the ideal, the truly beautiful, he can only feel that within himself, not outside himself in precepts that have been handed down. Let him find beauty in fidelity to the artistic whole of which he is part, in the integrated character he portrays. . . ." [214]

By 1894 Brahm knew that his temporary, often old-fashioned actors had to be assembled into a permanent company in order to work together without interruption at the new method. So, he applied for and got retiring L'Arronge's job as producer at the Deutsches Theater, which, founded in 1883 for the presentation of classical historical plays in the Meininger manner, had flourished because of the skills of such actors as Barnay (until 1887), Kainz, and newcomer Agnes (Zaremba) Sorma (1865–1927). A combined company was then formed with Cord Hachmann (1848–1905) and Emil Lessing (1857–1921) as stage directors.

Brahm promptly announced that at the Deutsches Theater he would produce, in addition to modern, naturalistic plays, the works of Shakespeare, Lessing, Goethe, Schiller, and so on. But he didn't plan to stage classics in the traditional and conventional way; his intention was to reinterpret them in a contemporary spirit, "to make them come to life by utilizing . . . the new naturalistic art of acting." Brahm wanted to prove "that modern realism . . . and the style of classical drama are not mutually exclusive," that only within the realistic style "can the nuances between previous periods and our own be skillfully brought out." The modern actor, he said, "cannot seek to preserve within himself the style of the past: he is a living artist, not an art-historian and antiquarian." He must "speak in the living speech of our time" and "quicken sluggish old forms with powerful modern feeling." [215]

In sensing that the great classic plays still contained the stuff of life for modern actors to capture and convey to modern audiences, Brahm was perceptive; but in assuming that the various forms into which that still vibrant and revealing content had been shaped could be changed by acting and directing into the realistic form, or changed without essential loss, he made a grievous error. And quickly, perhaps grudgingly, he discovered it. In order to illustrate clearly the potency of the realistic method Brahm started his new venture with a modernized *Intrigue and Love*, the same play that had opened the same Deutsches Theater eleven years before. He asked the cast—at only six rehearsals, to be sure—to read the flights of Schiller's language, the swing and the fire of his lines, naturally. Some of them wouldn't, some tried but couldn't; only two succeeded in being simple, almost true-to-life, and ordinary —and were lambasted by the critics. The production, as Brahm admitted, was an unmistakable failure. Four weeks later he again tried to apply the realistic method to the poetry and artifice of *The Merchant of Venice*. Again it just didn't serve. Again Brahm failed to vivify an old play by trying to make it like life. Thereafter he shied away from staging classic plays and assigned their direction to Hachmann. Although earlier he had condemned "the extreme historical naturalism of the Meininger as representing a confusion between reality and art" and had charged them "with bringing reality itself on the stage instead of selected bits of reality," Brahm couldn't in actual practice be anything else but thoroughly realistic. So, he centered his attention on the presentation of modern scripts and their "denial of all that is theatrical." No nonrealistic plays by Strindberg, Wilde, Wedekind, Maeterlinck, or Shaw were offered at his theater. And, according to one severe critic, "All dramas, born in the realm of the imagination . . . were murdered, died in and of his sober dullness, which barred as unnatural all things of beauty, any rising flame, anything aglow with the fire of youth, with festive joy or with wrath." [216]

Yet for ten years (until 1904) Brahm as an intelligent, attentive, nearly pedantic rehearsal critic bossed the more-or-less-easy-because-near-to-life staging of realistic plays at the Deutsches Theater, determining their "basic mood, the tempo, and the rhythm," and insisting that "First and foremost, the actor is the faithful interpreter of the dramatist's intentions (*"der treue Interpret dichterischer Absichten"*). With Teutonic thoroughness "He corrected mistakes in individual delivery, . . . he brought about the coordination of the dialogue, and . . . achieved unsurpassed unity in the interaction of the characters. . . . He never inspired the actors by communicating passion and ecstasy to them; he simple restrained [them] from doing too much. . . ." In essence, and ahead of Stanislavski, he urged his actors to live their parts onstage (*"Man deklamiert nicht mehr, man lebt die Rollen"*). "As a result of his strict and objective criticism, the style [of the Deutsches Theater actors] crystallized more and more; it became increasingly an exhibition of people just as they were in real life." "Nevertheless, as a cure for the bad tricks of 'virtuosity' and for weaning the actors from meaningless posing [and elocution], this style turned out to be a blessing for the German stage. And if, at bottom, the result was only negative, still, it cannot be denied that it rendered service by sweeping away abuses and thus making a real art of playing possible again." [217]

Among the new actors who worked under Brahm toward achieving a logical, everyday, sometimes heavy, lack-luster believability in playing was twenty-one-year-old Max (Goldmann) Reinhardt (1873–1943); "but he had too clear an eye, too much imagination, too much inborn longing for movement, change, surprise, to tolerate for any length of time the monotony and drabness of naturalism." [218] After two seasons he left the Deutsches Theater.

IV

By 1889, when at a private showing Janet Achurch (1846–1916) impersonated Nora in *A Doll's House*, as translated by William Archer (1856–1924), a few Englishmen began to ask, "Why have we not a Théâtre-Libre" to encourage the writing of plays that are better than merely conventional and bland, of plays close to life, even like life? So, Dutchman Jacob T. Grein (1862–1935), playwright and critic, founded in 1891 the Independent Theatre for the presentation each year of at least four stimulating plays of an artistic rather than a commercial value. In early March he produced, under another's direction, a "remarkably well acted" *Ghosts* for one "invitation" performance by an unpaid, almost unknown cast of semi-professionals. Ibsen, however, was immediately called "an egotist and a bungler" who had written "a dull, undramatic, verbose, tedious, and utterly uninteresting play"; and Grein was chastised for daring to assume "that the Continental stage was far ahead of our own in literary production." Nevertheless he persisted. Seven months later the Independent Theatre, with less than two hundred subscribers and only £88 in the bank, presented one performance of Zola's *Thérèse Raquin;* "and again the air was pregnant with abusive language." But "England had at last its revolutionary theater, patterned on a foreign playhouse, introduced by a foreigner," [219] and offering works by foreign, realistic playwrights. The only flaw was the fact that the English didn't care for foreign plays too close to life for comfort.

In December 1892 George Bernard Shaw (1856–1950) bounced onstage and saved the day for England with the Independent Theatre production of his first play, *Widowers' Houses.* Then in April 1894 his *Arms and the Man* was given an eleven week, financially unsuccessful, but full-fledged professional production at the Avenue Theatre. And his *Candida* was tried out by the Independent Theatre on provincial tours in 1897 and 1898. Shaw, however, wasn't a naturalistic playwright, and only partly a realistic one. He wasn't interested in presenting people onstage just as they are in real life; instead, he centered his penetrating wit on exhibiting ideas, and on exhibiting them theatrically. Shaw therefore shocked and puzzled not only audiences but also conventional colleagues like former actor (with the Bancrofts), Arthur Wing Pinero (1855–1934), author of the politely scandalous *The Second Mrs. Tanqueray* (1893); Henry Arthur Jones (1851–1929), who weighed religion in *Michael and His Lost Angel* (1896); and James M. Barrie (1860–1937), who sentimentalized in *The Little Minister* (1897).

Grein's sporadic Independent Theatre, having experimented with twenty-two productions, and having ignited Shaw, faded away after the tour of *Candida.* But it made its point: it circulated the notion that a play's content, though not its form, ought to be realistic. It convinced some English writers that "a play's business is to interpret life, not to imitate other plays." [220]

In due time English actors started thinking, imagining, feeling, talking, and moving a little less in terms of the theater and more and more in terms of life. They practiced "mimetic realism, the minute and unconventional reproduction of observed idiosyncrasies," in an attempt to deceive audiences into halfway believing that they were everyday people behaving as if they weren't onstage. One actor-manager, Wilson Barrett (1874–1904), even went so far as to engage actual "denizens of frowzy courts and alleys" to appear in one of his productions.[221]

V

Most of the playwrights, producers, and actors in the United States during the final quarter of the century safely and profitably copied only the stagy realism of the British and the French. For instance, two of manager Albert Palmer's (1838–1905) big hits at the Union Square Theatre were an adaptation of Dennery and Eugène Cormon's (1811–1903) *The Two Orphans* (1874) and Bronson Howard's French-American *The Banker's Daughter*

(1878). A greater success, the domestic *Hazel Kirke* (1880), was written, produced, and acted by Steele Mackaye at the Madison Square Theatre for nearly 500 consecutive performances.

The year before, in 1879, tireless conservative Augustin Daly (bolstered by his brother Joseph) opened his own theater (plus another Daly's in London in 1893) and assembled stock companies of first-rate, politely real players such as arch comedienne and star Ada Rehan (1860–1916), John Drew, Mrs. Gilbert, Clara Morris, Fanny Davenport, Adelaide Neilson and E. H. Sothern (1859–1933) from England, James (Demming) Lewis (1837–1896), Charles Fisher (?–1891), Otis Skinner (1858–1942), and Maxine Elliott (1871–1940). Then by insisting that they only do exactly what he told them to do—by showing everyone just how to move, to speak, to look—he coached into existence a contrived, external, and yet genteel realistic ensemble. Once at rehearsal, for example, Daly directed Clara Morris to cross to a far side of the stage out of hearing of two other players—and told her to motivate the cross. "Here," as she later explained, "are a few of the many rejected ideas. There was no guest for me to cross to in welcoming pantomime; no piano on that side of the room for me to cross to and play on softly; ah, the fireplace! and the pretty warming of one foot? But no, it was summertime, that would not do. The ancient fancy-work, perhaps? no, [the character I was playing] was a human panther, utterly incapable of so domestic an occupation. The fan forgotten on the mantlepiece? Ah, yes, that was it! you cross the room for that—and then suddenly I reminded Mr. Daly that he had, but a moment before, made a point of having me strike a gentleman sharply on the cheek with my fan. 'Oh, confound it, yes!' he answered, 'and that's got to stand—that blow is good!' The old, old device of attendance upon the lamp was suggested; but the hour of the day was plainly given by one of the characters as three o'clock in the afternoon. These six are but a few of the many rejected reasons for that one cross of the stage; still Mr. Daly would not permit a motiveless action, and we came to a momentary standstill. Very doubtfully, I remarked, 'I suppose a smelling-bottle would not be important enough to cross the room for?' He brightened quickly—clouded over even more quickly. 'Y-e-e-s! N-o-o! at least, not if it had never appeared before. But let me see— Miss Morris, you must carry that smelling-bottle in the preceding scene, and —and, yes, I'll just put in a line in your part, making you ask someone to hand it to you—that will nail attention to it, you see! Then in this scene, when you leave these people and cross the room to get your smelling-bottle from the mantel, it will be a perfectly natural action on your part. . . .' " [222]

With that anemic brand of natural acting Daly's actors for a period of twenty years, from 1879 to 1899, appeared principally in a flock of outdated plays, in about thirty adaptations of silly German farces, in sixty-five more or less trivial French pieces (twelve by Sardou), and after 1886 in annual "fricassees" of Shakespeare. The most elaborate and highly praised of these rearrangements were *The Taming of the Shrew* in 1886, *As You Like It* in

1889, and *Twelfth Night* in 1892. In 1884, 1886, 1888, and 1890 Daly's company performed in London to appreciative audiences, although sometimes the actors were found to be lacking in "dignity of style" and "knowledge of the art of speaking blank verse." The Americans also appeared in Berlin and Hamburg, and twice in Paris where one critic reported: ". . . if all American actors play like those we are seeing, the American theater may be said to be naturalistic. . . . The propensity for naturalism shows itself in a thousand details. The fashion of entering, sitting, taking a chair, talking, taking leave, going out, coming in,—it is the usage of everyday life. With us there is always a little conventionality in the movement of the characters." And "I regret that the dialogue is delivered in a fashion so rapid and in a tone of such conversational intimacy as to lessen the effect of many points. I am one of those who believe that it is not necessary to speak on the stage as in a room or a *salon.*" [223]

While Antoine was advocating naturalism at the Théâtre-Libre another American manager, Charles Frohman (1860–1915), opened the Empire Theatre in 1893 with *The Girl I Left Behind Me*, co-authored by David Belasco (1859–1931). This stock company included Viola Allen (1869–1948), Effie Shannon (1867–1954), Henry Miller (1860–1926), Wilton Lackaye (1862–1932), and William Faversham (1868–1940). In 1895 Frohman produced Wilde's nonrealistic *The Importance of Being Earnest;* and in 1897 he discovered a new star, Maude Adams (1872–1953), in Barrie's *The Little Minister.*

A surface realism, however, was added to some of the conventional, well-made American plays. Bronson Howard recalled the Civil War with *Shenandoah* (1888), James R. Herne (1839–1901) was homey in *Shore Acres* (1892), efficient William Gillette (1855–1937) starred in his own *Secret Service* (1895), and Augustus Thomas (1857–1934) went West in *Arizona* (1899).

In 1896 Minnie Maddern Fiske (1865–1932) at three performances portrayed Nora in *A Doll's House* (first acted in New York by Mansfield's wife, Beatrice Cameron [1868–1940], in 1889), and then in 1897 created a stir in a dramatization of Thomas Hardy's *Tess of the D'Ubervilles.* That same year Mansfield produced and acted Dick Dudgeon in Shaw's *The Devil's Disciple* for fifty-six performances. But a flashier theatricality and a flashier though false realism was carefully, even sanctimoniously concocted to amaze the tired American business man and his wife by Belasco when he wrote, produced, and directed *The Heart of Maryland* (1895) with Maurice Barrymore and Mrs. Leslie Carter (1862–1937) for a run of 240 performances. In 1899 he starred the same actress in his adaptation of *Zaza.* That year also Klaw and Erlanger produced a highly successful, often revived dramatization of *Ben-Hur* (1880) by General Lew Wallace (1827–1905).

For a sharper, more artful realism Americans turned to *The Adventures of Huckleberry Finn* (1885) by Mark Twain (Samuel Clemens) (1835–1910) and to *McTeague* (1899) by Frank Norris (1870–1902).

VI

Things theatrical in Moscow were stimulated by the opening of a number of private theaters after the abolishment in 1882 of the Imperial monopoly, and then by the first visit of the Meininger to the city in 1885. Alexander Ostrovsky, like everyone else, praised their pictorial groupings of characters and their vitally realistic crowd scenes. But that's about all he found worthy of praise in their work. The Germans, he wrote in his diary, were mistakenly addicted to externals, to lifelike effects, to naturalism. Such trying for absolute authenticity in scenery, props, and costumes, he decided, was pedantry. Worse, the acting of the Meininger troupe was also external. It was more efficient than esthetic. For Ostrovsky the visiting players obviously performed at the word of command by the director. They were mechanically, technically expert. Often therefore they lacked that difficult-to-acquire fundamental of all acting: inner truth.[224]

Not so penetrating in their analysis of the Meininger actors were the young men who, inspired by them, eventually organized the Moscow Art Theatre. It was, in part, an outgrowth of the Society of Art and Literature, which was organized in 1888—a year after the start of Antoine's first full season at the Théâtre-Libre—for the general purpose of regenerating Russian dramatic art. Foremost among its amateur actors—foremost because he had been performing in private theatricals with his family and friends as a child and a teen-ager, because he'd "gone often to the French theaters in Paris," and because he'd furnished much of the financing—was Constantin Alexeyev or Alexieff (1863–1938), the son of a wealthy owner of a factory for making gold and silver thread. Three years earlier he'd taken the stage name (Polish) of Stanislavski "so as to dissociate his family from the rather outrageous parts he played" in public performances of farces and musical comedies. At the Society for more than two years he acted character roles in plays directed by Alexander F. Fedotov (1841–1895), and later by actress Fedotova; but he didn't always perform well because he was bumptious and untrained, because he believed "that *looking* the part was the best way of getting to live it." [225]

Then in 1890, when Stanislavski was twenty-seven, he was influenced strongly by the second visit of the Meininger to Moscow. He didn't miss a single performance; he studied each one; he swooned over all the little accuracies, the logically conceived, external actualities he saw onstage. Worse, he envied the despotic power of director Chronegk and decided that he, too, would be a big boss like that. So, unaware of "the difference between artistic and commonplace life on the stage," and unabashed at turning his amateurs into puppets by insisting that they imitate him, he next year directed for the Society, and assigned himself leading roles in, a private showing of Tolstoy's bitter comedy, *Plodi prosveshcheniya* (*The Fruits of Enlightenment*) (1891) and his own version of Dostoyevsky's "The Village of Stepanchikovo," called

Foma (Thomas). The first production was praised, as all amateur productions are praised by someone; therefore in 1894 Stanislavski was vested with full financial and artistic responsibility for the Society's stage presentations. In the autumn of that year he directed, like a despot and a puritan, the businessmen, civil servants, teachers, and students he had cast for Gutzkow's *Uriel Acosta*. He rehearsed them every evening in his study from eight until midnight, fined them for being late or for making mistakes in learning their lines, banished garish attire and flirting from the meetings, and then proceeded to demonstrate how every speech should be acted. For instance, he illustrated "the furious fanaticism of each member of the crowd in the synagogue . . . , screaming, weeping and storming all over the room" in an attempt to duplicate the Meininger effects. Since the play, finally presented in January 1895, was a stirring success, Stanislavski was easily persuaded to do some semi-professional directing and to portray, in 1896, Othello, a role which had tingled his anticipation ever since he saw Salvini act it in 1882. His impersonation was a flat failure. In tackling the character he overlooked the play as a whole and concentrated only on certain feelings which appealed to him. These he elaborated "irrespective of whether or not they had anything to do with the playwright's intentions or whether or not they distorted the playwright's ideas." Stanislavski couldn't or wouldn't identify himself with the larger-than-life, heroic Othello. He seemed, according to an actress, "to lack the inner force which enables an actor to identify himself with the heroic figure he is representing." He was interested only "in looking for realism. . . ." "All you need," Rossi told him, "is art." [226]

Returning to the Society of Art and Literature, Stanislavski continued to be too enamored with the tyranny of directing and too insensitive to the form of a play as he staged in the Meininger naturalistic manner, and acted in, scripts as widely different as Ostrovsky's *Bespridannitsa (The Girl Without a Dowry)* (1879), *The Polish Jew* (a version of *The Bells*), *Much Ado About Nothing*, *Twelfth Night*, Goldoni's *The Mistress of the Inn*, and Hauptmann's largely nonrealistic, verse *The Sunken Bell*. Consequently, he altered the whole ruling idea of *The Girl Without a Dowry* "so drastically that Ostrovsky himself would not have recognized it." As Benedick he attempted "to conceal his own unfitness for the part by foisting upon it an interpretation that was completely at variance with the character created by Shakespeare." And as Heinrich in *The Sunken Bell* he also failed: "Lyricism in that sweet effeminate sentimental way in which I then falsely understood it," he admitted, "romanticism which neither I nor any actor outside of a real genius could express simply, meaningfully and nobly, and at last pathos in strong places in which my stage director's hokum did not help me—all this was far above my strength and my ability." [227] *The Sunken Bell*, presented in January 1898, was the final Society of Art and Literature offering. By then, at the age of thirty-five, Stanislavski had acted seventy-five roles (and would add only twenty-eight more in all the later years). By then also he was co-founding the Moscow Art Theatre.

In June 1897—almost eight years after the opening of the Freie Bühne —thirty-eight-year-old Vladimir Nemirovich-Danchenko (1859–1943) had approached Stanislavski with a dream; and at a first meeting of about eighteen hours the two of them had talked into existence a new, professional Moscow Art (and Popular) Theatre which, financed by shareholders, would offer daily performances of perhaps ten plays per season. Nemirovich-Danchenko, a successful playwright, critic, director, and teacher of acting at the Moscow Philharmonic School, as the brain behind the enterprise, was made adminstrative head and given full power of veto in all literary matters; Stanislavski was given a veto in all artistic matters. The repertoire was to include plays "pervaded by a healthy feeling for the living truth," modern plays like those by Hauptmann and Ibsen which, Nemirovich-Danchenko declared, "are much more important than the trifles of great playwrights like Shakespeare and Molière." [228] The nucleus of the company of actors would include Stanislavski's wife Maria Lilina (1866–1943), Maria Andreyevna (1872–1953), Maria Samarova (1852–1919), Vasily Luzhsky (1869–1931), Alexander Artyom (Artemiev) (1842–1914), Alexander Vishnevsky (1861–1943), and Georgy S. Burdzhalov (1869–1924), all from the Society of Art and Literature; and Olga Knipper (1870–1959), who would become Chekhov's wife in 1901, Maria Roksanova (1884–1958), Margarita Savitskaya (1869–1911), Ivan Moskvin (1874–1946), and Vsevolod Meyerhold (1874–1942), all talented, well-trained graduates of the Philharmonic School. To this core a few professional players from Moscow, St. Petersburg, and the provinces were to be added.

Active preparations started in June 1898, four months before an October opening date, at a barn converted into a theater at summer resort Pushkino, about twenty miles from Moscow. Before then Stanislavski had devised production books for several of the plays. In each "everything was written down —how, where, and in what way one was to understand the role and the hints of the author, what voice one was to use, how to act and move. . . . There were special drawings in accordance with the principle worked out . . . for all the business of entrances, exits, and changes of position. There was a description of the scenery, costumes, make-ups, manners, ways of walking, methods and habits of the roles played." Then, book in front of him, demanding schoolroom discipline, and forcing the actors to follow in minute detail his prescription for interpretation—and no arguments!—Stanislavski conducted rehearsals that "began at eleven in the morning and ended at five in the afternoon. Until seven the actors were free to bathe in the river nearby, to dine, and to rest, but at seven they returned for the second rehearsal of the day which lasted until eleven at night. . . . And what plays! In the morning *Tsar Feodor* (*Ivanovich*), in the evening *Antigone*, or in the morning *The*

Merchant of Venice, and in the evening either [*The Sunken Bell*] or *The Seagull.*" And *The Mistress of the Inn, Samoupravtsy* (*Men Above the Law*) (1866) by Pisemski, *Hedda Gabler,* and a potboiler called *Greta's Joy.* Nine plays were put through 120 rehearsals. The opener, *Tsar Feodor,* was rehearsed seventy-four times (compared to maybe six or eight rehearsals given a new play at the Maly Theatre); and the sixth offering, *The Seagull,* was rehearsed twenty-six times—fifteen times by Nemirovich-Danchenko, nine by Stanislavski, and twice by Luzhsky—for a total of eighty hours.[229]

With *Tsar Feodor* Stanislavski tried for the New, for anything that led away from the Old, by emphasizing costumes, decorations, scenery, properties, and sound effects—anything "that might dazzle the spectator." We worked, he later confessed, toward "an outward and coarse naturalism." We donned "all sorts of costumes, footgear, stuffing . . . we glued on noses, beards, mustaches, we put on wigs . . . we visited art galleries. . . ." "The contents of the play and all its [acting] problems were often forgotten. . . ." And daily, as if to accent his indelible, insensitive pedantry, Stanislavski kept a record book "into which was entered all that had to do with the work of the theater—what play was being rehearsed, who rehearsed, what actors did not appear at the rehearsals, who was late and why, what disorder took place, and what was to be ordered or made to facilitate the work. The visit of any important guest and all the pleasant and unpleasant happenings of the day were also entered." [230]

The Moscow Art Theatre opened at the Hermitage on October 14, 1898, with Moskvin as Feodor. The play was a Meininger-like success because of such unusual treats as perspective scenes of the roofs of medieval Moscow, a river with boats on it and crossed by a practical bridge, the etiquette of court in front of museum trappings, the colorful costumes of the Boyars, servants moving about with large platters laden with geese, suckling pigs, and great slabs of beef, authentic goblets and dishes which Stanislavski had found in Nijny Novgorod, and finally, a number of expertly stage-managed crowd scenes.[231] *Tsar Feodor* was performed, at intervals, fifty-seven times the first season.

Then, following five failures in a row, the new company scored its second success—again a realistic director's success—on December 17 with *The Seagull* (which had flopped earlier at the Alexandrinsky Theatre in St. Petersburg). The play was performed nineteen times during the 1898–99 season with Maria Roksanova as Nina, Olga Knipper as Arkadina, Meyerhold as Treplev, and Stanislavski as Trigorin. As director, the latter copiously elaborated "the author's stage directions dealing with the environmental elements in the play" and "corrected" any that didn't coincide with his own interpretation. And by emphasizing "*the external characterization*" of each role, he perfected an ensemble, a rhythm, a mood "to the highest degree exact and naturalistic." He went so far, once, as to advise his actors "not to be afraid of the *most* glaring realism. . . ." Yet as early as September, when

Chekhov heard that the cast was trying to make everything in his play realistic, he had commented: "Realistic? . . . The stage is art. . . . the stage reflects the quintessence of life. Nothing superfluous should be introduced on the stage." Stanislavski, nevertheless, sought to overwhelm his audiences by many superfluous realistic devices: for instance, he "broke up" the traditionally bare stage with three-dimensional objects such as trees, bushes, little bridges, tables, various seats, and the like so that the actors could have something *to do* while speaking their lines, and thus exhibit a sort of naturalness; in the first act he placed a long bench downstage across the proscenium opening and directed his actors to sit there sometimes with their backs to the audience; and he cluttered the dialogue with a variety of sound effects: the croaking of frogs, the chirping of crickets, the clip-clop of horses' hooves in the distance, the tolling of a church bell, and so on.[232]

Stanislavski was so occupied with putting accurately onstage all sorts of lifelike details that he "remained completely in the dark as to the meaning of [*The Seagull*], and indeed, did not know what it was all about." As a result, he transformed the comedy into a tragedy; he "entirely misunderstood the [key] character of Nina, and in doing so distorted the ruling idea of the play"; and he "utterly failed to understand the character of Trigorin." According to Chekhov, who saw a performance of his script in May 1899, Stanislavski "walked about the stage and talked as though he were paralyzed"; he interpreted Trigorin "in such a way that it made me sick to look at him."[233] (The role was later acted by Vasily Kachalov [1875–1948], who came to the company in 1900.)

In its second season the new troupe first presented *Uncle Vanya* on October 26, 1899, with Stanislavski as Astrov ("wrong, absolutely wrong!" according to Chekhov, in his interpretation of the Act IV scene with Elena).[234] But the lukewarm, though long-lasting, success of the play firmly set the Moscow Art Theatre on its way to twentieth-century eminence.

❀ NONREALISM

Not everything onstage at the end of the nineteenth century, however, was realistic. Some people, less logical or pedestrian than Antoine, Brahm, or Stanislavski, but with more feeling for art, objected to the new excessive lifelikeness in playwriting, production, and acting; they opposed the exhibition of only an easy, pseudo-scientific, popular verisimilitude merely for the sake of verisimilitude. Perceptively they contended that plays and their representations ought even when realistic to be artfully instead of actually so. They also argued that theater fare oughtn't to be exclusively realistic, that it generously could be classic, romantic, realistic, symbolic, expressionistic, or whatever. And they believed that actors ought to search for truth, yes, but in addition ought to transform their awareness of it, their feeling for it, into the theatrical.

Some critics, in other words, were inclined to find something lacking in a narrowly naturalistic kind of acting that couldn't cope with, couldn't enliven, Greek tragedies, Shakespeare, Molière, or comedies. After all, they argued, the Moscow Art Theatre players in their first season had failed in *Antigone*, *The Merchant of Venice*, and *The Mistress of the Inn*.

As early as 1876 critic Francisque Sarcey (1827–1899) in an *Essai d'une esthétique de théâtre* (*A Theory of the Theater*) maintained that "it is not sufficient simply to affirm that drama is the representation of life. It would be a more exact definition to say that dramatic art is the sum total of the *conventions* [my italics], universal or local, permanent or temporary, by the aid of which in representing life in the theater, the audience is given the illusion of truth." "It is an indisputable fact," he continued, "that a dramatic work, whatever it may be, is designed to be listened to by a number of persons united and forming an audience, that this is its very essence, that this is a necessary condition of its existence." Therefore, since the theater's "business is to represent life to a crowd," a crowd that "thinks and feels differently from the individuals which compose it, . . . deceptions—conventions—are essential." Reality onstage would appear false. Therefore, Sarcey implied, an actor, like a playwright, must accept the condition that a play is something to be performed in a theater—*not* as if in an actual living room or a real street, and before an audience—*not* for only the stage partners. An actor, like a playwright, he said, may "omit all the needless details and all the extraneous particularities which would in real life delay and dilute the action." He should "depart from the fact" by suppressing or altering reality. He must, in order to make the events of life interesting to his audience, "find means [via his medium] to heighten and render more vivid [and more revealing] and more enduring the impression he wishes to create." [235]

Then in 1887 German philosopher Wilhelm Dilthey (1833–1911) decided that imitation in art (in playwriting, in acting) had become more and more untenable as "idealistic philosophy deepened the search into the subjective capacities of man and grasped their autonomous force." The poet, or actor, he claimed, "does not *imitate* nature (in the sense of *Nachahmung*); he *reproduces* his experience (in the sense of *Nachbildung*) in imagination. 'Here we enter into the most proper sphere of the poet [or actor]: an experience that has been lived (*Erlebnis*) and its expression or its reproduction in imagination'" and via a medium. In short, according to Dilthey, after he had messed around with semantics, "the alternative to 'imitation' (which means copying) is 'creation' (which means adding)." [236]

And English journalist C. E. Montague (1867–1928) was sure in 1899 that an artist must revel in his apprehension of fact, and then must add to it "a veritable passion for arresting and defining in words or lines and colors or notes of music [or whatever is his medium], not each or any thing that he sees, nor anybody else's sense of that thing, nor yet the greatest common measure of many trained or untrained minds' senses of it, but his own unique sense of it, the precise quality and degree of emotion that the spectacle of it breeds in him and nobody else, the net result of its contact with whatever in his own temperament he has not in common with other men. That is the truth of art [the truth Stanislavski never uncovered], to be true less to facts without you than to yourself as stirred by facts." Artistic expression for Montague is therefore "not merely a transcription of the artist's sense of fact but a perfecting of that sense itself." So the [actor as] artist is incessantly preoccupied in leading his sense of fact up to the point at which it achieves not merely expression but its own completion in [whatever way] can make it, simply as a feeling of his own, all that it has in it to be." In brief, then, "To find a glove-fit [of movements and tones, of tempo and rhythmic vitality] for your sense of 'the glory and the freshness of a dream,' to model the very form and pressure of an inward vision to the millionth of a hair's breath—" [237] that, he almost said, is the actor's essential and difficult task.

II

Some late nineteenth-century playwrights in their search for full, individual expression therefore refused to accept the restrictions of realism. Ibsen, for one, plunged into the secret recesses of motivation and came up with the symbolic *Rosmersholm* (1886), and soared in an unreal realm with *Bygmester Solness* (*The Master Builder*) (1892). Frank Wedekind (1864–1918) as early as 1890 in *Die junge Welt* (*The World of Youth*) belittled naturalists who could do no better than copy life. Then with Gertrud Eysoldt (1870–1955) he acted in his *Frühlings Erwachen* (*Spring's Awakening*) (1891), a mixture of naturalism and symbolism, a lyrically distorted, shocking depiction of adolescent sex imaginings; and with *Erdgeist* (*Earth Spirit*) (1895) he moved with a striking talent toward expressionism. Belgian symbolist Maurice Maeterlinck (1862–1949) transcended the limitations of external reality in 1891 with two tiny gems, *L'Intruse* (*The Intruder*) and *Les Aveugles* (*The Blind*). And in *Pelléas et Mélisande* (1893) and *L'Interieur* (*The Interior*) (1894) he continued to bypass fact and reason and to approach things we do not already know, mysteries we can only divine in that "terrible tranquillity watched by the stars." [238]

In 1894 Philippe Villiers de l'Isle-Adam (1838–1889) forsook the actual and with *Axël* wrote a "Bible of the idealists," who in contrast to the realists "proclaimed their faith in the validity of the suprasensible world. . . ." Oscar Wilde (1856–1900) with a glittering wit that demolished the real ("The real is dead, long live artifice!") composed a farcial masterpiece, *The Importance of Being Earnest* (1895), a script that thumbs its nose at believable acting and quickly separates skilled from would-be players. In that same year Paul M. Potter (1853–1921) dramatized the plushy novel *Trilby* (1894) by George Du Maurier (1834–1896) into a long popular British and American box-office success. Shaw concocted, with only "a certain admixture of reality," [239] three brainy, rhetorical fantasies: *Arms and the Man, Candida,* and *Caesar and Cleopatra* (1897). In them the ideas so cracklingly advanced are real enough, but the characters—always regulated by thought—who debate them are so unnatural, so volubly designed, and so supremely theatrical that actors who elect truly to "live" them are invariably defeated.

In 1896 Hauptmann wearied of naturalism and, fascinated by the dream conclusion of his *Hanneles Himmerlfahrt,* wrote a powerful, symbolic fairy tale in verse, *Die versunkene Glocke* (*The Sunken Bell*). Edmond Rostand (1868–1918) revived romanticism with a lilting *Cyrano de Bergerac* (1897). Next year Gabrielle D'Annunzio (1863–1938) flamboyantly rebelled against realism as he tried to modernize, emotionalize Greek tragedy in *La città morta* (*The Dead City*). And Strindberg, whose genius teetered near madness, imitated "the disconnected but seemingly logical form of the dream . . . in all its terrifying half-reality" [240] in *Till Damaskus* (*To Damascus*) (i and ii, 1898; iii, 1904).

Moreover, in Paris in 1891 the Théâtre d'Art was founded to fight naturalism by symbolist poet Paul Fort (1872–1960) and actor Aurélien-Marie Lugné-Poë (1869–1940), who had studied at the Conservatoire under traditional Gustave Worms and then worked with Antoine at the Théâtre-Libre. The pair staged a series of poetic performances that included Shelley's *The Cenci* (1818), Marlowe's *Dr. Faustus,* Maeterlinck's *The Intruder* and *The Blind, Les Flaireurs* (*The Smellers*) (1904) by Belgian Charles Van Lerberghe (1861–1907), and the like. Then in 1893 Lugné-Poë continued the revolt at the long-lasting Théâtre de l'Oeuvre by presenting such plays as Ibsen's *Rosmersholm* and *Peer Gynt,* Hauptmann's *The Sunken Bell,* Wilde's *Salomé* (1892), and Alfred Jarry's (1873–1907) surrealistic *Ubu Roi* (1896).

In England toward the end of the century Ben Greet (1857–1936), Frank Benson (1858–1939), and William Poel (1852–1937) retreated to Shakespeare and undertook to rediscover his verbal magic.

❦ ACTOR'S CHOICE?

Actors near the end of the nineteenth century could choose, it seems, to be either realistic or nonrealistic. They could concentrate on personable, believable underplaying; on doing little, everyday things—even irrelevant things—accurately; on the reproduction of observed naturalistic details in utterance, gesture, movement, byplay, and business. Or they could continue with traditional formalized techniques to "fill the scene" with large, artful idealities and to seize an audience's attention with *bravura* impersonations, ringing and rhythmic in voice, precise in diction, and graceful in motion.

Actually, of course, most actors had no such choice. They had been forced to surrender that prerogative; their days of dominance had ended. Ever since about 1880 they had been rudely, but correctly, demoted to the task of serving a script, of interpreting it. They could only be as realistic or as formal as a playwright prescribed. And most of the new plays were more or less realistic.

Yet when actors performed realistically, they *did* have a choice, a definite and fundamental choice, to make. They could then hope to deceive audiences into believing that they were creatures of daily life, behaving and talking as if they *weren't* onstage; or they could still refuse to disguise the fact that they were actors in front of an audience, actors exploring, exploiting, enjoying their medium. In short, they could live a role or act it; they could be real or theatrical; they could be representational or presentational.

II

Some European and American actors, especially the newer ones, emphasized the lifelike in their characterizations; but they did so without forfeiting an habitual, instinctive sense of the theatrical. They were more or less real only in terms of their medium.

Most real in due time were the Russians. With naive gusto, intense soul-searching, and some heaviness they advanced toward "a profound and exalted simplicity in their truthfulness and realism." Among the actors at the Moscow Art Theatre who best evinced "the quality of naturalness in its most complete and inclusive sense" [241] were Moskvin, Olga Knipper-Chekhov, Kachalov, and Leonid Leonidov (1873–1941), who joined the company in 1903.

Some British actors politely worked at surface realism, at a well-articulated, emotionally restrained, genteel sincerity in playing that was equally inhospitable to French calculation and design and to Russian explorations of psychological truthfulness. The Bancrofts, for instance, advanced to realistically powdered-and-painted but hollow adaptations from Victorien Sardou (1831–1908) called *Peril* in 1876 with Madge Kendal in the cast, *Diplomacy* in 1878, *Odette* in 1882 at the Haymarket (where the team moved in 1880), and *Fédora* in 1883. That year also the Bancrofts failed dismally, with their society naturalness, their underplaying, and their love for coyly observed external details in the nonrealistic *The Rivals.* (Yet, over-all, the Bancrofts were so continuously triumphant as realistic actor-managers that in twenty years, from 1865 to 1885, they produced only thirty-one plays. And Bancroft was knighted in 1897.)

Comedienne Madge Kendal until long after she retired in 1908—she was made a Dame Commander of the British Empire in 1926—served as the adored, eminently respectable model of a realistic player. Hers was a "stalwart British-matron sort of conscientious acting . . . distinguished in the main by a constantly crystallizing technical skill" in copying the minutiae of normal behavior in normal Victorian living rooms, by underplaying, and by an "increasing emphasis upon a self-conscious display of her own personality."

Because she was so "natural" onstage, so interested in self-reproduction, and so unconcerned with traditional methods and magnifications Madge Kendal failed, of course, "to make sparkling and pointed the wit" of Goldsmith's Kate Hardcastle and failed as Rosalind "to do justice to the language of Shakespeare." [242] But no matter: plays of that sort were outmoded. Arch verisimilitude was the fashion.

In Italy a more audacious realism was added to impersonation by new players Ermete Zacconi (1857–1948), Alfredo de Sanctis (1867–1954), Ferruccio Garavaglia (1870–1912), Virginia Reiter (1868–1937), Irma Gramatica (1870–), Emma Gramatica (1875–), Tina Di Lorenzo (1872–1930), Ruggero Ruggeri (1871–1954), Giovanni Grasso (1875–1930), and especially by Duse. She was the supreme artist. Her power of conveying a sense of radiant reality was unequalled as she relived a role evening after evening, "always with new and surprising variations, but always with the same essential line." By 1885, when Duse was only twenty-six, she had found, and almost perfected, what the Russians were searching for. She had felt her way into and worked out with cryptic skill a new method of acting, a rarefied realistic style that did "not accept the surface of things," nor her own body and voice, but forced them "toward a more intricate and luminous expression of the life hidden within." She illustrated the fundamentals of all art,[243] and particularly of realism as an art.

III

Other actors near the end of the nineteenth century were relatively sure that a psychological understanding of a character helped, helped considerably, in effecting a truthful interpretation. No argument on that score. But they weren't convinced that psychological insight could be substituted for theatrical techniques. That, the majority of the stars of the period believed, was only something extra added to content, not necessarily to form, not to the way in which matter is conveyed to an audience. Therefore, they did far less, or more, than live their roles. They continued to act them, to be more theatrical than real.

For instance, Ristori in her old repertoire, Salvini chiefly with the indispensable Othello, and Rossi in Shakespeare continued to tour and to impress the world as classic actors modern enough to stoop to some "naturalism in delivery, while bringing into relief the poetic beauties" of their roles. (Ristori retired in 1885, Salvini in 1890, and Rossi died in 1896.) In Russia Yermolova and Lensky with their attractive individualities, their expert speaking, and their studied techniques stood more for romanticism than for realism. And Vera Komisarjevskaya (1864–1910), first at the Alexandrinsky and then at her own theater, pushed the belief that the actor should find "theatrical" forms, independent of everyday life, in characterizations. She was, "for lack of a better name, . . . 'symbolical.'" [244]

German actors were, in general, too studied, too academically esthetic in their realism to be realistic. They were stagy. "One might imagine," wrote Salvini, "that they were guided by a mathematical study, as it were, of their art, and that they had undertaken to put it into methodical practice." But soon enough under Reinhardt new actors, especially Alexander Moissi (1880–1935), "all lightning and flame" as Oedipus, Everyman, Romeo, Oberon, Hamlet, Mephistopheles, and Oswald in *Ghosts*, would soar acting above logic and daily levels. In the meantime, Polish Helena Modjeska (1844–1909) in the United States and occasionally in England until she retired in 1905, portrayed Mazeppa, Mary Stuart, and Lady Macbeth with "a quiet and violent intensity, right away from naturalism, much bigger than actual life, becoming universal, a symbol." [245]

In England, oddly enough, dedicated and autocratic Henry Irving—who took over the management of the Lyceum Theatre at the end of 1878—was hailed by his countrymen for his realistic playing of tragedy; but Coquelin found fault with him "for not seeming sufficiently natural." Irving was lifelike, all right, just as many British actors by, say, 1885 were more lifelike onstage than ever they'd been. He was well aware of "the growth of naturalism in dramatic art," and tritely announced that "A grain of nature is worth a bushel of artifice," that an actor must lure an audience "into the fleeting belief that they behold reality" upon the stage. And, disdaining to make traditional, applause-getting "points" in performance, he studiously made new, difficult, natural ones. For example, as Othello telling Iago to have Desdemona watched, he very humanly "turned away that his ensign might not see his face"; as Richard III saying the line "And if I die no soul shall pity me" he dropped his hands "as it were unconsciously about a crucifix on the table in the tent—a master touch"; as director he instructed Peter "not to stand grinning meaninglessly at Romeo and the Nurse, but to sit himself down against a wall and stretch out lazily in the Italian sunshine"; and so on.[246] In short, Irving intellectually molded his productions, and especially his own roles—since he carried the star system as far as it could be carried—out of a serviceable number of realistic details.

But Irving wasn't a realistic actor. He was always emphatically theatrical. "To appear to be natural," he said, the actor "must . . . be much broader than nature. To act on the stage as one would in a room, would be ineffective and colorless." "Nature may be overdone by triviality in conditions that demand exaltation. . . ." The actor, Irving was sure, ought to rise with his sentiment "Like the practiced orator," and should always know "that he is a figure in a picture." Consequently, Irving's realistic details were exaggerated and pointed up until his characterizations exuded a "romantic flamboyant *baroque* quality." With a compelling virtuosity of execution they were almost Gothic. His Mathias in *The Bells*, for instance, was "pre-eminently a haunted murderer" while Coquelin's was "pre-eminently an Alsatian innkeeper." [247]

"To Irving," as Arthur Symons observed, "acting is all that the word literally means." He acts. He crosses the stage, he gestures, with theatrical intent; "he intentionally adopts a fine, crabbed, personal, highly conventional elocution of his own; he . . . acts, keeping nature, or the too close semblance of nature, carefully out of his composition. . . . his acting is no interruption of an intense inner life, but a craftsmanship into which he has put all he has to give. It is . . . wholly rhetorical, that is to say, wholly external; his emotion moves to slow music, crystallizes into an attitude, dies upon a long-drawn-out word." Irving, you can say, "turned his back on the realistic art of the new dramatists, . . . and concerned himself with Shakespeare, with melodrama, and with romantic poeticizing. . . . and as a result he represents the apotheosis of romantic realistic acting and is hardly to be regarded as allied to the true realism of the naturalistic theater." [248]

Until 1902, for thirty-one years at the Lyceum (twenty-five seasons under his own management), with excursions into the provinces and eight tours to the United States, Irving magnetized audiences with his skills at rearranging instead of copying nature. Moreover, while saying that "The actor's business is primarily to reproduce the ideas of the author's brain," he inevitably made them subservient to his own ideas and compelled the public to accept his conceptions even when they were in flat contradiction to the texts.[249]

Among his abler characterizations were the title role in a revival of Boucicault's *Louis XI* in 1878; Shylock for the first time in 1879; Othello and Iago shared with Booth in 1881; Benedick in a seven month run of *Much Ado About Nothing* in 1882; Dr. Primrose in *Olivia* (1878), an adaptation of Goldsmith's *The Vicar of Wakefield*, in 1885, Mephistopheles in a new version of *Faust* (1885), a "consummate confection of . . . claptrap and culture" [250] which ran for 496 performances, or two full seasons; Cardinal Wolsey in *Henry VIII*, which ran for the full seven-month season of 1892–93; and the title role in Tennyson's *Becket* (1893), which opened on his fifty-fifth birthday. Then in 1895 Irving was knighted, the first actor (actor-manager) to be so honored; and three years later the University of Cambridge conferred upon him the degree of Doctor of Letters.

Ellen Terry's acting was more glowing, more spontaneous than Irving's. "When we act," she wrote, "we must *feel*, not necessarily with our own personal feelings. Your voice, your movement, your whole body, are only an instrument for this *feeling*." But Ellen Terry, like Irving, presented "nature sublimated to the ideal." Although she lacked the temperament of a tragic actress, her instinctive timing and subtlety, her "surprising picturesqueness of aspect, pose, and movement," [251] and her superb speech conferred on all her characterizations a warmly feminine distinction. (She continued to perform until 1925—sixty-nine years after her debut—when she was made a Dame Grand Cross.)

Three newer English players also chose not to be too realistic. Johnson Forbes-Robertson (1853–1937) worked under Phelps in 1874, then with the

Bancrofts and with Irving, and became by the end of the century essentially a classic actor, a well-nigh perfect Hamlet. He used his voice "as if for song or recitative"; but he restricted himself to the tones of natural speaking "produced with greater resonance, intensity and flexibility than they have in the ordinary speaking voice." Because he never tried, "as naturalistic actors do, by some sudden turn of queer, incontestable veracity, to shake you into a troubling and importunate consciousness of the presence of life," and because he deprecated unemotional "acting down," which tempts one, he said, "to do no acting at all," Forbes-Robertson "belonged to a tradition that was doomed." Imaginative, erratic Herbert Draper Beerbohm Tree (1852–1917) produced and acted in a number of Shakespeare's plays plus such items as *The Dancing Girl* (1891) by Henry Arthur Jones, *A Woman of No Importance* (1893) by Wilde, Gilbert Parker's (1862–1932) *The Seats of the Mighty* (1897), and *The Musketeers* (1898) taken from Dumas. As an actor he trailed "with him into the twentieth-century clouds of romanticism, from which . . . the glow and color had in a measure departed." And Mrs. Patrick (Stella Tanner) Campbell (1865–1940) realistically blew her nose right in the middle of her most emotional scene in Pinero's *The Second Mrs. Tanqueray*" for which she was discussed at every dinner table for months after"; but her "irresistible physical gifts and her cunning eye for surface effects" [252] marked her as being, in most instances, a vibrantly theatrical actress instead of a realistic one.

(In early 1891, incidentally, a British Actors' Association was organized principally for the purpose of protecting members of the profession from the increasing danger of absconding managers who left companies penniless and stranded in the middle of tours. In 1907 Granville-Barker proposed to the Association "That all salaries be paid on the weekly basis of six performances, with every additional performance paid for at the rate of one-sixth of the weekly salary. That special salaries be paid during rehearsals. That no actor or actress be employed . . . except as an understudy, who was not qualified to be a member of the Actors' Association." [253] The proposals, however, were shelved, the managers withdrew from the organization, and it almost expired. The American Actors' Equity Association was formed in 1912, the British Actors' Equity in 1929.)

In the United States Edwin Booth continued until 1891, two years before his death, to spurn realism, to deliver all his lines facing the audience, and to diminish each standard play he appeared in to "the monologue of a star for whom the performances of the rest of the company existed only as a figured base." He was much more traditional than Irving. Booth's Iago, for example, was "clear, cool and precise, admirably thought out [along conventional lines], never deviating a hair's breadth from the preconceived play—design and execution marching hand in hand with ordered steps from the first scene to the last; a performance of marvellous balance and regularity, polished to the very fingernails." Irving's Iago, in contrast, was "startling, picturesque, irregular, brilliant—sometimes less brilliant than bizarre—but always fresh and suggestive, always bearing that peculiar stamp of personality which . . . so often saved the actor in his sorest straits." [254]

Other American actors who didn't subscribe to the new realistic acting included Richard Mansfield (1857–1907), who won romantic fame in *Dr. Jekyll and Mr. Hyde* (1887), *Richard III* in 1889, *Beau Brummel* (1890) by Clyde Fitch, and *Cyrano de Bergerac* in 1898; James O'Neill (1847–1920), the father of Eugene, who began portraying the long-run *Monte Cristo* in 1883; Robert Mantell (1854–1928); E. H. Sothern; Julia Marlowe (1865–1950); and Margaret Anglin (1876–1958).

French actors, of course, excelled all others in being just realistic enough without forfeiting, however, an iota of their long-ingrained feeling for theatrical style, style that "derives from a combination of sensibility and calculation, and moves toward the ideal of distinction with a touch in it of conscious elaboration or artifice." French acting, though strengthened by Antoine, continued to illustrate that in the theater "no word spoken, no gesture made, [need be] carried through *in* the time, with the force, or *through* the special extent and direction of actual life." [255] Everything natural was to some degree reshaped in terms of the medium. Coquelin, Bernhardt, Mounet-Sully, high comedienne Réjane (Gabrielle Charlotte Réju) (1857–1920), Lucien Guitry (1860–1925), Edouard de Max (Alexandre) (1869–1925), and others didn't thrill audiences by "living" their roles onstage; they thrilled them by their "instrumentalism," by the vocal and visual skills with which they conveyed an idea, not merely familiar behavior.

"To be natural," Sarah Bernhardt wrote, "does not mean that an actor should exhibit the passions in the manner they are exhibited by everybody. . . ." So, with a passionate drive toward the glamorous, with fierce egotism and mesmerizing power, with a voice "like a thing detachable, . . . like a musical instrument," in short, with sheer acting, she molded larger than life, and electrified, such characters as the Queen in *Ruy Blas* at the Odéon in 1872 when she was twenty-eight, Phèdre in 1874 and Doña Sol in *Hernani* in 1877 with the Comédie-Française, Adrienne Lecouvreur and Marguerite in *La Dame aux camélias* in 1880, Sardou's first Fédora at the Vaudeville in 1882, Théodora in 1884 and La Tosca in 1887 at the Porte-Saint-Martin, Magda in 1895, de Musset's Lorenzaccio in 1896, Hamlet in 1899, and in 1900, when she was fifty-six, Rostand's L'Aiglon and Roxanne opposite Coquelin in *Cyrano de Bergerac*. And always consciously, skillfully the actress as well as the part, she "amazed, thrilled, defeated" audiences; "she dominated even if she taxed them; she delighted, exalted, and made them shiver with ice on their spines." [256]

After her triumph in London in 1879—along with Coquelin, Gôt, and Mounet-Sully—Bernhardt left the Comédie-Française in order to seek independent fame and riches as "an international institution." That year she first came to the United States with a miraculous contract which "guaranteed a hundred performances in four months" at "one thousand dollars . . . for each performance, plus fifty percent of all receipts above four thousand dollars. . . ." In addition, she received two hundred dollars a week for hotel expenses and a private railroad car containing a drawing-room, a dining-room and kitchen, and bedrooms. In 1881 Bernhardt toured Europe. In 1893 she managed the Théâtre Renaissance. Then she competed with Duse in 1895 in London and in 1897 in Paris, and her Marguerite and Magda were more popular than her rival's. In 1899 she opened her own Théâtre Sarah Bernhardt. There and on tours until her death in 1923, on one leg after 1919, she continued to enslave the world, not with her very "limited range of ideas, such ideas, for instance, as amorous seduction, pain and anger—the famous rage through tears—and the infinite throes of dying," and not with her naturalness, but with her resonant and magnetic theatricality "that was easily detected by the average audience as art." [257]

Coquelin also was theatrical, a presenter rather than a representer. He preferred "stage-convention" to the new realism or "naturalism, as it is now called." In a huge theater, he maintained, nature must be enlarged in order to produce a lifelike effect on, say, fifteen to eighteen hundred people. (But, one may ask, is that same enlargement needed today in films and on television? And if not, is it therefore no longer needed onstage?) Moreover, and more important, Coquelin insisted that actors "have a special and peculiar medium; [and they] must use it in an appropriate manner" (even in films and on television). They "must not destroy . . . the theatrical illusion by too great fidelity to fact." People attend plays, he said, for theatrical pleasure, a unique sort of pleasure "partly composed indeed of the illusion that they are seeing a reality, but mingled" with esthetic distance "and a sincere conviction that they are assisting only at an illusion." "I refuse to believe in art without nature," he summed up, but "I will not in the theater have nature without art." Art, Coquelin maintained, is "the interpretation of nature and of truth, more or less tinged by a peculiar light, which does not alter the proportion, but yet marks the salient features, heightens their colors, displays their fidelity to nature, so that our minds are more deeply and forcibly affected by them. . . ." And since acting is "an art . . . analogous to that of the portrait-painter . . . , nature can be reproduced by it only with . . . luster and relief," with "the fragrance of poetry, the vision of the ideal." In short, the reproducing must have style. "Where style is wanting there is no art." [258]

Although Coquelin was not handsome, was, indeed, a type formed for the broadest comedy, his gamut ranged from the pathetic to the extravagantly droll, and in a pinch from the heroic to the romantic. After his fabulous success as Figaro in Le Barbier de Séville in 1861, and his election as a sociétaire of the Comédie-Française in 1864 when he was twenty-three, he acted a horde of parts for the company, many of them in unremembered plays, until his resignation in 1886. Coquelin was, for instance, a brilliant

Mascarille in Molière's *Les Précieuses ridicules* and a perfect Tartuffe. He acted César de Bazan in *Ruy Blas*, Adolphe in Augier's *Paul Forestier* (1868), the Duc de Septmonts in the realistic *L'Étrangère* (*The Strange Woman*) (1876) by Dumas *fils*, the title role in the tragic *Jean Dacier* (1876) by Charles Lomon (1852–1923), *Luthier de Crémone* (*The Lute-maker of Cremona*) (1876) by François Coppée (1842–1908), the old rabbi in *Ami Fritz* (1876) by Erckmann and Chatrian, Don Annibal in *L'Aventurière* (*The Adventuress*) (1880) by Augier, and Thouvenin in *Denise* (1885) by Dumas *fils*. On his own after 1886 he impersonated such roles as Duval in *Les Surprises du Divorce* (1888) by Alexandre Bisson (1848–1912) and Antony Mars (1862–1915), Octave Feuillet's (1821–1890) *Chamillac* (1889), swaggered to immortality as Cyrano at his Porte-Saint-Martin in 1897, and tried Jean Valjean in a version of *Les Misérables* (1899).

Always his "acting was nothing but acting; unfortified by any separable thrill or lure of beauty, sex, or intellectual ascendancy; his power was simply the sum of the three strict elements of great acting—a plastic medium, a finished technical cunning, and a passion of joy in the thought of the character he acted." The defect of Coquelin's genius may have been "a certain technical hardness, an almost inhuman perfection of surface"; and occasionally he may have lost the idea while he listened to the form. Nevertheless, he was a superlative speaker. He could, it's true, "time and modulate and animate the most familiar gesture into a novel expressiveness; when his Tartuffe, in the first shock of being exposed, felt in the air behind for a chair to lean on, the hackneyed trick looked like the fruit of fresh observation of life." But audiences got "the cream of his talent, or at least of his virtuosity," when he had "a very long and composite speech to utter, be it verse or prose." They listened, for instance, to his four-page speech in the last act of *Denise* "not altogether perhaps to hear what Thouvenin would say . . . , but certainly to hear how Coquelin would bring Thouvenin through." And he could "shed over . . . stiff-seeming lines [of verse] such color, diversity, warmth, colloquial quickness, that hearers . . . half wondered whether perhaps the use of rhymed couplets was what human speech, in its longing for heightened expression at crises of feeling, had really been groping for always till now." Coquelin, in short, could excitingly *say* things onstage at a time when that skill was nearly out of fashion. "To *do* them," as Henry James observed, "with a great reinforcement of chairs and tables and articles of clothing . . . is the most that ever occurs to our Anglo-Saxon stars of either sex." [259]

❈ COQUELIN'S METHOD

At the end of 1880 in *L'Art et le Comédien* (*Art and the Actor,* or less confusingly *The Actor as Artist*) Coquelin claimed that actors are artists like painters or musicians and therefore "are entitled to hold honorable rank . . . in the annals of our country." The actor is an artist, he claimed, because he uses himself as his material, "he works upon himself . . . , he molds himself like wet clay" in order to make a likeness, a designed likeness. And even though he's assigned an already created character, he still creates. He creates the actual living body "laughing, crying, walking, breathing, talking, and moving; and all these modes of being . . . must fit together—form a real individuality, such a person as we meet every day" and recognize as a type.[260] So, because the actor imaginatively adds to and physically enlivens an original creation he, too, is a creator. Call him a subsequent co-creator.

(In 1882, two years after the appearance of this article, active actors were officially honored when Gôt, twenty-ninth Doyen of the Comédie-Française, was elected to the Legion of Honor. Coquelin, however, always refused to accept that accolade "in order that it might not be supposed that he had made his appeal on his own behalf.")[261]

In *The Actor as Artist* Coquelin explained, as already noted, his opposition to naturalistic acting. In addition, he agreed with Diderot that the actor as artist need not experience emotions during a performance in order truly to convey them. That is as unnecessary, he wrote, "as it is for a pianist to be in the depths of despair to play the Funeral March of Chopin or of Beethoven aright. . . . I would lay a heavy wager, on the contrary, that if he should give way to any personal emotion, he would play but ill; and by analogy, that an actor who regarded his own emotions otherwise than as material to be utilized [to be worked upon, molded, made expressive of an idea] . . . would be likely to fare badly." [262]

Some years later in "Actors and Acting" (1886–87), reworked, enlarged, and retitled *L'Art du Comédien* (*The Art of the Actor*) in 1889, and published separately in 1894, Coquelin more thoroughly studied his art, "inquiring into its conditions, laying down the principles of its rightful practice—those at least which I consider to be such from my own experience, an experience extending . . . over a period of thirty years." The premise of his practice, sired by Diderot, is simple. Since, Coquelin said, the actor's medium is himself, since the actor's own voice, his "face, his body, his life is the material of his art, the thing he works and molds [in order] to draw out . . . his creation, . . . it follows that the existence of the actor must be dual." In fact, "the characteristic gift of the actor is . . . this dualism." "One part of him is the performer, the instrumentalist; another, the instrument to be played on. . . . 'Number One' conceives the character to be created, or rather, since it is in fact the creation of the author, sees it as the author has drawn it"; and then " 'Number Two' realizes [this character] in his own person." And " 'Number One' must be master of 'Number Two' . . . at all times, but especially during the actual performance of a play. In other words, the actor must remain master of himself even in those moments where the public, carried away by his acting, thinks him most absolutely distracted; he must *see* what he is doing, [never forget his medium, never "forget that he is before the public"], judge himself, and retain his self-possession." Coquelin overstressed his point by reiterating that an actor "must not experience a shadow of the sentiments he is expressing—at that very moment when he is expressing them with the greatest truthfulness and power." More temperately, more correctly, he might have said that an actor *need* not experience *completely* the sentiments he's expressing. An actor at his best can and ought to fill the form he makes—and yet not forfeit it—with the truth, the life, from which it is derived. Even so, however, Coquelin would insist that the greater the mastery of "Number Two," the instrument, by "Number One," the instrumentalist, or the more the feeling is controlled and designed, the greater the artist.[263]

The Coquelin method of acting differs from the later Stanislavski method essentially. The latter, at least as practiced in the United States, ignores, or does not emphasize, this dualism, the actor's "Number One" and his "Number Two." Stanislavski students from the start of their training, and exclusively for years afterward, admittedly work in almost a Freudian way only on the vague, very generalized lumps of themselves. They try to find and to understand themselves, to feel into and out of themselves, to dig down into their own experiences, emotion memories, honesties, peculiarities, and so on. They carry on self-love affairs. The characteristic gift of the actor, they try to demonstrate, is an achingly true knowledge of self. They exhibit mostly that.

Coquelin followers would agree, of course, that actors, painters, musicians, and writers need to explore and to know and to be themselves. And especially all would-be artists, they would add, need to know whether or not they are imaginative. So far so good. But, the Coquelin people would continue, knowing yourself and being yourself, even being brilliantly imaginative, doesn't necessarily mean that you can act. Maybe you can paint—once you learn what painting is and then go on to master the special skills required. If you wish to act—well, you must learn what acting is and then go on to master different special skills. Surely an actor should exhibit more than his own analysis of himself or his own fancying of himself. An actor, expert or novice, ought primarily to exhibit an awareness of the play as a whole, of the scene (even when it's rehearsed in class) as part of the whole. (After all, in *An Actor Prepares*—"prepares," mind you—Stanislavski talks about "Units and Objectives," "The Unbroken Line," and "The Super-Objective.") An actor ought from the very beginning of his training to exhibit an awareness of his unique medium, its distinctive techniques, and an awareness of the audience. As Coquelin might sum up, the actor must concentrate on and exhibit more than himself.

So, you deduce, a follower of the Coquelin method finds the fundamentals of acting by first dividing himself into "Number One" and "Number Two." "Number One" always reminds him that his chief stage task is "to respect the text," to search out "the accent of the author." "Every dramatist," Coquelin insisted, "has his own peculiar mental outlook, his works reveal it, and the actor must reflect it. . . ." You do not act "Molière . . . like Beaumarchais, nor Augier like Meilhac," Shakespeare like Ibsen, or Anouilh like O'Neill. The actor as "Number One" therefore practices sensing the quality of the play-wright. Eventually he learns, for instance, that "When you play Molière, take on his breadth, his admirable precision, so indifferent to the mere sparkle of wit, so fascinated, on the contrary, by the broad, open countenance of truth. Take on his gaiety, so completely the natural state of his soul . . . that gal-lant laughter, devoid, whatever men may say, of all admixture of misanthropic bitterness. Speak with fitting breadth that glorious language of comedy, the finest in the theater." But "Beaumarchais is something quite different; no sap flowing spontaneously from a naturally joyful soul. Witty, combative, carping, provocative; so rich in all these things that he lavishes them on his characters. . . . poise, audacity, *brass!* that is what you need to play Beaumarchais." And "Hugo must be played lyrically. He is that above all. And he treated lyrically the most dramatic situations he could find, so much so that they sometimes seem nothing but opportunities for a magnificent outpouring of poetry. . . . Who are Don César and Ruy Blas? Fantastic lyrists." Next, the actor as "Number One" practices understanding, or feeling his way into, *a specific script* since all plays by one dramatist aren't always alike. He finds that the style of, say, *Les Fourberies de Scapin* differs from the style of *Le Misanthrope;* and he knows that he can't act the one like the other any more than he can "play melodrama on the same lines as comedy." [264] Finally, the actor as "Number One" practices finding the idea in each play and conceiv-ing his character as an harmonious, functional part of it.

Simultaneously, "Number Two" constantly reminds the actor that he must assist in conveying the playwright's idea to an audience. The actor there-fore practices admitting its presence in the theater, going out to it, seizing and controlling its attention. He practices conveying his matter in distinctive, well-executed, theatrical ways. He practices communicating courteously, perhaps gracefully, via a voice, a diction, and a motion more special than ordinary. As "Number Two," according to Coquelin, the actor perfects his voice into an instrument "most flexible, most glowing, most rich in the power of variety"; he also perfects his "articulation, . . . the A B C . . . of our art." "Ah! but what about speaking naturally, I shall be asked—is that not essential? Don't talk to me of the natural speech of those who will not take the trouble to articulate. They chat before the public as they might do at meals, interrupting and repeating themselves, correcting themselves, chewing their words as they might the end of a cigar; gabbling, that is the right term. . . ." No, no, no! We actors must not talk onstage "as we talk every day; we must *speak,*" which implies "giving to the phrases and to all essential words their true [or revealing] value, here with the lightness of a feather, there, on the contrary, with the whole weight of a vocal inflection; distributing the planes of speech, its reliefs, its light and shadow, modeling our utterance." [265]

But what about the actor as a person, the Stanislavski adherents scream. Does he ignore himself, his own individuality, his own creativeness? Oh, no. When Coquelin portrayed a character he wasn't the least bit interested in erasing his individuality. He gloried in displaying his own uniqueness. (What artist doesn't, shouldn't?) Always he was indubitably and fully Coquelin in every role he impersonated. But he minimized exhibiting only *his* personality, or habits, or psyche. That demands no skill. Without half trying anyone can reveal himself. Everyone always does. Coquelin, as an artist, exhibited what *he* had *made*. "Character," he said in *The Art of the Actor*, "is the basis of everything in acting," and "the inward study of characterization [is] the most important of all studies. . . ." [266] Therefore Coquelin made characters; he made in terms of the theater a Mascarille, a Gringoire, a Cyrano, and so on. And in each of them was found his uniqueness.

In other words, Coquelin was emphatically himself as "Number One," the instrumentalist, when he dissected, analyzed, and assimilated a character. But he was widely, not narrowly, so. Unlike the Stanislavski actor, he didn't prepare to rehearse by looking into a mirror or into his own case history to find attributes he possessed, or personal feelings he could recall and re-experience, which could be transferred to the assigned character. No. He did more, much more than that. He began with the script. With *his* instinct, *his* intelligence, and *his* imagination he pieced together the author's character in *his* mind's eye. He blended his individuality with the playwright's. He obtained his model. He saw and heard the character as it *must* be. And always it was as much his own, as different from anyone else's, as it could possibly be.

Then Coquelin proceeded to bring his concept to life. But as "Number One," the instrument, he tried to get away from himself. He didn't force the playwright's character to fit him—his voice, movements, habits, motives, actions, and so on—in order to be easily, fashionably, and safely natural or believable. Instead, he forced himself to fit the model he had imagined. With his perfected technique he transformed his personality into the very idiosyncrasies of the role. He assumed it. For example, he endowed Tartuffe with an utterance and a gait unlike his own; he changed his features to match those of the ideal Tartuffe; he went beyond himself to select traits from among those he'd collected in his observation of others; he tried to convey not his own inner self, but Tartuffe's inner self, Tartuffe's very soul; and over all he used "whatever can be made effective in the theater." As Thouvenin in *Denise*, for another example, Coquelin tried strenuously *not* to be himself. Thouvenin, he wrote, "talks [and] argues just as . . . I should do every day myself. Well, there was the snag. Just because I was near akin to the character in everyday life I might be tempted to overlay him with my physical habits, to make him speak with my voice, to play him, in fact, as M. Coquelin. . . . I had to watch myself all along, correct my behavior, supple my movements, moderate the power of my voice . . . ; in a word, work on my whole physiognomy so as to give Thouvenin just his right carriage. . . ." [267] In short, Coquelin believed that the genuine actor's stage task isn't merely to be; it's to exhibit what he is by what he can make.

Because of the actor's basic duality, according to Coquelin, there should not be, there cannot be, any such thing as being the character, as living the role. Stanislavski himself noted that Coquelin actors live their parts only in rehearsals "as a preparation . . . for further artistic work, . . . for perfecting an external form. . . ." And Stanislavski knew that "You can receive great impressions from this [Coquelin brand of] art, . . . this acknowledged . . . creative art." But, he warned, "they will neither warm your soul nor penetrate deeply into it. Their effect is sharp but not lasting." All "delicate and deep human feelings are not subject to such technique. They call for natural emotion *at the very moment* in which they appear before you in the flesh." ". . . *in our art you must live the part every moment that you are playing it, and every time.*" Coquelin might ask: But if you only live the role, how do you find the significant pattern, the idea? How do you perfect its external embodiment, its style, its theatrical form? How, since they aren't identical, do you transmute life into art? Stanislavski would reply: That will all happen in due time. "Time . . . not only purifies; it also transmutes even painfully realistic memories into poetry," into art. Eventually the actor will "find a beautiful form and expression, appropriate to the theater." [268] Coquelin might retort that actors aren't likely to find the theatrically designed idea without trying for it.

II

In "Actors and Acting" Coquelin implied that Irving was one of those actors, possibly inferior, in whom "the *ego* . . . exerts so much influence that they can never put it aside, and instead of . . . going to [a] role and clothing themselves in its semblance, . . . they make the role come to them and clothe itself in theirs." Irving bristled. "The individual force of the actor," he proudly announced, "must find its special channel." But, Coquelin replied, by being yourself you neglect the true study and digestion of the character and, oddly enough, try only for the external and the extraneously picturesque. If "picturesque means beauty," said Irving, or "the selection of what is pleasing and harmonious in illustration—then by all means let us be picturesque." Let us, said Coquelin, above all else be the character. And, still clinging to his "unattainable ideal," his belief that "an actor must modify his gait, his general bearing, and if he can his voice" in making a character, Coquelin boldly advised Irving "in certain roles to efface as much as possible his own personality in order to bring forward conspicuously the personality of the character he is playing." And lose my own nature? protested Irving. By no means, Coquelin assured him. As an actor you "never set aside your own individuality." Every actor is a character (say, for example, Becket) *and also* the artist (Irving) who uniquely designs and controls it. (The actor, for a modern example, is Astrov the doctor or a vastly different Shallow the justice, and yet in both instances is indisputably Olivier.) And audiences respond to the character while they simultaneously perceive the individuality and skill of the artist. They can even hiss the character at the same time as they applaud the actor—or vice versa.[269]

Irving missed the point. Rachel, he countered, didn't owe her success to any transformation of physique. She owed it to her electric quality, to her divine fire. In acting, he continued with weird logic—because Rachel was a studied performer, and Irving himself was an excessively studied one—experience, study, and absolute self-possession count for little without inspiration, or those flashes of feeling that happen spontaneously onstage. Coquelin significantly answered that he by no means denied the value of inspiration, that "when one is sure of a role, when . . . one leaves nothing to hazard, then indeed one can without inconvenience try some of those traits which are suggested by the heat of representation." But he couldn't agree to set up inspiration "as the essential mark which distinguishes superior artists." Inspiration, for instance, can't teach an actor how to compose a role or how to speak it properly. The actor as artist "criticises his inspiration. He revises, he judges, cuts out here, amplifies there," and so on. But, Coquelin concluded, the problem "is of small importance to the public. By what token shall the spectator know whether such and such a thrilling cry has just been hit upon by the actor there on the spot, or whether it has been tried, thought over, learned, and repeated a hundred times beforehand? Does Mr. Irving mean to maintain that the cry found on the stage by inspiration [truly feeling or living the part] will be for that reason infallibly truer and finer than the other? The whole history of dramatic art would rise in protestation against such an assertion." [270]

Irving had no opportunity at rebuttal on that point. He dismissed Coquelin for lacking soul, for being prosaic. Realistic portraiture, he declared as he grasped for a straw, may be important in the comic drama, but "in [poetic] tragedy it has a comparatively minor place." (Boucicault, in his contribution to the Coquelin-Irving duel, agreed that "the heart is inartistic [and] must be controlled and molded by the brain . . . in comedy," but not in tragedy.) Coquelin replied, "Man is the end and aim of tragedy, as of comedy; and the tragedian, like the comedian, having to render man, I do not see why their methods should differ so radically. The tragedian must be master of himself quite as much as the comedian." [271]

In summary, then, Coquelin's main point wasn't that the actor mustn't feel during a performance, but that always he must "see and hear himself play" [272] in order to preserve the design of his characterization.

Salvini, Stanislavski's idol, ambiguously agreed with Coquelin's premise. True, in his commentary on the Coquelin-Irving discussion he wrote that "The actor who does not feel the emotion he portrays is but a skillful mechanician" who tempts the audience "to exclaim 'How marvelous! Were it only alive 'twould make me laugh or weep.' He who feels, on the contrary, and can communicate this feeling to the audience, hears the cry: 'That is life! [Instead of art?] That is reality! See—I laugh! I weep!'" Yet at the time Salvini particularly wished to impress on his readers the significant point "that while I am acting I am leading a dual life, crying or laughing on the one hand, and simultaneously so dissecting my tears and laughter that they appeal most forcibly to those whose hearts I wish to reach." [273]

III

English critic and Ibsen translator William Archer missed the central point about acting when he read Coquelin [274]—and, in addition, Walter Herries Pollock's 1883 translation of Diderot's *Paradoxe*. Instead of perceptively asking "Should actors design their roles?" and if so, "How, in allegiance both to the playwright and to the theater medium, do they shape their feelings?" Archer asked the old, obvious, and incidental questions, "Do actors feel?" and if so, "How do they feel?" He beat a dead horse by preparing a lengthy questionnaire about weeping, blushing, blanching, laughing, perspiring, and the like onstage, submitted it to leading actors and actresses of the day, and then systematized the answers into a plodding, scholarly article, "The Anatomy of Actors" in the January, February, and March 1888 issues of *Longman's Magazine*. Later that same year it was expanded, largely with quotations from actors of former times, as *Masks or Faces? a study in the psychology of acting*.

Archer's findings provide interesting reading of a gossipy sort, but they are indecisive. For instance, in Chapters IV and V, the most essential sections of his interrogatory, Archer discovered that an actor's personal emotions can be used "sometimes to the advantage, sometimes to the detriment of the . . . performance." In Chapter IX he was impressed with the value of concentration in acting (and may have set Stanislavski to churning about that topic). In Chapter X he inquired into "the multiplex action of the mind whereby the accomplished actor is ennabled to remain master of himself even in the very paroxysm of passion," and "was able to deduce many cases in which double and treble strata of mental activity were clearly distinguishable, but very few examples of that total and somnambulistic absorption in a part which the antiemotionalists assume to be the normal condition of the emotional actor." Then in Chapter XII Archer learned that some actors insist "on rigorous predestination of every detail of position, gesture, and inflection; while others . . . leave a wide margin for impulse, spontaneity, free-will. The latter sect is probably the more numerous and influential." He "also ascertained that the 'foreknowledge absolute' of the necessitarians is by no means inconsistent with the keenest susceptibility to the emotional influence of their characters." [275]

Finally, Archer tended to believe "that even the greatest virtuoso of mechanical mimicry [cannot] attain to the subtle and absolute truth of imitation which is possible to the actor who combines artistically controlled sensibility with perfect physical means of expression." [276] But "artistically controlled sensibility" isn't quite the same thing as mere sensibility, or only feeling the part.

So, Archer, despite the fact that as a spectator he was usually wounded by every element "which interferes with the credibility of a scene," agreed in part, although perhaps reluctantly, with Coquelin. "Acting," he found, "*is* imitation; when it ceases to be imitation it ceases to be acting and becomes something else—oratory perhaps, perhaps ballet-dancing or posturing. Everyone knows that the actor is not necessarily a mere copyist of nature; he may sing, for example, or he may talk alexandrines; but he must always preserve a similarity in dissimilarity; he must always imitate, though we permit him to steep his imitation, so to speak, in a more or less conventional atmosphere. 'He plays naturally,' or, in other words, 'He imitates well,' is our highest formula of praise even for the operatic tenor or the French tragedian, who may not deliver a single word or tone exactly as it would be uttered in real life." [277]

IV

Coquelin wasn't influential enough. Neither he nor those who in varying degrees accepted his premises could stop the rush toward a fashionable and easy lifelikeness in acting. By the close of the nineteenth century the majority of actors decided perforce to be more real than theatrical onstage, to be representational instead of presentational. When they characterized, they accurately copied everyday behavior. They "put in everything," even immaterial tidbits. Anything was justified, was perfection, so long as it was "natural." Acting was more and more popularly defined as the "faithful, photographic imitation of the figures before us in real life, with all their ways, tones, peculiarities of speech, gestures, dress, and the rest." This idea, according to critic Percy Fitzgerald (1834–1925), "is born of the gross realism so popular in our day—for it is a day of servile copying and imitation, and realism reigns in every art." In 1892 Fitzgerald wrote that nowadays "it will be generally admitted that there is little attempt at formal *elocution* on our stage. Every one says his say, as best he can, and in his own way. And curiously enough this neglect appears to be of a set purpose, and carried out with intention. . . ." He also complained that "Gesture on our stage is . . . chiefly prompted by the *instinct* of the moment" instead of being studied and regulated as a subtle, swift, and potent means of expression. "The mere imitative actor," he noted sadly, "can 'get on the stage' without study or preparation." [278]

Shaw turned his fireworks on this new acting, which he called "more a picked up habit than an art," a kind of "slip-shod carelessness of speech and action [that] would not be tolerated from a parlor-maid. . . ." As the weekly reviewer of plays for *The Saturday Review* from 1895 to mid-1898 he agreed, that an actor ought above all else to convey to an audience a "sense of humanity," that his business is "to supply an idea . . . with a credible, simple, and natural human being to utter it. . . ." "In France," he joked, "an actor is a man who has not common sense enough to behave naturally." But Shaw also knew that the art of acting required more than a "mere abandonment" to being natural. It demands, he continually insisted, "technical skill, . . . at least some scrap of trained athleticism of speech and movement." It "can only be made tolerable by sheer beauty of execution. . . ." Even for natural speaking he was "on the side of smart execution." Unless "the lines are spoken by voices of which the ear never tires, with gestures and action which never lose their fascination, the result can be no better than a disagreeable experience, drawing a crowd and holding it only as a street accident does." [279]

Shaw maintained that speaking naturally was not the end-all of acting. For example, he explained, "It is no use to *speak* [Othello's] 'Farewell the tranquil mind'; for the more intelligently and reasonably it is spoken the more absurd it is. It must affect us as '*Ora per sempre addio, sante memorie*' affects us when sung by Tamagno." "Shakespeare," he said, "is so much the word-musician that mere practical intelligence, no matter how well prompted by dramatic instinct, cannot enable anybody to understand his works or arrive at a right execution of them without the guidance of a fine ear. At the great emotional climaxes we find passages which are Rossinian in their reliance on symmetry of melody and impressiveness of march to redeem poverty of meaning. . . . Wreck that beauty by a harsh, jarring utterance, and you will make your audience wince as if you were singing Mozart out of tune. Ignore it by 'avoiding singsong'—that is, ingeniously breaking the verse up so as to make it sound like prose— . . . and you are landed in a stilted, monstrous jargon that has not even the prosaic merit of being intelligible." It is "only in music, verbal or other, that the feeling which plunges thought into confusion can be artistically expressed. Any attempt to deliver such music prosaically would be as absurd as an attempt to speak an oratorio of Handel's, repetitions and all. The right way to declaim Shakespeare is the singsong way. Mere metric accuracy is nothing. There must be beauty of tone, expressive inflection, and infinite variety of *nuance* to sustain the fascination of the infinite monotony of the chanting." [280]

In summary, Shaw pointed out that the portrayal of a role can be "true to nature" and yet lack "artistic character," that the actor as artist, in addition to vivifying his sense of humanity, must awaken in himself "the artistic conscience," or "a sense of beauty," and cultivate it "to such a degree of sensitiveness that a coarse or prosaic tone, or an awkward gesture, jars instantly . . . as a note out of tune jars on the musician." [281]

But to Stanislavski, and to the twentieth century, nothing in acting could possibly be inartistic which was spontaneous and natural.

❊ REALITY REPRODUCED

A new invention was soon to satisfy the craving for greater realism in the theater and to prove more influential than either Coquelin or Stanislavski in shaping acting. That was the camera. In late 1889—fifty years after Frenchman Louis Daguerre (1789–1851), with the earlier help of Joseph Nicéphore

Niepce (1765–1833), had demonstrated a complete, practical photographic process—American Thomas Alva Edison (1847–1931) and his assistant, William Dickson (1860?–1935), were experimenting at East Orange, New Jersey, with a Kinetoscope and making some first, very brief moving pictures. (The latter actually invented the process.) Four years later Edison produced *The Execution of Mary, Queen of Scots* (1893). The film, "running just under a minute, begins as Mary approaches the chopping block. She kneels, the headsman swings his ax—and the audience is rewarded with the edifying spectacle of Mary's head rolling in the dust. At the crucial moment, of course, the film was stopped in the camera and a dummy substituted for Mary; but the gruesome bit of action continues on the screen without interruption." [282]

By 1895 Louis Lumière (1864–1948), and others in France, in England, and in Germany, were perfecting the mechanics of shooting and projecting animated pictures. One Lumière film, *Arrival of the Paris Express* (1895), offered views that might be witnessed on a journey to or from the Riviera, and was praised for its "realism that seemingly defies improvement." That same year Edison photographed Joseph Jefferson performing bits from *Rip Van Winkle* amid the natural scenery of his summer home on Buzzard's Bay, Massachusetts. Eight episodes were billed and sold as separate catalog items, such as: "No. 45. *Rip's Toast*, 25 feet," or No. 48. *Rip's Passing over the Mountain*, 26 feet." [283] Then on April 23, 1896, Edison first presented his projecting Kinetoscope to the public as part of a vaudeville show at Koster & Bial's Music Hall in New York City.

In Paris in 1899 professional magician Georges Méliès (1861–1938) notably added narrative to motion pictures. By 1900 he'd prepared over two hundred subjects, each about one hundred feet in length. Among his longer films were *L'Affaire Dreyfus* (1899); the pantomime-spectacle *Cinderella* (1900), filmed on 2,000 feet of celluloid, but released by Pathé in 900 feet; and *Jeanne d'Arc* (1900) in twelve tableaux using "about 500 persons . . . all superbly costumed . . . with pictures of the greatest beauty in the production of which nothing has been economized." Méliès "exploited not only the narrative but also the trick possibilities of the motion picture camera. He quickly learned how to stop it in the middle of a scene and create miraculous appearances, disappearances, and transformations. He mastered the technique of double exposure and superimposition, producing truly extraordinary effects. . . . He was without question the movies' first creative artist." [284]

Most of the subsequent makers of motion pictures, however, were not interested in the new medium's potentialities for the fantastic or the artificial. They were businessmen who set out to make a profit by photographing the real; and they rapidly attracted mass audiences to a new kind of acting so truthful, or personable, that often it was hardly acting at all.

PART IV-

THE VARIETY

OF ACTING ~ ~

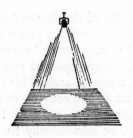

9- The Mass-Culture Century

The first half of the twentieth century was a world-changing time. In 1900 the powerful nations were Great Britain, France, the United States, Germany, Austria-Hungary, Imperial Russia, Turkey, and Japan. Then by mid-century, after two world wars, the United States and Soviet Russia dominated the others—including a new Communist China and a new, multinationed Africa—and engaged in a nuclear-armed cold war. Under such uneasy conditions any examination of the theater, especially of acting, might seem unimportant. But one traces the evolution of an art through the centuries, or, as Granville-Barker observed, "One follows a calling for thirty years and forgets its comparative unimportance; how could it hold one otherwise?" [1]

The present century is also the time of the average man—either in a democracy or in a totalitarian state. The masses are all-important; the results are mass-culture, mass standards of what is best. And recently, especially in the United States, the average man has been fascinated by what makes him tick individually, and conform or not conform. Via psychoanalysis as developed after 1910 by Austrian Sigmund Freud (1856–1939) he has turned inward. Today, as a consequence, playwrights and actors are furnished with models who, in most instances, are lost amid huge events, smaller than they were, and fearfully complex.

II

Over all, the characteristics of the theater from 1900 to 1950 are at least four. First, a big majority of the world's playwrights embraced realism. Influenced by Ibsen's triumph in announcing "not merely social change but the disintegration of an intellectual and spiritual world" [2] into one teeming with irrational and often neurotic people, and by his careful depictions of reality in which people behave as we do and converse in prose almost like ours, they discarded idealism. No longer did they represent the world around us according to traditional standards, or intellectually transform life into something superior to what it is, into something more perfect than nature, something ideally beautiful. Instead, they tried to record as truthfully as possible what their senses perceived.

A talented minority of playwrights, however, was dissatisfied with realism—even when selected, rearranged, heightened. The illusion of actuality, they maintained, does not provide the best theater, the most fully expressive, the most artistic. So, they turned to various types of symbolism, a mode of seeing life not objectively but from a singular or special point of view. As symbolic or poetic writers they shaped their findings "in an arbitrary, mostly nonrealistic" way. They used whatever expressed what was desired, "whether or not it [was] possible or even seen or heard" in life. By the start of the century this antirealistic or "symbolist movement in the drama was already in full swing . . . with Maeterlinck in Belgium, von Hofmannsthal in Austria, Yeats in Ireland . . . , D'Annunzio in Italy," [3] Andreyev in Russia.

Other antirealistic playwrights went beyond approving symbolic or poetic plays and held that true theater ought to be presentational rather than representational. They objected to the realist's *and* to the symbolist's aim of *representing* "a true image of life existing outside and quite independently of the theater," or of *representing* "an illusion of a life going on which is apart from the audience, but at which the audience is allowed to look on." They believed that playwrights as artists ought to forsake aiming at illusion and *present* life "as an image existing in the theater and finding its expression in the forms of the theater," in forms revived in part from an older time, forms that audiences, undeceived, could enjoy as such. They asked: "Should the play appear as something existing outside the theater? Or as a make-believe world, which derives its reality not from its power of deceiving the spectator but from its frank recognition that it is nothing but make-believe? Likewise, should the actors impersonate real characters, and incarnate beings of symbolical significance? Or should they present them through the prism of their own individuality and acting-craft?" [4]

Such questions, too concerned with form to be popular, may before long become crucial if plays written for the theater are to differ essentially from plays written for films and television. And if acting onstage is to be distinguished from acting on the screen.

Second, in the first half of the twentieth century a new and huge emphasis was placed upon directing. As early as 1905 Gordon Craig, for one, was proclaiming that the dominant artist of the theater must be the director. Quickly enough, primarily because of the intricacies of modern staging, the director replaced the star or the actor-manager as mid-wife. Today each script has its director who, like an orchestra conductor, controls all the ingredients of production and, when successful, "brings the theater work into being, its parts justly related and its idea expressed." [5]

Moreover, in our time it seems that "directors have made a more creative contribution to the theater than the dramatists." Most of "the innovations and changes which have transformed the theater" [6] have been due primarily to Stanislavski, Adolphe Appia, Craig, Max Reinhardt, Harley Granville-Barker, Jacques Copeau, and Vsevolod Meyerhold rather than to Strindberg, Chekhov, Shaw, Pirandello, Claudel, Giraudoux, or O'Neill. And it's significant to note that all but one of those directors and all but one of the playwrights were most often antirealist.

Third, since about 1925 the realistic system of acting as collated by Stanislavski has "exerted incomputable influence throughout the Western Hemisphere." His system is not perfect; it meanders into hocus-pocus; it has its limitations. But when the arguments reverently pro and violently con have subsided it can be agreed that "whatever errors Stanislavski was led into by his theories, he . . . nevertheless . . . erected certain signposts which every genuine actor has to follow. . . ." Or maybe, since few of his disciples teach the same kind of acting, it is more accurate to say that the "most respected acting method of our time . . . [is] Stanislavski, a modification of Stanislavski, or an improvement on Stanislavski, as you will. . . ." [7]

Fourth, the mass popularity of moving pictures has had a tremendous effect on acting. On the credit side, films have begun to unify acting throughout the world. Slowly they have been seducing Orientals to forsake their ancient, esoteric, deliberately dancelike and formal styles of performing for the Occidental realistic style. On the debit side, films (and television) have definitely weakened stage acting—have, according to some, murdered it. The screen actor, "magnified many times life size by a camera that sees everything, must . . . always underplay and, at all costs, be casual [or natural, or lifelike]. He can't rearrange, heighten, design, or project his behavior in character." He can't *act* as he does onstage. Once, for instance, when Fredric March (1897–) was rehearsing for the cameras he stopped and said, "Sorry, I did it again. I keep forgetting—this is a movie and I mustn't act." [8]

The screen, unfortunately, "has a built-in preference for the two varieties of nonactor": for "the Hollywood star, who always plays the same person, himself," and for "the amateur who knows no better than to behave naturally." [9] Italian film director Vittorio de Sica, for example, can take a soccer player and a schoolgirl, neither of whom has had any training in acting, and get from them persuasively real performances. On the screen, in short, the only thing that counts is a recognizably, believably real performance.

Onstage, therefore, by some weird logic, almost the only thing that counts any more is that same "real" performance.

❀ FROM SWEDEN TO DUSE

A detailed examination of the twentieth-century theater, and the changes in acting, begins in Sweden. There Strindberg, probing deeper in his nearly maddened search for "the essential life," continued his break with standard dramatic techniques and experimented with expressionism, or the "outward expression of inner feelings." He attempted to capture and convey his own emotions "at any cost—the cost being usually an exaggeration or distortion of natural appearances. . . ." (Like symbolism, expressionism is thus antirealistic; and it can be representational or presentational.) In two opaque but powerful plays, *Ett Drömspel* (*The Dream Play*) (1902) and *Spöksonaten* (*The Spook Sonata*) (1907), Strindberg depicted man's appalling knowledge of himself and his struggles with himself; and by employing characters that "split, double, multiply, vanish, solidify, blur, clarify" [10] he challenged actors to impersonate in ways beyond the easy and the popular.

But Strindberg's most typical, perhaps greatest play is the brutally realistic *Dödsdansen* (*The Dance of Death*) (1901). And among his most popular creations are the gently religious and symbolic *Pask* (*Easter*) (1901), and the unreal fairy and folk plays, *Svanevit* (*Swanwhite*) (1902) and *Kronbruden* (*The Bridal Crown*) (1902). When one adds to them *Gustavus Vasa*, *Folkungasagan* (*The Saga of the Folkungs*), and *Erik XIV*, all written in 1899, and among the best of recent historical plays, one rightly concludes that no modern dramatist's "range is wider or more provocative." [11] In his something near seventy scripts Strindberg re-emphasized in our time the fact that it takes all kinds of plays, from the realistic to the surrealistic, to make a vibrant theater. And he had no qualms whatsoever about pushing acting beyond the realistic.

II

In France from 1900 through 1910 no revolutionary playwright challenged actors. Drama drooped. The naturalistic and realistic rebels of yesteryear had become manufacturers of thesis and triangle plays. "The dramatic range . . . narrowed down in form to the ingenious and reliable well-made play, and in substance chiefly to themes on adultery, jealousy, and divorce, with sometimes some pallid excursion into ideological and sociological realms." Brieux, for instance, studied venereal disease in *Les Avariés* (*Dam-*

aged Goods) (1902) and discussed childbearing in *Maternité* (1903). Henry Bataille (1872–1922), in reaction against "brutal realism, easy to master, which gives readily to the public the illusion of life," aimed for the poetic but compromised in *Maman Colibri* (1904), *La Marche nuptiale* (*The Wedding March*) (1905), and *La Femme nue* (*The Naked Woman*) (1908) and put onstage "a clinic of morbid and erotic passions that adjoins the boudoir on one side and the morgue on the other." [12] Henri Bernstein (1876–1953) satisfied thrill-seekers with ingenious melodramas like *Le Voleur* (*The Thief*) (1906).

Some playwrights, however, disdained clever, titillating, and pat realism. Rostand followed his enormously successful *Cyrano de Bergerac* with the poetic *L'Aiglon* (1900), about the "eaglet" son of Napoleon, impersonated by Bernhardt, and with *Chantecler* (1910), in which Lucien Guitry acted the Cock. Maeterlinck, who earlier had subtly "transferred the stage to the *terra incognita* of the soul," [13] abandoned some but not all of his mysticism in the popular *Monna Vanna* (1902), and then escaped to childhood in *L'Oiseau bleu* (*The Blue Bird*) (1908).

Monna Vanna was first staged at the Théâtre de l'Oeuvre. There until 1927 Lugné-Poë, representing "an antidote to Antoine's realism," created "a theater of dreams and poetry and intellectuality" by introducing to Paris the plays of D'Annunzio, Strindberg, von Hofmannsthal, Shaw, and Claudel. Even Antoine as director of the Odéon from 1906 to mid-1914 "had the delicacy not to obtrude his [naturalistic] Théâtre-Libre plays by French authors"; and, as a state functionary, he was obligated to include in his presentations works by Aeschylus, Sophocles, Shakespeare, Calderón, Goethe, Schiller, and the great French classic writers. "We have . . . been . . . determined," as Michel Saint-Denis explained, "to avoid presenting a photograph of real life on the stage." [14]

The quartet of great French actors—Coquelin, Bernhardt, Mounet-Sully, and Réjane—were also antirealistic. "It would have been impossible for Bernhardt to play a Chekhov heroine, because her conception, not so much of the role as of the whole purpose of acting, would have been alien and inappropriate." She and her colleagues were unconvinced that acting should be more or less identical with everyday behaving. They believed that actors ought to have "great stage presence," ought to use "a precise and fluent diction," and ought to move with design; that actors ought to bring onstage a *tradition*, and make audiences aware "of all actors and of the theater as a whole"; [15] that, above all else, actors ought to make audiences feel their art (or artifice) as well as their truth.

But Stanislavski didn't care for that brand of acting. He wrote of the Frenchmen: "Artists of the Coquelin school reason this way: The theater is a convention, and the stage is too poor in resources to create the illusion of real life; therefore the theater should not avoid conventions. . . . This type of art is less profound than beautiful, it is more immediately effective than truly powerful; in it the form is more interesting than its content. It acts more on your sense of sound and sight than on your soul . . . . delicate and deep human feelings are not subject to such technique. . . ." [16]

Hogwash, the French retorted.

III

Spain, undynamic in its acting, did not contribute anything influential during the first half of the twentieth century. For the record, however, Echegaray, essentially a romanticist, received half a Nobel Prize in 1911 for having enlivened his country's stage with over sixty plots of intrigue, surefire theatrical tricks, and conventional rhetoric. His contemporary, Benito Pérez Galdos (1845–1920), a novelist and critic, limned for actors some first-rate realistic characters in Electra (1900) and El Abuelo (The Grandfather) (1904). And prolific, intelligent Jacinto Benavente (1866–1954) with a wide variety of scripts including a social study, La Gobernadosa (The Governor's Wife) (1901), a satirical Los Malhechores del bien (The Evil Doers of Good) (1905), a romantic La Princesa sin corazon (The Heartless Princess) (1907), a picaresque commedia, Los Intereses creados (The Bonds of Interest) (1907), and a realistic peasant drama, Señora Ama (1908), mildly modernized the Spanish theater (and won the Nobel Prize in 1922).

Also for the record it should be noted that two expert Spanish players, Fernando Diaz de Mendoza (1862–1930) and his wife, María Guerrero (1868–1928), managed the Teatro Español from 1896 to 1909 and won for their profession a solid respect.

During this period a worthy South American Spanish theater was inaugurated by Florencio Sánchez (1875–1910), a Uruguayan, with M'Hijo el Dotor (My son the Doctor) (1903) and Los Muertos (The Dead) (1905).

IV

In Italy, playwrights tried during the first decade of the century to be modern by trading their native theatricality for "truth in art." Not many of them were as vividly naturalistic as Sicilian Verga with his Dal Tuo al mio (From Thine to Mine) (1903) or Neapolitan Salvadore di Giacomo (1862–1934) and his 'O Voto (The Vow) (1909) and 'O Mese Marino (The Month of Mary) (1909). But society was probed realistically in mild plays like Come le foglie (Like Falling Leaves) (1900) and Il Più forte (The Stronger) (1904) by Giuseppe Giacosa (1847–1906), the librettist for three Puccini operas, in La Crisi (The Crisis) (1901) by Marco Praga (1862–1929), in Fantasmi (The Phantoms) (1906) and Il Piccolo Santo (The Little Saint) (1909) by Roberto Bracco (1862–1943).

But, as elsewhere, there were antirealists. In Italy they were led by popular, even notorious, D'Annunzio. In the medieval *Francesca da Rimini* (1902), the peasant *La Figlia di Iorio* (*The Daughter of Jorio*) (1904), first acted by Ruggeri and Irma Gramatica, and *La Fiaccola sotto il maggio* (*The Light Under the Bushel*) (1905) egos and primitive passions flare into "a winged and hyperbolic language." Influenced by those plays, Sem Benelli (1877–1949) ornately romanticized history in *La Maschere di Bruto* (*The Mask of Brutus*) (1908) and *La Cena delle beffe* (*The Jest*) (1909). Yet neither the poetic nor the realistic satisfied Filippo Marinetti (1876–1944). Disgusted with the modern theater "because it wavers stupidly between historic reconstruction . . . and photographic reproductions of our daily lives," he impotently demanded "an art which will reflect the mechanical civilization around us," [17] a so-called futurist art stylized into abstract forms.

Italian actors outshone Italian playwrights. Chief among them were the classical Novelli, the realists Zacconi, Ruggeri, Grasso, the two Gramatica sisters, and, of course, Eleanora Duse (1859–1924). In the 1900's, at her prime, she was hailed in her native land, Austria, South America, France, England, and the United States for bringing to the title roles of Sardou's *Fédora* and *Théodora*, *La Femme de Claude* (*Claude's Wife*) (1873) by Dumas *fils*, and Sudermann's *Magda* a "perpetual dilation of reality." Her subtle, apparently simple, "entirely beautiful" [18] performances were almost the antithesis of what before her time had been known as acting.

As Stark Young pointed out, Duse "could not . . . have recited as Bernhardt was able to do, in any elaborate, heroic diction and with any of that incomparable vocal spell that Bernhardt knew how to weave. . . . She could never have lifted a role to any classic fatality and splendor as Mounet-Sully could do in *Oedipus*. She had not a certain golden luster that Ellen Terry had. She could not have exhibited that wild animality, speed, passion and impetus" that Grasso did. "She had nothing of that romantic epic style that Chaliapin [brought] to Boris. She had none of the gusto and bravura of an actor like Coquelin. And Réjane had more brilliance." But Duse could render "by means of only actual or possible external details the inmost idea." Deep "sorrow, discontent, thwarted desires," as she may have hinted, "tortured and exalted her" into a passionate search for "beauty and the flame of life." [19]

How Duse acted remains almost a mystery. First, for sure, she went to herself—to her "sensitivity and power in feeling, in idea, in soul, in the education and fine culture of all these . . . to invent an art wholly personal, . . . wholly subtle, almost spiritual, a suggestion. . . ." She acted, as she tried to explain, "by pulling up all the rags of her own soul." By "her force of will, her mastery of herself, . . . by continually controlling nature into the forms of her desire, as the sculptor controls the clay under his fingers," she portrayed at home and abroad, until 1913 and a return to the stage in

1923, characters that ranged from Marguerite in *La Dame aux camélias* to Santuzza in Verga's *Cavalleria Rusticana* (*Rustic Chivalry*) (1884), from comic Mirandolina in *The Mistress of the Inn* to Paula Tanqueray, from Ibsen's Ellida in *Fruen fra havet* (*The Lady from the Sea*) (1888) and Mrs. Alving (whom she hated) to D'Annunzio's *La Gioconda* (1899) and *Francesca da Rimini.* Duse created all these "totally different women, none of them Duses, though Duse is all of them." Her art "arose from her life and what she was." [20]

Second, Duse brought to the play she appeared in an idea. Not a thesis, not anything as intellectual as that, but a deeply felt, pervasive oneness for the whole. She found in a character, or she put into it, her sensitive response to life, then simplified that response, and extracted from it something like a principle. She discovered "what is most significant, a right relation of the concrete to the ideal, of the phenomenon, the accident, to the permanent, the essential. . . . To her a drama or a character exhibited only some power of life that lay in it; and so [even] to hollow roles . . . she brought a devastating light; she acted out of herself some beauty and meaning that the dramatist had never imagined; and what he had not felt, of love, irony, radiance, she felt and created in the role." Duse did that despite the fact that she professed, when she so rarely talked at all about acting, that the actress "must be merely the faithful attentive collaborator, who forces himself to transmit, without deforming it, the poet's creation to the public." [21]

Third, Duse made for her idea "a form . . . inseparable from it," a form intrinsic to the medium in which she worked, to the motion and sound of a human being in the presence of an audience. She seldom used her strong mimetic gift merely to reproduce or counterfeit. Everything she presented had "a certain removal and restatement to it." Duse's acting, though realistic, wasn't "a copy of something which we may see in life and from which we may guess the inner thought; no, it exhibited—as great painting does or great sculpture—a visual design as free of or as faithful to actual nature as the artist chooses to make it." And always about her acting hovered the echoes of music. Duse looked not only to her own response to experience but "to every form of art for help, for sustenance, for inspiration" in the shaping of her expression. Acting that carefully designed served Duse ill, of course, in films. She made a few reels once, and destroyed them because disastrously she had used "'theatrical' techniques despite every effort to avoid them." They just didn't work on camera. Acting there—and then, not now—was different from acting onstage. To act beautifully in films, Duse said, "I would start afresh. . . . I should have to learn from the bottom up, forgetting the theater entirely, and concentrating on the special medium of this new art." [22] To her, as to all artists, including realists, the medium was of prime importance.

In the first years of this century, then, Duse luminously perfected the art of realistic acting by making the real poetic and the poetic real.

✿ TO THEATRICALIZE OR NOT?

In Germany in this period Hauptmann, despite his leanings toward fantasy, turned fashionably into a naturalist. His best work behind him, he wrote such true-to-life plays as *Michael Kramer* (1900), the comic *Der Rote Hahn* (*The Red Cock*) (1901), and *Rose Bernd* (1903). But, yearning for something less ordinary and more colorful than life, he also told a medieval legend in verse with *Der Arme Heinrich* (*Poor Heinrich*) (1902), and used the symbolism of a fairy tale in *Und Pippa Tanzt!* (*And Pippa Dances!*) (1906).

Also during these years Wedekind continued with an amazing but erratic imagination to break away from naturalism and to people his nightmares of sex with symbolic abstractions. His difficult, not widely popular plays included *Der Marquis von Keith* (1900), *So ist das Leben* (*Such Is Life*) (1902), *Die Büchse der Pandora* (*Pandora's Box*) (1903), and *Tod und Teufel* (*God and Devil*) (1906).

Austrian Arthur Schnitzler, an urbane realist, gently dissected the inner lives of people in four one-acters called *Lebendige Stunden* (*Living Hours*) (1901), in his most characteristic script, *Der Einsame Weg* (*The Lonely Way*) (1904), in *Der Ruf des Lebens* (*The Call of Life*) (1905), and *Der junge Mardardus* (*The Young Mardardus*) (1910). More floridly, Hugo von Hoffmannsthal (1847–1929), a librettist for Richard Strauss, "blew a retreat from naturalism with stirring words on the importance of poetic vision" [23] in a modernized, neurotic *Elektra* (1903), taken from Sophocles, a psychological *Das Gerettete Venedig* (*Venice Preserved*) (1905), recreated from Otway's tragedy, and an inspired translation of *Oedipus Rex* (1910).

In Hungary Ferenc Molnar (1878–1952) spurned realism to concoct playful, sophisticated theater pieces like *Äz Ördög* (*The Devil*) (1907) and the not initially successful *Liliom* (1909).

Max Reinhardt, however, who first staged *Elektra*, was more crowd-catching and immediately more important than any dramatist. Eclectic, energetic, and showy, he started producing plays in 1902, and by 1910 had made the director the most dynamic factor in the theater and Berlin the anti-realistic theater capital of Europe. Although he had been a naturalistic actor under Otto Brahm, Reinhardt believed that the theater "is the happiest loophole of escape" from a bourgeois life too "narrowly circumscribed, and poor in feeling." So, as a director he announced that "There is no one form of theater which is the only true artistic form"; [24] he exhibited all types of plays from all countries and periods on all sorts of stages; and by exploiting machinery, lighting, scenery, costumes, and music to their fullest he dazzled audiences with make-believe. He retheatricalized the theater.

Although Reinhardt sometimes staged realistic plays, he "put his heart and soul into the most ornate, . . . the baroque theater. . . ." In the nine productions he directed for his first season, 1902–03, at the Kleines and Neues Theaters, realism was best represented by Strindberg's *Brott och brott* (*There Are Crimes and Crimes*) (1899) and Gorky's *The Lower Depths* (1902), in which he acted Luka; antirealism was represented by Wilde's *Salomé*, Maeterlinck's *Pelléas et Mélisande*, and Wedekind's *Earth Spirit*. For his second season thirty-year-old Reinhardt staged twenty-four different plays, including a realistic *The Vultures* by Becque, *The Fruits of Enlightenment* by Tolstoy, and Schiller's *Intrigue and Love* along with a nonrealistic *Medea* by Euripides, Lessing's *Minna von Barnhelm*, and Shaw's *Candida*. Then early in 1906 at the Deutsches Theater, seating 1,000, he inventively, sensationally staged *A Midsummer Night's Dream* and "did away in one evening with all the voluptuous pessimism and sordidness of the preceding fifteen or twenty years of naturalism." For the 1909–10 season at the Deutsches and the Kammerspiele, seating only 300, Reinhardt directed thirteen new productions plus a repeat of *Hamlet,* and revived eleven more on tour in Budapest, Vienna, and Munich. The plays ranged from *Ghosts* to *Oedipus Rex,* from *Major Barbara* (1905) to an exotic, pantomimic *Sumurun* (1910) by Friedrich Freksa (1882–?) with music by Victor Hollaender (1866–1940), from *Lysistrata* to *Le Bon roi Dagobert* (1908) by André Rivoire (1872–1930) and Felix Salten (1869–1945).[25]

Yet in all his rich shuttling back and forth between realistic and nonrealistic plays magician and businessman Reinhardt apparently learned little about the complexities of acting and contributed next to nothing to its development. He found it "stagy"; he left it a bit more so. Yes, he could announce, to a roll of publicity drums, that "It is to the actor and no one else that the theater belongs"; but by that he meant "first and foremost, the actor as poet," and "likewise the actor as director, stage manager, musician, scene designer, and certainly not least of all, the actor as spectator," whose "contribution . . . is almost as important as that of the cast." Reinhardt's concern with acting went no deeper than "How will it contribute to the over-all theatrical effect I'm aiming at?" In most instances he persuaded actors "to surrender to the ensemble, . . . to the total picture he [had] worked out." His theory of acting, based on realism, which could be rather heavily stylized, was limited to a meager, martinet "Do as I tell you" or "Do as I do." When rehearsing with a cast, often at length and in Teutonic detail, Reinhardt usually demonstrated how he wanted each of them to speak and move. He compelled everyone to do what he did; and most of what he did was prepared in detail ahead of time and set down in a promptbook. As one of his players typically reported, "Reinhardt's personality dominates one to such an extent that one must copy all his intonations, all his emphases," all his movements. He even "shows the actor a ready-made feeling. . . ." In short, he disallowed his actors a method of working out their characterizations, and thus nearly erased their individualities. Many "who came to Reinhardt without name, often won a reputation in a short time, which they . . . lost as soon as they left Reinhardt." [26]

Alexander Moissi was the most gifted and praised "Reinhardt actor." A dozen others were Max Pallenberg (1859–1934), Rudolph Schildkraut (1865?–1930), Albert Bassermann (1867–1952), Friedrich Kayssler (1874–), Paul Wegener (1874–1948), Camilla Eibenschütz (?–1958), Else Heims (1878–), Tilla Durieux (1880–), Lucie Höflich (1883–1956), Werner Krauss (1884–1959), Emil Jannings (1887–1950), and Elizabeth Bergner (1900–).

Georg Fuchs (1868–1949?) was another German antirealist. In 1908, while he was directing *Faust* and *Twelfth Night* at the München Künstler Theater, he adopted as his motto: "Retheatricalize the theater." Then in his *Die Revolution des Theaters* (1909) he blasted actors who, "like monkeys, . . . have been trained to ape the empty clutter and inane behavior of the everyday world," to reproduce "a fleeting fragment of the accidental and obvious so that those of vulgar and complacent mind may sigh, 'Ah, such is life.'" Fuchs urged actors to shun the literary, the psychological, the naturalistic in an attempt to "give complete physical expression to intellectual and emotional concepts." In the actor's art, he wrote, "the most fundamental and essential element [is] rhythm, in movement, in speech, and in gesture." [27]

II

In mid-1900, when the Moscow Art Theatre began its third season, and waited for Chekhov's third script, Stanislavski directed Ostrovsky's *The Snow Maiden* and Ibsen's *An Enemy of the People*; his coleader, Nemirovich-Danchenko, directed Ibsen's symbolic *Naar vi doede vaagner* (*When We Dead Awaken*) (1899). An autocrat like Reinhardt, Stanislavski handled his actors like puppets in working on Ostrovsky's fairy play for almost three months (103 rehearsals). And though he professed to find it "engaging to invent something that has never happened in life, but is nevertheless true," he was too much the copyist, the naturalist, to succeed with fantasy. He overloaded the production with realistic touches, and emphasized each one so strongly that the play was submerged in a plethora of details. It was withdrawn after only twenty-one performances. Stanislavski was happier with his role in *An Enemy of the People*. Not "a great actor, as indeed he himself stated many times," he nevertheless felt a deep affinity with Stockmann, believed in him, and proceeded to incarnate him by making-up like the composer Rimsky-Korsakov, by remembering how a scholar he'd met in Vienna manipulated his fingers, by copying a "sawing the air" gesture of Gorky's, by shifting from foot to foot like a well-known Russian musician and critic, and so on.[28]

Next, with hopes high, Stanislavski prepared a detailed promptbook for Chekhov's *Tri sestri* (*The Three Sisters*), setting down "who must cross to

where and why, what he must feel, what he must do, how he must look.
. . ." But since he didn't quite understand the script, didn't know how to
capture and express its subtle, *inner* reality, the play "only just scraped
through the rehearsals" [29] and flopped its first night in January 1901. *The
Three Sisters* was rerehearsed and revived that autumn, but never found its
true form until about three years later. After that it remained a permanent
gem in the repertoire.

Late in 1902 Stanislavski produced Leo Tolstoy's *The Power of Darkness*
on the lines of ordinary, everyday life. "We made," he wrote, "an expedition
for the purpose of studying village life to the estates of Stakhovich in the
Government of Tula, the place where the action was supposed to have tran-
spired. We lived there for two weeks and visited the nearest villages. . . .
We studied the buildings, and yards, barns, outhouses, and main structures
on the estate. We studied the customs, the marriage ceremonies, the run of
everyday life, the details of husbandry. We brought back with us from the
village clothes, shirts, short overcoats, dishes, furniture. Not only that—we
also brought two living specimens of village life with us, an old man and an
old woman . . . [who] were to direct the play from the viewpoint of village
customs." But all this "unjustified naturalism was a mistake," and the play
failed. Stanislavski also failed as Mitrich even though he pasted bumps on
his forehead and disfigured his hands, feet, and body in order to look like
a mujik.[30]

Still enamored with external realism, however, and "guided by living
memories and not by invention or guesswork" or imagination, Stanislavski
and Nemirovich-Danchenko scored a triumph in December 1902 with *Na
dna* (*The Lower Depths*) by Maxim Gorky (1868–1936). The play was
presented sixty-one times that season. But Stanislavski admitted that as
Satine he "overacted romanticism and fell into ordinary theatrical pathos
and declamation." [31]

On that same successful realistic basis the Moscow Art Theatre in
October 1903 produced *Julius Caesar*. Nemirovich-Danchenko journeyed to
Italy to look for inspiration and historical details on the actual site of the
Roman Forum, while Stanislavski prepared a promptbook crammed with
lifelike details and told the actors that they must play Shakespeare "in Chekhov tones." The presentation, of course, was a dud. Stanislavski failed
miserably as Brutus; the unreal lines, the poetry, were beyond his grasp. He
was forced to admit that "we do not possess a technique for the saying of
the artistic truth in the plays of Shakespeare." [32]

With a sigh of relief the company welcomed Chekhov's realistic *Vish-
nyoviy sad* (*The Cherry Orchard*). On its first night in January 1904 the
play was only "a mediocre success," probably because Stanislavski had overlooked its comedy and again had missed its inner truth. After some time,
however, he found the latter, the cast expressed it, and the play became the
most popular Moscow Art Theatre production. And the inner truth that

Stanislavski discovered "served as the foundation for what was later called the Stanislavski System." [33]

That same year, 1904, Valery Bryussov (1873–1924), a poet and leader of the symbolist movement in Russia, boldly attacked the naturalistic methods of production at the Moscow Art Theatre. In an article, "Unnecessary Truth," published in *The World of Art*, he ridiculed Stanislavski for attempting to reproduce faithfully the environment of a Chekhov play, for pretending that his stage rooms had four walls, through one of which the audience might eavesdrop, and for stressing trivial, pointless realistic details, such as, curtains of an opened window blowing in the wind. The theater must stop copying life, Bryussov argued, because the art of the stage is in essence, and by distinction, unrealistic.[34]

Stung by such criticisms, Stanislavski and Nemirovich-Danchenko extended their theatrical researches "toward the fashionable influence of symbolism." But they were wary. They knew, after some of their Ibsen failures, that "It is a hard nut to crack—the Symbol." In 1904 they experimented with an evening of Maeterlinck one-acters, *The Blind* and *The Interior*. Then near the end of 1905 the two leaders set up an experimental studio under Vsevolod Meyerhold, who'd left the company in revolt against its realistic methods. The Studio functioned on the principle "that realism and local color had lived their life and no longer interested the public. The time for the unreal on the stage had arrived. It was necessary to picture not life itself as it takes place in reality, but as we vaguely feel it in our dreams, our visions. . . ." For a while the actors rehearsed Maeterlinck's *Le Morte de Tintagiles* (1894), Hauptmann's fantastic masque, *Schluck und Jau* (1899), and Ibsen's *Love's Comedy*. But when Stanislavski didn't understand or appreciate the new abstract stagings and ways of performing, the Studio was abandoned. As the First Revolution broke out he was more firmly convinced that the naturalistic line of acting was the only line, and that it has to "become one with the more important line of the intuition of feelings." [35]

At the start of 1906 the Moscow Art Theatre gave sixty-two performances in Berlin, Dresden, Prague, Vienna, Frankfurt-on-Main, Hannover, Karlsbad, Wiesbaden, and Warsaw. Five realistic plays were acted: the company's initial success, *Tsar Feodor Ivanovich*, *An Enemy of the People*, *Uncle Vanya*, *The Three Sisters*, and *The Lower Depths*.

Back in Moscow the company tried Ibsen's symbolic *Brand*; it failed. Then in 1907 Stanislavski, perplexed, even agonized by his failures with non-realistic plays, tried Knut Hamsun's (1859–1952) abstract *Livets spil* (*The Game*, or *Drama*, *of Life*) (1896). With this play, which demanded "a different and specialized form of acting," Stanislavski said, "I first consciously applied all my attention as a stage director almost entirely to the inner character of the play and its roles." He taught his actors to forget the external and to search for the inner, "unseen, unembodied passion" of the soul. The play met with a mixed reception and ran for only twenty-seven performances.

The conjecture is that Stanislavski tried for the impossible by urging his actors "to live" abstractions. Undaunted, however, he decided to devote his work and attention from then on "to the study and teaching of inner creativeness," to "the superconscious through the conscious!" [36]

Then, paradoxically, the Moscow Art Theatre presented in stubborn succession three nonrealistic plays: in 1907 the mystic allegory, *Zhizn cheloveka* (*The Life of Man*) (1906) by Leonid Andreyev (1871–1919), and in 1908 Ibsen's symbolic *Rosmersholm* and Maeterlinck's *The Blue Bird*. Only the latter (which the author sniped at) was a success. At the end of that year, with Gogol's *The Inspector General*, the theater "returned to realism, to a deeper, more refined and more psychological realism." [37]

All this while Stanislavski was puttering with his notions of acting. He had become magnetized by "the feeling for truth." At times when he acted *he forgot he was onstage*; and "it was especially at such times," he remembered, "that my creative mood was most pleasant." He decided that "The art of actors consists in living the part." [38]

In May 1908 Stanislavski wrote to a close friend about his new system of acting "which during the last few years I have got sufficiently ready." Then in December of that year, after four months of rehearsing, he "scored the first victory for his 'system'" [39] with a brilliant production of the quietly psychological *A Month in the Country* by Turgenev. His system, however, was far from complete. He was still adding basic principles and hunting for exercises. As a matter of fact, he still didn't know how to direct or act nonrealistic plays. To learn something about that he asked Gordon Craig to stage a production of *Hamlet* for the Moscow Art Theatre.

III

Vsevolod Meyerhold could have taught Stanislavski what he wanted to know: that art isn't life, that the theater isn't meant to be a copy of anything, that acting is more than living a role. After the closing of the Moscow Art Theatre's experimental Studio in 1906, Meyerhold went to St. Petersburg to work at the theater of Vera Komizarjevskaya, the antirealistic actress. There, searching for purely theatrical forms of expression, he directed a highly stylized *Hedda Gabler*; Maeterlinck's *Soeur Béatrice* (*Sister Beatrice*) (1899), in which the acting was "stylized as regards the intonations, gestures and movement," [40] the premiere of the symbolic, *commedia dell' arte*-styled *Balaganchick* (*The Booth*, or *The Puppet Show*, or *Farce*) (1906) by Alexander Blok (1880–1921), Wedekind's lyrically lurid *The Awakening of Spring*, the premiere of the medieval *Pobeda smerti* (*The Triumph of Death*) (1907) by Feodor Sologub (1853–1926), and finally *Pélleas et Mélisande*.

At Vera's theater Meyerhold was succeeded by Nicolai Evreinov (1879–1953) and her brother, Theodore Komisarjevsky (1883–1954), who continued to battle the Moscow Art Theatre's objective method of representation which allowed audiences no opportunity of using their imaginations. Two of their striking productions were Wilde's *Salomé* and Andreyev's nightmarish *Cherniya maski* (*The Black Maskers*) (1908). Evreinov, in particular, and often with ridicule, hoped to drive the last nail "into the coffin of (external) realism," sure that "no one will go so far as to deny the rightfulness of at least certain conventionalities in the existence of the theater." [41]

In 1910 at the Alexandrinsky Theatre in St. Petersburg Meyerhold caused a considerable buzz of excitement with his production of Molière's *Don Juan*. He abolished the curtain, used the forestage, kept the house lights on during the entire performance, and compelled his actors frankly to *act* a play that was frankly pretense: "Blackamoors inundating the stage with intoxicating perfumes. . . . Blackamoors flitting over the stage to pick up a lace hankerchief dropped by Don Juan or to offer a chair to a tired actor. Blackamoors tying the laces on the shoes of Don Juan as he argues with Sganarelle. Blackamoors passing lanterns to the actors when the stage is in darkness. Blackmoors removing from the stage the cloaks and sabers after the desperate fight between Don Juan and the brigands. Blackamoors ringing a silver bell to summon the audience and . . . announcing intermissions. . . ." [42] In short, he offered audiences presentational theater, and they loved it: *Don Juan* was performed thirty times that season and repeatedly thereafter.

Also in 1910 producer-writer Evreinov staged at his Theatre of the Crooked Looking-glass an evening of five condensed versions of *The Inspector General*. "The first was a classical production of the play. The second was an ultrarealistic version in the spirit of Stanislavski. The third was a grotesque performance in the style of Max Reinhardt. The fourth was a mysterious conception of it in the style of Gordon Craig. Finally the fifth was a parody of what a film version of it might be. . . ." [43]

Proof enough, therefore, wasn't lacking—except to the narrow-minded —that the theater needn't be, can't be, limited to only the naturalistic. Stanislavski, however, may have agreed that "Naturalism isn't everything." Possibly he believed only that it is "a good starting point, without which the artifice of dramatic convention, essential in art, cannot exist." [44]

❀ ENGLISH-SPEAKING ACTORS

The British and American theater of the first ten years of the century can be quickly summarized since the happenings there were not as experimental as they were elsewhere.

In London the top players were studied, fading Henry Irving, Ellen Terry, John Hare, Madge Kendal, classical Johnson Forbes-Robertson, Charles Wyndham, romantic Herbert Beerbohm Tree, comic Charles Hawtrey (1858–

1923), George Alexander (1858–1918), Shakespearean Frank Benson, John Martin-Harvey (1863–1944), who was to be Irving's successor, Janet Achurch (1864–1916), Marie Tempest (1864–1942), and Mrs. Patrick Campbell. Of this group only a third might be called realists: Madge Kendal, Hare, and Hawtrey performed, mostly in comedies, with a sort of genteel natural- ness, and Janet Achurch in serious plays could match the truthfulness of the Russians.

Yet during this period English acting moved grudgingly toward the realistic—without forsaking theatricality or "staginess"—in such plays as Pinero's well-made Iris (1903) and Mid-Channel (1909), in Barrie's The Admirable Crichton (1902) and What Every Woman Knows (1908), in Galsworthy's The Silver Box (1906), Strife (1909), and Justice (1910), in The Playboy of the Western World (1907) by John M. Synge (1871–1909), and in Granville-Barker's (1877–1946) The Voysey Inheritance (1905), Waste (1907), and The Madras House (1910), in which he "sought to ex- tend the realistic form beyond its Ibsenite bounds." [45]

Some plays, however, weren't realistic. Shaw's Man and Superman (1903, first staged in 1905), Major Barbara (1905), The Doctor's Dilemma (1906), Misalliance, and Fanny's First Play (both 1910) can't be performed correctly by actors who must live their roles. Neither can the Barrie fantasies, Quality Street (1902) and Peter Pan (1904).

The best British acting in the early 1900's was monitored by Barker, eminently a director, who "handled drama in terms of an actor." [46] He entered the theater as an actor, and between 1891 and 1904 impersonated nearly thirty characters. In 1899, when he was twenty-two, Barker first attracted at- tention as Shakespeare's Richard II. Next year he was the perfect March- banks in Candida, in 1903 he impressed critics as Marlowe's Edward II, and in 1904 his reading of the Messenger in the Hippolytus of Euripides, as translated by Gilbert Murray (1866–1957), confirmed the high opinion of his skills. He was on his way to becoming a first-rate nonrealistic actor.

Then from mid-1904 to mid-1907, with business associate John Vedrenne (1863–1930), and with considerable help from Shaw, Barker managed the small, "out-of-town" Court Theatre as an experiment in battling the censor and commercialism—especially the long-run system. New plays were per- formed a week or two, at first only at matinees, taken off, and revived if the demand warranted. The "aim of the Court was freedom from the dom- ination of 'the witless majority' on one side of the curtain, and from the bonds of stereotyped social comedy and melodrama, from commercial specu- lation, and from domination by the actor-manager on the other." In three years the Court unprofitably offered "nearly a thousand performances of thirty-two plays by seventeen authors, and although critics were fond of referring to it as a Shavian temple (Barker produced eleven of his plays), plays of Euripides, Galsworthy, Yeats, Ibsen, Hauptmann bore out Barker's declaration that it was rather a place 'for the production of anything and everything that has genuine art about it.'"[47] About twenty of the plays were nonrealistic.

Barker acted Keegan in Shaw's *John Bull's Other Island* (1904), Valentine in *You Never Can Tell*, Tanner in *Man and Superman*, Adolph Cusins in *Major Barbara*, Dubedat in *The Doctor's Dilemma*, and General Burgoyne in *The Devil's Disciple*, as well as Pierrot in his and Laurence Housman's (1865–1959) *Prunella* (1904), Hjalmar Ekdal in *The Wild Duck*, and Edward Voysey. Some of his players were his first wife, the expert Lillah McCarthy (1875–1960), Mrs. Patrick Campbell, Edith Wynne Matthison (1872–1955), William Poel, Louis Calvert (1859–1923), Nigel Playfair (1874–1934), Edmund Gwenn (1875–1959), Lewis Casson (1875–), Robert Loraine (1876–1935), Henry Ainley (1879–1945), Harcourt Williams (1880–1957), and Godfrey Tearle (1884–1953). And audiences "were able to say, with new meaning, how excellent London actors are."[48]

In 1904 Barker found that British acting was falling between two stools —the rhetorically conventional, "a technique outworn and discarded," and the naturalistic, "an attempt to do without any technique at all." At the Court he tried to remedy that mishap. But, unlike Stanislavski, he didn't turn the actor in on himself. He wasn't the least bit interested in anyone's living a role, or in the actors feeling natural. Like most English actors, even today, Barker probably held that "an actor cannot afford what is loosely called living the part, than which there is no greater trap. If he does live the part he is liable to live it differently, and perhaps wrongly, three nights out of four. What he must do is acquire the emotional attributes of the character, then discipline himself to the job of reproducing them with regularity."[49]

Barker turned the actor's attention toward the script, the play. "All acting," he said some years later, "is interpretation" and "demands a technique of interpretation." Actors, he continued, echoing Coquelin, "must continue what the dramatist has begun by methods as nearly related to his own in understanding and intention as the circumstances allow." The "traits of each dramatist mold and pervade his work and should dictate a related method for its interpretation."[50] In brief, Barker insisted that the actor must sense the meaning and the form, realistic or nonrealistic, of the words as set down by the author, and go on from there to increase the richness of his characterization.

At the Court, Barker battled the "no technique" naturalists by advocating an intelligent, calculated, designed realism in acting. When he directed, each character's every action was not only felt, and never lived, but "exactly worked out, timed, and detailed" for its contribution to the whole structure of the play. At the same time Barker avoided the external, empty sights and sounds of old-fashioned "staginess" by emphasizing underplaying. He preferred "the muted, subtle, sensitive, and delicate air." According to Shaw, Barker's "fault was to suppress his actors when they pulled out all their stops and declaimed. . . . They underacted, or were afraid to act at all lest they should be accused of ranting or being 'hams.' " Barker's "style and taste were as different from mine as Debussy's from Verdi's. With Shakespeare and with me he was not always at his happiest and best." [51]

Thus Granville-Barker, despite his failure in establishing a repertory theater first at the Court, then in 1907 at the Savoy in the West End, and finally with the American Charles Frohman at the Duke of York's in 1910, indelibly contributed to the modernization of British acting in ways quite different from Stanislavski's. In due time, and significantly, he would become an outstanding preceptor of poetic acting with his discerning *Prefaces to Shakespeare* (1927–47).

Ellen Terry's son, Gordon Craig (1872–), however, was more widely, though indirectly, influential than Barker. As a theorist, a dreamer (although he did stage a few productions), he railed against realism in the theater, against "the blunt statement of life, something that everybody misunderstands while recognizing." The fact that the modern actor "attempts to make a picture to rival a photograph . . . , tries to reproduce Nature," made Craig wish "that photography had been discovered before painting, so that we of this generation might have had the intense joy of advancing, showing that photography was pretty well in its way, but there was something better!" In 1907 he wrote that "to train a company of actors to show upon the stage the actions which are seen in every drawing room, club, public house or garret must seem to everyone nothing less than tomfoolery." "This tendency towards the natural," he continued, "has nothing to do with art, and is abhorrent when it shows in art, even as artificiality is abhorrent when we meet it in everyday life. We must understand that the two things are divided, and we must keep each thing in its place. . . ." [52]

All art, all acting, Craig maintained, not newly, has to do with calculation that creates the *spirit* of the thing. And the person who disregards calculation "can only be but half an actor. . . . The perfect actor would be he whose brain could conceive and could show us the perfect symbols of all which his nature contains. He would not ramp and rage up and down in *Othello*, rolling his eyes and clenching his hands in order to give us an impression of jealousy; he would tell his brain to inquire into the depths, to learn all that lies there, and then to remove itself to another sphere, the sphere of the imagination, and there fashion certain symbols which, without exhibiting the bare passion, would none the less tell us clearly about them. And the perfect actor who should do this would in time find out that the symbols are to be made mainly from material which lies outside his person." [53]

If, then, Craig continued, "Art arrives only by design," acting can't be an art when "the mind of the actor . . . is less powerful than his emotion," when only living the role counts, as Stanislavski would soon teach. For then "emotion is able to win over the mind to assist in the destruction of that which the mind creates," and "accident upon accident must be continually occurring." [54]

Therefore, Craig teasingly announced that the all too human actor who can't, or won't, *design his expression via his medium* "must go, and in his place comes the inanimate figure—the Über-marionette we may call him. . . ." Then these marionettes, like the members of an orchestra, can be controlled and guided by the director—the only possible restorer of the true Art of the Theater—toward the creation of "a *noble* artificiality." [55]

II

In the United States during the first decade of the century nobody cared much about theories of acting; the theater flourished more as business than as art. At the forty-three playhouses in New York City in 1900 (sixty-eight in 1926), with companies "on the road," and at countless resident stock companies throughout the land managers profited by offering audiences glamorous escapes into classics, romances, melodramas, slightly realistic comedies, and musicals. From the start Americans were expert and creative in the musical branch of presentational theater. Some of the early twentieth-century successes in this field were: the Weber and Fields *Fiddle-dee-dee* (1900), with De Wolf Hopper (1858–1935), Lillian Russell (1861–1922), Fay Templeton (1865–1939), and David Warfield; *Floradora* (1900), which originally ran for 505 performances; *Robin Hood* (1902) by Reginald De Koven (1861–1902); Fred Stone (1873–1959) in *The Wizard of Oz*, (1903); Victor Herbert's *Babes in Toyland* (1903), *Mlle. Modiste* (1905), and *The Red Mill* (1906); and the *Ziegfield Follies* of 1907, 1908, 1909, 1910.

Regular plays offered during this period weren't much. *Ben-Hur* ran the 1899–1900 season and part of the next, and was revived in 1903 and 1907; two productions of *Quo Vadis* opened the same night in April 1900. In 1903 Hoosier George Ade (1866–1944) tried for comic, rural color in *The County Chairman*. In 1905 the topical, big business *The Lion and the Mouse* by Charles Klein (1867–1915) scored 686 performances; London-born William Faversham won a solid success in *The Squaw Man* by Edwin Milton Royle (1862–1942); and Bertha Kalich (1874–1938) briefly emoted in *Monna Vanna*.

Three hits next year, in 1906, were the political *The Man of the Hour* by George Broadhurst (1867–1952) with Douglas (Ulman) Fairbanks (1883–1939), the trashy *The Chorus Lady* by James Forbes, and a Western *The Three of Us* by Rachel Crothers (1878–1958). Augustus Thomas added telepathy to melodrama in *The Witching Hour* in 1907. And in 1908 the funny, patriotic, Hoosier bragging of Booth Tarkington (1869–1946) and Harry Leon Wilson (1867–1939) in *The Man From Home* was sandwiched between the two chief foreign hits of the period, Bernstein's *The Thief* in 1907 and Molnar's *The Devil* with English George Arliss (1868–1946) in 1908. Finally, Edward Sheldon with *The Nigger* (1909) seriously explored an American problem.

Clyde Fitch (1865–1909) was the prolific, popular playwright. In 1900–01 ten of his plays were running in New York City and on tour. Among them were *The Climbers* and *Captain Jinks of the Horse Marines* in which Ethel Barrymore (1879–1960) dazzled her way to stardom. At his death at the age of forty-three Fitch had written some fifty highly skilled, but superficial, scripts like *The Girl with the Green Eyes* (1902), *The Truth* (1907), and *The City* (1910).

Actor-writer George M. Cohan (1878–1942) also pleased the public with a batch of enormously popular, intrinsically light musicals, among them *The Governor's Son* (1901), *Little Johnny Jones* (1904), in which he first became a star, *George Washington Jr.* (1906), and *The Talk of New York* (1907) plus some straight plays such as *Forty-five Minutes from Broadway* (1906). Cohan was the typical American man of the theater. He possessed "undoubted talent and a great knowledge in the means by which his ends [were] wrought. But this is a thin region after all, boyishly abundant on the prose side and covering a wide, but not very deep, section of our popular life." [56]

Saintly faced, priest-garbed David Belasco was the most successful man of the theater at this time. When he came east from San Francisco in 1880, he reputedly had "acted 170 parts, directed almost as many plays and written or adapted over one hundred plays." In New York he became an independent producer in 1890, and ten years later, at the age of thirty-one, was acclaimed for his fidelity to sensational realism in staging. His allegiance to truth, however, went no deeper than "what he thought his audiences would accept as truth," such as, blood dripping from the ceiling in his own *The Girl of the Golden West* (1905), real tulips growing in the garden in *The Return of Peter Grimm* (1911), or sizzling wheatcakes served in an exact duplication of Child's Restaurant in *The Governor's Wife* (1912).[57]

Belasco's carefully cultivated, long-lasting theater wizardry was no more than an instinct for writing, rewriting, or selecting poor scripts, a Stanislavski skill at decking them out with all sorts of naturalistic details and showmanship gimmicks, and a Reinhardt martinet way of bossing his actors ("who almost invariably played better for him than they did before or after being with him") in "big" scenes that pandered to primitive passions. The best you can say of him is that he had an uncanny, dedicated sense of the theater, that "again and again he . . . devoted his rich resources to doing the lesser thing perfectly." [58]

Some of his shows were: the one-act *Madame Butterfly* (1900) written in collaboration with John Luther Long (1861–1927) and starring Blanche Bates (1872–1941); *The Auctioneer* (1901) by Charles Klein and Lee Arthur (1876–1911), in which David Warfield (1866–1951) became a star; *The Darling of the Gods* (1902), another highly profitable collaboration with Long; Warfield again in Klein's long-running *The Music Master* (1904); Richard Walton Tully's (1877–1945) *The Rose of the Rancho* (1906), with

Frances Starr (1886–); William C. De Mille's (1879–1955) *The Warrens of Virginia* (1907) with Cecil B. De Mille (1881–1959) and Mary (Gladys Smith) Pickford (1893–) in the cast; and a realistic, melodramatic *The Easiest Way* (1909) by Eugene Walter (1864–1941).

During this period American acting was influenced largely by the British and continually nourished through visits to this country by Irving and Terry, Hawtrey, Hare, Wyndham, Forbes-Robertson, Ben Greet, Mrs. Patrick Campbell, and others. It was also stimulated by the playing of Polish Modjeska, Bernhardt and Coquelin, Réjane, Duse, Novelli, Komisarjevskaya, and Alla Nazimova (1879–1945).

Mrs. Patrick Campbell helped widen the interests of the American theater by acting in Björnson's *Beyond Human Power*, Echegaray's *Mariana* (1892), *Pelléas et Mélisande*, *Hedda Gabler*, and von Hoffmannsthal's *Electra*. Nazimova, a Moscow-trained leading lady from St. Petersburg, exhibited in English a kind of acting that was deeper and more intensely psychological in its approach to characterizations, and therefore more pervasively real, than Jefferson's had been. Her work in 1906 and 1907 as Hilda in *The Master Builder*, as Hedda, and as Nora in *The Doll's House* was new enough to startle some audiences at first; but slowly it commanded admiration.

At the start of the century the great Joseph Jefferson, most often as Rip Van Winkle, tottered out his long life onstage. James O'Neill was more often than not still rhetorically portraying Dantes in *Monte Cristo*. Dapper John Drew starred in such polite pieces as Pinero's *His House in Order* (1906), with Billie Burke (1885–) in the French derived *My Wife* (1907), and with Mary Boland (1880–) in Somerset Maugham's (1874–) *Jack Straw* (1908). Scot Robert Mantell recited the plays of Shakespeare in 1904, 1907, and 1909. Gillette underplayed his *Sherlock Holmes* (1899) through most of 1900, revived it in 1902, appeared in *The Admirable Crichton* in 1903, returned as Sherlock in 1905, and then performed in Frenchman Henri Bernstein's *Samson* (1907) in 1908.

Romantic Richard Mansfield now and then revived *Cyrano* and *The Devil's Disciple*, was King Henry V in 1900, Tarkington's (*Monsieur*) *Beaucaire* in 1901, Brutus in 1902; then in 1904 he tackled (*The Death of*) *Ivan the Terrible* by Alexei Tolstoy plus a dramatization of Robert Louis Stevenson's (1850–1894) *Dr. Jekyll and Mr. Hyde*, in 1905 *Le Misanthrope*, and finally in 1907 *Peer Gynt*. Otis Skinner acted in his own adaptation of Stevenson's *Prince Otto* in 1900, was Petruchio in 1904, starred in *The Duel* (1905) by Henri Lavedan (1859–1940) in 1906, and found a long-lasting hit in *The Honor of the Family* (1908), a dramatization taken from Balzac. English born E. H. Sothern, after trying Hauptmann's *The Sunken Bell* and *Hamlet* in 1900, triumphed in 1901 as Villon in *If I Were King* by Justin McCarthy (1861–1950), and then played repertory, mostly Shakespeare, with Julia Marlowe in 1904, 1905, 1908, and 1909.

Henry Miller moved from Armand in *Camille* in 1904 to the hero in the first modern American play, *The Great Divide* by William Vaughn Moody (1869–1910). James K. Hackett (1869–1926) pleased in *The Walls of Jericho* (1904) by English Alfred Sutro (1863–1933). (Peter) Arnold Daly (1875–1927) turned Shavian as Valentine in *You Never Can Tell* and Marchbanks in *Candida* in 1905, then as Bluntchli in *Arms and the Man* in 1906. Walter Hampden (1879–1955) as Solness joined Nazimova in *The Master Builder* in 1907, and next year with English Edith Wynne Matthison was praised in *The Servant in the House* by Charles Rann Kennedy (1871–1950).

Seven American actresses stood out among many—too many to list here—who were both charming and competent. Ada Rehan was Portia in *The Merchant of Venice*, Katharine in *The Taming of the Shrew* and Lady Teazle in *The School for Scandal* in 1905. Intelligent, modern Minnie Maddern Fiske tried Nora in *A Doll's House*, *Hedda Gabler*, Rebecca West in *Rosmersholm*, Lona Hessel in *The Pillars of Society*, and Hauptmann's poetic *Hannele*, but won her biggest successes in Langdon Mitchell's (1862–1933) satire on divorce, *The New York Idea* (1906) and *Salvation Nell* (1908) by Sheldon. Viola Allen played Viola in *Twelfth Night*, both Hermione and Perdita in *A Winter's Tale*, and Imogene in *Cymbeline*. Beautiful Maxine Elliott became an independent star in Fitch's *Her Own Way* (1903), and built her own theater in 1908.

Maude Adams, after acting *L'Aiglon* in 1900, took to Barrie with *Quality Street* in 1901, *The Little Minister* in 1904, *Peter Pan* in 1905, and *What Every Woman Knows* in 1908. Margaret Anglin, leading Lady in Charles Frohman's Empire Theatre Stock Company (starting its thirteenth season in 1900), appeared in *Mrs. Dane's Defense* (1900) by Henry Arthur Jones and *Diplomacy* (or *Dora*) (1877) by Sardou in 1901, and then was Camille in 1903 and the heroine in *The Great Divide* in 1906. Ethel Barrymore acted with her brother John (1882–1942) in Barrie's *Alice-Sit-By-the-Fire* in 1903, briefly was Nora in *A Doll's House* in 1905, and then appeared in Galsworthy's *The Silver Box* in 1907.

Some of the American acting at this time was less "stagy" than it had been. A number of players agreed with Gillette who said that "Drama can make its appeal only in the form of simulated life as it is lived—not as various authorities on grammar, pronunciation, etiquette, and elocution happen to announce . . . that it ought to be lived." [59] But they still knew how to project to the galleries and to gesture boldly, to face three-quarters front, to begin a cross with the upstage foot, to upstage others, and to take center stage.

Mansfield, for one, was sure in theory if not in practice that "Declaiming is not acting." Yet the voice was valued by Mrs. Fiske and others as "the beginning and the end" of the art. "Three hours of voice practice every day of the season—that, properly, is the actor's chore. He *must* have such practice at least one hour a day," she said. "With any less time than that it is absolutely impossible to keep the instrument in proper condition, absolutely impossible." And Nazimova believed that "Sincerity and the correct use of voice are the greatest things in the art of acting. . . ." [60]

No American actor was as deeply concerned as Stanislavski was at this time with feeling the role, or "living the part." Mrs. Fiske, for instance—who, incidentally, told an interviewer once that On Actors and the Art of Acting by Lewes was "the soundest and most discerning treatise on the subject I have ever read"—was opposed to an actor's only feeling or living a role anew at every performance. She insisted that there ought to be a science, "a complete technic of acting." Like the Lunts in our time she worked for "a precision of performance." "Any one," she argued, "may achieve on some rare occasion an outburst of genuine feeling, a gesture of imperishable beauty, a ringing accent of truth; but your scientific actor knows how he did it. He can repeat it again and again and again. He can be depended on. Once he has thought out his role and found the means to express his thought [and his emotion?] he can always remember the means." Relying on that memory in later performances, he need not feel so keenly again. "The greater the artist, the less keenly need he feel. The actor with no science must keep lashing at his own emotions to get the effect a master technician would know how to express with his thoughts at the other end of the world." [61]

Belasco, taking his cue from Diderot and Coquelin, agreed. "In acting," he maintained, "there never can be, in the very nature of things, any real feeling." When "sensibility is permitted to hold sway," the actor loses "complete self-control, dominion, poise, authority. . . ." [62]

"A good actor," as Nazimova explained, "should be able to make an audience, any audience, feel what he wants it to feel. That is his assignment. . . . But no losing yourself in the part! No being transported into other worlds by the emotion of the play! . . . One watches oneself always." [63]

Finally, Gillette, fully aware that playwriting was more closely approximating life, and that consequently "the merest slip from true life-simulation [by the performer] is the death or crippling of the character involved," strongly emphasized an old notion about acting and advocated a new one. First, he was sure that every presentation of a play "must have that indescribable life-spirit or effect which produces the illusion of happening for the first time." [64]

Second, he disagreed with Mansfield, Belasco, and Nazimova who believed that an expert actor ought to be able to impersonate an unlimited number of totally different roles "often most unlike himself." Nazimova, for instance, remarked that always "I have to reconstruct my whole self into this woman I am to portray—speak with her voice, laugh with her laughter, move with her motion." Gillette, however, argued that the new verisimilitude forced the actor to delineate only those characters "within the limited scope of his [own] personality," or to transfer his own unique individuality to each and every assigned role. [65] In short, he used only his own voice, laughter, and motion in all his impersonations. His reason for saying and doing that was simple. Gillette was a run-of-the-mill, highly competent actor. Never a great one. He *couldn't possibly* imagine anyone except himself. In that respect he resembled so many film players of today—and some Stanislavski disciples.

III

Motion pictures were only four or five years old in 1900, but they were catching on. In France, George Méliès continued to experiment with pictorial fantasies like *Blue Beard* (1901) in 690 feet, *A Trip to the Moon* (1902) in 845 feet, and *The Palace of Arabian Nights* (1905) in 1,400 feet.

Americans, however, weren't as yet interested in fantasy. They at once knew that films could capture living reality in direct representation. So, in 1903 Edwin S. Porter (1870–1941) directed for the Edison Company, with Gilbert "Bronco Billy" Anderson (1882–) in the cast, *The Great Train Robbery*. Partly filmed outdoors on 740 feet (eight minutes running time), the wholly cinematic quality of this realistic melodrama excited interest everywhere. Porter, looking for more and more realism, made in 1906 *A Desperate Encounter between Burglar and Police* which accurately depicted "scenes and incidents of a noted crime in New York City . . . , and the same night-watchman and the same policemen who took part in the real tragedy are seen in the picture." [66]

David Wark Griffith (1875–1948), a stock company actor since 1897, pantomimed for $5 a day in 1907 in another Porter film, *Rescued from an Eagle's Nest*. Next year, for the Biograph Company, he directed his first movie, a brief *Adventures of Dollie*, and thereafter "an average of two films a week, one roughly a reel long, the other shorter." In 1909, when he was thirty-four, Griffith directed *The Lonely Villa*, with a vague script by New York bit player, Mack Sennett (1884–1960), and with Mary Pickford in the cast. That same year he used new technical devices, took ten days to shoot *A Corner in Wheat*, and "tried to make his characters resemble people in real life and to reveal them intimately." [67]

❀ AFTER 1910: COPEAU

World War I (1914–18) consumed almost half of the next decade. In Spain, before its outbreak, Benavente continued to pour out his plays, among them the realistic *La Malquerida* (*The Passion Flower*) (1913) and *Campo de armiño* (*Field of Ermine*) (1916). And Gregorio Martínez Sierra (1881–1947) with the mild *Canción di cuna* (*Cradle Song*) (1911), *El Reino de Dios* (*The Kingdom of God*) (1916), and *Sueño de una noche de Agosto* (*A Dream of an August Evening, or The Romantic Young Lady*) (1918) attracted some international attention. So did Serafín (1871–1938) and Joaquín (1873–1944) Quintero with the gentle realism of such pieces as *Papá Juan, centenario* (*A Hundred Years Old*) (1909) and *La Malvaloca* (1912).

In Italy several searching playwrights moved away from realism to the "teatro del grotesco," among them Luigi Chiarelli (1884–1947) with a first-rate satire, *La Maschera e il volto* (*The Mask and the Face*) (1916). And one of the most original playwrights of the century, Luigi Pirandello (1867–1936), philosophically examined the very nature of reality. His not very lifelike characters in *Così èse vi pare* (*Right You Are—If You Think So*) (1916), *Il piacere dell' onesta* (*The Pleasures of Honesty*) (1917), and *L'uomo, la bestia e la virtù* (*Man, Beast, and Virtue*) (1919) either seriously or humorously debate the question, "Where and what is truth?"

In France Sacha Guitry (1885–1957) was technically skilled in pleasing Boulevard audiences with unfailing "wit and sentiment, gayety and melancholy, realism and fantasy, delicacy and vulgarity, poetry and cynicism." His scripts ranged from the frivolous *La Veilleue de nuit* (*The Night Watchman*) (1911), *Faisons un rêve* (*Sleeping Partners*) (1916), and *L'Illusioniste* (1917) to biographies like *Deburau* (1918) and *Pasteur* (1919). In contrast, Paul Claudel (1868–1955) used the stage "as a vestibule to the altar" and musically, mystically exhalted the "passion of the universe." His theme was the eternal relationship between man and woman and between man and God. In expressing it he "marvelously profited from the achievements of the symbolists, from thirty years of poetic acrobatics, in order to create his own eloquence, with its remarkable suppleness and abundance and weight." His glory was to have his plays compared, by some, with those of Aeschylus and Shakespeare.[68] Claudel's *Portage de midi* (*The Break of Noon*), written in 1906, wasn't staged until 1921. But the greatest modern Christian drama, his *L'Annonce faite à Marie* (*The Tidings Brought to Mary*), was produced in 1912 at Lugué-Poë's Théâtre de l'Oeuvre. And *L'Ôtage* (*The Hostage*), written in 1911, was staged there in 1914. That same year *L'Échange* (*The Exchange*) was first performed at the Théâtre du Vieux-Colombier.

To Jacques Copeau (1878–1949), however, French actors are fond of saying, "goes the honor of raising the theater to the level of the other arts; of restoring to our profession a certain greatness. . . ." Today there is "not an author or an actor that is not heir to his labors, who is not his debtor." [69]

In 1907, before he was thirty, Copeau served as dramatic critic for *La Grande Revue*, and later was one of the founders of *La Nouvelle Revue Française*. At that time naturalism was dead in France. And classicism was petrified, symbolism "was full-blown like a flower whose petals prepare to fall," and realism was superficially purveyed in well-made marital plays produced with profitable but boring regularity. Copeau lashed out at all such commercial and middle-class pretences at art. He hoped "to . . . rescue . . . reality from the disorder and shrinkage of an industrial world." [70]

To do that, however, Copeau had to get *in* the theater. So, in 1911 he co-dramatized Dostoyevsky's *Les Frères Karamazov*, which was staged at the Théâtre des Arts with Charles Dullin (1885–1949) as Smerdyakov and Louis Jouvet (1887–1951) as Father Zossima. And by 1912 he'd written the first

act of *La Maison natale* (*The House into Which We Are Born*), not produced until near the end of 1923.

Then in mid-1913, indignant at a theater "suffering from a lack of guidance and discipline, from greediness for profit, and the absence of a common
ideal; disgusted with "the great 'stars' who . . . throw stage-productions out
of balance, attract the audience's attention to themselves rather than to the
play, and cheapen the playwright's talent by using their plays only as vehicles
for their stardom"; and determined "To put an end to 'ham-acting,' " Copeau
set out to prove "that for the theater to regain its touch with life and all that
was newly alive in art . . . it must cut free from the hectic Boulevard."
He founded the Théâtre du Vieux-Colombier as a "rallying point for those
who . . . are tormented by the need of restoring once more . . . beauty to
the stage." With some personally selected actors—ten of them, including
Dullin and Jouvet—he imitated Stanislavski's example by retiring to the
country, to Le Limon, an hour's ride from Paris, to study and rehearse plays
for more than two months in a small woodshed. There every day for five
hours the group worked on several productions. Two further hours each day
were devoted to "sight readings as exercises in mental alertness and voice
training, to analyses of literary texts . . . , and to physical exercises." [71]

During these preparations Copeau clung to a simple, almost chaste
ideal, namely, that "the literary drama must remain the soul of the theater." [72]
For him, first, the playwright is the prime and essential creator. Here, of
course, he was diametrically opposed to Craig.

Second, in his "opposition to the realistic theater," Copeau searched not
for more naturalness but for style, for "the poetry proper to the theater." "The
word *poetry* served him as a passport in acting, staging, and writing. . . ." [73]
Here he differed from Stanislavski.

The problem of production, Copeau felt, is how to recreate a script *into
form*, not necessarily into something resembling life; and the correct form,
he knew, can be found only in the text as set down by the author, not elsewhere. Certainly not in nature. "We have found that a good script," he
wrote, "contains time-spans—movements and rhythms—comparable to those
in music and, as in music, capable of generating space. The question of what
space or playing area to choose in a given play, or in a given scene from a
play, is therefore not an unimportant matter. For there is a stage economy
that corresponds to dramatic economy, a performing style engendered by a
literary style; and indeed, a theater's physical structure may serve to heighten
and enhance the intellectual structure of a play or, on the contrary, to distort
and destroy it." Copeau believed, it seems, that the director as artist "is
always a creator of essential form, and the more purely this form is real, the
more it is abstracted and remote from the reality of the realists." [74]

Third, Copeau was convinced that "the actor . . . is the very warp and
woof of the play, the living presence of the author, giving substance and life

to his design. Everything is done by the actor and for the actor; all the rest is superfluous." [75]

Therefore, Copeau tried to school actors "in the *métier* of the mind, . . . in the school of poetry," and toward simplicity of expression. He taught them "their essential and primordial function: no more and no less than to serve the author's idea, to make it legible, intelligible, in form and rhythm, convention and reality, keeping what is natural without the banality or corruption of the naturalistic school, preserving style without the pomposity and absurdity of the Conservatory fossil. . . ." [76]

And, fourth, Copeau followed the theories of Swiss Adolphe Appia (1862–1928) by stripping his stage of all the then fashionable machinery and decoration in order to emphasize the presence of the actors in space.

At the start of September 1913 Copeau and his actors returned to Paris, and nearly two months later, on October 22, in an entertainment hall seating scarcely five hundred (the Athénée Saint-Germain on the Rue du Vieux-Colombier on the Left Bank), performed Heywood's *A Woman Killed With Kindness* (1603) and Molière's *L'Amour médecin*. The opening scene of the former consisted of "a table, two high-backed chairs, and a sun-gold background"; another scene was limited to "an iron fence and dark blue drapes." Next month the group acted a new script, *Les Fils Louverné* by Jean Schlumberger (1877–). Among other plays presented were Molière's *L'Avare* and *La Jalousie du Barbouillé*, de Musset's popular *Barberine* (1835) with only a chair, a table, and a cushion on the proscenium, *The Brothers Karamazov*, and in February 1914 the season's highly successful closer, *Twelfth Night*, in which Olivia's room, for instance, was represented by only a green semi-circular bench, two flowering bushes, and a staircase in front of blue drapes. [77]

The outbreak of the War in August 1914 scattered the troupe. Copeau, however, was eager to open a school for actors. Near the end of 1915, after conferring with Gordon Craig and eurhythmic Emile Jaques-Dalcroze (1865–1950), he started teaching "a dozen pupils, boys and girls, under the age of twenty. The initial training began with the students imitating animal sounds, assuming the shapes of trees, benches, and other inanimate objects in order to make their bodies supple and adaptable for any theatrical purpose. Varied improvisations, rhythmic attitudes, and the use of masks were part of the training." [78]

In June 1917 Copeau was sent by the French Ministry of Fine Arts to lecture in New York City; he returned there with a subsidized company of actors in November, opened at the Garrick Theatre, and remained for two seasons to stage nearly fifty productions in French. The opening bill consisted of Copeau's *Impromptu du Vieux-Colombier* and *Les Fourberies de Scapin* (with Copeau in the title role), both acted on a bare stage with a platformlike structure at the center in front of an orange velvet curtain.

The farce was a dismal failure. Mild successes of the first season, however, included *L'Avare, The Brothers Karamazov* (with Copeau as Ivan), and *Twelfth Night*. For his second season Copeau, yielding to American tastes, staged a number of standard, popular scripts—by Augier, Brieux, Rostand, Hervieu, and Dumas *fils*. However, *Le Mariage de Figaro* (1784) by Beaumarchais (with Copeau in the title role), Molière's *Le Médecin malgré lui* and *Le Misanthrope*, de Musset's *Les Caprices de Marianne* (1833), and *Rosmersholm* were presented in a fairly profitable season. But Copeau complained that in the United States he had found again, "with all his heads complete, and more threatening than ever," the dragon he had sallied forth to kill in 1913. Yet "Despite the misunderstandings and sometimes obtuse criticisms in New York, the body of critics realized, after the termination of its visit, that this French theater had in some way been wonderful. . . ." [79]

Back in Paris in 1919, Copeau enlarged the stage at the Vieux-Colombier into a permanent, almost Elizabethan, architectural platform and early in 1920 reopened his theater, now seating only about three hundred, with *The Winter's Tale*. Parisians were indifferent to it, however, and to such plays as *Le Paquebot Tenacity* (*S. S. Tenacity*) by Charles Vildrac (1882–). "On July 17, 1920, Copeau declared a deficit of 116,000 francs." [80] But, undaunted, he continued his search for style and purity in acting at his theater and at his school, in charge of playwright Jules Romains (1885–), until the middle of 1924.

Beginning in 1919 Russian actor-director Georges Pitoëff (1887–1939), assisted by his actress wife Ludmilla (1896–1951), also battled the commercial theater in Paris by staging simply at various theaters plays by Chekhov, Shaw, Ibsen, and Shakespeare. He also first produced *Le Temps est un sorge* (*Time Is a Dream*) (1919) and *Les Ratés* (*The Failures*) (1920) by Henri-René Lenormand (1882–1951) who in dialogue between the conscious and the subconscious exposed the abnormal tragedies of modern individuals.

❊ EXPRESSIONISM

In Germany between 1910 and 1920 much of the theater was excitingly nonrealistic. Reinhardt, in his ninth season (1910–11) at the Deutsches and Kammerspiele Theaters, directed seventeen productions. Among his typical successes were *The Comedy of Errors* and *Othello*, Molière's *Le Mariage forcé*, and Goethe's *Faust II*. In addition, he brought *Oedipus Rex* to Vienna and Budapest in 1910 and *Sumurun* to London in 1911. For the next season he directed nineteen productions, including the *Oresteia* and *Jedermann* (*Everyman*) as adapted by von Hoffmannsthal in the Zirkus Schumann. He also staged *The Miracle*—based partly by Karl Vollmöller (1878–1948) on *Sister Beatrice*—in London in 1911, and *Oedipus Rex* in both London and Moscow as well as *Sumurun* in New York City in 1912. In 1913–14 he toured Cologne, Paris, Prague, Hamburg, Vienna, and Budapest. In 1916–17 one of his twenty offerings was the American Mitchell's *The New York Idea*. In 1919–20 at Berlin's Grosses Schauspielhaus "for the five thousand" he presented massive productions of *Danton* (1901) by Romain Rolland (1868–1944), the *Oresteia*, *Helios* by Hauptmann, *Antigone* (1917) by Walter Hasenclever (1890–1941), and *Julius Caesar*.

Reinhardt's well-organized energies and talents were endless. In twenty-five years at Berlin he directed 452 plays for a total of 23,374 performances distributed as follows among his ten favorite playwrights: Shakespeare, 2,527; Shaw, 1,207; Wedekind, 1,171; Hauptmann, 974; Goethe, 746; Strindberg, 491; Tolstoy, 473; Molière, 333; Sternheim, 318; and Ibsen, 306.[81] Of these playwrights, Carl Sternheim (1878–1943) gained attention by forging a satirical weapon out of naturalism to knife middle-class viciousness and hypocrisy. Two of his best plays are *Die Hose* (*The Underpants*) (1911) and *Der Snob* (1913).

II

Reinhardt's only competitor for audience attention in these years was a weird Expressionism as introduced in Germany by Reinhard Sorge (1892–1916) with *Der Bettler* (*The Beggar*) written in 1912, produced in 1917, Hasenclever's *Der Sohn* written in 1914, produced in 1916, and *Die Verfuehrung* (*The Seduction*) written in 1913, produced in 1916, and *Himmel und Hoelle* (*Heaven and Hell*) (1919) by Paul Kornfeld (1889–1944) of Prague. Then Georg Kaiser (1878–1945) popularized the new form with *Von Morgens bis Mitternacht* (*From Morn to Midnight*) (1916) and *Gas*, in two parts (1918, 1920).

Expressionism, like Reinhardt's theatricality, was primarily a reaction against realism. Derived in part from Strindberg and Wedekind, and encouraged by Freud, it is essentially the projection in art of the inner self. The expressionist "seeks to give meaning to all that happens within the ego, to grasp into the chaos of the unconscious and bring to the light of consciousness whatsoever meaning there is to this existence of ours." In most instances, therefore, he's obliged to distort the objective world in an attempt to convey to others his own subjective responses to it. In Ernst Toller's (1893–1939) *Masse-Mensch* (*Man and the Masses*) (1921), for example, "the central figure (a woman . . . Sonia) is the direct autobiographical projection of the author's soul—his feminine, pacifistic, nobly humanitarian, all-embracing soul, not symbolized but, rather, concretely objectified." [82] In fact, all the characters in an expressionistic play are usually dreamlike abstractions, figments of the brain of the author (or of a central character); and their actions, often fragmentary and disconnected, take place not in nature but amid symbolic forms or in space.

The actors, consequently, forget their ties to everyday living, and often "chant and intone or . . . shout and bark; sound-effect is the main thing, rather than (primarily) meaning-effect. The element of sound, in acting, must have a direct emotional effect, utterly presentational, casting the connotational meanings of objective reality; it must be antinaturalistic and, hence, (theoretically) more theatrical, more abstractly artistic." Similarly, the "actors move and gesticulate with abrupt, studied, mechanical, almost marionettelike movements, reminding one at times of the two-dimensional profile figures on Egyptian . . . friezes." [83]

As Kornfeld wrote in his epilogue to The Seduction: "Let not the actor in this play behave as though the thoughts and words he has to express have only arisen in him at the very moment in which he recites them. If he has to die on the stage, let him not pay a visit to the hospital beforehand in order to learn how to die; or go into a bar to see how people act when they get drunk. Let him dare to stretch his arms out wide and with a sense of soaring speak as he has never spoken in life; let him not be an imitator. . . . In short, let him not be ashamed of the fact that he is acting. If the actor builds his characters from his experience of the emotion or fate he has to portray and with gestures adequate to this experience, and not from his recollections . . . he will see that his expression of a feeling which is not genuine and which has really been artificially stimulated is purer, clearer, and stronger than that of any person whose feeling is prompted by a genuine stimulus." [84]

Leopold Jessner (1878–1945), German producer, became most famous "as an exponent of the expressionistic theater and the theater theatrical." [85] In 1919 he was appointed director of the Berlin State Theater where he stunningly staged Richard III, Othello, Macbeth, Schiller's The Robbers and Wilhelm Tell, Faust, Christian Grabbe's (1801–1836) Napoleon, oder die hundert Tage (Napoleon, or the Hundred Days) (1831), and Wedekind's Marquise von Keith.

Jessner's "technique of signification" employed only those details, however "unnatural," which could heighten the depiction of vital experience. He refused to be hindered "by obligations to faithful reproduction." Influenced by Appia, and like Copeau, he insisted that "the inner continuity of every play is best to be presented in the theatrical space arrangements of the actors," and he moved them arbitrarily, expressively left and right, forward and back, up and down, singly and in groups on various levels and stairs. Movement was meant to serve several functions. "It could, for instance, . . . serve to define the relations between characters; it could, on the other hand, have an emotional and symbolic significance. . . ." Jessner also energized his actors—notably Fritz Kortner (1892–)—into speaking, not naturally, but with an intensity and a rhythm that electrified audiences. Moreover, as a thoroughly presentational director, he set his "actors and their movements, the setting and its lights, talking directly to the audience." [86]

Some of Jessner's productions were "marred by excessive stylization, grotesqueness, caricature, ecstatics," [87] just as productions by Antoine and Stanislavski were marred by excessive attention to lifelike details. But the point is that Jessner believed that the theater must not aim to reproduce life. Stanislavski believed that it should.

❀ STANISLAVSKI PREPARES

Stanislavski had his troubles from 1910 to 1920—not entirely the result of the Revolution (1917–1920).

Following the realistic productions of Brat'ya Karamazovy (The Brothers Karamazov) in 1910 and of Tolstoy's Zhivoi trup (Redemption, or The Living Corpse [written in 1900]) in 1911, the Moscow Art Theatre finally offered Craig's production of Hamlet in December 1911. It wasn't a success. Rehearsals had disclosed a number of serious faults in Stanislavski's tentative system, especially between the motives of the actors' feelings and their expression onstage. And his dividing the play into small sections, into "Units and Objectives," resulted in the actors' losing sight of the play as a whole. Furthermore, the actors were so addicted to "humdrum naturalness and simplicity" they couldn't speak the verse. They "fell back upon declamation, a dead seesaw rhythm, and a methodical flow of monotonous voices and monotonous conventionalization of speech." Thus "Hamlet on the stage of the Moscow Art Theatre became a kind of realistic 'middle-class' drama." Stanislavski concluded that he still had to find "methods and means [to act] plays in the heroic and the grand style." [88]

At least five of the next productions, none of them quite successful, were nonrealistic: Peer Gynt and Andreyev's symbolic Katherina Ivanovna in 1912, Molière's Le Malade imaginaire in 1913, Goldoni's The Mistress of the Inn in 1914, and the poetic Mozart and Salieri as part of a bill of short Pushkin plays in 1915. Stanislavski claimed that he "felt and lived" Salieri. "But when it became necessary to incarnify all that was lived over inwardly by the sound of the voice, by the poetic phrase, by resonant and rhythmic words, by controlled motions, I saw myself that I had neither voice nor diction, plastics, nor rhythm, nor tempo. I was a mere dilettante." Stanislavski, and most of his actors, could impersonate only roles "which were near to their own lives." [89] They lacked an awareness of their medium. They lacked imagination.

For a while Stanislavski considered staging the premiere of the famous Jewish, mystic folk tragedy, The Dybbuk (written in 1914, first produced in 1920) by S. (Solomon A. Rappaport) An-sky (1863–1920); but for some reason he didn't. During the 1917–18 season the Moscow Art Theatre presented only one new play, a realistic adaptation from Dostoyevsky, "The Village of Stepanichikovo," which Stanislavski had first staged in 1891. During the rehearsals director Nemirovich-Danchenko, dissatisfied with Stanislavski's interpretation of Colonel Rostanev, took the part away from him and effected a break between the co-founders.

The Revolution began in late 1917, all theaters were nationalized in

1919, and near the middle of 1920 Stanislavski produced Byron's Biblical *Cain* (1821). It failed.

Here it is important to note that in 1912 Stanislavski, smarting from "the lukewarm, if not hostile, reception" of his tentative system by the leading actors of the company, had set up a First Studio, or laboratory theater, under his close friend, Leopold Sulerzhitsky (1872–1916), who was assisted by Eugene Vakhtangov (1883–1922). There his ideas about acting were tried out on students. The First Studio opened in January 1913 with a performance of the realistic *Op Hoop van Zegen* (*The Good Hope*) (1899) by Dutch Herman Heijermans (1864–1924). It was directed by Richard Boleslavsky (1889–1937). In 1914 Sulerzhitsky, who vaguely disagreed with Stanislavski and believed that creativeness "was more than the recalling by the actor of intuitive or experienced emotions," [90] directed a successful production of *The Cricket on the Hearth*, an adaptation of the Dickens story.

When Sulerzhitsky died in 1916, Vakhtangov took over as head of the Studio, and slowly turned it out of the realistic path of the Moscow Art Theatre. "He worked toward three things: the releasing of the theater from obsession with verisimilitude, the unifying of thought and feeling in the actor, and the freeing of acting from 'the power of subconscious and elemental perceptions.' In other words, he drew away from some of the Stanislavski system, placing his stress upon more instead of less 'theatricality' on the stage." Vakhtangov was certain that under Stanislavski's method of "becoming" the character "the actor failed to master feelings and really became subject to them, and so taught that 'the truth of the theater consists in *enacting* the character.'" Therefore, his chief actor, Anton's nephew, Michael Chekhov (1891–1955), "presented not himself metamophosed into the character, but the *idea* of the character." [91] In 1918 the First Studio successfully performed *Twelfth Night*.

II

In 1911 Stanislavski continued to experiment with his system, "notwithstanding that the majority of these experiments," as he confessed, "were incorrect." That same year he became interested in Hindoo philosophy and especially in the yoga system of abstract meditation and mental concentration. This evidently led him to phrasing one of the fundamentals of his own system—the "*circle of public solitude*." Then near the middle of the year he wrote out "The first sketch of the System . . . a typescript of forty-six pages. . . . It was not published." [92]

In the autumn of 1912 Stanislavski "decided to collate his own conclusions on the art of acting with the conclusions reached by the old European masters of stagecraft, and in a letter to [friend and woman dramatic critic Lyubov] Gurevich (1866–1940) in September he asked her to go through all their works in the Petersburg libraries and have the relevant passages translated and typed out for him." [93]

In 1913 at the First Studio Sulerzhitsky supervised the students in exercises for relaxing the muscles, entering the circle of attention (public solitude), and for attaining the feeling of truth and belief. He also worked with them on improvisations. Stanislavski supplemented this work by reading a course of lectures on acting.

Then in the summer of 1914, when he was fifty-one, Stanislavski met Lyubov Gurevich at his vacation spot, Marienbad, and collated the material she'd gathered. "This work," he said later, "clarified many things to me and helped me to lay out the facts I had learned from experience on the shelves of my mind." He was enthusiastic about the "Reflections upon Declamation" by Luigi Riccoboni, and about The Art of the Theatre by Riccoboni's son, Antonio Francesco—even though the two men didn't agree on several basic points. Stanislavski was also greatly interested in Diderot's Paradoxe sur le comédien, the Mémoires of Clairon and Dumesnil, and the "Reflections" by Talma. He liked, in particular, the extracts from the books—perhaps the Mémoires (1825) and the Über meine theatralische Laufbahn (1886)—by Iffland.[94]

You wonder if Stanislavski read the writings on acting by Coquelin, or the books on the subject by Lewes and by Archer. He must have; yet nowhere is there any mention of them. Nor did he take any notice, it seems, of the writings of Craig.

At the end of 1914 Stanislavski wrote that he had "evolved a great deal that is new especially in the sphere of the subconscious and the methods of stimulating the activity of those feelings which are beyond the reach of the conscious mind." [95] Evidently by this time he'd read the Psikholigiia chuvstv, a translation of Théodule Ribot's (1839–1916) Psychologie des sentiments (1896), and become fascinated by the theory of "emotion memories."

Then, while he was slowly trying to put his system of acting into some sort of shape, Stanislavski stubbornly tackled another nonrealistic play, poet Blok's medieval and symbolic Roza i krest (The Rose and the Cross) (1912). He rehearsed it for almost two years—from March 1916 through December 1918. But for some reason it was never performed for the public.

After that, Stanislavski returned to his first love, music, and began working at the Opera Studio of the Moscow Bolshoy Theatre. Starting in 1918 he established there, he said, "a system of classes in subjects that had never been taught in other schools before, the theory and practice of what is called the System of Stanislavski, various exercises in the development of the feeling of rhythm not only in movement, but in the inner sensations and in sight, and so on." [96] He also discoursed to the singers on his findings about acting, findings which he organized eighteen years later into An Actor Prepares. One of the students, K. Antarova, took down in shorthand some of what he said between 1918 and 1922; her transcript, or portions of it, was published after Stanislavski's death as "The System and Methods of Creative Art."

III

While readying his system of acting Stanislavski curiously paid little attention to the work of any of his Moscow colleagues: Komisarjevsky, Tairov, Meyerhold. They might just as well have been producing plays in far away Rio de Janeiro. He didn't stoop to examine, to fathom, or even to find fault with symbolic or presentational performing. He completely ignored them. From this time on he concentrated only on realistic acting. He'd gotten hold of a tiger's tail, and he couldn't or wouldn't let go. He was carried along. He simply had to force all acting into "living the part." Whatever couldn't be made into that wasn't acting.

But the three other Russians can't be that blindly ignored. They, too, were intelligent and dedicated to the theater, to acting. At the Moscow Nezlobin Dramatic Theatre from the autumn of 1910 through 1913, and then at the Imperial Theatres in St. Petersburg until the Revolution, Theodore Komisarjevsky staged a number of well-received, purely theatrical productions. For instance, instead of reproducing a sordid courtyard for Ostrovsky's *Ne bylo ni grosha—i vdrub altyn* (*Not a Copper—and Suddenly a Goldpiece*) (1871) he aimed for the scenic effect of an imaginative, romantic colored print, and then "prettified" the acting to harmonize with it. In his presentational offering of Gozzi's *Turandot* "the interpreters of the comic characters improvised their parts, talked to the audience, danced, produced acrobatic tricks. . . ." And both *The Merry Wives of Windsor* and Molière's *Le Bourgeois gentilhomme*, gaily stylized in settings and costumes, were "played as in a buffonade." [97]

Stanislavski probably judged those productions frivolous. He was so noble-minded, so terribly in earnest about acting. And, like most average audiences, he probably found little that appealed to him in the extremely formalized productions of Alexander Tairov (1885–1950), "the originator of Russian expressionism in the art of the theater." [98]

Influenced by Coquelin's insistence on the truth of Nature *plus* the truth of Art, by the theatricality of Fuchs and Meyerhold (with whom he served for a while as assistant director), and by Craig's longing for über-marionettes, Tairov founded at Moscow in December 1914 the Kamerny (Chamber, or Intimate) Theatre. It was his protest "against the standardized, static norms and forms of reality and their recreation in art," against the dilettantism of both the naturalistic theater and the symbolic theater. [99] Tairov was also against what he called the "bookish" theater. He maintained that a stage presentation ought to be more than a group recitation of literature, that its essence, its distinction, is movement. For him actors moving by design in costumes and amid scenic forms that accented those movements contributed largely to making the theater truly theatrical. And in direct contradiction to Stanislavski, who was telling his actors to forget that they were onstage, Tairov told his actors *never* to forget that fact.

As an innovator Tairov was much too sophisticated to stage merely Russian plays. He overstressed the novel, the esoteric. He whisked audiences out of life in order to show them art. His opening production was the fourth-century, Sanskrit *Sakuntala* by Kalidasa. And two of his attention-attracting presentations in 1917, with decorations derived from cubist painters, were Wilde's *Salomé*, *König Harlequin* (1900) by Rudolf (Spitzer) Lothar (1865–1933?) and *La Boîte à joujoux* (*The Play Box*) (1913), a pantomime-ballet by Claude Debussy (1862–1918). Later esthetic presentations, which seemed to minimize humanity, included *Adrienne Lecouvreur* by Scribe and Legouvé in 1919, and in 1920 *Princess Brambilla*, taken from a tale by E. T. A. Hoffmann (1776–1822), and *The Tidings Brought to Mary*.

At the Kamerny for more than twenty years Tairov fostered antirealism in acting. It "certainly . . . isn't enough," he wrote, "to ask the actor only to feel. . . ." Oh, no. The actor must be long and vigorously trained to *express*, to convey to an audience. He must learn how to use his body, hands, arms, legs, head, eyes (as a ballet dancer does), his voice and his speech. He must learn to use his unique medium—as a painter uses his medium, a musician his. Then "What craft, what tireless vigilance, what carefulness must be yours as an actor in order to subject your material to your creative will, in order to force it to take the necessary forms. . . ." [100]

"Two fundamental processes, interlaced in a thousand discoverable ways," Tairov said, "are involved in the creation of every work of art: the process concerned with the inner state, the artistic idea [or content], and the process concerned with its outward embodiment" (or form). [101] Therefore, the actor as artist must try to perfect both an inner and outer technique. (From Tairov Stanislavski may have learned to emphasize both an inner and an outer technique in acting. But on his own he confused the meaning of "inner state," and then capriciously changed inner technique-as-idea into inner technique-as-natural-truthfulness on the part of the performer.)

Meyerhold—born in Pensa of German parents, he dropped his given names of Karl Theodor-Kasimir for that of Vsevolod in honor of Russian author Vsevolod Garshin (1833–1888)—was more potently antirealistic, anti-Stanislavski than Tairov. He refused "plenary faithfulness to the minutiae of life," and "sought to unearth an absolute reality . . . independent of photographic exactness. . . ." He "sought to endow life on the stage with fuller implications than any individual's senses conceived in life itself." [102]

Is it possible, he asked, to call someone who appears onstage as he really is an "actor"? What *art* is there in that? The public expects make-believe, acting, craftmanship, and gets, instead, either life, or a slavish imitation of it." "The modern actor," he continued, "never 'acts,' but merely 'lives' on the stage. He does not understand the theater's magic word: 'acting.'" Or that the purpose of acting "is to lead the audience into the realms of imagination and to entertain it on its way by his technical brilliance," by "invented gesture, suitable only in the theater; [by] conventional movement, possible only in the theater, [and by] the artificiality of stage elocution," permitted only in the theater. Let those who desire to look at and to listen to naturalness go to the movies. "The kinematograph," he wrote, "is the realized dream of those who have been striving to obtain a photographic impression of life, a striking instance of extreme attachment to quasi-naturalness." [103]

So, Meyerhold decided that "in the theater we must translate everything into theatrical terms." Like Copeau, he began "a search for style." And by 1912, when he was thirty-eight, he had found "in the theater of the Greek mimes or the old Roman comedy of masks, [in] the medieval histrion-jongleurs, . . . the old Russian zanies, the Italian Commedia dell' arte, . . . the wandering actors of England and Spain, . . . [and in] the folk theater of Japan and China . . . a single style of folk theater common to all." Its distinguishing features were: "(1) Independence from literature and gravitation toward improvisation; (2) the prevalence of movement and gesture over the word; (3) the lack of psychological motivation in acting; (4) a rich and trenchant comic quality; (5) easy transitions from the lofty-heroic to the base and the ugly-misshapen and comical; (6) the spontaneous combination of ardent rhetoric with exaggerated buffonade; (7) an effort at generalization, synthesizing of the characters by singling out sharply a given feature of the character, leading thus to the creation of conventional theatrical figures—masks; (8) the lack of any differentiation of the functions of the actor: the coalescence of the actor with the acrobat, jongleur, clown, juggler, mountebank, songster, fool; (9) the universal technique of acting conditioned by this versatility, built upon the mastery of one's own body, upon an innate rhymicality, upon an expeditious and economical use of one's movements." [104]

That style of acting, somehow modernized, Meyerhold set out to revive. "No one who was interested in being himself, no one whose ideal in the theater was feeling his or her own part, no one who brought a personal relationship to the role or the play, no one who could say 'I don't feel comfortable in this position or with this piece of business,' no one who looked at the theater as a place where life was mirrored, no one who had ideas as to what kind of role he or she would play, could possibly find asylum in his theater." Meyerhold rarely told his actors "This is what you'd do if you were this character in these circumstances." Instead, he said to them, "This is what an actor might do." [105]

In short, Meyerhold advocated the presentational theater. Disagreeing with Stanislavski, who'd "placed the center of gravity of the production on the stage," he "transferred it to the audience." "Here in the theater," he might have said, "we are spectators and actors. Let us admit this fact and make the best of it." [106]

By 1912, Meyerhold was teaching the new-old principles of acting at his studio and experimenting with the production of "theatricalized" plays in St. Petersburg. Among the many scripts he staged were Blok's allegorical *Neznakomka* (*The Unknown*) (1906) in 1914, for which he introduced "practicables" and levels in order to accent the movements of his actors; Ostrovsky's realistic *The Thunderstorm* in 1915; and Lermontov's romantic *Masquerade* in 1917. Then in 1918, on the first anniversary of the Revolution, he electrified audiences by directing, at the Party's request, "An Heroic, Epic, and Satiric Representation of Our Epoch," the propaganda-pageant, *Misteriya-Buf* (*Mystery-Bouffe*) by Vladimir Mayakovski (1893–1930). His fame thus assured, Meyerhold in 1920 was appointed head of the Theater Section of the Commissariat of Education. At once, after accusing the academic producers of "deliberately and systematically destroying the traditions of the great masters of the theater, of diligently cultivating the theatrical rubbish of the second half of the nineteenth century," [107] he tried to revolutionize Russian staging and acting.

IV

To sum up: while Stanislavski was determined to prove that the best acting is like living, or behaving naturally, both Tairov and Meyerhold were just as determined to prove that it isn't. And the latter had on their side critic Alexander Bakshy (1855–1929) who pointed out in 1916 that acting "must be distinguished from other activities of life by something that is peculiar to itself"; otherwise, we'd be justified in calling anything that anyone does in everyday life acting. And "this peculiarity" that separates acting from living, he said, "is its *form*." [108] Acting is human behavior *designed* in terms of the theater. Or in terms of the camera.

It is necessary to note, however, that there can be too much design in acting. First, design can interfere with communication. It can become so "pure," so esoteric, it has no meaning for average audiences. Too often it appeals only to specialists in love with significant form. Second, "in the distortion, the abstraction, and the exaggeration which are the necessary tools of the radicals and modernists in art, there lies the danger of supposing that design and technique are an end rather than a means, that most human attributes are unnecessary or irrelevant. There is more to the meaning of art than the perception of abstract relations between the various parts of a design. . . ." [109]

Many of us can agree with Thomas Craven who, in his *Men of Art*, paid tribute "to the power and the glory of artists whose work is impregnated with human meanings and interwoven with the fabric of the social structure as opposed to the futile practitioners of art for art's sake." And we can understand critic Kenneth Tynan when he writes: "I became aware that art, ethics, politics, and economics were inseparable from each other; I realized that theater was a branch of sociology as well as a means of self-expression. . . . I learned that all drama was, in the widest sense of a wide word, political; and that no theater could sanely flourish unless there was an umbilical connection between what was happening on the stage and what was happening in the world." [110]

Acting, for sure, should never be *only* design. *What* the actor designs is the essential thing. But design he must. Shape his timely matter he must.

❀ MOSTLY BOX-OFFICE

Neither British nor American men of the theater had much time from 1910 through 1920 to think about design in acting. Most of them were too busy making money. Shaw, for instance with *Androcles and the Lion* (1912), *Pygmalion* (1913), and *Heartbreak House* (1920), first produced by the American Theatre Guild, was well on his way to becoming the richest playwright ever. And box-office successes were recorded for Barrie's *A Kiss for Cinderella* (1916) and *Dear Brutus* (1917), for Galsworthy's *The Pigeon* (1912), Maugham's *Our Betters* (1917), A. A. Milne's (1882–1956) *Mr. Pim Passes By* (1919), and the like. At least one expert new performer, Edith Evans (1888–), attracted attention in 1912.

The standard examination of most acting in English at this time was Louis Calvert's *Problems of the Actor* (1918). From his long experience in both Great Britain and the United States he offered students advice about "The Voice," "Getting Inside One's Part," "The Eye and the Hands," "The Emotions," "The 'Tone' of a Performance," and so on.

On this side of the Atlantic, Belasco, having "gauged the American *esthetik* as probably no other showman . . . has gauged it," [111] continued to thrill audiences with his elaborately tricky realism. Among his triumphs were his own long-running *The Return of Peter Grimm* (1911), 384 performances of *Tiger Rose* (1917) by Willard Mack (1873–1934), Ina Claire (1895–) in *Polly With a Past* (1917) by George Middleton (1880–) and Guy Bolton (1881–) and in *The Gold Diggers* (1919) by Avery Hopgood (1882–1928), and Granville-Barker's version of Sacha Guitry's *Deburau* in 1920.

Incidentally, during the run of *Peter Grimm* the star, David Warfield, "kept all members of his fine cast constantly on edge with his tricks and his pranks. On one occasion he spread limburger cheese inside the petals of a bowl of tulips," and when the leading lady buried her face in them "she almost became ill onstage." In another scene of the play freshly made waffles and coffee were served—since this was a Belasco production—and "one evening the prankful Warfield, carrying whimsy to quite an extreme, substituted castor oil for the maple syrup." [112]

Belasco, according to George Jean Nathan (1882–1958), "contributed

one—and only one—thing for judicious praise to the American theater. He
. . . brought to that theater a standard of tidiness in production and matura-
tion of manuscript, a standard that has discouraged to no little extent that
theater's erstwhile not uncommon frowzy hustle and slipshod manner of
presentation. But what else? His plays, in the main, have been the sentimental
vaporings of third- and fourth-rate writers. He has produced none of the
classics; he has produced not a single modern first-rate British play or French
play or German play; he has encouraged no young American talent and those
young Americans whom he has encouraged, he has encouraged to write not
dramatic literature but so-called sure-fire shows, lending to their manuscripts
his fecund aid in devising superficial hokums and punches and other such
stuffs of the two-dollar vaudevilles; he has developed, in all his career, but
one actress, Miss Frances Starr; he has developed, in all his career, but a
single actor, David Warfield." [113]

A baker's dozen of American plays presented by other producers during
this period were: *The Scarecrow* (1911) by Percy MacKaye (1875–1956),
Jane Cowl (1890–1950) in 541 performances of the shopgirl *Within the
Law* (1912) by Bayard Veiller (1869–1943), 441 showings of *Potash and
Perlmutter* (1913) by Montague Glass (1877–1933), the sweet *Peg O' My
Heart* (1912) by J. Hartley Manners (1870–1928), which Laurette Taylor
(1884–1946) acted for an original run of 603 performances, Cohan's *Seven
Keys to Baldpate* (1913), *On Trial* (1914) by Elmer Rice (1892–), the fluffy
Good Gracious Annabelle by Clare Kummer (1873–1958), *Why Marry?* by
Jesse Lynch Williams (1871–1929), *Lightnin'* by Winchell Smith (1871–
1933) and star Frank Bacon (1864–1922), which set a record of 1,291 per-
formances, Lionel Barrymore (1878–1954) in *The Copperhead* (1918) by
Augustus Thomas, Tarkington and Wilson's *Clarence* (1919) with Alfred
Lunt (1893–) and Helen Hayes (1902–), Ethel Barrymore in *Déclassée*
(1919) by Zoë Akins (1886–1958), and the realistic *Miss Lulu Bett* (1920)
by Zona Gale (1874–1939).

Winthrop Ames (1871–1937), a producer more interested in taste
than in receipts, staged Schnitzler's *The Affairs of Anatol* (1893) in 1912
with John Barrymore and Doris Keane (1885–1945) in the cast, *Prunella*
in 1913, and in 1914 revived Fitch's *The Truth* with Grace George (1879–
1961) as star. And stage-manager Guthrie McClintic (1893–1961) "For the
first time . . . heard an actress (Miss George) saying to a director, 'I have
no feeling yet that this is *my* drawing room. Why is it? What can I do?'
(And Mr. Ames would think up some business that would unmistakably
stamp her as mistress of the house.) Or another player saying, 'I don't
feel I can say that line sitting down.' " [114]

In early 1915 Granville-Barker came from London to please some New
Yorkers with his stagings of *The Man Who Married a Dumb Wife* (1912)
by Anatole France (1844–1924) and on the same bill Shaw's *Androcles and
the Lion*, followed by *A Midsummer Night's Dream*. Partly influenced by his

work a group, mostly amateurs, that year formed the Washington Square Players to produce scripts of "artistic merit" ignored by commercial managers. In four years the organization presented inexpensively on a subscription basis sixty-two one-act plays plus six long dramas. Among the latter were *The Sea Gull, Ghosts,* and *The Life of Man.*

For the 1917–18 and 1918–19 seasons Copeau and his company were in New York City.

Art became profitable when John Barrymore portrayed Falder in 106 showings of Galsworthy's *Justice* in 1916, and again the following year when he and Lionel appeared in Du Maurier's *Peter Ibbetson* (1895). Then John acted Fedya in Leo Tolstoy's *Redemption* (*The Living Corpse*) in 1918, brilliantly designed by Robert Edmond Jones (1887–1954) and produced by Arthur Hopkins (1878–1950). "Overnight several rings were added to the American theater oak." [115] Next, for the same team, both Barrymores starred in Benelli's *The Jest* in 1919, and John played Richard III in 1920.

In April 1919 the Theatre Guild, a commercial expansion of the Washington Square Players, began its long, notable career with Benavente's *The Bonds of Interest.* It flopped. But the next production, realistic *John Ferguson* (1915) by Irish St. John Ervine (1875–), cost less than $1,000 and earned nearly $50,000.[116] The third Guild offering was the Japanese *The Faithful* (1915) by British poet John Masefield (1875–). It was followed by a dramatization of William Dean Howells' 1885 novel, *The Rise of Silas Lapham,* and then in 1920 by Tolstoy's *The Power of Darkness* and Ervine's *Jane Clegg* (1913). (For the 1923–24 season the Guild's season-ticket subscriptions numbered 12,000, and for 1925–26 rose to 20,000. By 1929, after the Guild opened subscription seasons in Cleveland, Chicago, Pittsburgh, Baltimore, Philadelphia, and Boston, the figure passed 60,000, evenly divided between New York and the road.)

During this upswing in good things theatrical American plays were noticeable by their scarcity. But Eugene O'Neill (1888–1953), who had had eleven of his one-acters produced by the Provincetown Players off Broadway in New York (and one by the Washington Square Players) between 1916 and 1920, arrived on Broadway early that year with the full-length, Pulitzer Prize winner, *Beyond the Horizon.* Months later the Provincetown Players won fame and fortune with his bold, stunning *The Emperor Jones* (later brought uptown), and followed it with his New England *Diff'rent* (also later brought uptown). While an early version of his *Anna Christie* was being tested on the road, Americans, after a long waiting, hailed O'Neill as the first truly great native playwright.

II

Also in 1920 the radio broadcasting of speech and music in regularly scheduled programs for the public was introduced over station KDKA in

Pittsburgh. Within a few years short plays, paid for by commercials, and slickly read by actors, would be aired to millions of homes across the country.

But motion pictures fast became the most popular and profitable form of entertainment for the masses. In France Réjane, limited by the absence of speech, exaggerated her theatrical gestures in *Madame Sans-Gêne* (1911); and Bernhardt, trying for her "one chance of immortality," was statuesque in acting *Queen Elizabeth* (1912). *Tatters* (1912), an English film, charmed largely because of "its highly stylized acting, . . . acting in a now vanished tradition of the theater, as formal as a ballet routine, as unnatural and expressive."[117]

Americans, however, were quickest to sniff out the money-making potentialities of motion pictures. With rapidly developing technical skills, and an inclination for trying to copy life, they soon monopolized the new medium. Theda Bara (Theodosia Goodman) (1890–1955) became famous overnight as a "vamp" in *A Fool There Was* (1914), William S. Hart (1870–1946) left the New York stage for his first Western, *The Last Card* (1915) directed by Thomas H. Ince (1882–), and Griffith astounded the world with *The Birth of a Nation* (1915), *Intolerance* (1916), *Broken Blossoms* (1919), and *Way Down East* (1920).

Mention also ought to be made of the soundly realistic *The Outlaw and His Wife* (1917), made in Sweden, the German expressionistic *The Cabinet of Dr. Caligari* (1919), and the Danish historical *Hamlet* (1920).

The genius actor in this new medium was, of course, the comic, non-realistic Charlie Chaplin (1889–). A Londoner, trained in pantomime in its music-halls, he toured the United States from late 1910 until 1913. Then he was hired by Keystone Films, and in his first year in Hollywood improvised thirty-five short comedies—about one a week—plus the six reel *Tillie's Punctured Romance*, adapted from a Broadway farce, and starring Marie Dressler (1869–1934). This major effort used up fourteen weeks. In 1915 Chaplin was signed by the Essanay Company at $1,250 a week. Next year when he was twenty-nine he moved to the Mutual Company for a salary of $10,000 a week, plus a bonus of $150,000 or a total annual income of $670,000. In 1918 for a million dollars and a bonus of $15,000 he agreed to make at First National eight feature pictures in eighteen months. Two of them, both exhibited that year, were *A Dog's Life* and *Shoulder Arms*. In 1920 he created *The Kid*.

Chaplin was much more than a big business, however. Stark Young saluted him in 1920 for being "very easily . . . the greatest actor in English." You have, he wrote, "a technic completely finished for your needs so far; an absolute accuracy of the body and the idea, a perfect identification of gesture and intention. You have the musical quality without which no acting is consummate; it appears in your incomparable fluidity of action and in your beautiful, unbroken continuity of style. You have precision and extraordinary economy. You have invention. And—what is the last test—you have been able to give all this craft and abundance of technical resource that final genius of vitality that makes it really universal, makes it of the people. . . ." [118]

❀ AMERICAN ACCENT IN THE 1920'S

In the 1920's American playwrights broke the bonds of inherited stage convention, evolved new forms of expression, and used "the theater to a greater extent than other writers had previously used it in this country, to reflect the life and thought of the people of their day." Eugene O'Neill was the pioneer with eight diverse, powerful major works: the realistic *Anna Christie* (1921); the antirealistic, almost expressionistic *The Hairy Ape* (1922), whose leading character is "a symbol of man, who has lost his old harmony with nature"; the overwhelming chronicle of a Negro in a white society, *All God's Chillun Got Wings* (1924); the unpretty, moving exposure of passion and greed, *Desire Under the Elms* (1924); an abstract mystery of masks, *The Great God Brown* (1926); the extravaganza satire on Western hardheadness, *Marco Millions* (1928); the nine-act *Strange Interlude* (1928), whose asides and monologues explored the complexities of the human heart; and a philosophical pageant "for an imaginative theater," [119] the exultant *Lazarus Laughed* (1928).

It is believed by some that O'Neill's amazing achievement and quick world-wide recognition had "nothing to do with intellect [or] verbal beauty; he could not think . . . he was no poet"; his dialogue is almost always heavy, stagy. But O'Neill could feel, and with skillful audacity he experimented in shaping those feelings theatrically. Behind much that's trite, adolescent, melodramatic in his plays there is—as Stark Young, and most audiences, discovered—"a torment of spirit," "a feeling [that] is close and genuine and personal. It arises from the author's own . . . emotional necessity." And "we are stabbed to our depths by the importance of this feeling to him, and we are all his, not because of what he says but because it meant so much to him." [120] O'Neill is, in short, one of the world's great playwrights.

A dozen representative, meritorious popular scripts by O'Neill's American contemporaries were the expressionistic *The Adding Machine* (1923) and the realistic *Street Scene* (1929) by Elmer Rice, the tough *What Price Glory?* by Maxwell Anderson (1888–1959) with Laurence Stallings (1894–), and the former's would-be poetic *Elizabeth the Queen* (1930); *They Knew What They Wanted* (1924) by Sidney Howard (1891–1939), George Kelly's (1887–1957) *Craig's Wife* (1925), S. N. Behrman's (1893–) intellectual *The Second Man* (1927), *The Road to Rome* (1927) by Robert Sherwood (1896–1946), Philip Barry's *Holiday* (1929), the expressionistic, German-derived *The Beggar on Horseback* (1924) by George S. Kaufman (1889–1961) and Marc Connelly (1890–), the movie satire, *Once in a Lifetime* (1930) by

Kaufman and Moss Hart (1904–1961), and *The Green Pastures* (1930), a dramatization by Connelly of some stories by Roark Bradford (1896–1948).

During this decade England could boast about Shaw's *Saint Joan* (1923), Galsworthy's *Loyalties* (1922), Maugham's *The Circle* (1921), and Noel Coward's (1899–) *Private Lives* (1930). In Ireland Sean O'Casey (1884–) contributed *Juno and the Paycock* (1924) and *The Plough and the Stars* (1926). Other first-rate European plays included *Sei personaggi in cerca d'autore* (*Six Characters in Search of an Author*) (1921) and *Enrico Quarto* (*Henry IV*) (1922) by Pirandello; the lyric symbolism of Frederico García Lorca's (1899–1936) *El maleficia de la mariposa* (*The Butterfly's Crime*) (1920) and *La zapatera prodigiosa* (*The Shoemaker's Prodigious Wife*) (1930); *Martine* (1922) by Jean-Jacques Bernard (1888–) in which "poetry catches up with realism and psychology," *Antigone* (1922) and *Orphée* (1926) by Jean Cocteau (1891–), "the spearhead of writers who demand that the theater should turn from the realistic style to evolve fresh forms of expression," and *Siegfried* (1928) and *Amphitryon 38* (1929) by Jean Giraudoux (1882–1944), whose "art is a perpetual firework of intellectual and verbal virtuosity that ascends to the stratosphere of human thought and sensibility." [121]

Other plays worth mention are Swedish Pär Lagerkvist's (1891–) imaginative *Den osynlige* (*The Invisible*) (1923) and *Han som fick leva om sitt liv* (*The Man Who Lived His Life Again*) (1928), Czech Karel Capek's (1890–1937) *R.U.R.* (1921), Austrian Franz Werfel's (1890–1945) *Bocksgesang* (*The Goat Song*) (1921), the Russian *Dhi Turbinikh* (*The Days of the Turbines* (1926) by Michael Bulgakov (1891–1940). And it is impossible to forget *Im Dickicht der Städt* (*In the Jungle of Cities*) (1923), *Mann ist Mann* (*Man Equals Man*) (1926), *Die Dreigroschenoper* (*The Threepenny Opera*) (1928)—with music by Kurt Weill (1900–1950), and *Die Massnahme* (*The Measures Taken*) (1930) by Bertolt Brecht (1898–1956), one of the most puzzling and controversial of modern writers.

In short, between 1920 and 1930 all sorts of playwrights all over the world generated a new excitement in the theater. That was fortunate, because in those years it was forced to compete with moving pictures.

In the 1920's the United States dominated that new industry. Bankers and Hollywood producers acquired virtual control of film distribution throughout the world and proceeded to deluge it with their pictures. A few of the better-than-average mass entertainments were: Rudolph Valentino (1895–1926) in *The Four Horsemen of the Apocalypse* (1921), which, made at a cost of $640,000, grossed by the end of 1925 more than $4,000,000; *Tol'able David* (1921) with Richard Barthelmess (1897–); Douglas Fairbanks as *Robin Hood* (1922); Robert J. Flaherty's (1884–1951) documentary *Nanook of the North* (1922); Cecil B. De Mille's *The Ten Commandments* (1923); *Salomé* (1923) with Nazimova; Erich von Stroheim's (1885–1957) *Greed*

(1923–24); *The Navigator* (1924) with Buster Keaton (1896–); Ernst Lubitsch's (1892–1947) *The Marriage Circle* (1924); and Greta Garbo (1905–) in *Flesh and the Devil* (1927).

Alongside those were German Emil Jannings in both F. W. Murnau's (1889–1931) *The Last Laugh* (1924) and E. A. Dupont's (1891–1956) *Variety* (1925), Sergei Eisenstein's (1899–1948) *Potemkin* (1925) and Vsevolod Pudovkin's (1893–1953) *Storm Over Asia* (1928), René Clair's (1898–) *The Italian Straw Hat* (1927), and Carl-Theodor Dreyer's (1889–) *The Passion of Joan of Arc* (1928). The list, of course, is only a sampling.

Then in 1928 the first full-length, all-talking picture, *The Lights of New York*, was exhibited. Soon audiences were being thrilled by the Negro *Hallelujah!* (1929), Clair's *Sous les Toits de Paris* (1929), *All Quiet on the Western Front* (1930), *Little Caesar* (1930), and so on. Their "enthusiasm for sound was so strong that attendance leaped from 60 million paid admissions per week in 1927 to 110 million in 1929." [122]

The theater, without quite knowing it, was engaged in a battle for survival.

II

In France Copeau apparently failed in his crusade against commercialism and realism in the theater. Near the middle of 1924, with religion occupying a larger and larger place in his mind, he abandoned the Vieux-Colombier and fled with a few students to Burgundy. He had struggled against the epoch, André Gide (1869–1951) wrote, "as any good artist must do. But dramatic art has this frightful disadvantage, that it must appeal to the public, count with and on the public," despite the fact "that truth is not on the side of the greatest number. Copeau, though claiming not to, was working for a select few. He wanted to lead to perfection, to style, to purity, an essentially impure art that gets along without all that." [123]

But his experiments, his dreams, were not fruitless. Ever since Copeau and the Théâtre du Vieux-Colombier, it's said that "the actor has been looked upon in France as a man trained to interpret a script, as an instrument in the service of a literary text." [124]

Copeau's labors were continued by actor-directors Charles Dullin and Louis Jouvet. In 1921 the former, at the age of thirty-six, opened his own theater, L'Atelier, and for seventeen years staged the classics of France, translations of famous foreign plays, and scripts by newcomers Armand Salacrou (1900–), Marcel Achard (1899–), Jean-Paul Sartre (1905–), and Jean Anouilh (1910–). Endorsing "the unreality of the theater," Dullin emphasized in his productions "the mysterious, poetic, and fantastic quality of the literary text." [125]

Thirty-five year old Jouvet left Copeau in 1922 and settled at the Comédie des Champs-Élysées to concentrate on "a verbal theater in which the text is given first place." Only by knowing the total environment of an author at the time of composition, he believed, can interpreters arrive at the true and complete meaning of a play. Jouvet also believed that sincerity in the actor —the foundation of the Stanislavski system—is unnecessary, even harmful. The actor must forget self, he declared. True sincerity onstage is the search for deception. This is the essence of theater.[126]

With the help of Monroe Stearns, we can summarize, too baldly perhaps, Jouvet's theory, his solution to the enigma of acting. It isn't easy . . . In the actor's first phase, his period of "sincerity," he is "totally ignorant about himself. To be something other than himself disturbs him violently. In order to acquire a new identity he naively believes that Orestes or Hamlet is waiting for him to bring them to life by lending them his own soul. Everything in the theater begins and ends in him and exists because of him." In his second phase, the actor "begins to see that his taking possession of a character . . . has deceived no one but himself. . . . His mind becomes a labyrinth in which he strays until he encounters the wall which is himself. After he has met himself, found out what he really is, he becomes conscious of what he is doing. He "discovers the Convention of the theater and the restrictions of his profession. He sees his position as both instrument and instrumentalist. He perceives that his existence on the stage is composed of the audience, his fellow actors, the character he must play. Thus, he learns the art of pretending. . . . He acknowledges now his own 'insincerity,' understands that he has a double nature, that he must live in the limbo of half being and half seeming. What he used to call his art, he recognizes as a craft, a trade." In his third phase, the actor "finally masters his feelings" and, by a vibrant sensitivity which may be called intuition, becomes "one with the private and inexpressible intention of the author." And when he knows that onstage, in theater terms, he must be "the link between the author and the public," the actor "has found the meaning of his profession; now he can give meaning to his life." [127]

At the Comédie des Champs-Élysées, Jouvet achieved his first great success at the end of 1923 when he designed, directed, and acted the title role in Knock; ou, Le Triomphe de la Médecine by Romains. Then for nearly five years, constantly in financial difficulties, he staged and acted in many new French scripts, as well as two foreign ones, Outward Bound (1923) by Sutton Vane (1888–) and Gogol's The Inspector General. In mid-1928, after two months of rehearsing, he treated Paris to Siegfried by Giraudoux. The offering, according to one critic, "marks a date, a point of departure, a new hope. It marks the theater's escape from naturalism and psychologism into poetry. . . . It marks the rebirth of style in the theater. . . ." [128] Near the end of 1929 the Jouvet-Giraudoux partnership was cemented with the production of Amphitryon 38; and as director, actor, scene designer, lighting expert, and script editor Jouvet was well on his way to becoming the most expert man of the theater since Molière.

In Paris at this time important director Gaston Baty (1885–1952) did not agree with Dullin and Jouvet's reverence for the playwright. Like Gordon Craig, "He feared the domination of the text of the play over the production." For him the words must be only the pit, and the staging the fruit around it. At the Studio des Champs-Élysées Baty wished in his presentations "to render externally sensible through scenic patterns the language the text speaks, and sometimes does not, thus raising staging on a par with the writing of the play." [129]

Baty, of course, was not an actor. No matter. There is always room in the theater for men of different theories, different talents. One can agree with Baty or with Jouvet, with Coquelin or with Stanislavski. Who cares? The important point is to allow, even to encourage, each artist to create in his own way in the theater. Their differences will engender vitality.

III

German examinations of acting were not as visionary, as mystical, as Jouvet's. They were heavier, more earthbound. In 1925, for instance, Lorenz Kjerbühl-Petersen (1891–), actor and director of the Mannheim Theater, continued the studies begun by Martersteig, Kerr, Hagemann, Gregori, and Winds with *Die Schauspielkunst*, translated as *Psychology of Acting*. His book, divided into two parts, "The Illusion of the Audience" and "The Creative Work of the Actor," attempts to cull from many opinions of German actors and writers on acting something "intended to be first of all of practical service." [130]

Kjerbühl-Petersen uncovers a danger in the evolution of acting, an evolution "characterized and conditioned by the emancipation of the actor's individuality." He is afraid that "an extreme individualism leads ultimately to complete annihilation of the factors that are essential to acting." For him "self-portrayal does not signify true art" because acting "means at least the art (of the author) seen through a temperament (of the actor)." An actor who "lives" his role by transferring to it his own feelings is consequently only himself onstage and "not capable of characterization." [131]

Therefore, Kjerbühl-Petersen believes that theorists—from Sainte-Albine and his *Le Comédien* to Stanislavski—who overemphasize the actor's individuality by insisting that he must truly feel onstage, and *be* the character, make two errors: (1) they transfer "to the actor the emotion which should be awakened in the spectator"; and (2) they wrongly conceive "this emotion which is awakened in the spectator to be an actual emotion arising from a complete illusion, thus misunderstanding its fictional character." [132]

Finally, Kjerbühl-Petersen is disinclined to accept the testimony of actors who assert that during a performance they have complete empathy with the characters they impersonate. They can be mistaken, he suggests.

They can confuse the excitement and tension of being an artist—an interpreter performing in public—with the emotions of the role. So, indeed, an actor may feel during a performance, but his feeling isn't only the emotion of the part.[133]

Another German, Erwin Piscator (1893–), introduced in Berlin in 1924 a new, practical, didactic, and decidedly political kind of acting, acting meant to be a branch of sociology, acting umbilically connected with actual, large happenings in the world. The war and the Russian Revolution gave birth to it. In his *Das Politische Theater* (1929) Piscator reports that once in 1915 he was asked what his occupation had been before the war. "At that moment, as I uttered the word 'actor,' with shells bursting around me, my profession seemed . . . so stupid, such a ridiculous caricature, so little related to . . . life and the world, that my fear of the oncoming shells was less than the shame I felt at my profession." [134] That shame festered.

By 1922, along with Bertolt Brecht, he was convinced that so-called stage realism was too subjective and thin, too illusory and pointless and dated, usually too narrow in focus, and always cowardly in not facing up to vital, even world-changing social issues. Both men were to some extent fascinated by the bold, vigorous disregard of conventionalities in expressionism, by the frankly theatrical, presentational work of Jessner, Meyerhold, and Tairov (some of whose productions had been seen in Berlin). But they objected to "the isolated aims of expressionism, with all its escapism and screaming." They envisioned a new kind of theater which could "create a common, communal feeling," [135] which in almost a journalistic way would examine the historical process, and which in so doing would use the inventions and discoveries of modern science. Piscator, after viewing films like *Potemkin*, was excited by their potentialities for giving scope and emphasis to the messages he intended to deliver as from a tribunal. He was certain that productions ought to teach while entertaining.

In 1924 thirty-one-year-old Piscator was put in charge of the Volksbühne in Berlin. There he applied "the principles of fluidity, simultaneity and cinematic cutting" to such documentary plays as *Fahnen* (*Flags*) (1924) by Alfons Paquet (1881–), which analyzed the Chicago anarchists' trial of 1886, and *Das Trunken Schiff* (1925) by Paul Zeck (1881–), a biography of the rebel French poet, Arthur Rimbaud (1854–1891). Three years later at his own theater, where he was sometimes helped scriptwise by Marxist Brecht, Piscator startled the city by employing unpretty scenic constructions, films, graphs, slides, photographs, captions, and charts to convey political and sociological backgrounds for "the education of the audience even against its will." [136] Two of his 1927 unliterary, "epic" productions were Toller's *Hoopla, wir leben* (*Hurrah! We Live!*) and *Rasputin*—a retitling of *Zagavor imperatritsy* (*The Plot of the Empress*) (1925) by Alexei Tolstoy—in which three different films were projected simultaneously. In 1928 Piscator triumphed with his and Brecht's adaptation of Jaroslav Hasek's (1883–1923) comic novel *Die Abenteuren des braven Soldaten Schweik* (*The Good Soldier Schweik*).

For these reportage productions Piscator needed "a new kind of acting which estranges the events being presented on the stage from the spectator and makes the audience assume an inquiring and critical attitude. . . ." He simply couldn't accept "the Chekhovian actor, hypnotizing himself behind 'the fourth wall.' " [137] He wanted his actors to demonstrate the action of each scene, to see the characters they represented from without (as if in a mirror), to forget instinct and impulse, and to reason out movements, gestures, and utterances.

Furthermore, Piscator directed his actors to know audiences, to concentrate their whole attention "out there," and, in a sense, to narrate the play, to serve as "a kind of guide" to its meaning, and to comment, yes, even comment, on their characterizations. "We don't want the modern actor improvising his emotions," he wrote (in 1949, to be sure), "but we want him to give us commentaries on these emotions—playing not only a result but the thought which caused the result. . . . To do this, the modern actor needs a superior control so that he will not be overcome by his emotions. He needs what I have called 'the new objectivity.' " [138]

Stanislavski's opinion of this "Objective Acting" is unknown. Probably he winced. And went on wincing. So, surely, did Copeau, Granville-Barker, and possibly Stark Young. But if you erase the quality of the ideas and look at the *form* used by Piscator in vivifying them, you will perhaps admit that it was, even with its crudities, highly theatrical. Actors ought to act from an idea (not necessarily political, however), ought to convey it to an audience, and ought to be allowed to make their own comments on it.

IV

At this time Granville-Barker was the only Englishman who cared so much for acting he thought about it. In *The Exemplary Theatre* (1922), "a plea for the recognition of the theater as an educational force," he wrote that "the whole art of acting . . . remains in these days most sadly in the dumps." The average critic knows little or nothing about it; "The average audience knows less and cares hardly at all, demands sensation, the stirring to tears or laughter; by what means effected is no matter." So, actors, bound to approximate their work to audience expectations, easily and popularly resort to mere self-expression or self-exhibition. And the art of acting, "as a whole, is neither studied, practiced, nor appreciated . . . with any sustained intelligence." [139]

Ahead of Kjerbühl-Petersen, Barker particularly objected to the modern emphasis placed upon the individual performer. Acting, he argues, "does not consist simply [of] *self*-expression, though that is part of the training for it."

Self-expression is too often only self-assertion. Inevitably, then, even when actors possess a trained technique for asserting themselves—and precious few of them do—the crucial question must be asked: what sort of self is expressed, asserted? [140] Almost always it's only ordinary.

To the service of a play, Barker asked the actor to "bring far more than a crude power of self-expression." After all, he explains, the acted play "is the working out . . . not of the self-realization of the individual but of society itself": along one idea and in one style (or form) by this playwright, along another idea and in another style by another playwright, and so on. Therefore, the actor must bring to each script a technique of *interpretation*. "All acting," Barker firmly declares, "is interpretation; it can have no absolute value of its own." An actor must truly interpret not himself but an assigned character. His work must be "looked at in its due relation to the play!" Interpretations, he continues, "must follow the lines the creators have traveled. If Shakespeare wrote rhetorically, wove his effects out of strands of unrepressed individual emotion, if Sheridan cared greatly for the set of his prose, Robertson for sentiment, Pinero in his farces for well-bitten comic figures, if the work of Ibsen is most strongly marked by the involute process of revelation of character, that of Chekhov by the way in which his men and women are made to seem less like independent human beings than reflections in the depths of the circumstance of his plays—these traits of each dramatist mold and pervade his work and should dictate a related method of interpretation." [141]

And since plays will continue to be written in various styles—not only in the realistic one—Barker maintains that what is most needed by actors today is a greater virtuosity of interpretation. In other words, just as an actor can't "contentedly approach a performance of, say, Hjalmar Ekdal [in *The Wild Duck*], bringing to bear upon it the same technical equipment that he has cultivated for Romeo," neither can he hope to interpret characters in plays by Shaw, Pirandello, O'Neill, Anouilh, or Brecht in the same way he would interpret characters in, say, a play by Arthur Miller. In short, Barker concludes, "This interpretative method of acting that we desiderate will certainly differ so much in degree as almost to seem different in kind from the crude impersonative realism which belongs, properly enough no doubt, to crudely realistic plays. . . ." His blunt point is that acting shouldn't be praised only when it's lifelike. "There will be great hope for the theatre," he writes, "on the day that a play [and, by extension, an actor's performance] is soundly hissed for its artistic demerits." [142]

The difference between Barker's and Stanislavski's ideas about acting is clear. For Barker—if we can put things almost too simply—acting is essentially the product of only two trainings: First, he advises, let actors "break their shins, so to speak, . . . over voice production, elocution, dialectics, eurythmics. . . ." Let them learn the technique of their special medium. Second, let them participate "upon the lines of a seminar" in "the cooperative study" of widely different plays.[143] (And his exposition of this training, long overlooked, is still worth studying by teachers of acting in colleges and universities.)

For Stanislavski, on the other hand, acting is the product of virtually only one training: self-expression. Now and then, of course, he mentions the importance of effective speech and movement (especially later on, in *Building a Character*), and he sometimes mentions the importance of the playwright and his designed idea. But in the main Stanislavski minimizes Barker's first and second trainings, expands on his notation that self-expression is part of the training for acting, inserts it between the other two, and then enlarges its importance excessively. Primarily, narrowly, and endlessly, he teaches actors to work on themselves: to explore their own qualities, their peculiarities, their psyches, their memories more than their imaginations, their five senses, and so on. He overstresses *self*-expression to such an extent that his disciples tend to ignore their medium as well as the content and form of a script. Most members of the Actors Studio, for instance, work for two or three years only on themselves. They rarely go beyond doing that.

V

We have already glanced at the bloom of new playwrights in the United States in the 1920's, and at the change-over from moving to talking pictures. What happened to acting in those years? Well—something basic and, in due time, far-reaching. Many players, of course, rushed to Hollywood for high money and wide popularity. And that, in a way, was the end of some acting. Enough players, however, stayed in New York. And some of the young ones, not yet successful, began criticizing the commercial theater's conventional themes and its hit-or-miss methods of production.

They were sure that acting must be extricated from all the external fripperies and trickeries lavished, for instance, on such productions as Belasco's 1921 *Kiki* (1918) by André Picard (1874–1926) and on Reinhardt's 1924 *The Miracle*—which out-Belascoed Belasco, and went about as far as anyone could go with well-publicized, dazzling stage effects. They believed that the ability to act should not be confused with a radiant personality, which seemed, typically, to have happened when Katharine Cornell (1898–) became a star overnight in *A Bill of Divorcement* (1921) by English Clemence (Winifred Ashton) Dane (1878?–). They insisted that fundamentally acting should be less traditional, less formal, and less escapist than John Barrymore's eminently satisfying Hamlet in 1922 and Jane Cowl's vibrant Juliet in 1923. And they rejected all acting that was fashionably empty of meaning, cliché-ridden, superficial, and slick. They decided to nourish a new kind of acting, one based on truth.

These perceptive, thoroughly right dissenters, or dreamers, were ordinary people, this was their century, and they wanted to be heard. They were convinced that their acting ought to be truly American. They turned for help to Stanislavski. If that seems inconsistent, where else could they turn? They had heard and read about his search for truth in acting; and they sensed that his findings were universal.

The young Americans learned nothing from Duse when she acted *Ghosts* and *The Lady from the Sea* in New York in 1923. She was single, special. Nobody knew how she did what she did. She never worked out and set down for others to follow a "do-it-yourself" method of acting. They learned little or nothing from Copeau, from Barker. Or from the Habima players of Moscow in the Vakhtangov production of *The Dybbuk* as seen in New York in 1926. They learned nothing much from the Theatre Guild company whose members subscribed to no single method of acting and let honest reality emerge when and if it could. The Guild-Copeau offering of *The Brothers Karamazov* in 1927, for instance, even with Alfred Lunt and Lynn Fontanne (1887?–) in the cast, "created nothing by which what goes on before our eyes is true." [144] It couldn't compare with the powerful Moscow Art Theatre rendering and flopped.

Having been teased by inklings of Stanislavski's "truthful" system, and after attending the Moscow Art Theatre productions in New York, they were positive that his way of acting, of teaching acting, was for them.

The Russian company, after appearing for more than a month in Berlin and Paris, came to New York in January 1923. For three months, mostly to full houses, it acted *Tsar Feodor*, *The Lower Depths*, *The Three Sisters*, *The Cherry Orchard*, scenes from *The Brothers Karamazov*, and Turgenev's *A Provincial Lady*. The actors next performed for three weeks in Chicago, two weeks in Philadelphia, another two in Boston, and a "farewell" in New York. In November 1923 the company returned for a second three-month run in New York and followed that with three weeks in Chicago, plus one week each in Philadelphia, Boston, Washington, D.C., Pittsburgh, New Haven, Hartford, Newark, Cleveland, and Detroit. In all, the Moscow Art Theatre performed in the United States more than forty weeks.

Audiences everywhere raved about the Russian acting. And rightly so. After all, this was "a group of sincere artists, created by their art, rich by their intense living in it, and sure of all art's importance and duration." Its members had worked together thoroughly for a long, long time "under a distinguished and sympathetic leader. . . ." They'd been acting *Feodor*, *The Lower Depths*, and the two Chekhov plays off and on for nearly twenty years, the *Karamazov* scenes since 1910, and *The Provincial Lady* since 1912. Americans could boast of no native acting so deeply studied, well-rehearsed, integrated, mellowed. The young onlookers swooned over impersonations which professed "the intention of ignoring the presence of spectators and of producing an effect of life as life would be seen going on if the fourth wall of a room were removed. . . ." [145]

Critic Stark Young, however, did not follow the fad of praising everything the Russians exhibited. He liked and he disliked. He sat "quite un-moved, indifferent" at *Tsar Feodor*, feeling that the actors' "studied natural-ness" failed to achieve "the form, the magic of distance and scope, the con-scious arrangement, the artifice and logic that would create . . . the idea. . . . The effort and theory of making the past as natural as if it were the present," he wrote, "seems to me only a deficiency in cultural perspective." He liked some of the frank, inherent theatricality in *The Lower Depths*, and wished for more of it; but the actors "worked on an assumption of exact realism, and so mixed matters up." He cheered the *Karamazov* scenes be-cause the cast "exhibited an understanding, a perfection of ensemble and an inexhaustible study and elaboration of the characters that must certainly be unequalled. . . ." And he lauded the two Chekhov productions, calling them "the rarest of events in the theater anywhere," and praising the actors for carrying realism "to an honest and spiritual depth and candor and to a relentless, poignant perfection and truth." [146]

In Young's opinion the Russians failed in the non-Russian, comic *The Mistress of the Inn* by Goldoni. He found Stanislavski's production to be "amazingly thorough without being infectious. Judged by itself that was. Judged by the quality of the play it was pretty much all wrong." Young also decided that Stanislavski, "as compared to several others in the company, [was] not an important actor at all but more like a teacher or illustrator of what would be done in acting [a] role." [147]

In March 1923 when Stanislavski was sixty and in the United States, he began writing *My Life in Art*, finished it eleven months later, and the book was published in Boston, May 1924. (In 1925 a revised version was published in Moscow.) At once actors on Broadway, on tour, in stock companies, in little theaters, in dramatic schools, and in universities read and reread it to learn more about the new system of acting.

Some of them immediately announced that they were practicing it. Well, surely, "There must have been hours of devoted talk about it, of discipleship too, and, at the worst, of that particular kind of philosophic art argument that is characteristic of small talents especially." But what possibly could they have practiced? Stanislavski said in 1924 that "There is no actual *method* yet; there are only a number of basic principles and exercises"; but "continuous exercises . . . have never been performed even up to the present day, either by the actors or the pupils of the Studio. This is why I claim that my system has not yet shown any of its real results." The things many Ameri-cans did practice were vague. They intoned "The superconscious through the conscious," wooed the "creative mood" by forgetting they were onstage, and tried to "feel . . . truth at all times." They completely ignored Stanislavski's warning that "In the sphere of rhythm, plastics, the laws of speech, the plac-ing of the voice, breathing, . . . there is much that is incumbent upon all." [148]

In October 1923, however, Richard Boleslavsky, a Stanislavski "pupil and disciple for fifteen years," had published in *Theatre Arts Monthly* a

"First Lesson in Acting," on "Concentration." (He followed it with the "Second Lesson," on "Memory of Emotion," in July 1929.) Also in the fall of 1923, with the assistance of Maria Ouspenskaya (1881–1949), an actress from the Moscow Art Theatre, he began teaching New York students, "for the first time, the [Stanislavski] technique of acting" [149] at the Theatre Arts Institute—which next year was renamed the American Laboratory Theatre. (Instruction was also offered in eurhythmics and in diction.)

In 1924 Boleslavsky staged *The Sea-Woman's Cloak* by Amélie Rives Troubetzkoy (1863–1945), in 1925 *Twelfth Night* and a dramatization of Hawthorne's *The Scarlet Letter*, in 1926 Eugène Labiche's (1815–1888) *Le Chapeau de paille d'Italie* (*The Italian Straw Hat*) (1851) and a Civil War play, *The Trumpet Shall Sound* by Thornton Wilder (1897–). In 1927 and 1928, in a remodeled brewery, leased for six years, the students acted seven more plays, including *Big Lake* by Lynn Riggs (1899–1954), *Martine, Doctor Knock*, and *Much Ado About Nothing*. Most of the offerings were non-realistic.

Then in 1928 minor actor Lee Strasberg (1901–), who'd attended courses at the American Laboratory Theatre, and minor actor Harold Clurman (1901–) collected a group of young unknowns and, on their own, as a schooling in vague elements of the new system, rehearsed *New Year's Eve* by Waldo Frank (1889–) for seventeen weeks and *Balloon* by Padraic Colum (1881–) for another six weeks.[150]

Finally, in 1930, when the Theatre Guild decided to present experimental scripts for its subscribers at special Sunday performances, the young actors found an opportunity for exhibiting their work. Clurman, the Guild's new play-reader, chose *Konstantin Terekhin* (or *Red Rust*) (1927) by Russian Vladimir Kirshon (1902–1937), which was given a regular production with Franchot Tone (1904–), Strasberg, "and a number of the Lab Theatre contingent" in the cast. After this initial offering, however, the Guild abandoned its Studio project. But the actors didn't abandon their dream. Clurman, Strasberg, Guild casting director Cheryl Crawford (1902–), and others met frequently to discuss the formation of a permanent company of actors dedicated to "A technique . . . founded on life values." [151] Dedicated, in others words, to the Stanislavski system.

Out of this ferment came, in 1931, the Group Theatre.

❀ STARK YOUNG

Stark Young wasn't too happy about the vague, so-called new system of acting. He mistrusted Stanislavski's tendency in *My Life in Art* to rely on "true," "inner," "sincere," and similar terms. Worse, he commented, "in the whole volume there is not one remark that gave me any sense of the creative surprise, the authentic right, the illumination, that comes from a man inside an art." [152]

But the new American actors didn't listen to Young, didn't weigh his opinions, didn't turn to him for help. And their reasons for not doing so were perhaps two. First, they probably agreed that his opinions on art were aristocratic, esoteric. And it's true that for some his writings are so far "out of this world" that—like Plotinus, his abiding influence—he often seems to regard as a misfortune the descent of his soul into his body. Actually, however, Young insists that we must "relate this art [of the theater] to life and read its significance from life." [153] That is the starting point of his theories. And if he was not too interested in current social and political issues, well, neither was Stanislavski—who was right in the middle of a revolution. Second, Americans never quite understood Young and could not easily use his findings about acting because he neglected to arrange them into the patness of a system, a practical formula.

Yet Stark Young has examined acting with more love, more perception, more lucidity, and more stimulating challenge than any writer on the subject. Of his analysis it may be said

> As of Plato's position in relation to the culture of the race,
> That it is unique, and he owes it
> Not to the closeness of his reasoning,
> Not to the extent of his knowledge,
> Not even to his great passion for truth,
> Or any specially firm grasp of it,
> But to the unparalleled fecundity of his thought,
> That is, to the breadth and length of his view.

From "The Kind of Poetry I Want" by Hugh MacDiarmid. Reprinted by permission from The Hudson Review, Vol. XIV, No. 1 (Spring 1961). Copyright © 1961 by The Hudson Review, Inc.[154]

Because Young has come nearest to setting down final truths about the art, his thirty-seven page chapter on "Acting" in The Flower in Drama (1923), or better, his twenty-three page chapter on "The Actor" in The Theater (1927) ought to be required study. Either article furnishes actors with what they need most today: philosophic guidance.

Stark Young, unlike Stanislavski, knows that the "question of the relation of art to reality is the greatest of all questions with regard to art." That "It parallels—to employ the terms closest to us humanly—the relations of the spirit to the body, or, to go the other way round, the relation of the passing to the permanent, of the casual in the moment to the flower in it." [155]

"The underlying principles of all arts," according to Young, "are the same; what is essentially true of one is true of all." And the purpose of any work of art is not to record the objective world around us; it is, rather, "to arouse in us the experience that the artist had and strives to re-create, . . . to arouse the life in it"; it is to capture, isolate, convey, or even immortalize it. That experience, that resultant "state of mind and spirit," that thought-felt thing, is his idea; and as idea it holds together and shapes the symphony, the painting, the tale, the script as acted. More important, it gives to the art work a point. Therefore, "To see anything as art means that you do not see it as a duplicate of something in life. It means that you see it complete in itself. You judge it by its . . . essential idea" [156] as expressed in this or that medium.

It follows, then, that "Acting is not an art until it ceases to be life." It is not expert (1) until it takes the reality it portrays and molds it into idea, until it "adds to it something that was not there before." For example: "What conception of love do you find in Shakespeare, in Aeschylus, in Molière, in Ibsen?" Or in Shaw, in Giraudoux, in O'Neill, in Tennessee Williams? Well, then, isn't it idea instead of mere naturalness that should "determine the form and treatment of the love-scenes in *Romeo and Juliet, Agamemnon, L'Amour dépit, Rosmersholm?*" Or in *Man and Superman,* Giraudoux's *Intermezzo* (*The Enchanted*) (1933), *Anna Christie, A Streetcar Named Desire* (1947). And part of acting from an idea "consists in an ability to perceive the quality of the thing acted, to perceive its school, its genre, its characteristic necessity; the ability to act it, in sum, in its own kind." Another example: As actor what idea do you have of, say, *Macbeth?* (Or rather, what idea does the director have?) Well, "merely to glimpse the idea with a descriptive word—we may inquire if you wish to create primitive archaisms or baroque complexities or a sense of powers of evil, or what? What is it that you will try to create with this play as the material and with your theater as the medium? You must know. With this clear to you, you can set about finding a body for your idea." Young suggests that an actor "if he had power behind the idea and the expression of it, . . . could, if he chose, do a beggar, not in whining rags but in the most exalted declamation and elegance. . . . On the other hand he could do a king in . . . homely cotton and the simplest realism, as in certain beautiful and moving folk dramas and rituals." [157]

Acting is is not an art, is not expert, (2) until it recreates its idea via the theater medium, or vocally and visually in frank cooperation with an audience. Put this another way: acting isn't acting when the player "lives his part." Mere sincerity, emotion *per se,* and naturalness do not make acting, "which finally depends on expression, and expression arrives only through the acting medium and technique." And the actor as artist has the right—at his own peril, of course—to use his medium "as realistically or as remotely, as photographically or as abstractly, as he likes." [158]

In sum, then, from Young one learns that the first problem in acting, is to find, recognize, and capture the reality to be expressed. The second problem is to find in the actual matter its point. And the third problem is to find ways of conveying that point in theater terms.

Young admits that an actor can impersonate realistically. His appreciation is catholic. He knows that the instinct for imitating the actual is potent, and that acting "arouses . . . more than any other art a strong demand for likeness." He knows that realism, "as much as any other method in art, selects, arranges, breathes into its material the idea that will preserve it from universal welter and chaos." He also knows that "a realistic actor may be great, just as a drama that employs realism may be great." Finally, he can't deny that in the United States today the "main body of theater is natural, is based on resemblance, reproduction, photography. Realism reigns. . . ." And this "realistic method turns on external possibility in its details; there is no other basis on which to distinguish it." [159]

But the fact remains, Young reminds us, "that realism, even great realism, is not the only way of life in the theater." And the danger is that the American addiction to realism "confuses our notions with regard to the theater's style." [160]

Let us examine that danger as it applies, first, to audiences. Their desire for illusion, says Young, "is too much like a monkey's delight in front of a mirror. Deception as an end in art brings us to nonsense. And from the confusion on this point acting suffers more than any other art; for this mania that people have, to find in art the illusion of the actual, pursues the actor to the last ditch. Many people who have got over thinking that the painting is art in which ears of corn are rendered so that under a strong light you cannot tell them from real corn, and who know that the rumbling at the bottom and tweedling at the top of the piano to reproduce the thunder and the shepherd's bells is not music, know nothing of the sort when it comes to acting." Their only basis for judging whether or not it is expert is to compare it with everyday behavior. Everyone, "being naturally familiar with things as they are and being born equal to anyone else, is a born judge" [161] of the art. Everyone can compare the way actors walk, talk, sneeze, hate, turn off a faucet, cry, and so on with the ways people have been observed doing those things in life; and if the actors in their copyings are accurate and sincere, why, of course, they are first-rate artists! Consequently, the actors, limited by this only measuring-rod of success, and tutored by Stanislavski, try for acclaim and security by exhibiting more and more recognizable behavior in front of bankers, salesmen, cab drivers, and their wives whose notion of art is narrow, whose appreciation of it is dull and rambling, and whose response to forms other than the realistic is impeded.

The danger in realism is that it can make actors too narrow. First, they are reduced (often unwillingly, to be sure) to the mere expedient of being type-cast, which "spoils acting as an art. . . . The mere superficiality of likeness in an actor to a character will often satisfy" a playwright, his director, and the audience. Second, realism induces the easy belief in actors that onstage, as lifelike characters, they must *be* persons other than themselves. This, declares Young, is all wrong: "exactly as acting is not life but art, the actor is not some other person but always himself, . . . in every role he is himself. But he is himself only as a medium for his idea. He uses himself, his body, his voice, and the elusive personal quality that goes with these, . . . to create a form for his idea." Third, via realism the actor is taught, particularly by Stanislavski disciples, the deadly principle of exhibiting to audiences "the emotions he has experienced by putting himself in the character's place. This implies sincerity, naturalness, and the rest of that familiar list of qualities. . . ." But "Mere sincerity of intention does not necessarily put an actor into the character's place; nor does mere genuineness of emotion on the actor's part give us the right emotion for the character. After all, what we are interested in is the role, not the actor's feeling natural." [162]

In summary, then, Young believes that the actor should concentrate on his idea and his medium as much as on himself. He agrees, of course, with Stanislavski that the actor must work on himself as a person. The ideas an actor may have—or use—depend on what sort of person he is, on the intelligence, sensitivity, imagination he possesses. Furthermore, the actor's personal quality "is part of the material that art works in, precisely as is a voice, or a hand, or a mind." But the person who hopes to be an artist— which isn't quite the same thing as an aware, fully functioning, estimable person—or, more specifically, the person who wants to be an actor—which isn't the same thing as a painter, a musician, or a writer—ought, according to Young, to work less on being sincerely believable, on truly feeling the emotions, on "living the part" and more on five aspects of his special medium: (1) on a "personal theatricality" which "corresponds to what a real singing voice . . . is to the singer, good or bad": (2) on his natural assets, especially his voice; (3) on "the time sense, . . . a sense of rhythm and an instinct for pause, cues and general tempo . . .'"; (4) on a "sense of movement and line"; and (5) on mimicry, which "will give him a kind of solid reality [to] begin with and which he can alter and force to his own ends." [163]

❈ VARIOUS RUSSIANS

While Stanislavski was trying from 1920 to 1930 to pull together his system of realistic acting his contemporaries, Tairov and Meyerhold, stunned, then baffled, and finally angered Party officials with their flagrantly antirealistic productions. Both were called too "esthetic" for the new Communist state. In 1923 playwright and Commissar of Education, A. V. Lunacharsky (1875–1933) defensively coined the phrase, "Back to Ostrovsky," an official call for a return to nineteenth-century realism as the proper mode for the Soviet theater.

Sophisticated, esoteric, theatrical Tairov at first had enunciated the slogan: "Art is without a party: it is like air, like water, like the sun, it lights everyone with its ways. . . ." In 1921 he produced Phèdre on a stage whose "space was broken—one might almost say smashed and splintered—in Cubist style, into crystalline forms" while retaining "such classic elements as simple round columns. The costumes and make-up were similarly treated, in strongly emphasized but abstract high lights and shadows." The acting, both utterance and movement, was rhythmically formalized. In 1923 Tairov staged a dramatization of G. K. Chesterton's (1874–1936) novel, *The Man Who Was Thursday* (and opened a school where his brand of abstract acting was taught), in 1924 Ostrovsky's *The Storm* and Shaw's *Saint Joan*, in 1926 O'Neill's *The Hairy Ape* and *Desire Under the Elms*, and in 1927 *Antigone* (1919) by Hasenclever. Party critics screamed: "The Kamerny is a theater of decadence." "The Kamerny has lost contact with the masses." "The Kamerny is ideologically unsound." [164]

Consequently Tairov was forced to renounce some of his theatricality. In 1928 he presented Bulgakov's allegorical satire on Soviet dictatorship, *Bagrovyi ostrov* (*The Purple Island*). The play was promptly banned, and the author ostracized. Next year, after O'Neill's *All God's Chillun Got Wings*, Tairov staged *Natalya Tarpova* by Sergei Semyonov (1893–); but because a few of the play's speeches, delivered from a rostrum directly to the audience, were rabidly anti-Soviet and met with applause, the production was quickly canceled. In order to save himself and his theater Tairov agreed to produce only Soviet agitation plays. First, however, he took his company on a triumphant tour of Italy, Switzerland, Czechoslovakia, Uruguay, Argentina, and Brazil.

II

For more than a dozen years Meyerhold successfully promulgated his notions of nonrealistic acting because he was shrewd enough to use as his slogans: "Art cannot be nonpolitical," "Art is class Art," and "The theater is the tribune of agitation." An opportunist, he saw in the smashing of capitalistic traditions a chance for smashing theatrical traditions. And in inaugurating a new, scientific, class-conscious dramatic art this "frenzied Maestro" became "in many respects the Picasso of the theater." He explored and emphasized the medium until the theater became "something beyond what really happened." And despite his eventual failure, and mysterious death, Meyerhold was surely "one of the very few masters of the regisseur's technique of the anti-naturalistic modern theater," "the only one of all the Russian directors who [had] the feel of theatricality." [165]

In 1920 Meyerhold directed *Les Aubes* (*The Dawn*) (1898) by Belgian Émile Verhaeren (1855–1916) and introduced "into the performance reports of the progress of the Civil War as the news arrived in Moscow; the glorious achievements of the partisan bands, of Chapayev and his army, etc. Such an intensity of emotion was galvanized into action . . . that the play became a living thing, a struggle between life and death, the future life and the future death of those very people sitting in the theater. To them it was an emotional call to action as direct as any speech, any distribution of leaflets or any newspaper report." [166]

Then in 1922, with his production of the satirical *Le Cocu magnifique* (*The Magnificent Cuckold*) (1920) by Franco-Belgian Fernand Crommelynck (1888–), Meyerhold clearly and boldly began his personal revolution. The offering in no way resembled the initial presentation at Lugné-Poë's Théâtre de l'Oeuvre. Western "bourgeois" society was lampooned by actors whose "speech was not the speech of ordinary conversation but a kind of standardized, syncopated recitative carefully calculated in its vowel and consonant accents and in its syllabic and phrase measures." And the cast—all clad in blue denim overalls—moved, ran, danced, turned somersaults and cartwheels on an almost bare stage, on and around "an arrangement of platforms whose scaffoldings were completely unmasked," under "three wheels of different sizes hanging above the highest platform which were later to revolve, apparently at will," in revolving doors, and on ladders, stairs, ramps, and slides (instead of furniture)—and all for a purpose. Norris Houghton suggests this purpose by describing the entrance of the lover: "At another theater there would be a knock at the door, the man would enter, see the object of his affection, move toward her with eager steps, smile and take her in his arms. They would both register 'joy' at the meeting. Meyerhold places the lady at the foot of a tin slide, the lover climbs up a ladder to the top of the slide, zooms down it, feet first, knocks the lady off onto the floor, and shouts something that sounds like Russian for 'Whee!' Thus does Meyerhold express the effect of an eager lover meeting his mistress. The spirit of the scene is established directly by this completely abstract action. Of course, Meyerhold knows that lovers don't enter down slides in real life, but he believe[d] . . . that the emotion of abandonment and joy with which the man is filled can much more accurately be revealed if he slides down a ten-foot S curve to meet his lady than if he follows the dictates of natural movement. When this is understood there is some meaning to Meyerhold's work." [167]

Another of fifty-year-old, "Artist of the People" Meyerhold's startling attempts to be both presentational and pro-Soviet, "to arrive at verity without being a slave to verisimilitude," was his 1924 reinterpretation of Ostrovsky's *The Forest*. The classic was freely cut, reorganized, and "changed from the original five acts into thirty-three episodes" (Meyerhold always mauled every script he used); it was acted in a set that consisted "of a simple, hanging, bridgelike, winding-road, rising from the foreground to the back, on an incline, to a height exceeding the human figure"; and it became a grotesquery of the degenerate nobility and the petty merchants. This time the lovers used a seesaw and made a Freudian comment; and then the lady stood on the bridge, as the man climbed into a swing and rose higher and higher toward her. ("The mood is very lyric.") "The leading lady's lewdness was emphasized by her burning red wig and sentimental whining voice, the unctuous priest had a gold wig and beard, a young sap wore green hair, etc." Only sympathetic characters (the workers) were shown in normal guise. And all the actors continually concentrated on "physical actions." "Every person was shown in association with some object characteristic of him. During the performance something was always being done: shaving, cleaning the rifle, hanging laundry, swinging around the maypole, exercising on the trapeze, playing the accordion." [168]

Soviet audiences, of course, were bewildered by all these Meyerhold stunts, but they liked the novelty, and they were compelled to like the ideology.

"Motion," Meyerhold instructed them, "is the most powerful means of expression in creating a theatrical presentation. The role of motion on the stage is more important than the role of the other elements. . . . The audience learns the thoughts and motives of an actor through his movements. . . ." [169] And in the theater those movements should not be, must not be, merely lifelike.

In order to emphasize actors in physical action Meyerhold abolished old-fashioned, "decadent," decorative or photographic settings and, like an engineer, in tune with the scientific and machine age, demanded purely functional ones. They were called Constructivist. A "typical constructivist setting may be described as a skeleton structure . . . an agglomeration of . . . stairs, platforms, runways, . . . stripped to their basic and structural forms, held together by plain scaffolding, and arranged to permit the running off of a play at its fullest theatrical intensity. It is all the scenes of a play simplified to the bone and woven into one scene. Always the true constructivist setting is conceived for use without a curtain and to stand in space from the time the audience arrives until it leaves. It is utterly unnatural, in its grouping together of many elements detached from life, and in its bareness, its lack of every casual detail of nature and of such usual elements as walls and ceilings. Every plank and post of it is tested by the rigid question of its functional use. It is the 'practicables' of the old pictorial scene plucked out of the picture, skeletonized and nailed together for safe usage. What 'design' is expended on weaving these naked structural things into one whole theoretically has the sole purpose of capitalizing movement as a revealing theatrical element." [170]

For such settings Meyerhold devised a completely new kind of movement, a new kind of acting, called Bio-mechanics—derived, for sure, from the studies in conditioned reflexes by Ivan Pavlov (1849–1936). He eliminated the actor's feelings and demanded "physicalizations." He brazenly turned acting outward by replacing psychological or emotional nuances with gymnastic dexterities whose purpose was to make the *audience* feel. "To be as general as may be, . . . bio-mechanics is built on the premise that life is an entirely physiological condition and accordingly man is simply an animal a little more highly developed in certain directions than some other animals. His contact with the outside world is maintained through the elaborate mechanism of the nervous system which reacts automatically to external in fluences. All of what we are prone to consider his emotional life, all of what yesterday was thought to be the center and core of man, his immortal soul, is merely the aggregation of these impressions of the nervous system, just as the feeling of pain, to use an elementary illustration, is the result perhaps of pricking the finger. This is to state the situation very crudely, but clearly enough at any rate to make apparent the breadth of the chasm between the old method and the new." [171] Thus bio-mechanic actors were taught at Meyerhold's school to ignore in most instances subjective feelings, taught that the nucleus of expression is the action and reaction of nerves and muscles, and transformed via exercises in boxing, tumbling, "physical jerks," running, jumping, dancing, and climbing into alert, agile, functional men and women of the Communist regime. (The only acceptable actor of the company was Igor Ilyinsky [1901–], who at best was a comic, gymnastic puppet.)

Bio-mechanics and constructivism in various guises (sometimes muted, and then definitely made less and less abstract as Party officials began to condemn formalism) shaped most of Meyerhold's productions during this period. Some of them were: in 1924 D. E. Daesh Evropu (The Destruction of Europe), a dramatization of Ilya Ehrenburg's (1891–) novel, in which the Bolsheviks bored a tunnel between Leningrad and New York City and through it marched a triumphant army; in 1925 Uchitel Bulbus (Teacher Bulbus) by Alexei Faiko (1893–), which developed the theme of class vigilance; in 1926 a daring, inventive, brilliant interpretation of The Inspector General; and in 1929 Kommandarm 2 (The Second Army Commander) by Ilya Selvinski (1899–) and Mayakovsky's Klop (Bedbug).

III

Tolstoyan and then Marxist Eugene Vakhtangov was dissatisfied with the theatrical abstractions of Tairov and Meyerhold, primarily because they weren't very human, and with the naturalism of Stanislavski, primarily because it wasn't theatrical. By 1920, when he was thirty-seven, he was teaching at the First Studio of the Moscow Art Theatre, where Michael Chekhov was a leader; at the Second Studio, founded in 1916, and headed by Vakhtang Mchedelov (1884–1924); at several other studios in the city; and at his own school, where now and then he performed (as "an average actor") in order to perfect his directing. And he was dreaming of having his own theater some day, a "people's theater," where he could stage Hamlet, Faust, the Sukhovo-Kobylin trilogy, Hugo's Les Misérables, Byron's tragedies, and plays by Gorky, Lunacharsky, Romain Rolland.[172]

In 1920 Vakhtangov's school evolved into the Third Studio of the Moscow Art Theatre. This group, after working on Chekhov's one-acters, Svadba (The Wedding) (1889) and Yubiley (Jubilee, or The Anniversary) (1891, 1902), soon presented for the public a revival of an earlier Vakhtangov production, Maeterlinck's *Le Miracle de Saint Antoine*. With future director Yuri Zavadsky (1894–) as the saint, it "struck Moscow as an absolute revelation" of pure theatricality.[173]

Also in 1921 Vakhtangov staged for the First Studio Strindberg's *Erik XIV* with Chekhov in the title role. The production was propagandistic because Sweden's ruler was transformed into a "generalization of kingly power"; but more important, it vividly made the point that in the theater everything should be theatrical. "Up to now," Vakhtangov announced, "the Studio, true to Stanislavski's teaching, has doggedly aimed at obtaining mastery of inner experience; now the Studio is entering a period of search for new forms. . . . This is the first experiment. . . . The Revolution demands of us significance and vividness." [174]

Thus Stanislavski's "most brilliant, best" pupil broke sharply with his teacher's insistence that the audience should forget that it is in the theater. Stanislavski, he said, "rejoiced in the fact that the audience used to come to the Moscow Art Theatre to *The Three Sisters*, not as to a theater, but as if invited to the Prosorov house. This he considered to be the highest achievement of the theater." That formula and that attitude, Vakhtangov argued, "led him to a dead end, a tragic dead end. The audience should not forget for one single instant that it is in a theater." The Moscow Art Theatre, he continued, "does not give birth to artistic works, for creativeness is absent there. There is only a refined, skillful, keen result of one's observations of life. Carried away "by the need for ferreting out vulgarity, Stanislavski also removed a certain genuine, necessary theatricality, and genuine theatricality consists in presenting theatrical works in a theatrical manner. . . ." He forgot "that the actor's inner experience must be conveyed to the auditorium with the help of theatrical means." Moreover, he forgot that the "few great actors—Duse, Chaliapin, Salvini—in acting *show* that they act." [175]

"Vakhtangov took from Stanislavski's method: (1) concentration; (2) justification of everything one does on the stage; (3) the process of finding every shade of meaning of the author's reading between the lines; (4) the development of the biography of each character . . . ; (5) the rooting out of moldy acting clichés." [176] Then he aded theatricality, and did so brilliantly with An-sky's *The Dybbuk* and Gozzi's *Turandot* in 1922.

After working for an entire year with the Habima (stage) Players, who spoke the classical Hebrew language, Vakhtangov transformed them into admirable, imaginative, stylized actors; commissioned a setting that consisted of "Prismatic walls, warped stairways, chairs and tables slanting toward the audience, spotlights hidden in strategic corners of the stage"; and created with *The Dybbuk* "a complete work of art" which "cannot be too highly praised." From it audiences got "the extreme stylization that ritual can go to and at the same time the truth that worshippers bring to ritual." [177]

Then just before he died, "to his everlasting glory," Vakhtangov directed *Turandot* at the Third Studio. With it he displayed "his love of comedy—

broad slap-stick children's comedy and the light fantasy tinged with irony which drew a modern moral from a familiar fairy story without ever being sententious—his romantic, bravura color and sweep in the costumes, and his delicious understanding of music as a theatrical medium. Rhythm was the keynote of the acting" by a large cast headed by Zavadsky, Boris Shchukin (1894–1939), and Reuben Simonov (1899–). Before the play began the actors in formal attire appeared before the curtain and, to a haunting waltz, told the audience what it was to see. Next, with bright colored, silk scraps picked up onstage they costumed themselves in oriental garments, sashes, turbans, wigs and trooped off. Then stagehands—"young men and girls in dark blue kimona suits with colored caps"—to the same waltz set the scenery. Doors and windows, pillars and arches, counterweighted with gaily colored little sandbags, sailed gracefully into position. The crew bowed, left, and the story was performed, maintaining throughout the "let's pretend and have fun" attitude.[178]

How long Vakhtangov might have continued—or have been allowed by Party officials to continue—being that fantastic, that theatrical, is an unanswered question. But before his early death (he never saw the opening of Turandot) he had thought deeply about the stage, about the widely different ways in which Stanislavski and Meyerhold used it, and arrived at a few dabs of theory which guided his crowd of followers in evolving with their productions a unique, highly successful theatrical style.

"Stanislavski," he wrote, "in his enthusiasm for real truth, brought naturalistic truth to the stage. He sought theatrical truth in the truth of life," and "found only a harmony with the mood of the Russian society of his period; but not everything that is contemporary is eternal." "Meyerhold, carried away by theatrical truth, removed the truthfulness of feelings. . . ." Both, Vakhtangov decided, were wrong, or only half right. Yes, one must seek truth in the theater; but *also* one must seek "a form [with] a theatrical ring to it." Theatricality meant to Vakhtangov the way in which scenes and behavior onstage differ from scenes and behavior in life. He explained, "Feeling is the same in theater and life, but the means and methods of presenting them are different. The grouse is the same, whether served in the restaurant or at home. But in the restaurant it is served and prepared in such a manner as to have a theatrical ring to it, while at home it is just a homemade piece of meat." [179]

"In the theater," Vakhtangov concluded, "there should be neither naturalism nor realism. . . ." Both should take from life only what is needed, "only what has histrionic value." "In the theater . . . the form must be created, and it must be created by one's fantasy [imagination]. This is why I call it fantastic realism. . . . The means must be theatrical." [180]

"Stanislavski and Meyerhold—content and form, truth of feeling and theatricality—these Vakhtangov wanted to unite in his theater. He intended that this theater should express the organic unity of the 'eternal' basis of art with theatrical form, directed by a sense of the contemporary." And Stanislavski admitted that Vakhtangov finally discovered what "he himself had sought for years and could not find." [181]

✿ FINDING A SYSTEM

Elated with his foreign success, Stanislavski in the autumn of 1924 returned to Moscow and to his disappointment in the new order and the "new" theater of Meyerhold, Tairov, Vakhtangov, and Michael Chekhov which, having found a vivid form, was being compelled to find a social content. Immediately, and to his sorrow, he presided over the liquidation of the Studios of the Moscow Art Theatre. The Second Studio disappeared when most of its actors were taken into the main company as replacements for those who had remained abroad as political émigrés. Prominent among the new members was Nikolai Khmelyov (1901–1945) who, after the death of Nemirovich–Danchenko in 1943, was appointed Artistic Director of the Moscow Art Theatre. Also in 1924 the Fourth Studio (formed in 1921) went its independent way under that name until 1927 when it was called the Realistic Theatre. (Beginning in 1932 Nikolai Okhlopkov [1900–], a Meyerhold student, served as its director.)

The two other Studios definitely deflected from Stanislavski's teachings. During his absence the First Studio, like Vakhtangov's Third Studio, had abandoned much of his system of acting "the life of the human soul" and had moved from psychological realism to theatricality in the production of such plays as Synge's *The Playboy of the Western World* (retitled *Geroi, The Hero*), *The Taming of the Shrew,* and *King Lear.* In 1924 it became by government decree the Second Moscow Art Theatre with Chekhov as its director. For its initial production this brilliant actor, who believed that "Naturalism is not art, for the artist can add nothing of his own to the naturalistic 'work of art' since his task is limited to knowing how to copy 'nature' more or less accurately," portrayed Hamlet with a "vivid theatricality"; and in 1925 the new organization successfully presented Eugene Zamyatin's (1884–1938) dramatization of Leskov's *Blokha (The Flea)* as an ingenious piece of "local fair" buffoonery (like *Turandot*). But Party critics attacked it for being too esthetic. (Because of continued political pressures like that Chekhov in 1927 "refused a special 'Michael Chekhov Theatre' in which to do nothing but the clasics, [and] deserted to foreign countries.") [182] The Third Studio in 1924 was reorganized into the Vakhtangov Theatre, and three years later reached maturity with the presentation of Leonid Leonov's (1899–) psychological, partisan *Barsuki (The Badgers).*

This new theatricality, "beautiful and sharp in form" but largely external, distressed Stanislavski. It hasn't produced, he wrote in his revised *My Life in Art (Moia zhizn'v iskusstve),* "a single actor-creator who is strong in portraying human emotion, nor has it worked out a single new method, instituted anything resembling a search in the sphere of inner technique or built up a brilliant ensemble. In a word, there is not a single achievement in the sphere of spiritual creativeness." [183] So, nearing sixty-two, he went to work again with his Moscow Art company—soon, however, delegating most of the production chores to assistants. More important, he worked on his realistic, "inner" system of acting.

In 1924 Stanislavski supervised student rehearsals of an adaptation of *The Battle of Life* (1846) by Dickens; next year he directed and acted the role of Famusov in a revival of the company's 1906 *Woe From Wit* by Griboyedov. Then in September 1925 the Moscow Art Theatre offered its first new production in eight years, its first play by a contemporary dramatist in ten years, the historical *Pugachovshina* (*The Time of Pugachov*) by Constantin Trenyev (1878–). It flopped. But in January 1926 the actors achieved their first genuine success since the Revolution with Ostrovsky's *Goryacheye serdtse* (*A Warm Heart*) (1869) in which Ivan Moskvin performed expertly. "Stanislavski here applied the method of 'artistic maximalism' for the first time, that is, realism, scenic truth, and . . . theatrical brilliance—all to the maximal limit. Characterizations of the cast were sharpened almost to the point of the grotesque." Also that year the company was hailed for presenting with "careful psychological interpretation of character" [184] Bulgakov's *The Days of the Turbines*, a Chekhovian study of an old-time family confronted by the Revolution.

Productions in 1927 of *The Marriage of Figaro* and *The Two Orphans* (retitled *The Sisters Gerard*) were followed on the tenth anniversary of the Revolution by the presentation of *Bronepoezd 14–69* (*Armored Train 14–69*) by Vsevolod Ivanov (1895–). Its realism was "bright and definite, its sense of communal history broad and fervent." This premiere marked a turning point in the history of the company. It "began the 'Sovietization' of that theater and Stanislavski's acceptance of the existing government." [185] Then, in 1928 at a celebration of the thirtieth anniversary of the Moscow Art Theatre, Stanislavski performed for the last time, as Vershinin, in the first act of *The Three Sisters*.

In 1930 Nemirovich–Danchenko directed a very popular farce, *Kvadratura kruga* (*Squaring the Circle*) by Valentin Kataev (1897–), Stanislavski directed Leonidov in *Othello*, which failed, and Danchenko staged a truly human yet presentational version of Tolstoy's *Voskresen've* (*Resurrection*) (1889–90). "In a simple dark blue jacket, without make-up, with a pencil in his hand, and without any theatricality, Kachalov walked among the first rows of the orchestra" and talked the actual words with which Tolstoy begins the novel—words describing the coming of spring in a big city. Then, as if illustrating the story, separate scenes of the story were acted for the audience, with Kachalov now and then relating the hero's thoughts. "As the play went on he wandered in and out among the actors, from time to time interrupting their dialogue with Tolstoy's descriptions or philosophical comments on their actions." [186]

II

Some of Stanislavski's slow, confused, and verbose putterings with his system can be traced and summarized. In the recently printed "The System and Methods of Creative Art," a shorthand record of his talks at the Opera Studio between 1918 and 1922, he began by announcing quite definitely that nobody can be taught to act. All that he could do, he said, was teach those with talent how to expunge hackneyed stage conventions from their impersonations, and how to avoid the traps of becoming only external and mechanical onstage. And his "system" for doing that, he assured the student singers, wasn't anything newly invented by him; it was merely the gist of all he had learned from life and from men of the theater.[187]

Acting, Stanislavski declared, can theoretically be split into two processes: "work on oneself and work on the part." In the 1925 Russian version of My Life in Art he expanded that point as follows: "My 'system' falls into two main parts: (1) the actor's inner and outer work on himself; (2) inner and outer work on the role. Inner work on oneself consists in developing psychic technique which enables the actor to work up a creative mood in which he finds inspiration. Outer work on oneself consists in preparing one's body apparatus to incarnate the role and fully bringing out its inner life. [Inner] Work on a role consists in studying the spiritual content of the drama, the core around which it is built and which determines its meaning as well as the meaning of each of its roles." [188] But outer work on the role, curiously enough, he did not define.

The actor working on himself, Stanislavski then continued, should first discover the beautiful in everyone around him, and also in himself. From that wholesome premise he should proceed carefully to observe himself and others in order to learn the true expression of each emotion in given circumstances. Then he should practice mastering that essential of all acting, relaxation, which can be attained by achieving public solitude, by entering "the creative circle," by concentrating. In other words, Stanislavski believed that an actor must forget he is onstage and that people are looking at him, listening to him. To be an artist instead of a stage hack, he said, "you must try to be the person you are acting . . . throughout the whole day of the performance" and especially during its entire length. Anyone "who during the intervals in the wings powders his face or smooths his hair when that is not, according to his part, the business of his creative circle, or who has a cup of tea, or puts drops into his nose, has not only broken his circle, dissociated himself from his part, and distracted his attention, but also gone back to the preoccupations of his private life, and will never be able to enter afresh into the life of his hero." [189]

This creative circle of repose can best be induced, Stanislavski taught, if the actor while working on his part will concentrate on his "physical actions," on whatever his five senses are perceiving, and on the smallest concrete details of whatever he is in character actually *doing*.

Later, the actor should advance to understanding those actions and to grouping them logically into a *series* of truthful actions, into larger "units and objectives." By doing that, he will become aware of "the ruling idea of the play." (And then more carefully reshape all the actions of his part.)

But, Stanislavski wisely warned, "to be able to digest a character in your mind does not mean that you are a talented actor," [190] that you can therefore express your matter or convey it to others. "You need technique," he probably wanted to say, "a special technique for the theater." But he *didn't* say that. He ducked emphasizing or even mentioning it, or the theater medium, and blithely, fatally, advised each student only to use "as if" and naturally to live each of his roles. To be able to do that, he inferred, meant that you were a talented actor.

At least two of Stanislavski's points in this 1918–22 period appear inconsistent with the system as he finally set it down in 1936. Or at least they are inconsistent with the system as taught by many of his American disciples. First, he suggested that an actor in rehearsal and performance "must forget all about himself as an individual and yield his place to the character in the play, [or otherwise] he will paint all the different characters he is representing in the colors of his own personality" or "transfer his personal idiocyncrasies to every part. . . ." In short, Stanislavski once was opposed to the actor's impersonating only himself onstage. Second, he assured his students: an audience will believe in you as an actor *"only if your life on the stage bears no resemblance, however true or subtle, to ordinary life"* [my italics], but instead has been transformed into a high degree of "heroic tension." [191] That term seems to have been Stanislavski's synonym for theatricality. He was, this once anyway, well aware of its value in acting.

In 1923–24, according to Nikolai Gorchakov (1901–   ), one of his student directors, Stanislavski continued to insist that the "correct state of being on the stage . . . is the normal state of a human being in life." To help students arrive at that state he instructed them to prepare detailed biographies of the characters they acted, to answer such questions as the following: "(1) Who am I? How old am I? My profession? Members of my family? What is my disposition? (2) Where do I live in Moscow? (You must be able to draw the plan of your apartment and the furniture in the rooms.) (3) How did I spend yesterday? How did I spend today until this evening? (4) Whom do I know among those present [in a scene] and what is my relationship to them?" And then at rehearsals he would say: "Don't fix anything before the scene. This is the surest way to deaden the scene and your parts. The true adjustment will come on the stage as a result of the correct state of the actor in the character, from his desire to fulfill the problems of the part in the given circumstances. . . . Act, but don't plan your action among yourselves beforehand." [192]

But, aware of the importance of outer creative effort, Stanislavski announced that "It is not enough to know how to live your role on the stage. You must have a strong, well-trained voice of pleasant—or, in any case—expressive timbre, perfect diction, plasticity of movement—without being a poseur—a face that is beautiful and mobile, a good figure, and expressive hands." Also aware that the "audience is concerned with the author's idea and [the] presentation and interpretation of it," he admitted that the actor "needs a developed technique, . . . the ability to communicate, to 'come across' to" it.[193]

In 1929 Stanislavski wrote for the *Encyclopaedia Britannica* a brief article on "Direction and Acting," in which he declared that "an actor must without let-up work on the development of his *sense of truth* which supervises all of his inner and physical activity both when he is creating and also when he is performing his part. It is only when his sense of truth is developed that he will . . . express the state of the person he is portraying and . . . not merely serve the purposes of external beauty, as all sorts of conventional gestures and poses do." He also said, taking another crack at his "theatrical" contemporaries, that "the director and actors must try to achieve an exact and profound understanding of the spirit and thought [and style?] of the playwright and not replace them by their own inventions." [194]

On the subject of feelings Stanislavski insisted that the actor must not voluntarily evoke them in himself. He should play his actions and let the emotions arise from them. Moreover, by his imagination he can stir up his "emotion memory," luring "from its secret depths, beyond the reach of consciousness, elements of already experienced emotions," and then *regroup* them to fit each specific instance. But Stanislavski was wise enough to warn the actor, rather unemphatically, to be sure, that during a performance a portion of his consciousness "must remain free from the trammels of the play in order that it [can] exercise some supervision over whatever he is feeling and doing. . . ." [195]

In the *Encyclopaedia* article Stanislavski also briefly mentioned "Units and Objectives," "The Unbroken Line," and "The Super-Objective," topics he treated more fully seven years later in *An Actor Prepares*.

In mid-1929, after a serious illness, and on leave from the Moscow Art Theatre, Stanislavski went to southern France to recuperate and "to cast into final form the long prepared book" on acting. Originally it was planned to cover both aspects of his method—the inner preparations of an actor and the external means of bringing a character to life before an audience. Because Stanislavski—but few of his American followers—believed that "the student-actor must keep moving along parallel lines of inner and outer creative effort," the two parts "were side by side" in the first drafts worked out on the Riviera.[196]

Back in Moscow in the autumn of 1930 Stanislavski, assisted by Lyubov Gurevich as literary adviser, decided to give the book a semifictional character. But even then the writing wasn't easy. He spent much time reorganizing, rewriting. "His main trouble was that he frequently changed his ideas about the importance of certain elements of his system. Thus, at first he regarded the emotional memory of the actor as of paramount importance and treated it quite independently of the actor's imagination. It was only later that he began to regard the 'magic if,' that is to say, the actor's imagination, as of much greater importance; and this view, too, . . . he subsequently modified. . . . All this made his work on the book a very slow and at times rather painful business, and it is perhaps not surprising that in the end Gurevich gave up her collaboration with Stanislavski." [197]

Undaunted, however, Stanislavski in December 1930, when he was almost sixty-eight, outlined four books he intended to write on the subject of Acting. The first (after *My Life in Art*, which he called a "Preface . . . leading to the 'system,' ") was to be titled *Working on Oneself*: "Divided into 'Living One's Part' and 'Embodiment.' " The second was to be called *Working on One's Role*: "In this book I shall deal in detail with excerpts and tasks and through-action." The third book "will treat of creating a polished role, leading to Creative Mood." The fourth book, *Three Trends in Art*, "will be about the art of performance and trade tricks (to be dealt with considerably more comprehensively)." [198]

❧ 1930–1950

During the depression in the United States in June 1931, thirty-three years after Stanislavski had taken his newly organized Moscow Art Theatre actors to Pushkino for four months to rehearse a number of plays, a group of intense young Americans—"twenty-eight actors, some wives, two children, . . . three directors [Clurman, Strasberg and Cheryl Crawford], and a few friends" went from New York to Brookfield Center, Connecticut, for three months to rehearse *The House of Connelly* by Paul Green (1898–). Strasberg, as director of the play, used what he knew of the Stanislavski system, making it something "peculiarly his own," and causing at least one of the actors, Morris Carnovsky (1898–), to ask "What is this hocus-pocus?" [199]

Principally it was work in improvisation and with emotion, or affective, memory. In improvisation exercises the actors did "extemporaneous scenes based on situations emotionally analogous to those in the play, but not actually part of the play's text"; they also ad-libbed the play's scenes in their own words. In the "memory of emotion" exercises each actor "was asked to recall the details of an event from his own past. The recollection . . . would stir [up] . . . some of the feeling involved in the original experience, thus producing 'mood.'" All summer "Strasberg was a fanatic on the subject of true emotion. Everything was secondary to it. He sought it with the patience of an inquisitor, he was outraged by trick substitutes, and when he had succeeded in stimulating it, he husbanded it, fed it, and protected it. Here was something new to most of the actors, something basic, something almost holy. It was revelation in the theater; and Strasberg was its prophet." [200]

Next summer at Dover Furnace, New York, after Broadway productions of *The House of Connelly*, *1931*— by Paul (1897–) and Claire Sifton (1897–), and *Night Over Taos* by Maxwell Anderson, Strasberg initiated for the Group Theatre "classes designed to stimulate the actors' imagination and resourcefulness"; along with truth of emotion, "theatricality and clarity of interpretation" were emphasized. He also "asked the actors to prepare dramatic scenes based on well-known paintings"; Clurman played records of classical music, "and the actors improvised scenes suggested to them by the music." Some evenings Strasberg, hoping to learn more about Stanislavski's system from newly arrived publications on the Soviet theater, "had a Russian acquaintance, who worked in [the] kitchen, translate these volumes for those who were interested. . . . The books were mostly esthetic and technical, but the quality of the listening was, for the most part, one of romantic awe." [201]

In the fall of 1933 Strasberg expertly directed the Group Theatre's first popular success, *Men in White* by Sidney Kingsley (1906–). Stella Adler (1904–) and Alexander Kirkland (1904–) were down for $200 a week, Carnovsky and J. Edward Bromberg (1903–1951) for $175, Luther Adler (1903–) for $140, Clifford Odets (1906–) for $50, and Elia Kazan (1909–) for $40. That summer Stella Adler, who had spent five weeks in France studying daily with Stanislavski, returned to the company to report that its "use of the . . . system had been incorrect." Too much emphasis had been placed on emotion memory. Action, she said, is more important; actions lead to correct emotion. To prove her point she exhibited a chart she'd copied; on it "ACTION" was placed ahead of "Truth of feeling or passion" in the scheme of things. "Strasberg's first reaction to this declaration was the charge that Stanislavski had gone back on himself. Later, however, he decided to take advantage of the suggestions furnished by Stella's report. . . ." Also, because he'd been in Moscow briefly and been impressed "with the Meyerhold productions," he displayed in staging *Gold Eagle Guy* (1934) by Melvin Levy (1902–) "a greater concern with movement and the expressive value of physical materials than he ever had before." [202]

In 1935 some of the Group members became fascinated with the performances of Michael Chekhov, who "observed all of the 'externals' as well as the 'internals' in his acting." They "felt that they had achieved some measure of honesty and truth in their work, but [that] Chekhov's gift for combining these with sharply expressive and yet very free color, rhythm, and design was something in which they knew themselves to be deficient, and which they therefore envied." At once agitation was started—"led by Stella Adler—to take group lessons from the Russian. . . ." Nothing came of it. That summer Clurman, who in February had made a vigorous hit of *Awake and Sing* by Odets, went with Cheryl Crawford to Moscow, saw thirty-five productions in five weeks, liked Meyerhold's versions of *The Inspector General* and *The Forest*, and put questions both to him and to Stanislavski for hours.[203]

At about this time the Group Theatre appears to have gotten from someone, possibly Vakhtangov, the notion that the "principal aim of a theatrical school" must be the "liberation and disclosing" of the actor's individuality. It "must remove all the conventional rubbish which prevents the spontaneous manifestation of the student's deeply hidden potentialities." It must "bring out within the pupil the singular qualities which predetermine the possibility of creative work." (That was the prime aim of the Actors Studio—founded in 1947 by Elia Kazan, Cheryl Crawford, and Robert Lewis (1909–). In the 1950's Lee Strasberg, the Studio's perceptive teacher, was trying, according to one student, "to make you find things in yourself that you can use." The training was "not unakin to analysis.") Furthermore, Group actors came to believe, again apparently from Vakhtangov, that "it is necessary to live your own temperament on the stage and not the supposed temperament of the character. You must proceed from yourself," they argued, "and not from a conceived image; you must place yourself in the position of the character." [204] (But not a word about Vakhtangov's insistence on "theatricality.")

Some of the Group's confusion about acting (according to Stanislavski, Meyerhold, M. Chekhov, or Vakhtangov?) was lessened by the publication in New York in 1936 of *An Actor Prepares*. In this book Stanislavski did not have room enough to emphasize the importance of vocal and visual techniques onstage. But with a portion of his "System" he furnished these Americans a "Method"—as Strasberg soon called it.[205]

In 1936 the Group Theatre produced *The Case of Clyde Griffiths*, a dramatization of Dreiser's novel co-authored by Piscator, in 1937 Green's *Johnny Johnson* and *Golden Boy* by Odets, in 1938 the latter's *Rocket to the Moon*, in 1939 *The Gentle People* by Irwin Shaw (1913–), an experimental *My Heart's in the Highlands* by William Saroyan (1908–), poetically staged by Lewis, and Robert Ardrey's (1908–) *Thunder Rock* directed by Kazan. In 1941, two years after the outbreak of World War II, the Group Theatre disbanded.

II

Now we must go back a few years, and return to Russia. In the newspaper *Pravda* (*Truth*) in April 1932 the Party Central Committee published its decree "On the Reorganization of Literary and Artistic Organizations," in which Stalin's "Socialist Realism," a concept which had been bandied about for several years, received official formulation. "Socialist Realism," it was announced, "demands of the artist a truthful and historically concrete representation of actuality in its revolutionary development." In other words, he must express lifelike truth, but in such terms "that the worker-audience . . . gets a perspective of either the socialism it is helping to build or of the factors of the past out of which that socialism has come." [206]

In other words, the government, "aware that the truth of life and the truth of art may be phrased differently," banished all formalism—called something that "never happened and could never happen in life"—from the Russian stage.[207] Inevitably, in a few years, the Second Moscow Art Theatre, Meyerhold's Theatre, and the Kamerny were closed. (The Vakhtangov Theatre escaped because for a while it had safely retreated to realism.)

Meyerhold bitterly fought the Party dictum. In 1939 he dared to yell at his censors: "That miserable and pitiable thing which pretends to be called the theater of Socialist Realism has nothing in common with art! Go to the theaters in Moscow and look at the dry and boring plays, one like the other. . . . There, where only recently the creative idea was the key; there, where there were the best theaters in the world, there now rules dismal mediocrity. . . . Wanting to throw out the dirty water, you have thrown the child out with it! Hunting down formalism, you have destroyed art!" [208] Shortly afterwards, he mysteriously disappeared.

The Soviet insistence on realism encouraged Stanislavski (who earlier had been called too "mystic") to continue writing his book on acting while he directed or supervised plays and operas. In January 1933 he wrote to Gorky that he was at work on his "grammar of dramatic art." "I have been doing my utmost," he explained, "to put down on paper what a young actor ought to know. Such a book is a necessity, if only because it would put an end to all the silly talk about my so-called 'system,' which in the form it is taught now merely cripples the actor. . . . Oh, if only I could throw off ten years of my life and get rid of my constant illnesses!" [209]

In 1935 he said, "our art is based entirely on the actor who is exchanging living currents with the auditorium. . . . If real life is born on the stage, the audience does not demand anything else. . . ." Because films destroy "this direct communication between the actor and the audience" he disliked them. The next year he reiterated his principal points: that "theatrical style arise[s] out of being natural," and that the actor "must always be himself." (If at other times Stanislavski contradicted those points, well, it's true "that for any assertion about his art theories one can always find in his statements or his practice sufficient basis for a counterstatement.") [210]

Stanislavski was seventy-three when An Actor Prepares was published in the United States. This first publication in 1936 was, however, "a mere fragment; the complete work, published in Russia after Stanislavski's death in 1938, . . . bears an entirely different title, namely, Actor and Self: Personal Work in the Creative Process of Re-Living. The text is almost three times as extensive" as that of the American edition. "In a preface, Stanislavski . . . emphasizes that the volume [either edition] deals merely with the actor's preparatory work and not with problems of rehearsal and performance." [211]

Scads of American would-be actors bought the 1936 book. (In twenty-five years, in eighteen printings, some 90,000 copies were sold; and it continues to be sold at the rate of about 4,000 copies annually in the United States.) Students especially latched onto Stanislavski's indelible, flattering "main proposition . . . that nothing ought to be imposed on the actor from without, . . . that everything must come from within the actor himself. . . ." They were hypnotized by the assertions that the "basis of our school of acting . . . is . . . living your part"; that "Nature's laws are binding on all, without exception"; that *in our art you must live the part every moment that you are playing it, and every time*"; that the actor "lives the part, not noticing *how* he feels, not thinking about *what* he does. . . ." They especially revered the instructions: "you must play yourself," and "*never allow yourself externally to portray anything that you have not inwardly experienced*" (remembered, that is, not imagined). At once actors began refusing to play roles not consonant with their own personalities. They changed the playwright's words whenever sentences were not written the way they would say them. They ruined the rhythm of a scene with pauses in which they could uniquely and ponderously "react." They just couldn't cross stage right on this speech or that in accordance with a director's design because they "didn't feel it." And, in speaking with everyday naturalness, they didn't much care whether audiences could hear them. In short, they performed not to serve a playwright and not to entertain an audience but only to "realize" themselves.[212]

But, back in Moscow in that brief time before his death, Stanislavski was stressing—even more strongly than Stella Adler had noticed—the importance of onstage actions. "Action is the very basis of our art," he insisted, "and with it our creative work must *begin*" [my italics]. Formerly, he admitted, he had taught by working on the actor's feelings, had attempted to draw them out truly. Now he decided to proceed differently. "We shall create the line of his action, the life of his body, and then the life of his spirit will be created indirectly by itself." Stanislavski did even more to emphasize the essential potency of action. He curiously began to doubt the worth of most preliminary study of a script by a cast around a table, the discussion, for instance, of "Units and Objectives." That practice, he held, leads the actor into the sphere of abstract reasoning and thus muddles his concentration on the concrete, on the specific. "My theory," he announced, "is to take away the text from the actor and make him work on [physical] actions." [213]

In Stanislavski's last years, "movement, voice, and acting techniques became increasingly a matter of concern and importance to him." [214] In his *Building a Character*, which he was writing just before his death, and which was published in the United States eleven years later in 1949, he included such topics as "Toward a Physical Characterization," "Making the Body Expressive," "Plasticity of Motion," "Diction and Singing," "Tempo-Rhythm in Movement," and "Speech Tempo-Rhythm."

In 1938, Stanislavski frequently voiced the regret that even in his revised *Actor and Self* "he had dealt with the ruling idea and through-action at the end of it instead of at the beginning. He regarded that as the greatest flaw of the system as formulated by him in the book." Action onstage, he said, can be creative only when it is governed and shaped by an idea. The "smallest detail [however sincere, or natural, or believable], if . . . not related to the ruling idea, becomes superfluous and harmful and is liable to divert the attention from the essential point of the play." "Never forget," he warned, "that what keeps the theater alive is . . . the idea of the playwright." Directors and actors, he once told Leonidov, who brilliantly analyze a play but forget through-action and the ruling idea are like a cook who tries to make an omelet with eggs, salt, a frying-pan—and no heat.[215]

By 1950 all Russian acting was soundly based on Stanislavski's system; but the egoism of "playing yourself" and "living the part" was minimized, if not ignored, and emphasis was placed on through-action, the ruling idea, and theatrical techniques. Today at the Moscow Art Theatre Studio School, for instance, the instructors initially and for a while try to get the first-year student "to improvise in terms of his own person, [but] then they take him on to more difficult characters away from his own personality." Moreover, the first-year student is required to attend "one class in movement each day and also one in voice." At the Moscow Art Theatre itself "direction is overtly technical and is as much concerned with the actor's technique as with the subjective inner life of the characters." One of the directors, Victor Stanitsyn, trained by Stanislavski, "not only omits basic aspects of 'the method' but also demands of his actors a high level of technical competence in voice and movement, an adherence to the director's *blocking* and a complete fidelity to the text as written. Unlike some American practitioners of 'the method,' the Russian directors . . . do not indulge actors in rehearsal or in performance by permitting inaudibility; license to wander, to rewrite the dialogue, or to alter radically the pace and line readings." [216]

By mid-century in the United States the ardent, controversial, often violently prejudiced adherents of the Stanislavski system had truly vitalized American acting. "Like it or lump it," critic Walter Kerr wrote, "the Actors Studio has literally given birth to the clearest, most carefully defined, most virile approach to the player's craft that the American theater has produced." "It has taught us to respect character, to seek penetration in depth, to deal accurately with environment, to avoid obvious sham, and so on." Most conspicuously it contributed, even in shoddy scripts, many lifelike characterizations for television (which spurted into easy popularity between 1948 and 1950, when the amount of money spent by advertisers on the new medium "leaped 1,044 percent from $8,700,000 to $90,629,000.") [217]

But blind adherence to the system "also created something of a bottle-neck. It . . . led to an intolerance of other and broader styles. It . . . led to a considerable overemphasis on the actor's personal processes, as though these in themselves were the main concern of the theater. And it . . . had the unfortunate effect of equating, in many performers' minds, everything that is genuinely theatrical with 'sham.'" What is lacking in today's acting, according to Clurman, "is originality . . . , grandeur, passion, daring, sweep, color, brilliance, grace, above all, the magic gift for inner and outer trans-formation." [218]

Lately some of the variously instructed Stanislavski actors have paused to think twice on learning that often among the French, and especially among the British, "mistrust of 'Method' acting verges on hysteria." Pugnaciously or innocently they have asked why? The answers are many. In the opinion of German director Willi Schmidt (1910–) the American actor is "too pre-occupied with the naturalistic drama, is afraid to be unnatural." He has the habit of playing inwardly instead of outwardly. "He doesn't trust his body. He doesn't know that his whole body, his hands, head and his features are able to express just as much as his voice." Furthermore, Schmidt continues, the idea that "we must be on the stage as we are in real life is wrong. . . . If . . . the theater would be just like life (with its boundless and diffuse con-tradictions and its formless and unmanageable aspects) then we would not need art. We can go further and say that art would not exist if it were like life." According to Jacques Charon (1920–) of the Comédie-Française the young American actor is "easy prey to theories adopting 'truthfulness' as a criterion of interpretation." Almost exclusively his work "consists in dis-covering and exploring himself . . . (and sometimes with detriment to his text). The annoying part of this is that anyone can reach his own truth; so if this is the only quality required, then anybody can be an actor." And Michael Chekhov in *To the Actor, on the technique of acting* (1953)—valued by many as the best textbook on the subject—advises the player that he "can-not give his audiences new revelations by unvaryingly displaying only himself on the stage." Fundamentally, and excitingly, the actor ought to ask, Chekhov instructs, "What is the *difference* . . . between myself and the character as it is described by the playwright?" Finally, Laurence Olivier (1907–), along with many English actors, is sure that the American performer needs to work more on the vocal and visual techniques of his medium. After all, he declares, "One cannot play poetic drama, with its conventions of syllables, accents, and caesuras . . . , by means of intuition or spontaneity." [219]

III

Fervid pro and con attention awarded the Stanislavski system in the 1940's tended to obscure the peculiarly French theories of acting practiced by Jean-Louis Barrault (1910–). He centered his attention on the theater medium; he valued the actor primarily as a vocal and visible *instrument*. For him an actor ought to be more than a true, aware, and imaginative person. A novelist or a poet ought to be that; but the novelist and poet must also know how to *write*. Likewise, the actor must know how to *act*, how to use his voice and his body onstage in order to convey the playwright's text to an audience.

From 1931 to 1935 Barrault acted at Dullin's Théâtre de l'Atelier where he learned "the essential importance of *living a situation sincerely*, and from Stanislavski's teachings the necessity of "concentration, . . . observation, self-control, and *decontraction*." "When one plays comedy, straight drama or tragedy," he wrote in his *Réflexions sur le théâtre* (1949), "it is *indispensable* that the CHARACTER should always be SINCERE. It is not indispensable that the actor, who is playing the Character, should be so." "If the play that is being interpreted belongs to a theater-form that is technically easy," he elaborated, "then the actor can give himself up to sincerity side by side with his Character (who will be all the better for it). This is the case of the typical 'boulevard' play. If on the other hand the play that is being interpreted belongs to a technically difficult theater-form—such as the classics in general— the actor must forego a little of his sincerity (like dropping ballast) so as better to supervise what he is doing." Barrault also arrived at the belief that no player "can act convincingly with his own genuine emotion." Instead, he wrote, in some agreement with Stanislavski, that the actor must concern himself "with actions," with "only DEEDS." [220]

Significantly, Barrault learned from Dullin the importance to the actor of "his body and its expression." "It was through the study of the Body," he explained, "that I was to approach the technique of the actor." Not that he minimized voice and speech training. On the contrary, he stated, "it would be useful if there were a solfeggio of voice-positions by which the actor could train himself and acquire greater vocal-agility," by which he "might gain a deeper awareness of the *crescendo*, of the *sforzando*, the *staccato*, the *legato*; of a tied note, a dotted note, a quaver, etc." But for Barrault the visual was the neglected, essential ingredient of theater. Under the further influence of mime Étienne Decroux (1898–) and rebel Antonin Artaud (1896–1948), he maintained that the actor who rightly aims "to imitate nature *by means of the artificial*" must train himself to employ movement and gestures "calculated, chosen, rhythmic." [221]

In mid-1935 Barrault left the Atelier, appeared in some films, and then in 1937 offered his first independent production, fifteen performances of the tragic *Numancia* (c. 1587) by Cervantes, and for three months "floundered among Alceste's 900 lines" in *Le Misanthrope*. In 1940 Copeau engaged him for the Théâtre-Français where he acted Rodrigue in *Le Cid*, Hippolytus in *Phèdre*, and directed Claudel's *Le Soulier de satin* (*The Satin Slipper*) (1924). In 1946 he resigned from the Comédie-Française and formed the Compagnie Madeleine Renaud (1900–)–Jean-Louis Barrault to stage and act in André Gide's (1869–1951) translation of *Hamlet* (1944), Marivaux's *Les Fausses confidences*, Molière's *Amphitryon* and *Les Fourberies de Scapin*; in 1947 Gide's version of Franz Kafka's (1883–1924) twenty-two-year-old *Der Prozess* (*The Trial*), Salacrou's *Les Nuits de la colère* (*Nights of Wrath*) (1947), *L'Etat de siège* (1948) by Albert Camus (1913–1960) as "an experiment in the combining of many theatrical forms (lyric monologue, dialogue, movement of large groups on the stage, farce, chorus, panto-mime)," [222] and also in 1948, forty-two years after it was written, Claudel's *Partage de midi*.

If, as some have complained, Barrault's antirealistic method "has led him into an increasing preoccupation with manner and an increasing care-lessness of matter," he would probably answer, "What matter? There is matter and matter." Theoretically he has followed Artaud in asking "who ever said the theater was created to analyze a character, to resolve the con-flicts of love and duty, to wrestle with all the problems of a topical and psy-chological nature that monopolize our contemporary stage?" Who ever said that its aim is to serve literature, to copy actuality, "to resolve social or psychological conflicts, to serve as battlefields for moral passions . . . ?" He may agree with Artaud that its aim can be to reassert aspects of "the internal world, that is, of man considered metaphysically." And now and then it can dare, not popularly, to explore an "archetypal and dangerous reality, a reality of which the Principles, like dolphins, once they have shown their heads, hurry to dive back into the obscurity of the deep." [223]

The vogue of the Stanislavski system also obscured for a while another theory of acting, a very practical system antagonistic to Barrault's concern with philosophy and theatrical form and to the Russian's primary concern with actors' feelings. It placed first emphasis upon the script, the historical fact, the idea to be conveyed to an audience, and was variously advocated by Bertolt Brecht, who, despite his "resistance to emotional impulse," has been called "the greatest poet Germany has produced since [Johann Christian] Hölderlin [1770–1843], and the most remarkable playwright since Büchner." "I am the Einstein of the new stage form," he announced, proud of the fact that he reflected "the scientific and analytical spirit of modern society, as well as the specially materialistic dialectic of Marxism." Yet he was viewed by Communists "with considerable reserve and caution" because he "be-lieved himself a better Marxist than the Party." [224]

By 1931, when he was thirty-three, Brecht was convinced, in Ernest Borneman's words, that "The Ibsen theater with its evocation of conflict between the protagonists, its invitation to the audience to identify itself with the characters and laugh or cry with them, its attempt to direct the actors as if they *were* the figures they portrayed, . . . was dead and could never be revived. The time now had come for a theater in which exactly the opposite had to be attempted." And for the next seventeen years "Brecht worked with phenomenal ingenuity at devising an infinitely complex and most thoroughly integrated technique which broke with almost every theater tradition from Ibsen to Stanislavski." [225]

In 1930 Brecht's "rational" opera *Aufstieg und Fall der Stadt Mahagonny* (*Rise and Fall of the City of Mahagonny*) with music by Kurt Weill shocked Leipzig audiences with its depiction of bourgeois society "as a lawless frontier town, where everything is permitted according to the principle of *laissez-faire* and the only crime is lack of money." [226] In 1932 he wrote and staged a primer of revolutionary method, *Die Mutter*, adapted from Gorky's 1907 novel; and that same year he produced on radio in Berlin his anticlassical, anticapitalist *Die Heilige Johanna der Schlachthoefe* (*St. Joan of the Stockyards*), set in Chicago.

In February 1933 Brecht fled from Hitler's Germany to live principally in Denmark and Sweden and to write plays often derived from other plays. Among them were *Furcht und Elend des Dritten Reiches* (*Fear and Misery of the Third Reich*, or *The Private Life of the Master Race*) (1935–38); a conventional script on the Spanish Civil War, *Die Gewehre der Frau Carrar* (*Señora Carrar's Rifles*) (1937); the powerful *Mutter Courage und ihre Kinder* (*Mother Courage and Her Children*) (1937, first staged 1941); *Leben des Galilei* (*Galileo*) (1938–39, first staged 1943), "an incomparable theatrical statement of the social responsibilities of the intellectual"; and *Der Gute Mensch von Sezuan* (*The Good Woman of Setzuan*) (1938–40, first staged 1943). Then for six years from mid-1941 Brecht lived in southern California and wrote more plays, including *Der Aufhaltsame Aufstieg des Arturo Ui* (*The Resistible Rise of Arturo Ui*) (1941, first staged 1958), a story of Hitler told in mock-heroic blank verse and in terms of Chicago gangsters, and the excellent *Der Kaukasische Kreidekreis* (*The Caucasian Chalk Circle*) (1944–45, first staged 1948). In 1947 Brecht went to Switzerland, returning to Germany (East Berlin) the following year to direct a production at the Deutsches Theater of *Mother Courage* with his wife Helene Weigel (1900–) in the title role. Then in November 1949, Brecht's Berliner Ensemble took stage in his *Herr Puntila und sein Knecht Matti* (*Puntila and His Hired Man Matti*) (1940–41). (In 1954 Brecht achieved one of the greatest ambitions of his life when the East Berlin government gave him a large subsidy, his own Theater am Schiffbauerdamm, and "a company of about sixty actors and actresses, a total personnel of more than two hundred and fifty—actors, designers, directors, Dramaturgen, mechanics, musicians, scene painters." Finally "When the Berliner Ensemble visited Paris—in 1954 with *Mother Courage* and in 1955 with *The Caucasian Chalk Circle*—its European fame was assured." [227] After Brecht's death in mid-1956 the group was directed by his wife.)

With his so-called "epic" theater Brecht demonstrated for audiences "how the world works, to the end that the world may be changed." (The term "epic," later discarded, "comes from Aristotle, who used it to describe a poem of vast historic events as contrasted with a story of private or family fortunes.") "Today," Brecht wrote in 1931, "human character must be understood as the 'totality of all social conditions.'" And only his kind of playwriting and staging, he claimed, "could present the complexity of the human condition in an age in which the life of individuals could no longer be understood in isolation from the powerful trend of social, economical and historical forces affecting the lives of millions." He did not believe in allowing audiences to eavesdrop on real events or to identify themselves and empathize with his characters lest they "fail to observe them, assess them, and draw objective conclusions." "If the theater is to do more than pander to emotionalism," he wrote, "it must teach. It must teach in its own fashion, brilliantly, colorfully, entertainingly—but teach it must." Audiences today, he was certain, must use their minds and "reach a verdict." They must find a *"guide to action."* They must learn "how to survive." [228]

Audiences at a traditional production, according to Brecht, forget that they are in a theater, attending an illusion of something currently happening, and say: "Yes, I have felt the same. . . . I am just like this. . . . This is only natural. . . . It will always be like this . . . . This human being's suffering moves me because there is no way out for him." But audiences at a Brecht production admittedly sit *in a theater* watching and listening to a group of *actors* recount "things that have happened in the *past* at a certain time in a certain place." They attend not a photograph of reality but reality "arranged for the purposes of an analysis." "They . . . sit back, relax, and reflect on the lessons to be learned from . . . events. . . ." They say: "I should never have thought so. . . . That is not the way to do it. . . . This is most surprising, hardly credible. . . . This will have to stop. . . . This human being's suffering moves me, because there would have been a way out for him." The audience's reaction is "the pleasure we feel when we discover new truths, the exhilaration we experience when we enlarge our understanding, . . . the exaltation felt by the scientist who has uncovered one of the mysteries of the universe." (Brecht regarded the "instinct of inquiry as a social phenomenon not less pleasurable, nor less imperious, than the instinct of procreation.") [229]

Brecht hoped, of course, that his detached, critically minded audiences would see facts as he saw them. That worried or riled the Communists who insisted that audiences must remain uncritical and see only facts altered to fit the Party line. Nevertheless, the Russians admitted that Brecht's work, although not representative of Social Realism, "enriched and fructified the theater of Social Realism." [230]

For his unconventional, anti-"well made" scripts—"cool, unemotional presentation[s] of a case offered for contemplation"—Brecht propounded a naive *"Verfremdung"* or "alienation" theory of acting (derived from "old theatrical conventions and traditions: the Elizabethan, Chinese, Japanese and Indian theater, the use of the chorus in Greek tragedy, the techniques of clowns and fairground entertainers, the Austrian and Bavarian folk play, and many others").[231] In order to prevent the intrusion of audience empathy he instructed his actors to separate themselves from the characters they portrayed and from the things they did. He trained them to be almost lecturers, or better, demonstrators.

The Brecht actor therefore resists letting "himself be transformed into the man he presents so that nothing of himself is left." He doesn't try to *be* another person. He virtually exorcises his feelings, relies only on his powers of observation, and then "not as self-expression, but as history" realistically demonstrates for an audience what his character specifically *did*. "*Die Wahrheit ist konkret*," or "The truth is concrete." (Thus a cast strips down a script to actions, to essential *story*, to "the social behavior of human beings toward each other.") The actor shows what his assigned character did in the same way that an eyewitness to a street accident describes for others what happened: "he wants to *indicate* [my italics] that the old man who has been run over walked very slowly, so he will imitate his gait to show exactly what he means. He is in fact *quoting* the old man's walk. And he is quoting only *those elements* of the old man's movements which are *relevant* to the situation he wants to describe. The eyewitness concerned is far from wanting to *impersonate* the victim: 'He never forgets, nor does he allow anyone to forget, that he is not the one whose action is being demonstrated, but the one who demonstrates it.' The character who is being shown and the actor who demonstrates him remain clearly differentiated." And the actor uses empathy only "to the extent that anyone without histrionic talent or ambition would use it" in illustrating some happening. But that empathy is never allowed to well up spontaneously in performance; it must be jelled "at some point in the course of rehearsals while the role is still being learned." [232]

By not living his part, by standing beside it, as it were, the Brecht actor is free to be frankly presentational, pridefully theatrical. At "all essential points" he is able to show, for instance, not only what Galileo or Mac the Knife did but also what they did *not* do; by "hesitation or by starting the action one way and then finishing it another," he proves to an audience the possibility of alternatives, the crucial importance of decisions. The Brecht actor turns at times "directly to the audience" and talks to it. He avoids putting it into a trance, or melting it "together into a single emotional lump" by imagining it "a divided group of friends and enemies," and therefore addresses himself "to one part of the audience now, to another part the next moment." He comments on his character's actions, evincing approval or disapproval. "And he underscores the fact that this is his, the actor's account, version, opinion of the events." [233]

Finally, the Brecht actor presents his character to an audience realistically instead of poetically or as an abstraction. In speaking his lines "not as improvisation [an illusion of the first time] but as a *quotation*," he still must render "all the undertones, all the concrete, plastic detail of full human utterance." And in moving and gesturing in obviously studied ways, and while

visibly observing his physical effects (sometimes in front of a mirror at rehearsals), he must still aim for full human corporeality.[234]

Such were the theories best, and compellingly, practiced by the Berliner
Ensemble. Yet toward the end of his life Brecht was told again and again
that his working-class audience "simply could not follow his logic, his style
of presentation, his theatrical objectives." In the opinion of one observer,
"Every play that was successful . . . succeeded for the wrong reasons: only
those passages that did not conform to his theories, that were unextruded
remnants of conventional theater, really moved his audience, while those
passages . . . which most lucidly demonstrated his theories of the epic stage
pleased no one except his fellow-artists" and the intelligentsia. Nevertheless,
as Tynan reported in 1959, "Wherever you go in Germany, Brecht is inescapable." His ubiquity and influence have been growing. "In the 1957–58
season he set a record; for the first time in the history of the German theater
a contemporary native playwright was among the four dramatists whose works
were most often performed in the German-speaking countries. Shakespeare,
as always, came first, with 2,674 performances, and he was followed by
Schiller, with 2,000; Goethe, with 1,200; and Brecht, with 1,120. (Molière,
Shaw, and Hauptmann, in that order, were the runners-up.)" [235]

❀ THE YEARS AHEAD

Other men will follow Brecht, Meyerhold and Stanislavski, Young,
Barker, and Copeau in propounding philosophies and methods of acting.
They may offer little that is new; their findings will certainly be derived in
part from preceding theories. Subsequent thinkers on the subject will continue variously to emphasize communication of revealing matter either in
terms of the verisimilar or in terms of the theater medium. They will desire
a greater emphasis on nature or on art, on what is representational or what is
presentational. One guess is that some of them will more persuasively than
ever champion that lively contagion of the moment which differentiates
acting onstage from acting on motion picture or television screens. Another
guess is that someone, starting afresh as Duse suggested, will forget the stage
(if that is possible), concentrate on the new media dominated by the camera,
and work out a particular theory for film and television acting. Undoubtedly
such a theory will conclude that expert screen performing requires more than
a photogenic personality.

II

Theories aside, what happens in acting before the year 2000 may depend
largely on what happens in the remainder of this mass-culture century to the
so-called legitimate theater. There acting is purest: happening now—alive for
palpable audiences. But average men in a sizable majority are likely to forsake

the theater for relatively inexpensive motion pictures and for free or small-pay television. Actors seeking higher remuneration and national acclaim are therefore also likely to desert the stage. And the natural acting (or nonacting) on screens could influence and reshape what remains of stage acting until it loses its distinction, its essential design.

Ever since the 1930's, since the first wide popularity of films, the theater in the United States intermittently has been called "the fabulous invalid." In 1960 the condition of the patient was critical. According to a study made by O. Glenn Saxon and summarized in the *New York Times*, the United States was the only major nation (excluding Norway) which had not experienced a rise in theater popularity after World War II. In New York—almost the only habitat of the vast country's professional theater—there were 66 playhouses in 1931, and only 33 in 1960. In 1928, 264 plays were produced on Broadway; in 1960, a mere 57. Between 1930 and 1960 the total attendance fell from 12,300,000 to 8,100,000, a decline of more than a third. Meanwhile, as Dr. Saxon pointed out, the population of the United States increased 46 percent and the "disposable personal income" rose 355 percent. Additional statistics showed that between 1944 and 1959 the "average maximum" box-office price of dramas had risen 105.5 percent, and the price of musicals 77.1 percent.[236] In short, the American professional theater appeared to have been very nearly priced out of popularity.

In other countries motion pictures and television had not by 1960 seriously diminished the theater. In France, especially in Paris, the theater was as nationally and culturally important as it always had been: the government, adhering to a long tradition, granted an annual subsidy of 600,000,000 francs ($1,200,000) to the Théâtre-Français (deducting 130,000,000 francs for the Compagnie Renaud–Barrault). The theater flourished also in divided Germany because both governments supported it generously. Every town big enough to have an art gallery and a public library had in addition a municipal playhouse which automatically received a civic subsidy, "since the Germans believe that if a citizen has a right to good paintings, good sculpture, and good books, he has a right to good drama as well. . . . West Germany, with a population of 53,000,000 [had] 121 theaters, or one to every 430,000 people. The equivalent figures for the East [were] 18,000,000 inhabitants and 86 theaters, or one to every 209,000." In West Berlin specifically, the joint Intendant of the Schiller Theater and its affiliated surburban house, the Schlosspark, received "an annual grant of 4,000,000 marks—just over $950,000 —on which to struggle through the season." In East Berlin, Brecht's Ensemble was given "more than 3,000,000 marks"—over $700,000—for the year by the Ministry of Culture.[237]

In Russia in 1960 the theater succeeded because under government control it was popularly priced. Moscow regularly attended 25 legitimate theaters (three of them entirely devoted to the production of plays for children); and permanent professional theaters were located in other cities of the Union.

Only Moscow's Maly Theatre, the repository of Russian stage traditions, was directly subsidized by the government; but the government assured the economic health of all the others by eliminating playhouse rentals and entertainment taxes. Consequently, each principal theater boasted "a permanent company of between 80 and 100 actors, recruited in most cases from an affiliated drama school; and a repertoire of some twenty plays, so alternated that the same piece [was] never performed for more than two consecutive nights." Any Moscow resident or visitor could choose in any given week from 150 different shows [238]—a majority of which, however, were strictly, dully propagandistic.

Is some financial aid from the federal government really needed to support the professional theater in the United States? Perhaps. But most observers "have little hope that either the Republicans or the Democrats will do anything for the arts"—and especially for the theater. Creative talent, "the very articulation of democracy, will always be a minority and therefore at a peculiar disadvantage with the electorate." [239]

Only once has the American theater been government-supported: following the depression of 1929–35, when, concurrently, the sudden changeover from live to photographed entertainment caused a high rate of unemployment among stage actors and their associates. From mid-1935 until mid-1939 a Federal Theatre, under the Works Progress Administration, provided employment for a yearly "average 10,000" experienced theater workers who "supported an average of four dependents." The total gross cost was $46,207,779. During those four years well over 1,000 assorted productions, exclusive of radio, were presented throughout the country. Among them were more than 100 original scripts, 32 new plays for children, 30 new Negro dramas, 28 new musicals, 24 new dance dramas, 20 new religious dramas, 11 pageants and spectacles, and 9 "living newspapers"—plus 31 classical and 346 modern (post-1860) plays.[240]

Hopes that this Federal Theatre might be continued, might indeed be the basis of a government-supported national theater, were dashed when the project was abruptly abolished. In the opinion of Hallie Flanagan (1890–), its dynamic head, "Congress, in spite of protests from many of its own members, treated the Federal Theatre not as a human issue or a cultural issue, but as a political issue." Since 1939 the professional American theater has been left to cherish its "competitive independence, . . . left free to continue to earn and pay its own way—free from all governmental subsidies, free from all Socialistic controls. . . ."[241]

III

Happily, the American theater in its stiff competition with films and television has been supported and will continue to be supported whenever it needs outside help by some of the foundations, or by public contributions and subscriptions. In 1926, for instance, actress–director Eva Le Gallienne (1900–), encouraged by a small endowment and campaigning for public memberships, selected a permanent company of young professional actors to appear in a repertory (mainly of famous plays) to be offered audiences at a top price of $1.50. In October of that year she opened the off-Broadway Civic Repertory Theatre with Benavente's *La Noche del sábado* (*Saturday Night*) (1903), and followed it the next evening with Chekhov's *The Three Sisters*; the next week she increased the repertory with Ibsen's *The Master Builder*. Thereafter a new production was added every five or six weeks—Ibsen's *John Gabriel Borkman*; Goldoni's *La Locandiera*; *Twelfth Night*; Sierra's *Cradle Song* (a hit); and a new American play, *Inheritors*, by Susan Glaspell (1882–1948)—until at season's end the envied company was acting eight plays.

For the second season, when the Civic Repertory Theatre's public memberships, at one dollar each, totaled 50,000, the repertory was increased by five more plays, including a lauded *Hedda Gabler*. For the third (1928–29) season six more plays were staged, the most successful of which starred Nazimova in *The Cherry Orchard* and Miss Le Gallienne in the title role of *Peter Pan*; in 1929–30 five more plays were added, notably *Romeo and Juliet*; and in 1930–31 another five, among them a provocative Giraudoux *Siegfried* and a box-office-record-breaking *Camille*.

In December 1932 *Alice in Wonderland*, one of the three new presentations, drew large, enthusiastic audiences; but by then, after six years, the expenses incident to the repertory idea were too high, the play was moved uptown, and the Civic Repertory Theatre was abandoned. Nevertheless, the experiment, even in failure, was a glorious one.

In the early 1960's the slightly endowed, more cautious Living Theatre proved that repertory could succeed off Broadway. Moreover, a sum of three million dollars was donated for the building of a Repertory Theater at the Lincoln Center for the Performing Arts in New York, scheduled to open in 1963. As part of "an enduring symbol of America's cultural maturity," according to John D. Rockefeller, III, chairman of the over-all project, this could mark the beginning of a National Theater—the first in an English-speaking country.

According to some, however, that theater should not in two years be compelled to balance its books, to compete with Broadway on Broadway's terms any more than the Metropolitan Opera House, the Metropolitan Museum of Art, or the Public Library should be compelled to pay all of their expenses. According to Kenneth Tynan, "It should be demanded of the new theater that it should lose a solid, whacking sum of money each year" [242] so long as it exhibits at moderate prices the best plays expertly acted.

According to others, a true national theater will come into being only when all sections of the large, diverse United States participate in and derive benefits from the institution. It ought to have branches in, say, Boston, Washington, D.C., Atlanta, Detroit, Chicago, Minneapolis, Omaha, New Orleans,

Denver, San Francisco, and Seattle. It might be a circuit theater, partly supported by foundations and municipalities, and simultaneously presenting some plays and constantly exchanging others.

IV

Much of the vitality of the future American theater will surely come from off Broadway, away from the economic bottleneck of the Times Square area. By the end of the 1948–49 season more than 150 off-Broadway producing groups, ranging from professional to amateur and collegiate, were listed. Best known were the ANTA (American National Theatre and Academy) Experimental Theatre, which staged *Hippolytus*, a dramatization of Melville's *Billy Budd*, and some original scripts; New Stages, which imported such works as *Mort sans sépultures* (*The Victors*) (1946) by Jean-Paul Sartre (1905–) and Lorca's *Bodas de sangre* (*Blood Wedding*) (1933); and the Equity Library Theatre, which—with brief, free revivals of both classical contemporary plays —provided beginning professionals with a showcase for their talents. In mid-1950 New York's first theater-in-the-round, or arena theater, was installed in a hotel, and Broadway–film star Lee Tracy (1893–) appeared there in George Kelly's *The Show-off* (1924).

Since the "urge to act is immeasurably stronger than the urge to make money by acting," [243] enthusiasm for the theater ran high among amateurs off Broadway. By the 1952–53 season some of these groups began to attract both critical and popular attention. Made up mostly of young people with little money but a large ache to act and a large urge to revive certain commercial failures, to experience the classics, and to appear in plays less conventional than those which appealed to Broadway audiences, the amateurs presented their wares in crudely renovated movie houses, cafés, meeting halls, studios, basements, lofts, or wherever they could. At least two dozen of their offerings drew enough interested audiences for good runs. The New York Repertory Company, for instance, began with *Othello*; the Living Theatre staged several "bohemian" plays, among them *Doctor Faustus Lights the Lights* by Gertrude Stein (1874–1946); and the Circle in the Square expertly revived *Summer and Smoke* (1943) by Tennessee Williams (1914–), which quickly made Geraldine Page (1925–) a Broadway star.

In 1953–54 the off-Broadway amateurs, abetted by professionals who forfeited high salaries so long as they could act somewhere and could also escape type-casting, went "from the 'little theater' class to big business." [244] The Circle in the Square consistently presented sound productions to larger and larger houses; the Theatre de Lys sponsored first-rate plays like Mackaye's *The Scarecrow*, *The Little Clay Cart*, *The School for Scandal*, and the Brecht-Weill *The Threepenny Opera*, as adapted by Marc Blitzstein (1905–), which set a long-run record; the professional Phoenix Theatre started its first annual subscription season (continued for eight years at the original location) with Sidney Howard's unproduced *Madam, Will You Walk?* (1931) and also tackled *Coriolanus* and *The Sea Gull.*

For the 1955–56 season more than 90 off-Broadway productions were staged, many of them skillfully. Not quite half that number were originals, the remainder revivals; and well over half of the latter were classic or semi-classic. In 1957–58 off Broadway had at least 40 theaters of one kind or another where more than 100 plays were presented. Again in 1959 and in 1960 (when Broadway could squeeze out only 57 productions) the total number of off-Broadway productions exceeded 100—including some city-sponsored, free, outdoor Shakespeare in Central Park. By 1961 off Broadway was more or less regularly creating some of the most stimulating—though not always the most expert—theater experience in the United States.

From there may come original, imaginative, and enriching playwrights, actors, directors, and designers whose aim—like the aim of those dedicated to other arts, or to medicine, to science, and to teaching—will not be only or even primarily to stash up a fortune larger than a colleague's or a neighbor's. Then, in due time, perhaps an inspired, hard-working group headed by another Antoine, or Barker, or Stanislavski and Nemirovich-Danchenko, or Clurman, Strasberg, and Crawford might help renovate the current Broadway setup and inaugurate a less materialistic one.

The only worry is that off Broadway can be seduced into being only commercial. By 1961, theater rentals, union impositions, advertising expense, a costly itch for elaborate externals in staging, and producer-backers avid for quick profits had raised prices nearer and nearer to those prevailing on Broadway.

V

Farther off Broadway, outside of New York City, amateurs have been trying for more than thirty years to revitalize the American theater—to decentralize it, to divorce it from commercialism, to improve it as "neighborly ritual." In some measure they have succeeded. Community and college theaters, well over 2,500 of them in the fifty states, entertained in 1960 an audience that ran into the millions, an audience made up of people who rarely came to New York and seldom had the opportunity of attending productions by professionals.

After the breakup of resident stock companies in the late 1920's (because of the popularity of motion pictures) professional actors converged on New York or Hollywood and only now and then ventured into the hinterlands. Sometimes they toured in Broadway hits, but in some instances these shows relaxed into tepid copies of the originals. Inevitably, of course, some professionals each year acted for ten weeks in hectic summer stock, sometimes testing new scripts, but many of the productions were quickly and therefore sloppily prepared. Recently professionals have participated in such regional celebrations as the Old Globe Shakespeare Festival at San Diego, California, and the American Shakespeare Festival at Stratford, Connecticut. In the main, however, they have toured the country only on motion picture or television screens.

Therefore, average people from Florida to Washington, from New Mexico to Vermont created their own "live" theater. Busy-during-the-day Americans hustled at night to community and civic groups to participate in play productions as actors, set and costume designers, electricians, prop boys or girls, box-office managers.[245] They did so not to make money but simply because they loved to spend their leisure time making theater. Simultaneously, colleges and universities—from Yale to the University of California, serving the arts as well as the sciences—began instructing would-be workers in the theater and regularly exhibiting the best classic and contemporary plays. The sum total of these efforts created the largest people's theater in the world.

Not all of this theater was first-rate. Many community groups used play production as an excuse for social high-jinks; frequently their performances were inept. Most universities forgot or were afraid to lead the way by experimenting: often the plays and stagings were dully academic. Worse, a majority of community and university theaters inexcusably tended to copy Broadway. (Lacking faith in their own creativity, many of them unfortunately still do.)

Nevertheless, much of the work offered to the public across the United States—in playhouses newer and superior in every respect to those on Broadway—showed integrity, individuality, and amazing skills. At least fifteen civic theaters, and perhaps another fifteen campus theaters, have been a credit not only to their country but to their art. Among the former, for two examples, are the hardy Cleveland Playhouse, founded in 1916, with its three auditoriums and a large company of permanent professionals, local volunteers, and staff apprentices; and the semiprofessional San Francisco Actors Workshop, started in 1951, with a repertory ranging experimentally from Shakespeare to Samuel Beckett (1906–), Jean Genet (1909–), and Eugène Ionesco (1912–).

Attracted by the excellent work done away from New York, professionals by 1960 were regularly returning to the various states—for a season or a summer at one community theater, as guest stars for a single attraction at another. For the 1960–61 season the San Francisco Actors Workshop was one of several community groups enabled through the generosity of the Ford Foundation to hire ten professional actors from New York at a salary of $200 a week for a period of ten months. (The Foundation was trying to ascertain whether experienced professional actors would forsake Broadway for long intervals, and what stimulation, if any, they might bring to local groups.) Professional actors have even been invited to take up brief residence at some colleges and universities.

Also by 1960 new theaters continued to be built everywhere: as imposing and flexible as the $2,000,000 Loeb Theater at Harvard, and as intimate as the $75,000 civic theater for amateurs in Waco, Texas. In 1961 Washington, D.C.'s Arena Stage began its twelfth season in a new, privately financed (with foundation help), 796-seat $850,000 theater, and on a budget of $240,-000 offered the Capital eight productions directed by professionals and acted by partly professional casts. And Minneapolis consolidated its position as a leading American city by erecting a municipal theater for a permanent company of professional players to be directed by internationally famous Tyrone Guthrie (1900–).

VI

Thus, in its own highly individual, democratic way the theater in the United States will withstand the competition of mass-culture movies and television. Thus in all countries that theater, created by a minority for a minority, will continue to attract and to reveal the "inscapes of things" to more and more of the majority. But it will do that only in so far as its partisans are aware of its values, its distinctions, and stubbornly refuse to forfeit them.

Playwrights for the world's theater will be more than intellectually honest in dramatizing the central themes of today's shaky world. They will also be imaginative in expressing them; they will explore and master their unique medium. For instance, they will halt the current "retreat from the word" by doing something about language which "no longer articulates, or is relevant to, all major modes of action, thought, and sensibility." They will use "their greatest weapon against the cosy naturalism of television and the cinema—the imaginative scope of the theater." And they will write with a will to discover in live performances in the presence of audiences that public spirit, that mass adhesion, that collective expression known to older theaters.[246]

Then stage actors as interpreters will learn that only third-rate acting, like third-rate writing, "is all microscope—all examination of the minutiae of everyday life." [247] They will be unafraid of selected, rearranged, heightened speech and movement. They will advance beyond self-expression to the expression of idea. They will search for style, which is the knack of feeling a play as artifact, of feeling a character as an harmonious part of the whole, and of feeling its behavior onstage as *performance*.

Of the best of these actors in the theater it will be said: "Seeing the point, they imagine and design."

SOURCES

The full citation of each source is given at its first listing for each chapter.

The epigraphs are from STARK YOUNG, *The Flower in Drama* (New York, 1923),
pp. 61–62, and ANDRÉ MALRAUX, *The Psychology of Art, Museum Without Walls* trans.
by Stuart Gilbert (New York, 1929), p. 76.

The quotations in the Preface are from GEORGE HENRY LEWES, *On Actors and the
Art of Acting* (London, 1875), p. vi, and GEORGE JEAN NATHAN, *The Theatre of the Moment* (New York, 1936), p. 51.

✿ CHAPTER 1

1. ARISTOTLE, *Poetics*, 4, 1448^b.
2. ALEXANDER BAKSHY, *The Theatre Unbound* (London, 1923), p. 82; FRANCIS FER-
   GUSSON, *The Idea of a Theatre* (Princeton, 1949), pp. 236, 238.
3. ROBERT EDMOND JONES, *The Dramatic Imagination* (New York, 1944), pp. 46–48.
4. GEORGE THOMSON, *Aeschylus and Athens* . . . (London, 1941), p. 382.
5. ROY C. FLICKINGER, *The Greek Theatre and Its Drama* (Chicago, 1918), p. 17.
6. DIOGENES LAERTIUS, iii, 56, cited *ibid.*, p. 18; see ARTHUR PICKARD-CAMBRIDGE, *The
   Dramatic Festivals of Athens* (Oxford, 1933), pp. 131–132; PLUTARCH, *The
   Lives of the Noble Grecians and Romans*, trans. by John Dryden (1749), rev.
   by Arthur Hugh Clough (1859) (New York, n.d.), p. 115.
7. H. D. F. KITTO, *Greek Tragedy* (1939, rev. 1950) (New York, 1954), p. 34.
8. *Ibid.*, p. 56.
9. See *Poetics*, 4, 1449^a (Cooper, p. 87); see G. F. ELSE, "The Case of the Third
   Actor," *Trans. American Philosophical Ass.*, LXXVII (1945), 1–10.
10. DONALD CLIVE STUART, *The Development of Dramatic Art* (New York, 1928), p. 49;
    Kitto, GT, pp. 80, 70, 87, 72.
11. *Ibid.*, pp. 86, 84, 86, 85.
12. AESCHYLUS, *Oresteia, The Libation Bearers* trans. with Int. by Richmond Lattimore
    (Chicago, 1953), lines 904–930, pp. 125–126.
13. *Poetics*, 25, 1460^b; Plutarch, *De Prof. in Virt.*, 7; WERNER JAEGER, *Paideia: the ideals
    of Greek culture* trans. by Gilbert Highet (New York, 1939), I, 268.
14. HENRY BAMFORD PARKES, "Home and Hellenism," *Partisan Review*, XXI (September–
    October 1954), fn. p. 563.
15. Kitto, GT, pp. 69, 156, 144.
16. *Ibid.*, pp. 160, 161, 162.
17. *Ibid.*, p. 163.
18. ARISTOTLE, *Rhetoric* (Cooper), III, 1, 1403^b.
19. Stuart, DDA, p. 100; Kitto, GT, p. 383.
20. Fergusson, *Idea*, p. 34.
21. *Poetics*, 25, 1460^b; ARISTOPHANES, *The Frogs* trans. by Dudley Fitts (New York,
    1955), p. 101; GILBERT MURRAY, *Euripides and His Age* (New York, 1913),
    p. 82; DAVID GRENE, "Introduction to *Hippolytus*," in *Complete Greek Tragedies*

ed. by DAVID GRENE AND RICHMOND LATTIMORE, *Euripides I* (Chicago, 1955), p. 159; DAVID GRENE, *Three Greek Tragedies in Translation* (Chicago, 1942), p. 165.

22. RICHMOND LATTIMORE, "Introduction to Alcestis," in *Euripides I*, p. 3; ALLARDYCE NICOLL, *World Drama from Aeschylus to Anouilh* (New York, 1950), pp. 76–77; Kitto, *GT*, pp. 340–341; Trans. by F. M. Stawell in Nicoll, pp. 88–89.

23. Jaeger, *Paideia*, p. 343; *The Frogs* (Fitts) p. 103.

24. Kitto, *GT*, p. 244; Murray, *Euripides*, pp. 132–133; Kitto, pp. 215, 230.

25. Jaeger, *Paideia*, p. 360.

26. H. D. F. KITTO, *The Greeks* (Harmondsworth, England, 1951), p. 213.

27. JOHN GASSNER, *Masters of the Drama* (New York, 1940), p. 93.

28. Pickard-Cambridge, *DFA*, p. 314.

29. *Rhetoric*, III, 2, 1405ᵃ; Flickinger, *Greek Theatre*, p. 185; Pickard-Cambridge, *DFA*, p. 95.

30. *Rhetoric*, III, 1, 1403ᵇ; Pickard-Cambridge, *DFA*, pp. 313, 101; *Poetics*, 26, 1461ᵇ; Flickinger, *Greek Theatre*, p. 191.

31. PLATO, *Gorgias*, 502b–d; *Laws*, 659b, c; *Republic*, III, 398a; Aristotle, *Politics*, viii, 7; Aristotle, *Problems*, xxx, 10; Pickard-Cambridge, *DFA*, p. 314; A. E. HAIGH, *The Attic Theatre* (Oxford, 1889), p. 255.

32. *Poetics*, 6, 1450ᵇ; also 14, 1453ᵇ and 26, 1462ᵃ, and see *Rhetoric*, III, 12, 1413ᵇ; JAMES TURNEY ALLEN, "Greek Acting in the Fifth Century," *Univ. California Pub. Classical Philology*, II (March 3, 1916), 289.

33. LANE COOPER, *Aristotle on the Art of Poetry* . . . (New York, 1913), p. xvii; LANE COOPER, *The Rhetoric of Aristotle* . . . (New York, 1932), pp. vii, xvii, xx, xxii, 3.

34. PLATO, *Phaedrus*, 269.

35. PLATO, *Ion*, 535; *Meno*, 82; *Phaedrus*, 245.

36. GEOFFREY RANS, "London Letter," *Hudson Review*, V (Autumn 1952), 425; BURGES JOHNSON, "Inspired and Uninspired Writers," *Saturday Review*, XXXVI (April 25, 1953), 44–45, 13; CONSTANTIN STANISLAVSKI, *An Actor Prepares* trans. by Elizabeth Reynolds Hapgood (New York, 1936), p. 14.

37. *Rhetoric*, III, 1, 1404ᵃ; *Poetics*, 19, 1456ᵇ.

38. STARK YOUNG, *The Theater* (New York, 1927), p. 106; *Ellen Terry and Bernard Shaw, a correspondence* ed. by CHRISTOPHER ST. JOHN (1931) (New York, 1949), p. 171.

39. Young, *Flower*, p. 92; Haigh, *AT*, pp. 246–247.

40. Young, *Flower*, pp. 89, 86.

41. See ARISTOTLE, *On the Generation of Animals*, v, 7, 786ᵇ, and *On the Soul*, ii, 8, 420ᵇ–421ᵃ; *Rhetoric*, III, 9, 1409ᵇ; 12, 1413ᵇ; 7, 1408ᵇ; III, 2, 1404ᵇ.

42. *Poetics*, 2, 1448ᵃ; STARK YOUNG, *Glamour* . . . (New York, 1925), pp. 80–81.

43. *Poetics*, I, 1447ᵃ (Cooper, p. 2); 2, 1448ᵃ (p. 6); 3, 1448ᵃ (pp. 8, 9); 6, 1450ᵃ; Stanislavski, *AP*, pp. 34, 35.

44. *Rhetoric*, I, 13, 1373ᵇ, (see I, 11–12); *Poetics*, 25, 1461ᵃ; 24, 1460ᵇ.

45. *Rhetoric*, I, 5, 1360ᵇ; also I, 10, 1368ᵇ–1369ᵃ; *Poetics*, 6, 1450ᵃ.

46. *Poetics*, 15, 1454ᵃ; 6, 1449ᵇ–1450ᵃ.

47. *Rhetoric*, I, 9, 1368ᵃ; *Poetics*, 6, 1450ᵇ; *Rhetoric*, I, 12, 1372ᵃ; II, 12–17, 1389ᵃ–1391ᵇ; *Poetics*, 25, 1461ᵃ.

48. See *Rhetoric*, II, 2–11, 1378ᵃ–1388ᵇ; 2, 1378ᵃ.

49. *Poetics*, 17, 1455ᵃ.

50. AULUS GELLIUS (*c.* A.D. 123–*c.* 165), *Attics Nights* trans. by John C. Rolfe (London, 1927), VI, 5, pp. 25–27.

51. *Poetics*, 17, 1455ᵃ (Cooper, p. 58).

52. *Ibid.*, p. xxv.

53. KENNETH BURKE, "A 'Dramatistic' View of 'Imitation,'" *Accent*, XII (1952), 230.
54. PHILOSTRATUS (fl. c. A.D. 217), *The Life of Apollonius of Tyana* trans. by F. C. Cony-beare, VI, 19; GEORGE PLIMPTON, "The Art of Fiction XXI, Ernest Hemingway," *Paris Review*, 5 (Spring 1958), 88–89.
55. Plato, *Ion* (Jowett), 530; *Phaedrus*, 268.
56. *Poetics*, 6, 1450ᵃ; ROBERT MARSH, "Aristotle and the Modern Rhapsode," *Quarterly Journal Speech*, XXXIX (December 1953), 497, 498.

❀ CHAPTER 2

1. LIVY, *Ab Urbe Condita* trans. by B. O. Foster, Loeb Classical Library (Cambridge, Mass., 1924), VII, 2; see W. BEARE, *The Roman Stage* (Cambridge, Mass., 1951), p. 11.
2. *Ibid.*; see Beare, RS, pp. 13–14; ATHENAEUS, *Deipnosophistai* ed. by G. Kaibel (Leipzig, 1925), p. 26; Livy, VII, 2; see Beare, pp. 13–14, 133; MARGARETE BIEBER, *The History of the Greek and Roman Theatre* (Princeton, 1939), p. 313; Beare, p. 143.
3. TENNEY FRANK, *Life and Literature in the Roman Republic* (1930) (Berkeley and Los Angeles, 1956), 35; Beare, RS, p. 22.
4. Frank, LLRR, p. 90; PHYLLIS HARTNOLL (ed.), *The Oxford Companion to the Theatre* (London, 1951), p. 673; CICERO, *de Oratore* (Sutton and Rackham), I, xxviii, 129; Frank, p. 96.
5. Cicero, *de Oratore*, I, v, 18; lxi, 259; v, 18; lix, 251; xi, 51.
6. TERENCE, *Phormio*, lines 9–10; QUINTILIAN, *Institutio Oratoria* (Butler), II, x, 8; I, xi, 2–3; x, 31; XI, iii, 4.
7. Beare, RS, p. 61.
8. WILLIAM BLANCKÉ, *The Dramatic Values in Plautus* (Geneva, N. Y., 1919), pp. 20, 32.
9. HORACE, *Epistles*, II, 1, 176; GILBERT NORWOOD, *The Art of Terence* (Oxford, 1923), p. 1; GILBERT NORWOOD, *Plautus and Terence* (New York, 1932), p. 58.
10. *Ibid.*, p. 12; Blancké, *Dramatic Values*, p. 59.
11. *Casina*, III, 683–685; *Aulularia*, IV, 715–720; *Poenulus*, III, 550–554, and V, 1224; *Pseudolus*, II, 720–721.
12. Norwood, PT, pp. 133, 113.
13. Beare, RS, p. 126.
14. *Ibid.*, p. 129; Frank, LLRR, p. 127.
15. *Ibid.*, p. 126; see Beare, RS, p. 135.
16. DIOMEDES, *Artis grammaticae libri*, III, 1 (in H. Kein, I, 491).
17. Beare, RS, pp. 141, 145.
18. *Ibid.*, p. 231; see also ALLARDYCE NICOLL, *Masks Mimes and Miracles* (New York, 1931), pp. 111, 116–118.
19. *Ibid.*, pp. 85–86; Choricius cited in HERMAN REICH, *Der Mimus* . . . (Berlin, 1903), p. 142, and in Nicoll, MMM, p. 99.
20. Frank, LLRR, pp. 127–128.
21. GRACE FRANK, *The Medieval French Drama* (Oxford, 1954), p. 1.
22. E. K. CHAMBERS, *The Medieval Stage* (Oxford, 1903), I, 8, 7.
23. TERTULLIAN, *De Spect.*, 30, quoted *ibid.*, I, 11; Chrysostom, *Hom. VI in Matt.*, xxxviii, quoted in Nicoll, MMM, p. 138; Chambers, MS, I, 14; Cassiodorus, *Var.* ix, 21, cited *ibid.*, p. 21.
24. *Ibid.*, I, 24–25.
25. Cicero, *de Oratore*, I, xxviii, 129–130; JAMES TURNEY ALLEN, *Stage Antiquities of the Greeks and Romans* (New York, 1927), p. 51.

26. Cicero, *Sest.*, 120–124; see Beare, *RS*, p. 158.
27. Quintilian, *I.O.*, XI, iii, 178–180.
28. Cicero, *de Oratore*, III, xxii, 83.
29. Beare, *RS*, p. 175.
30. GILBERT MILLSTEIN, "A Comic Discourses on Comedy," *N.Y. Times Magazine*, March 31, 1957, p. 62.
31. Cicero, *de Oratore*, II, vii, 30, 33; Quintilian, *I.O.*, I, Pr., 26; I, Pr., 27.
32. *Ibid.*, XI, iii, 14; 63, 62.
33. *Ibid.*, XI, iii, 39; I, viii, 1; VIII, iii, 52; XI, iii, 43–51; VIII, iii, 83; I, x, 25; I, viii, 2.
34. *Ibid.*, IX, ii, 30; III, viii, 49; XI, i, 39–40; Cicero, *de Oratore*, I, li, 223, quoted in *I.O.*, II, xxi, 6; LUCIAN, *Works*, II, 261, 81; II, 257, 67.
35. Quintilian, *I.O.*, VIII, Pr., 9; V, x, 32; VI, v, 11; XII, x, 70.
36. *De Oratore*, II, xlvii, 195; xlvi, 194; *I.O.*, VI, ii, 26, 28; HORACE, *Art of Poetry*, lines 102–103 (Conington); the second trans. is by Smart.
37. PLUTARCH, "Symposiacs," in *Miscellanies and Essays*, III, v. 314–316.
38. Lucian, *Works*, II, 261–262, 83–85.
39. DIDEROT, *The Paradox of Acting* (1773–78) trans. by Walter Herries Pollock (London, 1883), p. 16; CONSTANTIN STANISLAVSKI, *An Actor Prepares*, trans. by Elizabeth Reynolds Hapgood (New York, 1936), p. 18.
40. *I.O.*, VIII, iii, 88; X, vii, 15; VI, ii, 29–30; II, iv, 7; XII, x, 71.
41. *De Oratore*, III, lix, 221; *I.O.*, X, v, 6; Lucian, *Works*, II, 259.
42. *I.O.*, XI, iii, 65; XI, iii, 85–87; XI, iii, 119; II, xii, 9–10.
43. *De Oratore*, III, lvii, 216.
44. *I.O.*, IV, i, 57; IV, i, 60; V, x, 125; X, vii, 8.
45. *Ibid.*, XI, iii, 180; VIII, Pr., 15; XII, ix, 16.
46. *Ibid.*, II, x, 12–13.
47. DHANAMJAYA quoted in Int. to NANDIKEŚVARA, *Abhinaya-darpana* (13th century?) trans. by Ananda Coomaraswamy and Gopālakristnaya as *The Mirror of Gesture* (New York, 1936) p. 21; DHANAMJAYA, *Daśarupa (Ten Forms)* (10th century) trans. by G. C. O. Haas (New York, 1912), p. 3; CHANDRA BHAW GUPTA, *The Indian Theatre* . . . (Benares, 1954), p. 151.
48. Cited in ARTHUR B. KEITH, *The Sanskrit Drama in its origin, development, theory & practice* (Oxford, 1924), p. 322; DHANAMJAYA, IV, 52, and VIŚVANĀTHA, *Sāhitya-darpana* (14th century) trans. by Pramadasa Mitra from james R. Ballantyne rev. by E. Roer (1851) as *The Mirror of Composition* (Calcutta, 1875), III, 49–50; see ANANDA COOMARASWAMY, *The Transformation of Nature in Art* (1934) (New York, 1956), pp. 14, 51.
49. Dhanaṃjaya, *Daśrupa*, p. 3; Gupta, *Indian Theatre*, p. 13; Nandikeśvara, *Abhinaya-darpana*, p. 19; Gupta, p. 97; MANOMOHAN GHOSH, *Abhinaya-darpana* . . . (Calcutta, 1934), pp. xxvii, xxviii.
50. Nandikeśvara, *Abhinaya-darpana*, pp. 17, 18; Viśvanātha, *Sāhitya-darpana*, III, 20.

✻ CHAPTER 3

1. Quoted by ALLARDYCE NICOLL, *Masks Mimes and Miracles* (New York, 1931), p. 142; see HERMAN REICH, *Der Mimus* . . . (Berlin, 1903), Ch. II, viii, pp. 204–222.
2. E. K. CHAMBERS, *The Medieval Stage* (Oxford, 1903), II, 179–180.
3. Cited *ibid.*, II, 232, and in Nicoll, *MMM*, p. 151; Chambers, *MS*, II, 179; I, 25; Nicoll, pp. 165, 159, 152.
4. GRACE FRANK, *The Medieval French Drama* (Oxford, 1954), p. 5; Chambers, *MS*, I, 44, 48.

5. L. C. ARLINGTON, *The Chinese Drama* . . . (Shanghai, 1930), p. 39.
6. ANANDA COOMARASWAMY, *The Transformation of Nature into Art* (1934) (New York, 1956), pp. 14, 15; F. S. C. NORTHROP, *The Meeting of East and West* (New York, 1946), pp. 317–318; STARK YOUNG, *Immortal Shadows* (New York, 1948), p. 118.
7. See *ibid.*, pp. 114, 118, 116.
8. ROGER FRY, *Transformations* (1926) (New York, 1956), pp. 102–103, 106–107.
9. Frank, *MFD*, pp. 20–21; *The Regularis Concordia* of St. Ethelwold quoted by Chambers, *MS*, II, 14–15; see 306–309.
10. Frank, *MFD*, p. 24; ERICH AUERBACH, *Mimesis, the representation of reality in Western literature* (1946) trans. by Willard Trask (1953) (New York, 1957), p. 175; Frank, pp. 25, 27–28.
11. KARL YOUNG, *The Drama of the Medieval Church* (Oxford, 1933), II, 19.
12. Frank, *MFD*, pp. 33, 35–36.
13. *Ibid.*, p. 75.
14. *Ibid.*, p. 76; DONALD CLIVE STUART, *The Development of Dramatic Art* (New York, 1928), pp. 163, 166.
15. Auerbach, *Mimesis*, p. 131.
16. Cited in Chambers, *MS*, II, 80–81.
17. Frank, *MFD*, p. 99.
18. *Ibid.*, p. 97; see Chambers, *MS*, II, 88, 258.
19. *Ibid.*, pp. 147, 99–101, 102.
20. *Summa Theologia* (1274) cited *ibid.*, I, 58.
21. Frank, *MFD*, p. 112; see pp. 106–112; Chambers, *MS*, I, fn. 48, 65; Frank, pp. 226–227, 229, 234.
22. Chambers, *MS*, II, 211–212; C. S. BALDWIN, *Renaissance Literary Theory and Practice* (New York, 1939), p. 44.
23. Chambers, *MS*, II, 258.
24. Frank, *MFD*, p. 166; ALLARDYCE NICOLL, *World Drama* . . . (New York, 1949), p. 162.
25. *Ibid.*, p. 151; Frank, *MFD*, pp. 168–169; Chambers, *MS*, II, 114; see HARDIN CRAIG, *English Religious Drama of the Middle Ages* (Oxford, 1955), p. 167; Chambers, *MS*, II, 139.
26. THOMAS WALTON, "Staging Le Jeu de la Feuillée," *Modern Language Review*, XXXVI (1941), 345–346; quoted in Nicoll, *WD*, p. 151; Frank, *MFD*, pp. 169, 168; Chambers, *MS*, II, 139.
27. Quoted by ALLARDYCE NICOLL, *The Development of the Theatre* (London, 1927), p. 80.
28. Frank, *MFD*, pp. 167, 168.
29. Chambers, *MS*, II, 197, 214, 185–186.
30. ARTHUR WALEY, *The Nō Plays of Japan* (1921) (New York, 1957), pp. 23, 24, 25, 23; T. NOGAMI, *Zeami and His Theories on Noh* trans. by Ryōzē Matsumoto (Tokyo, 1955), pp. 7, 1, 23; *Seami-juroku-bu-shu*, p. 25, quoted by Waley, p. 29; Nogami, pp. 21–22.
31. ERNEST FENOLLOSA AND EZRA POUND, "*Noh*," or *Accomplishment; a study of the classical stage of Japan* (New York, 1917), p. 5; A. C. SCOTT, *The Kabuki Theatre of Japan* (London, 1955), pp. 51–52; see Waley, *Nō Plays*, p. 28.
32. Nogami, *Zeami*, p. 79; Umewaka Ninoru reported by Fenollosa-Pound, "*Noh*," pp. 31, 49, 47; Seami, p. 60, cited by Waley, *Nō Plays*, p. 47; Fenollosa-Pound, p. 120; Seami, p. 133, cited by Waley, p. 46; Osward Sickert quoted *ibid.*, p. 307; Seami, p. 102ff. quoted *ibid.*, p. 44.
33. See Nogami, *Zeami*, Ch. VIII, "Imitation (Monomane)," pp. 35–50; 36, 50; Fenollosa-Pound, p. 51; Nogami, p. 49.

34. See *ibid.*, Ch. IV, "Transcendental Phantasm (Yūgen)," pp. 51–61; 53, 54, 35, 16, 15, 23, 54.
35. Waley, *Nō Plays*, p. 51; STARK YOUNG, *The Flower in Drama* (New York, 1923), pp. 138–139, from Seami, pp. 12 and 54ff. as quoted by Waley, p. 46. See also ELSIE FOGERTY's Int. to her trans. of COQUELIN's *The Art of the Actor* (1894) (London, 1932), pp. 15–16.
36. Young, *Flower*, p. 138, from Seami, p. 54, quoted by Waley, *Nō Plays*, p. 46.
37. See Nogami, *Zeami*, Ch. V, "The Flower (*Hana*)," pp. 62–67; 62, 66, 63, 62.
38. See *ibid.*, Ch. VI, "The Returned Flower (Kyahurai-ka) and The Attained Skill (Ran-i)," pp. 68–74; 69, 69–70.
39. WALTER F. KERR, *N.Y. Herald Tribune*, June 12, 1960, Sect. 4, p. 1.

✿ CHAPTER 4

1. See E. K. CHAMBERS, *The Medieval Stage* (Oxford, 1903), II, 180–181; E. K. CHAMBERS, *The Elizabethan Stage* (Oxford, 1923), I, 269, 3.
2. ROSAMOND GILDER, *Enter the Actress* . . . (London, 1931), p. 84; GRACE FRANK, *The Medieval French Drama* (Oxford, 1954), pp. 182, 192, 193 from L. Petit de Julleville, *Les Mystères* (Paris, 1880), II, 133.
3. CHARLES NIEMEYER, "The Hôtel de Bourgogne, France's first popular playhouse," *Theatre Annual* (1947), p. 69.
4. Tallement des Réaux quoted by Gilder, *Actress*, p. 89.
5. Chambers, *MS*, II, 260, 186, 183, 186.
6. *Ibid.*, 187; Chambers, *ES*, II, 78, 79.
7. *Ibid.*, I, 81; see also 83, 84–85.
8. Chambers, *MS*, II, 226, 193; Chambers, *ES*, II, 28, 29, 11; see *MS*, II, 193–195; B. L. JOSEPH, *Elizabethan Acting* (Oxford and London, 1951), p. 13; Chambers, *MS*, II, 192.
9. Chambers, *ES*, I, 239, 271.
10. *Ibid.*, III, 2–3, see 3–5; Gilder, *Actress*, p. 52.
11. ALLARDYCE NICOLL, *World Drama* . . . (New York, 1950), p. 201; DONALD CLIVE STUART, *The Development of Dramatic Art* (New York, 1928), p. 343; Erasmus, *De Ratione Studii* (1511) cited by Joseph, *EA*, p. 28; Chambers, *ES*, III, 19, 20; GILBERT HIGHET, *The Classical Tradition* (New York, 1949), pp. 134, 133; Stuart, pp. 343–344; cited by Highet, pp. 231–232.
12. JOHN ADDINGTON SYMONDS, *The Renaissance in Italy* (1881–98) (New York, 1935), II, 265, 268, 265; see also p. 239.
13. Gilder, *Actress*, p. 50.
14. Chambers, *ES*, IV, 239; WINIFRED SMITH, *Italian Actors of the Renaissance* (New York, 1930), pp. 15–16.
15. K. M. LEA, pp. 399–401, in PHYLLIS HARTNOLL (ed.), *The Oxford Companion to the Theatre* (London, 1951); Nicoll, *WD*, pp. 184–185. See K. M. LEA, *Italian Popular Comedy* . . . (Oxford, 1934), I, "Ruzzante," 233–238; "Calmo," 239–245; and "Zan Polo and Cimedor," 245–251.
16. Smith, *Actors*, p. 5; see also pp. 6, 21–22, 22–24; ALLARDYCE NICOLL, *Masks Mimes and Miracles* (New York, 1931), p. 299.
17. Smith, *Actors*, pp. 36, 35.
18. GIRALDI CINTHIO, *Discorso sulle Comedie e sulle Tragedie* (1543) quoted by Stuart, *DDA*, p. 261; *ibid.*, pp. 242, 264.
19. *Ibid.*, p. 246; T. S. ELIOT, "Seneca in Elizabethan Translation" (1927) in his *Selected Essays 1917–1932* (New York, 1932), p. 54.
20. Cervantes's Preface to *Ocho comedias y ocho entreméses nuevos* (1615) cited by

HUGO ALBERT RENNERT, *The Spanish Stage in the Time of Lope de Vega* (New York, 1909), p. 17.

21. *The Spiritual Exercises of St. Ignatius* trans. by Louis J. Puhl (Westminster, Maryland, 1951), Section 65, "Fifth Exercise of the First Week," pp. 32–33, and "The Second Contemplation of the Same Week," pp. 52–53; see also "The Fifth Contemplation," pp. 54–55, and "The First Contemplation of the Third Week," pp. 81–82.

22. FRANCIS FERGUSSON, *Idea of a Theatre* (Princeton, 1944), p. 238.

23. Niemeyer, "Hôtel," pp. 66, 67.

24. Stuart, *DDA*, pp. 349, 300.

25. THOMAS WILSON, *Rhetorique* (London, 1553), p. 218.

26. Chambers, *ES*, II, 82, 83.

27. *Ibid.*, II, 356.

28. *Ibid.*, II, 85, 91–92; IV, 84; II, 92.

29. Trans. and quoted by Rennert, *Spanish Stage*, pp. 151–154; see also A. M. NAGLER, *Sources of Theatrical History* (New York, 1952), pp. 57–60.

30. See *Oxford Companion*, p. 492, 711; ALESSANDRO D'ANCONDA, *Origini del Teatro Italiano* (Turin, 1891), II, 405, cited by Smith, *Actors*, p. 150.

31. Quoted by ALLARDYCE NICOLL, *The Development of the Theatre* (London, 1927), Appendix B, pp. 250–253; also see TOBY COLE AND HELEN KRICH CHINOY (ed.), *Actors on Acting* . . . (New York, 1949), pp. 45–49, and Nicoll, *DT* (1948 ed.), pp. 237–262.

32. Cited in Gilder, *Actress*, p. 58; A. NERI, "Fra i comici dell' arte," *Revista teatrale italiani* (1906), pp. 55–56, quoted in Smith, *Actors*, p. 26.

33. Scaliger's *Poetices Libri Septem* (1561), iii, 96, quoted by J. E. SPINGARN, *A History of Literary Criticism in the Renaissance* (1899) (New York, 1925), pp. 94–95.

34. Giraldi Cinthio, *Discorso*, ii, 10ff. quoted by Spingarn, *Literary Criticism*, p. 91; Castelvetro cited in H. P. CHARLTON, *Castelvetro's Theory of Poetry* (Manchester, 1913) and reprinted in BARRETT H. CLARK (ed.), *European Theories of the Drama* (Cincinnati, 1918), p. 64; Spingarn, pp. 97–98, 90.

35. *Ibid.*, pp. 85, 86.

36. MICHELE SCHERILLO, "The Commedia dell' arte," *The Mask*, III (1910–11), 113, cited by PIERRE LOUIS DUCHARTE, *The Italian Comedy* . . . (1924) trans. by Randolph T. Weaver (New York, 1929), pp. 19, 18–19, 19.

37. Nicoll, *MMM*, p. 302; Smith, *Actors*, pp. 28, 33; Nicoll, pp. 303–304; Charles Sorel cited in Ducharte, *Italian Comedy*, p. 22; Smith, pp. 40–41; Baschet cited by Nicoll, p. 306.

38. FREDERICK HAWKINS, *Annals of the French Stage* (London, 1884), I, 44. See HENRY LANCASTER, *A History of French Dramatic Literature in the Seventeenth Century* (Baltimore, 1929–42), Part I, Vol. II, 727–728; W. L. WILEY, *The Early Public Theatre in France* (Cambridge, Mass., 1960), pp. 43–44.

39. Geoffrey Fenton quoted in Chambers, *ES*, IV, 195; see I, 269–382; II, 87–88.

40. *Ibid.*, II, 305, 86, 87, 85.

41. See *ibid.*, I, 283; W. MACQUEEN-POPE, p. 789, in *Oxford Companion*.

42. Chambers, *ES*, II, 88–89; see *Oxford Companion*, pp. 386–387.

43. Chambers, *ES*, II, 4; I, 217; II, 97–98, 134, 93, 4; I, 348.

44. Chambers, *MS*, II, 226; *ES*, I, 254, 287.

45. Stuart, *DDA*, pp. 308, 364.

46. Ducharte, *Italian Comedy*, p. 74; cited by Niemeyer, "Hôtel," p. 70.

47. Ducharte, *Italian Comedy*, pp. 60, 89, 87; see also Nicoll, *MMM*, pp. 315–316; Ducharte, p. 90; Nicoll, *MMM*, p. 244, and also pp. 310, 311, 241, 373.

48. M. M. REESE, *Shakespeare* . . . (New York, 1953), fn. p. 47; Chambers, *ES*, I, 288.

49. *Ibid.*, I, 289; Stephen Gosson quoted in IV, 218–219.

50. *Ibid.*, I, 291; II, 104–105; Reese, *Shakespeare*, p. 188; Chambers, *ES*, II, 104, 106–107.
51. *Ibid.*, I, 293, 309, 358; Reese, *Shakespeare*, p. 69; Chambers, *ES*, II, 296, 307.
52. *Ibid.*, II, 110, 135–136; J. DOVER WILSON, Int. to *The Second Part of King Henry VI* (Cambridge, 1952), p. xii.
53. Eliot, "Seneca," pp. 75–76.
54. Niemeyer, Hôtel," p. 70; see Lancaster, *HFDLSC*, Part I, Vol. 2, 728–730; Wiley, *EPTF*, pp. 48–50.
55. ANGEL FLORES, *Lope de Vega* (New York, 1930), p. 126.
56. HUGO ALBERT RENNERT, *The Life of Lope de Vega* (Glasgow, 1904), pp. 128, 132, 133.
57. Reese, *Shakespeare*, p. 191; see Dover Wilson, *Second Part Henry VI*, p. xiii, xix; Green's *Works* ed. by Grosart, xii, 144, cited p. xv; J. DOVER WILSON, Int. to *The First Part of King Henry VI* (Cambridge, 1952), p. xiv, from *Henslowe's Diary* ed. by Greg, I, 13–15; read pp. xlviii–xlix.
58. Delp, p. 307, in *Oxford Companion;* see also p. 102, and Chambers, *ES*, II, 137–138.
59. Henslowe cited in Chambers, *ES*, II, 193; *ES*, I, 201; see II, 197–199.
60. *Ibid.*, II, 143.
61. Wilson, *Second Part Henry VI*, p. x; Chambers, *ES*, II, 141, 142; see 139.
62. *Ibid.*, II, 143.
63. Thomas Nashe quoted *ibid.*, I, 297; 300–301, 309.
64. *Ibid.*, II, 156, 159–160, 165–171; BORIS FORD (ed.), *The Age of Shakespeare*, Penguin Books (1955), p. 44.
65. Chambers, *ES*, I, 356; II, 417; Reese, *Shakespeare*, pp. 152, 152–153. For additional material on the "shares," see *ES*, I, 352–358, or Reese, pp. 209–214.
66. Chambers, *ES*, II, 528, 526; Reese, *Shakespeare*, p. 129.
67. Chambers, *ES*, I, 309; Green's *Groatsworth of Wit* . . . cited by Reese, *Shakespeare*, p. 91; Francis Meres quoted in G. G. SMITH (ed.), *Elizabethan Critical Essays* (London, 1904), II, 313.

❁ CHAPTER 5

1. BENEDETTO CROCE, from his *Poesia populare e poesia d'arte* (1933) trans. as "Commedia dell' Arte" by Phyllis deKay Bury, *Theatre Arts*, XVI (December, 1933), 929, 929–930; WINIFRED SMITH, *Italian Actors of the Renaissance* (New York, 1930), p. 14.
2. Croce, "Commedia," p. 933; JOHN V. FALCONIERI, "The Commedia dell' Arte, the Actors' Theatre," *Theatre Annual* (1954), p. 39; Croce, p. 929; Falconieri, p. 47.
3. CARLO GOLDONI, *Memoirs* (1737) trans. from French by John Black (1814) (New York, 1926), pp. 364, 188.
4. K. M. LEA, *Italian Popular Comedy* . . . (Oxford, 1934), I, 136; EVARISTO GHERARDI, "On the Art of Italian Comedians," from the preface to the six volume *Le Théâtre Italien de Gherardi* . . . (Paris, 1694, 1700, 1741), *Theatre Arts*, X (February 1926), 109–110, and quoted in TOBY COLE AND HELEN KRICH CHINOY (ed.), *Actors on Acting* . . . (New York, 1949), p. 58; ANDREA PERRUCCI, *Dell arte rappresentativa, premeditata ad all' improviso* (Naples, 1699), in ENZO PETRACCONE (ed.), *La Commedia dell' arte; storia, technica, scenari* (Naples, 1927), pp. 69–72, and quoted in Cole and Chinoy, p. 56; PHILIPPE MONNIER, "The Venetian Theatre and Italian Comedy in the Eighteenth Century," *The Mask*, III (1910–11), 104; Perrucci cited by Cole and Chinoy, p. 56.
5. Carlo Gozzi quoted by PIERRE LOUIS DUCHARTE, *The Italian Comedy* . . . (1924)

    trans. by Randolph T. Weaver (New York, 1929), p. 51; Monnier, "Venetian Theatre," p. 105.

6. Perrucci, *Dell arte rappresentativa*, cited by Cole and Chinoy, AA, p. 56.

7. Falconieri, "Commedia dell' Arte," pp. 46, 45; Gherardi, "Italian Comedians," p. 109, and quoted in Cole and Chinoy, AA, p. 58.

8. Croce, "Commedia," p. 934; Falconieri, "Commedia dell' Arte," p. 30; PIER MARIA CECCHINI, *Frutti delle moderne comedie et avisi a chi recita* . . . (Padua, 1628) in Petraccone, *Commedia*, pp. 8–18, and quoted by Cole and Chinoy, AA, pp. 50–51; Gherardi, "Italian Comedians," p. 110, and cited *ibid*., p. 59; Perrucci, *Dell arte rappresentativa* cited in ALLARDYCE NICOLL, *Masks Mimes and Miracles* (New York, 1931), p. 234; Ducharte, *Italian Comedy*, pp. 145, 141, 245.

9. CONSTANT MIC (Miclascefsky), *La Commedia dell' Arte* (1914) trans. from Russian (Paris, 1927) and quoted by Falconieri, "Commedia dell' Arte," p. 43; Gherardi cited by Ducharte, *Italian Comedy*, p. 243; J. CASANOVA, *Mémoires* (Paris, 1843) quoted from Mic by Falconieri, p. 43; JOHN H. MCDOWELL, "Some Pictorial Aspects of Early *Commedia dell' Arte* Acting," *Studies in Philology*, XXXIX (1942), 59.

10. STARK YOUNG, *The Theater* (New York, 1927), pp. 50–51, 45.

11. See MICHELE SCHRERILLO, "The Commedia dell' Arte," *The Mask*, III (1910–11), 115; Nicoll, MMM, p. 253; ROSAMOND GILDER, *Enter the Actress* . . . (London, 1931), p. 71.

12. Nicoll, MMM, pp. 265, 258; Ducharte, *Italian Comedy*, p. 185; see also Nicoll, p. 255.

13. Monnier, "Venetian Comedy," p. 104; Nicoll, MMM, p. 219.

14. Ducharte, *Italian Comedy*, p. 36; Riccoboni quoted in Nicoll, MMM, p. 220; Petraccone cited *ibid*.; M. G. (GUELLETTE), *Tradution du scenario de Joseph Dominique Biancolelli, dit Arlequin* . . . (Paris, 1759?), I, 386, quoted *ibid*., p. 221.

15. Falconieri, "Commedia dell' Arte," p. 45; Perrucci, *Dell arte rappresentativa*, from Petraccone, pp. 193–196, trans. by Salvatore J. Castiglione in A. M. NAGLER, *Sources of Theatrical History* (New York, 1952), pp. 258–259.

16. *Ibid*., p. 258.

17. *Ibid*., p. 257; the scenario trans. by Cesare Levi, *The Mask*, VI (1913–14), 353–356.

18. Riccoboni cited in WINIFRED SMITH, *Commedia dell' Arte* . . . (New York, 1912), p. 216; Lea, IPC, I, 132; Ducharte, *Italian Comedy*, p. 51; JOHN GASSNER, *Masters of the Drama* (New York, 1940), p. 171.

19. See Nicoll, MMM, pp. 228–229.

20. Ducharte, *Italian Comedy*, pp. 236, 19, 288, 229, 179, 200, 134; Croce, "Commedia," p. 937.

21. ROY MITCHELL, *Creative Theatre* (New York, 1929), p. 158.

22. *Ibid*., p. 157.

23. CONSTANTIN STANISLAVSKI, *An Actor Prepares* trans. by Elizabeth Reynolds Hapgood (New York, 1936), p. 134.

24. Gherardi cited by Ducharte, *Italian Comedy*, p. 31; see Cole and Chinoy, AA, p. 58.

25. Riccoboni quoted by Ducharte, *Italian Comedy*, p. 32; Gherardi, "Italian Comedians," p. 110, and see Cole and Chinoy, AA, p. 59; CHARLES DE BROSSES (1709–1777) cited by Ducharte, p. 34; see also Nicoll, MMM, p. 230.

26. Ducharte, *Italian Comedy*, p. 88; Smith, *Actors*, p. 53; Gilder, *Actress*, pp. 67, 72, 79; Smith, p. 52.

27. Ducharte, *Italian Comedy*, p. 90; see Nicoll, MMM, pp. 317–321, 320.

28. *Ibid*., pp. 323–324; Smith, *Actors*, pp. 79, 85; A. BASCHET, *Les Comédiens italiens à la cour de France sous Charles IX, Henri III, Henri IV, et Louis XIII* (Paris, 1882), pp. 114ff., cited *ibid*., p. 80; 84–85.

29. *Ibid.*, pp. 83–84, 168; Lea, *IPC*, I, 306; Nicoll, *MMM*, pp. 331–332; Baschet, *Comédiens*, p. 270, cited in Smith, *Actors*, p. 166; "Jarro," p. 40, cited *ibid.*, p. 157.

30. *Ibid.*, p. 173; Rasi quoted *ibid.*, p. 100; 103; see also p. 125; 179, 180–181; 181; D'ANCONA, *Lettere de comici italiani del sec XVII* (Pisa, 1893), pp. 27–29, quoted *ibid.*, pp. 182, 185.

31. See "The Later Mantuan Troupes and the Troupes of Parma and Modena," pp. 335–342, in Nicoll, *MMM*. Consult A. F. BADER, "The Modena Troupe in England," *Modern Language Notes*, L (June 1935), 367–369, and IFAN KYRLE FLETCHER, "Italian Comedians in England in the 17th Century," *Theatre Notebook*, VIII (July–September 1954), 87–89.

32. See Ducharte, *Italian Comedy*, Ch. VIII, "The French-Italian Comedy, or the Italian Comedy in France," pp. 102–108, and Nicoll, *MMM*, "The Italian Comedians in France," pp. 342–346; PERCY A. CHAPMAN, *The Spirit of Molière* (Princeton, 1940), p. 64.

33. Scherillo quoted by Ducharte, *Italian Comedy*, p. 100; *ibid.*, p. 53; *Oxford Companion*, p. 143.

34. Nicoll, *MMM*, pp. 345–346.

35. *Ibid.*, p. 374; Riccoboni cited by Ducharte, *Italian Comedy*, p. 32; PIERRE RAMÉS, *The Mask*, III (1910–11), 175, cited *ibid.*, p. 309; see GEORGE FREEDLEY AND JOHN A. REEVES, *A History of the Theatre* (New York, 1941), p. 233.

36. Ducharte, *Italian Comedy*, p. 114; see FREDERICK HAWKINS, *The French Stage in the Eighteenth Century* (London, 1888), I, 121, and compare with Ducharte, pp. 115–116; Hawkins, I, 121; Ducharte, p. 114.

37. Hawkins, *French Stage*, I, 122, 121–122; Ducharte, *Italian Comedy*, p. 115.

38. Goldoni, *Memoirs* cited by BARRETT H. CLARK (ed.), *European Theories of the Drama* (Cincinnati, 1918), p. 247, and by Nagler, *Sources*, p. 276; VIOLET M. SANDERS, p. 404, in *Oxford Companion*; Goldoni cited by Nagler, p. 278, and Clark, p. 247; see Nicoll, *MMM*, pp. 383–384.

39. F. C. L. VAN STEENDEREN (ed.), *Goldoni on Playwriting, Discussions of the Drama II*, Dramatic Museum Columbia University (New York, 1919), p. 11; Nicoll, *WD*, p. 383; *Il Teatro comico* trans. by H. C. CHATFIELD-TAYLOR and cited by Clark, *European Theories*, p. 246.

40. Goldoni, *Memoirs* (Black), pp. 188, 181; see also pp. 239, 368.

41. *Ibid.*, cited by Nagler, *Sources*, p. 275; cited in van Steenderen, *Goldoni*, pp. 13–14.

42. *Il Teatro comico* quoted by Clark, *European Theories*, p. 246; van Steenderen, *Goldoni*, p. 13.

43. Goldoni cited by Nagler, *Sources*, p. 278, and by Clark, *European Theories*, p. 247.

44. K. M. Lea, p. 402, in *Oxford Companion*; CYRIL W. BEAUMONT, *The History of Harlequin* (London, 1926), cited by Ducharte, *Italian Comedy*, fn. p. 21; Gozzi quoted by Nicoll, *WD*, p. 379; Ducharte, p. 117.

45. Lea, p. 403, in *Oxford Companion*; D. NEVILE LEES, "Carlo Gozzi and the Venetian Drama of the Eighteenth Century," *The Mask*, VI (1913–14), 289.

❊ CHAPTER 6

1. MILDRED ADAMS, "Spanish Theatre Then and Now," *Theatre Arts*, XIX (September 1953), 690, 691; JOHN GARRETT UNDERHILL, Int. to his *Four Plays by Lope de Vega* (New York, 1936), p. xiii; ALLARDYCE NICOLL, *World Drama . . .* (New York, 1949), p. 212; Underhill, p. xxiii; DONALD CLIVE STUART, *The Development of Dramatic Art* (New York, 1928), p. 323; Cervantes cited by ROSAMOND GILDER, "Lope de Vega," *Theatre Arts*, XIX (September 1935), 660; Adams, p. 691.

2. JOHN GASSNER, *Masters of the Drama* (New York, 1940), p. 185.

3. Underhill, *Four Plays*, p. xxiii.

4. Cited by Adams, "Spanish Theatre," p. 697.

5. GERMAIN BAPST, *Essai sur l'histoire du théâtre* . . . (Paris, 1893), p. 280; see KARL MANTZIUS, *A History of Theatrical Art* . . . , V, *Great Actors of the Eighteenth Century* trans. by Louise von Cossel (London, 1909), 6–7; and W. H. BRUFORD, *Theatre, Drama and Audience in Goethe's Germany* (London, 1950), p. 32.

6. CHARLES NIEMEYER, "The Hôtel de Bourgogne . . . ," *Theatre Annual* (1947), pp. 70–71; JOHN LOUGH, *Paris Theatre Audiences in the Seventeenth & Eighteenth Centuries* (London, 1957), p. 44; BRUSCAMBILLE, *Oeuvres* (Rouen, 1626), p. 332.

7. Lough, *PTA*, pp. 8–9; W. L. WILEY, *The Early Public Theatre in France* (Cambridge, Mass., 1960), pp. 50–51; see S. WILMA DEIERKAUF-HOLSOBER, "Vie d'Alexandre Hardy, poeté du Roi," *Proceedings American Philosophical Society*, 91 (1947), 341–354, 349, 393–394.

8. Wiley, *EPTF*, pp. 52–53; Lough, *PTA*, p. 9.

9. Wiley, *EPTF*, p. 51; ROSAMOND GILDER, *Enter the Actress* . . . (London, 1931), p. 90.

10. Wiley, *EPTF*, pp. 92, 93, 103, 53; see Deierkauf-Holsober, "Hardy," pp. 348, 355, 383, 393; and *ibid.*, cited by HENRY C. LANCASTER, *French Tragedy in the Time of Louis XIV and Voltaire 1715–1774* (Baltimore, 1950), II, 631.

11. Stuart, *DDA*, p. 364; Wiley, *EPTF*, p. 252.

12. Lough, *PTA*, p. 39.

13. Wiley, *EPTF*, p. 107; Ogier cited in BARRETT H. CLARK (ed.), *European Theories of the Drama* (Cincinnati, 1918), p. 119.

14. Niemeyer, "Hôtel," p. 73.

15. S. WILMA DEIERKAUF-HOLSOBER, *Théâtre du Marais* (Paris, 1954), I, 149.

16. Wiley, *EPTF*, pp. 86, 87; Stuart, *DDA*, p. 389.

17. PERCY CHAPMAN, *The Spirit of Molière* . . . (Princeton, 1940), p. 18; Wiley, *EPTF*, pp. 104, 103; Tristam quoted by FREDERICK HAWKINS, *Annals of the French Stage* (London, 1884), I, 72; Wiley, p. 99.

18. See HENRY C. LANCASTER, *A History of French Dramatic Literature in the Seventeenth Century* (Baltimore, 1929–42), Part I, Vol. 1, 21; and Hawkins, *Annals*, I, 83; Tallemant cited by Chapman, *Molière*, p. 17; Stuart, *DDA*, p. 384; Nicoll, *WD*, p. 302; Stuart, pp. 383–384.

19. Trans. *ibid.*, pp. 393–394.

20. Nicoll, *WD*, p. 302.

21. Chapman, *Molière*, p. 17; Hawkins, *Annals*, I, 149; Deierkauf-Holsober, *Marais*, p. 150.

22. See Hawkins, *Annals*, I, 135–137; and Palmer, *Molière*, pp. 46–47.

23. *Ibid.*, p. 33.

24. Hawkins, *Annals*, I, 147–148.

25. E. K. CHAMBERS, *The Elizabethan Stage* (Oxford, 1923), I, 304; ALFREL HARBAGE, *Shakespeare and the Rival Traditions* (New York, 1952), p. 47.

26. See Chambers, *ES*, II, 176, 186, 188, 190; GERALD E. BENTLEY, *The Jacobean and Caroline Stage* (Oxford, 1941), I, 136, 137, 139.

27. See M. M. REESE, *Shakespeare* . . . (New York, 1953), pp. 562–563 for speculations drawn from E. K. CHAMBERS, *William Shakespeare* . . . (Oxford, 1930), I, 57–91, II, 71–87; Chambers, *ES*, II, "The Lord Chamberlain's Men," pp. 192–220, and Ch. XV, "The Actors," pp. 295–360; Bentley, *JCS*, I, "The King's Company," 1–134, and II, "Players," 343–628; for sharers Condell, Sly, and Ostler see Chambers, *ES*, II, 213–214, 331.

28. *Ibid.*, II, 214; Gerald E. Bentley, "Shakespeare and the Blackfriars Theatre," pp. 40, 47, in *Shakespeare Survey 1* (1948) ed. by ALLARDYCE NICOLL.

29. L. G. SALINGAR, "The Decline of Tragedy," p. 430, in BORIS FORD (ed.), *The Age of Shakespeare*, Penguin Books (1955); THOMAS MARC PARROTT AND ROBERT HAMILTON BALL, *A Short View of Elizabethan Drama* (New York, 1943), p. 202.

30. Bentley, *JCS*, I, 2; Wright quoted by A. M. NAGLER, *Sources of Theatrical History* (New York, 1952), p. 161; Chambers, *ES*, I, 349–350.

31. *Ibid.*, I, 370; ALWIN THAYER, "The Elizabethan Dramatic Companies," *Pub. Modern Language Ass.*, XXXV n.s. (1920), 156; see T. W. BALDWIN, *The Organization and Personnel of the Shakespearean Company* (Princeton, 1927), pp. 90–117.

32. Bentley, *JCS*, I, 43–45; see also Chambers, *ES*, II, 425–426, 310.

33. Reese, *Shakespeare*, p. 210.

34. *Ibid.*; ALWIN THAYER, "Minor Actors and Employees in the Elizabethan Theatre," *Modern Philology*, XX (1922), 50.

35. Thayer, "EDC," p. 146; see Chambers, *ES*, II, 236–238, and Bentley, *JCS*, I, 158; Webster cited by William Armstrong, "Shakespeare and the Acting of Edward Alleyn," p. 87 in *Shakespeare Survey* 7 (1954), ed. by ALLARDYCE NICOLL; Bentley, *JCS*, II, 363, 353.

36. *Ibid.*, I, 16.

37. *Ibid.*, I, 67; 68–69; LESLIE HOTSON, *The Commonwealth and Restoration Stage* (Cambridge, Mass., 1928), p. 32.

38. Bentley, *JCS*, II, 597; Chambers, *ES*, I, 306–307; see Wright, *Historica Histrionica*, pp. 1–10, quoted by Bentley, II, 695.

39. A. C. SCOTT, *The Kabuki Theatre of Japan* (London, 1955), pp. 35–36, 277, 36, 37.

40. *Ibid.*, p. 38, 54, 38.

41. *Ibid.*, pp. 32–33; DONALD KEENE, *Japanese Literature* (New York, 1955), p. 65; Gassner, *Masters*, pp. 129–130.

42. Scott, *Kabuki*, pp. 19, 117–122, 18, 167, 83.

43. *Ibid.*, p. 37; see pp. 172–175.

44. *Ibid.*, pp. 91, 105–106, 108–109.

45. *Ibid.*, pp. 169; *Ayame-gusa* quoted *ibid.*, pp. 173, 174.

46. *Ibid.*, pp. 74–76.

47. See *ibid.*, pp. 157, 113–114, 115, 112–113, 114–115, 99–100, 110, 157.

48. Chikamatsu quoted by DONALD KEENE, *The Battles of Coxinga* (London, 1951), pp. 95–96.

49. JOHN PALMER, *Molière* (New York, 1930), p. 108; see Hawkins, *Annals*, I, 80; GEORGE FREEDLEY AND JOHN A. REEVES, *A History of the Theatre* (New York, 1941), p. 134.

50. Chapman, *Molière*, p. 60.

51. *Ibid.*, p. 61. "Preface of 1682" cited *ibid.*, p. 62; La Grange quoted *ibid.*

52. Palmer, *Molière*, p. 133.

53. *Ibid.*, pp. 154, 137; Chapman, *Molière*, p. 74; Stuart, *DDA*, p. 334.

54. MORRIS BISHOP, Int. to *Eight Plays by Molière*, Modern Library (New York, 1957), pp. ix, vii.

55. Chapman, *Molière*, p. 108; Stuart, *DDA*, p. 336; Chapman, p. 122.

56. *Ibid.*, p. 136; Palmer, *Molière*, p. 265; BRANDER MATTHEWS, *Molière* (New York, 1910), p. 127; Bishop, *Eight Plays*, p. 115.

57. La Serre (1734) cited by Palmer, *Molière*, p. 193; the "mysterious" Sieur Neufvillaine cited *ibid.*, p. 176.

58. Bishop, *Eight Plays*, p. 20; see pp. 131, 135, 134 and 141, 131.

59. *Ibid.*, p. 127; Hawkins, *Annals*, II, 75–76.

60. Lancaster, *HFDL*, V, fn. p. 22; Hawkins, *Annals*, II, 171.

61. WYLIE SYPHER, *Four Stages of Renaissance Style* (New York, 1955), pp. 288, 295; MARTIN TURRELL, "For Jean Racine," *Horizon*, II (August 1940), 32, 38; ELEANOR JOURDAIN, *The Drama in Europe . . .* (New York, 1924), p. 69;

FRANCIS FERGUSSON, *The Idea of a Theatre* (Princeton, 1949), p. 48; Jourdain, p. 70.

62. Nicoll, WD, pp. 309–310; GEOFFREY BRERETON, *Jean Racine* . . . (London, 1951), p. 101; Stuart, DDA, p. 410; Fergusson, *Idea*, p. 50.

63. The *Entretiens Galants* (1681) cited by Brereton, *Racine*, p. 152; Stuart, DDA, p. 410.

64. Gassner, *Masters*, p. 230; Fergusson, *Idea*, p. 48; Gassner, p. 281; Fergusson, p. 53.

65. Hawkins, *Annals*, II, 138, 139.

66. See HENRY C. LANCASTER, *Comédie Francaise, 1680–1701* . . . (Baltimore, 1941), pp. 9–10.

67. Lough, PTA, p. 48; Lancaster, CF, cited *ibid.*, p. 49; 51, 49, 52–53.

68. JOHN LOUGH, "The Earnings of Playwrights in Seventeenth Century France," *Modern Language Review* (1947), p. 331; see also Lancaster, CF, pp. 19, 22, and HFDL, V, fn. 22.

69. Hotson, cited by Bentley, *JCS*, II, 370; ALLARDYCE NICOLL, A *History of English Drama 1660–1900*, I, *Restoration Drama 1660–1700* 4th ed. (Cambridge, 1952), p. 291; Bentley, II, 374, 373. See also Nicoll, pp. 287–289, 291; "Some Notes on William Beeston," *Times* (London) *Literary Supplement*, November 22, 1923; and Bentley, II, 270–374.

70. Nicoll, *Rest.*, p. 29; see Gilder, *Actress*, p. 133; *Roscius Anglicanus* (1708) ed. Knight cited by ROBERT W. LOWE, *Thomas Betterton* (New York, 1891), p. 8; W. MACQUEEN-POPE, *Ladies First* (London, 1952), p. 26; Nicoll, *Rest.*, p. 287.

71. *Ibid.*, pp. 289, 293; Macqueen-Pope, *Ladies*, p. 28; see JOHN H. WILSON, *All the King's Ladies* (Chicago, 1958), p. 7; Macqueen-Pope, p. 39.

72. Nicoll, *Rest.*, p. 301; ELIZABETH G. SCANLAN, "Reconstruction of the Duke's Playhouse in Lincoln's Inn Fields, 1661–1671," *Theatre Notebook*, 10 (January–March 1956), 50; *Oxford Companion*, p. 201. See also Nicoll, *Rest.*, pp. 81, 82–83.

73. *Ibid.*, p. 311; see pp. 308–313, and MONTAGUE SUMMERS, *The Playhouse of Pepys* (London, 1935), pp. 118–120.

74. RICHARD SOUTHERN, *The Georgian Playhouse* (London, 1948), p. 20; *Oxford Companion*, p. 201; Nicoll, *Rest.*, pp. 323–325; Gildon quoted in COLLEY CIBBER, *An Apology for the Life of Colley Cibber* . . . (1740) ed. Bellchambers (London, 1822), p. 172.

75. JOHN DOWNES, *Roscius Anglicanus* ed. Summers, pp. 21, 24. See also Nicoll, *Rest.*, pp. 301, 303, 296, 299.

76. JOHN H. WILSON, *Nell Gwyn, royal mistress* (New York, 1952), pp. 44–45.

77. Nicoll, *Rest.*, p. 236; JOSEPH WOOD KRUTCH, *Comedy and Conscience after the Restoration* (New York, 1924), p. 22.

78. Wilson, *King's Ladies*, p. 47; Ravenscroft's *The Canterbury Guests* (1694) cited *ibid.*, p. 72; 46.

79. Nicoll, *Rest.*, p. 64; Wilson, *King's Ladies*, pp. 33, 34, 35.

80. Downes, *Roscius* cited in Cibber, *Apology* ed. Bellchambers, fn. p. 73; Rymer quoted *ibid.*, fn. pp. 73–74; Wilson, *King's Ladies*, p. 37; *Tatler* No. 99 quoted in Cibber, fn. p. 82, fn. p. 80, 82; Pepys quoted by Nicoll, *Rest.*, p. 69; Cibber cited *ibid.*, fn. p. 68; Downes cited by MacQueen-Pope, *Ladies*, p. 22; Cibber, p. 124.

81. Pepys quoted in MacQueen-Pope, *Ladies*, p. 70; Wilson, *Gwyn*, pp. 95, 117.

82. Nicoll, *Rest.*, p. 66; Cibber, *Apology*, pp. 88, 108, 89, 94, 91; Wilson, *King's Ladies*, p. 37.

83. Nicoll, *Rest.*, p. 67; Cibber, *Apology*, pp. 148, 163, 156, 134, 144.

84. MacQueen-Pope, *Ladies*, p. 46. *Tatler* No. 20; MacQueen-Pope, p. 94; Cibber, *Apology*, pp. 171, 186; Wilson, *King's Ladies*, p. 21.

85. *Ibid.*, p. 38.

86. Nicoll, *Rest.*, pp. 342, 331, 333.

87. Cibber, *Apology*, pp. 87–88, 189.

88. [Gildon] *A Comparison between the Two Stages* cited by Nicoll, *Rest.*, p. 333; Henry Morley quoted in W. CLARK RUSSELL, *Representative Actors* (London, c. 1872), p. 38.

89. Nicoll, *Rest.*, p. 341.

90. A. INGEGNERI, *Della Poesia Rappresentativa* (1598) cited by B. L. JOSEPH, *Elizabethan Acting* (Oxford, 1951), p. 84; THOMAS WRIGHT, *The Passions of the Mind* (1604) cited by SYPHER, *Four Stages*, p. 275.

91. Joseph, *EA*, pp. 148, 130, 51; BULWER, *Chironomia* (1644), pp. 20–21, quoted *ibid.*, p. 150.

92. See Reese, *Shakespeare*, p. 128; Dekker, *The Gull's Hornbook* (1605) quoted in Nagler, *Sources*, p. 134; H. GRANVILLE-BARKER, *Prefaces to Shakespeare, second series* (London, 1935), pp. 249–250; Daniel's *Musophilus* (1599) cited in *Age of Shakespeare*, p. 43.

93. WILLIAM J. LAWRENCE, "Old-Time Rehearsing," p. 94, in his *Old Theatre Days and Ways* (London, 1935); Robert Greene, *Francescos Fortunes* (1590) cited in ALFRED HARBAGE, "Elizabethan Acting," *Pub. Modern Language Ass.*, LIV (September 1939), 700.

94. Heywood, *Apology* [p. 17]; Heywood cited in Joseph, *EA*, p. 15; JOHN BRINSLEY, *Ludus Literarius: or the grammar school* (1612) cited *ibid.*, p. 12; B. L. Joseph, "The Elizabethan Stage and Acting," in *Age of Shakespeare*, p. 157.

95. JOHN BARTON, *The Art of Rhetorick* . . . (1634) cited in WILBUR S. HOWELL, *Logic and Rhetoric in England, 1500–1700* (Princeton, 1956), pp. 275, 274; DUDLEY FENNER, *The Artes of Logick and Rhetorike* (1584) quoted *ibid.*, p. 256; see Joseph, *EA*, pp. 35, 131–132; Howell commenting on George Puttenham's *The Art of English Poesie* (1589), p. 327; Flecknoe cited in Chambers, *ES*, IV, 569–570; H. GRANVILLE-BARKER, *Prefaces to Shakespeare, II, [Coriolanus]* (Princeton, 1947), p. 277.

96. Joseph, "ESA," p. 154; Abraham Fraunce, *Arcadian Rhetorike* (1588) ed. Seaton, p. 106, cited in Howell, *Logic*, p. 258; Fraunce, Bk. II, Ch. 3; Heywood, *Apology* cited by Joseph, *EA*, p. 17; Wright, *Passions*, p. 179, cited *ibid.*, p. 3; Bulwer, p. 44, cited Joseph, p. 76; p. 16 cited *ibid.*, p. 39; pp. 16–17 cited *ibid.*, p. 43; *ibid.*, pp. 41, 43.

97. *Ibid.*, p. 60; John Webster (?), "Of an Excellent Actor," quoted by Chambers, *ES*, IV, 257–258.

98. Flecknoe cited *ibid.*, pp. 369–370.

99. ELMER EDGAR STOLL, *Shakespeare and Other Masters* (Cambridge, Mass., 1940), pp. 339, 25; Henri Fluchère, *Shakespeare & the Elizabethans* (1947) (New York, 1956), p. 131; SAMUEL L. BETHELL, *Shakespeare & the Popular Dramatic Tradition* (London, 1944), p. 79; G. WILSON KNIGHT, *The Wheel of Fire* (1930) (London, 1937), p. 16.

100. Joseph, "ESA," p. 158; JOHN JAY CHAPMAN, *A Glance toward Shakespeare* (New York, 1923), cited by Stoll, *SOM*, p. 248. See Fluchère, *Shakespeare*, pp. 139–140.

101. Stoll, *SOM*, p. 242; Fluchère, *Shakespeare*, p. 132; Stoll, p. 248; J. I. M. STEWART, *Character and Motive in Shakespeare* . . . (London, 1949), p. 108; H. GRANVILLE-BARKER, *Prefaces to Shakespeare, first series* (London, 1933), pp. 27, 75; see Stewart, pp. 108, 110.

102. Bethell, *SPDT*, p. 87; Stewart, *Character*, p. 117; LIONEL TRILLING, "Freud and Literature," *Horizon*, XVI (September 1947), 92, cited *ibid.*, p. 144.

103. Bethell, *SPDT*, p. 79; Stoll, *SOM*, p. 97; MURIEL C. BRADBROOK, *Elizabethan Stage Conditions* . . . (Cambridge, 1932), p. 86.

104. Fluchère, *Shakespeare*, p. 133; see Joseph, *EA*, pp. 125–130; Gielgud in ROSAMOND GILDER, *John Gielgud's Hamlet* . . . (New York, 1937), pp. 66–67.

105. Erasmus, *De Ratione Studii* (1511) trans. by Woodward as *Desiderius Erasmus concerning the Aim and Method of Education* (1904), pp. 173–174, quoted in Joseph, *EA*, p. 28; Barton cited by Howell, *Logic*, p. 275; see ROBERT SPEAIGHT, *William Poel and the Elizabethan Revival* (Cambridge, Mass., 1954), pp. 62–66.

106. Wright, *Passions*, quoted in Joseph, *EA*, p. 70; see STARK YOUNG, "Eugene O'Neill, notes from a critic's diary," *Harper's* 214 (June 1957), 63; see Joseph, "*ESA*," p. 148.

107. Samuel de Sorbière (1664) cited by STARK YOUNG, *Immortal Shadows* (New York, 1948), p. 275; see Young, "O'Neill," p. 68; J. Cocke "A Common Player" (1615) in Chambers, *ES*, IV, 256; Granville-Barker, *Prefaces, first series*, p. xxvi.

108. Niemeyer, "Hôtel," p. 72; WILLIAM L. SCHWARTZ, "Molière's Theatre in 1672–1673," *Pub. Modern Language Ass.*, LVI (June 1941), 398–399; Lough, *PTA*, pp. 49, 51; Nagler, *Sources*, p. 285, and Lewis [Luigi] Riccoboni, *An Historical and Critical Account of the Theatres in Europe* . . . (London, 1741), pp. 144–149, cited *ibid.*, pp. 285–286; Charles Sorel, *La Maison de Jeux* (1642) cited by Niemeyer, p. 73; Lough, p. 52.

109. Samuel Chappuzeau, *Le théâtre françois* . . . (1674), pp. 54, 61, cited by Nagler, *Sources*, pp. 181–182; ABBÉ D'AUBIGNAC, *La pratique du théâtre* (1657) trans. as *The Whole Art of the Stage* (London, 1684), Bk. III, p. 14; Bk. II, p. 68; ANTOINE FOCLIN, *La Rhetorique françoise* (1555) cited by Howell, *Logic*, p. 168; Bernard Lamy, *De l'Art de Parler* (1675) English trans. 1676 cited by Joseph, *EA*, p. 68; Howell, pp. 170–171.

110. Jourdain, *Drama Europe*, p. 70; John Dryden, *An Essay of Dramatick Poesie* (1668) in Clark, *European Theories*, p. 189; SOMERSET MAUGHAM, *The Razor's Edge* (New York, 1944), pp. 200–201.

111. WILBUR SAMUEL HOWELL, "Sources of the Elocutionary Movement in England: 1700–1748," *Quarterly Journal Speech*, XLV (February 1959), 8.

112. Sypher, *Four Stages*, pp. 274, 275–276, 278.

113. D'Aubignac, *Whole Art*, Bk. III, p. 50; Stuart, *DDA*, pp. 404, 378, 377, 399.

114. Jean Chapelain, *Les Sentimens* . . . (1637) in Clark, *European Theories*, p. 126; cited by Stuart, *DDA*, p. 378; Chapelain, *Sommaire d'une Poétique dramatique* in Clark, p. 127; Stuart, p. 379; Clark, p. 127.

115. D'Aubignac, *Whole Art*, Bk. II, pp. 81, 115; III, p. 60; I, p. 53; III, pp. 12, 22, 37.

116. *Ibid.*, Bk. I, p. 30; III, p. 39; I, p. 30; III, pp. 57, 59; II, p. 23; III, p. 29.

117. *Ibid.*, Bk. III, pp. 44, 6, 40, 42; Bk. II, p. 76.

118. Sypher, *Four Stages*, p. 181.

119. Corneille, *Examen de la Galerie du palais* quoted in Stuart, *DDA*, p. 322; Corneille, *Premier discours* . . . (1660) in Clark, *European Theories*, p. 139.

120. Racine, *Preface Bérénice* (1674) cited *ibid.*, p. 156; ERICH AUERBACH, *Mimesis* . . . (1946) (New York, 1957), pp. 343, 331, 340, 337.

121. UNA ELLIS-FERMOR, *The Frontiers of Drama* (London, 1945), p. 108; Boileau, *Art Poétique* (1674) in Clark, *European Theories*, p. 162; Fergusson, *Idea*, p. 53.

122. LOUIS JOUVET, "Molière," *Theatre Arts*, XXI (September 1937), 694, 696, 697.

123. Auerbach, *Mimesis*, pp. 318, 320, 317, 321.

124. Howell, *Logic*, p. 396; Sypher, *Four Stages*, pp. 261, 260; Nicoll, *WD*, p. 342; Sypher, p. 261.

125. Anthony Ashton (c. 1682–1749?), *A Brief Supplement to Colley Cibber* . . . cited in TOBY COLE AND HELEN KRICH CHINOY, *Actors on Acting* . . . (New York, 1949), p. 15; CHARLES WILLIAMS, *Rochester* (London, 1935), p. 117; Nicoll, *Rest.*, p. 27, fn. p. 63; pp. 65, 32.

126. Dryden, *EDP*, in MARK SCHORER, JOSEPHINE MILES, GORDON MCKENZIE (ed.), *Criticism* . . . (New York, 1948), p. 232; Cibber, *Apology*, pp. 94–95; Ashton in Cole and Chinoy, *AA*, p. 114; Cibber, p. 95; MONTAGUE SUMMERS, *The Playhouse of Pepys* (New York, 1935), p. 45; Cibber, p. 94; Chetwood, *History of the Stage* (1749) cited in ROBERT HITCHCOCK, *Historical View of the Irish Stage* . . . (Dublin, 1788), I, 34, and Russell, *Representative Actors*, p. 20; Dryden, *Macflecknoe* (1682) cited by Nicoll, *Rest.*, p. 313.

127. W. A. DARLINGTON, *The Actor and His Audience* (London, 1949), p. 36; Dryden, *EDP* (in *Criticism*), pp. 221, 247, 246; Dryden, *Defence of an Essay of Dramatic Poesy* (1668) ed. Ker, I, 113–114.

128. Congreve, *Concerning Humor in Comedy* (1696) in Clark, *European Theories*, pp. 214, 213–214; Dryden, *EDP* (in *Criticism*), p. 246.

129. Sprat, *The History of the Royal-Society of London, For the Improvement of Natural Knowledge* (1667), pp. 112, 328, cited in Howell, *Logic*, pp. 389–390; Glanvill, *An Essay concerning Preaching* (1678), pp. 23, 24–25, cited ibid., 394.

130. Dryden, *EDP* (in *Criticism*), p. 232; *Defence* in Clark, *European Theories*, pp. 198, 195, 201.

131. Dryden, *EDP* (in *Criticism*), p. 232; *Defence* in Clark, *European Theories*, p. 196; *EDP*, p. 226.

132. Dryden, *Defence*, in Clark, *European Theories*, pp. 194, 202.

133. Cibber, *Apology*, pp. 132, 182.

134. JOHN DORAN, *Annals of the English Stage* (London, 1887), p. 18; Davies quoted in Russell, *Representative Actors*, p. 32.

135. Cibber, *Apology*, pp. 127, 131.

136. Ashton in Cole and Chinoy, *AA*, p. 116.

✻ CHAPTER 7

1. ALFRED NORTH WHITEHEAD, *Science and the Modern World* (New York, 1939), p. 86; JOHN MASON BROWN, *The Art of Playgoing* (New York, 1936), p. 183; EARL R. WASSERMAN, "The Sympathetic Imagination in Eighteenth-Century Acting," *Journal English and Germanic Philology*, XLVI (July 1947), 272.

2. THOMAS WILKES, *A General View of the Stage* (London, 1759), p. 92; Wasserman, "Sympathetic Imagination," p. 272.

3. The Abbé de Bellegarde cited in E. B. O. BORGERHOFF, *The Evolution of Liberal Theory and Practice in the French Theatre 1680–1757* (Princeton, 1936), p. 93; FREDERICK HAWKINS, *The French Stage in the Eighteenth Century* (London, 1888), I, 13.

4. Borgerhoff, *Liberal Theory*, p. 2; KARL MANTZIUS, *A History of Theatrical Art*, V, *The Great Actors of the Eighteenth Century* trans. by Louise von Cossel (London, 1909), pp. 233–234; Devisé quoted in Hawkins, *French Stage*, I, 15.

5. Lee Strasberg, Int. to TOBY COLE (ed.), *Acting, a handbook of the Stanislavski Method* (New York, 1947), p. 12.

6. Borgerhoff, *Liberal Theory*, p. 12; La Motte, *Discours sur la poesie* (1707), cited ibid., p. 11.

7. Johnson quoted in JAMES J. LYNCH, *Box, Pit, and Gallery* (Berkeley, 1955), p. 345; ALLLARDYCE NICOLL, *World Drama* . . . (New York, 1949), p. 372; Lynch, p. 149; E. CURLL, *The Life of that Eminent Comedian Robert Wilks* (London, 1733), p. 8; see ALLARDYCE NICOLL, *A History of English Drama 1660–1900*, II, *Early Eighteenth Century Drama* 3rd ed. (Cambridge, 1952), p. 47.

8. Doran cited in W. CLARK RUSSELL, *Representative Actors* (London, c. 1872), p. 42; Davies, *Dramatic Miscellanies* quoted in COLLEY CIBBER, *An Apology* . . . ed.

Bellchambers, p. 470; Lewis Melville, *Stage Favorites of the Eighteenth Century* (London, 1929), p. 26.

9. POPE, *An Essay in Criticism* (1709).

10. [CHARLES GILDON] *The Life of Mr. Thomas Betterton* (London, 1710), pp. v, 1–3.

11. *Ibid.*, pp. 17, v, 3, 18.

12. *Ibid.*, pp. vi, ix; see WILBER SAMUEL HOWELL, "Sources of the Elocutionary Movement in England: 1700–1748," *Quarterly Journal Speech*, XLV (February 1959), 9–11.

13. Gildon, *Betterton*, pp. x, 12.

14. *Ibid.*, pp. 32, 34.

15. *Ibid.*, pp. 66, 88, 41.

16. *Ibid.*, pp. 41, 16, 139, 83, 55, 58, 54, 27.

17. *Ibid.*, pp. 97, 94 and 98, 137, 105, 113, 83, 27, 32, 28, 102, 93.

18. *Ibid.*, pp. 39, 70, 71, 68.

19. *Ibid.*, p. 86.

20. *Ibid.*, pp. 139, 62–63, 40.

21. *Ibid.*, pp. 92, 43, 75.

22. Hawkins, *French Stage*, I, 102; *Memoirs of Hyppolite Clairon . . .* (London, 1800), I, 52–53.

23. HENRY C. LANCASTER, *French Tragedy in the Time of Voltaire 1715–1774* (Baltimore, 1950), I, 6, 5.

24. *Ibid.*, p. 6.

25. *Ibid.*, pp. 8, 90, 89.

26. Georges Monval, *Lettres de Adrienne Lecouvreur*, quoted in Mantizius, V, 244–245.

27. Elena Riccoboni quoted *ibid.*, pp. 240–245, and in TOBY COLE AND HELEN KRICH CHINOY (ed.), *Actors on Acting . . .* (New York, 1949), pp. 159–160.

28. BENEDETTO CROCE, *Aesthetic* (1907) trans. by DOUGLAS AINSLIE (New York, 1909, rev. ed. 1953), p. 196; DU BOS, *Critical Reflections on Poetry, Painting and Music . . .* trans. by Thomas Nugent (London, 1748), I, 343, 342, 341.

29. See ERNEST CASSIER, *The Philosophy of Enlightenment* (1932) trans. by Fritz C. A. Koell and J. P. Pettegrove (1951) (New York, 1955), pp. 300–302; Du Bos, CRPPM, I, 337; cited in LORENZ KJERBÜHL-PETERSEN, *Psychology of Acting* (1925) trans. by Sarah T. Barrows (Boston, 1935), p. 159; Du Bos, I, 338, 339. See Borgerhoff, *Liberal Theory*, p. 39.

30. Cited by Croce, *Aesthetic*, pp. 196 and 445.

31. See JOHN LOFTIS, *Steele at Drury Lane* (Berkeley and Los Angeles, 1952), pp. 22, 66, 162; CHARLES H. GRAY, *Theatrical Criticism in London to 1795* (New York, 1931), p. 54.

32. JOHN GASSNER, *Masters of the Drama* (New York, 1940), p. 285; PHYLLIS HARTNOLL (ed.), *The Oxford Companion to the Theatre* (London, 1951), p. 202; ARTHUR C. SPRAGUE, "Did Betterton Chant?" *Theatre Notebook*, I (October 1946), 54–55; see Gray, *Criticism*, pp. 99–100; Pope and Victor cited in HENRY BARTON BAKER, *English Actors from Shakespeare to Macready* (New York, 1879), I, 104; see AARON HILL, *Works* (London, 1754), I, 292–296, or II, 140–144; STEELE, *Tatler* No. 182, and *Spectator* No. 546; Davies cited in Baker, I, 107.

33. Chetwood cited in Russell, *Representative Actors*, p. 53; see also Baker, *English Actors*, I, 115; WILLIAM COOKE, *Memoirs of Charles Macklin* (London, 1804), pp. 98–99, and JOHN GENEST, *Some Account of the English Stage, from the Restoration in 1660 to 1830* (London, 1832), IV, 311.

34. See PAUL SAWYER, "John Rich; a biographical sketch," *Theatre Annual*, XV (1957–58), 55–68; THOMAS DAVIES, *Memoirs of the Life of David Garrick* (London, 1808), I, 370; all figures are from EMMET L. AVERY, "The Finances of an Eighteenth-Century Theatre," *Theatre Annual* (1955), p. 52. See A. M. NAGLER, *Sources of Theatrical History* (New York, 1952), pp. 344–351.

35. Playwright Charles Johnson (1679–1748) in the preface to his *The Successful Pyrate* (D. L. 1712) cited by Nicoll, *Eighteenth Century*, p. 45; *ibid.*, p. 119; Loftis, *Steele*, pp. 193, 196, 197; Nicoll, pp. 192–193.

36. JAMES T. KIRKMAN, *Memoirs of the Life of Charles Macklin Esq. . . .* (London, 1799), I, 159; see Loftis, *Steele*, p. 108.

37. DAVID MAGARSHACK, *Stanislavsky, a life* (New York, 1951), p. 336.

38. "Riccoboni's Advice to Actors" trans. and epitomized by Pierre Ramés, *The Mask*, 3 (April 1911), 177, 179.

39. *Ibid.*, pp. 178, 179.

40. LEWIS [LUIGI] RICCOBONI, *An Historical and Critical Account of the Theatres in Europe . . .* [with] *An Essay on Acting, or, The Art of Speaking in Public . . .* (London, 1741), pp. 3, 4, 8, 9, 25–26, 26, 25.

41. *Ibid.*, pp. 19–20, 21–22, 21.

42. *Ibid.*, pp. 28–29, 29–30, 31, 30–31.

43. Nicoll, WD, p. 364.

44. See OSCAR J. CAMPBELL, *The Comedies of Holberg* (Cambridge, Mass., 1914), pp. 27–32, 38–41.

45. BETSY AIKIN-SNEATH, *Comedy in Germany in the First Half of the Eighteenth Century* (Oxford, 1936), pp. 14–15; Mantzius, V, 20; W. H. BRUFORD, *Theatre, Drama and Audience in Goethe's Germany* (London, 1950), pp. 35, 19–20; R. Lothar, *Das Wiener Burgtheater* (1899) cited *ibid.*, p. 28.

46. Mantzius, V, 37, 38, 41; Aikin-Sneath, *Comedy*, p. 17; Bruford, *Theatre*, p. 55.

47. *Ibid.*, pp. 15–16, 51; F. J. VON REDEN-ESBECK, *Caroline Neuber*, pp. 107ff., cited *ibid.*, p. 120.

48. Mantzius, V, 77, 78; Bruford, *Theatre*, p. 13, but Mantzius, V, 34, says that Frau Schröder was paid about double as much as Ekhof; Bruford, p. 12; see Aikin-Sneath, *Comedy*, pp. 71–72, and Bruford, pp. 89–90; *ibid.*, p. 93.

49. Mantzius, V, 80; *Oxford Companion*, p. 217.

50. Bruford, *Theatre*, p. 97; Aikin-Sneath, *Comedy*, pp. 32, 33, 31; Bruford, p. 68; Aikin-Sneath, p. 38.

51. DONALD CLIVE STUART, *The Development of Dramatic Art* (New York, 1928), p. 458.

52. See Lynch, *Box*, pp. 57–59, and MRS. CLEMENT PARSONS, *Garrick and His Circle* (London, 1906), p. 95; Nicoll, *Eighteenth Century*, p. 14; for a synopsis of *The London Merchant* see Stuart, DDA, pp. 432–435; see Gray, *Criticism*, p. 77.

53. HARRY WILLIAM PEDICORD, *The Theatrical Public in the Time of Garrick* (New York, 1954), p. 5; JOHN GALT, *The Lives of the Players* (London, 1831), I, 192; *The Life of Mr. James Quin . . .* (London, 1887), p. 28; "James Quin," by ROBERT W. LOWE, pp. 29–30, in BRANDER MATTHEWS AND LAURENCE HUTTON (ed.), *Actors and Actresses of Great Britain and the United States*, I, *Garrick and his Contemporaries* (New York, 1886).

54. *Memoirs of Richard Cumberland* (1806) cited in Lowe, "Quin," p. 36; Barry Cornwall, *Life of Kean* quoted *ibid.*; the *Museum*, XXV (February 28, 1747) cited in Gray, *Criticism*, p. 100; see Lynch, *Box*, pp. 160 and fn. p. 328; CHARLES CHURCHILL, *The Rosciad* (London, 1761), p. 47; Tobias Smollett, *Peregrine Pickle* (1751) cited by EDWARD A. PARRY, *Charles Macklin* (London, 1891), pp. 42–43, and by Nagler, *Sources*, pp. 356–357.

55. The *Prompter* No. 66 cited by Gray, *Criticism*, p. 91; DOROTHY SENIOR, *The Life and Times of Colley Cibber* (London, 1928), p. 56; see AUSTIN DOBSON, "Aaron Hill," pp. 229–262, in his *Rosalba's Journal and other papers* (London, 1915); Nicoll, *Eighteenth Century*, pp. 335–336, 438; LESLIE STEPHEN, article on Aaron Hill, DNB, and Thomas Lounsbury, *Shakespeare and Voltaire* (New York, 1902), p. 83, cited by HAROLD L. BRUCE, *Voltaire on the English Stage*, Uni. *California*

Pub. Modern Philology, 8 (June 20, 1918), 23, 5; Cibber, *Apology* ed. Bell-chambers, fn. pp. 379–380.

56. DOROTHY BREWSTER, *Aaron Hill* . . . (New York, 1913), p. 136; Hill, *Works* (1754), I, 214; the Prologue, III, 119–122; I, 194.

57. *Ibid.*, I, 217, 221, 219, 275–276.

58. *The Prompter*, Nos. 3, 51, 56, 62, 64, 66, 67, 79, 92, 95, 99, 100, 103, 104, 113, 117, 118, and 129; Gray, *Criticism*, pp. 104, 89; Hill, *Works*, I, 284, 285.

59. See LEO HUGHES, "The Actor's Epitome," *Review of English Studies*, XX (October 1944), 306–307; Hill, *Works*, IV, 76–80.

60. Cooke, *Macklin*, pp. 98–99.

61. Parsons, *Garrick*, p. 45; Cibber, *Apology* ed. Bellchambers, p. 189; Boswell, *Johnson*, IV, 243; W. A. DARLINGTON, *The Actor and His Audience* (London, 1949), p. 41; Cibber, p. 62; BENJAMIN VICTOR, *History of the Theatre* (London, 1761), II, 164.

62. See Parry, *Macklin*, p. 21; Kirkman, *Macklin*, I, 364–365. See also Cole and Chinoy, *AA*, p. 122.

63. Parry, *Macklin*, p. 63; FRANCIS A. CONGREVE, *Authentic Memoirs of the late Mr. Charles Macklin, Comedian* (London, 1798), p. 12, quoted in the *Connoisseur*, and cited in WILLIAM ANGUS, "An Appraisal of David Garrick: Based Mainly Upon Contemporary Sources," *Quarterly Journal Speech*, XXV (February 1929), 34; see (George) *Lichtenberg's Visits to England as Described in His Letters and Diaries* trans. by Margaret L. Mare and W. H. Quarrell (Oxford, 1938), p. 40, cited in Baker, *English Actors*, I, 183–184, and in Nagler, *Sources*, p. 358; see Kirkman, *Macklin*, I, 253–265.

64. JOHN HILL, *The Actor* (1755), p. 239; (1750), pp. 194, 195.

65. See J. FITZGERALD MOLLOY, *Peg Woffington* (New York, 1897), I, 99–100; Davies quoted in Parsons, *Garrick*, p. 44; Davies, *Garrick*, I, 39–41, cited in Nagler, *Sources*, p. 362; the *Daily Post* (October 22, 1741) cited in Parsons, p. 42; Gray quoted *ibid.*, p. 57; see FRANK A. HEDGCOCK, *A Cosmopolitan Actor: David Garrick and his French Friends* (London, 1911), p. 38.

66. JAMES BOADEN, *The Private Correspondence of David Garrick* (London, 1831–32), I, 7; ARTHUR MURPHY, *The Life of David Garrick* (London, 1801), II, 174, 176–177; the *Champion* quoted in Angus, "Appraisal," p. 41.

67. Kirkman, *Macklin*, I, 248.

68. Davies, *Garrick*, I, 154; Russell, *Representative Actors*, p. 119; Boswell, *Johnson*, IV, 243, and see III, 184; Hannah Moore quoted in Baker, *English Actors*, I, 145; Murphy, *Garrick*, I, 28–30.

69. Melville, *Stage Favorites*, p. 65; Lowe in Matthews-Hutton, I, *Garrick*, p. 30.

70. Pedicord, *Theatrical Public*, pp. 13–14; *Memoirs of Richard Cumberland* (1806), p. 41; see Russell, *Representative Actors*, p. 99; Johnson cited in Melville, *Stage Favorites*, p. 71; 64; Doran quoted in *Oxford Companion*, pp. 633–634; Johnson quoted in Russell, p. 105; *ibid.*, pp. 200, 121; Parsons, *Garrick*, pp. 120–121; Pedicord, pp. 16, 17.

71. ALAN S. DOWNER, "Nature to Advantage Dressed: Eighteenth Century Acting," *Pub. Modern Language Ass.*, LVIII (December 1943), 1023; Cibber, *Apology*, fn. p. 14; LILY B. CAMPBELL, "The Rise of a Theory of Stage Presentation During the Eighteenth Century," *Pub. Modern Language Ass.*, XXXII (n.s. XXV) (June 1917), 170; see Wasserman, "Sympathetic Imagination," p. 204.

72. Hill, *Works*, II, 233–234; the poem "The Art of Acting," in III, 387–408; see Hughes, "Epitome," pp. 306–307; Hill, III, 395; II, 278; see II, 211; IV, 396; II, 351; IV, 339.

73. *Ibid.*, I, 293–296 or II, 140–144; II, 262; Hill in his advertisement to *Merope* (1749) quoted in Bruce, *Voltaire*, p. 50; *ibid.*, pp. 40–41, 56.

74. See, for example, *The Actor, or, guide to the stage, exemplifying the whole art of acting in which the dramatic passions are defined, analyzed, and made easy of acquirement, the whole interspersed with select and striking examples from the most popular pieces* (London, 1821), 29 pp., and the *Art of Acting; or, Guide to the stage in which the dramatic passions are defined, analyzed, and made easy of acquirement* (New York, 1855), 24 pp.

75. Le Motte, *Oeuvres*, IV, 277–308, 48–68, mentioned in Borgerhoff, *Liberal Theory*, pp. 42, 77–78; *ibid.*, pp. 49–50; Lancaster, *Voltaire*, I, 129; JAMES LOUGH, *Paris Theatre Audiences* (London, 1957), p. 178; see Lancaster, I, 147.

76. Stuart, *DDA*, p. 427; quoted by Borgerhoff, *Liberal Theory*, p. 20; Laurroument cited *ibid.*, p. 21; Nicoll, *WD*, p. 403.

77. *Silvie* (1742), p. 7, quoted by Borgerhoff, *Liberal Theory*, p. 26; Stuart, *DDA*, pp. 436, 437, which also furnishes a synopsis of the play.

78. Cited by Croce, *Aesthetic*, pp. 257–258.

79. Hawkins, *French Stage*, I, 310; Diderot cited by Lancaster, *Voltaire*, I, 17; Collé and Bachaumount cited *ibid.*, p. 19.

80. WILLIAM ARCHER, *Masks or Faces?* (London, 1888), p. 12, or (New York, 1957), p. 82; Wasserman, "Sympathetic Imagination," p. 267; Strasberg, Int. to Cole, *Acting*, p. 14; MARIE-FRANÇOISE DUMESNIL, *Mémoires* . . . (Paris, 1799), pp. 8–9. Consult also Borgerhoff, *Liberal Theory*, pp. 56–58, and Kjerbühl-Petersen, *Psychology Acting*, pp. 159–163.

81. P. R. DE SAINTE-ALBINE, p. 23, and Hill, p. 3; S-A, p. 26, and H, p. 7; H, p. 10; Quintilian, for instance, *I.O.*, III, iii, 4–6; S-A, p. 23, and Hill, p. 5; H. Caudwell, *The Creative Impulse* (London, 1951), p. 99; see *ibid.*, pp. 108, 55; S-A, p. 23, and Hill, p. 5.

82. Hill, p. 14; Sainte-Albine, p. 48, and H, p. 41; S-A, p. 91, and H, p. 106; see Cole and Chinoy, *AA*, p. 32; S-A, pp. 91–92, and H, pp. 106–107; see S-A, p. 33, and H, p. 16; S-A, pp. 37–38, and H, p. 24; S-A, p. 32, and H, p. 16.

83. Hill, p. 43.

84. Sainte-Albine, p. 44, and Hill, p. 36; see, for instance, Cicero, *de Oratore*, I, xlv, 188, 190; I, xlvi, 193, 194, etc.; Quintilian, *I.O.*, XI, iii, 2, 3; Chappuzeau, *Théâtre français*, cited in Nagler, *Sources*, pp. 61–62; Brumoy, *Le Théâtre des Grecs*, mentioned in Borgerhoff, *Liberal Theory*, p. 17; S-A, p. 47, and H, p. 40; S-A, p. 44, and H, p. 36.

85. Sainte-Albine, pp. 54–55, and Hill, p. 57; S-A, p. 60, and H, p. 61; H, pp. 75–76.

86. S-A, p. 71, and H, p. 32.

87. S-A, p. 108, and H, p. 125.

88. S-A, p. 112, and H, pp. 129, 128.

89. S-A, p. 132, and H, p. 153; S-A, p. 134, and H, p. 155.

90. S-A, p. 135, and H, p. 156; S-A, p. 136, and H, p. 156.

91. S-A, p. 137, and H, p. 157.

92. S-A, p. 139, and H, p. 158; S-A, p. 142, and H, p. 161; S-A, p. 143, and H, p. 161.

93. S-A, pp. 147–148, and H, p. 165; S-A, pp. 155–156, and H, pp. 178–179.

94. S-A, p. 158, and H, p. 181; S-A, p. 159, and H, p. 182; S-A, p. 162, and H, p. 184; S-A, p. 160, and H, p. 183.

95. S-A, pp. 164–165, and H, p. 187; S-A, p. 166, and H, p. 188; H, p. 18.

96. S-A, p. 167, and H, p. 193; S-A, p. 168, and H, p. 195.

97. S-A, pp. 170–171, and H, p. 197; S-A, p. 174, and H, p. 210; S-A, p. 173, and H, p. 208; S-A, p. 175, and H, p. 211; H, pp. 211–212; S-A, p. 215, and H, p. 184.

98. *Ibid.*, p. 214; S-A, p. 183, and H, p. 214; S-A, p. 183, and H, p. 215.

99. S-A, fn. p. 167.

100. *Ibid.*, p. 216, and H, p. 236; S-A, p. 226, and H, p. 245; S-A, p. 255, and H, p. 259; S-A, pp. 248–249, and H, p. 259; S-A, p. 256, and H, p. 265; S-A, p. 260.

101. Ibid., p. 229, and H, p. 247; S-A, pp. 230–231, and H, p. 248; S-A, p. 246, and H, p. 247.

102. S-A, p. 280, and H, p. 279.

103. Ibid., pp. 298–299; see S-A, p. 293.

104. See ibid., pp. 263–264, and H, p. 271, then H, p. 291.

105. S-A, p. 294, and H, pp. 299–300; S-A, p. 288, and H, p. 287.

106. S-A, p. 295, and H, p. 300; S-A, p. 299, and H, p. 303; S-A, p. 305, and H, pp. 306–307.

107. Magarshack, Life, pp. 332, 335–337.

108. Ibid., p. 337; Grimm cited in DIDEROT, The Paradox of Acting (1773–78) trans. by Walter Herries Pollock (London, 1883), fn. p. 83; FRANCESCO RICCOBONI, Die Schauspielkunst trans. by Gotthold Lessing (1750) ed. by Gerhard Piens (Berlin, 1954), pp. 7, 54–55.

109. Borgerhoff, Liberal Theory, pp. 64, 108, 65; see in Piens, Schauspielkunst, Schröder's "Extracts from L'Art du Théâtre, with Additional Remarks" (1810), pp. 111–147.

110. Piens, Schauspielkunst, pp. 14, 17, 18, or F. Riccobini, L'Art (Lessing), p. 110.

111. Ibid., pp. 70, 76, 76–77.

112. See Borgerhoff, Liberal Theory, p. 65; see Riccoboni, L'Art, pp. 70–73, 100–104.

113. Ibid., pp. 76, 100, 101; see Borgerhoff, Liberal Theory, p. 28.

114. Riccoboni, L'Art, p. 76. See the same quotation credited to Beck in the Mannerheim Protokolle and cited by Kjerbühl-Petersen, Psychology Acting, p. 117.

115. Riccoboni, L'Art, pp. 73, 73–74, 74–75; see also Borgerhoff, Liberal Theory, p. 65, and Kjerbühl-Petersen, Psychology Acting, p. 164.

116. Riccoboni, L'Art, fn. p. 75.

117. Ibid., p. 76; see Kjerbühl-Petersen, Psychology Acting, pp. 164–165.

118. Some Remarks on the Life and Writings of Dr. J—— H——, Inspector-General of Great Britain . . . (London, 1752), p. 13; LORANDE LOSS WOODRUFF, "The Versatile Sir John Hill, M.D.," American Naturalist (Lancaster, Penn., 1926), p. 439; D'Israeli, Curiosities, I, 201, cited in Boswell, Johnson, II, fn. 39; Some Remarks . . . , p. 16; see Woodruff, pp. 417–442; A Letter from Henry Woodward . . . (London, 1752), p. 7; Parsons, Garrick, p. 179; JOHN PIKE EMERY, Arthur Murphy . . . (Philadelphia, 1946), p. 13; Fielding quoted in Woodruff; Boswell, II, 39.

119. Parry, Macklin, p. 79; Gray, Criticism, p. 112.

120. Hill, The Actor (1750), "Dedication," pp. 1, 4.

121. Archer, Masks, pp. 17, 16–17.

122. Hill, The Actor (1755), p. 1.

123. Ibid., pp. 6, 12, 7, 17.

124. Ibid., pp. 13, 14, 7.

125. Ibid., pp. 20, 22, 41.

126. Ibid., pp. 32–33, 34, 35, 34.

127. Ibid., p. 21.

128. Ibid., pp. 49, 51–52, 52, 58.

129. Ibid., pp. 54, 55; see also p. 56.

130. Ibid., pp. 61, 93, 99.

131. Ibid., pp. 93–94, 78, 95, 102, 98, 95, 102.

132. Ibid., pp. 79, 87, 103, 90.

133. Ibid., pp. 108, 119.

134. Ibid., p. 110.

135. Ibid., pp. 221, 196, 177–178.

136. Ibid., pp. 239, 212, 231, 227–228.

137. Ibid., pp. 160–161.

138. *Ibid.*, pp. 252, 249, 252, 260, 278.

139. *Ibid.*, pp. 174, 176.

140. JAMES BOADEN, *Private Correspondence of David Garrick* (London, 1831–32), I, 617, cited in Hedgcock, *Cosmopolitan Actor*, p. 258; Grimm, *Correspondence* (1765) cited *ibid.*, p. 234; see Parsons, *Garrick*, p. 131.

141. *Ibid.*; JOHN TAYLOR, *Records of My Life* (London, 1832), I, 350, quoted in MATTHEWS-HUTTON, I, *Garrick*, p. 75; Jean Georges Navarre (1727–1810) quoted in DERYCK LYNHAN, *The Chevalier Navarre, father of modern ballet* (London, 1950), p. 141; *Lichtenberg Visits* cited in Nagler, *Sources*, p. 365; Kirkman, *Macklin*, II, 260; *Theophilus Cibber to David Garrick, Esq.* . . . (1759) cited in Hedgcock, *Cosmopolitan Actor*, p. 55; Lichtenberg quoted *ibid.*, p. 55; ROSAMOND GILDER, *John Gielgud's Hamlet* . . . (New York, 1937), pp. 107–108.

142. Grimm quoted in Hedgcock, *Cosmopolitan Actor*, pp. 233–234; Kirkman, *Macklin*, II, 268, 269.

143. See Diderot, *Salon de 1767, Oeuvres* ed. Assezat and Tourneaux, XI, cited in Hedgcock, *Cosmopolitan Actor*, fn. p. 56.

144. See Parsons, *Garrick*, p. 84; HENRY ANGELO, *Pic-nic* (1834) cited in Hedgcock, *Cosmopolitan Actor*, pp. 52–53.

145. *Garrick's Correspondence*, I, 359, quoted in Archer, *Masks*, p. 180.

146. Parsons, *Garrick*, pp. 85, 405. See also FREDERICK W. HILLES (ed.), *Portraits by Sir Joshua Reynolds* (New York, 1952), p. 97.

147. THEOPHILUS CIBBER (1703–1753), *The Lives and Characters of the Most Eminent Actors* . . . (1753), p. viii. See Gray, *Criticism*, p. 154.

148. T. Cibber, *Lives*, p. ix; RENÉ WELLEK, *A History of Modern Criticism 1750–1950*, I, *The Later Eighteenth Century* (New York, 1955), 118, 115, 79.

149. See Gray, *Criticism*, pp. 182, 173.

150. PAUL HIFFERNAN, *Dramatic Genius* (London, 1770), p. 71; JAMES BOSWELL, *On the Profession of a Player* (1770) (London, 1929), p. 26; Lloyd, *Actor*, pp. 1, 3, 4; Churchill, *Rosciad* in *Poems* 3rd ed. (London, 1766), I, 50, 17, 31.

151. Boswell, *Profession*, pp. 3, 33, 14, 16, 18.

152. Burgh, p. 6; see W. M. PARRISH, "The Burglarizing of Burgh . . . ," *Quarterly Journal Speech*, XXVIII (December 1952), 431–434; Sheridan, *Lectures*, pp. 121, 4–5; CHARLES A. FRITZ, "From Sheridan to Rush: the beginnings of English Elocution," *Quarterly Journal Speech*, XVI (February 1930), 76.

153. See DONALD J. RULFS, "Entre'acte Entertainment at Drury Lane and Covent Garden, 1750–1770," *Theatre Annual*, XII (1954), 17–27; CHARLES B. HOGAN, "An Eighteenth-Century Prompter's Notes," *Theatre Annual*, X (January–March 1952), 44; Lynch, *Box*, p. 157; also pp. 146–148.

154. *Ibid.*, pp. 142, 143; Rulfs, "Entre'acte," p. 27.

155. Hogan, "Prompter's Notes," p. 43; Lynch, *Box*, pp. 17 and 19.

156. Hogan, "Prompter's Notes," p. 42.

157. Postboy quoted in ARTHUR HORNBLOW, *A History of the Theatre in America* (Philadelphia, 1919), I, 64; see BARNARD HEWITT, *Theatre USA* (New York, 1959), pp. 8–9.

158. Bruford, *Theatre*, p. 99; Sainte-Albine trans. in *Theatralische Bibliothek*, 1, 209–226; Lessing's *Werke*, XI, 301–331; Wilhelmina Delp, p. 479, in *Oxford Companion*, p. 459; Bruford, pp. 100–101.

159. Bruford, *Theatre*, pp. 94, 95; Mantzius, V, 83, 84.

160. Bruford, *Theatre*, p. 96; *Oxford Companion*, p. 94; Mantzius, V, 135–136; Bruford, pp. 97–98; for Döbbelin see Mantzius, V, 136–139.

161. Schröder quoted *ibid.*, V, 88; Lessing's *Werke*, IX, 252, and VI, 152, cited by OTTO

G. GROF, "Lessing and the Art of Acting," *Michigan Academy Science, Arts Letters*, XI (1955), 295, 298.

162. Quotations cited by Kjerbühl-Petersen, *Psychology Acting*, pp. 192–193.

163. See Mantzius, V, 104–108, 100.

164. See J. G. Robertson, *Lessing's Dramatic Theory* . . . (Cambridge, 1939), p. 26.

165. Bruford, *Theatre*, pp. 171–172.

166. *Ibid.*, pp. 174–175.

167. B. V. VARNEKE, *History of the Russian Theatre* (1939) trans. by Boris Brasol, ed. by Belle Martin (New York, 1951), pp. 68–71.

168. *Ibid.*, p. 71.

169. *Ibid.*, pp. 83, 77.

170. Hedgcock, *Cosmopolitan Actor*, p. 214; see ARTHUR M. WILSON, *Diderot: The Testing Years, 1713–1759* (New York, 1957).

171. Lough, PTA, p. 174; Lancaster, *Voltaire*, II, 368; Hawkins, *French Stage*, II, 57–58, 91.

172. See Lancaster, *Voltaire*, II, 410, and Lough, PTA, p. 180; Lancaster, *Voltaire*, I, 417–418; Hawkins, *French Stage*, II, 88.

173. For "Clearing the Stage of Spectators," see Voltaire, *Works*, XIII, 28–29, cited in Nagler, *Sources*, pp. 324–325; Stuart, DDA, p. 445; Lough, PTA, pp. 188, 264–265; Lancaster, *Voltaire*, II, 578, 581.

174. Goldoni, *Memoirs* (Black), p. 367; Dorat, *Art de la déclamation* quoted by Hedgcock, *Cosmopolitan Actor*, p. 158; PERCY FITZGERALD, *Life of David Garrick* (London, 1899), p. 284.

175. Lancaster, *Voltaire*, I, 3, 21; Huchon, *Mrs. Montagu* quoted in Hedgcock, *Cosmopolitan Actor*, p. 258; Boaden, *Private Correspondence*, I, 617, cited *ibid.*, pp. 257–258.

176. See *ibid.*, pp. 266–267.

177. Mercier cited by Lough, PTA, p. 170.

178. Maillet-Duclairon, *Essai*, pp. 42–43, 50–54, 55, quoted by Borgerhoff, *Liberal Theory*, pp. 63, 28, 63.

179. Marmontel, *Mémoires* (London, 1805) II, 43–49, quoted by Nagler, *Sources*, pp. 294–296; Parsons, *Garrick*, p. 310.

180. Archer, *Masks*, pp. 17–18.

181. Diderot, *Paradox* (Pollock), p. 83; LEE STRASBERG, Int. to (Diderot) *The Paradox of Acting* and (Archer) *Masks or Faces?* (New York, 1957), p. x.

182. *Les Bijoux indiscrets* (1748) in F. C. GREEN (ed.), *Diderot's Writings on the Theatre* (Cambridge, 1936), p. 224; "Lettre de Madame Riccoboni" (1758) in Green, p. 213. For the "Entretiens," see Green, pp. 17–109; for the "Poesie," pp. 111–210. A large portion of the letter is translated in BARRETT H. CLARK (ed.), *European Theories of the Drama* (Cincinnati, 1918), pp. 286–299.

183. Diderot, *Paradox*, pp. 65, 66, 61; cited by Strasberg, Int. p. x; *Paradox*, pp. 101, 103.

184. Diderot cited by Stuart, DDA, p. 440; "De la Poesie," in Clark, *European Theories*, pp. 298, 299; see Stuart, pp. 435–441.

185. "Genie" by Diderot in the *Encyclopédie* cited by Strasberg, Int. pp. x–xl; "Entretiens" in Green, *Diderot's Writings*, p. 43.

186. "Extracts from Diderot's Letters to the Young Actress Mlle. Jodin," *ibid.*, pp. 245–246. For a guess at Garrick's influence, see Hedgcock, *Cosmopolitan Actor*, pp. 228–229, 306.

187. Diderot, *Réfutation d'Helvétius*, II, 330–331, quoted in JAMES DOOLITTLE, "Criticism as Creation in the Work of Diderot," *Yale French Studies*, 2 (Spring–Summer 1949), 17; 16, 15.

188. Diderot, *Paradox*, p. 4.

189. *Ibid.*, 8; see Grimm's *Correspondence* (1812–14) ed. Tourneux, IX, 33, 149, or Green, *Diderot's Writings*, pp. 227–242; Hedgcock, *Cosmopolitan Actor*, pp. 336–337; Archer, *Masks*, p. 19; Hedgcock, p. 337.

190. Diderot, *Paradox*, pp. 17; 5 and 7, 16, 23.

191. Riccoboni, *Die SchauspielKunst*, pp. 73–74, and see Kjerbühl-Petersen, *Psychology Acting*, p. 164; Gildon, *Betterton*, p. 86; Hill, *The Actor* (1755), pp. 54, 55, 6; Sticotti, *Garrick*, p. 68 from Hill, p. 54, and p. 96 from Hill, p. 90; Boswell, *Profession*, p. 18.

192. *Paradox*, p. 56; Sainte-Albine, p. 32; Hill (1750), p. 15; Sticotti, *Garrick*, p. 65 from Hill, p. 51.

193. *Paradox* (Pollock, London ed.), pp. 14, 7, 43–44.

194. *Ibid.*, pp. 12–13.

195. *Ibid.*, p. 46.

196. *Ibid.*, pp. 16, 95.

197. *Ibid.*, pp. 100–101; 95–96, 16.

198. *Ibid.*, p. 11.

199. *Ibid.*, pp. 8, 9.

200. *Ibid.*, p. 108.

201. *Ibid.*, pp. 25, 22, 20, 22, 19, 74, 5, 102, 5.

202. *Ibid.*, p. 80.

203. *Ibid.*, pp. 17, 49, 92, 10, 60.

204. Archer, *Masks*, p. 180.

205. Strasberg, Int. p. xii.

206. CONSTANTIN STANISLAVSKI, *Building a Character* trans. by Elizabeth Reynolds Hapgood (New York, 1949), pp. 70, 19.

207. Varneke, *Russian Theatre*, pp. 78–81.

208. *Ibid.*, pp. 88, 90, 94, 92, 161–162.

209. Bruford, *Theatre*, p. 252; F. L. W. MEYER, *Friedrich Ludwig Schröder* (Hamburg, 1819), p. 337, cited in Mantzius, V, 163, and in Cole and Chinoy, AA, p. 257.

210. Bruford, *Theatre*, pp. 172, 255; Kjerbühl-Petersen, *Psychology Acting*, pp. 185–186; Bruford, p. 258; Kjerbühl-Petersen, p. 185; see also Mantzius, V, 207.

211. Kjerbühl-Petersen, *Psychology Acting*, p. 167.

212. Bruford, *Theatre*, p. 251.

213. Meyer, *Schröder*, II, 193, quoted by Kjerbühl-Petersen, *Psychology Acting*, p. 195; *ibid.*, p. 196; Jens Baggesen, *Labrinthen*, I, 171ff., quoted in Mantzius, V, 180–181.

214. *Ibid.*, p. 180; Devrient cited in Bruford, *Theatre*, p. 254.

215. See *ibid.*, p. 165; THEODORE KOMISARJEVSKY, *The Theatre* . . . (London, 1935), p. 67; Mantzius, V, 215.

216. Siddons, *Rhetorical Gesture*, pp. 15, 54.

217. *Ibid.*, pp. 15, 27, 21, 194.

218. *Ibid.*, pp. 120, 16, 98; see "Lettre," I, 123–124.

219. MANTZIUS, VI, *Classicism and Romanticism* trans. by C. Archer (London, 1921), 240.

220. Bruford, *Theatre*, p. 296; Mantzius, VI, 239, 240.

221. Quoted from Eduard Devrient, III, 254, in Kjerbühl-Petersen, *Psychology Acting*, p. 184; Bruford, *Theatre*, pp. 301–302.

222. *Ibid.*, pp. 302–303, 305, 304–305; Welleck, *Criticism*, p. 150.

223. Devrient quoted in Bruford, *Theatre*, p. 310.

224. Hawkins, *French Stage*, II, 217; Beaumarchais, *Lettre Modérée* . . . quoted in Clark, *European Theories*, p. 308.

225. STARK YOUNG, *The Flower in Drama* (New York, 1923), p. 31; STARK YOUNG, *Glamour* . . . (New York, 1925), p. 37.

226. Mantzius, VI, 102; Nicoll, WD, p. 436.

227. Hawkins, *French Stage*, II, 210; Samson, *Mémoires* cited in Mantzius, VI, 126, 104.

228. *Ibid.*, pp. 98–99.

229. *Ibid.*, pp. 104–105, 105–106.

230. Hawkins, *French Stage*, II, 353.

231. *Ibid.*, p. 355; Mantzius, VI, fn. p. 140; Hawkins, *French Stage*, II, 364.

232. CLAIRON, *Memoirs* trans. into English (London, 1800), I, 42, 148, 35, 41–42; Dumesnil, *Mémoires*, p. 19; Clairon, I, 47, 46; Dumesnil, p. 23. See Cole and Chinoy, AA, pp. 170–176, and pp. 176–177.

233. Woodfall cited in YVONNE FRENCH, *Mrs. Siddons* (1936) rev. ed. (London, 1954), p. 28.

234. *Ibid.*, pp. 45, 46.

235. *Ibid.*, p. 58; Davies, *Dramatic Miscellanies* cited in LEWIS MELVILLE, *More Stage Favorites of the Eighteenth Century* (London, 1929), p. 95; Thomas Holcroft in the *English Review* (1783) reprinted in JAMES AGATE (ed.), *The English Dramatic Critics* (1932) (New York, 1958), pp. 65–66, 63–64; French, *Siddons*, pp. 66, 76; WILLIAM HAZLITT, "Mrs. Siddons" (1816), p. 272, in *Criticisms and Dramatic Essays of the English Stage* (1851) (1854).

236. Melville, *MSF*, p. 125; see Macready quoted in BRANDER MATTHEWS AND LAURENCE HUTTON (ed.), *Actors and Actresses*, II, *The Kembles* (New York, 1886), p. 43; see H. C. FLEEMING JENKIN, *Mrs. Siddons as Lady Macbeth* (1878) and *as Queen Katharine* (1882) reprinted as *Papers on Acting III*, Dramatic Museum Columbia University (New York, 1915), pp. 25–68. For Mrs. Siddons's own analysis of the character see THOMAS CAMPBELL, *Life of Mrs. Siddons* (London, 1834), pp. 10ff. But of her representation "the essay . . . gives not the faintest idea," Jenkin, p. 11; see also p. 37.

237. See French, *Siddons*, pp. 251–253, and Hazlitt, *Criticisms*, p. 272; FANNY KEMBLE, *On the Stage* (1863) reprinted as *Papers on Acting III*, Dramatic Museum Columbia University (New York, 1926), p. 13; JOHN MASON BROWN, "Sarah Siddons to Katharine Cornell," in *Letters from Greenroom Ghosts* (New York, 1924), p. 20.

238. From "The Devil's Pocket-Book" (1786) in Agate, *Critics*, p. 80; Melville, *MSF*, p. 96; Walpole cited *ibid.*, p. 93; Campbell cited in Russell, *Representative Actors*, p 22; Hazlitt in the *Examiner* (1814) cited by ERNEST BRADLEE WATSON, *Sheridan to Robertson* . . . (Cambridge, Mass., 1926), p. 288; ARTHUR COLBY SPRAGUE, *Shakespearian Players and Performers* (Cambridge, Mass., 1953), p. 68; Lord Erskine cited in Russell, p. 228; Leigh Hunt, *Autobiography*, I, Ch. 6, cited in Matthews-Hutton, II, *The Kembles*, p. 51.

239. JOHN MASON, *An Essay on Elocution* . . . (London, 1748) cited by W. M. PARRISH, "Elocution—A Definition and a Challenge," *Quarterly Journal Speech*, XLIII (February 1957), 2; French cited by Sprague, *SPP*, p. 68; Holcroft quoted by Agate, *Critics*, pp. 64–65; Parrish, "Elocution," p. 3.

240. Holcroft quoted by Agate, *Critics*, p. 68; LEIGH HUNT, *Critical Essays* . . . (London, 1807), p. 20.

241. *Leigh Hunt's Dramatic Criticism 1803–1831* ed. by L. H. and C. W. Houtchens (New York, 1949), pp. 301, 103, 104, 103; Matthews-Hutton, II, *The Kembles*, p. 93; Hunt, *Autobiography* cited *ibid.*, p. 79; Hazlitt, *Criticisms*, p. 280.

242. Mantzius, VI, 31; Sprague, *SPP*, pp. 186, 44; Hazlitt, *Criticisms*, p. 295; Hunt, *Essays*, p. 12.

243. Hazlitt, *Criticisms*, pp. 280, 285, 286, 282; see JAMES BOADEN, *Memoirs of the Life of John Philip Kemble* (London, 1825), I, 175ff; Hazlitt, p. 285; *The Thespiad* (London, 1809) quoted in Matthews-Hutton, II, *The Kembles*, p. 83.

244. See a critic, possibly George Steevens, in the *London Chronicle* (1783) cited in Gray, *Criticism*, p. 261; *The Devil* (1786) quoted *ibid.*, p. 301; see William Woodfall

in the *Morning Chronicle* mentioned in Gray, pp. 272, 276–277; Sprague, *APP*, p. 41; Hunt, *Essays*, p. 15.

245. *The Devil* quoted in Gray, *Criticism*, p. 301.

246. REYNOLDS, *The Discourses* (Oxford, 1907), III (1770), pp. 23–24; X (1780), p. 149; VIII (1778), p. 136; XIII (1786), pp. 202, 206, 210, 204, and see 205ff.

247. MORGANN, *Essay . . . Falstaff*, in *Shakespeare Criticism* (1916) ed. by D. Nichol Smith (Oxford, 1941), fn. p. 193; fn. p. 184, 197.

248. Whately quoted *ibid.*, p. 151; WILLIAM RICHARDSON. *Philosophical Analysis . . .* (London, 1779), I, 117; Morgann, *Essay*, in Smith, p. 185.

249. Hogan, "Prompter's Notes," p. 39; George Frederick Cooke in the *N. Y. Mirror* (1833) cited in Matthews-Hutton, II, *The Kembles*, p. 87.

250. French, *Siddons*, pp. 142–143; Galt, *Players*, II, 264.

251. See Pedicord, *Theatrical Public*, pp. 6, 4.

252. The *Commercial Advertiser* (1799) cited in Nagler, *Sources*, p. 535; see LAEL J. WOODBURY, "The American Theatre's First Star: Thomas Abthorpe Cooper," *Theatre Annual*, XV (1957–58), 7–14.

❊ CHAPTER 8

1. JACQUES BARZUN, *Romanticism and the Modern Ego* (New York, 1943), p. 132.

2. See *ibid.*, pp. 137–138.

3. M. H. ABRAMS, *The Mirror and the Lamp, romantic theory and the critical tradition* (New York, 1953), p. 22; Schleiermacher quoted in BENEDETTO CROCE, *Aesthetic* (1907) trans. by Douglas Ainslie (New York, 1909, rev. ed. 1953), p. 317; Goethe quoted in RENÉ WELLEK, *A History of Modern Criticism: 1750–1950, The Later Eighteenth Century* (New Haven, 1955), p. 207.

4. B. V. VARNEKE, *History of the Russian Theatre* (1939) trans. by Boris Brasol, ed. by Belle Martin (New York, 1951), p. 170.

5. *Ibid.*, pp. 164, 161, 162, 165–166; Belinsky cited *ibid.*, p. 175; 176; Kalikov quoted *ibid.*, p. 296.

6. *Ibid.*, p. 248; Hertzen cited *ibid.*, p. 251; 249; Belinsky quoted *ibid.*, pp. 251–252.

7. *Ibid.*, Shakovskoy quoted p. 259; 258, 260, 262–263; Belinsky quoted p. 257.

8. *Ibid.*; Kryukov cited *ibid.*, p. 260.

9. CONSTANTIN STANISLAVSKY, *My Life in Art* (1924) trans. by J. J. Robbins (Boston, 1927), p. 10; Hertzen quoted in Varneke, *Russian Theatre*, p. 290; Stanislavsky, p. 80.

10. Varneke, *Russian Theatre*, p. 280; Shchepkin quoted *ibid.*, pp. 290, 291; DAVID MAGARSHACK, *Stanislavsky, a Life* (New York, 1951), p. 141.

11. Varneke, *Russian Theatre*, p. 215.

12. KARL MANTZIUS, *A History of Theatrical Art*, VI, *Classicism and Romanticism* trans. by C. Archer (London, 1921), 264, 266; see Wellek, *Criticism*, pp. 208–212.

13. *Ibid.*, p. 249; W. H. BRUFORD, *Theatre, Drama and Audience in Goethe's Germany* (London, 1950), p. 270; Wellek, *Criticism*, pp. 249–250.

14. See Bruford, *Theatre*, p. 309; Mantizius, VI, 247.

15. "Goethe's Rules for Actors: a Translation with an Introduction," by ARTHUR WOEHL, *Quarterly Journal Speech*, XIII (June 1927), 243–264; partly reprinted in TOBY COLE AND HELEN KRICH CHINOY (ed.), *Actors on Acting . . .* (New York, 1949), pp. 248–256.

16. Bruford, *Theatre*, p. 304; Wolff quoted by J. WAHLE, *Das Weimarer Hoftheater unter Goethes Leitung*, p. 166, and J. PETERSEN, *Das deutsch Nationaltheater*, p. 69, cited *ibid.*; F. L. W. Meyer quoted in Mantzius, VI, 268.

17. *Ibid.*, pp. 249, 268.

18. See Bruford pp. 252–253; A. W. Schlegel quoted *ibid.*, p. 334; and see Mantzius, VI, fn. 287.

19. *Ibid.*, p. 324.

20. *Ibid.*, pp. 312, 314–315.

21. *Ibid.*, pp. 318, 320, 322.

22. *Ibid.*, pp. 332–333.

23. PHYLLIS HARTNOLL (ed.), *The Oxford Companion to the Theatre* (London, 1951), p. 610.

24. Mantzius, VI, 214, 212.

25. GEORGE HENRY LEWES, *On Actors and the Art of Acting* (London, 1875), p. 74.

26. Mantzius, VI, 225; Lewes, *AAA*, p. 79.

27. See MATTHEW JOSEPHSON, *Stendhal* . . . (New York, 1946), pp. 292–294.

28. See Mantzius, VI, 163, and FRANCISQUE SARCEY, *A Company of Actors* (1879) reprinted as *Papers on Acting IV*, Dramatic Museum Columbia University (New York, 1926), pp. 44–45; Mantzius, VI, 179.

29. *Ibid.*, p. 183; Oehlenschläger quoted *ibid.*, p. 184; 184; Eduard Devrient cited p. 186; *Macready's Reminiscences* ed. Pollock (New York, 1875), p. 180; Jal cited in Mantzius, VI, 188; 188.

30. *Ibid.*, pp. 170, 165, 166; Geoffroy cited *ibid.*, pp. 167, 166; fn. p. 168.

31. See LORENZ KJERBÜHL-PETERSEN, *Psychology of Acting* (1925) trans. by Sarah T. Barrows (Boston, 1935), p. 189; *The Journal of Eugène Delacroix* (1822–1863) trans. by Walter Pach (New York, 1937), p. 268.

32. Irving, Introduction to *Reflexions on the Actor's Art* (1825) reprinted as *Papers on Acting IV*, Dramatic Museum Columbia University (New York, 1925), p. 1.

33. Talma, *Reflections*, pp. 15, 13, 25–26.

34. *Ibid.*, pp. 7, 24, 21.

35. *Ibid.*, pp. 19, 18, 49, 20–21.

36. *Ibid.*, pp. 19, 21, 51–52, 8.

37. *Ibid.*, pp. 24, 29.

38. *Ibid.*, pp. 34, 35, 35–36.

39. *Ibid.*, p. 39.

40. LEIGH HUNT, *Dramatic Essays* ed. by William Archer and Robert W. Lowe (London, 1894), p. 213; FANNY KEMBLE, *On the Stage* (1863) reprinted as *Papers on Acting III*, Dramatic Museum Columbia University (New York, 1926), pp. 14–15.

41. *Leigh Hunt's Dramatic Criticism 1808–1831* ed. by Laurence and Carolyn Houtchens (New York, 1949), p. 88; *Hazlitt on Theatre* ed. by William Archer and Robert W. Lowe (1895) (New York, 1958), p. 62; Lamb cited in BRANDER MATTHEWS AND LAURENCE HUTTON, *Actors and Actresses* . . . , II, *The Kembles* (New York, 1886), p. 104; Joseph Cowell cited *ibid.*, p. 114, 104; *Hazlitt*, p. 154; Hunt, *DC*, p. 98; Hunt, *Critical Essays* . . . (London, 1807), pp. 180–181, 200; *Hazlitt*, p. 58.

42. Hunt, *CE*, pp. vi–viii; cited in Archer-Lowe, Int. to *DE*, p. xxvi.

43. Hunt, *CE*, pp. 51, 54, 1, 11.

44. *Ibid.*, pp. 49, 50–51, 2, 1–2, 34–35, 54.

45. Hunt, *DC*, pp. 72, 114, 330.

46. Hunt, *CE*, p. 77; "Appendix," *ibid.*, pp. 1, 60–61.

47. *Ibid.*, fn. p. 50, 51.

48. Hunt, *DC*, pp. 202, 203, 25, 5.

49. *Hazlitt on Theatre*, pp. 30, 1; GILES PLAYFAIR, *Kean* (1939) (London, 1950), p. 92.

50. *Hazlitt*, Int., p. xx.

51. *Ibid.*, pp. 110, 28, 53, 137–138.

52. W. CLARK RUSSELL, *Representative Actors* (London, c. 1872), fn. p. 346; Playfair, *Kean*, pp. 106, 121.

53. Ibid., p. 99; Hazlitt, p. 3; BERTRAM JOSEPH, The Tragic Actor (New York, 1959), pp. 282–283, 275.
54. Hazlitt, pp. 4, 8, 198, 21–22.
55. Lewes, AAA, p. 6; Hazlitt, pp. 205, 69, 70, 52, 33.
56. Ibid., pp. 130, 125–127, 102.
57. Joseph, TA, p. 272; Dame Madge Kendal, by Herself (London, 1933), p. 7, cited ibid., p. 275; JOHN FINLEY, Miscellanies (Dublin, 1835), p. 210, quoted by ARTHUR COLBY SPRAGUE, Shakespearian Players and Performers (Cambridge, Mass., 1953), p. 74.
58. Joseph, TA, p. 269; Hazlitt, p. 22.
59. Ibid., pp. 35, 34.
60. Hunt, DC, pp. 113–114, 180; Hunt, DE, pp. 199, 224.
61. Ibid., p. 225.
62. Playfair, Kean, p. 181; quoted ibid., p. 222.
63. Hazlitt, p. 65; Macready cited in Matthews-Hutton, II, The Kembles, p. 291; Hazlitt, pp. 65, 152, 207, 208.
64. Ibid., p. 98; Hunt, DC, pp. 219, 223.
65. Macready's Reminiscences, p. 45.
66. Quoted in Joseph TA, p. 302; Macready's Reminiscences, p. 130.
67. Ibid., pp. 32, 42, 72.
68. Ibid., p. 78.
69. Ibid., p. 109.
70. Ibid., 87.
71. ALAN DOWNER, "The Making of a Great Actor—William Charles Macready," Theatre Annual, VII (1948–49), 63.
72. Coleridge, "Progress of the Drama" (1818) in BARRETT H. CLARK (ed.), European Theories of the Drama (Cincinnati, 1918), p. 426; JOHN MASON BROWN, "Lamb as a Critic," Saturday Review, XXXI (July 31, 1948), 27, 26; Lamb, "The Artificial Comedy of the Last Century" (1823) in PERCY FITZGERALD, The Art of the Stage as set out in Lamb's Dramatic Essays (London, 1885), pp. 72, 80.
73. Lamb, "Stage Illusion" (1833) in Fitzgerald, Art of Stage, pp. 47, 50, 51, 48; "Artificial Comedy," p. 79; "Stage Illusion," p. 48; Lamb, "The New Style of Acting," Examiner (July 1813).
74. Lamb, "The Tragedies of Shakespeare . . ." (1811) in Fitzgerald, Art of Stage, pp. 12, 5, 28.
75. WILLIAM DUNLAP, Memoirs of G. F. Cooke (New York, 1813), I, 123.
76. Playfair, Kean, pp. 252, 255.
77. Cited in MONTROSE J. MOSES, The Fabulous Forrest (Boston, 1929), p. 74.
78. ALLARDYCE NICOLL, World Drama . . . (New York, 1949), p. 488; see NEIL C. ARVIN, Eugène Scribe and the French Theatre 1815–1860 (Cambridge, Mass., 1924), p. 14; DONALD CLIVE STUART, The Development of Dramatic Art (New York, 1928), p. 520.
79. ERNEST LEGOUVÉ, "Eugène Scribe" (1872) trans. by Albert D. Vandam in Papers on Playmaking ed. by BRANDER MATTHEWS (New York, 1957), pp. 271, 270, 270–271.
80. Clark, ETD, pp. 379, 372, 369, 381, 380–381.
81. Stuart, DDA, pp. 502–503.
82. Ibid., p. 507.
83. A. Bournonville cited in Mantzius, VI, 225; Janin quoted in ROBERT BALDICK, The Life and Times of Frédérick Lemaître (Fair Lawn, N.J., 1959), p. 54.
84. Ibid., p. 97; Méry quoted ibid., p. 132; Gautier cited ibid., p. 179; 195; Hugo to Jules Clarétie quoted ibid., p. 244.
85. Dumas cited in Nicoll, WD, p. 489.

86. HENRI (VANGEON) GHÉON, *The Art of the Theatre* (1925, 1938) trans. by Adele M. Fiske (New York, 1961), pp. 46, 49; Nicoll, *WD*, pp. 489, 497.

87. Stuart, *DDA*, p. 513.

88. Lewes, *AAA*, p. 26.

89. *Ibid.*, p. 23.

90. *Macready's Reminiscences*, p. 553; Sampson, *L'Art Théâtral* trans. by Helen Burlin in Cole and Chinoy, *AA*, pp. 189, 188, 189, 188.

91. *Ibid.*, p. 189.

92. *Macready's Reminiscences*, p. 504; Lewes, *AAA*, pp. 24, 29, 24.

93. Sarcey, *Company Actors*, pp. 49, 49–50.

94. C. E. MONTAGUE, *Dramatic Values* (New York, 1925), p. 116; Lewes, *AAA*, p. 194.

95. GENEVIEVE STEBBINS, *Delsarte System of Expression* 4th ed. (New York, 1892), p. iv; *Delsarte System of Oratory* . . . trans. by Abby L. Alger (New York, 1893), cited in Cole and Chinoy, *AA*, pp. 192, 193 (Stebbins, p. 66); 193; Stebbins, p. 99; and see Cole and Chinoy, p. 194.

96. Stebbins, *Delsarte*, p. 11; see 17–28.

97. *Ibid.*, pp. 121 and 187, 47, 48–49, 93, 137, 156, 138.

98. *Ibid.*, pp. 190, 191, 209–210, 194.

99. *Ibid.*, pp. 206–207.

100. *Ibid.*, p. 216.

101. *Ibid.*, p. 64.

102. ADELAIDE RISTORI, *Studies and Memoirs, an autobiography* (Boston, 1888), p. 15.

103. *Leaves from the Autobiography of Tommaso Salvini* (New York, 1893), pp. 25, 45, 70–71.

104. Varneke, *Russian Theatre*, pp. 203, 207, 236.

105. VLADIMIR NOBOKOV, *Nikolai Gogol* (Norfolk, Conn., 1944), pp. 35–36, 153; Varneke, *Russian Theatre*, pp. 312, 314; THEODORE KOMISARJEVSKY, *The Theatre* . . . (London, 1935), pp. 63–64, 63.

106. Varneke, *Russian Theatre*, p. 303.

107. P. O. Morozov quoted *ibid.*, p. 402.

108. JOHN GASSNER, *Masters of the Drama* (New York, 1940), p. 503.

109. Varneke, *Russian Theatre*, p. 297.

110. *Ibid.*, p. 367.

111. Bazhenov quoted *ibid.*, p. 274.

112. See Komisarjevsky, *Theatre*, p. 65; see Varneke, *Russian Theatre*, p. 290; Stanislavsky, *MLA*, pp. 88, 65, 292, and Magarshack, *Life*, p. 156.

113. Shchepkin letter to Shumsky (1848) in Varneke, p. 287; S. P. Solovyov citing Shchepkin *ibid.*, p. 293; 286; Shchepkin to actress Shubert (1848) quoted in Cole and Chinoy, *AA*, p. 423; Varneke, pp. 293, 286; Cole and Chinoy, p. 422; Varneke, p. 293. For other translations of the Shumsky letter see Stanislavsky, *MLA*, pp. 85–86, and Cole and Chinoy, pp. 422–423.

114. Shchepkin quoted in Cole and Chinoy, *AA*, pp. 423, 422. See Komisarjevsky, *Theatre*, p. 53.

115. *Ibid.*, pp. 91–92, 90–91.

116. Mantzius, VI, 215, 216; Devrient, *Bermerkungen zur Novelle* (1834–50) cited in Cole and Chinoy, *AA*, p. 262.

117. Hunt, *DE*, pp. 148, 171.

118. FRANCIS HODGE, "Yankee in England: James Henry Hackett and the Debut of American Comedy," *Quarterly Journal Speech*, XLV (December 1959), 382; ALFRED BUNN, *The Stage* (Philadelphia, 1840), II, 34–35, cited *ibid.*, p. 389.

119. *Macready's Reminiscences*, fn. p. 259; 287; Hunt, *DE*, pp. 193, 211; WHATELEY, *Elements of Rhetoric* (1828) 7th ed. (London, 1846), p. 35.

120. ERNEST BRADLEE WATSON, *Sheridan to Robertson* . . . (Cambridge, Mass., 1926), p. 307; Joseph, *TA*, pp. 297–298.
121. *Macready's Reminiscences*, pp. 265, 285, 289, 356, 337, 339, 364.
122. *Ibid.*, p. 326; RICHARD LEE, "Samuel Phelps," *Theatre* (September 1886), p. 150; Nicoll, *WD*, p. 505.
123. Watson, *Sheridan*, pp. 196, 197; ALLARDYCE NICOLL, *A History of English Drama 1660–1900, II, Early Eighteenth Century Drama* 3rd. ed. (Cambridge, 1952), pp. 53, 38.
124. *Macready's Reminiscences*, pp. 301, 498, 534; see Joseph, *TA*, p. 286.
125. MOY THOMAS, "The Late Mr. Phelps," *Academy*, XIV (1878), 485; E. J. WEST, "The Victorian Voice on the Stage: Samuel Phelps, 'faultless elocutionist,'" *Quarterly Journal Speech*, XXXI (February 1945), 29; Lewes in *Dramatic Essays* [by Lewes and John Forster] ed. by WILLIAM ARCHER AND ROBERT W. LOWE (London, 1896), p. 124.
126. Marston quoted by Joseph, *TA*, p. 303.
127. Marston quoted in Watson, *Sheridan*, p. 309.
128. GARFF B. WILSON, "The Acting of Edwin Forrest," *Quarterly Journal Speech*, XXVI (December 1950), 486, 487; Moses, *Fabulous Forrest*, p. 326; see *The American Theatre as Seen by Its Critics* ed. by MONTROSE J. MOSES AND JOHN MASON BROWN (New York, 1934), pp. 84–85; Wilson, "Forrest," pp. 489, 490; Whitman quoted in Cole and Chinoy, *AA*, p. 467.
129. Dumas, *Préface Un Père prodigue* (1868) reprinted in Clark, *European Theories*, pp. 388, 386; Dumas in a letter to Sarcey cited *ibid.*, p. 382.
130. Lewes, *AAA*, pp. 189, 194.
131. SAMUEL M. WAXMAN, *Antoine and the Théâtre-libre* (Cambridge, Mass., 1926), p. 9; Dumas, *Préface Thérèse Raquin* (1873) in Clark, *European Theories*, pp. 401–402.
132. Gassner, *Masters*, p. 399; *Préface Thérèse Raquin* in Clark, *European Theories*, p. 401; Nicoll, *WD*, p. 511; Waxman, *Antoine*, p. 17.
133. PERCY FITZGERALD, *Principles of Comedy and Dramatic Effect* (London, 1870), p. 351; Henry James, Int. (1887) to COQUELIN, *Art and the Actor* (1880) trans. by Abby Langdon Alger (1881) reprinted as *Papers on Acting II*, Dramatic Museum Columbia University (New York, 1915), p. 16.
134. Domenico Vittorini, "Italy," pp. 320, 321, in BARRETT H. CLARK AND GEORGE FREEDLEY (ed.), *A History of Modern Drama* (New York, 1947).
135. Ristori, *Studies and Memoirs*, pp. 91, 31, 56, 58, 109.
136. *Macready's Reminiscences*, p. 709; Lewes, *AAA*, pp. 174, 166, 170.
137. Salvini, *Leaves*, pp. 73–74, 82, 167; Lewes, *AAA*, pp. 264–265, 267, 271, 274, 275, 278.
138. Salvini, *Leaves*, pp. 152–153.
139. Varneke, *Russian Theatre*, pp. 336–337.
140. *Ibid.*, pp. 355, 357.
141. *Ibid.*, 378, 379.
142. Stanislavsky, *MLA*, p. 92; *Oxford Companion*, p. 851; *MLA*, p. 129.
143. *Ellen Terry's Memoirs* (1908) ed. by EDITH CRAIG AND CHRISTOPHER ST. JOHN (New York, 1932), p. 40.
144. Watson, *Sheridan*, pp. 234, 225; *Ellen Terry*, pp. 14, 13.
145. TOWNSEND WALSH, *The Career of Dion Boucicault*, Dunlap Society (New York, 1915), p. 43; Watson, *Sheridan*, pp. 251, 39; *Theatre Journal* (1852) cited *ibid.*, p. 228.
146. *Ibid.*, pp. 370–371, 234, 370; Lewes, *AAA*, p. 15; Lewes in the *Leader* (1852) quoted in Watson, *Sheridan*, p. 368; Lewes, *AAA*, p. 13.
147. *Ellen Terry*, p. 12; Lewes, *AAA*, p. 13; *Theatrical Journal* (1853) cited in Watson, *Sheridan*, p. 369.

148. *Ibid.*, pp. 231, 232.
149. JUSTIN MCCARTHY, *Portraits of the Sixties* (New York, 1903), p. 251; Watson, *Sheridan*, pp. 237, 238; McCarthy, p. 248; Watson, p. 372; CHARLES DICKENS, "Fechter's Acting," *Atlantic Monthly*, XXIV (August 1869), 244; CLEMENT SCOTT, "Two Dramatic Revolutions," *North American Review*, CLII (October 1893), 479.
150. Watson, *Sheridan*, pp. 235, 377–378.
151. Lewes, AAA, p. 133.
152. *Ibid.*, pp. 132, 134, 148, 134.
153. *Ibid.*, pp. 147–148.
154. Watson, *Sheridan*, p. 240.
155. *Ibid.*, p. 220.
156. E. J. WEST, "The London Stage, 1870–1890," *Uni. Colorado Studies*, series B, 2 (May 1943), 78.
157. Watson, *Sheridan*, p. 250.
158. *Ibid.*, p. 249.
159. HENRY BARTON BAKER, *A History of the London Stage 1576–1903* (London, 1904), p. 231; DUTTON COOK, *Nights at the Play* (London, 1883), II, 69.
160. Watson, *Sheridan*, p. 418; Mr. & *Mrs. Bancroft On and Off the Stage* (1885) 7th ed. (London, 1889), pp. 383, 139. *On and Off the Stage* became *Recollections of Sixty Years* (London, 1909).
161. *Ibid.*, fn. pp. 96–97, 97, 390, 106, 390, 113, 390, 140, 390–391.
162. *Ibid.*, pp. 384, 383.
163. *Ibid.*, pp. 384–385.
164. Quoted by Watson, *Sheridan*, p. 221; Walsh, *Boucicault*, p. 116.
165. West, "London Stage," p. 33; George Freedley, p. 160, in Clark and Freedley, *Modern Drama*; West, p. 33; Nicoll, WD, p. 505; West, p. 31.
166. *Ibid.*, p. 50 citing Pinero, "The Theatres in the 'Seventies," in *The Eighteen-Seventies; Essays of Fellows of the Royal Society of Literature* (Cambridge, 1929), p. 158; Watson, *Sheridan*, p. 413.
167. West, "London Stage," p. 76; JOHN MASON BROWN, *The Art of Playgoing* (New York, 1936), pp. 183–184; F. ALLEN LAIDLAW, "The New School of Acting," *Gentleman's Magazine*, CCXL (April 1876), 472.
168. W. S. Gilbert quoted in SIDNEY DARK AND ROWLAND GREEN, *W. S. Gilbert* (London, 1923), p. 59; Robertson, "Theatrical Types," *Illustrated Times* (1864) reprinted in A. M. NAGLER, *Sources of Theatrical History* (New York, 1952), p. 493; HARLEY GRANVILLE-BARKER, "Exit Planché—Enter Gilbert," in *The Eighteen Sixties* . . . (Cambridge, 1932), p. 187.
169. West, "London Stage," p. 56.
170. See *ibid.*, pp. 73, 69; HENRY MORLEY, *The Journal of a London Playgoer from 1851 to 1866* (London, 1891), p. 263; see FREDERICK WEDMORE, " 'The School for Scandal' at the Prince of Wales'," *Academy*, V (April 11, 1874), 412–413, mentioned by West, "London Stage," pp. 68–69; Cook, *Nights*, II, 69–70.
171. Mr. & *Mrs. Bancroft*, p. 315.
172. Lewes, AAA, pp. 45, 57, 67.
173. *Ibid.*, pp. 90, vii, ix.
174. *Ibid.*, pp. 106, xi, 94, 106, 96, 102–103.
175. *Ibid.*, pp. 99, 225, 105, 167, 95, 97.
176. *Ibid.*, pp. 90, 80, 98–99, 91, 168.
177. *Ibid.*, pp. 80, x, 267–268, 18–19, 98–99, 38, 179.
178. *Ibid.*, pp. 119–120, 121, 112–113.
179. *Ibid.*, pp. 115–116, 242, 125.
180. *Ellen Terry*, p. 351.

181. *Ibid.*, 61; see LAURENCE IRVING, *Henry Irving* . . . (New York, 1952), pp. 685–703.
182. *Ibid.*, p. 140.
183. *Ibid.*, pp. 190, 206, 234, 237.
184. *The Autobiography of Joseph Jefferson* (New York, 1889), pp. 428–454, quoted in Cole and Chinoy, AA, pp. 476, 478, 474–475, 475, 478, 479.
185. ELEANOR RUGGLES, *Prince of Players Edwin Booth* (New York, 1953), p. 91.
186. *Ibid.*, pp. 114, 117.
187. *Ibid.*, pp. 122, 206, 216.
188. *Ibid.*, pp. 209; *Oxford Companion*, p. 59.
189. Edwin Booth, "A Few Words about Edmund Kean," in BRANDER MATTHEWS AND LAURENCE HUTTON (ed.), *Actors and Actresses* . . . , III, *Kean and Booth* . . . , cited in Cole and Chinoy, AA, p. 483.
190. PERCY MACKAYE, *Epoch, the Life of Steele Mackaye* . . . (New York, 1927), I, 152; see also 157 and 164; II, 274.
191. ARGUS JOHN TRESIDDER, "The Meininger and Their Influence," *Quarterly Journal Speech*, XXI (November 1935), 468; LEE SIMONSON, *The Stage Is Set* (New York, 1932), p. 287; Tresidder, p. 469.
192. LEO WIENER, *The Contemporary Drama of Russia* (Boston, 1924), p. 77, cited by Joel Trapido, "The Meininger," *Quarterly Journal Speech*, XXVI (October 1940), 383; Simonson, *Stage Set*, pp. 286, 273.
193. Trapido, "Meininger," p. 380; Tresidder, "Meininger," p. 469.
194. Simonson, *Stage Set*, p. 277.
195. *Ibid.*, pp. 277, 294.
196. *Ibid.*, pp. 300, 301, 301–302.
197. See Max Grube, *Geschichte der Meininger* (Berlin, 1926), pp. 129–131.
198. Simonson, *Stage Set*, p. 302; Stanislavsky, MLA, pp. 197–198.
199. *Mr. & Mrs. Bancroft*, p. 317; Tresidder, "Meininger," p. 474.
200. THEODORE KOMISARJEVSKY, *Myself and the Theatre* (New York, 1930), p. 63; and his *Theatre*, p. 106.
201. Stuart, DDA, p. 574; William Archer cited *ibid.*
202. Nicoll, WD, p. 526; Alrik Gustafson, "The Scandinavian Countries," p. 46, in Clark and Freedley, *Modern Drama*; THEODORE JORGENSON, *Henrik Ibsen* . . . (Northfield, Minn., 1945), p. 292.
203. HALVDAN KOHT, *The Life of Ibsen* (London, 1931), II, 58, 127; Jorgenson, p. 292, in Clark and Freedley, *Modern Drama*.
204. ELIZABETH ROBINS, *Ibsen and the Actress* (London, 1929), pp. 10–11.
205. See Antoine quoted in Waxman, *Antoine*, pp. 137–139; Strindberg cited in Gassner, *Masters*, p. 392.
206. Antoine, "Causerie sur la mise en scène," *Revue de Paris*, 10 (April 1, 1903), quoted in TOBY COLE AND HELEN KRICH CHINOY (ed.), *Directing the Play* . . . (Indianapolis and New York, 1953), p. 81; Waxman, *Antoine*, pp. 65, 71, 73; Antoine quoted in Cole and Chinoy, AA, p. 217; Waxman, p. 89; Sarcey cited *ibid.*, p. 91; 97.
207. Antoine, *Le Théâtre Libre* (Paris, 1890) trans. by Joseph M. Bernstein and cited in Cole and Chinoy, AA, p. 217; Waxman, *Antoine*, p. 85; Antoine, *Théâtre Libre* in Cole and Chinoy, AA, p. 217; Waxman, p. 89; Sarcey cited *ibid.*, p. 91; 97.
208. Cole and Chinoy, AA, pp. 219, 220, 221; Cole and Chinoy, *Directing*, p. 88; Cole and Chinoy, AA, p. 218.
209. *Ibid.*, p. 219; see Waxman, *Antoine*, p. 139; Cole and Chinoy, AA, p. 220, and Waxman, p. 98; *ibid.*, p. 138; Cole and Chinoy, AA, p. 221.
210. Cole and Chinoy, *Directing*, p. 89.
211. Antoine cited in Waxman, *Antoine*, p. 175.
212. *Ibid.*, pp. 155–156.

213. Kerr quoted *ibid.*, p. 211; HERBERT HENZE, *Otto Brahm und das Deutsch Theater* (Berlin, 1930) abridged and trans. as "Otto Brahm and Naturalistic Directing," *Theatre Workshop*, 1 (April–July 1937), 16, 17.

214. *Ibid.*, pp. 16, 14; Brahm, *Kritische Schriften über Drama und Theater* (Berlin, 1913), in Cole and Chinoy, *Directing*, p. 96; the same in Cole and Chinoy, *AA*, pp. 273, 272, 273.

215. Henze, *Brahm*, p. 18; Brahm, *KS* in Cole and Chinoy, *Directing*, pp. 97, 94; the same in their *AA*, pp. 271, 272.

216. See Henze, *Brahm*, pp. 21–25; Brahm, *KS*, I, 11, cited in MAXIM NEWMARK, *Otto Brahm, the man and the critic* (New York, 1938), p. 193; Henze, p. 25; Maximilian Hardy, "The Genius of Max Reinhardt," in OLIVER M. SAYLER (ed.), *Max Reinhardt and His Theatre* (New York, 1924), p. 233.

217. Henze, *Brahm*, p. 26; Brahm, *KS*, I, 187, cited in Newmark, *Brahm*, p. 205; Henze, p. 26; Hermann, "The Spiritual Sources of Reinhardt," in Sayler, *Reinhardt*, p. 40.

218. *Ibid.*, p. 41.

219. George Moore quoted in Waxman, *Antoine*, p. 212; Clement Scott, *Daily Telegraph* (March 14, 1891) reprinted in A. C. WARD (ed.), *Specimens of English Dramatic Criticism* . . . (Oxford, 1945), pp. 183, 185, 183; Waxman, p. 214.

220. HARLEY GRANVILLE-BARKER, "A Letter to Jacques Copeau" (1940) reprinted in *Theatre Arts Anthology* (New York, 1950, 1960), p. 17.

221. Archer, "The Drama," in T. H. WARD, *The Reign of Queen Victoria* (London, 1887), II, 590, cited in West, "London Stage," p. 55; LEWIS WINGFIELD, "Realism Behind the Footlights," *Fortnightly Review*, XLI (April 1884), 477, cited *ibid.*, p. 71.

222. CLARA MORRIS, *Life on the Stage* (New York, 1902), pp. 326–329, reprinted in Nagler, *Sources*, pp. 562–563.

223. See MARVIN FELHEIM, *The Theatre of Augustin Daly* (Cambridge, Mass., 1956), pp. 249, 288; JOHN FRANCIS DALY, *The Life of Augustin Daly* (New York, 1917), pp. 419–420.

224. See Magarshack, *Life*, pp. 40, 41, 42.

225. Stanislavsky, *MLA* (American ed.), p. 201; see Magarshack, *Life*, pp. 19, 30, and *MLA*, p. 146.

226. *MLA*, p. 207; Magarshack, *Life*, p. 87; Maria Andreyeva quoted *ibid.*, p. 110; Rossi quoted in *MLA*, p. 286.

227. Magarshack, *Life*, pp. 117, 125; Stanislavsky, *MLA*, p. 263.

228. Magarshack, *Life*, pp. 157, 160.

229. *MLA*, pp. 322, 301; Magarshack, *Life*, p. 162; see *The Seagull Produced by Stanislavski* ed. with Int. by S. D. Balakhaty and trans. by David Magarshack (New York, 1952), p. 56.

230. *MLA*, pp. 332, 308, 331, 333, 332, 301.

231. Magarshack, *Life*, p. 177.

232. Balakhaty in *Seagull Produced*, pp. 103–104, 87, 109, 59–60; see Magarshack, *Life*, pp. 172, 182, 172.

233. *Ibid.*, p. 181; see David Magarshack, *Chekhov the Dramatist* (London, 1952), p. 188; Magarshack, *Life*, p. 181; see *Seagull Produced*, pp. 72, 80; Magarshack, p. 181; *Seagull Produced*, p. 80; see also pp. 83–84.

234. Magarshack, *Chekhov*, p. 222.

235. SARCEY, *A Theory of the Theatre* (1876) trans. by Hatcher Hughes and reprinted as *Papers on Playmaking IV*, Dramatic Museum Columbia University (New York, 1916), pp. 30, 24–25, 26, 27, 28, 31, 12, 10, 40.

236. See RICHARD MCKEON, *Thought Action and Passion* (Chicago, 1954), pp. 282, 203, 285.

237. C. E. Montague, "F. R. Benson's Richard II" (1899) reprinted in Ward, *Specimens*, pp. 224, 225, 226, 225.

238. MAURICE MAETERLINCK, "The Tragical in Daily Life," in his *The Treasure of the Humble* trans. by Alfred Sutro (New York, 1900), p. 99.

239. S. A. Rhodes, p. 246, in Clark and Freedley, *Modern Drama*; A. B. WALKLEY, *Drama and Life* (New York, 1908), p. 216.

240. Preface to *The Dream Play*; Geijerstam quoted by Gustafson, p. 34, in Clark and Freedley, *Modern Drama*.

241. STARK YOUNG, *The Flower in Drama* (New York, 1923), p. 32, or *The Flower in Drama and Glamour* (New York, 1955), pp. 27, 26.

242. Henry Labouchere quoted in E. J. WEST, "Actress Between Two Schools: the case of Madge Kendal," *Speech Monographs*, XI (1944), fn. 111; 109; Percy Fitzgerald cited *ibid.*, p. 108.

243. Silvio D'Amico cited in Cole and Chinoy, AA, p. 394; Young, *Flower*, p. 161, or *FG*, p. 84; STARK YOUNG, *Immortal Shadows* (New York, 1948), p. 34.

244. Salvini, *Leaves*, p. 239; Komisarjevsky, *Myself*, p. 67.

245. Salvini, *Leaves*, pp. 176–177; DAME SYBIL THORNDIKE, "The Great Actress Ladies," *N.Y. Times*, September 27, 1959, p. x3.

246. COQUELIN, "Actors and Acting" (1887) reprinted as *The Art of Acting* in *Papers on Acting II*, Dramatic Museum Columbia University (New York, 1926), p. 37; HENRY IRVING, *The Drama* (Boston, 1892), "The Art of Acting" (1885), pp. 71, 69; and "The Art of Acting" (1891), p. 178; Charles Pascoe, *The Dramatic List*, p. 199, and *The Theatre* (1897), I, 15, cited in Joseph, TA, pp. 375, 380.

247. Irving, *Drama*, pp. 74–75, 70, 82; A. B. WALKLEY, *Pastische and Prejudice* (New York, 1921), p. 170; *Theatre* (1895), I, 130, cited in Joseph, TA, p. 368.

248. Symons in Agate, *Critics*, p. 320; Joseph, TA, p. 363.

249. Irving, *Drama*, p. 178; see AUGUSTIN FILON, *The English Stage* (London, 1897) trans. by Frederic Whyte, cited in Bernard Shaw, *Our Theatres in the Nineties* (London, 1932), III, 154.

250. LAURENCE IRVING, *Henry Irving, the actor and his world* (New York, 1952), p. 470.

251. *Ellen Terry's Memoirs*, p. 337; *The Theatre* (1891) cited in Joseph, TA, p. 381.

252. *Ibid.*, p. 395; Montague, *Dramatic Values*, p. 60; Forbes-Robertson quoted in Joseph, TA, p. 387; 393; DESMOND MACCARTHY in *Herbert Beerbohm Tree* (London, 1920), p. 221, quoted *ibid.*, p. 385; see Shaw's Int. to LILLAH MACCARTHY, *Myself and My Friends* (London, 1933), reprinted in *Shaw on Theatre* ed. by E. J. West (New York, 1958), pp. 222, 223; Joseph, TA, p. 380; Shaw, OTN, II, 146.

253. C. B. PURDOM, *Harley Granville Barker* (Cambridge, Mass., 1956), p. 24.

254. Irving, *Irving*, p. 375.

255. Young, *Flower*, p. 31; ELSIE FOGERTY, Int. to COQUELIN's *The Art of the Actor* (1887, 1889, 1894) (London, 1932), pp. 28, 20.

256. SARAH BERNHARDT, *The Art of the Theatre* trans. by H. J. Stenning (London, 1924), pp. 98–99; Symons quoted in Agate, *Critics*, p. 322; Young, *Glamour*, p. 20.

257. LOUIS VERNEUIL, *The Fabulous Life of Sarah Bernhardt* trans. by Ernest Boyd (New York, 1942), p. 121; Young, *Glamour*, p. 4, or *FG*, pp. 162, 159.

258. COQUELIN, *Art and the Actor* (1880) trans. by ABBY LANGDON ALGER (1881), reprinted as *Papers on Acting II*, Dramatic Museum Columbia University (New York, 1915), pp. 64, 67; Coquelin, *The Art of the Actor* (Fogerty), p. 81; Alger, pp. 39, 63, 46, 63; Fogerty, pp. 77, 46.

259. Montague, *Dramatic Values*, p. 42; HENRY JAMES, Int. (1886, 1915) to Coquelin, *Art and Actor* (Alger), pp. 36, 15; Montague, pp. 43–44; James, pp. 19, 21; Montague, p. 44; James, p. 21.

260. Coquelin, *Art and Actor* (Alger), pp. 88, 40, 44.

261. Brander Matthews, *ibid.*, p. 98.
262. *Ibid.*, p. 61.
263. Coquelin, *Art of Actor* (Fogerty), pp. 30, 31, 71, 72, 71, 35.
264. *Ibid.*, pp. 46, 89, 87, 90, 91, 94–95, 87.
265. *Ibid.*, pp. 58, 44, 44–45, 55.
266. *Ibid.*, p. 38.
267. *Ibid.*, pp. 33, 34, 33, 40, 59; see also "Actors and Acting" (below), pp. 19–20.
268. CONSTANTIN STANISLAVSKI, *An Actor Prepares* trans. by Elizabeth Reynolds Hapgood (New York, 1936), pp. 18, 22, 18, 163, 151.
269. COQUELIN, "Actors and Acting," in *The Art of Acting, a discussion* . . . Dramatic Museum Columbia University (New York, 1926), pp. 10–11; Irving, "M. Coquelin on Actors and Acting," *ibid.*, p. 51; Coquelin, p. 11; Irving, p. 50; Coquelin, "A Reply to Mr. Henry Irving," *ibid.*, pp. 73, 78; Irving, p. 52; Coquelin, pp. 29, 79.
270. *Ibid.*, Irving, pp. 46–47, 47–48; Coquelin, pp. 70–71, 72, 90, 85, 72.
271. *Ibid.*, Irving, pp. 46, 52, 52–53; Boucicault, "Coquelin-Irving," *ibid.*, pp. 57–58; Coquelin, p. 87.
272. *Ibid.*, Coquelin, p. 88.
273. SALVINI, "Some Views on Acting" (1880), *Theatre Workshop*, I (October–December 1936), 74, 77.
274. See Archer, *Masks*, pp. 23, 184–185.
275. *Ibid.*, p. 37, 203, 206, 206–207.
276. *Ibid.*, p. 208.
277. Shaw, OTN, I, 91; Archer, *Masks*, p. 196.
278. PERCY FITZGERALD, *The Art of Acting* . . . (London, 1892), pp. 72–73, 77, 36–37, 50–51, 67.
279. *Ellen Terry and Bernard Shaw, a correspondence* ed. by Christopher St. John (1931) (New York, 1949), p. 3; BERNARD SHAW, *Dramatic Opinions and Essays* (New York, 1906, 1922), I, 204, or OTN, I, 224; DOE, II, 1, or OTN, II, 145; DOE, II, 256, or OTN, III, 128; DOE, II, 17, or OTN, II, 157; DOE, II, 273, or OTN, III, 141; DOE, I, 197, or OTN, III, 141; DOE, I, 197, or OTN, I, 219.
280. Shaw, DOE, II, 281, or OTN, III, 148; DOE, II, 213–214, or OTN, III, 76–77.
281. Shaw, DOE, I, 15, or OTN, I, 12; DOE, I, 207, or OTN, I, 212; DOE, I, 207, or OTN, I, 211–212.
282. ARTHUR KNIGHT, *The Liveliest Art* (1951), Mentor Books (New York, 1959), p. 22.
283. A. NICHOLAS VARDAC, *Stage to Screen* (Cambridge, Mass., 1949), pp. 166, 169.
284. *Ibid.*, p. 176; Knight, *Liveliest Art*, pp. 23–24.

❊ CHAPTER 9

1. HARLEY GRANVILLE-BARKER, *The Exemplary Theatre* (Boston, 1922), p. 1.
2. JOSEPH WOOD KRUTCH, *'Modernism' in the Modern Drama* (Ithaca, N.Y., 1953), p. 17; for "idealism" see, for instance, "Discourse III" (1770) by SIR JOSHUA REYNOLDS; see HERBERT READ, *The Meaning of Art* (1931) 3rd rev. enlg. ed. (London, 1951), p. 137.
3. ALEXANDER BAKSHY, *The Theatre Unbound* (London, 1923), p. 95; STARK YOUNG, "Realism in the Theatre," *Yale Review*, XVI (October 1926), 115; H. W. L. Dana, "Russia," p. 430, in BARRETT H. CLARK AND GEORGE FREEDLEY (eds.), *A History of Modern Drama*.
4. Bakshy, *Theatre Unbound*, p. 92; STARK YOUNG, *The Flower in Drama* (New York, 1923), p. 10, and reprinted as *The Flower in Drama and Glamour* (New York,

1955), pp. 8–9, and in his *Theatre Practice* (New York, 1926), p. 8; Bakshy, pp. 92, 100–101.

5. STARK YOUNG, *The Theater* (New York, 1927), p. 121.

6. MICHEL SAINT-DENIS, *Theatre* . . . (New York, 1960), pp. 72–73.

7. MICHAEL REDGRAVE, *Mask or Face* (New York, 1958), p. 171; Theodore Komisarjevsky quoted in DAVID MAGARSHACK, *Stanislavski on the Art of the Stage* (London, 1950), p. 84; WALTER F. KERR, "Acting Techniques Discusses," *N.Y. Herald Tribune*, August 17, 1952, p. 4-1.

8. ERIC LARRABEE, commenting on Siegfried Kracauer's *Theory of Film* . . . (Oxford, 1960), in *Harper's*, 222 (January 1961), 31.

9. *Ibid.*

10. Herbert Read, *Art*, pp. 222, 225; a prefatory note for *To Damascus*.

11. ALLARDYCE NICOLL, *World Drama* . . . (New York, 1949), p. 563.

12. S. A. Rhodes, "France and Belgium," pp. 274, 269, in Clark and Freedley, *Modern Drama*.

13. *Ibid.*, p. 249.

14. WALLACE FOWLIE, *Dionysus in Paris, a guide to contemporary French theatre* (New York, 1960), p. 37; SAMUEL WAXMAN, *Antoine and the Théâtre-Libre* (Cambridge, Mass., 1926), p. 193; Saint-Denis, *Theatre*, p. 28.

15. KENNETH TYNAN, *Curtains* (New York, 1961), p. 414; see HAROLD CLURMAN, "The Paradox of the French Stage," *Theatre Arts*, XLIV (December 1960), 79.

16. CONSTANTIN STANISLAVSKI, *An Actor Prepares* trans. by Elizabeth Reynolds Hapgood (New York, 1936), pp. 21–22.

17. Mario Pucci quoted by Domenico Vittorini, "Italy," p. 347, in Clark and Freedley, *Modern Drama*; Marinetti cited in TOBY COLE AND HELEN KRICH CHINOY (ed.), *Actors on Acting* . . . (New York, 1949), p. 395.

18. Young, *Flower*, p. 158; A. B. WALKLEY, *Drama and Life* (New York, 1908), p. 254.

19. STARK YOUNG, *Glamour* (New York, 1925), pp. 5–6, reprinted in *FG*, p. 164; STARK YOUNG, *Immortal Shadows* (New York, 1948), p. 35, or *FG*, p. 174; ARTHUR SYMONS, from *Eleanora Duse* (New York, 1926) reprinted in JAMES AGATE (ed.), *The English Dramatic Critics* (New York, 1958), p. 316; Symons cited in Cole and Chinoy, *AA*, p. 159.

20. Young, *Shadows*, pp. 34–35; Symons, *Duse*, pp. 320, 315; Young, *FG*, p. 161; BERNARD SHAW, *Dramatic Opinions and Essays* (New York, 1906, 1922), II, 329, or his *Our Theatres in the Nineties* (London, 1932), III, 210; Young, *FG*, p. 159.

21. Young, *Shadows*, p. 31; Young, *Glamour*, p. 17; JEANNE BORDEUX, *Eleanora Duse* . . . (London, 1924), cited in Cole and Chinoy, *AA*, p. 413.

22. Young, *Shadows*, p. 31, or *FG*, 173; Young, *Glamour*, pp. 18–19, 11; Symons, *Duse*, p. 315; Duse quoted in Cole and Chinoy, *AA*, p. 412.

23. JOHN GASSNER, *Masters of the Drama* (New York, 1940), p. 460.

24. MAX REINHARDT, "The Actor," *Encyclopaedia Britannica* (1929), XXII cited in Cole and Chinoy, *AA*, pp. 278, 275; Max Reinhardt, "On the Living Theatre," p. 64 in *Max Reinhardt and His Theatre* ed. by OLIVER M. SAYLER (New York, 1924).

25. ERIC BENTLEY, *In Search of Theatre* (New York, 1953), p. 263; Rudolf Kommer, "The Magician of Leopoldskron," in Sayler, *Reinhardt*, p. 7. See Appendix III, "Chronology of Reinhardt's Productions," pp. 346–372.

26. Reinhardt, "The Actor," in Cole and Chinoy, *AA*, pp. 274–275; Carl Heine, "The Actor of Reinhardt's Ensemble," in Sayler, *Reinhardt*, p. 112; R. BEN-ARI, "Four Directors and the Actor" trans. by Harry Elion, *Theatre Workshop*, I (January–March 1937), 72; Richard Beer-Hofmann, "Reinhardt Preceptor of Poet and Player," in Sayler, p. 106.

27. GEORG FUCHS, *Die Revolution des Theaters* (*Revolution in the Theatre*) (Munich,

1909) condensed and adapted by Constance Connor Kuhn (Ithaca, N.Y., 1959), pp. 48–49, 49, 65.

28. See DAVID MAGARSACK, *Stanislavsky, a life* (New York, 1951), p. 207; CONSTANTIN STANISLAVSKY, *My Life in Art* (1924) trans. by J. J. Robbins (Boston, 1924, 1927), p. 340; Magarshack, p. 209; *ibid.*, p. 213; see pp. 212–214, and MLA, pp. 404–407.

29. *Ibid.*, p. 371; Magarshack, *Life*, p. 220.

30. Stanislavsky, MLA, pp. 401, 403.

31. *Ibid.*, p. 398.

32. See Magarshack, *Life*, pp. 247, 246; MLA, p. 350.

33. *Ibid.*, pp. 422, 351.

34. See Magarshack, *Life*, p. 265.

35. MLA, pp. 344, 434, 403.

36. *Ibid.*, pp. 473, 474, 481, 483.

37. Stanislavski quoted in Magarshack, *Life*, p. 294.

38. MLA, pp. 467, 464; Stanislavski quoted in Magarshack, *Life*, p. 310.

39. *Ibid.*, p. 507; NIKOLAI A. GORCHAKOV, *The Theatre in Soviet Russia* trans. by Edgar Lehrman (New York, 1957), p. 38.

40. THEODORE KOMISARJEVSKY, *Myself and the Theatre* (New York, 1930), p. 76.

41. NICOLAS EVREINOFF, *The Theatre in Life* (1912–17) ed. and trans. by Alexander I. Nazaroff (New York, 1927), p. 136.

42. Vsevolod Meyerhold, *O Teatre* (1913), excerpt reprinted in TOBY COLE AND HELEN KRICH CHINOY (ed.), *Directing the Play* . . . (New York, 1953), p. 140.

43. Dana, p. 443, in Clark and Freedley, *Modern Drama*.

44. HENRI GHÉON, *The Art of the Theatre* (1923) trans. by Adele M. Fiske (New York, 1961), p. 60.

45. Nicoll, WD, p. 667.

46. C. P. PURDOM, *Harley Granville Barker* . . . (Cambridge, Mass., 1956), p. 21.

47. ALAN S. DOWNER, "Harley Granville Barker," *Sewanee Review*, LV (Autumn 1947), 631–632; see Purdom, *Barker*, pp. 290–291.

48. *Ibid.*, p. 66.

49. Barker, *Exemplary Theatre*, p. 83; JOSEPH MORGENSTERN, "Advocate for a 'Strong Play,'" quoting Leo Genn, *N.Y. Herald Tribune*, March 5, 1961, Sect. 4, p. 4.

50. Barker, *Exemplary Theatre*, pp. 87, 213–214, 87.

51. Purdom, *Barker*, pp. 166, 41; BERNARD SHAW, "Barker's Wild Oats," *Harper's*, 1160 (January 1947), 53, 52.

52. GORDON CRAIG, "The Actor and the Über-Marionette" (1907) in *On the Art of the Theatre* (1911) (Boston, 1925), pp. 89, 62, 71–72; "The Artists of the Theatre of the Future" (1907), *ibid.*, pp. 36, 35.

53. *Ibid.*, pp. 10, 11.

54. "Actor and Über-Marionette," pp. 55, 57.

55. *Ibid.*, p. 81; see "The First Dialogue" (1905), pp. 147, 178. See also BERNARD BARSHAY, "Gordon Craig's Theories of Acting," *Theatre Annual* (1947), pp. 55–63.

56. Young, *Flower*, p. 26.

57. "David Belasco," *Theatre Arts Monthly*, XXVII (August 1943), 495; see Ward Morehouse, *Matinee Tomorrow, fifty years of our theatre* (New York, 1949), p. 15.

58. "David Belasco," p. 496; *Mrs. Fiske, her views on actors, acting* . . . recorded by ALEXANDER WOOLLCOTT (New York, 1917), p. 124.

59. WILLIAM GILLETTE, *The Illusion of the First Time in Acting* (1913), reprinted as *Papers on Acting I*, Dramatic Museum Columbia University (New York, 1915), p. 44; see Cole and Chinoy, AA, p. 488.

60. RICHARD MANSFIELD, "Concerning Acting," *North American Review*, CXCVII (September 1894), 337–340, partly reprinted in Cole and Chinoy, AA, p. 490; *Mrs. Fiske*, pp. 82, 95–96; Nazimova quoted in MORTON EUSTIS, *Players at Work* (New York, 1937), p. 56. See Fiske in Cole and Chinoy, pp. 506–509, and Nazimova, *ibid.*, pp. 512–513.

61. *Mrs. Fiske*, pp. 104, 76, 79, 100.

62. DAVID BELASCO, "About Acting," *Saturday Evening Post*, CXCIV (September 24, 1921), partly reprinted in Cole and Chinoy, AA, p. 503.

63. Nazimova quoted in Eustis, *Players*, p. 57; see Cole and Chinoy, AA, p. 513.

64. Gillette, *Illusion*, p. 43, and in Cole and Chinoy, AA, p. 487.

65. See Mansfield, "Acting," cited in Cole and Chinoy, AA, p. 490; Belasco, "Acting," quoted *ibid.*, p. 500; Nazimova in Eustis, *Players*, p. 53, and in Cole and Chinoy, p. 512; Gillette, *Illusion*, p. 47, in Cole and Chinoy, p. 489.

66. *Edison Catalogue* (1906) cited in A. NICHOLAS VARDAC, *Stage to Screen* . . . (Cambridge, Mass., 1949), p. 186.

67. *Film Notes*, Bulletin Museum Modern Art, XVI (1949), 11, 12.

68. Rhodes, pp. 299, 253, in Clark and Freedley, *Modern Drama*; Fowlie, *Dionysus*, pp. 144, 143.

69. JEAN-LOUIS BARRAULT, *Reflections on the Theatre* (1949) trans. by Barbara Wall (London, 1951), p. 20. Louis Jouvet quoted in ERIC BENTLEY, *In Search of Theatre* (New York, 1953), pp. 261–262.

70. WALDO FRANK, "The Art of the Vieux Colombier," in his *Salvos* . . . (New York, 1924), pp. 126, 124.

71. COPEAU, "Un Essai de rénovation dramatique," *Nouvelle Revue Française*, September 1, 1913, and in *Etudes d'art dramatique, critiques d'un autre temps* (Paris, 1923), reprinted in extract in Cole and Chinoy, AA, p. 223; GRANVILLE BARKER, "A Letter to Jacques Copeau" (1940) in *Theatre Arts Anthology* (New York, 1950, 1960), p. 14; Rhodes, p. 275, in Clark and Freedley, *Modern Drama*; Copeau "Essai," in Cole and Chinoy, AA, p. 224.

72. Frank, "Vieux Colombier," p. 137.

73. Ghéon, *Art Theatre*, pp. 93, 63; Rhodes, p. 273, in Clark and Freedley, *Modern Drama*.

74. Frank, "Vieux Colombier," p. 157; Copeau, "La Mise en scène," *Encyclopédie Française*, December 1935, reprinted in Cole and Chinoy, *Directing*, p. 156; Frank, p. 166.

75. Ghéon, *Art Theatre*, p. 73.

76. Bentley, IST, p. 262; Ghéon, *Art Theatre*, p. 75.

77. BETTINA LIEBOWITZ KNAPP, *Louis Jouvet, man of the theatre* (New York, 1957), pp. 26, 31, 39.

78. *Ibid.*, p. 42.

79. Rhodes, p. 275, in Clark and Freedley, *Modern Drama*; Knapp, *Jouvet*, p. 55.

80. *Ibid.*, p. 61.

81. *Theatre Arts Monthly*, XXVII (January 1944), 51–52. For a "Chronology of Reinhardt's Productions" (1902–1923) see Sayler, *Reinhardt*, pp. 346–370.

82. CARL DAHLSTRÖM, *Strindberg's Dramatic Expressionism* (Ann Arbor, Michigan, 1930), pp. 51–52, cited by William Angus, "Expressionism in the Theatre," *Quarterly Journal Speech*, XIX (November 1933), 480, 482.

83. *Ibid.*, p. 491; H. G. SCHEFFAUER, *The New Vision in the German Arts* (1924), p. 193, cited *ibid.*, p. 491.

84. PAUL KORNFELD, "Nachwort an den Schauspieler," *Die Verfuehrung* (Berlin, 1921), quoted in Cole and Chinoy, p. 279.

85. COLBY LEWIS, "Leopold Jessner's Theories of Dramatic Production," *Quarterly Journal Speech*, XXII (April 1936), 197.

86. *Ibid.*, p. 201; KARL TH. VON BLUTH, *Leopold Jessner* (Berlin, 1928) cited by H. Darkes Albright, " 'Design' in the Theatre," *Quarterly Journal Speech*, XX (April 1934), 260; KENNETH MACGOWAN, *Continental Stagecraft* (New York, 1922), p. 143.

87. Arthur Kutscher cited by Lewis, "Jessner," p. 205.

88. See Magarshack, *Life*, pp. 328, 329; Stanislavsky, *MLA*, pp. 523, 522; Komisarjevsky, *Myself*, p. 73; *MLA*, p. 524.

89. *Ibid.*, pp. 549, 524.

90. Magarshack, *Life*, p. 330; ARGUS TRESIDDER, reviewing *The First Studio* . . . by P. A. Markov and *The Theatre of the Social Mask* by B. Alpers, *Quarterly Journal Speech*, XXII (April 1936), 317.

91. *Ibid.*

92. *MLA*, p. 527; see Magarshack, *Life*, p. 322; Gorchakov, *Theatre Soviet Russia*, fn. 27, p. 411.

93. Margarshack, *Life*, p. 332.

94. *Ibid.*, pp. 336; see p. 337.

95. *Ibid.*, p. 343.

96. *MLA*, pp. 561–562.

97. Komisarjevsky, *Myself*, pp. 91, 93, 95.

98. RENÉ-FÜLÖP MILLER AND JOSEF GREGOR, *The Russian Theatre* . . . (1928) trans. by Paul England (Philadelphia, 1930), p. 57.

99. ALEXANDER TAIROV, "Structural Realism," *Soviet Theatre*, II (March 1934), 28.

100. ALEXANDER TAIROV, *Zapiski Rezhissera* (*Notes of a Director*) (1921) trans. as *Das Entfesselte Theater* (*The Emancipated Theatre*) (1923) (Potsdam, 1927), pp. 37, 35.

101. *Ibid.*, p. 38.

102. HERBERT J. BIBERMAN, "Meierhold at Work," *Theatre Guild Magazine*, VI (January 1929), 25.

103. VSEVOLOD MEYERHOLD, "The Booth" (1912) trans. by Alexander Bakshy, *The Drama*, 26, 27 (May, August 1917), 429, 213, 427, 436. See *Tulane Drama Review*, 4 (September 1959), 139–149.

104. BRYLLION FAGIN, "Meyerhold Rehearses a Scene," *Theatre Arts*, XVI (October 1932), 834, 836; LEE STRASBERG, "The Magic of Meyerhold," *New Theatre*, I (September 1934), 15 and 30.

105. Biberman, "Meierhold," p. 30.

106. ALEXANDER BAKSHY, *The Path of the Modern Russian Stage* . . . (London, 1916), pp. 57–58, 94.

107. Meyerhold quoted by Strasberg, "Magic Meyerhold," p. 15.

108. Bakshy, *Path Russian Stage*, p. 142.

109. Albright, "Design," p. 25.

110. THOMAS CRAVEN, *Men of Art* (New York, 1931), p. xix, cited *ibid.*; Tynan, *Curtains*, p. viii.

111. GEORGE JEAN NATHAN, "Legend's End," in *Mr. George Jean Nathan Presents* (New York, 1917), p. 78.

112. Ward Morehouse, *Matinee Tomorrow*, p. 169.

113. Nathan, "Legend's End," pp. 76–77.

114. GUTHRIE MCCLINTIC, *Me and Kit* (Boston, 1955), p. 124.

115. ARTHUR HOPKINS, *Reference Point* (New York, 1948), p. 110.

116. Morehouse, *Matinee Tomorrow*, p. 169.

117. *Film Notes*, pp. 14, 11.

118. Young, *Flower*, pp. 48–49, and *FG*, p. 72.

119. Barrett H. Clark, pp. 681–682, in Clark and Freedley, *Modern Drama*; O'Neill quoted *ibid.*, pp. 686, 689.

120. Tynan, *Curtains*, p. 223; Young, *Shadows*, pp. 61, 91.
121. Rhodes, p. 285, in Clark and Freedley, *Modern Drama;* Nicoll, *WD*, p. 775; Rhodes, p. 307.
122. ARTHUR KNIGHT, *The Liveliest Art* (1957) (New York, 1959), p. 142.
123. *The Journals of André Gide, III: 1928–1939* trans. by Justin O'Brien (New York, 1940), 140.
124. Fowlie, *Dionysus*, p. 53.
125. *Ibid.*, p. 42.
126. *Ibid.*, p. 45; MONROE STEARNS, "Louis Jouvet: The Master of Deceit," *Theatre Arts*, XXXVII (January 1953), 93, 18, 20.
127. *Ibid.*, pp. 20, 93.
128. Benjamin Crémieux quoted in Knapp, *Jouvet*, p. 131.
129. Fowlie, *Dionysus*, p. 44. Rhodes, p. 277, in Clark and Freedley, *Modern Drama.*
130. LORENZ KJERBÜHL-PETERSEN, *Die Schauspieler* (1929) trans. as *Psychology of Acting* by Sarah T. Barrows (Boston, 1935), p. ix.
131. *Ibid.*, pp. 135, 141, 142, 143, 175.
132. *Ibid.*, p. 163.
133. *Ibid.*, see p. 232.
134. Cited in MORDECAI GORELIK, *New Theatres for Old* (New York, 1940), pp. 442–443; see also Cole and Chinoy, *AA*, pp. 285–286.
135. *Arnolt Bronnen gibt zu Protokoll* (1954) cited in JOHN WILLETT, *The Theatre of Bertolt Brecht* . . . (London, 1959), p. 109.
136. *Ibid.*, p. 110; Piscator quoted in Cole and Chinoy, *AA*, p. 285.
137. Piscator, "Objective Acting," *ibid.*, p. 288.
138. *Ibid.*, pp. 286, 290, 289.
139. Barker, *Exemplary Theatre*, pp. 1, 82, 89, 90, 37.
140. GRANVILLE-BARKER, *The Study of Drama* (Cambridge, 1934), p. 16; his *Exemplary Theatre*, p. 46.
141. *Ibid.*, pp. 47, 46, 87.
142. *Ibid.*, pp. 85, 155, 67.
143. *Ibid.*, pp. 103, 115.
144. Young, *Shadows*, p. 81.
145. *Ibid.*, pp. 19, 15.
146. *Ibid.*, pp. 16, 18, 39, 18, 19.
147. *Ibid.*, p. 37; STARK YOUNG, "His Art in Life," review of *My Life in Art, New Republic*, 94 (March 30, 1938), 223.
148. *Ibid.*, p. 222; NIKOLAI M. GORCHAKOV, *Stanislavski Directs* (1950) trans. by Miriam Goldina (New York, 1954), p. 119; Stanislavsky, *MLA*, pp. 529–530, 483, 461, 464, 465, 565; see also p. 569. In MLA Stanislavski did write that "the so-called Stanislavski System . . . at present has already reached definite form," p. 483.
149. RICHARD BOLESLAVSKY, "Stanislavsky—the Man and his Methods," *Theatre Magazine* (April 1923), p. 27; HAROLD CLURMAN, *The Fervent Years* . . . (New York, 1945), p. 11.
150. *Ibid.*, pp. 11, 24.
151. *Ibid.*, pp. 27, 34.
152. Young, "His Life in Art," pp. 222, 223.
153. STARK YOUNG, *Theatre Practice* (New York, 1926), p. vii.
154. HUGH (CHRISTOPHER GRIEVE) MACDIARMID, "The Kind of Poetry I Want," *Hudson Review*, XIV (Spring 1961), 16.
155. Young, *Shadows*, p. 117.
156. Stark Young, "Realism," p. 121; Young, *Theater*, pp. 32, 26, 20.
157. Young, *Flower*, p. 11, or *FG*, p. 10; *Theatre Practice*, p. 126; *Flower*, p. 19; *Theater*, pp. 96–97, 118.

158. See Young, *Flower*, p. 12; *Theater*, p. 115; "Realism," p. 123.
159. Young, *Theater*, pp. 119, 161, 101–102, 160, 161.
160. *Ibid.*, pp. 163, 160.
161. Young, *Flower*, pp. 8–9; *Theater*, p. 163.
162. Young, *Flower*, pp. 20, 13; *Theater*, pp. 112, 103, 104.
163. Young, *Flower*, p. 4; *Theater*, pp. 106, 108, 110.
164. *Soviet Theaters 1917–1941* ed. by MARTHA BRADSHAW (New York, 1954), p. 94; Gorelik, *New Theatres*, p. 299, *Soviet Theaters*, p. 91.
165. ANDRÉ VAN GYSEGHEM, *Theatre in Soviet Russia* (London, 1943), p. 13; B. ALPERS, *Teatr Sotsialnoi Maski* (*The Theatre of the Social Mask*) (1931) trans. by Mark Schmidt (in mss. for the Group Theatre) (New York, 1934), p. 3; LOUIS LOZOWICK, "V. E. Meyerhold and his Theatre," *Hound and Horn*, IV (October–November 1930), 95; Biberman, "Meierhold," p. 52; Komisarjevsky, *Theatre*, p. 147; Vakhtangov cited in "Fantastic Realism," p. 161, in Cole and Chinoy, *Directing*.
166. Van Gyseghem, *Soviet Russia*, p. 13.
167. Lozowick, "Meyerhold," p. 99; NORRIS HOUGHTON, *Moscow Rehearsals* (New York, 1936), pp. 20–21.
168. Lozowick, "Meyerhold," pp. 100, 101; Strassberg, "Magic Meyerhold," p. 14; Lozowick, p. 101.
169. Meyerhold quoted in Gorchakov, *Theatre Soviet Russia*, p. 412.
170. SHELDON CHENEY, "Constructivism," *Theatre Arts*, XI (November 1927), 857.
171. JOHN MARTIN, "How Meyerhold Trains His Actors," *Theatre Guild Magazine*, VII (November 1930), 27–28.
172. NIKOLAI GORCHAKOV, *The Vakhtangov School of Stage Art* trans. by G. Ivanov-Mumjiev (Moscow, 1960), pp. 10, 9, 27, 20, 32, 66.
173. *Soviet Theatres*, p. 14.
174. *Ibid.*, p. 42.
175. Houghton, *Moscow Rehearsals*, p. 126; Magarshack, *Life*, p. 356; see Gorchakov, *Vakhtangov*, p. 9; VAKHTANGOV, *Zapiski, Pisma, Stati* (*Notes, Letters, Articles*) (1922) (Moscow, 1939) trans. as "Fantastic Realism," and reprinted in part in Cole and Chinoy, *Directing*, p. 160; V. [OR B.] ZAKHAVA, "The Creative Method of the Vakhtangov Theatre," *Soviet Theatre*, 12 (1931), 6–16, trans. (and abridged) by Mark Schmidt and ed. by MOLLY DAY THATCHER as "Can We Use Stanislavsky's Method?" *New Theatre*, II (August 1935), p. 16; Vakhtangov, *Zapiski*, pp. 162, 160, 164.
176. R. BEN-ARI, "Four Directors and the Actor," trans. by Harry Elion, *Theatre Workshop*, I (January–March, 1937), 67; see Gorchakov, *Theatre Soviet Russia*, p. 439.
177. Gorelik, *New Theatres*, p. 301; Young, *Shadows*, pp. 70, 71.
178. Gyseghem, *Soviet Russia*, pp. 98, 99; see p. 100.
179. Vakhtangov, *Zapiski*, pp. 161, 162, 161, 162, 161.
180. *Ibid.*, p. 165; "Eugene Vakhtangov: 1883–1922" (extracts from his diary), *Theatre Arts*, XX (September 1936), 679.
181. BORIS ZAKHAVA, *Vakhtangov i evo studiya* (*Vakhtangov and His Studio*) (Moscow, 1930), p. 139, cited in *Soviet Theatres*, p. 42; Ben-Ari, "Four Directors," p. 67.
182. Chekhov quoted in Gorchakov, *Theatre Soviet Russia*, p. 436; see *Soviet Theatres*, pp. 37–39; JOSEPH MACLEOD, *The New Soviet Theatre* (London, 1943), p. 98.
183. STANISLAVSKI, MLA (Moscow, 1925) trans. by G. Ivanov-Mumjiev (Moscow, 1960), p. 457.
184. *Soviet Theatres*, p. 53; Gyseghem, *Soviet Russia*, p. 39.
185. Macleod, *New Soviet Theatre*, p. 1131 Gorchakov, *Theatre Soviet Russia*, p. 183.
186. *Soviet Theatres*, p. 62; Dana, p. 397, in Clark and Freedley, *Modern Drama*.
187. See K. ANTAROVA, "The System and Methods of Creative Art," in *Stanislavski on the*

Art of the Stage trans. by DAVID MAGARSHACK (London, 1950), pp. 91, 92, 113, 130.

188. *Ibid.*, p. 120; Stanislavski, *MLA* (1925), p. 466.
189. See Antarova, pp. 123, 92, 189–190, 179, 178–179.
190. *Ibid.*, p. 149.
191. *Ibid.*, pp. 117, 195.
192. NIKOLAI M. GORCHAKOV, *Stanislavski Directs* (*Rezhisserskie Uroki K. S. Stanislavskogo*) (1950) trans. by MIRIAM GOLDINA and ed. by VIRGINIA STEVENS (New York, 1954), pp. 119, 23 and see 148, 94.
193. *Ibid.*, pp. 193–194, 41, 49.
194. STANISLAVSKI, "Direction and Acting," *Encyclopaedia Britannica* (1929), pp. 22, 35–38, but given a different trans. by ELIZABETH REYNOLDS HAPGOOD in *Stanislavski's Legacy* . . . (New York, 1958), pp. 177, 170.
195. *Ibid.*, pp. 175, 176. The original *Encyclopaedia* trans., unidentified, appears in TOBY COLE (ed.), *Acting, a handbook of the Stanislavski method* (New York, 1947), pp. 22–32.
196. CONSTANTIN STANISLAVSKI, *Building a Character* trans. by Elizabeth Reynolds Hapgood (New York, 1949), pp. vii–viii; Antarova, "System," p. 221; Stanislavski, *BC*, p. viii.
197. Magarshack, *Life*, pp. 380–381.
198. Stanislavski, *MLA* (1925), p. 499.
199. Clurman, *Fervent Years*, pp. 39, 139; see p. 194, 42.
200. *Ibid.*, pp. 43–44, 44–45.
201. *Ibid.*, pp. 87, 91–92.
202. *Ibid.*, p. 139; see ROBERT LEWIS, *Method—or Madness?* (New York, 1958), pp. 23, 26, 57; Clurman, p. 139.
203. Lewis, *Method*, p. 55; Clurman, *Fervent Years*, pp. 158, 160.
204. "Preparing the Role" (from the Diary of E. Vakhtangov), "adapted from a translation made for the use of the Group Theatre," and reprinted in Cole, *Acting*, p. 116; Lewis, *Method*, p. 15; Ben Gazzara quoted by ROBERT RICE, "Actors' Studio," *N.Y. Post*, May 14, 1957, p. M4; Vakhtangov, "Preparing the Role," p. 120.
205. HENRY HEWES, " 'The Method's' Mouth," *Saturday Review*, XLII (January 24, 1959), 25.
206. *Soviet Theatres*, p. xiv; Macleod, *Soviet Theatre*, pp. 20–21.
207. *Ibid.*, p. 19; *Soviet Theatres*, p. 58.
208. See JURI JELAGIN, *Taming of the Arts* (New York, 1951), pp. 171–173.
209. See *Soviet Theatres*, p. 42; Magarshack, *Life*, p. 384.
210. *Ibid.*, p. 389; STANISLAVSKI, "Work With Actors" (1936), *One Act Play Magazine*, I (December 1937), 762, 761; Zakhava, "Creative Method," p. 16.
211. HENRY SCHNITZLER, "Truth and Consequences, or Stanislavsky Misinterpreted," *Quarterly Journal Speech*, XL (April 1954), 161–162.
212. Magarshack, *Life*, p. 393; Stanislavski, *AP*, pp. 28, 295, 18, 13, 167, 28, and see p. 48; see *Stanislavski's Legacy*, pp. 129, 134.
213. Magarshack, *Life*, pp. 397, 389; Gorchakov, *Stanislavski Directs*, p. 375; see Magarshack, p. 375.
214. Mikhail Khedrov quoted in "The Moscow Art Theatre in Rehearsal," by JOHN D. MITCHELL, GEORGE DREW, MIRIAM P. MITCHELL, *Educational Theatre Journal*, XII (December 1960), 281.
215. Magarshack, *Life*, pp. 372, 373, 372; Gorchakov, *Stanislavski Directs*, p. 390; see Magershack, p. 373.
216. Mitchell, Drew, Mitchell, "Moscow Art Theatre," pp. 282, 280, 284.
217. WALTER F. KERR, "Earnest Players," *N.Y. Herald Tribune*, June 17, 1956, Section 4,

p. 1; see his *Pieces at Eight* (New York, 1957), p. 236; WALTER F. KERR, "Acting Techniques Discussed," *N.Y. Herald Tribune*, August 17, 1952, Section 4, p. 1; book digest of STAN OPOTOWSKY, *TV: The Big Picture* (New York, 1961), *N.Y. Post*, May 29, 1961, p. M21.

218. Kerr, "Acting Techniques," p. 1; HAROLD CLURMAN, "Actor in Style—and Style in Actors," *N.Y. Times Magazine*, December 7, 1952, p. 38.

219. Tynan, *Curtains*, p. 163; Willi Schmidt quoted *N.Y. Times*, February 13, 1960, p. 13; JACQUES CHARON, "As Others See Us," *Equity*, XLV (June 1960), 9; MICHAEL CHEKHOV, *To the Actor* . . . (New York, 1953), pp. 85, 86; OLIVIER quoted *N.Y. Times*, (February 7, 1960), Section 2, p. 3.

220. Barrault, *Reflections*, 18, 19, 119, 126, 127, 129.

221. *Ibid.*, pp. 19, 21, 112, 114, 113.

222. *Ibid.*, p. 73; Fowlie, *Dionysus*, p. 189.

223. Tynan, *Curtains*, p. 391; ANTONIN ARTAUD, *Le Théâtre et son Double* (1938) trans. by Mary Caroline Richards (New York, 1958), pp. 41, 70, 72, 48.

224. ERNEST BORNEMAN, "Two Brechtians," *Kenyon Review*, XXII (Summer 1960), 481, 470; MORDECAI GORELIK, "Brecht . . . ," *Theatre Arts*, XLI (March 1957), 73; JOHN GASSNER, "A Modern Style of Theatre," *Quarterly Journal Speech*, XXXVIII (February 1952), 71; MARTIN ESSLIN, *Brecht, the man and his work* (New York, 1961), p. 195.

225. ERNEST BORNEMAN, "Credo Quia Absurdam: an epitaph for Bertolt Brecht," *Kneyon Review*, XXI (Spring 1959), 192.

226. Esslin, *Brecht*, p. 46.

227. Tynan, *Curtains*, p. 468; Esslin, *Brecht*, p. 92.

228. Borneman, "Two Brechtians," p. 466, and Esslin, *Brecht*, p. 144; BERTOLT BRECHT, "Neue Technik der Schauspielkunst" (1940, published 1952) trans. by Eric Bentley as "A New Technique of Acting," *Theatre Arts*, XXXIII (January 1949), 38–40, and reprinted as "The Alienation Effect," Cole and Chinoy, AA, p. 285; Gorelik, "Brecht," p. 86; Brecht, "Anmerkungen zur *Dreigroschenoper*" (1931), *Schriften zum Theater*, p. 35, cited by Esslin, *Brecht*, p. 123; *ibid.*, p. 126; Gassner, "Modern Style," p. 69; Gorelik, p. 86; EDMUND FULLER, "Epic Realism . . . ," *One Act Play Magazine*, I (April 1938), 1127; Borneman, "Credo," p. 193; Tynan, *Curtains*, p. 461.

229. Brecht, "Vergnuegungstheater oder Lehrtheater" (1936), *Schriften zum Theater*, p. 63, quoted by Esslin, *Brecht*, p. 129; see *ibid.*, p. 125; Gassner, "Modern Style," p. 68; Esslin, pp. 125, 129, 127; 27; Brecht, "Anmerkungen zu *Leben des Galilei*," *Stuecke* VIII, p. 205, cited *ibid.*, p. 127.

230. Official directive to *Pamietnik Teatralny* (1955) cited by Esslin, *Brecht*, p. 207.

231. Borneman, "Credo," p. 191; Esslin, *Brecht*, p. 121.

232. Brecht, "Neue Technik," in Cole and Chinoy, AA, p. 282; Eric Bentley, "German Stagecraft Today," *Kenyon Review*, XI (Winter 1949), 642; Brecht quoted by Tynan, *Curtains*, p. 461; Esslin, *Brecht*, pp. 134, 130, and Brecht, "Die Strassenszene" (1940), *Schriften zum Theater*, p. 99, cited *ibid.*; Brecht, "Neue Technik," p. 282.

233. *Ibid.*; Borneman, "Credo," p. 194; Brecht, "Neue Technik," p. 282; Borneman, "Credo," p. 194; "Neue Technik," p. 284.

234. *Ibid.*, p. 283; see Tynan, *Curtains*, p. 461.

235. Borneman, "Credo," pp. 196, 197; Tynan, *Curtains*, pp. 459–460.

236. *New York Times*, April 3, 1961, p. 32.

237. See Tynan, *Curtains*, pp. 413, 414, 455, 456, 470.

238. *Ibid.*, pp. 425–426.

239. Sterling North, *New York World-Telegram*, February 24, 1956, p. 22.

240. See HALLIE FLANAGAN, *Arena* (New York, 1940), pp. 377–436.

241. *Ibid.*, pp. 334–335; Saxon report, *New York Times*, April 3, 1961, p. 32.
242. Tynan, *Curtains*, p. 375.
243. *The Burns Mantle Best Plays of 1949–50* ed. by JOHN CHAPMAN (New York, 1950), p. 382.
244. Garrison P. Sherwood, p. 356, in *The Best Plays of 1953–54* ed. by LOUIS KRONEN-BERGER (New York, 1954).
245. See Carl Glick, "The Community Theater Movement," p. 169, in *The Theatre Handbook* . . . ed. by BERNARD SOBOL (New York, 1940).
246. George Steiner, "The Retreat From the Word," *Kenyon Review*, XXIII (Spring 1961), 196, 203; Peter Hall quoted, *New York Times*, October 11, 1960, p. x7; see Fowlie, *Dionysus*, p. 288.
247. Colin Wilson, "Speaking of Books," *New York Times Book Review*, February 17, 1957, p. 2.

IMPORTANT WRITINGS
ON ACTING

ANCIENT TIMES

ARISTOTLE (384–322 B.C.). *Poetics* and *Rhetoric* (both *c.* 335–322 B.C.).
Butcher, S. H. *Aristotle's Theory of Poetry and Fine Art with a critical text and translation of the Poetics* (1894), 4th ed. (London, 1907); reprinted 1948, 1957. The *Poetics*, pp. 5–111; the Commentary, pp. 113–407.
Cooper, Lane. *Aristotle on the Art of Poetry, an amplified version with supplementary examples for students of composition and public speaking* (New York, 1913) 100 pp.; reprinted 1947.
See Books I, II, and IV. (And Marsh.)
The Rhetoric of Aristotle, an expanded translation with supplementary examples for students of composition and public speaking (New York, 1932), 259 pp.
For action and motives see especially Book I, 5–6, 10–13; for emotions, Book II, 1–11; for types of characters, Book II, 12–17; for delivery, Book III, 1.
Rhetoric trans. by W. Rhys Roberts (1924); *Poetics* trans. by Ingram Bywater (1909) with Int. by Friedrich Solmsen, Modern Library (New York, 1954), 289 pp.
BHARATA. *Nātya-śāstra (Dramatic Science)* (*c.* 3rd century) *with the commentary of Abhinavagupta* ed. in Sanskrit by M. Ramakrishna Kavi [with the Preface, pp. 5–12, in English] (Baroda, 1926), 2 vols.
Ch. I–XXVII trans. by Manomohan Ghosh, Royal Asiatic Society of Bengal (Calcutta, 1951); Ch. IV, together with a glossary of the technical dance terms from Ch. VIII, IX, X, trans. by Bijayeti Venkata Narayanaswami Naidu and Ongole Venkata Rangayya Pantulu (Madras, 1936), 177 pp.
CICERO (106–42 B.C.). *De Oratore* (*c.* 55 B.C.). English opposite Latin, Books I, II trans. by E. W. Sutton; completed, with Int. by H. Rackham; Book III trans. by Rackham. Loeb Classical Library (Cambridge, Mass., 1942; rev. 1948), 2 vols.
"I do not take a very different line when I am discussing the orator from the line I should take if I had to speak about the actor," III, xxii, 83.
Material relevant to acting is scattered throughout; see, for instance, Book I, lv, 14; v, 18; xi, 51; xxiii, 107–109; xxv, 113–115; xxvi, 124–215; xxviii, xxxii, xxxiii, 149–150; xxxiv, 156; l, 219; li, 223; lviii, 251–252; lix, 251–252; lxi, 259. Book II, vii, 30–33; xxii, 90ff.; xxxiv–xxxv, 145–151; xlii, 178; xlv, 188–197; li–lii, 206–211; lxxxvii, 356. Book III, xi, 40–43; xii, 45; xxii, 83; xxvi, 101–103; xlviii, 184–186; l, 195; lvi–lx, 213–225.
COLE, TOBY and HELEN KRICH CHINOY (ed.). *Actors on Acting; the theories, techniques, and practices of the great actors of all times told in their own words* (New York, 1949).
Ch. I, "Greece," with an introduction, "The Artists of Dionysus," and excerpts from Plato, Aristotle, Plutarch, Gellus, and Pollux, pp. 3–18; and II, "Rome," with an introduction, "Actors, Slaves, and Orators," and excerpts from Cicero, Quintilian, and Lucian, pp. 19–33.

MARSH, ROBERT. "Aristotle and the Modern Rhapsode," *Quarterly Journal Speech*, XXXIX (December 1953), 491–498.

Brings together "the general outlines of what an Aristotelian might suggest as foundation for carrying out the task of re-creating an imitated action."

PICKARD-CAMBRIDGE, A. W. *Dithyramb Tragedy and Comedy* (Oxford, 1927).

Ch. II, iii, "Thespis," pp. 97–120.

The Dramatic Festivals of Athens (Oxford, 1953).

The sections on the actor's contests, pp. 93–96, 100–103; Ch. III, "The Actors," pp. 127–174, with discussions of terminology, the number of actors and distribution of parts, delivery-speech-recitative and song, voice and enunciation, gesture; and VII, "The Artists of Dionysus," pp. 286–315, are indispensable in this field.

PLATO (429–347 B.C.). *Ion* (*c.* 390 B.C.) trans. by Shelley, Jowett, Cooper, *et al.*

QUINTILIAN (*c.* A.D. 35–95). *Institutio Oratoria* (*c.* A.D. 90). English opposite Latin trans. by H. E. Butler. Loeb Classical Library (Cambridge, Mass., 1921–22), 4 vols.

In this work on the education of the perfect orator, the section most applicable to acting is Book XI, iii, 1–124, pp. 243–309, on delivery; the best known excerpt is Book VI, ii, 22–36. Additional pertinent remarks appear in Book I, Pr. 26–27; viii, 1–3; xi, 1–19. Book II, x, 13–14; xii, 8–11; xiii, 15–17; xvii, 5–6, 41–43. Book III, v, 1; viii, 50–51. Book IV, ii, 36–39. Book V, x, 32ff. Book VII, x, 14–15. Book VIII, Pr. 15; iii, 83. Book X, i, 65–71, 119; ii, 1–6ff. Book XI, i, 4, 39, 43, 46–47; iii, 150, 178–184. Book XII, x, 42–45.

See Martin T. Cobin, "An Oral Interpreter's Index to Quintilian," *Quarterly Journal Speech*, XLIV (February 1958), 61–66.

REICH, HERMAN. *Der Mimus; ein litterar-entwichelungsgeschichlicher Versuch* (Berlin, 1903), 900 pp.

A list of critical works on the subject printed by 1900 is included on pp. 6–10.

SHISLER, F. L. "The Use of Stage Business to Portray Emotion in Greek Tragedy," *American Journal Philology*, LXVI (October 1945), 377–397.

Material on "actions, gestures, appearances, etc."

SPITZBARTH, A. *Untersuchungen zur Spieltechnik der griechischen Tragödie* (Zurich, 1946), 109 pp.

An examination of the texts for evidence of gesture, action, and the representation of emotions.

THE MIDDLE AGES TO 1600

CHAMBERS, E. K. *The Medieval Stage* (Oxford, 1903), 2 vols.

The author's intent was to give "some short account of the origins of play acting in England and of its development during the Middle Ages. Unfortunately it soon became apparent that the basis for such a narrative was wanting," I, v. Consequently, his account is swelled beyond that topic of acting, but what it includes is valuable. Especially recommended are the books on "Minstrelsy," I, 1–86, and on "The Interlude," II, 179–226.

COHEN, GUSTAVE. *Histoire de la mise-en-scène dans le théâtre religieux français du moyen age* (1906) (Paris, 1951), 354 pp.

Ch. VII, "Les Acteurs," pp. 196–243.

COLE and CHINOY. *Actors on Acting.*

Consult Ch. III, "The Middle Ages," pp. 34–40.

DI SOMI, LEONE (1517–1592). *Dialoghi in materia di rappresentazione sceniche* (*Dialogues on Stage Affairs*) (*c.* 1560).

The Third Dialogue, on acting, is included in Luigi Rasi, *I Comici italiani: biografia, bibliografia, inconografia* (Florence, 1897–1905), I, 107–116; "a translation of the entire text of these interesting disquisitions" appears in Allardyce Nicoll, *The Development of the Theatre* (1948 ed.), pp. 237–262. Cole and Chinoy, AA, reprint 23 of the original 32 speeches of the Third Dialogue, pp. 44–49, from Nicoll, DT (1927 ed.), pp. 250–253. See also Winifred Smith, *The Commedia dell' arte* . . . (New York, 1912), pp. 70–78, and A. M. Nagler, *Sources of Theatrical History* (New York, 1952), p. 103; reprinted 1959.

FRAUNCE, ABRAHAM (fl.1587–1633). *The Arcadian Rhetorike* (London, 1588). See *The Arcadian Rhetorike by Abraham Fraunce* ed. by Ethel Seaton (Oxford, 1950).
A translation of the *Rhetorica* (*c.* 1550) of Audomarus Talaerus (Omer Talon) (*c.* 1510–1562), a colleague of the celebrated Frenchman, Pierre de la Ramée, better known as Petrus Ramus (1515–1572). The work is a collection of Ramistic precepts for style and delivery, with illustrative passages designed "to exhibit a trope, a figure, a kind of voice, or a motion of head, eyes, lips, arms, hands, and feet," Wilbur S. Howell, *Logic and Rhetoric in England*, 1500–1700 (Princeton, 1956), p. 258.

GAUTIER, LEON. *Les Épopées françaises* (1865–68) 2nd ed. (Paris, 1878–1892), 3 vols. II, Ch. XIV, "De l'Execution des chansons de geste," pp. 386–411.

HSIU-LING CH'ÊNG (Cecelia S. L. Zung). *Secrets of the Chinese Drama* . . . (Shanghai, 1937).
Part II examines traditional acting "Technique," pp. 77–148.

NANDIKEŚVARA. *Abhinaya-darpanam* (13th century?) trans. by Ananda Coomaraswamy and Duggirāla Gopālakrishnāya as *The Mirror of Gesture* (1917) (New York, 1936), 81 pp.
See also the *Abhinaya-darpanam, a manual of gestures and postures used in Hindu dance and drama* trans. by Manomohan Ghosh (Calcutta, 1934), 55 pp.

PETIT DE JULLEVILLE, L. *Histoire de Théâtre en France. Les Comédiens en France au moyen age* (Paris, 1885).
Ch. I, "Les jongleurs," pp. 15–28; IV, "Les confréres," pp. 55–87; V, "Les Basochiens," pp. 88–142; VI, "Les Enfants-sans-Souci," pp. 143–191; VII, "Les sociétés joyeuses," pp. 192–261; X, "Les comédiens," pp. 324–352.

REICH. *Der Mimus.*
Ch. IX, "Der Mimus im Occident während des Mittelalters," pp. 744–859.

SEAMI or ZEAMI (1363–1443). *Kadensho (The Instructions on Flower)* or *Fūshi-Kaden (The Instructions on the Posture of Flower)* (1400–1418) which includes *Nenrai-Keiko-Jōjō (Matters concerning the Training and Ages)*; *Monomane-Jōjō (Matters concerning Imitation)*; *Mondo-Jōjō (Questions and Answers on the Essentials of Noh)* (1400); *Shingi (The Origin and the History of Sarugaku)*; *Ogi (The Fundamentals of Noh)* (1402); *Kashū (The Acquisition of Flower)*; and *Besshi-Kuden (Supplementary and Particular Oral Instructions)* (1418).
The *Hachijyōbon-Kadensho (Instructions on Flower in Eight Volumes)*, an extremely altered ed. of the original *Kadensho* (1665); and *Zeami-jūrokubu-shū (Collection of Sixteen Treatises by Zeami)* ed. by Togo Yoshida (1909).
See *Seami Jûroku Bushû (Seami's Sixteen Treatises), Kadensho (The Book of Flower)* trans. by Michitaro Shidehara and Wilfred Whitehouse, *Monumenta Nipponica*, IV (July 1941), 204–239; V (1942), 218–239.
Consult passages from Seami's writings in Arthur Waley, *The Nō Plays of Japan* (1921) (New York, 1957), pp. 21ff., and Toyoichirō Nogami, *Zeami and His Theories on Noh* trans. by Ryōzē Matsumoto (Tokyo, 1955), 89 pp.
The oldest complete statements of an actor concerning his art and his theories of acting that have come down to us, though his kind of acting was quite unlike that exhibited in the West.

COMMEDIA DELL' ARTE (c. 1560–1765)

BARBIERI, NICOLÒ (?–c. 1640). *La Supplica: discorso famigliare diretta a quelli che scrivendo o parlando trattano de comici trascurando i meriti della' azzioni virtuose* . . . (1634) (Bologna, 1636), 233 pp.

 See Enzo Petracconi (ed.), *La Comedia dell' arte; storia, tecnica, scenari* (Naples, 1927), pp. 19–51, and a brief selection in Cole and Chinoy, AA, pp. 53–54.

 An actor's "kind of *apologia* for the stage of his time."

CABANELLOS, A. CUNILL. "El estilo del actor en la comedia del arte," *Cultura*, II (1950), 41–76.

CECCHINI, PIER MARIA (1563–c. 1645). *Frutti delle moderne comedie et avisi a chi le recita* . . . (Padua, 1628).

        Discorso sopra l'arte comica con il modo di ben recitare (n.d.).

 For the first work see Petraccone, *La Commedia*, pp. 8–18; a selection is included in Cole and Chinoy, AA, pp. 50–52. The second work is a ms. in the Library of Turin.

COLE AND CHINOY. *Actors on Acting.*

 Ch. IV, "Italy I, The Commedia dell' Arte," with excerpts from Di Somi, Cecchini, Barbieri, Perrucci, Gherardi, and Riccoboni, pp. 41–63.

DUCHARTE, PIERRE-LOUIS. *The Italian Comedy; the improvisation scenarios lives attributes portraits and masks of the illustrious characters of the commedia dell' arte* (1924) trans. by Randolph Weaver (New York, 1929).

 Ch. III, "The Technique of the Improvisators," pp. 30–40; VII, "The Actors and the Troupes of the Commedia dell' Arte," pp. 70–101; XII–XXII, The Characters, pp. 123–292. Bibliography, pp. 313–324.

 A later ed. is titled *La Commedia dell' Arte et ses enfants* (Paris, 1955).

GHERARDI, EVARISTO (1663–1700). *Le Théâtre italien, ou le recueil général de toutes les comédies et scènes françaises jouées par les comédiens italiens du roi, pendant tout le temps qu'ils ont été au service* (1694) (Paris, 1741), 6 vols. containing 17 scripts.

 See Gherardi, "On the Art of Italian Comedians," an excerpt from the *Avertissement* of the 1741 ed., *Theatre Arts*, X (February 1926), 109–111, and in Cole and Chinoy, AA, pp. 58–59. See also "The Introduction to 'Le Théâtre Italien of Evaristo Gherardi,' written by himself; translated with a Biographical Note upon the Author" by D. Nevile Lees, *The Mask*, III (1910–11), 164–168.

 Isadore A. Schwartz in his *The Commedia dell' Arte and its influence on French Comedy in the Seventeenth Century* (Paris, 1933) examines in Ch. VI, "The Gherardi Repertoire," pp. 129–172.

 Gherardi's collection "is . . . emphatically an actor's book completed by an actor. In it we have the scenes, the dialogues, the *lazzi*, the little songs and the music which went with them . . . ," Lees, p. 166.

GOLDONI, CARLO (1707–1793). *Il Teatro Comico* (1750) in his *Opere Teatrali* . . . (Venice, 1788), I, 1–72.

 A play about actors and acting.

McDOWELL, JOHN H. "Some Pictorial Aspects of Early Commedia dell' Arte Acting," *Studies in Philology*, XXXIX (1924), 47–64.

PERRUCCI, ANDREA (1651–1704). *Dell' arte rappresentativa, premeditata, e dall' improviso. Parti due giovevole non solo a chi si diletta di rappresentare; ma a' predicatori, oratori, accademici e curiosi* (Naples, 1699).

 See Petraccone, *La Commedia*, pp. 69–201; an excerpt is included in Cole and Chinoy, AA, pp. 56–57; another appears in Nagler, *Sources*, pp. 257–259. See also "The

Commedia dell' Arte, or Professional Comedy," another selection, *The Mask*, IV (1911–12), 113–115.

ZANNONI, ATANASIO. *Raccolta di vari motto arguti, allegorical e satirici ad uso del teatro* (c. 1760), 122 pp.

An actor's collection of humorous and sententious speeches for commedia performers.

THE SEVENTEENTH CENTURY

English

ARMSTRONG, WILLIAM A. "Shakespeare and the Acting of Edward Alleyn," *Shakespeare Survey* 7 ed. by Allardyce Nicoll (Cambridge, 1954), pp. 82–89.

BACHRACH, A. G. H. "The Great Chain of Acting," *Neophilologus*, XXXIII (1949), 160–172.

A discussion of Elizabethan acting.

BETHELL, SAMUEL L. *Shakespeare & the Popular Dramatic Tradition* (London, 1944).

Ch. I, "Conventionalism and Naturalism," pp. 13–30; II, "Planes of Reality," pp. 31–41; IV, "The Treatment of Character," pp. 62–107, with sections on "Soliloquy," "Direct Address," "Depersonalization," and "Characters of Double Nature."

"Shakespeare's Actors" (1948), *Review of English Studies*, n.s. 1 (July 1950), 193–205.

Insists that the acting was fundamentally formal, but "might be shaded by naturalism from time to time."

BROWN, JOHN RUSSELL. "On the Acting of Shakespeare's Plays," *Quarterly Journal Speech*, XXXIX (December 1953), 477–484.

Argues that it aimed at an illusion of life, although some vestiges of an old formalism remained.

BULWER, JOHN (fl. 1644–1654). *Chirologia*, 187 pp.; *Chironomia*, 146 pp. (London, 1644).

Chirologia: or, the natural language of the hand. Composed of the speaking motions, and discoursing gestures thereof. . . .

(*Chironomia: or, The art of Manuall Rhetorique. With the canons, lawes, rites, ordinances, and institutes of rhetoricians, both ancient and moderne, touching the artificiall managing of the Hand in Speaking. . . .*)

See excerpts in Lester Thonssen (ed.), *Selected Readings in Rhetoric and Public Speaking* (New York, 1942), pp. 189–206; Joseph, *Elizabethan Acting*; and James W. Cleary, "John Bulwer: Renaissance Communicationist," *Quarterly Journal Speech*, XLV (December 1959), 391–398.

"The work [based on Quintilian and Crésol] enjoys the historical distinction of being the first systematic and thorough treatise in English . . . ," Cleary, p. 395.

Pathomyotomia: Or, a Dissection of the Significative Muscles of the Affections of the Minde (London, 1649).

"Bulwer becomes the first to explain in English the subject of 'metaposcopy' or the study of the muscles of the face and their relation to emotion," Cleary, p. 399.

Philocophus: Or, the Deafe and Dumbe Mans Friend (London, 1648).

Ch. I–VII discuss the production and management of voice; VIII–XIV examine pronunciation.

COLE and CHINOY. *Actors on Acting.*

Ch. VI, "England, The Elizabethan Actor," with excerpts from Shakespeare, Jonson, *The Return from Parnassus II*, Heywood, *The Cyprian Conqueror* (c. 1633), and Flecknoe, pp. 75–91.

DAVIES, WILLIAM R. *Shakespeare's Boy Actors* (London, 1939), 207 pp.

EICH, LOUIS M. "Ned Alleyn versus Dick Burbage," *Speech Monographs*, VI (1939), 110–126.

FLATTER, RICHARD. *Shakespeare's Producing Hand, a study of his marks of expression to be found in the first folio* (New York, 1948), 184 pp.
    Considers "Aside," Entries, Pauses, Metrical Gaps, Irregular Stress, Simultaneousness, Line-division, Punctuation.

FOAKES, R. A. "The Player's Passion, some notes on Elizabethan psychology and acting," in *Essays and Studies* (English Association), n.s. 7 (1954), 66–77.

GREG, W. W. *Dramatic Documents from the Elizabethan Playhouses* (Oxford, 1931), 2 vols.
    Stage plots, actors' parts, prompt books, etc.
           "Edward Alleyn," in *Shakespeare and the Theatre* (London, 1927), pp. 1–34.

HARBAGE, ALFRED. "Elizabethan Acting," *Pub. Modern Language Ass.*, LIV (September 1939), 685–708.
    An "attempt to define two alternate styles of acting—formal acting and natural acting: to attack the case for natural acting on the Elizabethan stage and to defend the case for formal acting."

JOSEPH, BERTRAM. *Acting Shakespeare* (London, 1960), 199 pp.
    "The problem of speaking Shakespeare's score is twofold; on the one hand the actor has to give his audience an experience of the lines as poetry, and on the other he must sound natural, like a real human being . . . ," p. 55.
           Elizabethan Acting (Oxford and London, 1951), 157 pp.
    A scholarly examination.
           "The Elizabethan Stage and Acting," in *A Guide to English Literature: II, The Age of Shakespeare* ed. by Boris Ford (Penguin Books, 1955), pp. 147–161.
           The Tragic Actor (New York, 1959).
    English acting from the age of Shakespeare to Irving and Forbes-Robertson. See "The Age of Shakespeare," pp. 1–27, and "The Age of Betterton," pp. 28–66.

McNEIR, WALDO F. "Gayton on Elizabethan Acting," *Pub. Modern Language Ass.*, LVI (June 1941), 579–583.
    Concludes that the acting was "simplified, strenuous, and to a large degree formalized."

MATTINGLY, ALETHA S. "The Playing Time and Manner of Delivery of Shakespeare's Plays in the Elizabethan Theatre," *Speech Monographs*, XXI (March 1954), 29–38.

NAGLER. *Sources Theatrical History.*
    Selections on "Elizabethan Acting," pp. 122–128, and on acting during the Restoration, pp. 213–230.

ROSENBERG, MARVIN. "Elizabethan Actors: Men or Marionettes?" *Pub. Modern Language Ass.*, LXIX (September 1954), 915–927.
    Argues for a kind of "natural" acting.

SACKTON, ALEXANDER H. *Rhetoric as a Dramatic Language in Ben Jonson* (New York, 1948).
    See Ch. II, "The Tradition of Rhetoric in the Age of Jonson," pp. 11–32.

WILSON, JOHN H. "Rant, Cant, and Tone on the Restoration Stage," *Studies in Philology*, LII (October 1955), 592–598.

WRIGHT, THOMAS. *The Passions of the Mind* (London, 1604).

French

AUBIGNAC, ABBÉ D' (François Hédelin) (1604–1676). *La Pratique du théâtre* (1657) trans. as *The Whole Art of the Stage, containing not only the Rules of the Dramatick Art, but many curious observations about it. Which may be of great use to the authors, actors, and spectators of plays . . .* (London, 1684), 135, 176 pp. New ed. 1927.

The unknown "translator has made some Alterations in the Authors method & order of his Chapters . . ."

Book III, Ch. 1–9, pp. 1–65, consists of instructions to the poet about his use of Persons that are about to appear upon the Stage." Topics include "Of Discourses in general," "Of Narrations," "Of Deliberations," "Of Didactick Discourses or Instructions," "Of Pathetick Discourses, or of the Passions and Motions of the Mind," "Of the Figures," "Of Monologues," "Of a-Partes, or Discourses made to ones self in the presence of others."

COLE and CHINOY. *Actors on Acting.*

Ch. VIII, "France, Tradition and Revolt," with material on "The Comédiens of the Hôtel de Bourgogne," a bit from *The Impromptu at Versailles*, and "My Opinion of Michel Baron," by Elena Riccoboni, pp. 153–160.

CONRART, VALENTIN. See Le Faucheur.

CRÉSOL, LOUIS (Cresollius Ludovicus). *Vacationes Autumnales sive De Perfecta Oratoris Actione et Pronunciatione . . .* (Paris, 1620), 706 pp.

A massive compilation of all the doctrine of the ancients on the subject of voice and gesture in oratory.

One of Le Faucheur's, Bulwer's, and Gildon's sources.

LE BRUN, CHARLES (1619–1690). *The Conference of Monsieur Le Brun . . . Upon Expression general and particular* (1667) (London, 1701), 47 pp.

LE FAUCHEUR, MICHEL (?–1657). *Traitté de l'action de l'orateur, ou de la Prononciation et du geste* (Paris, 1657), 243 pp.

The author's name seems never to have been attached to "one of the most respectable works of scholarship in the whole elocutionary movement and one of the finest treatises on delivery in the history of rhetorical theory," Wilbur S. Howell, "Sources of the Elocutionary Movement in England 1700–1748," *Quarterly Journal Speech*, XLV (February 1959), 8.

"This work received several editions in French before the end of the seventeenth century, and in 1690 at Helmstedt it was published in Melchior Schmidt's Latin version, thus being made available to the entire European world of learning. Some dozen years after this latter event, it was given an anonymous English translation and published at London under the title, *An Essay Upon The Action of an Orator; As To His Pronunciation & Gesture . . .*" (c. 1702), Howell, "Sources," p. 6.

Japanese

ERNST, EARLE. *The Kabuki Theatre* (London, 1956).

Ch. VII, "The Actor," pp. 164–204.

SCOTT, A. C. *The Kabuki Theatre of Japan* (London, 1955).

Ch. VII, "The Actor's Technique," pp. 105–156, and VIII, "The Actor," pp. 157–198.

Spanish

COLE and CHINOY. *Actors on Acting.*

Ch. V, "Spain, The Actor as Playwright," with excerpts by Cervantes on Lope de Rueda, Alonzo Lopez Pinciano on "Actors and Playing," a selection from de Rojas, etc., pp. 64–74.

THE EIGHTEENTH CENTURY

English

ANGUS, WILLIAM. "An Appraisal of David Garrick Based Mainly upon Contemporary Sources," *Quarterly Journal Speech*, XXV (February 1939), 30–42.

A study in the changes from chant to "natural" speaking.

"BETTERTON, Mr. Thomas" (probably Edmund Curll (1675–1747). *The History of the English Stage, from the Restauration to the Present Time. Including the Lives, Characters and Amours, of the most Eminent Actors and Actresses. With Instructions for Public Speaking; wherein The Action and Utterance of the Bar, Stage, and Pulpit are Distinctly considered,* 167 pp. (together with) *Memoirs of Mrs. Anne Oldfield,* 86 pp. (London, 1741).

A potboiler hodge-podge of "The Memoirs of Mrs. Barry," "Some farther Memoirs of Nell Guyn," "Memoirs of Mr. Wilks," "Memoirs of Mr. Booth," and assorted squibs on other performers. The material on acting is filched from Gildon's *Betterton.*

BOSWELL, JAMES (1740–1795). *On the Profession of a Player, three essays now first reprinted from the London Magazine for August, September, and October 1770* (London, 1929), 43 pp.

The second essay, pp. 11–24, is especially worth reading.

CAMPBELL, LILY B. "The Rise of a Theory of Stage Presentation During the Eighteenth Century," *Pub. Modern Language Ass.,* XXXII, n.s. XXV (June 1917), 163–200.

A survey of the changes in English acting styles from about 1690 to 1814: the mechanical recitative of Betterton, the "natural" acting of Macklin and Garrick, and the "grand style" of Kemble and Mrs. Siddons.

CIBBER, COLLEY (1671–1757). *An Apology for the Life of Mr. Colley Cibber . . . Written by Himself; and interspersed with Characters and Anecdotes of his Theatrical Contemporaries; the whole forming a Complete History of the Stage for the Space of Forty Years* (1740). *New ed. with critical and explanatory notices by Edmund Bellchambers* (London, 1822), 514 pp. plus index.

A shortened, popular version: *History of the Stage. In which is included the Theoretical Characters of the most celebrated actors . . .* (London, 1742).

Also *An Apology,* etc., A *new edition with notes and supplement by Robert W. Lowe* (London, 1889), 2 vols. The commentary is exhaustive, and includes a supplementary chapter which completes Cibber's record up to his death. Included also is a reprint of Anthony Aston's (c. 1682–1749?) *Brief Supplement to Colley Cibber, Esq.; his lives of the late famous actors* (London, 1747), together with "Memoirs of the Actors and Actresses Mentioned by Cibber," taken from Bellchambers' ed. Cibber hopes that his account "may in some degree show what talents are requisite to make actors valuable," p. 189. Read especially Ch. IV and V.

See Cole and Chinoy, AA, pp. 102–114; (Aston), pp. 114–116.

COLE and CHINOY. *Actors on Acting.*

See Ch. VII, "England II, The Great Names," for selections from Gildon, Cibber, Aston, Aaron Hill, Macklin, John Hill, Garrick, Catherine Clive, and Mrs. Siddons, pp. 92–145.

DOWNER, ALAN S. "Nature to Advantage Dressed: Eighteenth Century Acting," *Pub. Modern Language Ass.,* LVIII (December 1943), 1002–1037.

Divides eighteenth-century acting into four schools: Betterton, Cibber-Booth-Wilks, Macklin-Garrick, and the Kembles.

GENTLEMEN, FRANCIS (1728–1784). *The Dramatic Censor; or The Critical Companion* (London, 1770), 2 vols.

Play reviews. See "Theatrical Representation and Performers," II, 475–497, for critical comments and comparative notes on various players.

[GILDON, CHARLES (1665–1724)]. *The Life of Mr. Thomas Betterton, the late Eminent Tragedian. Wherein the Action and Utterance of the Stage, Bar, and Pulpit, are distinctly consider'd. With the judgment of the late ingenious Monsieur de St. Evremond, upon the Italian and French music and opera's . . . To which is added, The Amorous Widow . . . written by Mr. Betterton.* (London, 1710), 176 and 87 pp.

Not a biography, it should perhaps more properly be titled *The Duty and Qualifications of Actors*. Gildon, a hack writer, uses Betterton in the ways that "Plato and Xenophon introduce Socrates in their Discourses" because "he may reasonably be thought a competent Judge" of acting, p. 3. "I flatter myself, that, as I am (as far as I know) the first, who in English has attempted this subject, in the Extent of the Discourse before you, so I am apt to believe, that I have pretty well exhausted the Matter," pp. vi–vii. "I . . . allow, that I have borrowed many of . . . [the rules for acting] from the French, but then the French drew most of them from [Cicero] Quintilian and other Authors," p. ix.

Gildon names as one of his sources the *Onomastikon* by Pollux; but he doesn't name the two substantial French ones: Louis Crésol's *Vacationes Autumnales sive De Perfecta Oratoris Actione et Pronunciatione Libri III* (Paris, 1620) and Michel Le Faucheur's *Traitté de l'action de l'orateur, ou de la Prononciation et du geste* (Paris, 1657) trans. into English as *An Essay Upon The Action of an Orator; As To His Pronunciation & Gesture* (London, c. 1702). See Howell, "Sources," pp. 9–12.

Acting is examined on pp. 15–142. An excerpt is included in Cole and Chinoy, AA, pp. 97–102.

GRAVES, S. T. "Some Aspects of Extempore Acting," *Studies in Philology*, XIX (October 1922), 429–456.

HILL, AARON (1685–1750). *The Prompter*, issued twice-a-week November 12, 1734, to July 2, 1736, with the assistance of William Popple (1701–1764) and possibly James Ralph (?–1762).

> The numbers dealing principally with acting are 3, 51, 56, 62, 64, 66, 67, 79, 92, 95, 99, 100, 103, 104, 113, 117, 118, 129. They constitute "the most important body of criticism of the period"; and Hill and Popple "deserve to be called the first professional theatrical critics," Charles H. Gray, *Theatrical Criticism in London to 1795* (New York, 1931), pp. 104, 96–97. The Yale University Library lacks Nos. 24, 84, 93, 116, 138, 152; the British Museum lacks 138, 158.

See also W. O. S. Sutherland Jr., "Polonius, Hamlet, and Lear in Aaron Hill's *Prompter*," *Studies in Philology*, LXIX (October 1952), 605–618 (No. 57 by Popple, and 95, 100 by Hill).

> *The Art of Acting, Part I, Deriving Rules from a new Principle, for Teaching the Passions in a Natural Manner . . . Adapted, in Particular, to the Stage; with a view to quicken the delight of audiences, and form a judgment of the actors, in their good, or bad, performances* (London, 1746), 22 pp. A poem of 416 lines. See *The Works of the late Aaron Hill, esq.; . . . Consisting of letters on various subjects, and of original poems, moral and facetious, with an essay on the art of acting* (London, 1754), 4 vol., III, 387–408.
>
> *An Essay on the Art of Acting*, in prose, *Works*, IV, 337–396.

See Cole and Chinoy, AA, pp. 116–120.

Hill, a sometime actor, teacher of acting, and playwright, apparently finished the essay c. 1749, but decided not to print it, *Works*, II, 351. After 1754 it was variously pirated and printed: *The Art of Acting; an Essay; to which is prefixed The Actor's Epitome, a poem*. 2nd ed. (London, 1801); *The Actor, or guide to the stage; exemplifying the whole art of acting: in which the dramatic passions are defined, analyzed, and made easy of acquirement. The whole interspersed with select and striking examples from the most popular modern pieces* (London, 1821), 29 pp.; *Art of Acting; or, Guide to the stage in which the dramatic passions are defined, analyzed, and made easy of acquirement* (New York, 1855), 24 pp.

See Leo Hughes, "The Actor's Epitome," *Review of English Studies*, XX (October 1944), 306–397, which arranges in sequence the five versions of Hill's statements on acting.

The *Works* contain additional material on acting: advice to a would-be actress, I, 199–204; advice to an actor, 213–216, 216–219; to an actress, 220–222; on playing Tamerlane, 222–225; on acting Bajazet, 225–228; to another actor, 228–230; to another actress, 243–246 (1773); to an actor as Othello, 272–276 (1734); on the acting of Barton Booth, 292–296 (identical with II, 120–144); on how to raise claps in an audience by phrasing and pauses, II, 182–186 (1741); on Garrick, 233–234 (1744); to Garrick on his acting, 260–265; to Garrick again, 349–353 (1746); again on claps, 359–360; and to Garrick again, 378–386 (1749). In III see the "Prologue . . . at . . . the *Tuscan Treaty*," pp. 119–122, and in IV, "The Actor's Epitome," a poem, 76–80.

In his *Life of Garrick*, Davies says that Hill was "almost the only gentleman who labored assiduously to understand the art of acting, and who took incessant pains to communicate his knowledge of it to others," I, Ch. 13.

HILL, JOHN (c. 1716–1775). *The Actor: a Treatise on the Art of Playing. Interspersed with Anecdotes, Critical Remarks on Plays, and Occasional Observations on Audiences* (London, 1750), 326 pp.

An expanded translation of Rémond de Sainte-Albine's *Le Comédien* (1747).

See Cole and Chinoy, AA, pp. 122–131.

"Dr. Hill's Actor, or a Treatise on the Art of Playing, is none of the worst productions of that multifarious arthor; and if I am not mistaken, players may learn many useful lessons from it," Boswell, *Profession*, Essay III, p. 26.

"The Inspector," in the *London Daily Advertiser and Literary Gazette*, October 3, 16, 25, 30, and December 17, 18, 30, 1751; reprinted (London, 1753), 2 vols.

The Actor: or, a Treatise on the Art of Playing. A New Work, written by the author of the former, and adapted to the present state of the theatres. Containing impartial observations on the performance, manner, perfections, and defects of Mr. Garrick, Mr. Barry, Mr. Woodward, Mr. Foote, Mr. Havard, Mr. Palmer, Mr. Ryan, Mr. Berry, &c. Mrs. Cibber, Mrs. Pritchard, Miss Nossiter, Mrs. Gregory, Mrs. Woffington, Mrs. Clive, Mrs. Green, Miss Bellamy, &c. in their several capital parts (London, 1755), 284 pp., plus an index of 19 pp.

JOSEPH. *The Tragic Actor.*

"From Quin to Garrick," pp. 103–172, and "The Kembles," pp. 173–239.

MORGANN, MAURICE (1726–1802). *An Essay on the Dramatic Character of Sir John Falstaff* (London, 1777).

NAGLER. *Sources Theatrical History.*

Consult Ch. X, "Eighteenth Century England," pp. 343–422.

PICKERING, ROGER (1718–1753). *Reflections upon Theatrical Expression in Tragedy . . .* (London, 1755), 81 pp.

Sections III–XI treat of figure, of voice, of ear, of memory, of the movement of the feet and legs, of the management of the hands and arms, of the management of the head, of the management of the face, and of the management of the eyes, pp. 22–46; Section XII treats of Silence by artificial Pauses, pp. 46–51; Section IX (an error for XIII) treats of Silence, when attending to the Parts of other Actors, pp. 51–56; and Section XVI treats of variety in Acting, at Different Times, the same Part, pp. 61–66.

POLLOCK, WALTER H. (1850–1926). "Garrick's Acting as Seen in his Own Time," *Longman's Magazine*, VI (August 1885), 371–384.

Testimonies by Georg Lichtenberg (1742–1799) and Davies on *Hamlet*, and by Murphy briefly on *Romeo and Juliet* and *Macbeth*.

See also Lichtenberg in Nagler, *Sources*, pp. 364–372.

SHERIDAN, THOMAS (1719–1788). *A Course of Lectures on Elocution* (1762). New ed. (London, 1781), 320 pp.

For Sheridan the actor see Daniel E. Vandraegen, "Thomas Sheridan and the Natural School," *Speech Monographs*, XX (March 1953), 58–64, and J. Yoklavich, "Hamlet in Shammy Shoes," *Shakespeare Quarterly*, III (July 1952), 209–218.

SIDDONS, HENRY. See Engel under "German."

SIDDONS, SARAH. See under "Nineteenth Century."

SPRAGUE, ARTHUR C. *Shakespeare and the Actors, the stage business in his plays* (1600–1905) (Cambridge, Mass., 1944), 440 pp. See also his *The Stage Business in Shakespeare's Plays, a postscript* (London, 1954), 35 pp.

> *Shakesperian Players and Performances* (Cambridge, Mass., 1953).

Ch. I, "Betterton as Hamlet," pp. 9–20; II, "Garrick as King Lear," pp. 21–40; III, "Kemble as Hamlet," pp. 41–56.

WASSERMAN, EARL R. "The Sympathetic Imagination in Eighteenth-Century Theories of Acting," *Journal English and German Philology*, XLVI (July 1947), 264–272.

An examination of "sensibility," or the systematic power of the imagination, as first developed into a critical principle by Rémond de Sainte-Albine and John Hill's *The Actor*; an introduction to the theory of "living a role" versus imitating "gracefully a reality molded into art."

WILKS, THOMAS. *A General View of the Stage* (London, 1759), 335 pp. The book is often attributed to Samuel Derrick (1724–1769).

Part II, "Of the Art of Acting," consists of 7 chapters, pp. 81–171; Part III, Ch. V, "Of Ancient Actors, " pp. 198–204; VII, "Of the most eminent British Actors from Queen Elizabeth's time to the Restoration," pp. 218–228; Part IV, "A Critical Examination of the Merits and Demerits of the principal Performers in England and Ireland," consists of Ch. II, "Of Garrick's different Excellencies," pp. 241–263; III, "Of Woodward, Mossop, &c," pp. 263–304; and IV and V, on the principal performers of the Irish stage.

French

BORGERHOFF, E. B. O. *The Evolution of Liberal Theory and Practice in the French Theatre 1680–1757* (Princeton, 1936), 117 pp.

An excellent study of the changes in the theater which affected acting, with notes on the two Riccobonis and Rémond de Sainte-Albine.

CHARPENTIER, LOUIS. *Causes de la Décadence du Goût sur le Théâtre, ou l'on traité des droits des talens, & des fautes des auteurs; des devoirs des comédiens, de ce que la société leur doit, & de leurs usurpations funestes à l'art dramatique* (Paris, 1768), 2 vols. in one.

CLAIRON, HYPPOLITE (1723–1803). *Mémoires, et réflexions sur la déclamation théâtrale* (Paris, 1798) trans. as *Memoirs of Hyppolite Clairon, the celebrated French actress: with reflections upon the dramatic art: written by herself* (London, 1800), 2 vols.

The "Reflections upon the Dramatic Art" in Vol. I are concerned with such topics as "Enunciation, Strength, Memory, Exterior, Kings, Vehement and impassioned Characters, Dress, On the Danger of Traditions, On the Use of White Paint, Portrait of Mademoiselle Dumesnil," and the characters of Monime, Hermione, Orosmane, Pauline, Roxane, Cornelie, Phèdre, Blanche, Two Electras, etc., pp. 33–234.

See Cole and Chinoy, AA, pp. 169–173.

COLE and CHINOY. *Actors on Acting.*

VIII, "France, Tradition and Revolt," and selections by Diderot, Clairon, and Dumesnil, pp. 146–150, 160–177.

DIDEROT, DENIS (1713–1784). "Lettre de Mme. Riccoboni" (1758), in F. C. Green, *Diderot's Writings on the Theatre* (in French) (Cambridge, 1936), pp. 210–222.

See also "Extracts from Diderot's Letters to the Young Actress Mlle. Jodin," in Green, pp. 243–247.

"Observations sur une Brochure intitulée *Garrick ou Les Acteurs Anglais* . . ." (1770), in Green, pp. 227–242. (See Sticotti under "Italian.")

Le Paradoxe sur le comédien (written 1773–1778; published 1830), in Green, pp. 249–317. See Walter H. Pollock, *The Paradox of Acting* trans. with annotations (London, 1883), 108 pp., reprinted with Archer's *Masks or Faces?* (New York, 1957); and *Denis Diderot, Paradoxe sur le Comédien, étude critique avec introduction, notes facimile* par Ernest Dupuy (Paris, 1902), 178 pp. This latter ed. juxtaposes the Naigeon mss. and the text of the Saint-Petersburg ed., and gives all the important passages of Diderot's correspondence with Grimm. See Cole and Chinoy, AA, pp. 160–169.

Diderot "was among the first to assert with emphasis that actors were not merely public amusers, but artists, men of genius," Robert L. Cru, *Diderot as a Disciple of English Thought* (New York, 1913), p. 328.

DORAT, CLAUDE J. (1734–1780). *La déclamation théâtrale* (1766), *poème didactique en quatre chants* 4th ed. (Paris, 1771), 238 pp. (The original ed. contained only three chants.)

"Discours Préliminaire," pp. 3–42, "La Tragedie, chant premier," pp. 73–99; and "La Comédie, chant second," pp. 101–128. The book is filled out with six "Letters."

DU BOS, J. B. (1670–1742). *Réflexions critiques et historiques sur la poésie et sur la peinture* (1719) trans. by Thomas Nugent as *Critical Reflections on Poetry, Painting and Music, with an inquiry into the rise of and progress of the theatrical entertainments of ancients* 5th rev. enlg. ed. (London, 1748), 3 vols.

I, Ch. XLI, "Of Simple recitative and declamation," pp. 332–340; XLII, "Of the French Manner of reciting tragedy and comedy," pp. 340–349; Bk. III, "Which contains a dissertation on the theatrical representations of the ancients," 244 pp. Ch. V through VIII, pp. 61–94, insist that the theatrical declamation of the ancient actors was composed and written with notes; see also X, 116–131; XVIII, "Reflections on the advantages and inconveniences arising from the composed declamation of the ancients," pp. 234–244.

Much of Du Bos was trans. by Lessing in the third part of *Theatralische Bibliothek* (1755).

DUMESNIL, MARIE-FRANÇOISE (1713–1803). *Mémoires de Marie-Françoise Dumesnil, en reponse aux mémoires d'Hyppolite Clairon* . . . (Paris, 1798–99), 411 pp. (Probably written by Coste d'Arnobat). An 1823 ed. includes "une notice sur cette comedienne par M. Dussault."

See Cole and Chinoy, AA, pp. 173–177.

HANNETAIRE. See Servandoni.

MARMONTEL, JEAN FRANÇOIS (1723–1799). "Déclamation," in *l'Encyclopédie* (1754), IV; *Oeuvres complètes* (1818), XIII, *Élements de Littérature* (1787), II, "Déclamation," 17–47. See also "Recitatif," IV, 179–193.

The first article is reprinted in Servandoni.

RÉMOND DE SAINTE-ALBINE, PIERRE (1699–1778). *Le Comédien* (Paris, 1747), 312 pp. The first original European book on acting.

"Part the First," pp. 17–130, is titled "Of the principal Advantages which a Player ought to have from Nature"; "Part the Second," pp. 131–307, is titled "Of those Assistances which Players ought to receive from Art."

Part I, Bk. I deals with the "Necessary qualifications of Performers in General," listing them as a good Understanding (judgment or discernment), Sensibility (or a dispossession to be affected by the passions), Fire (power, spirit, or vivacity), and a distinguished Figure (though merit should be valued above personal charms).

Bk. II deals with the necessary qualifications of Leading Players, divided into Section 1 on interior qualifications, and Section 2 on external qualifications. The former includes a "gaiety of Temper" in comedy, "an elevated Soul" in tragedy, Tenderness or Feeling, and naturally amorous propensities in those who act the roles of lovers. The latter includes a majestic voice in tragedy, and an easy and graceful one in comedy.

Part II asks "In what the Truth of a Representation on the Stage Consists?" and examines "Truth of Action" and "Truth of Recitation." Other chapters discuss "Of Natural Playing," "the Finesses [or the actor's personal creative work] in Playing," "Variety" (in characterization), "Graces in Playing," etc.

The book, while still separating tragedy from comedy, stresses a kind of naturalism and a strong emotionalism in acting; it newly emphasizes the importance of characterization.

RICCOBONI. See under "Italian."

ROLLIN, CHARLES (1661–1741). *Traité des études* (Paris, 1726–28). Reprinted 1740, 1805, 1823, 1846.

Almost 400 pp. are reprinted verbatim in Graverelle (?), *Traité de l'eloquence dans tous les genres* (Paris, 1757). Trans. into English as *Instructions with regard to the eloquence of the pulpit, the bar, and the stage* (London, 1734) 4th ed. 1749, 6th 1765, 10th 1804, 11th 1810. Also trans. into German, Italian, and Russian.

SERVANDONI, JEAN N. (d'Hannetaire) (1718–1780). *Observations sur l'art du comédien, et sur d'autres objets concernant cette profession en général: avec quelques extraits de différens auteurs et des remarques analogues au même sujet ouvrage destine à de juenes acteurs et actrices* 2nd ed. augmented (Paris, 1774), 348 pp. 4th et derniere ed. augmentée (1776), 467 pp.

Contains "Abrégé du comédien, ouvrage de M. Rémond de Sainte-Albine," pp. 77–146, with "Notes ou observations pour servir de Supplement aux différens articles de l'abrégé precédent," pp. 147–336.

"Observations de M. de Marmontel, sur l'art de la déclamation, tirées de *l'Encyclopédie*," pp. 369–386.

"Des Pensées sur la déclamation, bei Louis Riccoboni," pp. 394–408.

STICOTTI. See under "Italian."

German

COLE and CHINOY. *Actors on Acting.*

Ch. X, "Germany." Material from "The Hamburg Dramaturgy" plus selections by Goethe, Schröder, and Iffland, pp. 240–261.

ENGEL, JOHAN JAKOB (1741–1802). *Ideen zu einer Mimik* (Berlin, 1785–86), 2 vols. Later ed. 1802, 1804, 1812.

His "Idées sur le geste et l'action théâtrale" run through three vols. of *Recueil de pièces intéresante concernant les antiquités, les beaux-arts, les belles-lettres, et la philosophie; traduits de différentes langues* (Paris, 1788), 5 vols. The first French ed. is dated 1795.

See also Engel, *Lettere intorno Alla Mimica. Versione dal Tedesco* (G. Rasori). *Aggiuntoyi I Capitoli Sei Sull' Arte Rappresentativa di L. Riccoboni* (pp. 183–229) (Milano, 1818), 2 vols. in one, 251, 182 pp.

The English version is by Henry Siddons (1775–1815), *Practical Illustrations of Rhetorical Gesture and Action adapted to the English Drama from a work on the same subject by M. Engel* (London, 1807,), 387 pp. The 1822 2nd and improved ed. contains Sharpe's "Essay on Gesture."

LESSING, GOTTHOLD S. (1729–1781). *Beiträge zur Historie und Aufnähme des Theaters* (Stuttgart, 1750).

Lessing's trans. of Francesco Riccoboni's *L'Art du Théâtre* appears in the fourth part of this journal as "Die Schauspielkunst." See *Werke* ed. by K. Lachmann and F. Muncker (Stuttgart, 1886), IV, 180ff. See Riccoboni under "Italian."

Theatralische Bibliothek (Berlin, 1754–58). Lessing translates and includes fairly full extracts, with comments, from Rémond de Sainte-Albine's *Le Comédien;* see *Werke*, VI, 120–152.

Hamburgische Dramaturgie (1767–69).

See III, IV, V.

"The views which Lessing sets forth in the *Dramaturgie* are largely in agreement with Sainte-Albine's," Robertson, p. 474.

For Lessing's merest outline of a projected book on acting, *Der Schauspieler*, see *Werke*, XIV, 179. In 1754 he intended to prepare *Ein Kleines Werk Über die Körperliche Beredsamkeit;* see *Werke*, VI, 152.

Consult Otto G. Graf, "Lessing and the Art of Acting," *Michigan Academy of Science, Arts, and Letters*, XI (1955), 293–301, for Sainte-Albine's influence; Carl Michel, *Lessing und die heutigen Schauspieler* (Hamburg, 1888), 54 pp.; and J. G. Robertson, *Lessing's Dramatic Theory, being an introduction to & commentary on his Hamburgische Dramaturgie* (Cambridge, 1939), Ch. XVII, "The Art of the Actor . . . ," pp. 471–486.

NAGLER. *Sources Theatrical History.*

See Ch. XI, "Weimar Classicism," pp. 425–444.

SCHRÖDER, FRIEDRICH LUDWIG (1744–1816).

"Auszuge aus Franz Riccobonis Vorschriften über die Kunst des Schauspielers mit hinzugefügten Bemerkungen" (1810) in Francesco Riccoboni, *Die Schauspielkunst "L'Art du théâtre 1750"* Übersetzt von Gotthold Ephraim Lessing (Berlin, 1954), pp. 111–147.

Italian

RICCOBONI, ANTONIO FRANCESCO (1707–1772). *L'Art du Théâtre, à Mme. X.* (Paris, 1750), 102 pp.

The Italian trans. *L'arte del Teatro* (Venice, 1762). *Die Schauspielkunst . . . Übersetzt von Gotthold Ephraim Lessing . . .* (1750) *herausgegeben, eingeleitet und mit Anmergkungen versehen von Gerhard Piens* (Berlin, 1954), 167 pp., which includes "Einleitung," pp. 5–49; *Die Schauspielkunst*, pp. 51–110; Friedrich Ludwig Schröder, "Auszuge aus Franz Riccobonis Vorschriften uber die Kunst des Schauspielers mit hinzugefügten Bemerkungen" (1810), pp. 11–147.

RICCOBONI, LUIGI (c. 1675–1753). *Dell' Arte rappresentativa, capitoli sei* (1728).

In Engel, II, 183–229. See also a version trans. and paraphrased by Pierre Ramés, *Mask*, III (April 1911), 175–180, quoted in Cole and Chinoy, AA, pp. 50–63.

An Historical and Critical Account of the Theatres in Europe. Viz. The Italian, Spanish, French, English, Dutch, Flemish, and German Theatres. In which is contain'd A Review of the Manner, Persons and Character of the Actors . . . Together with . . . An Essay on Action, or, The Art of Speaking in Public . . . (1738) (London, 1741).

The "Reflections upon Declamation, or, The Art of Speaking in Public, &c," pp. 1–36. As *Pensées sur la déclamation* the essay was published separately (Paris, 1738), 47 pp.

See Servandoni under "French."

STICOTTI, ANTONIO FABIO (?) or ANTON GIOVANNI (1739–c. 1772), *Garrick, ou Les Acteurs Anglois; Ouvrage contenant des Observations sur l'Art Dramatique, sur l'Art de la Représentation, & le Jeu des Acteurs. Avec des notes historiques & critiques, & des anecdotes sur les différens théâtres de Londres & de Paris. Traduit de l'Anglois* (Paris, 1769), 200 pp.

A trans. with changes of Hill's 1755 *The Actor* back into French!
See Diderot.

THE NINETEENTH CENTURY

American

BOUCICAULT, DION (1822–1890). *The Art of Acting* (1882) reprinted as *Papers on Acting I*, Dramatic Museum Columbia University (New York, 1926), pp. 19–54; reprinted 1958.
See Cole and Chinoy, AA, pp. 469–473.
"Coquelin–Irving," *North American Review*, CCCLXIII (August 1887), 158–161, reprinted in *The Art of Acting, Papers on Acting II*, Dramatic Museum Columbia University (New York, 1926), pp. 54–62; reprinted 1958.
COLE and CHINOY. *Actors on Acting.*
Ch. XII, "America, Native Players and International Stars," with material on Forrest, and by Boucicault, Jefferson, Booth, Gillette, Mansfield, pp. 459–490.
CURRY, SAMUEL S. (1847–1921). *Imagination and Dramatic Instinct* (Boston, 1896), 369 pp.
The Province of Expression; a search for principles underlying adequate methods of developing dramatic and oratoric delivery (Boston, 1891), 461 pp.
DOWNER, ALAN S. "Players and Painted Stage—Nineteenth Century Acting," *Pub. Modern Language Ass.*, LXI (June 1946), 522–576.
JEFFERSON, JOSEPH (1820–1905). *The Autobiography of Joseph Jefferson* (New York, 1889).
Ch. XVI, "Reflections on the Art of Acting," pp. 425–463.
See Cole and Chinoy, AA, pp. 473–479, and *Theatre Workshop*, I (January–March 1937), 60–64.
MAMMEN, EDWARD W. *The Old Stock Company School of Acting, a Study of the Boston Museum* [1843–1893] (Boston, 1945).
Ch. III, "Acting Experience of Beginners," pp. 35–48; IV, "Instruction of Beginners," pp. 49–65; V, "Effectiveness of Training," pp. 66–70.
MANSFIELD, RICHARD (1857–1907). "Concerning Acting," *North American Review*, CXCVII (September 1894), 337–343.
See Cole and Chinoy, AA, pp. 489–492.
"Man and the Actor," *Atlantic Monthly*, XCVII (May 1906), 577–583.
MURDOCH, JAMES (1811–1893). *Analytic Elocution, containing studies theoretical and practical of expressive speech* (Cincinnati, 1884), 504 pp.
RUSH, JAMES (1786–1869). *The Philosophy of the Human Voice* . . . (1827) 4th ed. enlg. (Philadelphia, 1855), 559 pp.

English

ARCHER, WILLIAM (1856–1924). *Masks or Faces? a study in the psychology of acting* (London, 1888), 227 pp. Reprinted with Diderot's *Paradoxe* (New York, 1957).
A summary is reprinted in Cole and Chinoy, AA, pp. 339–346.
First printed as "The Anatomy of Acting," *Longman's Magazine*, XI (January, February, March 1888), 266–281, 375–395, 498–516.
A plodding, indecisive rejoinder to Diderot's *Paradoxe*. From historical material and from answers to a questionnaire, Archer tries to answer the questions "do actors feel? and ought they to feel?"

"A valuable study" for which "I have a particular regard," Gordon Craig, *Henry Irving* (New York, 1930), fn. p. 171.

AUSTIN, GILBERT. *Chironomia; or a treatise on rhetorical delivery; comprehending many precepts, both ancient and modern, for the proper regulation of the voice, the countenance, and gesture; together with an investigation of the elements of gesture, and a new method for the notation thereof* (London, 1806), 583 pp.

BELL, ALEXANDER M. (1819–1905). *A New Elucidation of the Principles of Speech and Elocution* . . . (Edinburgh, 1849), 311 pp.

BELL, CHARLES (1774–1842). *The Anatomy and Philosophy of Expression* (1806) 3rd ed. with corrections (London, 1844).

Essay III, "Of those sources of expression in the countenance which cannot be explained on the direct influence of the mind upon the features," pp. 76–90; IV, "Of the muscles of the face in man," pp. 90–111; VI–VII, "Of expression in the countenance," pp. 131–170; VIII, "Of expression in reference to the body," pp. 171–182.

COLE and CHINOY. *Actors on Acting.*

Ch. X, "England and Ireland, The Vicissitudes of Realism," with selections on Kean, and by Macready, Fanny Kemble, George Henry Lewes, the Bancrofts, Irving, Ellen Terry, Madge Kendal, Archer, Shaw, pp. 292–352.

DARWIN, CHARLES (1809–1882). *The Expression of the Emotions in Man and Animals* (1899) (New York, 1955), 372 pp.

FITZGERALD, PERCY (1834–1925). *The Art of Acting, in connection with the study of character, the spirit of comedy and stage illusion* (London, 1892), 194 pp.

Considers such topics as "Tone," "Distinction," "Breadth," "Should an Actor Feel?" "Facial Expression," "Elocution," "Gesture," "Stage Business," Realism, The Study of Character, "Double Intention," "Of Comedy."

See Lamb.

GARCIA, GUSTAVE. *The Actor's Art, a practical treatise on stage declamation, public speaking, and deportment, for the use of artists, students and amateurs* (1882) (London, 1888), 286 pp.

The topics are "The Voice," "On Articulation," "How to Walk the Stage," "Action of the Arms and Hands," "On Passions and Feelings," etc.

Jenkin in his review of Talma's *Réflexions* said that "Mr. Garcia explains what small actors can be taught and do learn."

GRANT, GEORGE. *An Essay on the Science of Acting* . . . (London, 1826), 201 pp.

HAMMERTON, JOHN A. (ed.) (1871–1949). *The Actor's Art, theatrical reminiscences, methods of study and advice to aspirants especially contributed by leading actors of the day* (London, 1897), 267 pp.

HAZLITT, WILLIAM (1778–1830). *Hazlitt on Theatre* ed. by William Archer and Robert W. Lowe (1895) (New York, 1957), 211 pp.

Contains all his "theatrical essays that have any abiding interest for the general reader" collected from his *View of the English Stage* (1818) and *Criticisms and Dramatic Essays* (1851) ed. by his son.

"On Actors and Acting," pp. 133–141, plus 19 essays on Kean, 6 on Miss O'Neill, 4 on Kemble, 3 on Macready, 2 on Mrs. Siddons, etc.

HUNT, LEIGH (1784–1859). *Critical Essays on the Performers of the London Theatres* (from the *News*) *including general observations on the practice and genius of the stage* (London, 1807, actually 1808), 229 pp. plus an Appendix of 58 pp. and an Index.

See William Archer and Robert W. Lowe (ed.), *Dramatic Essays by Leigh Hunt* (London, 1894), 241 pp., for a selection from the above with additional Hunt contributions to the *Tatler* (1830–32).

Leigh Hunt's Dramatic Criticism 1808–1832 ed. by Lawrence H. Houtchens and Carolyn W. Houtchens (New York, 1849), 347 pp.

"For the life of the theater he looked to the actors rather than to the authors. . . . ," A. C. Ward (ed.), *Specimens of Dramatic Criticism XV–XX Centuries* (London, 1945), p. 7

IRVING, HENRY (1838–1905). "The Calling of the Actor," *Fortnightly Review,* LXXXIII (May 1905), 820–829.

The Drama (addresses) (Boston, 1892).

"The Art of Acting," (1885), partly written by his secretary, Louis F. Austin (1852–1905), pp. 49–104; reprinted in part in Cole and Chinoy, AA, pp. 328–334; and "The Art of Acting" (a reworking) (1891), pp. 175–201; reprinted in Laurence Irving, *Henry Irving . . .* (New York, 1952), pp. 675–684.

"M. Coquelin on Actors and Acting," *Nineteenth Century,* XXI (June 1887), 800–803; reprinted in *The Art of Acting, Papers on Acting I,* Dramatic Museum Columbia University (New York, 1926), pp. 43–53; reprinted 1958.

JENKIN, H. C. FLEEMING. "Mrs. Siddons as Lady Macbeth" (1878) and "Mrs. Siddons as Queen Katharine" (1882), reprinted in his *Papers Literary, Scientific, &c.* (London, 1887) and as *Papers on Acting III,* Dramatic Museum Columbia University (New York, 1915), with Int. and notes by Brander Matthews, 113 pp.; reprinted 1958.

JOSEPH. *The Tragic Actor.*

"The Kembles and Edmund Kean," pp. 240–283; "The Age of Macready," pp. 284–320; "The Age of Phelps," pp. 321–359; "Irving and Forbes-Robertson," pp. 360–397.

LAMB, CHARLES (1775–1834). See *The Art of the Stage as set out in Lamb's Dramatic Essays with a Commentary* by Percy Fitzgerald (London, 1885).

The Essays, pp. 1–166, include "The Tragedies of Shakespeare, Considered with Reference to their Fitness for Stage Presentation" (1811), "On Some of the Old Actors" (1823), "On the Artificial Comedy of the Last Century" (1823), "On the Acting of Munden" (1823), "Stage Illusion" (1833), etc. with "A Commentary," pp. 167–276.

LEWES, GEORGE HENRY (1817–1878). *On Actors and the Art of Acting* (London, 1875), 278 pp. German trans. (Leipzig, 1878); American ed. 1878, 1958; reprinted 1961. See Cole and Chinoy, AA, pp. 312–323.

A reprinting of expert "remarks made at various times and in various periodicals" on Edmund Kean, Charles Kean, Rachel, Macready, Farren, Lemaître, The Two Keeleys, plus "Shakespeare as Actor and Critic" (reprinted in *Theatre Workshop,* I [October–December 1936], 41–50), "On Natural Acting," "Foreign Actors on Our Stage," and "First Impressions of Salvini."

Dramatic Essays [by John Forster (1812–1876) and George Henry Lewes] ed. by William Archer and Robert W. Lowe (London 1896).

The criticisms by Lewes, from the *Leader* (1800–54), pp. 73–280.

MACREADY, WILLIAM CHARLES (1793–1873). *Macready's Reminiscences, and selections from his diaries and letters* ed. by Frederick Pollock (New York, 1875), 750 pp. See Cole and Chinoy, AA, pp. 304–308.

In these volumes, "we see the incessant study which this eminently conscientious man to the last bestowed on every detail connected with his art; we see also how he endeavored by study to make up for natural deficiencies, and how conscious he was of these deficiencies. We see him over-sensitive to the imaginary disrespect in which his profession is held, and throughout his career hating the stage, while devoting himself to the art," Lewes, AAA, p. 50.

The Diaries of William Charles Macready,
1833–1851 ed. with int., notes, and commentaries by William Toynbee (London, 1912), 2 vols.
A fuller record.

MARSTON, JOHN WESTLAND (1819–1890). *Our Recent Actors . . .* (London, 1888), 2 vols.

NAGLER. *Sources Theatrical History.*
Ch. XII, "Nineteenth Century England," pp. 447–506. Excerpts on Kemble, Edmund Kean, Vestris, Macready, Phelps, Charles Kean, etc.

SHAW, BERNARD (1856–1950). *Dramatic Opinions and Essays* selected by James Huneker (New York, 1922), 2 vols., or his complete *Our Theatres in the Nineties* (London, 1932), 3 vols. Some of the reviews reappear in the briefer *Plays and Players*, essays on the theatre ed. by A. C. Ward (London, 1953).
Shaw is a clever, contradictory, unfeeling critic of acting. Read especially "Mr. Irving Takes Paregoric" (April 4, 1895), "Two Plays" (June 5, 1895), (June 17, 1895), "The Chili Widow" (October 12, 1895), "The Old Acting and the New" (December 7, 1895), "The Immortal William" (April 23, 1896), "Henry IV" (May 8, 1896), "Ibsen Ahead" (November 4, 1896), "Ibsen Without Tears" (December 12, 1896), "Shakespeare in Manchester" (March 20, 1897), "Mr. Grundy's Improvements on Dumas" (June 10, 1897), and "Hamlet Revisited" (December 18, 1897).
See Shaw's "High Comedy," *Theatre Arts*, XII (January 1928), 35–38; "From the Point of View of a Playwright," in *Herbert Beerbohm Tree: some memories of him and of his art* ed. by Max Beerbohm (London, n.d.), partly reprinted in Cole and Chinoy, AA, pp. 346–352; E. J. West, "G. B. S. and the Rival Queens—Duse and Bernhardt," *Quarterly Journal Speech*, LXIII (December 1957), 365–373; and "Bernard Shaw Talks About Actors and Acting" (1929), in E. J. West (ed.), *Shaw on Theatre* (New York, 1958), pp. 186–198.

SIDDONS, HENRY (1775–1815). *Practical Illustrations of Rhetorical Gesture and Action, adapted to the English drama from a work on the same subject by M. Engel* (London, 1807), 387 pp. plus index.
The 2nd. improved ed. (1822) contains an article on "Gesture" by Sharpe.

SPRAGUE. *Shakespeare and Actors.*
Shakespearian Players and Performances.
Ch. II, "Kemble as Macbeth," pp. 41–56; IV, "Mrs. Siddons as Lady Macbeth," pp. 57–70; V, "Edmund Kean as Othello," pp. 71–86; VI, "Macready as Macbeth," pp. 87–104; and VII, "Irving as Shylock," pp. 104–120.

WATSON, ERNEST B. *Sheridan to Robertson, a study of the nineteenth century London stage* (Cambridge, Mass., 1926).
See especially Ch. IV, "Histrionic Development of the Playhouse," pp. 80–96; V, "The Command of Audiences," pp. 97–134; and XIII–XVI, on Acting of Poetic Drama, Comic Acting, Acting in Burlesque and the Newer Comedy, Acting of Melodrama, pp. 281–379.

WEST, E. J. "Actress Between Two Schools" (Madge Kendal), *Speech Monographs*, XI (1944), 105–114.
"Ellen Terry—Histrionic Enigma," *Colorado College Pub.*, gen. ser. 226 (April 1940), (39–62).
"G. B. S. and the Rival Queens—Duse and Bernhardt," *Quarterly Journal Speech*, LXIII (December 1957), 365–373.
"Henry Irving, 1870–1890," pp. 166–196, in *Studies in Honor of Alexander M. Drummond* (Ithaca, N.Y., 1944).
"The London Stage, 1870–1890, a study in the conflict of the old and new schools of acting," *Uni. Colorado Studies*, 2 (May 1943), 31–84.

The article is summarized in "From a Player's to a Playwright's Theater, 1870–1890," *Quarterly Journal Speech*, XXVIII (December 1942), 430–436.

"The Original Robertsonians," *Speech Monographs*, XVI (1949), 253–271.

"The Victorian Voice on the Stage: Samuel Phelps, 'faultless elocutionist,'" *Quarterly Journal Speech* XXXI (February 1945), 29–34.

French

BERNHARDT, SARAH. See "Twentieth Century."

BERNIER DE MALIGNY, ARISTIPPE F. (?–1864). *Nouveau manuel théâtral, théorique et pratique, necessaire à tous les acteurs* . . . (Paris, 1854), 376 pp.

Théorie de l'art du comédien; ou, manuel théâtral (Paris 1826), 594 pp.

COLE and CHINOY. *Actors on Acting.*

Ch. VIII, "France, Tradition and Revolt," with selections by Samson, Delsarte, Coquelin, Bernhardt, Lucien Guitry, Antoine, pp. 186–222.

COQUELIN, CONSTANT (1841–1909). *L'Art et le Comédien* (1880) trans. as *Art and the Actor* by Abby L. Alger (1881); reprinted as *Papers on Acting II*, with Int. by William James (1887), Dramatic Museum Columbia University (New York, 1915), pp. 39–88.

"I attempted to demonstrate the claim of the actor to be considered an artist in the same sense as the painter and the musician; and to prove that the old-world prejudice which still attaches to his calling has no shadow of justification in the democratic times we live in," *The Art of the Actor*, p. 30.

"Actors and Acting," *Harper's Monthly*, LXXXIV (May 1887), 891–909, plus "A Reply to Mr. Henry Irving" and "A Reply to Mr. Dion Boucicault" trans. by Theodore Child, *Harper's Weekly*, XXXI (November 12, 1887), 830–832; reprinted as *Papers on Acting III, The Art of Acting, a discussion by Constant Coquelin, Henry Irving and Dion Boucicault*, Dramatic Museum Columbia University (New York, 1926), 93 pp.; reprinted 1958.

See Cole and Chinoy, AA, pp. 195–206.

Salvini contributed to the discussion with "Some Views on Acting," *Century Magazine*, XLI (December 1890), 194–196; reprinted in *Theatre Workshop*, I (October–December 1936), 73–78, and partly reprinted in Cole and Chinoy, AA, pp. 407–411. William Winter comments on "Irving and Coquelin," pp. 285–291, in *Shadows of the Stage, second series* (New York, 1893).

"L'Art du Comédien," *Revue Illustrée*, 9 (December 15, 1889), 12–40. Separately printed (Paris, 1894) and trans. as *The Art of the Actor*, with an Int., pp. 9–28, by Else Fogerty (London, 1932), 97 pp.

A newly translated enlargement of "Actors and Acting" (1887).

In "these present notes," Coquelin writes, "I wish to study . . . [the] art [of acting] in itself, inquiring into its conditions, laying down the principles of its rightful practice—those at least which I consider to be such from my own experience, an experience extending, I repeat, over a period of thirty years," p. 30.

L'Art de dire de monologue, written in collaboration with his brother Ernest, Coquelin *cadet* (1849–1909) (Paris, 1884), 210 pp.

"Les Comédiens . . . réponse à Octave Mirbeau" ("Le Comédien," *Le Figaro* October 26, 1862), *Le Temps* November 1, 1882; both reprinted (Paris, 1883), separately paged, Coquelin, pp. 5–11; Mirbeau, pp. 5–10.

DELSARTE, FRANÇOIS (1811–1871).

See *Delsarte System of Oratory, including the complete works of M. L'Abbé Delaumosne and Mme. Angélique Arnaud, with the literary remains of François Delsarte* (New York, 1893), 606 pp., and Genevieve Stebbins, *Delsarte System of Expression;*

with the address of François Delsarte before the Philotechnic Society of Paris (New York, 1894), 271 pp.

See Cole and Chinoy, *AA*, pp. 191–194, and Percy Mackaye, *Epoch, the life of Steele Mackaye* . . . (New York, 1930), I, V. "Aesthetic Expression," 132–167.

DUPONT-VERNON, HENRI (1844–1897). *L'Art de bien dire* (1888) 7th ed. (Paris, 1897), 263 pp.

A long-time textbook used at the Conservatoire de Musique et de Déclamation; written by an actor–teacher there.

> *Diseurs et comédiens* (Paris, 1891), 247 pp.
> *Principes de diction* (Paris, 1897), 158 pp.

GEOFFROY, JULIEN L. *Manuel dramatique, à l'usage des auteurs et des acteurs, et nécessaire aux gens du monde qui aiment les idées toutes trouvées, et les jugements tout faiths* (Paris, 1822), 404 pp.

HACKS, CHARLES. *Le Geste* (Paris, 1892), 492 pp.

LILLION-DAMIENS, LUCIEN-ELIE (ed.), *Le Bréviare des comédiens* (Paris, 1858), 312 pp. An anthology of extracts from great authors and actors on the art of acting with connecting notes by the compiler.

RIBOT, THÉODULE (1839–1916). *Psychology of the Emotions* (1896) trans. from the French (New York, 1897), 413 pp.

Part I, Ch. VII, "The Nature of Emotion," pp. 91–112; VIII, "The Internal Conditions of Emotion," pp. 113–123; IX, "The External Conditions of Emotion," pp. 124–129; Part II, Ch. X, "The Aesthetic Sentiment," pp. 228–267; XI, "The Intellectual Sentiment," pp. 368–379.

SAMSON, JOSEPH I. (1793–1871). *L'Arte théâtral* (vers) (Paris, 1863), 188 pp. Nouvelle edition, précédé d'une lettre d'Émile Augier et d'une preface de Coquelin *ainé* (Paris, 1889), 304 pp.

See Cole and Chinoy, *AA*, pp. 186–191.

TALMA, FRANÇOIS JOSEPH (1763–1826). "Réflexions sur Lekain, et sur l'Art Théâtral" included in the 1825 ed. of the *Mémoires de Lekain* ed. by his son (1801–02); trans. and reprinted in Richard Ryan, *Dramatic Table Talk* (London, 1825); printed in the *Theatre* (London) in 1877; reprinted as a pamphlet, *Talma on the Actor's Art* (London, 1883), 26 pp., with a preface by Henry Irving; reprinted as *Reflexions on the Actor's Art, Papers on Acting IV*, Dramatic Museum Columbia University (New York, 1915), 63 pp., with Int. by Irving, a review by H. C. Fleeming Jenkin, and Notes by Brander Matthews; reprinted 1958.

See Cole and Chinoy, *AA*, pp. 177–186.

TISSERANT, JEAN HIPPOLYTE (1809–1878). *Plaidoyer pour ma Maison* (Paris, 1866), 166 pp.

A treatise on acting by an actor of the Odéon and Gymnase theaters.

German

COLE and CHINOY. *Actors on Acting.*

Ch. IX, "Germany," with selections by Goethe, Schröder, Iffland, Eduard Devrient, and on the Meininger, pp. 247–267.

GREGORI, FERDINAND. *Das Schaffen des Schauspielers* (Berlin, 1899), 156 pp.

HELLBACH, R. *Die Kunst der Declamation* (Wien, 1871), 258 pp.

Italian

BAZZI, GAETANO (1771–1843). *Primi Erudimenti dell' Arte Drammatica per la recitazione e la Mimica* (Torino, 1845).

BLASIS, CARLO (1795–1878). *Studi sulle Arti Imitatrici* (Milan, 1844), 93 pp.

BUFFELLI, DOMENICO. *Elementi de Mimica* (Milan, 1829).

Buonsignori, Vincenzo. *Preccetti sull' Arte Mimica appliclicabili alla Coreografica ed alla Drammatica divisi in Quarto Lezioni Teoriche* (Siena, 1854).

Cole and Chinoy. *Actors on Acting.*
Ch. XI, "Italy, The Actor as Idol," with material by Ristori, Rossi, and Salvini, pp. 395–411.

Mantegazza, Paola (1831–1910). *Physiognomik und Mimik* (1880) trans. into French 1885, and into English as *Physiognomy and Expression* (London, 1890), 327 pp.

Morrocchesi, Antonio (1768–1838). *Lezioni di Declamazione e d'Art Teatrale* (Firenze, 1832), 366 pp.

Salvini, Tommaso (1829–1916). "Some Views on Acting," *Theatre Workshop*, I (October–December 1936), 73–78.
See Cole and Chinoy, AA, pp. 407–411.

Spanish

Bastús, Vicente J. (1799–1873). *Corso de Declamacio 6, arte dramático* (Barcelona, 1848), 406 pp.

THE TWENTIETH CENTURY

American

Boleslavsky, Richard (1889–1937). *Acting, the first six lessons* (New York, 1933), 122 pp.
"Fundamentals of Acting," *Theatre Arts*, XI (February 1927), 121–129.

Brown, John Mason. *The Art of Playgoing* (New York, 1936).
Ch. X, "On Judging Actors," pp. 173–195.

Clurman, Harold. "Actors in Style—and Style in Actors," *N.Y. Times Magazine* (December 7, 1952), pp. 26–27, 34–38.
"Interpretation and Characterization," *New Theatre*, III (January 1936), 21, 44.
"On Acting," in his *Lies Like Truth* (New York, 1958), pp. 242–249; reprinted from the *New Republic* (1949) and *7 Arts #2* ed. by Fernando Puma (New York, 1954), pp. 155–165.
"The Principles of Interpretation," pp. 280–302 in Gassner, *Producing the Play.*

Cole, Toby (ed.). *Acting, a handbook of the Stanislavski method* (New York, 1947).
Int. by Lee Strasberg, pp. 10–17; Stanislavski's "The Actor's Responsibility" (1911), pp. 18–21; "Direction and Acting" (from *Ency. Brit.* 1947), pp. 22–32; "To His Players at the First Rehearsal of *The Blue Bird*" (1908), pp. 218–223; Rapoport's "The Work of the Actor," pp. 33–68; Sudakov's "The Creative Process," pp. 69–104; M. Chekhov's "Stanislavski's Method of Acting," pp. 105–115; Vakhtangov's "Preparing for the Role," pp. 116–124; etc.

Cole and Chinoy. *Actors on Acting.*
Ch. XIII, "America, Native Players and International Stars," with selections by Belasco, Mrs. Fiske, Skinner, Nazimova, John Barrymore, Laurette Taylor, Chaplin, Judith Anderson, Muni, Huston, Massey, Stella Adler, José Ferrer, Howard Lindsay, and a condensation of Alexander Knox's "Acting and Behaving," pp. 498–550.

Eustis, Morton. *Players at Work, acting according to the actors* (New York, 1937).
Interviews with Helen Hayes, Lunt and Fontanne, Nazimova, Cornell, Ina Claire, Burgess Meredith, etc. reprinted from *Theatre Arts.*

Fenichel, Otto. "On Acting," *Psychoanalytic Quarterly*, XV (1946), 144–160; reprinted in *Tulane Drama Review*, 4 (March 1960), 148–159.

A psychiatrist's finding that part of the underlying basic instinct behind acting is exhibitionism.

FUNKE, LEWIS and JOHN E. BOOTH (ed.). *Actors Talk About Acting* (New York, 1961), 469 pp. Taped interviews with 14 modern actors.

GASSNER, JOHN (ed). *Producing the Play* . . . (New York, 1941).

III, "The Actor in the Theatre, The Actor's Art," pp. 121–127; "Acting and the Training of the Actor," by Lee Strasberg, pp. 128–162; "Supplementary Training" (rhythmic movement, gymnastics, voice, pronunciation, phonetics), pp. 163–179; "The Principles of Interpretation," by Harold Clurman, pp. 280–302.

GILLETTE, WILLIAM (1855–1937). *The Illusion of the First Time in Acting* (1913) reprinted as *Papers on Acting I*, Dramatic Museum Columbia University (New York 1915); reprinted 1958. The essay, pp. 21–48, with Int. by George Arliss and notes by Brander Matthews.

See Cole and Chinoy, AA, pp. 486–488.

KNOX, ALEXANDER. "Acting and Behaving," *Hollywood Quarterly*, I (April 1946), 260–269. Reprinted in Roger Manvell (ed.), *The Cinema 1951*, Penquin Books (1951), pp. 168–180. See Cole and Chinoy, AA, pp. 540–545.

KOFFKA, K. "The Art of the Actor as a Psychological Problem," *American Scholar*, II (Summer 1942), 315–326.

LANDIS, CARNEY. "The Interpretation of Facial Expression in Emotion," *Journal General Psychology*, II (1929), 59–72.

LEWIS, ROBERT. *Method—or Madness?* (New York, 1958), 165 pp.

Eight lectures on the Stanislavski method.

MATTHEWS, BRANDER (1882–1925). *On Acting* (New York, 1914), 90 pp.

MITCHELL, ROY. *Creative Theatre* (New York, 1929).

See especially Ch. VI, "Magic Restored," pp. 88–102; X, "The Art of Motion," pp. 155–169.

PARRISH, WAYLAND M. "The Concept of 'Naturalness,'" *Quarterly Journal Speech*, XXVII (December 1951), 448–454.

SKINNER, OTIS (1858–1942). "The Art of Acting after Booth," *Theatre Arts*, X (July 1926), 446–448.

"The Art of the Actor," *Theatre*, II (April 1902), 19–20.

"Kindling the Divine Spark," *Theatre Arts*, XXII (September 1938), 666–673; reprinted in *Theatre Arts Anthology* (New York, 1950, 1960), pp. 277–284.

STRASBERG, LEE. "Acting and the Training of the Actor," in Gassner, *Producing the Play*, pp. 128–162.

Theatre Workshop, I (October 1936), 93 pp.

Articles by Rapoport, Pudovkin, Lewes, Salvini, etc.

I (January–March 1937), 94 pp.

Articles by Sudakov, Galpern, R. Ben-Ari, etc.

WOOLLCOTT, ALEXANDER (1887–1943). *Mrs. Fiske, her views on actors, acting, and the problems of production* (New York, 1917).

Ch. III, "To the Actor in the Making," pp. 75–107.

See Cole and Chinoy, AA, pp. 506–509.

YOUNG, STARK. "Acting," in his *The Flower in Drama*, pp. 3–39.

This most perceptive and seminal examination of the subject appeared originally in *Theatre Arts*, VI (October 1922), 276–290; again in his *Theatre Practice*, pp. 1–27; and again, slightly revised, in *The Flower in Drama & Glamour* (New York, 1955), pp. 3–32.

"The Actor," in his *The Theater*, pp. 98–120.

Another prerequisite version of his esthetic of acting.

The Flower in Drama (New York, 1923), 162 pp. With *Glamour* rev. ed. (New York, 1955), 223 pp.

Articles on "Talent," "The Voice in the Theatre," "The Prompt-Book" (for actors), "Ben-Ami," "Dear Mr. Chaplin," a "Letter to Duse," etc.

> *Glamour, essays in the art of the theatre* (New York, 1925), 208 pp.

"Duse," pp. 3–31, "Madame Sorel," pp. 32–46, "The Moscow Art Theatre," pp. 47–68, "The Prompt Book" (for actors), with important notes on "Movement in Acting," "Seeing the Point," "Illusion in Acting," "Minor Exhibitionists," and "Wonder in Acting," pp. 63–107, plus "Letters from Dead Actors" (Rachel to Pauline Lord, La Corallina to Doris Keane, David Garrick to John Barrymore, Molly Nelson to Margalo Gillmore, and Mlle. Beauval to a Tea-Party at the Ritz), pp. 109–153.

> *Immortal Shadows* (New York, 1948), 290 pp.; reprinted 1959.

A selection of his dramatic criticism which includes expert comments on acting.

> *The Theater* (New York, 1927), 182 pp.; reprinted 1958.
> *Theatre Practice* (New York, 1926), 208 pp.

Mostly a collection of articles from *The Flower in Drama* and *Glamour*.

(Textbooks)

ALBERTI, MADAM EVA. *A Handbook of Acting, based on the new pantomime* (New York, 1932), 205 pp.

ALBRIGHT, H. DARKES. *Working Up a Part, a manual for the beginning actor* (New York, 1947), 224 pp.

BOSWORTH, HALLAM. *Technique in Dramatic Art* . . . (1926), rev. ed. (New York, 1934), 484 pp.

BRIDGE, WILLIAM H. *Actor in the Making, a handbook on improvization* . . . (Boston, 1936), 115 pp.

CHALMERS, HELENA. *Modern Acting* (New York, 1930), 151 pp.

CRAFTON, ALLEN and JESSICA ROYER. *Acting; a book for the beginner* (New York, 1928), 318 pp.

D'ANGELO, ARISTIDE. *The Actor Creates* (New York, 1939), 96 pp.

DOLMAN, JOHN. *The Art of Acting* (New York, 1949), 313 pp.
> See also "Theories of Acting," in his *The Art of Play Production* (New York, 1928), pp. 279–301.

FRANKLIN, MARIAM A. *Rehearsal, the principles and practice of acting for the stage* (1938) (New York, 1942), 457 pp.

GOODMAN, EDWARD. *Make-Believe, a primer of acting* (New York, 1957), 242 pp.

LEES, LOWELL. *A Primer of Acting* (New York, 1940), 188 pp.

McGAW, CHARLES. *Acting Is Believing, a basic method for beginners* (New York, 1955), 177 pp.

MACKAY EDWARD J. and ALICE B. *Elementary Principles of Acting, a textbook for teachers and students, based on F. F. Mackay's The Art of Acting* (1913) (New York, 1935), 253 pp.

PARDOE, E. Earl. *Pantomimes for Stage and Study* (New York, 1931), 395 pp.

ROSENSTEIN, SOPHIE, LARRAE A. HAYDON, and WILBUR SPARROW. *Modern Acting, a manual* (New York, 1936), 129 pp.

Selden, Samuel. *A Player's Handbook, the theory and practice of acting* (New York, 1934), 252 pp.
> *First Steps in Acting* (New York, 1947), 344 pp.
> *The Stage in Action* (New York, 1941), 324 pp.

Ch. I. "The Audience and the Actor," pp. 1–14; III, "The Player Dancing," pp. 41–98; IV, "The Player Singing," pp. 99–124; V, "Action," pp. 135–156.

STRICKLAND, F. COWLES. *The Technique of Acting* (New York, 1956), 306 pp.

English

ABERCROMBIE, LASCELLES. "Communication versus Expression in Art," *British Journal of Psychology*, XIV (July 1923), 68–77.

CALVERT, LOUIS (1859–1923). *Problems of the Actor* (New York, 1918), 274 pp.

COLE and CHINOY. *Actors on Acting.*

 Ch. X, "The Sovereignty of Words," by William Butler Yeats; "Advice from an Abbey Theatre Actor," by William Fay; "The Heritage of the Actor," by. H. Granville-Barker; "The Film as an Acting Medium," by Leslie Howard; "Creating My Roles," by John Gielgud; and "The Stanislavski Myth," by Michael Redgrave, pp. 362–390.

CRAIG, GORDON. *On the Art of the Theatre* (1911) (Boston, 1925).

 "The Actor and the Über-Marionette" (1907), pp. 54–94.

 Theatre Advancing (Boston, 1920).

 "On the Old School of Acting," pp. 209–219.

 See Bernard Barshay, "Gordon Craig's Theories of Acting," *Theatre Annual* (1947), pp. 55–63.

CRAUFORD, LANE. *Acting, its theory and practice* . . . (London), 248 pp.

GRANVILLE-BARKER, HARLEY (1877–1946). *The Exemplary Theatre* (Boston, 1922).

 See Ch. II, "The Educational Basis," pp. 36–95; III, "The Plan of the Theatre as School," pp. 96–143; IV, "The Theatre as Playhouse," pp. 144–206; V, "The Presentation of a Play," pp. 207–237.

 "Mr. Barker's chief interest in the stage is . . . in acting; though he is careful to render due lip-service to the art of the playwright. About acting, . . . what it is, how it is learnt, and still more what it ought to be and how it might be learnt—he has a great deal to say that everybody who is interested in the theatre should read," W. A. Darlington, *Literature in the Theatre* (London, 1925), p. 146.

       "The Heritage of the Actor," *Quarterly Review*, CCXXXIX (July 1923), 53–73.

 Reprinted in Cole and Chinoy, AA, pp. 366–373.

GUTHRIE, TYRONE. " 'Tamburlaine' and what it takes," *Theatre Arts*, XL (February 1956), pp. 21–23, 84–86.

HARDWICKE, CEDRIC. "An Actor Stakes His Claim," *Theatre Arts*, XLII (February 1958), 66–67, 92.

      "I Look at the Audience," *Theatre Arts*, XV (September 1931), 758–762.

      "The Moribund Craft of Acting," *Theatre Arts*, XXXIII (February 1939), 106–110; reprinted in *Theatre Arts Anthology*, pp. 285–292.

IRVINE, HARRY. *The Actor's Art and Job* (New York, 1942), 251 pp.

IRVING, HENRY. See "Nineteenth Century."

KNIGHT, G. WILSON. "On Imaginative Interpretation," in his *The Imperial Theme* . . . (London, 1931), pp. 1–13.

      "On the Principles of Shakespeare Interpretation," in his *The Wheel of Fire* . . . (London, 1930), pp. 1–18.

 Interpretation via the search for the pattern below the level of plot and character.

LABAN, RUDOLF. *Mastery of Movement on the Stage* (London, 1950), 190 pp.

LANE, YOTI. *The Psychology of Acting* (New York, 1960), 224 pp.

REDGRAVE, MICHAEL. *The Actor's Ways and Means* (New York, 1953), 90 pp.

      Mask or Face, reflections in an actor's mirror (New York, 1958), 188 pp.

      "The Stanislavsky Myth," *New Theatre* (London), III (June 1946), 16–18.

 Reprinted in Cole and Chinoy, AA, pp. 386–390, and in *Mask or Face*, pp. 171–180.

SEYLER, ATHENE. "A Series of Letters on the Art of 'Period Acting,'" *Theatre Arts*, XXXI (November 1947), 21–24; reprinted in *Theatre Arts Anthology*, pp. 317–323.

SEYLER, ATHENE and STEPHEN HAGGARD. *The Craft of Comedy, a correspondence* (London, 1943), 86 pp.

SPEAIGHT, ROBERT. *Acting; its idea and tradition* (London, 1947), 93 pp.

STEWART, J. I. M. *Character and Motive in Shakespeare* . . . (London, 1949).
> See especially Ch. V, "Steep Tragic Contrast," pp. 79–110, for a critical examination of Elmer Edgar Stoll's justification of Shakespeare's "unreal" characters.

TYNAN, KENNETH. *He That Plays the King* (London, 1950).
> See Ch. 2, "Heroic Acting Since 1944," pp. 32–113.

(Textbooks)

ARMFIELD, CONSTANCE (SMEDLEY). *Action. Greenleaf Theatre Elements I* (1925), 78 pp.
> *Speech. Greenleaf Theatre Elements II* (1925), 90 pp.

BEHNKE, KATE. *Speech and Movement on the Stage* (Oxford, 1930), 196 pp.

BLEACKLEY, J. ARTHUR. *The Art of Mimicry* (New York, 1911), 132 pp.

CARROLL, SIDNEY W. *Acting for the Stage* . . . (1938) (New York, 1948), 188 pp.

DUFF, JANET. *The Mirror of Acting, in practical lessons* (Edinburgh, 1934), 154 pp.

HICKS, E. SEYMOUR. *Acting, a handbook for amateurs* (London, 1931), 263 pp.

JENNINGS, HERBERT. *The Actor's Craft* (London, 1930), 258 pp.

LAWSON, JOAN. *Mime* (London, 1957), 208 pp.

MARASH, J. G. *Mime in Class and Theatre* (London, 1950), 116 pp.

MAWER, IRENE. *The Art of Mime* . . . (London, 1932), 244 pp.

NEWTON, ROBERT. *Acting Improvised* (London, 1937), 110 pp.

OXENFORD, LYN. *Design for Movement, a textbook in stage movement* (London, 1951), 96 pp.
> *Playing Period Plays* (London, 1955–57), 315 pp.
> Parts 1 and 2: Medieval (1066) through Stuart (1649); Parts 3 and 4: Restoration (1688) through Edwardian (1910).

PERUGINI, MARK. *Mime* (London, 1924), 64 pp.

PICKERSGILL, MARY G. *Practical Miming* (London, 1935), 117 pp.

ROSE, ENID. *First Studies in Dramatic Art* (London, 1926), 311 pp.

French

AUBERT, CHARLES. *L'Art Mimique, suivi d'un traité de la pantomime et ballet* (Paris, 1901) trans. as *The Art of Pantomime* by Edith Sears (New York, 1927), 210 pp.

BARRAULT, JEAN-LOUIS. *Reflections on the Theatre* (1949) trans. by Barbara Wall (London, 1951), 185 pp.
> *Nouvelles Réflexions sur le théâtre* (1959) trans. as *The Theatre of Jean-Louis Barrault* by Joseph Chiari (New York, 1961).
> See Ch. II, "About the Actor," pp. 32–63.
> "The Theatre and Its Instrument," trans. by Eric Bentley, *Kenyon Review*, XII (Spring 1920), 219–223.

BERNHARDT, SARAH. *L'Art du Théâtre; la voix, le geste, la pronunciation* (Paris, 1923), 232 pp. Trans. as *The Art of the Theatre* by H. J. Stenning (London, 1920), 224 pp.
> See an excerpt in Cole and Chinoy, AA, pp. 208–213.
> Also see West under "Nineteenth Century—English."

BREMONT, L. *L'Art de dire les vers* (Paris, 1903), 342 pp.

COLE and CHINOY. *Actors on Acting.*
> Ch. VIII, "France." "The Evolution of the Actor," by Sarah Bernhardt; "What I Would Say to Conservatory Students," by Lucien Guitry; "The Manifesto of the

Vieux Colombier," by Jacques Copeau; "Comédien and Actor," by Louis Jouvet; and "Pantomime," by Jean-Louis Barrault, pp. 208–233.

DOAT, JAN. *L'Expression corporelle du comédien* 2nd ed. (Paris, 1944), 72 pp.

JAQUES-DALCROZE, ÉMILE. *Eurhythmics, Art, and Education* trans. by Frederick Rothwell, ed. by Cynthia Cox (New York, 1930), 265 pp.

           Rhythm, Music, and Education trans. by Harold F. Rubinstein (New York, 1921), 334 pp.

JOUVET, LOUIS. *Le Comédien désincarné* (Paris, 1954), 280 pp.

           Réflexions du comédien (Paris, 1938), 208 pp.

VILLIERS, ANDRÉ (Bonnichon). *L'Art du comédien* (Paris, 1953), 128 pp.

           La Psychologie du comédien (Paris, 1946), 328 pp.

German

BAB, JULIUS. *Schauspieler und Schauspielkunst* (Berlin, 1926), 259 pp.

BRECHT, BERTOLT (1898–1950). "A New Technique of Acting" trans. by Eric Bentley, *Theatre Arts*, XXXIII (January 1949), 38–40.

    Reprinted as "The Alienation Effect" in Cole and Chinoy, AA, pp. 281–285.

BUSCHBECK, ERHARD (ed.). *Der Thespiskarren* . . . (Wien, 1943), 328 pp.

    A collection of writings on the art and technique of acting by critics.

COLE and CHINOY. *Actors on Acting.*

    Ch. IX, "Germany." "In Defense of Naturalism," by Otto Brahm; "The Enchanted Sense of Play," by Max Reinhardt; "Expressionism," by Paul Kornfeld; "The Alienation Effect," by Bertolt Brecht; "Objective Acting," by Erwin Piscator, pp. 269–291.

GREGORI, FERDINAND. *Der Schauspieler* (Leipzig, 1919), 132 pp.

HAGEMANN, CARL. *Der Mime. Die Kunst des Schauspielers und Opernsängers* (Berlin, 1916).

KERR, ALFRED. *Schauspielkunst* (Berlin, 1905), 84 pp.

KJERBÜHL-PETERSEN, LORENZ. *Die Schauspielkunst* (1925) trans. as *Psychology of Acting* . . . by Sarah T. Barrows (Boston, 1935), 260 pp.

MARTERSTEIG, MAX. *Der Schauspieler, ein kunstlerisches problem* (Leipzig, 1900), 81 pp.

MICHEL, KARL. *Korpersprache und toter Punkt der Schauspielkunst* (Leipzig, 1921), 143 pp.

WINDS, ADOLF. *Der Schauspieler: in seiner Entwicklung vom mysterien zum kammerspiel* (Berlin, 1919), 284 pp.

Italian

AUDISIO, ADOLFO. *Tratto teorico practico d'art dramatica* (Brescia, 1938), 278 pp.

CHIARINI, LUIGI and U. BARBARO (ed.). *L'Arte dell' attore* (Rome, 1950), 330 pp.

    A symposium on acting in films based on the writings of Diderot, Hegel, Jouvet, Pirandello, etc.

Russian

BAKSHY, ALEXANDER (1855–1929). *The Theatre Unbound* . . . (London, 1923).

    Ch. V, "The Aesthetic of the Theatre," pp. 65–107.

    "When Mr. Bakshy speaks of 'the art of the theatre' he frankly means acting. For him the playwright merely exists on sufferance as the man who provides something for the actor to perform," Darlington, *Literature in the Theatre*, p. 83.

BOLESLAVSKY. See under "American."

CHEKHOV, MICHAEL (1891–1956). *Put Aktera* (*The Path of the Actor*) (Leningrad, 1928), 176 pp.

           "Stanislavski's Method of Acting" trans. by Mark Schmidt and arranged by Molly Day Thatcher from Chekhov's notes (1922), New

Theatre, I (December 1934), 12–13, 29; (February 1935), 6–7; reprinted in Cole, *Acting*, pp. 105–115.

To the Actor; on the technique of acting (New York, 1953), 201 pp.

COLE and CHINOY. *Actors on Acting.*

XII, "Russia, The Moscow Art Theatre and Its Tradition," with selections by Shchepkin, Stanislavski, Nemirovich-Danchenko, Meyerhold, Vakhtangov, Khmelyov, Eisenstein, and Pudovkin, pp. 415–458.

EISENSTEIN, SERGEI M. (1898–1948) (and G. V. ALEXANDROV). "Doing Without Actors," *Cinema* (June 1930), pp. 18–56.

GALPERN, LASAR. "Body Training for Actors," *Theatre Workshop*, I (January–March 1937), 43–54.

LVOV, NIKOLAI and I. MAKSIMOV (ed.). *Masterstvo Aktera Krestomatiya (Chrestomathy of the Actor's Skill)* arr. by B. Alpers and P. Novitski (Moscow, 1935), 408 pp.

See Cole and Chinoy, AA, pp. 422–424.

PETROV, NIKOLAI. *Akter i Stsenicheski Obraz (The Actor and Stage Form)* (Leningrad, 1935), 100 pp.

PISARENKO, YU. *Krestomatiya Aktera (Actor's Chrestomathy)* (Moscow, 1930), 258 pp.

PUDOVKIN, V. I. (1893–1953). *Film Acting* trans. by Ivor Montagu (London, 1935), 153 pp.

See Cole and Chinoy, AA, pp. 455–458, for an excerpt from Ch. II; and "Film Acting: Two Phases," *Theatre Workshop*, I (October–December 1936), 53–67, for Ch. V and VI.

RAPOPORT, I. *Rabota Aktera* ("The Work of the Actor") trans. for the New Theatre School, *Theatre Workshop*, I (October 1936), 5–40; reprinted in Cole, *Acting*, pp. 33–68.

STANISLAVSKI (ALEKSEYEV), CONSTANTIN (1863–1938). *An Actor Prepares* trans. by Elizabeth Reynolds Hapgood (New York, 1936), 295 pp.

The book is "a mere fragment." The complete work, published in Moscow in 1938, just before Stanislavski's death, is titled *Rabota Aktera nad soboi (The Actor's Work on Himself*, or *Actor and Self; Personal Work in the Creative Process of Re-Living)*, and is almost three times as long as AP.

In his preface Stanislavski emphasizes the point that the book deals "merely with the actor's preparatory work and not with problems of rehearsal and performance."

Building a Character trans. by Elizabeth Reynolds Hapgood (New York, 1949), 292 pp.

According to the translator the book was "worked out side by side" in 1928–36 with AP. Elementary, it's notable only for the too long delayed attention Stanislavski gave to the external technical means of bringing a character *from a play* to life *in the theater*.

Creating a Role trans. by Elizabeth Reynolds Hapgood and ed. by Hermine Isaacs Popper (New York, 1961), 271 pp.

A combination of three drafts of a book which centers on the characters in *Othello*, Griboyedov's *Woe from Wit*, and Gogol's *The Inspector General* (1916–c. 1934).

My Life in Art trans. by J. J. Robbins (1924) (Boston, 1927), 586 pp. Reprinted 1956.

An excerpt is included in Cole and Chinoy, AA, pp. 430–435.

The revised, better illustrated Russian ed., *Moia zhizn'v iskusstve* (Moscow, 1925), has been trans. into English as *My Life in Art* by G. Ivanov-Mumjiev (Moscow, 195?), with a new, hodge-podge Appendix and (translator's) Notes, 503 pp.

In essentials, even in most of the language, the book is the same as the American ed. However, an editor (Lyubov Gurevich?) has improved organization of the material.

E.g., the original 61 chapters, most of them retitled, are lengthened to 72. Also, the first two sections, called "Artistic Childhood" and "Artistic Adolescence," pp. 13–116, are a new arrangement of the original pp. 3–147: Ch. III becomes Ch. I, Ch. IV follows Ch. V, becoming two chapters with enough left over for later pages, Ch. IX is pushed ahead of Ch. VI, which includes material from Ch. VII, etc. The third section, "Artistic Youth," pp. 119–342, while often newly paragraphed, briefly cut, rewritten, and expanded, more closely follows the original content, pp. 148–457. The fourth section, "Artistic Maturity," pp. 345–466, rearranged, briefly cut, rewritten, and expanded, contains much of the new material. Here Stanislavski significantly comments on voice and speech, and in a new chapter, "Departure and Return," pp. 448–458, reacts to the "theatrical" theater in 1925 Moscow.

The original *My Life in Art*, commissioned by Little, Brown and Co., was copyrighted in 1924 at Stanislavski's request in the United States and all Berne Convention countries so that the rights might be secure for him and his heirs. Stanislavski then allowed a reorganized, revised Russian translation to be published a year later when the international copyright had been established. The appearance in the United States and Berne Convention countries of the Soviet version translated into English has been ruled a violation of the copyright held in trust for Stanislavski's heirs.

Stanislavski's Legacy, a collection of comments on a variety of aspects of an actor's art and life ed. and trans. by Elizabeth Reynolds Hapgood (New York, 1958), 182 pp.

(About STANISLAVSKI)

DUERR, EDWIN. "Stanislavski and the Idea," pp. 31–53, in *Studies in Speech and Drama in Honor of Alexander M. Drummond* (Ithaca, N.Y., 1944).

GORCHAKOV, NICOLAI M. *Rezhisserskie Uroki K. S. Stanislavskogo* (1950) trans. as *Stanislavski Directs* by Miriam Goldina (New York, 1954), 402 pp.

Diary notes from 1924 to 1936.

GUTHRIE, TYRONE. "Is There Madness in 'The Method'?" N.Y. *Times Magazine* (September 15, 1957), pp. 23, 82–83.

MAGARSHACK, DAVID. *Stanislavski on the Art of the Stage* (London, 1950), 311 pp.

Contains "The System and Methods of Creative Art" (1918–22), pp. 89–253, "Five Rehearsals of Massenet's Opera *Werther*," pp. 255–284, plus Appendix I, "Stage Ethics" pp. 287–296, and Appendix II, "Melodrama: A Stanislavski Improvisation," pp. 297–304.

The first two articles weren't written by Stanislavski but by K. Antarova, based on notes she took in his classes between 1918 and 1922. The last article was written by Gorchakov.

Magarshack's "Introduction," pp. 11–87, furnishes an appraisal of the system.

MOORE, SONIA. *The Stanislavski Method* . . . (New York, 1960), 78 pp.

SCHNITZLER, HENRY. "Truth and Consequences, or Stanislavski Misinterpreted," *Quarterly Journal Speech*, XL (April 1954), 152–164.

An important article.

ZAKHAVA, V. [B. E.]. "Can We Use Stanislavski's Method?" trans. by Mark Schmidt and ed. by Molly Day Thatcher, *New Theatre*, II (August 1935), 16–18.

The article appeared originally as "The Creative Method of the Vakhtangov Theatre," *Soviet Theatre*, XII (1931), 6–16.

SUDAKOV, I. "The Actor's Creative Work," trans. for *Theatre Workshop*, I (January–March 1937), 7–42.

Probably Sudakov's *Osnovnye Elementy Akterskogo Masterstva* (*Basic Elements for the Mastery of Acting*) (1934).

TAIROV, ALEXANDER. *Das Entfesselte Theater, aufzeichungen eines regisseurs* (1921) (Potsdam, 1927).

"Der Schauspieler: Dilettantismus und Meisterschaft," pp. 32–39; "Die inner Technik des Schauspielers," pp. 40–48; "Die Äussere Technik des Schauspielers," pp. 49–58.

VAKHTANGOV. "Eugene Vakhtangov: 1883–1922," *Theatre Arts*, XX (September 1936), 679.

Very brief extracts from his notebooks.

"Fantastic Realism," in Toby Cole and Helen Chinoy (ed.), *Directing the Play* . . . (New York, 1953), pp. 160–165.

"Preparing for the Role, from his Diary," arranged by B. Zakhava, trans. and and adapted for use by the Group Theatre, in Cole, *Acting*, pp. 116–124, and partly reprinted in Cole and Chinoy, AA, pp. 444–446.

See Nikolai Gorchakov, *The Vakhtangov School of Stage Art* trans. by G. Ivanov-Mumjiev (Moscow, 1960), 206 pp.

ZAKHAVA, BORIS E. "Can We Use Stanislavski's Method?" (See under "Stanislavski.")

"Principles of Directing" trans. by Rose Siegel, *Theatre Workshop*, I (April–July 1937), 43–58; (September–October 1937), 14–33; and reprinted in Cole, *Acting*, pp. 182–218.

Scandinavian

SCHYBERG, FREDERIK (1905–1954). *Skuespillerens Kunst* (Copenhagen, 1954), 270 pp.

See "The Art of Acting" (1947, 1949) trans. by Harry G. Carlson, *The Tulane Drama Review*, 5 (Summer 1961), 56–76.

The essay is to be continued in subsequent issues.

Spanish (South American and Portuguese)

ALONSO, AMADO. "El ideal artistico de la lengua y la diction en el teatro," *Instituto nacional de estudios de teatro* (Buenos Aires), 2 (1938), 7–36.

FOLA IGÚRBIDE, JOSÉ. *El Actor; revision general de arte escenico y de valores de acte dramatico y literario* (Madrid, 1918), 291 pp.

PEREIRA DE AZEVEDO NEVES, JOÃO ALBERTO. *A mascara d'um actor; cabecas d'expressão* (Lisbon, 1914), 265 pp.

SANTOS, CARLOS. *Arte de representar; summario de licões* (Lisbon, 1951), 139 pp.

INDEX

*Limited to names, titles, and topics directly related to acting.
Principal omissions are playwrights and play titles.*

Abington, Frances, 278
Accesi, 126, 140
Achurch, Janet, 377, 426
Ackermann, Konrad, 218, 252–255
"Acting" (Young), 464ff.
Action, over-all; *see* Dominant urge
Action(s), 6, 15, 16, 17, 34–36, 37, 53, 57,
    80, 97, 118, 123, 134, 141, 145, 162,
    165, 179, 182–184, 187, 189, 195, 216,
    233–234, 245, 260, 278, 284, 373, 400,
    439, 477, 478, 479, 480, 483, 486, 490
Actions, physical, 55, 102, 124, 174, 246–
    247, 308, 366, 385, 396, 469–471,
    477, 483
Actor, The (Hill), 231ff., 242ff., 259
Actor, The (Lloyd), 250
"Actor, The" (Young), 464ff.
Actor Prepares, An, 202, 398, 443, 478–479,
    481, 482–483
"Actors and Acting," 397ff.
"Actor's Epitome, The," 222
Actors Equity Association, 393
Actors Studio, 460, 481, 484
Actresses, early, 41, 47, 65, 86, 92, 98–99,
    100, 106, 139, 140, 155, 170
Adams, Edwin, 364
Adams, John, 107
Adams, Maude, 380, 432
Adler, Luther, 480
Adler, Stella, 480, 481, 483
Admiral's Men, 104, 107, 108–109, 110,
    111, 112, 147–148, 153
Aeschylus
    as actor, 10–11, 12–13
    as director, 10
Aesopus, Claudius, 42, 50, 220
Affective memory; *see* Emotion memory
Aiken, George L., 361
Ainley, Henry, 427
Alexander, George, 426

Alexeyev, Constantin; *see* Stanislavski
Alizon, 142, 143
Allan, Louise Rosalie (Despreaux), 324
Allen, Viola, 380, 432
Alleyn, Edward, 108, 110, 113, 118, 139,
    147, 148
Amateur actors, 6–8, 18, 40–41, 46, 47, 64,
    68, 72, 74, 76–77, 84–90, 92–93, 94,
    95, 97, 98, 104, 105, 108, 254, 332,
    371–373, 381–382, 495ff.
Ames, Winthrop, 449
Anatomy and Philosophy of Expression, The,
    305
"Anatomy of Actors, The," 403–404
Anderson, Gilbert ("Bronco Billy"), 434
Andò, Flavio, 344
Andreini, Francesco, 118, 125, 139
Andreini, Giambattista, 126, 127
Andreini, Isabella, 125
Andreyevna, Maria, 383
Andronicus, 28
Anglin, Margaret, 394, 432
Anshültz, Heinrich, 296
Antarova, K., 443–444
Antoine, André, 371–374, 375, 380, 381,
    385, 388, 394, 415, 440, 496
Apology (Cibber), 223
"Apology for Actors" (Choricius), 63
Apology for Actors (Heywood), 147
Appia, Adolphe, 413, 437, 440
Aquinas, Thomas, 74
Arbuscula, 47
Archer, William, 242, 377, 402–403, 443
Arion of Corinth, 8
Ariosto, Lodovico, 91
Aristodemus, 29
Aristophanes, 22
Aristotle, 6, 27, 28, 29, 30, 32–33, 35–36,
    38, 39, 42, 53, 57, 73, 90, 94, 182, 187,
    189, 488

573

Arliss, George, 429
Armani, Vincenza, 100
Armin, Robert, 111, 148, 149
Arnobat, Coste d', 277
Arnould-Plessy, Jeanne-Sylvanie, 324, 360
Art, 188, 194, 203, 206, 219, 230, 233ff.,
    237, 250, 262, 268, 274, 277–278, 280,
    282, 283, 287, 292, 302, 310, 323, 325,
    330, 332, 335, 342, 357–358, 363, 364,
    382, 385, 386–387, 390, 395, 396–397,
    415–416, 418, 425, 427, 428, 435, 445,
    447–448, 456, 463ff., 473, 474, 482
Art, acting as an, 30–31, 52, 73, 179, 187,
    188, 192, 193, 205ff., 211, 221–222,
    241, 242ff., 249, 261, 266, 268, 269ff.,
    290, 301, 308, 311, 313, 356–357,
    397ff., 404–405, 454, 455, 458
Artaud, Antonin, 486–487
Art du Comédien, L', 397ff.
Art du Théâtre, L', 238–240, 443
Art et le Comédien, L', 396ff.
Arthur, Thomas, 87
"Art of Acting, The" (Hill), 227–228
Art of Elocution, The, 339
Art of Poetry (Horace), 90
Art of Speaking, The, 250
Art or nature, 19, 54, 66, 77, 82, 174, 179,
    181, 188, 190, 194, 196, 201–202, 204–
    205, 207ff., 214–215, 229, 230, 232,
    235, 238, 242ff., 249, 253, 262ff., 266–
    268, 270, 272, 274–275, 277–278, 283–
    284, 288, 290, 292, 300, 315–316, 319,
    335–336, 340, 357, 370, 375, 376, 381,
    387, 392, 402, 424ff., 428, 445, 464–
    465, 473, 482, 485, 491
Art théâtral, L' (Samson), 323, 342
Arte Rappresentativa in Italia, 327
Artyom (Artemiev), Alexander, 383
Asenkova, Barbara, 331
Ashbury, Joseph, 193
Astydamas, 28
Athenodorus, 28
Audience, actor and the, 29, 30, 42–43, 44–
    45, 51, 81–82, 99–100, 116, 120, 124,
    134, 141, 171, 176, 179, 182, 184–185,
    186, 190, 191, 192, 196, 201–202, 203,
    205, 212, 214–216, 222, 231, 232, 240,
    244, 247–248, 251, 260, 261, 268, 285,
    293, 306, 315–316, 332, 351, 372–373,
    386, 391, 395, 398–399, 401–402, 412,
    415
Augustine, St., 49, 187
Ausoult (Baron), Jeanne, 145, 164
Austin, Gilbert, 305
Auzillon, Mlle., 167
Ayame, Yoshizawa, 157
Ayame-gusa, 157

Bacon, Frank, 449
Bakshy, Alexander, 447

Baloré, Marguerite, 145
Bancroft, Marie (Wilton) and Squire, 353–
    356, 359, 378, 389, 393
Bannister, Henry, 306
Bara, Theda, 451
Barbieri, Niccolò, 128
Barker, Harley Granville; see Granville-
    Barker
Barnay, Ludwig, 368, 375, 376
Baron, André, 143, 145, 165, 203
Baron, Charlotte (La Thorillière), 168
Baron, Étienne, 202
Baron, Michel, 165, 166, 167, 168, 202, 210–
    211, 213, 229, 233, 235
Barrault, Jean-Louis, 132, 485–487, 492
Barrett, George, 317
Barrett, Lawrence, 364
Barrett, Wilson, 378
Barry, Elizabeth, 173, 176, 177, 178, 192,
    204, 212
Barry, Spanger, 226, 227, 241, 242, 244, 248
Barrymore, Ethel, 362, 430, 432, 449
Barrymore, John, 362, 432, 449, 450, 460
Barrymore, Lionel, 362, 449, 450
Barrymore, Maurice, 362, 364, 380
Barthelmess, Richard, 453
Bartolozzi, Lucia Elizabeth; see Vestris,
    Mme.
Bassermann, Albert, 421
Bates, Blanche, 430
Bathyllus, 48
Batteux, Charles, 230
Baty, Gaston, 456
Bazzi, Gaetano, 327
Beare, W., 51
"Beat," 374
Beaubourg, Pierre de, 203, 209
Beauchâteau, 141, 145
Beaulieu, 142
Beaupré, Mlle., 141, 160
Beauval, Jean Pital, 165, 167, 168
Beauval, Jeanne Olivier Bourgignon, 165,
    167, 168, 202, 203
Beaux Arts, Les, 230
Beck, Heinrich, 270
Becquerelle, François; see Firmin
Bedeau, François; see L'Espy
Bedeau, Julien; see Jodelet
Beeston, Christopher, 153
Beeston, William, 153, 169, 174, 193
Béguet, Marguerite, 142, 143, 145
Beil, Johann, 270
Béjart, Armande (Molière, d'Etriche), 163,
    165, 166, 167
Béjart, Genevieve; see Hervé, Mlle.
Béjart, Joseph, 161
Béjart, Louis, 161
Béjart, Madeleine, 146, 147, 161, 162, 191
Belasco, David, 380, 430–431, 433, 448–
    449, 460

Belinski, Vissarion, 290
Bell, Alexander, 338
Bell, Charles, 305
Bellamy, Mrs. George Anne, 226, 227, 241, 242
Belleau, Remy, 97
Bellecourt, 257
Belleroche; see Poisson, Raymond
Bellerose, 140, 141, 142, 145, 146, 147
Bélonde, Mlle., 167, 168
Benefits ended, 353
Benfield, Robert, 149, 151–152
Benini, Ferruccio, 344
Benson, Frank, 388, 426
Bentley, John, 107
Beolco, Angelo, 93
Bergner, Elizabeth, 421
Bernhardt, Sarah, 342, 394–395, 415, 417, 431, 451
Bernier, Aristippe F., 325
Bertinazzi, Carlo Antonio, 132
Betterton, Thomas, 157, 162, 170, 171, 172, 173, 175, 176, 177, 178, 192–193, 196, 204, 205ff., 212, 220, 222, 278, 349
Beyle, Henri; see Stendhal
Bianchi, Brigida, 128, 129
Bianchi, Giuseppe, 128, 129
Biancolelli, Domenico, 120, 129
Biancolelli, Isabella, 128
Biographies of characters, 472, 477
Bio-mechanics, 470–471
Birch, George, 97
Birch, John, 97
Bird, William, 112, 148
Blank verse, first, 91
Blassis, Carlo, 327
Blondel, 64
Blouin, Marie-Madeleine, 257
Blythe, Herbert; see Barrymore, Maurice
Bocage, 297, 320, 324, 333
Bodel, Jean, 72
Bodenstadt, Friedrich von, 365, 366
Boek, Johann M., 254, 255, 270, 271
Boileau-Despreaux, Nicolas, 211
Boland, Mary, 43
Boleslavsky, Richard, 442, 462–463
Booth, Barton, 212, 213, 214, 220, 225, 228
Booth, Edwin, 311, 339, 347, 360, 361, 362, 363–364, 392, 393
Booth, John Wilkes, 364
Booth, Junius, 364
Booth, Junius Brutus, 311, 363, 364
Borchers, David, 254
Borneman, Ernest, 487–488
Borozdina, Varvana, 345
Bosberg, Sarah von, 139
Boswell, James, 223, 250, 264
Boucicault, Dion, 337, 347, 351–352, 354, 402
Bouffé, Hugues-Désiré, 324

Boutet, Anne; see Mars, Mlle.
Box-set, early, 337
Boy actors, 88, 97–98, 104, 108, 147, 150, 152, 153
Bracegirdle, Anne, 177, 178, 204
Brahm, Otto, 374–377, 385, 419
Brandes, Johann, 253–255
Brecht, Bertolt, 453, 457–458, 487–491, 492
Brécourt, 165
Bressant, Jean, 342, 360
Brie, Edmé de, 161
Brissebard, Jean; see Joanny
Brizard, Jean-Baptiste (Britard), 257, 258
Brockmann, Johann, 269
Brodribb, John Henry; see Irving, Henry
Bromberg, J. Edward, 480
Brougham, John, 350
Brown, Elizabeth Ann; see Neilson, Adelaide
Browne, John, 97
Browne, Robert, 110
Brückner, Johannes, 253
Bruhl, Karl Moritz von, 295
Brumoy, 232
Bruscambille, 139
Bryan, George, 111, 148
Bryansky, Yakov, 289, 329
Bryussov, Valery, 423
Buckstone, John, 334, 346, 347, 360
Buffelli, Domenico, 327
Building a Character, 460, 483–484
Bullock, Jane, 212
Bullock, William, 212
Bulwer, John, 181–182, 188
Burbage, Cuthbert, 112, 149, 151, 152
Burbage, James, 103, 104
Burbage, Richard, 108, 110, 112, 118, 139, 147, 148, 149, 151, 152, 182, 349
Burdzhalov, Georgy S., 383
Burgh, James, 250
Burke, Billie, 431
Burke, Edmund, 248
Burke, Kenneth, 37
Butler, Charlotte, 177

Calculation, 248–249, 261–262, 270, 295, 302, 328, 344, 348, 357–358, 389, 394ff., 403, 427, 428, 486, 490–491; see also Design, acting as
Calderón, María, 138
Calderoni, Francesco, 128
Calmo, Andrea, 93
Calvert, Louis, 427, 448
Cameron, Beatrice, 380
Campbell, Mrs. Patrick, 393, 426, 427, 431
Canali, Isabella; see Andreini, Isabella
Cantú, Carlo, 128
Carnovsky, Morris, 479, 480
Carter, Mrs. Leslie, 380
Casson, Louis, 427

Castelvetro, 101, 189
Causes de la Décadence du Gout sur le théâtre, 259
Cazzola, Clementina, 343
Cecchini, Pier Maria, 117, 126, 140
Chaliapin, Feodor Ivanovitch, 417, 472
Chamberlain's (later King's) men, 110–111, 112, 147ff.
Chambers, E. K., 49–50, 64
Champmeslé, Charles, 166, 167, 168
Champmeslé, Marie Desmares, 166, 167, 168, 202
Chapelain, Jean, 188–189
Chaplin, Charlie, 37, 120, 451–452
Chappuzeau, 232
Characterization, 11, 13, 16–17, 21, 22, 27, 33–35, 38, 51, 53, 66, 100, 101, 118ff., 133–134, 143, 163, 164, 165, 175, 182–184, 191, 192, 195–196, 201, 208, 214, 216, 219, 224, 225, 233, 235, 243ff., 245–246, 247–248, 249, 250, 252, 258, 262, 272, 283, 284, 289–290, 302, 328, 331–332, 337, 339, 375, 390, 397ff., 401ff., 427, 433–434, 446, 456, 477, 486, 489–490; *see also* Impersonation
Charon, Jacques, 485
Charpentier, Louis, 259
Chastelet, François-Mathieu; *see* Beauchâteau
Chatterton, F. B., 354
Chekhov, Anton, 385
Chekhov, Michael, 442, 471, 472, 474, 480–481, 485
Chernikov, Vasily, 268
China, 65–67, 78–79
Chirologia, 181
Chironomia (Austin), 305
Chironomia (Bulwer), 181–182
Choricius, 48, 63
Chronegk, Ludwig, 366–368, 381
Chrysostom, 49
Churchill, Charles, 250
Cibber, Colley, 177, 195, 196, 204, 212, 213, 220, 222, 223, 225, 246
Cibber, Susanna Maria, 222, 226–227, 242
Cicero, 42, 50, 52ff., 56, 75, 88, 90, 97, 178, 180, 182, 184, 187, 206, 213, 232
Circumstances, 16, 17, 34, 35, 53, 124, 179, 182–183, 207–208, 233–234, 237, 243–245, 247–248, 278, 291, 313, 476–477
Clair, René, 454
Claire, Ina, 448
Clairon, Mlle., 230, 238, 248, 256, 257, 259, 265–266, 267, 277–278, 443
Clark, Bobby, 45
Cleander, 11–12
Cleidemides, 15, 17
Cleon (actor), 40
Clive, Catherine (Kitty), 226, 227, 242
Clurman, Harold, 363, 479–481, 485, 496

Coghlan, Charles, 356
Cohan, George H., 430
Coke, Richard, 97
Coleman, Mrs., 169
Coleridge, Samuel T., 315
Comédie-Française founded, 168
Comédien, Le, 228–238, 241, 253, 260, 301, 456
Comedy, derivation of, 18
Comic acting, 19, 26–27, 29, 43–45, 52, 56, 175–176, 191–192, 194, 196, 212, 231–232, 234, 236, 244, 248, 258, 266, 283, 301, 304, 305, 316
Commedia dell' arte, 95, 100, 101–102, 104, 105–106, 109, 110, 114–135, 137, 154, 161, 164, 184, 216, 217, 446
Comment, actor's, 236–237, 373, 458, 490
Communion or contact, 373
Comus, 18
Concentration, 96, 248, 279, 315, 332, 355, 442, 463, 467, 472, 476–477, 483, 486
Condé, Baudouin de, 64
Condé, Jean, 64
Condell, Henry, 111, 148, 149, 151
Condell, Mrs. Henry, 152
Confidenti, 106, 125–126
Confrérie de la Passion, 77–78, 82, 84, 85, 97, 102, 106, 109, 139ff.
Congreve, William, 194
Conrart, Valentin, 187
Constructivism, 470–471
Contat, Louise, 275, 276, 299
Conte, Valleran le, 109, 139–141
Control, 53–54, 208, 237, 240, 244, 248, 254, 263–266, 279, 290, 301, 363, 397ff., 402, 417, 433, 442, 456, 458, 478
Conventions, 179, 386, 425, 455
Conversational quality, 108–109, 163, 180–181, 194, 207, 210, 234, 251, 266, 280, 310–311, 335–336, 349, 368–370, 373, 380, 399, 412; *see also* Speech, natural
Cook, Dutton, 356, 361
Cooke, Alexander, 148, 149
Cooke, George Frederick, 316
Cooke, Leonard, 107
Cooke, Thomas, 334
Cooper, Thomas Abthorpe, 285, 286, 316
Copeau, Jacques, 413, 435–438, 440, 446, 450, 454, 458, 466, 491
Copying, 36–37, 82, 182, 214, 243, 247, 262, 265, 268, 283, 291, 292, 294, 305, 316, 354, 367–368, 386, 389, 392, 404, 418, 421, 423, 428, 440, 445, 451, 466, 474, 487
Coquelin, Constant, 324, 342, 360, 391, 394, 395–403, 404, 405, 415, 417, 427, 431, 433, 443, 444, 456
Cordon, Françoise; *see* Bélonde, Mlle.
Corey, Katherine, Mrs., 170, 174, 177

Coris, Bernardo, 128
Cornell, Katharine, 460
Correspondence littéraire, 263
Costantini, Angelo, 117, 128
Costantini, Costantino, 128
Costantini, Domenica, 128
Costantini, Giovan, 128
Costenoble, Karl, 296
Cours de déclamation, 301
Cours d'esthetique appliqué, 325
Course of Lectures on Elocution, A, 250–251
Couvin, Watriquet de, 64
Cowl, Jane, 449, 460
Cowley, Richard, 111, 148, 149
Crabtree, Lotta, 364
Craig, Gordon, 359, 413, 424, 425, 428–429, 436, 437, 441, 443, 456
Crates, 19
Cratinus, 19, 20
Craven, Thomas, 447
Crawford, Cheryl, 463, 479, 481, 496
Crésol, Louis, 206
Cresp, J., 325
Critical Essays . . . (Hunt), 305ff.
Criticisms and Dramatic Essays . . . , 308
Croce, Benedetto, 123, 231
Croisy, Angelique du, 168
Croisy, Philibert Gassot du, 161, 162, 163, 168, 191
Cushman, Charlotte, 338, 339, 362
Cytheris, 47

Daguerre, Louis, 405
Dalberg, Wolfgang von, 270
Dalcroze; see Jaques-Dalcroze
Daly, Arnold, 432
Daly, Augustin, 361, 379–380
Daly, Joseph, 379
Dancourt, Florent–Carton, 186, 202
Dangeville, Marie-Anne, 229, 257
Danjūrō I, Ichikawa, 157
Danjūrō IX, 157
Darbes, Cesare, 134
D'Aubignac, 189–190
Dauvilliers, Nicholas, 167, 168
Dauvilliers, Victoire (Poisson), 167
D'Avenant, William, 169, 172, 176, 177, 193
Davenport, Edward L., 338, 339, 361
Davenport, Fanny, 362, 379
Davenport, Hester, 170
Davydov, V. N., 346
Dazincourt, Jean (Albonis), 275, 276
Deburau (Jean-Gaspard), 297, 435
Decimus Laberius, 47
Declamation, 16, 25, 51–52, 94–95, 108, 133, 142, 143, 145, 178–196, 203, 209, 210–211, 212, 214–215, 219, 220–221, 222, 226, 227–228, 230, 231–232, 234, 239, 246, 253, 255, 257, 258,

Declamation (continued)
259ff., 265, 269, 275, 282, 289, 291, 292ff., 297, 300, 301, 311, 313–314, 320, 327, 331, 334–335, 422, 432, 465; see also Elocution
"Déclamation" (Marmontel), 259
Déclamation Théâtrale, La, 259
Decorum, 54, 94, 101, 179, 190, 194, 196, 211, 282, 290, 308, 330
Decroux, Étienne, 486
Dejazet, Pauline Virginia, 325
Delacroix, 231
Delane, Dennis, 226, 227
"De la Poesie Dramatique," 261
Delaunay, Louis Arsène, 324, 342, 360
Delaunay, Marie; see Dorvel, Mlle.
Delivery, 20–21, 30, 32–33, 34, 35, 179–181, 185, 209, 214, 227, 234ff., 300, 328, 337, 377, 399
Dell' Arte Rappresentativa (Gattinelli), 327
Dell' Arte Rappresentativa (L. Riccoboni), 131, 132, 214–215
Delsarte, François, 55, 325–327, 365
Demetrius, 50–51
Demetrius Phalerus, 30
De Mille, Cecil B., 431, 453
Demosthenes, 10, 32, 55, 187
Des Barres, Adrien; see D'Orgemont
Descartes, 188, 221
Desgilleberts, Guillaume; see Montdory
Design, acting as, 55, 58, 196, 201, 224, 236, 238, 240, 249, 265–266, 279, 280–281, 289–290, 292ff., 295, 311, 349, 357–358, 375, 391–392, 393, 399, 402, 403, 413, 415, 418, 427, 429, 447–448, 459, 480, 492, 498
Desiosi, 106, 126
Deslauriers, Jean; see Bruscambille
Desmares, Charlotte, 202, 203, 210
Desoeillets, Mlle., 163, 166
Desoeillets, Nicolas, 142
Devrient, Eduard, 270, 333
Devrient, Ludwig, 294–296, 297, 300, 333
Dialoghi in materia di rappresentazione scensche, 99–100
Diaz de Mendoza, Fernando, 416
Dickens, Charles, 349
Dickson, William, 406
Diderot, Denis, 54, 230, 231, 238, 250, 256, 260–268, 275, 357, 397, 403, 433, 443
Di Lorenzo, Tina, 390
Dilthey, Wilhelm, 386
Diogenes Laertius, 9
Directing, 332–333, 346, 355, 366–368, 372, 379, 381–382, 383, 413, 419ff., 421–422
"Direction and Acting," 478
Director, acting and the, 227, 352, 371, 374, 429, 436, 484
"Discourses" (Reynolds), 283

Distribution of Roles; see Roles
Dithyramb, 8–9
Dmitrevskaya, 256
Dmitrevsky, Ivan, 255–256, 268–269
Döbbeling, Karl, 253, 254, 255, 272
Doche, Eugenie, 340
Doggett, Thomas, 178, 204, 212
Dominant urge, 30, 34–35, 195, 237, 240, 284, 310, 314, 398, 478, 484
Donstone, James, 111
Dorat, Claude-Joseph, 259
D'Orgemont, 142
Dorimond, 146–147
Dorval, Mlle., 297, 298, 320, 324
Douglass, David, 252
Downton, Thomas, 111, 148
Dowton, William, 304
Dramatic Censor, The, 250
Dramatic Character of Sir John Falstaff, An Essay on the, 284
Dressler, Marie, 451
Drew, John, 362, 364, 379, 431
Drew, Mrs. Louisa, 339
Dreyer, Carl-Thedore, 454
Drive, Main; see Dominant urge
Drouin, Nicholas; see Dorimond
Dryden, John, 186, 193–194
Du Bellay, Joachim, 90
Du Bos, J. B., 211, 215, 231, 253
Dubus, Pierre Louis; see Préville
Duchesnois, Mlle., 299
Duclos, Marie (de Châteauneuf), 203, 210, 230
Dufresne, Charles, 147, 160, 161, 229
Dugazon, Jean Baptiste, 258, 276, 277
Dullin, Charles, 435, 436, 454, 456
Dumas fils, Alexandre, 340–341
Dumesnil, Mlle., 230, 231, 238, 257, 277–278, 443
Dunlap, William, 285–286, 316
Du Parc, Mme.; see Gorla, Marquise-Therése de
Du Parc, René Berthelot, 161
Dupin, 167
Dupin, Mme. (Montfleury), 167, 168
Dupont, E. A., 454
Durante, Jimmy, 45
Durieux, Tilla, 421
Duse, Eleanora, 344, 346, 390, 395, 417–418, 431, 461, 472, 491
Dutton, John, 107

Earnings, actors', 28, 50, 77, 85, 86, 87–88, 94, 97, 111, 127, 148, 151–153, 165, 167, 168–169, 174, 175, 177, 202, 209, 212–213, 218, 220, 226, 227, 230, 258, 269, 286, 289, 299, 308–309, 313, 324, 337, 362, 364, 395, 451, 480
Eccleston, William, 149
Edison, Thomas A., 406

Eibenschütz, Camilla, 421
Eisenstein, Sergei, 454
Ekhof, Konrad, 218–219, 238, 253–255, 270
Elementi de Mimica, 327
Elements of Criticism, 249
Elements of Elocution, 282–283
Elements of Rhetoric, 335–336
Elenson-Haack-Hofmann troupe, 217
Elevation (heightening, idealization), 33–34, 56, 190, 193–194, 202, 211, 214, 216, 219, 224, 228, 234, 236, 240, 268ff., 280, 282, 285, 292ff., 305ff., 334–335, 350, 364, 391
Elliott, Maxine, 378, 432
Elliston, Robert, 304, 307, 312, 313, 317
Elocution, 30, 55, 123, 148, 174, 175, 179, 180, 181, 185, 212, 223–224, 232, 250–251, 268ff., 278ff., 299, 301, 323–324, 326, 336, 338, 339, 341, 342, 348, 355, 356, 362, 364, 368, 377, 432; see also Declamation
Elocutione Libre, De, 30
Emery, John, 304
Emotion(s), 11, 17, 20, 22, 30, 33–34, 35–36, 38, 53–54, 57–58, 67, 80–81, 99, 145, 165–166, 181, 182, 184–185, 187, 188, 189, 195, 203, 204, 207–208, 211, 214–216, 221ff., 226, 227–228, 231ff., 239ff., 243–244, 248–249, 250, 254, 260ff., 272–273, 282, 283, 290, 291, 297, 302, 303, 309–310, 314, 337, 357–358, 365, 375–376, 382, 392, 397, 398, 403–404, 414, 423, 433, 442, 445, 448, 449, 456–457, 458, 467, 469, 470–471, 473, 476, 478, 479–480, 487, 490
Emotion memory, 36, 38, 232–233, 302, 327, 398, 400, 440, 442, 443, 456, 460, 463, 478, 479–480
Encina, Juan del, 95
Engagements
run of play, 353
single play, 352
Engel, Johann Jakob, 55, 272–273, 305
England, 76, 78, 87–89, 91, 97–98, 102–104, 106–109, 110–113, 145, 146, 147–155, 169–178, 179–185, 192–196, 202, 203–209, 211–214, 216, 217, 219–228, 241–252, 271, 278–285, 303–316, 333–338, 346–361, 362, 368, 371, 374, 377–378, 388–390, 391–393, 425–429, 448, 458–460
English, John, 87
Ennebault, Mme. (Montfleury) d', 168
Ensemble, 273ff., 293–294, 329, 355–356, 366ff., 373, 379, 420, 462, 475
"Entrétiens sur Le Fils naturel," 260–261
Enunciation, 31, 32, 100, 180, 191, 227, 251, 276, 293, 299, 328, 373, 399, 415; see also Speech
Epicharmus, 19

Epigenes of Sicyon, 8
Espéronnière, Antoine l', 86
Essai d'une esthétique de théâtre, 386
Essai sur la connaissance des théâtres-fran-çais, 258–259
Essai sur la Déclamation Oratoire et Dra-matique, 325
Essai sur la physiognomie, 282
"Essay on the Art of Acting, An," 228, 305
Essay of Dramatick Poesy, An, 193–194
Essay on the Dramatic Character of Sir John Falstaff, An, 284
Esslair, Ferdinand, 294
Ethos; see Dominant urge
Etriche, d', Mme.; *see* Béjart, Armande
Etriche, Guérin d', 167, 168
Eutyches, L. Acilius Pontius, 48
Evans, Edith, 448
Evans, Henry, 149
Evans, Thomas, 151
Evrienov, Nicolai, 424–425
Exemplary Theatre, The, 458ff.
Expression, 188, 221, 232, 239, 245, 264–265, 281, 288, 301, 352–358, 363, 373, 387, 403, 404, 418, 421, 433, 437, 441, 445, 465, 477
Expressionism, 414, 438ff., 457
Eysoldt, Gertrud, 387

Fabvre, Mathieu la; *see* Laporte
Fairbanks, Douglas, 429, 453
Fairet (Ferré), Marie, 86
Fanchon; *see* La Tuillerie
Farren, Elizabeth, 278
Farren the younger, William, 312
Fasset, Michael, 86
Faucit, Helen, 336
Faversham, William, 380, 429
Faviot, Alix; *see* Desoeillets, Mlle.
Fechter, Charles, 325, 340, 347, 348–350, 351, 364
Fedeli, 126–127, 128
Federal Theatre, 493
Fedotov, Alexander F., 381
Fedotova, Glikeriya, 345, 381
Feelings; *see* Emotion(s)
Félix, Elisa; *see* Rachel
Fergusson, Francis, 6, 96
Ferravilla, Edoardo, 344
Fidenza, Antonio, 127
Field, Nathan, 147, 149
Fields, W. C., 45
Figuero, Roque de, 138
Figure, 231ff., 258, 307
Filandre, 145, 146
Film acting, 413–414, 418, 434, 444, 446
Films, 405–406, 413, 434, 451–452, 453–454, 457, 482, 491, 492, 493, 496–497, 498
Films, talking, 454

Fiorilli, Tiberio, 117, 123, 128, 129, 161
Fire (spirit, energy), 231ff., 245, 309–310, 402
Firmin, 319
First time, illusion of; *see* Spontaneity
Fisher, Charles, 379
Fiske, Minnie Maddern, 380, 432–433
Fitzgerald, Percy, 404
Flaherty, Robert J., 453
Flanagan, Hallie, 493
Fleck, Johann, 272
Fletcher, Lawrence, 148
Fleury, Abraham-Joseph, 275, 276, 299
Floridor, 145, 146, 147, 160, 163, 166
Flower in the Drama, The, 464ff.
Fontanne, Lynn, 433, 461
Foote, Samuel, 242, 278
Forbes-Robertson, Johnson, 392–393, 425, 431
Form *vs.* content, 202, 436, 445, 447, 473; *see also* Art or Nature
Forrest, Edwin, 317, 338, 339–340, 362, 363
Fort, Paul, 388
France, 68–73, 74–76, 84, 85–86, 91, 97, 102, 104–105, 109–125ff., 139–147, 155, 159–169, 185–192, 202–203, 209–211, 216, 228–238, 260–268, 274–278, 296–303, 317–327, 340–342, 362, 371–374, 388, 394–403, 414–416, 435–438, 454–456, 485–487, 492
France, La; *see* Jadot
Franchini, Francesco, 128
Franz, Ellen, 365, 366
Freie Bühne, 374ff., 383
Freud, Sigmund, 411, 439
Frohman, Charles, 380, 428
Fuchs, Georg, 421, 444

Gabbrielli, Luisa, 129
Ganassa, Zan, 102
Garavaglia, Ferruccio, 390
Garbo, Greta, 454
Garland, John, 107
Garrick, David, 133, 223, 224–228, 241, 242, 243, 244, 246–249, 250, 251, 256, 257, 258, 259, 262, 263, 267, 271, 278, 279, 281, 282, 304, 307, 308, 311, 349, 352
Garrick, ou Les Acteurs Anglois, 260–262
Gassaud (Bellerose), Nicole, 141, 160
Gattinelli, Gaetano, 327
Gaulcher, le, 145
Gaultier-Garguille, 140
Gaussem, Jeanne-Catherine; *see* Gaussin
Gaussin, Mlle., 239, 257
Gautier, Théophile, 297
Geffroy, Edmond, 321
Gelosi, 102, 105, 125, 126, 129
Gémier, Firmin, 374
General View of the Stage, A, 250

Gentleman, Francis, 250
Geoffroy, Abbé, 300
George, Grace, 449
George, Mlle., 289, 299–300, 320
Germany, 84, 85, 87–89, 110, 139, 202, 217–219, 252–255, 269–274, 292–296, 332–333, 365–368, 374–377, 390, 419–421, 438–441, 456–458, 487–491, 492
Geschichte de Deutschen Schauspielkunst, 333
Gestu Histrionis, De, 51
Gestures, 34, 42, 50, 54–55, 57–58, 66–67, 80, 88, 100, 102, 110, 143, 156, 178–179, 180–182, 187–188, 192, 203, 206ff., 211, 212, 213–216, 231, 249, 251, 272, 291, 293, 303, 323, 325, 326, 332, 358, 362, 373, 375, 404, 446, 451; see also Movement
Gherardi, Evaristo, 115, 117, 124
Gibbon, Edward, 248
Gibson, Richard, 87
Gidayu, Takemoto, 156
Gide, André, 454
Gielgud, John, 247
Gilbert, Mrs. George H., 362, 379
Gilbourne, Samuel, 148, 149
Gildon, Charles, 205ff., 238, 264
Gillette, William, 380, 431, 432, 433–434
Glanville, Joseph, 194
Glaucon of Teos, 30
Godwin, Edward G., 359
Goethe, 273–274, 288, 292–294
    "Rules," 292–293
Gogol, Nikolai, 329
Goldoni, Carlo, 132–135
Gorbunov, I. F., 345
Gorchakov, Nikolai, 477
Gorelov, I. N.; see Davydov
Gorla (Du Parc), Marquise-Therése de, 161, 163, 165, 166
Gôt, Edmond, 324, 341, 360, 394, 397
Gottsched, Johann Christoph, 218
Gough, Robert, 149, 155
Gourgaud, Françoise; see Vestris, Mme.
Gourgaud, Jean Baptiste; see Dugazon
Gramatica, Emma, 390, 417
Gramatica, Irma, 390, 417
Granval, Charles de, 229, 257–258
Granville-Barker, Harley, 393, 411, 413, 426–428, 458–460, 461, 491, 496
Grasso, Giovanni, 390, 417
Gravelle, 259
Green, Thomas, 153
Greet, Ben, 388, 421
Gregori, Ferdinand, 456
Grein, Jacob T., 377–378
Grévin, Jacques, 97
Griffith, D. W., 434, 451
Grimaldi, Joseph, 312
Grimarest, Jean Leonor de, 203, 222

Grimm, Friedrich M., 263
Gros-Gaullaume, 140
Group Theatre, 463, 479–481
Guérin, Robert; see Gros-Guillaume
Guerrero, María, 416
Guéru, Hugues; see Gaultier-Garguille
Guilds, first actors', 27–28
Guillot-Gorgu, 142
Guiot, Mlle., 167, 168
Guitry, Lucien, 394, 415
Gunnell, Richard, 148
Gurevich, Lyubov, 238, 442–443, 479
Guthrie, Tyrone, 30, 498
Gwenn, Edmund, 427
Gwyn, Nell, 172, 174–175

Habima players, 461, 472
Hachmann, Cord, 376
Hackett, James Henry, 335, 338, 339
Hackett, James K., 432
Hagemann, Carl, 456
Hallam, Lewis, 252
Hallam, jr., Lewis, 285
hamartia (tragic flaw), 16
Hamburgische Dramaturgie, 254
Hammond, John, 87
Hampden, Walter, 432
Hare, John (Fairs), 353, 425–426, 431
Harrigan, Edward, 365
Harris, Henry, 171, 172, 175
Hart, Charles, 154, 169, 171, 172, 174–175, 196, 205
Hart, William S., 451
Hauteroche, Noel Jacques le Breton de, 160, 168
Havard, William, 226, 242
Hawtrey, Charles, 425–426, 431
Hayes, Helen, 449
Hazlitt, William, 281, 308–311, 313, 314
Hédelin, François; see D'Aubignac
Heims, Else, 421
Heldburg, Freifrau Helene von; see Franz, Ellen
Heminge, John, 11, 112, 148, 149, 151
Heminge, William, 152
Hemingway, Ernest, 37
Henderson, John, 278, 281, 282
Henry, John, 285
Hensel, Sophie, 254
Henslowe, Philip, 107, 110, 112, 113, 148
Heracleides, 20
Heredia, María de, 138
Heriot, Henry, 97
Herman, 31
Heron, Matilda, 365
Hervé, Mlle., 161
Heywood, Thomas, 147
Hilarius, 71
Hill, Aaron, 213, 214, 221–223, 227–228, 305

Hill, John, 231ff., 241–246, 259–260, 264
Histrio-Mastix, 154
"histrionic sensibility," 6
Hodgkinson, John, 286
Höflich, Lucie, 421
Holcroft, Thomas, 289
Hopkins, Arthur, 450
Hopper, De Wolf, 429
Horace, 43, 48, 90, 204, 208, 211, 231
Horton, Christina, 212
Hôtel de Bourgogne, 97, 102, 105, 109, 125, 126, 127, 129, 131, 139ff., 160ff., 185
Houghton, Norris, 469
Howell, Wilbur S., 206
Hubert, André, 165, 168
Hugo, Victor, 318–319, 321
Hunt, Leigh, 281, 304–308, 311, 313, 334–335
Hypokrites, 9, 12, 28

Ibsen, Henrik, 369–370, 370–371, 375, 412, 487–488
Idea in acting, 7, 24, 25–26, 33, 38, 42, 55, 66, 67, 79, 80–82, 118, 123, 129, 133, 182, 183, 185, 262, 265, 272, 274, 283, 292, 302, 305, 314, 315, 332, 338, 349, 368, 378, 382, 385, 387, 394–399, 401, 404, 413, 417, 418, 421, 437, 442, 445, 451, 458, 460, 462, 464–467, 477, 478, 484, 487, 498
Ideality, 274, 282, 283–284, 287, 290, 292, 301–302, 303, 322–323, 325, 335, 358–359, 392, 412
Ideas of the Sublime and Beautiful, 249
Ideen zu einer Mimik, 272
Idées sur le geste et l'action théâtral, 272
Iffland, August Wilhelm, 238, 270, 271, 272, 273, 294, 295, 443
Ignatius of Loyola, St., 96
I-Kher-no-fret, 7, 68
Illusion of the first time; see Spontaneity
Ilyinsky, Igor, 471
Imagination, 7, 30, 36–37, 38, 54, 66, 67, 96, 115, 163, 193, 203, 208, 221, 225, 231ff., 245, 247, 253, 262, 264, 266, 267, 283, 292, 294–295, 298, 302, 305–306, 375, 386, 397, 398, 400, 428, 441, 446, 467, 473, 478, 479, 480, 498
Imer, Giuseppi, 132
Imitative instinct, 6
Immermann, Karl, 332
Impersonation, 6, 8, 12, 13, 15, 18, 26, 33, 34, 46, 52–53, 70–71, 81, 178, 184, 195, 235, 247–248, 267, 412, 459, 490; see also Characterization
Impressionism, 288
Improvisation, 8, 18, 40, 46–47, 100, 101–102, 115ff., 128–134, 217, 218, 235, 437, 446, 458, 479–480, 484; see also Commedia dell' arte

Ince, Thomas H., 451
Independent Theatre, 377–378
India, 55, 56–58, 65
Ingegneri, Angelo, 105
Insight, 238–239; see also Understanding
Inspiration, 30–31, 116, 230, 262, 264–265, 267, 278, 288, 290, 297, 300–301, 302, 323, 343, 357, 363, 402, 433
Instinct, dramatic, 6
Institutio Oratoria, 51ff., 90, 94
Instrument, actor as, 250, 264, 268, 271, 357, 358, 374, 397ff., 403, 455, 478, 486ff.
Instrumentalist, actor as, 250, 263, 264, 268, 271, 302, 357, 394, 397ff., 403, 455, 478
Intellect, 35, 55, 191, 201–202, 203, 208, 213, 230, 231, 254, 260ff., 270, 279, 282, 283, 290, 300–301, 302ff., 344, 356–358, 400, 402, 405, 427, 428, 467, 489; see also Judgment, Understanding
Ion, 30, 37, 231
Irving, Henry, 301, 354, 359, 360–361, 391–392, 393–394, 401–402, 425, 431
Isocrates, 187
Italy, 40ff., 78, 84, 89–95, 99–102, 105–106, 109, 114–135, 137, 216, 327–328, 342–344, 390, 416–418, 435
Itchū, 79

Jacob, Zacharie; see Montfleury
Jadot, Jacquemin, 142
Jagermann, Caroline, 292
James, Henry, 396
Janin, Jules, 322
Jannings, Emil, 421, 454
Japan, 79–82, 155–159
Jaques-Dalcroze, Émile, 437
Jefferson I, Joseph, 317
Jefferson, Joseph, 339, 351, 352, 362–363, 364, 406, 431
Jeffes, Anthony and Humphrey, 112, 148
Jenkin, Fleeming, 302
Jessner, Leopold, 440–441, 457
Joanny, 319
Jodelet, 142, 143, 145, 146, 161, 163
Jodelle, Etienne, 97
Jodin, Mlle., 261
Johnson, Benjamin, 196, 212
Johnson, Samuel, 223, 226, 227, 241, 248, 249
Johnson, William, 103, 107
Jolly, George, 171
Jones, Richard, 111
Jones, Robert Edmond, 6, 450
Jordan, Dorothy, 304
Jouvet, Louis, 191, 435, 436, 454–455, 456
Juba II, 30
Juby, Edward, 111, 148

Judgment, 186, 193, 195, 207, 208, 231, 236, 244, 245, 263, 264–266, 268ff., 280, 357, 402; see also Intellect
Justification, 35, 184, 472; see also Motives

Kabuki, 155–159
Kachalov, Vasily, 385, 389, 475
Kadensho, 81
Kainz, Josef, 368, 376
Kalich, Bertha, 429
Kames, Lord, 249
Karatygin, Vasily, 289–290, 328, 329, 330
Kayssler, Friedrich, 421
Kazan, Elia, 480, 481
Kean, Charles, 334–335, 338, 347–348, 349, 351, 359, 364, 365
Kean, Edmund, 289, 294, 297, 300, 307–312, 313–314, 317, 319, 323, 324, 334–335, 343, 349
Keane, Doris, 449
Keaton, Buster, 454
Keeley, Mary Anne, 337, 360
Keeley, Robert, 337
Keene, Laura, 361
Kemble, Charles, 303–304, 312, 319, 334, 335
Kemble, Frances Anne, 314, 334, 335
Kemble, John Philip, 278, 281–282, 285, 289, 303–304, 308, 310, 311, 312, 313, 349
Kemble, Sarah; see Siddons, Mrs.
Kempe, Will, 110, 111, 112, 148
Kendal, Madge, 359, 389–390, 425–426
Kerr, Alfred, 456
Kerr, Walter F., 82, 484
Khmelyov, Nikolai, 474
Kiami, 79
Killigrew, Thomas, 170–172, 174, 177, 193
King, Thomas, 226, 278, 315
Kirkham, Edward, 149–150
Kirkland, Alexander, 480
Kitto, H. D. F., 18
Kjerbühl-Petersen, Lorenz, 456–457, 458
Knep, Mary, 174
Knight, Joseph, 361
Knipper (-Chekhov), Olga, 383, 384, 389
Koch, Charlotte, 253, 254
Koch, Christina, 253
Koch, Gottfried, H., 253
Koch, Siegfried (Eckhardt), 271
Kolosova, Aleksandra, 289, 328, 330
Komisarjevskaya, Vera, 390, 424, 431
Komisarjevsky, Theodore, 272, 424–425, 444
Korn, Maximilian, 296
Kornfeld, Paul, 440
Kortner, Fritz, 440
Krauss, Werner, 421
Kŕśaśva, 56
Krutitsky, Anton, 269, 288
Kummerfeld, Karoline, 254, 270

Kurz, Joseph F. von, 254
Kwanami, Kitosugu, 79
Kynaston, Edward, 170, 171, 174, 177, 196

Lackaye, Wilton, 380
Lacy, James, 226
Lacy, John, 153, 169, 174
Lafon, Pierre, 297
La Grange, Achille; see Verneuil
La Grange, Charles Varlet, 161, 162, 163, 165, 166, 168
Lahr, Bert, 45
Lamb, Charles, 315–316
La Motte, Houdart de, 203, 228
Laneham, John, 103, 107
La Péruse, Jean de, 97
Laporte, 140
Laroque, 145, 160, 167, 168
L'Arronge, Adolf, 375
La Thorillière, François Lenoir, 163, 165, 166, 167, 202, 324
La Thorillière, Pierre, 202, 324
La Tuillerie, Jean, 168, 202
Lavater, Johann Kasper, 283
Lavrova, Yekaterina, 345
Lecouvreur, Adrienne, 210, 235, 323
Le Faucheur, Michel, 187–188, 206
Le Gallienne, Eva, 494
Legouvé, Ernest, 318
Legrand, Henri; see Turlupin
Legrand, Marc, 210
Leicester's Men, 103, 107
Leigh, Anthony, 175–176, 177
Leigh, Elinor, 177
Lekain, Henri Louis, 256, 257–258, 259, 271, 288, 300, 301, 302–303
Lemaître, Frédérick, 297–298, 320–321, 324, 338
Lemoine, Madeleine; see Mlle. Beaupré
Le Noir, Charles, 140, 141, 142, 143
Lensky, Alexander, 346, 390
Leonidov, Leonid, 389, 475, 484
Léris de la Tude, Claire-Josèph-Hippolyte; see Clairon, Mlle.
L'Espéronnière, Antoine, 86
L'Espy, 142, 143, 145, 161
Lessing, Emil, 376
Lessing, Gotthold Ephraim, 219, 239, 253–254
Lettre intorno Alla Mimica, 272
Lewes, George Henry, 323, 341, 343–344, 348, 349–350, 356–359, 364, 433, 443
Lewis, James (Demming), 397
Lewis, Robert, 481
Lewis, William T., 307
Lezioni di Declamazione e d'Arte Theatral, 327
Life of Mr. Thomas Betterton, The, 205ff., 264
Lilina, Maria, 383

Listening, 8, 210, 222, 363
Liston, John, 312, 316, 334, 337
Living the role, 214, 225, 231, 235, 239ff.,
    243, 245, 247, 266–267, 291, 301, 341,
    357, 373, 377, 388, 394, 397, 400–401,
    402, 424, 426, 427, 428, 433, 441, 444,
    445, 456, 465–467, 476–478, 479, 483–
    484, 486, 487, 490
Livius Andronicus, 41, 73
Livy, 40, 91
Lloyd, Robert, 250
Locatelli, Basilio, 115, 128, 129
Lolli, 129
Long runs, 321, 334, 340, 347, 348, 350,
    352, 353, 354, 355, 359, 360–361, 362,
    364, 379, 380, 392, 426, 429, 448, 449,
    450
Longchamp (Raisin), François Pitel de, 168
Loraine, Robert, 427
Löwen, Johann, 254
Lowin, John, 148, 152, 154, 169, 172
Lubitsch, Ernst, 454
Lucian, 51, 53–54
Ludi Romani, 40, 41
Lugue-Poë, Aurelien-Marie, 388, 415, 435
Lumière, Louis, 406
Lunt, Alfred, 433, 449, 461
Luzhsky, Vasily, 383, 384
Lycon, 29

McCarthy, Lillah, 427
McClintic, Guthrie, 449
McCullough, John, 365
MacDiarmid, Hugh, 464
Mackaye, Steele, 365, 377
Macklin, Charles, 222–223, 225, 226, 241,
    246, 247, 252
Macready, William, 297, 299, 312, 313–
    315, 319, 323, 334–337, 343, 349
Maffeo (Zanini), 93–94
Maillet-Duclairon, Antoine, 258
Main drive; see Dominant urge
Make-believe, 6, 7, 96, 182, 412, 419ff., 473
Malcolmi, Amalia, 292
Mansfield, Richard, 380, 394, 431, 432, 433
Mantell, Robert, 394, 431
Marais built, Théâtre de, 143
March, Fredric, 413
Marchand, Marie Françoise; see Dumesnil,
    Mlle.
Marchionni, Carlotta, 327
Marcoureau, Guillaume; see Brécourt
Marcoureau, Pierre; see Beaulieu
Marinetti, Flippo, 417
Marlowe, Julia, 394, 431
Marmontel, Jean François, 259
Mars, Mlle., 298–299, 319, 329, 338
Marshall, Anne, 172, 174
Martersteig, May, 456
Martinelli, Drusiano, 102, 126–127

Martinelli, Tristano, 118, 126, 141
Martin-Harvey, John, 426
Martynov, Alexander, 329, 330
Masks or Faces?, 403–404
Massey, Charles, 112, 148
Matasaburō, 79
Mathews the younger, Charles, 337, 338,
    339, 352, 360
Matiness, early, 353
Matthison, Edith Wynne, 427, 432
Maudit-Larive, Jean, 258, 301
Maugham, Somerset, 186
Max, Edouard de, 394
May, Edward, 87
Mchedelov, Vakhtang, 471
Mecour, Sussanna (Preissler), 254
Medebac, 133, 134
Medium, 25, 36, 37, 56, 165, 247, 262, 264,
    302, 386, 389, 394–398, 418, 429, 441,
    445, 456, 459, 465–467, 468ff., 477,
    485, 486ff., 491, 498
Meininger, The, 365ff., 369, 373, 376, 381,
    382, 384
Méliès, Georges, 406, 434
Melody of Speaking Delineated, The, 283
Mémoires (Dumesnil), 277, 443
Mémoires (Molé), 300
Mémoires de Lekain, 301
Mémoires, et réflexions (Clairon), 277, 443
Memory, Affective; see Emotion memory
Mendoza, Fernando Diaz de; see Diaz
Men of Art, 446
Mengs, Anton, 202
Merry, Anne (Brunton), 285
Meshchersky, Prince, 291
Messier, Pierre le; see Bellerose
Mestivier, François, 142
Mestivier, Isabelle, 142, 143
"Method" as a term, 481
"Method," Stanislavski; see Stanislavski
Meyerhold, Vsevolod, 382, 384, 413, 423,
    424–425, 444, 445–447, 457, 467, 468–
    471, 472, 474, 480, 481, 482, 491
Mézieres, Marie-Jeanne Lalores de; see Ric-
    coboni, Mme. F.
Michaelot, Theodore, 319
Michau; see Jadot
Mikhilova, Avdotya, 268
Miller, Henry, 380, 431–432
Milward, Henry, 246
Mimes
    performers, 40, 46, 48–49, 63–64, 67, 446
    scripts, 19, 40, 46–48, 63, 73, 74, 118
Mimesis, 36–37, 64
Mimicry, 51, 53, 56, 81, 247, 294–295, 418,
    467
Minstrels, 64ff., 67, 69, 72–73, 74, 75, 77–
    78, 87, 102, 106, 446
Mitsutarō, 79
Mochalov, Paul, 290, 331

584 ✳ INDEX

Modena, Gustavo, 328
Modjeska, Helena, 391, 431
Mohun, Michael, 153, 169, 170, 171, 172, 174
Moissi, Alexander, 391, 421
Molé, François (Molet), 257, 258, 276, 301
Molière, 129, 131, 139, 146–147, 157, 160–165, 167–168, 172, 185, 191, 455
Moncalvo, Giuseppe, 327
Montague, C. E., 386–387
Montaigu, René, 216
Montdory, 139, 140–141, 142–143, 144–145, 146
Montfleury, 145, 163, 166
Monvel, Jacques, 258, 277, 299
Moral bent; see Dominant urge
Morgann, Maurice, 284
Morris, Clara, 362, 379
Morris, Mrs. Owen, 285
Morrocchesi, Antonio, 327
Moskvin, Ivan, 383, 384, 389, 475
Mossop, Henry, 246
Motion pictures; see Films
Motives, 16, 27, 34–35, 179, 182–183, 189, 192, 194–195, 284, 325, 328, 330, 331, 379, 400, 441, 446; see also Justification
Motoshige, 79
Mouchaingre, Jean Baptiste de; see Filandre
Mounet-Sully, 342, 373, 394, 415, 417
Mountfort (Verbruggen), Susanna, 177, 196
Mountfort, William, 177, 195–196
Movement, 42, 54, 58, 117–118, 124, 157, 176, 179, 188, 193, 204, 206ff., 212, 219, 223, 239, 293, 326, 356, 366, 373, 399–400, 440, 444–445, 446–447, 460, 467, 469ff., 478, 480, 483, 485, 486, 498; see also Gestures
Mowatt, Anna Cora, 338, 339
Muma no Shirō, 79
Murnau, F. W., 454
Munden, Joseph, 304
My Life in Art (1924), 462, 463, 479
My Life in Art (1925, Russian), 474–475, 476
Mylles, Thobye, 107
Mynniscus, 12, 13

Naharro, Bartolomé de Torres, 95
Naigeon, 263
Naseli, Alberto; see Ganassa
Natasūtra, 56
Nathan, George Jean, 448–449
"Natural" acting, 24, 100, 125, 175, 185, 186, 187, 189, 192, 194–195, 196, 201, 203, 204ff., 213, 219, 221–222, 229–230, 235–236, 240, 246, 248, 259, 261, 267, 268, 269, 282, 283, 289, 290–291,

"Natural" acting (continued)
297, 300, 305–306, 310–311, 313–315, 316, 333, 335–336, 336ff., 341, 348, 349, 356, 358–359, 362, 363, 372ff., 386, 394, 397, 404–405, 413–414, 421ff., 425, 427, 461–462, 467, 482, 485, 492
Naturalism, 13, 23, 51, 183, 188, 195, 222, 229, 256, 261ff., 274, 285, 292, 341, 349–350, 366ff., 370, 372, 374ff., 380, 381, 384, 391, 419–420, 421, 422, 435, 437, 455, 471, 473, 474, 498
Nature, 205ff., 215, 219, 220, 224, 226, 227, 228, 229–230, 231ff., 236, 238, 239, 242ff., 247, 250–251, 263, 268, 270, 272, 274–275, 279, 281–282, 284, 301, 304, 311, 319, 326, 335, 364, 375, 391–392, 395, 418, 436; see also Art or nature
Nātya-śāstra, 56
Nazimova, 431, 432, 433, 453, 494
Neilson, Adelaide, 359, 379
Nemirovich-Danchenko, Vladimir, 383–384, 421ff., 441, 474, 475, 496
Neoptolemus, 28, 32
Neuber, Carolina (Weissenborn), 217–219, 253
Neuber, Johann, 217–219, 253
New Elucidation of the Principles of Speech and Elocution, 338
Nicostratus, 15, 17
Niepce, Joseph Nicéphore, 405–406
Nikulina-Kositskaya, Lyubov, 345
Nō acting, 79–82, 155, 157
Nokes, James, 170, 172, 175–176, 177
Norway, 368–370, 492
Novelli, Ermete, 344, 417, 431
Nymphodoros, 40

"Objective acting," 458; see also Brecht, Piscator
Observation, 164, 194, 196, 207, 227, 239, 245, 265, 272, 291, 305, 307, 331, 357, 375, 400, 440, 472, 476, 486, 490
"Observations sur une Brochure intitulée Garrick," 263
Odets, Clifford, 480
Okhlopkov, Nikolai, 474
O Kuni, 155
Oldfield, Anne, 204, 210, 212, 213
Olivier, Laurence, 208, 401, 485
Olivier, Mlle., 276
On Actors and the Art of Acting, 356ff., 433
On the Profession of a Player, 250
O'Neill, Eliza, 312–313
O'Neill, Eugene, 394, 450, 452
O'Neill, James, 394, 431
Onomastikon, 30, 90, 206
Ook, Stone Age, 6–7, 8, 18, 68
Oratore, De, 51ff., 90, 94

Oratory, acting as, 29, 33, 38, 51–52, 55–56, 94, 123, 171, 178ff., 182, 185ff., 192, 206ff., 227, 280, 283, 391
Oriental acting, 57–58, 65–67, 79–82, 155–159, 446
Ostler, William, 147, 148, 149, 151
Ostrovsky, 381
Otway, Thomas, 173
Ouspenskaya, Maria, 463
Ovid, 47

Page, Geraldine, 495
Pallenberg, Max, 421
Palmer, Albert, 378
Palmer, John, 278, 279
Palmer, Joseph, 316
Pantomime, 40, 117–118, 123, 131, 227, 239, 246–247, 487; see also Gestures, Movement
Pantomimes, 48, 102, 116ff., 226
Panurgus, 50
Paradoxe sur le comédien, Le, 231, 260ff., 403, 443
Paulsen, Carl Andreas, 139
Pavlov, Ivan, 470
Payne, John Howard, 316–317
Pellesini, Giovanni, 126
Pellio, 50
Peñafiel, Damian Arias de, 138–139
Peñedo, Baltasar, 138
"Pensées sur la déclamation," 214–216, 238, 239, 443
Perez, Cosme, 138
Perkin, John, 103
Perkins, Richard, 153
Perrucci, Andrea, 116, 117, 120
Personal experience, using or exhibiting, 22, 24, 36, 55, 82, 164, 208, 240, 244–246, 247, 266–268, 269, 272, 279–280, 287, 294–295, 303, 306–307; see also Self
Personality, 118, 119, 155, 232, 235, 250, 297, 304, 309, 326, 373, 375, 389, 394, 399–400, 401–402, 413, 417–418, 433, 436, 445–446, 460, 466–467, 483, 484, 491; see also Self
Petit, Benoist, 109
Phaedrus, 37
Philosophy of the Human Voice, The, 339 350, 392
Pherecrates, 19
Phillips, Augustine, 111, 112, 148, 151
Philosophical Analysis . . . of Shakespeare's Remarkable Characters, 284
Philosophy of the Human Voice, The, 339
Philostratus, 187
Phrasing, 32, 52
Physical qualifications, 358; see also Figure
Piassimi, Vittoria, 106, 126
Picard, Louis, 296–297
Piccilini, Lorenzo, 343

Pickering, Roger, 250
Pickford, Mary, 431, 434
Pinero, Arthur Wing, 354, 378
Pinkethman, William, 212
Pisarev, Modest, 345
Piscator, Erwin, 457–458, 481
Pisistratus, 9
Pitoëff, Georges and Ludmilla, 438
Plato, 10, 29, 30, 205, 231, 464
Plautus
    as actor, 43
    as director, 44
Plavilshchikov, Peter, 269
Play as a whole, 37–38, 118, 179, 185, 227, 252, 310, 314, 373, 382, 398, 441, 459
Playfair, Nigel, 427
Playwright, actors and the, 24–25, 115ff., 134, 164, 185, 186, 192, 196, 231, 235, 237, 240, 243ff., 247, 261, 277, 302, 314, 351, 352, 377, 382, 388–389, 392, 397, 398–399, 418, 427, 436, 454–455, 456, 459–460, 478, 484
Plotinus, 464
Plutarch, 9, 53, 187, 207
Poel, William, 388, 427
Poetics (Aristotle), 30ff., 34, 90, 94, 189
Poetry, speaking, 182–184, 214, 302, 359, 396, 405, 441, 485
Poisson, Paul, 202
Poisson, Phillipe, 202
Poisson, Raymond, 160, 168, 202
Politische Theater, Das, 457ff.
Pollard, Thomas, 149, 151–152
Pollock, Walter Herries, 403
Pollux (Pollus), Julius, 30, 55, 90, 206
Polo, Zan, 92
Polus, 28, 36
Ponteuil I, 203, 209
Ponti, Diana, 106, 126
Pope, Thomas, 111, 112, 148, 151
Popov, Aleksey, 255
Popple, William, 222
Poquelin, Jean-Baptiste; see Molière
Porter, Edwin S., 434
Porter, Mary Anne, 212
Possart, Ernst von, 374
Potier, Charles-Gabriel, 297
Pouget (Beauchâteau), Madeleine de, 141, 145, 163
Powell, George, 178, 204
Power, Tyrone, 306
Practical Illustrations of Rhetorical Gesture and Action, 272, 305
Pratique du théâtre, La, 189–190
Praxiteles, 18
Preface to Cromwell, 318–319
Prefaces to Shakespeare, 428
Presentational acting, 44–45, 315–316, 389, 395ff., 404, 412, 414, 425, 440, 444ff., 457, 469ff., 473, 475–476, 489–491

Préville, 133, 257, 258, 275, 276, 324
Price, Stephen, 316, 317
Primi Erudimenti dell' arte Drammatica . . . , 327
Pritchard, Hannah, 226, 227, 242
Problems of the Actor, 448
Prompter, The, 222
Prosodia Rationalis, The, 251
Protagonist, 20
Protagoras, 16
Provincetown Players, 450
Provost, Jean-Baptiste, 321
Prynne, William, 154
Psychologie des sentiments, 443
Psychology of Acting, 456ff.
Pudovkin, Vsevolod, 454
Pushkin, Alexander, 289, 291
Pylades, 48

Queen's Men, 107, 108
Quin, James, 212, 220–221, 223–224, 226, 227, 228, 232, 242, 246, 258, 282
Quinault-Dufresne, Abraham, 209, 210
Quinault-Dufresne, Maurice, 210
Quintilian, 42, 50–51, 52ff., 56, 75, 90, 99, 181, 182, 187, 188, 206, 211, 222, 231

Rachel, 322–324, 338, 361, 402
Racine et Shakespeare, 298, 301
Radio, 450–451, 493
Rafuin, Catherine; *see* Duchesnois, Mlle.
Ragueneau (La Grange), Marie, 168
Raherus, 64
Raimund, Ferdinand, 294
Raisin, Jean Baptiste, 168
Rapin, René, 195
Rasas, 57
Raucourt, Mlle., 258, 299
Realism, 13, 22–23, 26, 38, 54, 70, 71–72, 75, 77, 82, 91–92, 101, 125, 156, 163, 172, 179, 182, 188, 190–191, 202, 204, 218, 220, 222, 224, 229, 235, 271, 273–275, 284, 287, 292, 300, 304, 320, 322, 330–331, 333ff., 336, 338, 339, 340ff., 349–350, 352ff., 359, 364, 365ff., 370ff., 374ff., 378, 382, 384–385, 388ff., 404ff., 412, 415, 418, 421ff., 426ff., 435–436, 457, 462, 465–467, 473, 482, 490–491
Reflections Upon Theatrical Expression, 250
Réflexions antique et historique, 211
Réflexions historiques et critiques, 214
Réflexions sur l'art théâtral (Maudit-Larive), 301
"Réflexions . . . sur l'art théâtral" (Talma), 301ff., 442
Réflexions sur la Poetique, 195
Réflexions sur le théâtre, 486
Regnault Petit-Jean, Pierre; *see* Laroque
Régnier, 321, 324, 342

Rehan, Ada, 379, 432
Rehearsing, 173, 176, 180, 222, 224, 252, 257, 265, 268, 269, 279, 284–285, 289, 302, 307, 314–315, 328, 332–333, 347, 353, 367, 376, 383–384, 401, 420, 421, 436, 443, 479–480, 484
Reicher, Emmanuel, 374, 375
Reinhardt, Max, 377, 391, 413, 419–421, 425, 430, 438–439, 460
Reiter, Virginia, 390
Réjane, 373, 394, 415, 417, 431, 451
Relaxation, 314, 326, 365, 476–477, 486
Remarks on some Characters of Shakespeare, 284
Rémond de Sainte-Albine, Pierre; *see* Sainte-Albine
Renaud, Madeleine, 132, 486, 492
Repertory, 251–252, 284–285
Representational acting, 315, 389, 404ff., 412, 414, 491
Revolution des Theaters, Die, 421
Reyes, Baltasara de los, 138
Reynolds, Joshua, 248, 283–284
Rhetoric (Aristotle), 30ff., 34, 35, 189
Rhetoric, 24–25, 29, 76, 108, 179–181, 184, 185, 186, 187, 190, 194, 216, 272, 335, 392
Rhetorical Grammar, A, 283
Rhetorique (Wilson), 97
Rhodes, John, 170
Rhymes, first, 43
Rhythm, 421
Ribot, Théodule, 443
Riccoboni, Antonio, 128, 130
Riccoboni, Elena (Mme. Luigi), 210
Riccoboni, Francesco, 132, 219, 238, 239–240, 260, 261, 263–264, 271, 443
Riccoboni, Mme. Francesco, 261, 262
Riccoboni, Luigi, 128, 130–132, 210, 214–216, 231, 232, 234, 238, 239–240, 260, 264, 443
Rice, John, 149
Rich, Christopher, 178, 212, 213
Rich, John, 212, 220, 226
Richardson, William, 284
Rios, Nicolás de los, 138
Riquier, Guiraut de, 64
Ristori, Adelaide, 327–328, 342–343, 390
Rituals, 7–8, 18, 41, 56, 77
Robertson, Agnes, 351
Robertson, T. W., 352–355
Robinson, Mrs., 152
Robinson, Richard, 149
Robit, Philibert; *see* Gaulcher, le
Rochester, Earl of, 176, 192
Rockefeller III, John D., 494
Roksanova, Maria, 383
Roles, distribution, 12–13, 15–16, 21, 26
Rollin, Charles, 259
Romagnesi, Marc' Antonio, 128

Romagnesi, Nicolas, 128, 129
Romains, Jules, 438
Romanticism, 287ff., 317ff., 333, 392, 393
Rosciad, The, 250
Roscius, Quintus (Gallus), 43, 50, 267
Rose (De Brie), Mlle. de, 161, 162, 168
Rosimond, 167, 168
Rossi, Ernesto, 328, 342, 344, 382, 390
Rowley, Samuel, 112, 148
Roze, Claude de; see Rosimond
Rozet, Catherine Leclerc du; see Rose, Mlle. de
Rueda, Lope de, 95–96
Ruggeri, Ruggero, 390, 417
Rules of Passion, 30
Rush, James, 339
Russell, Lillian, 429
Russia, 255–256, 268–269, 288–292, 328–332, 344–346, 367, 374, 381–385, 389, 390, 421–425, 441–447, 467–479, 481–484, 492–493
Rutebeuf, 74
Ruzzante; see Beolco
Ryan, Lacy, 212, 226, 242
Ryazantsev, 328

Sacchi, Antonio, 117, 133
Sadovsky, Prov, 331, 345
Sāhita-darpana, 57
Saint-Denis, Michael, 415
Sainte-Albine, Pierre Rémond de, 228–238, 239, 241ff., 247, 253, 254, 259–260, 301, 456
St. Jacques, Bertrame Hardouin de; see Guillot-Gorju
Saint-Val, Mlle., 257
Sainval (the elder), Mlle., 258
Sainval (the younger), Mlle., 258, 276
Salaries, actors'; see Earnings
Sallé, Jean, 203
Salvini, Tomasso, 328, 343–344, 356, 364, 382, 390, 391, 402–403, 472
Samarin, I. V., 331, 345
Samarova, Maria, 383
Samoilov, Vasily, 331, 345
Samoilova, Vera, 330, 331
Samson, Joseph Isidore, 297, 321, 322, 323, 324, 342
Sanctis, Alfredo de, 390
Sandford, Samuel, 176, 177, 178
Sarat, Agnan, 102
Sarcey, Francisque, 386
Sarrazin, Pierre-Claude, 229, 257
Saucerotte, Françoise; see Raucourt, Mlle.
Saunderson (Betterton), Mary, 172, 175, 176, 177
Savina, M. G., 346
Savitskaya, Magarita, 383
Saxe-Meiningen, Duke Georg II of, 365ff.
Saxon, O. Glenn, 492

Scala, Flaminio, 122, 125, 126
Schauspielkunst, Die, 456ff.
Schildkraut, Rudolph, 421
Schiller, Friedrich, 273–274, 292
Schlegel, Johann Elias von, 219
Schmidt, Willi, 485
Schöenemann, Johann Friedrich, 218, 253, 254
Schools for actors, 65, 140–141, 153, 156, 169, 171, 193, 221, 222, 253, 269, 276, 288, 297, 338, 360, 383, 437, 438, 443, 463, 468, 471, 484
Schreyvogel, Joseph, 296
Schröder, Friedrich, 219, 239, 253, 254–255, 269–270, 271, 294, 295
Schröder (Ackermann), Sophia, 218, 252–254
Schröder, Sophie (Burger), 294, 296
Schuch, Franz, 255
Schulz, Sophie, 253
Schulze, Sophie, 254, 255, 270
Scott, Clement, 349, 361
Seami (Zeami), 79–82
Self, use or exhibition of, 208, 220, 223, 238, 246, 273, 301, 358, 375, 390, 398, 399–400, 401–402, 412, 413, 417–418, 428, 433–434, 441, 442, 445–446, 455, 456, 458–459, 460, 466–467, 477, 479, 481, 482–484, 485, 490, 498; see also Personality
Semyonova, Catherine, 288–289, 329
Sennett, Mack, 434
Sensibility, 6, 54, 183, 201–202, 203, 211, 225, 227, 230ff., 243–245, 260ff., 295, 300–301, 302ff., 313, 358, 394, 403, 433, 498
Sentimental Spouter, The, 250
Seyler, Abel, 254, 255, 270
Shakespeare, 109, 110, 111, 112, 148, 149, 151
Shank, John, 149, 152
Shannon, Effie, 380
"Shares," 112, 148–149, 151–152, 168–169, 171, 174, 209
Sharpe, Richard, 149
Shaw, Bernard, 378, 404–405, 427–428
Shaw, Robert, 112
Shchepkin, Michael, 291–292, 329, 330–331, 345
Shchukin, Boris, 473
Sheridan, Richard B., 250
Sheridan, Thomas, 250–251
Shumsky, S. V. (Chesnokov), 330, 331, 345
Shumsky, Yakov, 268
Shusherin, Yakov, 269, 288
Shuter, Edward (Ned), 226, 227
Sica, Vittorio de, 414
Siddons, Henry, 272, 305
Siddons, Sarah, 278–282, 285, 286, 289, 303–304, 308, 313, 353

Siddons, William, 278
Siegler, Karoline, 270
Silālin, 56
Simonov, Reuben, 473
Sincerity, 290, 373, 389, 433, 455, 463, 465, 467, 484, 486
Singer, John, 107, 111, 148
Skinner, Otis, 379, 431
Skinner, Richard, 97
Slater, Martin, 111
"Slice of life," 249, 341
Sly, William, 111, 148
Smith, "Gentleman," 278, 279, 282
Smith, John, 197
Smith, William, 171, 173, 176, 178
Smollett, Tobias, 220
Snetkova, Fanya, 346
Socialist Realism, 481ff., 489
Socrates, 10, 30, 205
Sommi, Leone de', 99–100
Sophocles as actor, 12, 15
Sorma, Agnes, 376
Sosnitsky, Ivan, 289, 324, 330
Sothern, Edward A., 347, 352, 359, 360
Sothern, E. H., 379, 394, 431
Soulas, Josias de; see Floridor
South America, 416
Southey, Thomas, 97
Spain, 86–87, 98–99, 105, 109–110, 137–139, 155, 216, 416, 434
Spectator, The, 213
Speech, 32–33, 51–52, 72, 77, 100, 116–117, 157, 164, 166–167, 174, 176, 179ff., 186–187, 190–191, 192, 193, 194, 207ff., 212, 213, 214, 224–225, 226, 227, 234ff., 243, 250–251, 273, 275, 276, 279–280, 281–282, 293, 301, 302, 303, 304, 313–314, 326–327, 342, 344, 358–359, 376, 396, 404–405, 439, 440, 446, 460, 462, 486, 498
Speech, natural, 32, 39, 92, 122, 123–124, 133, 164, 183–184, 190, 194, 211, 223, 224, 234, 261; see also Conversational quality
Spencer, Gabriel, 112
Spielgelberg, C. J., 217
Spiritual Exercises, The, 96
Spontaneity, 55, 95, 100, 116, 124–125, 181, 194, 196, 215, 226, 235, 248, 267, 280–281, 309, 314, 363, 392, 402, 403, 404, 405, 433, 440, 485, 490
Sprat, Thomas, 194
Staël, Mme. de, 298
Stanislavski, Constantin, 31, 34, 36, 54, 124, 191, 201–202, 205, 208, 214, 215, 232, 233, 234, 235, 237, 238, 268, 280, 284, 291, 306, 325, 326, 331, 345, 346, 368, 374, 375, 377, 381–385, 387, 398, 399, 400, 401, 402, 403, 405, 413, 415, 421ff., 425, 427, 428, 430, 433, 434,

Stanislavski, Constantin (continued)
436, 440–444, 445, 446, 455, 456, 458, 459–460, 461–463, 464, 466, 467, 471, 472, 473–479, 480–481, 482–485, 486, 487, 488, 491, 496
Stanislavski "system" started, 423–424, 442ff., 462
Stanitsyn, Victor, 484
Stark, Joanne, 253
Starr, Frances, 431, 449
Stearns, Monroe, 455
Steele, Joshua, 251
Steele, Richard, 204–205, 211, 213, 221
Stendhal, 298, 301
Sticotti, Antonio, or Anton Giovanni, 238, 260, 262, 264
Stone Age Ook, 6–7, 8, 18, 68
Stone, Fred, 429
Stranitzky, Joseph Anton, 217
Strasberg, Lee, 231, 463, 479–481, 496
Stratocles, 50–51
Strepetova, P. A., 345
Strindberg, August, 370, 414
Stroheim, Erich von, 453
Studii sulle Arti Imitatrici, 327
Style, 38, 66, 134, 186, 247, 289, 292, 347, 380, 394, 395, 399, 401, 436–438, 446, 451, 454, 455, 466, 498
Subjectivity, 288, 292
Sulerzhitsky, Leopold, 442, 443
Sullivan, Barry, 359
Sumarokov, Alexander, 256
"Superconscious," 462
"Super-objective"; see Idea
Susarian, 19
Swanston, Eyllaerdt, 149, 151–152
Sweden, 414
Symons, Arthur, 391–392
Symbolic acting, 58, 66–67, 80, 182, 292, 357–358, 390, 391, 428, 440, 444
Symbolism, 287–288, 423
"System," Stanislavski; see Stanislavski
"System and Methods of Creative Art, The," 444, 476–477

Tairov, Alexander, 444–445, 447, 457, 467–468, 471, 474
Talma, François Joseph, 238, 275, 276–277, 297, 298, 299, 300–301, 313, 314, 319, 320, 321, 443
Talmy, Andrien, 109
Tarleton, Richard, 107, 108
Tatler, The, 204–205, 211, 221
Taylor, Joseph, 149, 152, 154, 169, 172
Taylor, Laurette, 449
Tearle, Godfrey, 427
Teatro comico, Il, 133, 134
Technique, 53, 55, 66, 80, 82, 96, 157–159, 248, 254, 261, 268, 271, 282, 289–290, 328, 343, 362–363, 374, 390, 396, 398,

Technique (continued)
  400, 401, 412, 416, 422, 427, 433, 451,
  484, 485
  inner, 423, 445, 446, 465, 472, 475, 479,
  480
  outer, 81, 445, 476, 478–479, 480, 483,
  485, 486
Telestes, 11
Television, 413, 484, 491, 492, 496, 498
Tempest, Marie, 426
Templeton, Fay, 429
Terence, 42
Terry, Ellen, 347, 359–360, 392, 417, 425,
  428, 431
Testelin, Henri, 188
Theatralische Bibliothek, 253
Théâtre-Libre, 371ff., 374, 377, 380, 381,
  388
Théâtre Libre, Le, 373ff.
Theatricality, 6, 21, 25–26, 33, 44–45, 56,
  67, 124, 172, 182–183, 190–191, 238,
  290, 292, 305, 315–316, 354–355, 359,
  372, 376, 378, 385, 390ff., 394ff., 416,
  418, 419ff., 421, 424ff., 426ff., 439,
  440, 442, 444ff., 451, 452, 457, 458,
  462, 467, 467ff., 472ff., 477, 480, 484,
  485, 487–488, 490
Theatriké Historia, 30
Theobald, Lewis, 211–212
Theodora, 49
Theodorus, 28, 33
Theodosius, 49
Theophrastus, 27
Theorie de l'art du comédien, 325
Thespis, 8–9, 12, 19, 38, 73
Thettalus, 28
Thrasymachus, 30
Timing, 32, 52, 248, 467
Timoneda, Juan de, 95
Tlepolemus, 15, 17
To the Actor, 485
Tójuró, Sakata, 157
Tone(s), 32, 33, 55, 100, 117, 188, 191,
  203, 211, 213, 223, 225, 226, 227,
  231, 234, 239, 251, 282, 283, 303, 311,
  312, 323, 337, 357, 358, 393, 405, 422
Tone, Franchot, 463
Tooley, Nicholas, 148
Tousez, François; see Régnier
Touzé, Pierre François; see Bocage
Towne, John, 107, 148
Towne, Thomas, 111
Tracy, Lee, 495
"Tragedies," derivation of, 8
Tragydos, 12
Traité de l'eloquence, 259
Traité des études, 259
Traité des Passions de l'ame, 221
Traité de Recitatif, 203
Traitté de l'action de l'orateur, 187–188, 206

Tree, Beerbohm, 393, 425
Tree (Kean), Ellen, 338, 347
Trépeau, Rachel, 140
Troyepolskaya, Tatyana, 256
Truth, sense of, 101, 124, 203, 214, 216,
  226, 233ff., 239, 245, 259, 291, 292,
  301–302, 350–359, 375, 381, 385, 386,
  390, 398, 415, 423, 460–461, 462, 463,
  473, 478, 480, 485
Turlupin, 140
Turpio, Ambivius, 50
Tynan, Kenneth, 448, 491, 494

"Unbroken line"; see Dominant urge
Underhill, Cave, 170, 175–176, 177, 178
Underplaying, 355, 356, 388, 389, 393, 427–
  428
Understanding, 37, 52, 185, 231ff., 243–
  245, 261, 374, 427
Underwood, John, 147, 148, 152
United States, 250, 252, 285–286, 311, 312,
  316–317, 325, 334, 335, 337, 339–340,
  343, 350, 351–352, 361–365, 371, 374,
  378–380, 392, 393–394, 411, 429–434,
  437–438, 448–454, 460–467, 479–481,
  483, 484–485, 492–498
Uniti, 106, 126
Unities, the three, 101, 143, 188, 202, 271
"Units and Objectives," 237, 398, 441, 477,
  478, 483

Vaca, Jusepa, 138
Vakhtangov, Eugene, 442, 461, 471–474,
  481, 482
Valentino, Rudolph, 453
Vallejo, Manuel, 138
Valleran; see Conte, le
Vandenhoff, George, 339
Vanhove, Charles Joseph, 275
Varlamov, K. A., 346
Vasilyev, S. V., 345
Vedrenne, John, 426
Velten, Catharina, 139, 217
Velten, Johannes, 139
Vendramin, 134
Venier, Marie, 140
Verbruggen, John, 196, 204
Verbruggen, Mrs.; see Mountfort, Mrs.
Verconus, 64
Verisimilitude, 33, 44, 66, 101, 182, 188,
  189ff., 194–195, 202, 228–229, 291,
  313, 355, 368, 370, 385, 390, 404ff.,
  433, 442, 459, 469, 491
Verneuil, 167, 168
Verse; see Poetry
Verviziotti; see Lensky
Vestris, Mme. (Bartolozzi), 337, 338, 339
Vestris, Mme. (Gourgaud), 258, 277
Vezin, Hermann, 359
Vezin, Mrs., 359

Viage Entretenido, 98–99
View of the English Stage, A, 308ff.
Villandrando, Augustin de Rojas, 98–99
Villiers, Claude Deschamps, 142, 145
Villiers, Jean de, 168
Vishnevsky, Alexander, 383
Viśvanātha, 57
Voice, 20, 31–33, 41, 42, 51–52, 55, 67, 77, 88, 97, 100, 117, 143, 145, 176, 178, 179, 180–181, 185, 187, 192–193, 195–196, 203, 204, 206, 208, 215, 221, 222, 223, 225, 227, 230, 232, 239, 249, 251, 265, 277, 280, 282–283, 289, 299, 302–303, 307, 314, 323, 326, 335–336, 339, 342, 343, 344, 370, 373, 375, 393, 394, 397, 399, 432–433, 436, 448, 462, 467, 478, 483, 484–485, 486
Volkov, Fedor, 255–256
Volkov, Grigóry, 255

Walker, John, 282
Walker, Thomas, 212
Wallack, Henry, 317, 337
Wallack, James, 337, 339
Wallack, Lester, 339
Wancourt, Jehanne de, 140
Warfield, David, 429, 430, 448, 449
Warner, Mrs., 338
Warren, William, 317
Washington Square Players, 450
Watts, George F., 359
Webster, Benjamin N., 346, 360
Wedekind, Frank, 387
Wegener, Paul, 421
Weigel, Helene, 488
Weissenborn, Carolina; *see* Neuber, Caroline

Weymer, Marguerite; *see* George, Mlle.
Whateley, Richard, 335–336
Whately, Thomas, 284
Whitman, Walt, 340
Whole, play as a; *see* Play as a whole
Wignell, Thomas, 285
Wilkes, Thomas, 250
Wilks, Thomas, 178, 204, 212, 213
Williams, Harcourt, 427
Wilson, Robert (Thomas), 103, 107
Wilson, Thomas, 97
Wilton, Marie; *see* Bancrofts
Winckelmann, Johann J., 202, 268, 272, 274
Winds, Adolf, 456
Winter, William, 339
Woffington, Margaret (Peg), 226, 227, 232, 242, 245–246
Wolff, Pius A., 292, 293, 296
Wood, William, 317
Woodward, Henry, 226, 227, 241, 242, 246
Worms, Gustave, 342, 388
Wyndham, Charles, 359, 425, 431

Yakovlev, Aleksey, 269, 288
Yates, Richard, 226, 227
Yermolova, Maria, 346, 390
Young, Charles Mayne, 312
Young, John, 97
Young, Stark, 33, 417, 451–452, 458, 461–462, 463–467, 491

Zacconi, Ermete, 390
Zanini; *see* Maffeo
Zavadsky, Yuri, 472, 473
Zeami; *see* Seami
Zola, Émile, 341, 372